# SUBSCRIBERS TO T

# 1989 FACSIMILE LIMIT



Margaret Ball, *8 Westrow Gardens, S*

Mrs S. Ballard, *"Holmleigh", Lyndock R* *on, Hampshire.*

James F. Barnes, *17 St Gabriel's Road, Bit* *Hampshire.*

Wendy M. Barrett, *6 Somerset Road, Portswoo* *n, Hampshire.*

G.A. Batchelor (City Crier, 1984-1989), *hurch Road, Warsash, Southampton, Hampshire.*

J.C. Beard, *33 Abbotts Ann Road, Winchester, Hampshire.*

Mr Christopher Bick, *"Domremy", 5 Sedgemead, Netley Abbey, Hampshire.*

Mrs June Andrea Bick, *"Domremy", 5 Sedgemead, Netley Abbey, Hampshire.*

Mr and Mrs Bird, *22 Chaucer Close, Fareham, Hampshire.*

Alfred David Bull, *4 Swift Hollow, Woolston, Southampton, Hampshire.*

Mr K.F. Burnet, *90 Northumberland Road, Southampton, Hampshire.*

C

A.E.R. and Mrs J.M. Cuerden, *85 Malwood Road West, Hythe, Southampton, Hampshire.*

D

Malcolm Paul Dalrymple, *26 Andover Road, Freemantle, Southampton, Hampshire.*

Mr and Mrs C. Doswell, *12 Redhill Close, Bassett, Southampton, Hampshire.*

F

Miss D.G. Le Faye, *16 Wilton Court, Wilton Road, Muswell Hill, London.*

The Rev. and Mrs G.D. Fuller, *South Stoneham Vicarage, Wessex Lane, Southampton, Hampshire.*

G

Mrs P.E. Gale, *47 Sydney Road, Shirley, Southampton, Hampshire.*

Mr Geof Golding, *17 Testbourne Road, Totton, Southampton, Hampshire.*

Mrs A. Gosling, *57 Charlton Road, Southampton, Hampshire.*

Frank J. Grayer, *18 Howard Road, Shirley, Southampton, Hampshire.*

Miss A.M. Green, *14 The Babbages, Bickington, Barnstaple, Devon.*

H

Mr D.A. Hall, *103 Farringford Road, Thornhill, Southampton, Hampshire.*

Mrs G.M. Hall, *Select Library, King Edward VI School, Kellett Road, Southampton, Hampshire.*

Hampshire County Library, *81 North Walls, Winchester, Hampshire.*

Mr David I.D. Harris, *"Woodlands", Petworth Road, Wormley, Surrey.*

Eric A. Harris, *"Fairwind", Grange Road, Netley Abbey, Southampton, Hampshire.*
Mr and Mrs M. Holloway, *27 Swift Gardens, Southampton, Hampshire.*
Miss Sylvia Horlock, *170 Howard's Grove, Shirley, Southampton, Hampshire.*
Rodney H. Howell, *7 Compton Close, Eastleigh, Hampshire.*

I

Sophie M. Ingledew, *10 Westfield Common, Hamble, Hampshire.*

J

Siân Jones, *Southampton City Museums, 125 High Street, Southampton, Hampshire.*

K

F.J. Kitney, *1 Culverley View, Armstrong Road, Brockenhurst, Hampshire.*

L

Professor G.M. Lilley, *"Highbury", Pine Walk, Chilworth, Southampton, Hampshire.*

M

Mrs A.T. Markwick M.A., Ph.D., *11 Deans Court, Milford-on-Sea, Hampshire.*
R.D. Martin, *48 Thorold Road, Bitterne Park, Southampton, Hampshire.*
Mr and Mrs Masters, *45 Romsey Road, Shirley, Southampton, Hampshire.*
Rev. Peter Matthews M.A., *St Marks Vicarage, Woolston, Southampton, Hampshire.*
M.J. Misselbrook, *121C Bassett Avenue, Southampton, Hampshire.*
Mr and Mrs John Mitchener, *"Pipers Wait", Balmer Lawn, Brockenhurst, Hampshire.*

N

Jean E. Nicklin, *Southampton, Hampshire.*

O

Gavin Ogilvie, *12 St Thomas Park, Lymington, Hampshire.*
J. Oliver, *Send Court, Send, Surrey.*

P

Stephen and Ruth Paddock, *35 Wellbrooke Gardens, Chandler's Ford, Eastleigh, Hampshire.*
Mr M.L. Pearce, *"Stonegarth", 11 Cedar Court, Willow Park, Langley Park, Co. Durham.*
Mr R.G.C. Pearce, *225 Butts Road, Sholing, Southampton, Hampshire.*

R

Adrian B. Rance, *12 Raymond Road, Southampton, Hampshire.*
Anne Richardson, *61 Launcelyn Close, North Baddesley, Southampton, Hampshire.*
Mr Trevor R. Richardson, *"Pine Ridge", 188 Midanbury Lane, Bitterne Park, Southampton, Hampshire.*
Mrs E.A. Rothery, *32 Hill Place, Bursledon, Southampton, Hampshire.*

S

Mrs E.M. Salmond, *4 Latimer Court, Brookvale Road, Southampton, Hampshire.*
Alec Samuels B.A., *14 Redhill, Bassett, Southampton, Hampshire.*

# A HISTORY

OF

# SOUTHAMPTON.

# Foreword to the Second Edition

The nineteenth century saw a considerable physical and intellectual growth in the city of Southampton, part of the greater national investment of intellect in works of art, architecture and literature. This brought about increased interest and awareness of the history of the area.

One tangible outcome of this was the publication in 1883 of the Rev J. Silvester Davies' *History of Southampton*. Davies' scholarship was recognised for generations to come and his work came to be regarded as the standard history of the city. A measure of our gratitude to the scholarship of that time is the extent to which we are now prepared to perpetuate it.

It is a matter of regret to local historians that the work has been out of print for many years and copies have only rarely been available on the secondhand book market. It was, therefore, with great pleasure that I learned that a new facsimile edition was proposed under the imprint of Hampshire Books. It is particularly fitting that this publishing venture, linking the Hampshire County Council and Wheaton Publishers, is making available to a wide audience of the twentieth century the scholarship of the nineteenth century.

The reprint includes the text and illustrations of the original edition with an added list of subscribers for this new edition. Published as part of the celebrations to mark 100 years of public library service in Southampton and the 100th anniversary of County Councils, it is hoped that it will give interest and pleasure to new generations of local historians.

F. A. J. Emery-Wallis, DL FSA Hon FRIBA
The Castle, Winchester

*TO THE WORSHIPFUL*

*THE MAYOR AND THE CORPORATION*

*OF*

**The Town and County of the Town of Southampton,**

*AND TO*

*ALL WHO HAVE FORWARDED THE PUBLICATION OF THIS WORK, AND HAVE AWAITED ITS PRODUCTION WITH A KINDNESS WHICH HAS NOT BEEN TRESPASSED UPON WITHOUT CAUSE,*

**This Volume**

*IS INSCRIBED.*

*October* 1883.

## ERRATA.

Page 132, line 31, *for* " Sir Edward " *read* " Sir Edmund."

Page 166, line 34, *for* " Aulnagar " *read* " Alnager."

Page 167, line 5, *for* " Scale " *read* " Seale."

Page 168, line 11, *for* " 1665 " *read* " 1655."

Page 187, line 2, *for* " translater " *read* " translator."

Page 200, line 2, *for* " de Vans " *read* " de Vaus."

Page 253, line 33, *for* " Toway " *read* " Fowey."

Page 392, line 1, *for second word* " of " *read* " at."

# PREFACE.

—o—

During a residence of several years in the immediate neighbourhood of Southampton free access to the Town Records was given me by the courtesy of the town authorities, of which I availed myself as opportunities offered ; and towards the close of 1877 it was suggested by the present publishers that I should undertake a history of the town, or at least, on obtaining permission, should edit the MS. of Dr. Speed's History among the Southampton Archives, continuing the work, and adding such matter as should bring it into conformity with present knowledge. I accepted the latter proposal as the less ambitious task, collated Speed's documents with the originals in view of publishing the texts, but soon found that I could construct no history by a reproduction of Dr. Speed's work without going to a length beyond all warrant, though much had to be cut out as inadequate or faulty. Under these circumstances I felt myself driven to greater freedom, and in the following pages I have produced substantially a new history, while all that is valuable in Dr. Speed's work has been preserved, either in his own words, within quotation marks, or condensed and acknowledged in the notes.

Dr. Speed's general plan has been adopted. The contents of his work are as follows :—(1.) The Name. (2.) Antiquity of Town. (3.) Situation of the Town. (4.) Liberties. (5.) Fortifications. (6.) Conduits and Waterworks. (7.) Quays. (8.) Market-house and Market. (9.) Pavement. (10.) Charters. (11.) Articles and observations which could not be inserted in their proper places without interrupting the course of the charters:—Of the Mayor, Recorder, Town-Clerk, Burgesses, Honorary Burgesses. Concerning offices: Bailiff, Sheriff, Constable, Steward, Discreets of Market, Alderman of Portswood, Sergeants, Porters, Bearers. The Staple, Exemption from Prisage, Admiralty, Petty Customs, Revenues of the Corporation, Charities, Almshouses, the Free School, the Town Seal, the Common, Members of Parliament, Fairs, Present State of Corporation, the Stewes, Style of the Corporation. (12.) The Churches. (13.) Trade of the Town. (14.) Mention of Southampton in our Histories, Bevis. (15.) Religious Houses: St. Denys, Chantry of St. Mary's, Hospital of St. Julian or God's House, Friars Minor, Hospital of St. Mary Magdalene for Lepers, Chapel, Chantries. (16.) Clausentum.

Appendix A. Expenses of Law-day (14 Hen. VII.). B. Compromise with Portsmouth (24 Hen. III.). C. Pedley's Waterworks. D. Dispute with New Sarum (2 Ed. III.). E. Dispute with Justices of the County (31 Hen. VI.). F. Expulsion of James Caplen, &c., from the Corporation, 1662. G. Agreement of Inhabitants to repair Banks at Saltmarsh, 1503. H. Order of Council (Lecture at Holy Rood), 1653. I. Holmage's Obit (14 Hen. VII.). K. List of Mayors. L. Laws of Guild. M. Form of Judgment in Quo Warranto against the Town (11 Car. I.). N. Act of Parliament about Prisage (22 Hen. VIII.), 1531. O. Release of Abbey Prisage (6 Jas. I.), 1609. P. Act of Parliament, foreign bought and sold (4 Jas. I.), 1606. Q. Sweet wine grant. R. Second sweet wine grant. S. Patent determining Malaga wines to be sweet wines, &c. Charter (16 Car. I.), 1640. Book of Rates and Rolls. Index.

This Table should be compared with that of the present volume, and any reference to articles in common will show, from the method of printing or from the notes, how far I have reproduced, and in what particulars I have excluded, Dr. Speed's work. The facilities given at the present day for consulting original records, and the constant publication of such, make it imperative that our town histories, of however small pretension, shall be to a great extent works of original research.

Dr. Speed was the fourth in direct descent from John Speed the chronologer, who died July 28, 1629. John Speed, M.D., the anatomist, son of the chronologer, died in May 1640, at the early age of forty-five, leaving behind him an anatomical work, *Σκελετὸς Πολυκίνητος*, which exists in duplicate, one copy being in the possession of St. John's College, Oxford. His son, John Speed, M.D., was the author of "Batt upon Batt," and of various other pieces which have never seen the light; among them a Latin poem on his old enemy, which he entitles, 'Batteidos: Battus in Battum, Clericum Parochialem, Fabrum Cultrarium, et Poetam South Antoniensem.' He was educated at Merchant Taylors' School and St. John's College, Oxford, and was ejected from his fellowship, when B.A., by the parliamentary visitors, October 17, 1648, after which he lived with his friend, Mr. Knollys, Grove Place, Nursling, near Southampton, till the Restoration, when he was reinstated in his fellowship, and graduated M.A. 1660, B. and M.D. 1666; he had been admitted burgess of Southampton January 20, 1658-59. In 1667 he settled in the town, and practised over an extended district. Humphrey Prideaux (Letters, pp. 32, 35), writing from Oxford in 1675, speaks of him, nevertheless, as a sad toper. He tells us that on one occasion Speed had remained in the city solely for the purpose of encountering Van Tromp, the 'drunkeing greazy Dutchman,' who, after a bout of many hours, fell vanquished before Speed's greater capacity for wine and brandy. He married firstly in 1667 the widow of Rev. William Bernard (see p. 407), who dying February 1677-78, he married, in 1680, Philadelphia, daughter of Thomas Knollys, Esq. of Grove Place. He became patron of the benefice of Eling, presenting Mr. Pinhorne (pp. 313, 401) in 1689. He was twice mayor (pp. 179, 180); died September 21, 1711, in his eighty-fifth year, and was buried at Holy Rood.

John Speed, M.D., eldest son of the last, was educated at Winchester and New College; B.C.L. October 1697, M.D. 1709. He settled at Southampton in his father's lifetime, marrying at Jesus Chapel, Peartree Green, January 19, 1701–1702, Anne, daughter of James Crosse, merchant, of Southampton. He was a zealous adherent of the Stewarts, and, as his son says of him, 'a man of excellent parts, and a most desirable companion over a bottle.' This latter circumstance, however, was found to diminish his practice, in which, otherwise, he had good success. He died 28th October 1747, aged seventy-seven, and was buried at Holy Rood, where memorials exist to his father and himself.

John Speed, M.D., the historian of Southampton, and son of the last, was born September 9, 1703, educated at Merchant Taylors' and St. John's, Oxford, being elected fellow, June 11, 1722. He proceeded M.A., March 21, 1729; B.M., December 7, 1732; M.D., July 11, 1740. He settled in the town during his father's life, and married after September 2, 1741, Anna Maria Crosse, his first cousin, daughter of James Crosse, Esq., barrister-at-law, and recorder of Winchester. In August 1732 the honour of burgess-ship was offered to him and to his brother Samuel, but declined by both: the compliment being subsequently renewed to Dr. Speed and accepted, he was elected November 10, 1752, and sworn in March 19, 1754. Dr. Speed at first resided, as his father had before him, in 'the great house' (p. 355) next to Holy Rood Church, but on November 8, 1751, he obtained from the Corporation license to alienate his lease to Mr. John Monckton, surgeon; he is then said to have lived at No. 1 High Street, but certainly afterwards in his own house in St.

Lawrence's parish, where he died March 8, and was buried at Holy Rood, March 15, 1781.

Dr. Speed had a large practice; but found time to be a constant writer. His largest work is a portentous folio of 830 pages, containing about 73,416 lines, with numerous notes, entitled 'Burnettus Restitutus, or Bp. Burnett's History, in Burlesque Verse, by Ferdinand MacPherson of that Ilk:' it is a marvellous work, not without its merits. Among his performances are medical, historical, and theological tracts, sonnets, &c. Some of his satirical pieces on the local government of Southampton should be mentioned. Dr. Speed was much averse to the local Acts (see pp. 117, 120) for lighting and paving the town, and spared no pains in exposing the authors of the schemes, and ridiculing the Corporation for surrendering their rights. In his 'Curious Account of a Nondescript Species of Negroes' he attacks the lighting scheme, and describes the manners of the town—the 'nocturnal rites,' that is, the balls, the dresses of the ladies, particularly the head-dresses; these latter are said to be frequently so complicated that they 'go untouch'd for months together,' and are swarming with vermin. Another piece, 'An Account of the Ancient Town of Gotham, and of some Transactions of the so-famous Wise Men there,' lashes the Corporation and the original promoters of the paving scheme, his characters evidently portraying the leaders in town politics.

But it is time to turn to Dr. Speed's History of Southampton. It is a small folio written in a printing hand, as was very common with him, the letters having been retouched with a pen the second time, probably towards the close of the author's life. The work is itself an expansion or second edition of one presented by him to the Corporation in February 1759, entitled 'The Charter of the Town of Southampton (16 Car. I.) in Latin and English, with remarks from the Journals.' This book was ordered November 30, 1810, to be fair copied, and it was handed in on April 9, 1813. The Corporation possess this volume; it is well written, but abounds in errors of transcription. The original appears to be lost.

The 'History of Southampton,' at the death of Dr. Speed in March 1781, passed with his other books and papers into the hands of his son, John Mylles Speed, Rector of Eling, who married, September 12, 1782, Harriot, daughter of Rev. Owen Davies, M.A., Rector of Exton and Curate of St. Mary's. On the death of Mr. Speed, October 8, 1792, his books[1] and other properties passed to his widow, who, on December 11, 1793, was married to John Silvester, Esq. (created a Baronet in 1814); thus the custody of the volume fell to Mr. Silvester, and on February 28, 1794, he presented it, through Mr. Ballard, to the Corporation of Southampton. The gift was acknowledged on March 28, and on April 4th Mr. Silvester received the honour of burgess-ship.

The book has been always valued by the Corporation, and has been constantly used. It had been prepared under difficulties from the want of arrangement in the Corporation documents; an inconvenience which has attended myself from no fault of the present custodians; happily the documents are now being arranged by a competent hand under the Historical MSS. Commission.

I have little to add concerning the following work, which, as explained above, may be said to be based on that of Dr. Speed. It presents for the first time much material which has not been worked up before. At the same time I am conscious of its defects, and its omission of some branches of

[1] Among these, in addition to the books and papers mentioned above, were a MS. by the Chronologer, and a fifteenth century Chronicle, a version of the Brute, with unique additions, which had been used by Speed, and previously by Stowe. The latter portion of this MS. was edited by me for the Camden Society, under the title of 'An English Chronicle of the Reigns of Richard II., Henry IV., Henry V., and Henry VI.'

inquiry which might reasonably be expected in a larger book; but as some extenuation of the latter point I may urge that the volume has already exceeded the space proposed.

No uniform method of spelling the names of persons and places has been adopted; they appear as they are found in the various contemporary documents; any difficulty in identification will probably be removed by consulting the Index.

Southampton is rapidly increasing, and one effort of its inhabitants must be to preserve its ancient monuments in these days of movement and prosperity. The study of archæology is growing, and towns will be valued and sought, among other things, for their associations with the past and the teaching power of their remains. No plea is offered here for 'restoration' in the too common acceptance of the term, but for intelligent and scrupulous preservation, even at apparent sacrifice, of every portion of what is historical. Southampton possesses remains some of which are believed to be unique; every fragment of the western walls should be rigidly guarded. A period of danger is possibly approaching; and should mischief happen, the time of regret will most certainly occur when reparation will be impossible.

I have to thank the Town Council for their permission to use Dr. Speed's MS., and the Town-Clerk, R. S. Pearce, Esq., for his unvaried courtesy and ready assistance in the midst of labours which appear unceasing; I have also received most willing attention in the office. My thanks are also due to Charles Wooldridge, Esq., Registrar of the Diocese for Hants, for kind accommodation and facility afforded me while examining the Episcopal Registers; to J. B. Lee, Esq., Secretary to the Bishop of Winchester, for access to the Registers in London; and to F. Bowker, Esq., Registrar of the Archdeaconry of Winchester, for permission to search the books under his care. It may be thought presumption to remark on the consideration which students invariably receive in our public departments; but I cannot forbear acknowledging the unvaried kindness and assistance of the authorities at the Record Office. To others also, both in Southampton and elsewhere, my thanks are due. To some I may have given trouble, I have taken much myself; and at length am able to leave to the kind judgment of my readers this imperfect contribution to local history.

J. SILVESTER DAVIES.

ENFIELD HIGHWAY, *October* 1883.

# CONTENTS.

## CHAPTER I.

### *INTRODUCTORY.*

Pre-historic—British and Romano-British—Clausentum: its History and Remains . . . . . . . . . 1–12

## CHAPTER II.

### *THE TOWN: ITS RISE AND EARLY HISTORY.*

SECTION I.—Origin and Name of Town—Ancient Site—Removal—Historical Notices—Domesday . . . . . . 13–28
SECTION II.—The Fee-Farm . . . . . . . . 29–40

## CHAPTER III.

### *LOCAL AND DESCRIPTIVE.*

SECTION I.—Liberties or Precincts: Account of Boundaries and Encroachments . . . . . . . . 41–48
SECTION II.—The Common and Common Lands . . . . 48–51
SECTION III.—Other Common Lands: the Saltmarsh: Old Controversies: Modern Transformations . . . . . . 51–59
SECTION IV.—The Fortifications: the Walls—The Castle—The Arcade—Norman Houses—Towers—Moats—Platform—Crosshouse . . . . . . . . . . 59–111
SECTION V.—The Quays . . . . . . . . . 111–113
SECTION VI.—Conduits and Waterworks . . . . . . 114–119
SECTION VII.—Pavement, Lighting, and Watching . . . . 119–125
SECTION VIII.—Audit-house and Markets—Municipal Buildings . 125–128
SECTION IX.—The Hartley Institute . . . . . . . 128–131
SECTION X.—The Ordnance Survey Office . . . . . . 131

## CHAPTER IV.

### *MUNICIPAL.*

| | PAGE |
|---|---|
| SECTION I.—The Guild Merchant and Ordinances . . . . . | 132–151 |
| SECTION II.—The Charters . . . . . . . . . . . | 152–163 |
| SECTION III.—Municipal Offices: of the Mayor—List of Mayors, Bailiffs, and Sheriffs—Of the Recorder—List—Of the Town-Clerk—List—Of the Burgesses—Honorary Burgesses—Burgesses of Parliament—Of the Sheriff—Of the Bailiffs—Of the Steward and Treasurer—Other Officers . . | 163–218 |
| SECTION IV.—The Staple . . . . . . . . . . | 219 |
| SECTION V.—Of Exemptions from Prisage . . . . . . | 219–220 |
| SECTION VI.—Of the Admiralty Jurisdiction . . . . . . | 221–225 |
| SECTION VII.—Petty Customs—Free Towns . . . . . | 225–230 |
| SECTION VIII.—The Fairs . . . . . . . . . . | 230–233 |
| SECTION IX.—The Courts of the Town and County—Of the Town: Court Leet—Town Court—County Court—Quarter Sessions—Orphans — Admiralty — Pie-powder — Pavilion Court (Winchester) . . . . . . . . . . | 233–245 |
| SECTION X.—The Seals, Arms, Coinage, and Sir Bevois . . | 245–247 |

## CHAPTER V.

### *THE TRADE OF THE TOWN.*

| | |
|---|---|
| SECTION I.—General . . . . . . . . . . . | 248–264 |
| SECTION II.—Trade Regulations . . . . . . . . | 264–279 |
| SECTION III.—Modern Trade . . . . . . . . | 280–292 |

## CHAPTER VI.

### *CHARITIES.*

| | |
|---|---|
| SECTION I.—The Almshouses . . . . . . . . | 293–294 |
| SECTION II.—Care of the Poor . . . . . . . . | 294–300 |
| SECTION III.—Benefactions . . . . . . . . | 300–309 |
| SECTION IV.—Medical Charities . . . . . . . . | 309 |

## CHAPTER VII.

### *EDUCATIONAL.*

| | |
|---|---|
| SECTION I.—The Grammar School—West Hall . . . . . | 310–323 |
| SECTION II.—Taunton's School . . . . . . . . . | 323–325 |
| SECTION III.—Other Schools and Educational Agencies . . . | 325–327 |

## CHAPTER VIII.

### *ECCLESIASTICAL.*

PAGE
SECTION I.—The Parish Churches—St. Mary's . . . . . 328–350
Parishes from St. Mary's: Trinity—St. Luke's—Christ Church, Northam—St. James's, Bernard Street—St. Matthew's—Christ Church, Portswood—St. Denys . . . . . 350–352
Holy Rood . . . . . . . . . . . . . 353–370
St. Lawrence and St. John . . . . . . . . . 370–382
St. Michael's . . . . . . . . . . . . 382–394
All Saints . . . . . . . . . . . . 394–402
Parishes from All Saints: St. Paul's—St. Peter's . . . . 402–403
French Church . . . . . . . . . . . . 403–422
SECTION II.—Chantries . . . . . . . . . . 422–427
SECTION III.—Nonconformist Congregations or Churches: Above Bar—Albion—Kingsfield—Belvedere—East Street, Baptist—Portland—Carlton—Particular Baptists—Bible Christians—St. Andrew's Presbyterian—Society of Friends—Synagogue—East Street, Wesleyan—Bevois Town—Kingsland, Primitive Methodists—Free Church—Catholic Apostolic—Unitarian—Roman Catholic . . . . . . . . 428–433
SECTION IV.—Religious Houses: Priory of St. Denys . . . . 433–442
Convent of Friars Minor . . . . . . . . . 442–447
Hospital of St. Mary Magdalene . . . . . . . . 448–450
Hospital of St. Julian of God's-house . . . . . . . 450–463

## CHAPTER IX.

### *EVENTS TILL THE PRESENT TIMES.*

Historical Notices . . . . . . . . . . . 464–517

# A
# HISTORY OF SOUTHAMPTON.

## CHAPTER I.

### *INTRODUCTORY.*

1. *Pre-historic.*—2. *British and Romano-British.*—3. *Clausentum: Its History and Remains.*

1. TRACES of a pre-historic population occur in a district part of which is now comprised within the Borough of Southampton. A few flint implements of the usual type have been found in gravel beds, once the valley gravels of the Test and the Itchen. We may make some probable conjectures as to the habits of those who used such tools or weapons, but we can form no trustworthy calculation as to the period when they lived. Their remains have become associated with geological formations, and with changes which must have required many ages for their completion. It is more than probable that the implements which have been found in the drift in the immediate neighbourhood of Southampton were in use when the configuration of the whole district was very different. The Test and the Itchen, between which rivers our Borough is situated, are remnants of another disposition of land and water. What is now the Southampton Water was itself then a river gathering the drainage of the country and emptying it into a still larger stream. This larger stream, now represented by the Solent, flowed from the west between the coasts of Hampshire and what is now the Isle of Wight, before that island was divided from Dorsetshire by the wearing away of the chalk rocks which connected it at the Needles with the bold white cliffs of Dorset, some twenty miles to the west.[1]

It is no part of our task to follow out this interesting subject, which has reference to a time far anterior to the birth of history. Suffice

[1] See Evans's Stone Implements, pp. 543, 603, &c.; Rev. W. Fox, Geologist, v. 452; Lyell's Antiq. of Man, p. 221, &c. The museum of the Hartley Institute contains several relics of the pre-historic period.

it to say, that these changes of land and water have made for our port one of the finest harbours in England. From Calshot Castle at its entrance to Southampton, the deep-water space embraces a channel five miles in length with a depth of from five to nine fathoms for three and a half miles of that distance at low water, and a breadth of half a mile with a considerable space of shallower water on either side, the mean distance from shore to shore being about two miles. A double tide at this port—a phenomenon also observed as far apparently to the west as Portland [1]—has attracted attention since the days of Bede,[2] and has given an important natural advantage to Southampton, the second high tide occurring about two hours and a quarter after the first, the fall between the two being only about nine inches; so that practically the high water is stationary for over two hours.

2. We have no distinct evidence of there having been any settlement at or near Southampton in the times preceding the Roman occupation, but it is not unlikely. During the Roman period a native population was probably gathered on the Southampton side of the river Itchen—a Romanised British town in connection with Clausentum, on the opposite bank. There had been a tradition of Roman coins having been found at Bevois Mount; and in 1852 Roman remains were discovered in the north-east of that locality, on the high ground in front of Portswood lawn, overlooking the river; and again in the same neighbourhood in 1868. Not very far from the same site other Roman or Romano-British relics have been brought to light mingled with those of the subsequent Old English population.[3]

Clausentum.

3. We must now devote a little space to Clausentum. This Roman fortress—the name of which probably enshrines the earlier local appellation—stood upon a peninsula formed by the winding of the river Itchen, about three miles from its junction with the Southampton Water. This peninsula, which faces due west, was cut across by two parallel fosses dividing it into two islands, the westernmost of these being nearly semicircular in form, the other and larger being nearly a parallelogram. A stream of fresh water flowing from the north-east discharged itself on the shore close to the southern end of the outer fosse, and may have contributed to the water supply of the station. One of the Roman wells, not discovered till the present century, is still in use on the inner island.

The main fortress of the station was built on the westernmost island. The fortifications consisted of a strong surrounding wall with

[1] See Notes and Queries, April 23, 1881.

[2] Bede, bk. iv. c. 16.

[3] Brit. Archæolog. Journ., vol. xi. p. 338, xxiv. 399, xxii. 350.

towers at intervals; but we know nothing of the buildings within this enceinte. Outside, at the foot of the wall, remains were found some years ago of the strong wooden frame or quay work which possibly served for the Roman galleys.

The gate of the main fortress was at or near the spot where the present Northam road crosses the inner fosse. From this gate a road led with a northerly inclination across the other island and the second fosse till it struck, nearly at right angles, the road from Venta (Winchester) on the north to Porchester on the south-east. The road out of Clausentum has not been laid open, but its direction is said to be observed by the difference in the growth of the crops along its supposed course. It seems doubtful whether the parallelogram-shaped island was in any part fortified by walls or towers.

No particular attention seems to have been paid to the site till the last century. Leland[1] and Camden mention it, the first as a 'ferme placed . . . caulled Bitherne,' belonging to the Bishops of Winchester, where yet 'remayne tokens and ruines of a castelle.' Camden was shown 'some rubbish and pieces of old walls, and the trench of an ancient castle half a mile in compass,' which at full tide was 'three parts surrounded by water.'[2] These remains he supposed to be either those of Clausentum or of one of the forts which, according to Gildas, the Romans built to check the Saxon piracies. Other writers since have given a few words to Bittern, but the place attracted no attention. It was well away from any public road; and until Northam Bridge was built in 1799, was only to be approached by a solitary farm-road from Wood Mill, or by a footpath through woods and fields along the river-bank from Itchen ferry, or by crossing the river in a boat.[3]

The Rev. Richard Warner, in 1792, is generally credited with having been the first to determine the position of Clausentum.[4] It is however certain that he was indebted to the labours of Dr. Speed, who had died in 1781, and whose work Warner had evidently used in every particular regarding Clausentum, without a word of acknowledgment.[5]

Clausentum is only known through the Antonine Itinerary, the date of which work may be about A.D. 320. From the probability of the case we should suppose this fortress on the Itchen to have been

[1] Itinerary, vol. iv. p. 21.

[2] Gibson's Camden's Britannia, i. p. 35.

[3] Buller's Englefield's Walk through Southampton, pp. 63, 64.

[4] Attempt to Ascertain the Situation of the Ancient Clausentum, 1792. In his preface of August 1, 1792, he states his discovery to have been just made.

[5] We have thought it necessary to reproduce but a small portion of Dr. Speed's chapter on Clausentum, or the indebtedness of Warner would be made manifest.

erected at the very earliest period at which the Romans effected a settlement, and wanted a safe water-way to Venta (Winchester); but the reduction of this neighbourhood was among the earliest of the Roman conquests in Britain. Dr. Speed, besides the probability of the case, has drawn an argument in favour of an early date for Clausentum from the *freshness* of large numbers of coins of the first period discovered on the spot. He says, "I have myself had from "thence the coins of Claudius, Nero, Vespasian, Sabina, Antoninus, "Commodus, Lucilla, Alexander Severus, Constantius, Constans, "Carausius, Aurelianus, Valentinianus, and Valens, which compre-"hend pretty nearly the whole time that the Romans were masters "of Britain." Hoards of coins, he observes, generally contain those only of a few emperors who lived near each other's times, and whose coins might well be current together. And from the finds of Claudius and other emperors of the earliest occupation containing many specimens of fresh money he infers the early existence of the settlement here.

As to inscriptions, he says, "I never could hear of any, great part "of the old buildings having been long ago taken down by Mr. "Mylles, the owner, under the Bishop of Winchester, to build a house[1] "and chapel upon another part of his estate, called Peartree, about a "mile distant from it."

Dr. Speed finishes his chapter on Clausentum by producing the Itinerary ascribed to Antoninus, the seventh Iter of which stands as follows, and by its general measurement points to Bittern as Clausentum:[2]—

"Iter a Regno Londinium, MP. XCVI. sic:
Clausentum, MP. XX.
Ventam Belgarum, MP. X.
Callevam Atrebatum, MP. XXII.
Pontes, MP. XXII.
Londinium, MP. XXII."

[1] Peartree House, afterwards inhabited by Captain Richard Smith, the builder of Peartree Green Church.

[2] Dr. Speed's text of the Iter is given, which is that of Surita, though it may not be considered the best reading now: no difference occurs in the distances from that of Wesseling. There is, however, a great variation as to the interpretation of the places at the present day. Dr. Speed followed the view of his time, and made Regnum, *Ringwood*, Calleva, *Wallingford*, Pontes, *Colebrook*. (See also Burton's Antoninus's Itinerary, pp. 217–225.) At the present time it is received that Regnum is *Chichester*, Calleva, *Silchester*, Pontes, *Staines*. Mr. Roach Smith has suggested that the figure opposite Clausentum was probably xxx. miles, the required distance from *Chichester*. Mr. Gordon M. Hills has lately attempted to reconstruct the Roman geography of South Britain, under whom Chichester becomes *Clausentum*, Havant, *Venta*, and the Bittern station, *Sorbiodunum*. (See Journal of Brit. Archæol. Assoc., Sept. 1878.)

From Dr. Speed's account we gather something of the condition of the fortress in the last century, though it is difficult from his description to say how much was Roman, how much medieval.

Remains about 1770.

" On the inner bank of this [westernmost or inner] ditch, towards " the north end of it, there is still standing an old stone building, now " converted into a barn, but which appears to me to have been part " of the old Roman fort, for in the upper part of the wall next the " ditch are slits to shoot arrows through, and within the barn are " plain marks of there having been a floor at such a height that men " standing upon it might conveniently shoot arrows through the slits. " At the north end of the barn are still to be seen some remains of the " foundation of the old wall of the fort, about four feet in thickness. At " the other end of the barn, adjoining to it, are the remains of a stone " gateway which consisted of two arches, one within the other, and " was, I suppose, the entrance into the fort by means of a drawbridge " over the ditch. There was a room over this gateway, for at that end " of the barn there is a door-case that leads to the top of the gate. " Within this barn is another old stone building, now a stable and " cart-house which reaches to the outside wall, next the river on the " east side, and on that side it has an arched window and slit like " those in the barn on each side of the window. From this building " there goes a wall to a square tower, still of some height, to the top of " which there is a stone staircase out of one of the upper rooms of the " manor-house which joins to it. At the bottom of this tower is a door- " case open to the shore from a small room, where perhaps a centinel " was placed to observe any signals that might be made from Bevois " Hill. Near this tower there still remain foundations of flint for a " considerable space, and many fragments of the same appear all round " the ground within the inner ditch, and on the bank of that ditch. " But many of the materials were removed in Queen Elizabeth's time " to build a house and chapel on another part of the owner's estate.[1]

" On the opposite side of the river southward is the place which " Bishop Gibson mentions in his additions to Mr. Camden to have " been converted into a dock for building men-of-war, and where he " says a gold coin had been then lately found. It is now called " Northam, and was probably a branch of Clausentum, for the channel " of the river runs so close under the shore here, that ships could " not pass up without being assailed from hence.

[1] See a previous note. Bishop Montague's license to Captain Smith of Peartree for enclosing ground on Ridgeway Heath for the purpose of a chapel and burial-ground bears date February 23, 1617–18. The consecration of the chapel and cemetery by Bishop Andrews took place on Sunday, September 17, 1620. The *house* may have been built in Queen Elizabeth's time.

" Opposite to Bittern, on the west side across the river, is a hill " called Bevois Hill, from a legendary tradition that Bevois of South- " ampton lies buried under it. It is now part of the beautiful gardens " made by the late Earl of Peterborough. Where the summer-house " now stands was a barrow, and in digging the foundation of the sum- " mer-house a human skeleton with bones of a large size was found; " but the compass of the foundation reaching no higher than the middle " of the thigh-bone, no search was made for the rest of the skeleton.

" The top of this hill was used to be ploughed, and I have heard " that Roman coins have been found there. The side of the hill next " the shore is very steep, and has a wet ditch at the bottom of it. I " suppose this hill to have been the *castrum exploratorum* or scout " watch to the station, and that the whole comprehended Bittern as " the principal fort, another fort at Northam, and this hill. And the " communication was easy, for about forty years ago a very old person, " being on evidence upon a trial, made oath that within his memory " the river had been fordable over against Bittern towards Bevois " Hill."

Englefield's discoveries.

It was at the beginning of the present century that the greatest light was thrown upon Clausentum by the investigations of Sir Henry Englefield, who had great facilities put in his way. That diligent antiquary left no stone unturned which might possibly have a history to divulge.[1] The remains discovered by him consisted of architectural fragments, some important inscriptions, fragments of Roman pavement and of Samian and coarser ware, some glass specimens, with a few other relics and coins, mostly of the Lower Empire. He also traced out the whole of the ancient wall, which was about nine feet thick and of the usual construction: it was, however, singular, though not unique, in having no foundation whatever, its base being protected by an earthen rampart.

The following inscriptions have been found at Bittern Manor:[2]—

I. *Gordian the younger*, A.D. 238–244.

| | |
|---|---|
| IMP C M | To the Emperor Cæsar Marcus |
| ANT GOR | Antonius Gor- |
| DIANO | -dianus, |
| PF AVG | the pious, the fortunate, the Augustus. |
| RP BI | (?) |

[1] Walk through Southampton, 1st ed. 1801, 2d ed. 1805; Bullar's ed. of Englefield's Walk, with Notes, 1841. See also Duthie's Sketches of Hampshire, pp. 417–421 (1839).

[2] See Mr. Roach Smith's paper in Winchester volume of Brit. Archæol. Assoc., 1845, pp. 163–170.

2. *Gallus and Volusian*, A.D. 252–254.

| | |
|---|---|
| IMPP CC | To the Emperors Cæsars |
| GALLO | Gallus |
| ET VOLVSI | and Volusi- |
| ANO AVG | -anus, the Augusti. |
| G | |

3. *Tetricus*,[1] A.D. 267–272.

| | |
|---|---|
| M C E S | To the Emperor Caius Es- |
| SVVIO | -suvius |
| TETRIC | Tetric- |
| VS PFAV | -us, the pious, the fortunate, the Augustus. |

4. *Tetricus.*[2]

| | |
|---|---|
| MP CA | To the Emperor Cæsar |
| CAESVIO | Caius Æsuvius |
| TETRICO | Tetricus, |
| PET AVG | the pious and the Augustus. |

5. *Tetricus the younger.*[3]

| | |
|---|---|
| IMP CC | To the Emperor Cæsar Caius |
| PIO ESVIO | Pius Esuvius |
| TETRICO | Tetricus, |
| PFAG | the pious, the fortunate, the Augustus. |

6. *Aurelian*, A.D. 270–275.

| | |
|---|---|
| IMP CAES LV | To the Emperor Cæsar Lu- |
| CIO DOMI | -cius Domi- |
| TIO AVRELIANO | tius Aurelianus. |

7. *To Ancasta*,[4] *a local divinity.*

| | |
|---|---|
| DEAE | To the Goddess |
| ANCA | Anca- |
| STA G | -sta G- |
| EMINV | -eminu- |
| S MANTI | -s Manti- |
| VS LM | -us [performs a vow] willingly, deservedly. |

8. *A defaced portion of a miliary column, now lost. No reading has been hazarded.*[5]

---

[1] The bad grammar on this stone will be observed. At the Numismatic Society in October 1875 a Gaulish coin was exhibited inscribed Esuios, a form of Esuvius, as in above inscriptions.

[2] See Archæologia, vol. xxix. 257.

[3] A miliary stone to Tetricus the younger, who was associated with his father as the Cæsar, has been discovered by M. Mowat of Rennes, and deposited by him in the museum of that place. He reads it thus, as given in a letter to Mr. Macnaghten, 'Caio Pio Esuvio Tetrico Nobilissimo Cæsari Civitas Redonum.'

[4] Of these inscriptions, Nos. 1, 2, 4, 6, 7, 8, were described by Englefield; Nos. 3, 5, and 7 are still preserved at Bittern Manor with other remains; the rest of the inscriptions are lost.

[5] Mr. Roach Smith thinks it may have had reference to the rebuilding some portion of the wall.

It will be seen that the inscriptions, as far as they can be assigned to a date, belong to the third century. The stones themselves, that is, such of them as are preserved at Bittern Manor, appear to have been quarried in the Isle of Wight, and the same has been observed of other stone about the place. The use of this stone would only show that the Romans had already subdued and were working quarries in the island when Clausentum was built; but the island was reduced by Vespasian in the middle of the first century.

History from the inscriptions.

We now turn to the period marked out by the inscriptions. That dedicated to the unfortunate young Emperor Gordian stands out simply as a relic of lost history, the affairs of Britain at this time being unrecorded by the ancient historians. The same may be said of the next inscription, that to Gallus and Volusian, father and son. This absence of record is sometimes taken to import a season of peacefulness and prosperity in Britain. But the inscriptions to Tetricus introduce us to another order of affairs, in which we find Britain wrested away from the imperial government, and its throne held by a series of usurpers. Tetricus, proclaimed emperor by the legions of Gaul with his son Tetricus as Cæsar, under the influence of Victoria the Augusta, reigned over Gaul and Britain some five years, a slave to those who had placed him on the throne. Able to bear this position no longer, he sought deliverance at the hands of the lawful emperor, Aurelian, against whom he was a rebel, imploring that victorious monarch in a secret letter to 'deliver him from his enemies.' He then feigned the appearance of war, led his troops against Aurelian, but in truth betrayed them, and himself deserted to the Emperor's camp. This was in 272. Two years after Tetricus and his son graced the triumph of Aurelian on his return to Rome, but subsequently were admitted to his friendship and advanced to wealth and dignity.[1] It seems likely, from the occurrence of these memorials to Tetricus at Bittern, that Clausentum was his chief station in this country.[2] Coins of Tetricus have been found in abundance there.

With the fall of Tetricus, Britain again passed under the Roman power, which remained undisputed for a short period. After the murder of Aurelian in 275, Roman affairs under Tacitus, Probus, Carus, and Carinus call for no special notice. Dioclesian succeeded to the imperial people in 284, and now again a rival empire became established in Britain. Carausius, a citizen of Menapia of singular ability and cunning, had been intrusted by Maximian, the associate of

[1] It is supposed that the memorials to Tetricus escaped the usual fate of those of conquered rebels by the special favour of Aurelian.

[2] See Wright's Celts, &c., pp. 138, 422.

Dioclesian, with the command of a fleet for protecting the British shores against Francs and Saxons;[1] but his honesty and fidelity becoming suspected, Maximian sent an order for his death. Carausius, however, who had acquired much wealth, for little of what he rescued from marauders had found its way to the imperial treasuries, bought over the forces, seized Gessoriacum (Boulogne), the chief station of the fleet, assumed the purple, and wrested Britain from the empire. This was in 287. The loss of Britain was deeply felt, but after vain attempts to overthrow the usurper, peace was made with him, and he has commemorated the event on some of his coins, the heads of Dioclesian, Maximian, and himself appearing surrounded by such legends as 'The peace of the Augusti,' 'Carausius and his brethren.' The coinage of Carausius has been found in great plenty at Bittern. He is believed indeed to have had a mint at Clausentum,[2] which may have always been one of his chief stations. He was slain at York in 294, by the treachery of his friend and minister Allectus, who succeeded him and held Britain for two years.

During this time Constantius Chlorus was preparing for the invasion of Britain. When all was ready, he divided his fleet into two squadrons, himself holding command of one at Boulogne, and intrusting the other at the mouth of the Seine to Asclepiodotus. The fleet of Allectus was riding off the Isle of Wight when the squadron of Asclepiodotus passed unnoticed in murky weather, and landed its troops upon the British shore. Allectus, who was awaiting Constantius in a different quarter, hastened to meet this unexpected foe. We do not know exactly where the battle was fought, but in it Allectus fell, and Britain passed again under the Roman power, A.D. 296. Coins of Allectus, with what is supposed to be the Clausentum mint mark,[3] have been found in some number at Bittern.

Reconstruction of the fortress.

No other historical events in any way connected with Clausentum have come down to us. The dates of the inscriptions carry us to about the end of the third century, after which it would seem there was some reconstruction of the fortress, fragments of ancient buildings and stones which before had occupied places of greater honour being worked into the wall; for in such a position Sir Henry Englefield found several, and apparently some of the above inscriptions. This rebuilding or strengthening of the fortress may have occurred in the latter

[1] Eutrop. ix. 21; Aurel. Victor de Cæsaribus, xxxix. 20, 21, 39.

[2] Wright's Celts, &c., pp. 140, 141; Akerman's Coins of the Romans relating to Britain, pp. 121, 136.

[3] Such as C (Clausenti), MC (Moneta Clausenti), SC (Signata Clausenti), MSC (Moneta signata Clausenti), SPC (Signata pecunia Clausenti). See Wright's Celts, &c., p. 431.

part of the fourth century, when the southern coasts were suffering more and more from Franc and Saxon depredations: it may have been after Theodosius had restored security to Britain for the time against Picts, Scots, and Saxons, and had seen generally to frontier walls and fortifications. Thus the date would be about A.D. 370.

Clausentum is not mentioned in the subsequent Notitia Imperii[1] as among the stations of the Count of the Saxon Shore, the westernmost of which was at Portus Adurni,—the mouth of the Adur in Sussex, probably at Bramber, some little way up the river, the outlet of which was broader in former times. Though the strengthening of the fortress may have been owing to the causes which had called into existence the Count of the Saxon Shore, whose duty it was to keep in check the invaders, yet it was apparently outside his jurisdiction, which did not stretch beyond our county of Sussex.

**Its subsequent fortunes.**

We may conclude that the Romans kept up the fortress till they left our land about 411; after which it may be taken for granted that it was occupied by the native Britons, though but for a short period. In little more than a century another kingdom—that of the West Saxons—was set up in these parts; and the old Roman fortress and town, possibly destroyed in some of the harrying raids of that period, may have been left under its new lords to ruin and desolation.

We next find it, after a great interval, under the name of Bittern, as an appendage of the See of Winchester, and in June 1284 the men of the Bishop's manors of Bitterne, Falele (Fawley), Ore (Ower), and Stoneham were permitted by royal license to answer with the Bishop's hundred of Wautham (Waltham).[2] In the middle ages it was a favourite manor and residence of the bishops. In 1286 we find Bishop Pontissara issuing mandates from 'Byterne;' Bishop Woodlock held ordinations in the chapel of the manor-house in July 1305, and again in August 1306 and April 1308. On the entrance of this Bishop the necessary repairs upon the house were put at £100, those upon the mills, &c., at £30. The appointments of bailiffs constantly occur, similar appointments having been made till the changes of a few years ago. The earliest extant seems to be that of Bishop Woodlock on his coming to the See, when he wrote to the bailiff and his men of Bytterne to receive Thomas le Eyr for his bailiff and to attend to him. These

[1] Date of this is the end of fourth or beginning of fifth century. The authority of the Count was confined to the counties of Norfolk, Suffolk, Essex, Kent, and Sussex; his stations and troops being settled at Branodunum (Brancaster), Garriannonum (Burgh), Othona (on the Blackwater, now covered by the sea), Regulbium (Reculver), Rutupiæ (Richborough), Dubris (Dover), Portus Lemanis (Lymne), Anderida (Pevensey), Portus Adurni (mouth of the Adur).

[2] Pat. 12 Ed. I. m. 11.

commissions, frequently issued in favour of the Bishop's valet (valectum nostrum) for good conduct, need not be further mentioned.

Bishop Fox let the place with the pasture called 'Bytterne Parke' for thirty-one years to John Tanner otherwise Mason of Weston, husbandman, for the yearly rent of £13, 13s. 4d. from Michaelmas 1520, Mason covenanting to keep in repair the house, with all the walls, ditches, gates, &c.[1] From this period Bittern may have ceased to be a residence of the bishops. In September 1551 it was alienated[2] by Bishop Poynet to Edward VI., together with the manors of Merdon, Twyford, Marwell, Waltham, and various other possessions, which were all restored to the See by Queen Mary[3] under Bishop Gardiner in 1553. Plundered from the See by the Commonwealth, it was sold[4] in June 1649 to John Barkstead, Esq., for £1716, 6s. 8d., and again restored in 1660. It does not appear when the possession of the manor-house (the old fortress) was separated from that of the manor. The latter continued to be held directly by the bishops till the death of Bishop Sumner, after which it passed to the Ecclesiastical Commissioners, while the manor-house has been for many years in private hands, its present proprietor being Steuart Macnaghten, Esq. Before taking leave of Clausentum or Bittern, it may be well to notice the changes which have occurred there since the time of Sir Henry Englefield. When he wrote, part of the gateway and the 'barn' spoken of by Dr. Speed were existing; but these buildings were demolished at the commencement of the present century.[5]

The manor-house was in Englefield's time a farm residence, which he describes as built into the remains of a 'stately Norman edifice.' Much of the history of the building is now totally covered from the eye, as necessarily in the case of a modern dwelling-house, but in the basement may still be seen eleventh-century work, if not that of an earlier period. One of the chambers in the first storey retains an ambry of the fourteenth or fifteenth century: there is also early medieval work immediately behind the new drawing-room, generally supposed to be some remains of the chapel.

A fragment of the Roman surrounding wall still exists at a little distance beyond the west end of the house. In Englefield's days there

[1] Reg. Pontiss, f. 5, &c.; Woodlock, f. 2, 10 † b., &c., 307 b., 311 b., 316; Fox, iv. f. 56 b.

[2] Records in Collier's Hist., No. lxvii.

[3] See in Milner, i. 271.

[4] See Doc. in Gale's Hist., p. 21; Winchester vol. Brit. Arch. Assoc. (1845), p. 47.

[5] They were medieval or medievalised. A drawing of one of the windows is given in the Hants Repository, vol. ii. plate iv.

were considerable remains of this fortification. But about the time that Northam Bridge and the new road were in construction, Clausentum was also undergoing reconstruction at the hands of its then proprietor. Every fragment of stone that could be utilised was turned to account,[1] walls were rooted out, aggers levelled to improve a kitchen garden and enrich a pasture. Little, in fact, was left but what could not well be destroyed. At the present day we have to lament the loss of five out of the eight inscriptions found on the spot.

It only remains to notice the alterations which have occurred in the ancient landmarks of Clausentum by the addition of soil reclaimed from the river. In Englefield's time, and for many years after, the boundaries remained as in the Roman period, and the tide washed nearly to the foot of the old manor-house and the fragments of the ancient walls.

The first alteration was effected by reclaiming a large portion of land on the north side, extending from the outer fosse to a point westward, nearly opposite what was then the island.

A further alteration has been made within the last few years by taking in a still larger portion of mud-land. Starting from or near the point just mentioned, the island itself has been included in the mainland, which now is extended towards a point near the foot of Northam Bridge.

It is necessary to bear in mind these alterations in any examination of the spot. A round tower, built a few years ago, marks the site of the island; while the old Roman boundary of the station is to be traced by the sudden fall of the land from the more ancient level to that of the soil reclaimed. On the east side of Northam Bridge the old coast-line is still preserved.[2]

---

1 See Duthy, p. 420.

2 A large number of Roman coins and some other relics found on the spot are preserved at Bittern Manor by Steuart Macnaghten, Esq., the owner of the estate, to whose courtesy archæologists visiting Southampton have been so constantly indebted.

# CHAPTER II.

## *THE TOWN: ITS RISE AND EARLY HISTORY.*

### SECTION I.

1. *Origin and Name of Town.*—2. *Ancient Site.*—3. *Removal.*—4. *Historical Notices.*—5. *Domesday.*

WITH the fall of the Roman power in Britain we lose the guidance of their writers, and the general history of our land passes through a semi-mythic period with the barbarian invaders: we take up our story where we can begin to deal with certainties.

1. "Cerdic and Cynric, his son, the founders of the West Saxon "kingdom, landed somewhere in this neighbourhood;" and the kingdom being founded in 519, after the battle of Cerdices-ford or Charford, near Breamore, Winchester was secured as the key to the old Roman roads; but it seems not improbable that Hampton, our town, was the earliest home of the invaders, and remained for some time the base of their work. Doubtless from this port the conquest of the Isle of Wight was undertaken in 530 by the West Saxons in conjunction with their Jutish allies, who thenceforth became settled in the island, and who probably at that period were admitted to occupy, as their descendants did in Bede's time, a little portion of West Saxon territory [1] opposite the Isle of Wight.

**Existence of town involved in name of shire.**

No distinct mention of the town occurs till the ninth century, but we meet with the name of the *shire*, which was derived from that of the town. Thus, to lay no stress on a doubtful writing of Cædwealha of Wessex, A.D. 680, in which mention is made of the 'territory of Heantun,' the name of Hamtun-scire occurs in the English Chronicle under 755, when Cynewulf and the West Saxon Witan deprived Sigebryht of his kingdom except Hamtun-scire. But the town must have had importance before it could give its name to the shire, and this was probably early. The recovery of Winchester after the

---

1 The places Meonstoke and East and West Meon preserve a memory of the settlement of the Jutish Meonwara. See Green's Making of England, 89. It was called 'the province of Meonwara, in the nation of the West Saxons,' and went in a grant with the Isle of Wight from Wulfere to Ædilwalch. Ibid. 90 and ref.

destruction of its civilisation by Cerdic was a matter of time; and though it became the residence of kings and the seat of a bishopric, still the 'home-town' of the conquerors by the sea was their own creation, and retained sufficient hold early in the West Saxon monarchy to give its name to the district before the great rise of the royal and episcopal city. The name continues as Hamtun-scire till about the middle of the tenth century, when the prefix *south* appears. We then begin to read of *Suthamtonia* and *Suthamtunensis provincia* and *Suthhamton-scire,* as well as the older form.[1] In Domesday the name is *Hantescire;* and from this probably the modern appellation of *Hants* is derived.

The name of the town thus passed on to the shire in the above forms was *Hám-tún,* a name purely English. *Hám* is the word *home,* and *tún* means an enclosure, a combination of which we have so many examples, blending the happy ideas of home and security. In relation to this Hamtun, the chief settlement, there was a 'home' a little to the north belonging to later times—the suburb we know as Northam.

The name of Hamtun or Hamtune first occurs under 837 in the English Chronicle. Æthelwulf of Wessex in 840 dates from the royal vill of Hamtun; and we get variations of this, such as Hamtone, Haamtun, Heantun, till the above-mentioned period, the middle of the tenth century, when the prefix *South* is met with. Thus in 962 the royal dues of *Suth-hamtune* were granted by King Eadgar, with other possessions, to the monastery of Abingdon, which he had restored. From this time the name of *Suthamtun* and its Latinised forms become very frequent, though by no means to the exclusion of the earlier, which still remained the common use. Thus in 1045 we read *Heantun* in a grant of the Confessor to Bishop Ælfwin; and in another gift from the same king to the same bishop, and dated in the same year, there is mention of the haye at *Hamtune,* that is, the hedge or enclosure at or near the town's limits.[2]

Judging, therefore, from the probabilities of the case and the evidence before us, as far as it goes, we conclude that the rise of the town was early in the English settlement; that here the conquerors first formed their hám-tún, which gave its name to the district round when it became necessary to distinguish it from other West Saxon principalities;[3] that in the tenth century the town became known as

[1] For numerous examples of all the above forms, see documents in Kemble's Codex Diplomat. Ævi Saxonici, the English Chronicle, Ethelwerd, Florence of Worcester, &c.

[2] For documents see Codex Diplomaticus.

[3] See Freeman (Norm. Conquest, i. 49), who suggests that the capital city may have been kept distinct from the shire.

Suth-hamtun, the prefix being added to distinguish it from other localities similarly named, and especially from the Hám-tún in Mercia (Northampton) after the annexation of that kingdom to Wessex in 920; that the change of the shire-name followed that of the town, though in each case the original appellation continued to be the one most frequently used.

2. We may now pass to the site of the town. Leland,[1] who presented his Itinerary to Henry VIII. in 1546, heard on his visit to Southampton that the town did not originally stand where it now does, but in the immediate neighbourhood of St. Mary's Church, some quarter of a mile or more to the north-east of the walled town, whence it stretched away to the river-side. Camden, the first edition of whose work appeared in 1586, heard the same account; and excavations made within the last forty-five years go to prove that these illustrious antiquaries had *so far* accepted and have handed down a true tradition. Old site.

In 1839 digging for clay was commenced in a field of eight acres in the parish of St. Mary, north-eastward of the town and extending towards the Itchen. The field had been hitherto used as arable and garden ground, and is now built over. It was found that the ground had been perforated over all its surface with large pits, over which there lay an accumulation of recent soil about two feet thick. Clay had been originally dug from these pits, which had been afterwards filled with all sorts of rubbish, amongst which were found the bones and teeth of various animals, such as deer, oxen, horses, sheep, pigs; there were boars' tusks, oyster shells, fish and fowl bones, &c. The bones were in such quantity that the labourers collected and sold them to the bone dealers in the neighbourhood, at the rate of twopence for a ballast basketful, containing about ten gallons. In two days,[2] a quantity sufficient to produce twenty-four shillings was obtained, so that one man of the party was afterwards employed to collect the bones and sell them for the benefit of the other labourers, and frequently got fifteen

[1] 'The Town of Old-Hampton, a celebrate Thing for Fisschar Men and sum Merchauntes, stoode a Quater of a Mile or ther above from New-Hampton by North Est and streachyd to the Haven syde. The Plotte wheryn it stoode berith now good corn and gresse, and is namyid S. Maryfeld by the chirch of S. Mary stonding hard by it.

'Sum Men yet alyve have seene dyvers Houses (especially up into the Lande of Old-Hampton) withyn the Feld self now caullyd S. Maryfeeld. Some thinke that the greate Suburbe standing a litle without the Est Gate of New-Hampton and joyning to S. Mariefeld was parte of Old-Hamptoun.'—*Itin.*, iii. 105.

[2] The late J. R. Keele, Esq., to whom we are indebted for the narration of these and similar discoveries; Collectanea Antiqua, vol. iv. (1857), pp. 58–62 and plates. See also Mr. Atherley's communication to Brit. Archæol. Journal, vol. v. (1850), p. 162.

shillings a week for his share. It was thought that at the end of 1849 fifty tons of bones had been obtained from these pits.

Quantities of old English coins were found in these investigations. There were sceattas of different types, pennies of Offa (Mercia), 757–796; Coenwulf (Mercia), 796–819; Ecbeorht, 800–836; Burgred, (Mercia), 852–874; Ceolwulf (Mercia), 874–877; Plegmund, Abp., 890–915; Ælfred, 871–901; Eadward the elder, 901–924; Æthelstan, 924–941; Eadmund, 941–946; Eadred, 946–955; Eadgar, 959–975; Æthelred, 978–1016. Coins of the above dates, and others which could not be read, were found while preparing for the foundations of the prison erected in the same field. Besides the pits above spoken of, *wells*, said to have been for water, were also observed; they had been sunk to a greater depth than the pits, and were filled with bones and rubbish.[1]

It appears that in digging out the clay the labourers came to as many as six or eight intersecting streets from twenty to thirty feet wide, the hard surface of the streets resting on the undisturbed clay.

In laying the foundation of Grove Street, immediately to the south of the field just spoken of, a large number of human bones were discovered; and in one of the graves a curious green glass vase, still preserved. This spot is believed to have been an early burial-ground of the settlement; the green vase, which was lying on the face of a skull, and some other objects discovered, belonging to a remote period.

Among the relics found in the rubbish-pits were several iron and bronze keys, and metal pins with ornamental heads. The bulk of the remains, including two spoons and one spoon and fork, were believed to range from the eighth to the tenth centuries. The household implements thus brought to light are examples of which few have been discovered of so early a date. The combination of spoon and fork in one implement is very rare, and may be compared with an example in the Londesborough Collection, which was found in Wiltshire together with coins of the eighth and ninth centuries.[2]

In March 1856 a similar discovery of bone-pits was made on the site of what is now called the Edinburgh Hotel in St. Mary's Road, about 150 yards from the pits described above, and forming a continuation of them. They were rectangular, from six to eight feet long, from four to six feet broad, and from six to seven and a half feet deep, though the depth was not always ascertained; above them the surface ground was about two feet in thickness. On examination the bones were found to be of a similar character to those in the other pits. There were also fragments of bricks and tiles which had been perforated by tubular

[1] Brit. Archæolog. Journal, vol. xx. pp. 68–73.
[2] Archæologia, vol. xxvii. pl. xxiv.

holes about an inch in diameter, and some pieces of Anglo-Saxon, that is, Old English pottery.[1] In December 1859 opportunity was afforded for examining the ground immediately above the inn just mentioned. Owing to the elevation of the road in front of the site, it was not necessary to excavate to any depth for building purposes, but enough surface ground was cleared away to discover the mouths of various pits, which, as far as they were entered, contained similar collections of bones to those previously found. There were also obtained from these pits two Roman coins, one of Constantine I., the other of Constantine II., and another penny of Offa. To these coins may be added a penny of Ceolnoth, Archbishop of Canterbury (830–871), found in the same locality; another of Burgred, one of Æthelbearht, and one of Ecgberht, son of Offa (796).

Subsequently to this, namely, in 1864 and 1866, further discoveries of bone-pits were made in the same locality, and in excavations prepared for the new streets on land to the east side of St. Mary's Road, belonging to Queen's College, Oxford, and long occupied as a market-garden; no coins were observed, but bones as before, and some Romano-British and Old English relics.[2] Besides the coins mentioned above, there have been found in the same neighbourhood a penny of Cuthred (Kent), 796–805; one of Æthelbearht, 860–866; one of Eadward the Confessor, 1042–1066; two of Charlemagne, 800; one of an uncertain Archbishop of Canterbury, bearing on the obverse 'Dorobernia civitas,' and on the reverse 'Luning moneta;' and in addition to these several coins of the post-Conquest kings.[3]

The evidence from these discoveries goes to prove the existence of an ancient town in the north and north-eastern districts of modern Southampton: on the other hand, the absence of such remains within the walls affords negative evidence as to there having been any settlement on the site of the medieval town. We are thus enabled to verify the old tradition of Hampton having been removed at some period to its present site within the walls.

**When was the town removed to its present site?**

3. The received tradition associates this removal with the burning of the town under Edward III. Thus Leland,[4] who represents the talk of his time: 'The old town of Hampton was brent in tyme of warre, spoyled and rasyd by French pyrates. This was the cause that the

[1] The late Rev. E. Kell in Brit. Archæolog. Journal, vol. xiii. (1857), pp. 207–210.

[2] Id., vol. xvi. (1860), p. 333; xvii. (1861), p. 231; xx. (1864), pp. 68–73; xxii. (1866), p. 455.

[3] Most of the above-mentioned coins were in the collection of the late Captain Bradby, R.N. Casts of several of them are in the Hartley Museum.

[4] Itin., iii. 106.

inhabitantes there translatid themself to a more commodious place and began with the kinges Licens and Help to build New-Hampton and to walle yt yn defence of the enemies.' The tradition may embrace an element of truth as to the cause of removal being invasion and spoliation, but the ravages were those of Danish, not French invaders.

The recollection of past weakness, and the knowledge that hard by existed a spot more capable of defence for the future, may have caused the migration from the old to the new site in the settled times of good King Cnut the Dane, whose memory has always been associated with the town. To the west and south-west there was ground on a slight elevation as compared with the level of the ancient occupation, which was scarcely above high-water mark; and towards the north-west portion of the area selected the ground reached its greatest altitude, offering the fitting centre for defence. On this elevation, easily adapted to warlike requirements, fortifications were constructed, under the shadow of which the new town grew up. No traces of these ancient works remain; but the stately keep of the Norman castle, the site of which is accurately known, must have been a replacement of the earlier fortress. The removal of the town, then, probably took place early in the eleventh century, or before the death of Cnut in 1035. By the end of that century we have evidence that the town was on its present site; and the remains of the population, described above, would seem to indicate an occupation in the ancient locality till about the period suggested. There is every probability that a large space of land was included in the ancient tún-scipe; and it seems likely that we have a remnant of the ancient relation between Old and New Hampton in the traditionary ecclesiastical connection between the churches of the borough. There has long been a doubtfulness as to the connection of St. Mary's with the other parishes of the town. Leland distinctly affirmed it to be the mother church, and this Dr. Speed denied.[1] But Leland was right and Speed wrong, for there is direct evidence of this relation, as will be seen farther on.

The tún-scipe was the sphere of the parish priest; and it is suggested that the sites of Old and New Hampton were both parts of the same civil and ecclesiastical township or parish; that when the town clustered for shelter near the newly erected fortification, no change was made in this relation; that St. Mary's occupies the site of the original ecclesiastical establishment for the whole neighbourhood, and is a witness to a history before the present town grew up.

---

[1] See under St. Mary's.

We have only general information to guide us as to the construction of the town in its earliest days. Stretching along the bank of the Itchen and inland, including perhaps the modern St. Matthew's Church on the north, and certainly St. Mary's on the south, near which was the cemetery of the settlement, we may see a wooden-built town or *home*—such was usual, the very word for *build* being *timbrian*, to construct of *timbor* (timber)—surrounded by its enclosure or *tun*, that is, a rampart of earth with a wooden stockade, the entrance through which was the géat or gate, outside all being a ditch. And when the town moved along to its new site, the general features were reproduced, excepting that possibly stone began to replace wood in some of the more prominent defences, as befitting the dignity of a place which had now become a burh or borough, as we shall see. A gerefa or reeve in the early times, who differed little from the steward of a manor, was the head of the community, and served for civil affairs on the part of the royal lord—our town being always the king's town or borough, and held directly from him, as the parish priest served in matters ecclesiastical. The town.

4. No earlier mention of the town occurs[1] than under 837, when a large force of Danes landed at Hampton from thirty-five ships, but were repulsed with great slaughter by the shire ruler, the Ealdorman Wulfheard.[2] Historical notices.

Upon the death of Æthelbald in 860, the Danes again landed at Hampton, and pressed on to Winchester, which they sacked; but on their return with the spoil, were met by Osric and Æthelwulf, Ealdormen of Hampshire, and Berkshire, and defeated with great loss. The remnant got to their ships and went into winter quarters in the Isle of Thanet.[3]

The next notice is of a more peaceful character. The town is classed 'with other burhs,' as having a mint, in the Constitutions of the Synod of Greatley in 925, which give the earliest English laws extant about coinage. One kind of money was to be current throughout the realm, and mints were appointed as follows:—At Canterbury, seven minters or coiners—four for the king, two for the bishop, and one for the abbot; at Rochester, three—two for the king and one for the

[1] Dr. Speed mentions this incident next after his account of the landing of Cerdic and Cynric, given above. Between this and the Norman Conquest, at which latter period he rightly places the real growth of the port, he gives four notices of Danish raids, one of them clearly belonging to Northampton, and no other historical reference. It has not been thought necessary to reproduce these notes.

[2] English Chron., sub ann.; Flor. Worcest., Hoveden, &c.

[3] English Chron., W. Malmesbury, Asser.

abbot; London, eight; Winchester, six; Lewes, two; Hampton, two; Wareham, Exeter, Shaftesbury, each two; Hastings and Chichester, each one; 'and other burhs,' one.[1] Ruding finds the mint mark of Southampton on coinage from the reign of Eadmund in 940 to that of Stephen, under the forms H, HA, HAM, AMTD, HAN, HAMT, HAMTV, HAMTVN, after which period it occurs no more.[2] In 1833 upwards of six thousand coins were found at Beaworth in Hants, bearing some of these mint marks and the moneyer's name, Sepine: they belong chiefly to the reigns of the first two Williams.[3] It has been questioned whether these mint marks may not refer to Northampton. But the geographical connection forbids this: added to which Northampton was but of little consequence at this period. The mint at Northampton perhaps appears NORT under William I., though possibly Norwich may be intended. It occurs under Henry I. as NORHA, the Southampton mark at the same period being HAM: just as in Domesday the same distinction had been drawn between these places, Southampton retaining the old appellation and appearing as Hantune, and the shire Hantescire, while the old Mercian town was written as Northamton and the county Northamtscire. No mention occurs in Domesday of any mint in either of these counties or towns.

The story of Northern raids has been somewhat interrupted; the interval represents a comparative quiet. For some period the Northmen had not ventured to attack the English shore, but with the unhappy reign of Æthelred (978–1016) the piratical descents were renewed. Hampton was ravaged by a sea force in 980, and suffered greatly in the loss of its citizens; many were slain, many taken captive.[4]

In the next year (981), the town suffered from those 'seven ships' which did so much damage and caused such talk throughout the country.[5] Apparently the Northmen met here with some successful resistance; we are told they fled to their ships, but not before they had committed their usual atrocities along the waterside.

Later in this reign (994), Southampton was made the head winter quarters of the Danes and Norwegians, who, under Svein, king of the former, and Olaf of the latter, had laid siege to London from as many as ninety-four ships. Repulsed by the citizens, they had scourged the coasts of Essex, Kent, Sussex, and Hampshire, 'burning, plundering, and murdering.' Finding themselves feebly opposed, they dashed into the interior of the country, and Æthelred and his Witan, equal to no

---

[1] Wilkins, Leges A.S., p. 59.
[2] Ruding, i. 251, &c., iii. 35.
[3] Archæologia, xxvi. 1.
[4] Eng. Chron., Flor. Worc.
[5] Eng. Chron.; Eulogium, iii. 24; Malmesb.

higher counsels, purchased immunity from the marauders at £16,000. They accepted the terms, and waited at Hampton with their whole army till the money should be paid.[1]

While their fleet was in harbour and the whole neighbourhood in deepest suffering, it occurred to Æthelred that a bond existed between the Norwegian king and himself which it might be well to acknowledge. Some time before, Olaf had received baptism at the hands of a hermit on one of the Scilly Isles; and the claims of Christian brotherhood were now made by Æthelred, who sent Ælphear, Bishop of Winchester (St. Alphage), afterwards murdered by the Danes, and Æthelweard the Ealdorman, inviting him to his court at Andover, hostages in the meantime being given to the fleet. Olaf met with a royal reception: he received confirmation from the Bishop of Winchester, and after many favours from the king, who had adopted him as his spiritual son, he returned to Hampton, having first sworn that he would never again come to England as a foe: and this promise he kept. In the following summer Olaf and Svein left our shores—Olaf to suffer ultimately through the enmity of Svein, possibly incurred at this period of Olaf's vow.

The greater portion of the army still remained behind, the burden becoming insupportable on the people of Hampton and Wessex; and finding the country impoverished, the marauders sailed westward to give the men of Hampton time to recover. They renewed their visit in 998, receiving their supplies as before from Hampshire and Sussex; but the siege of Rochester the following spring at length aroused Æthelred, and a fleet was prepared, which, though hindered in every way by incompetence and treachery, had the effect of warning off the foe from England to Normandy for the ensuing year.

In 1001 the Danes again ravaged Hampton and the Isle of Wight; and Æthelred and his Witan a second time purchased peace at the price of maintaining the invaders and a sum of £24,000. In the next spring came (1002) the marriage of Æthelred with Emma (Ælfgifu), the gem of Normandy, an alliance which might have strengthened the kingdom, but for the conduct of the worthless king. Whether or not this was feared by the Danes, we hear something of a secret conspiracy to murder the king and the Witan, a design, if real, terribly met by a counterplot, of which there is no doubt. Secret orders were issued to the cities and towns for a general massacre of the Danes, without regard to sex or age, on the following St. Brice's Day (November 13): a mandate faithfully obeyed and carried out with ferocity.

[1] Eng. Chron.; Malmesb., ii. 10; Huntingdon; Lappenberg's England under A.S. Kings, ii. 157, &c.

Among those who fell was an heroic Christian lady, Gunhild, the sister of Svein. She first saw her husband slaughtered and her son transfixed with four spears; then making no cry for mercy, she uttered with prophetic force a warning of the account which would soon be required of the land.

Svein, in answer to his countrymen's and his sister's blood, swore that he would conquer the realm within three years. He landed in Devonshire in the spring of 1003. Exeter, Wilton, and Salisbury soon fell before him. A powerful army gathered against him out of Hants and Wilts was neutralised by the treachery of its leader, Ælfric; and the Danish monarch, satiated with blood and plunder, was suffered to gain the sea, 'where he knew that his sea-horses were.'[1]

The next year's expedition (1004) was against East Anglia, where the Danes confessed they had never met worse hand-play among the English than Ulfcytel, the Ealdorman, had brought them, and for a brief season Hampton and Wessex were in quiet.

It was after midsummer 1006, when 'the great fleet' under Svein had put in at Sandwich, and the enemy had done their wont, ravaging, burning, destroying wherever they went, that Æthelred levied an army from Wessex and Mercia. But so little disciplined were the troops, that they proved hardly less disastrous to the unhappy people than the marauders themselves; and nothing was effected against the Danes, who passed to winter quarters in the Isle of Wight, levying their supplies from all Southamptonshire. At mid-winter they burst out again through Hampshire into Berkshire, to Reading, to Wallingford, and other places, 'doing as their wont, and lighting their war beacons as they went.' A band raised to cut them off was destroyed, and the terror-stricken citizens of Winchester saw them pass their city gates laden with spoil in the insolence of triumph and security. Wessex was now desolated, and the miserable Æthelred, who had fled into Shropshire, again, with the consent of his Witan, purchased peace at the price of £36,000 of silver, with rations as usual till payment.[2]

The brief interval of rest thus shamefully bought was occupied nevertheless by wise law-making, civil and ecclesiastical;[3] and another attempt was made at a fleet, with success so far, that in 1009 there rode before Sandwich a gallanter navy than England had ever

---

[1] Eng. Chron., sub ann.; Florence of Worcester, &c.

[2] Eng. Chron., sub. ann. 1006, 1007.

[3] The constitutions of the Witan, lay and clerical, under Æthelred, and the canons of the Witan at Ænham (perhaps the modern Ensham), are solemn reading, recalling our forefathers to righteousness in word and work, and to those efforts of patriotism which were specially needed.

seen—the willing effort of the whole nation under heavy taxation. But no sooner had the fleet been collected than misfortune, desertion, treachery, waited on it. 'We had not the good fortune or the worthiness that the ship-force should be of any more use than it had been before.' A panic seized the king, the ealdormen, the nobles: they fled to land, and the deserted seamen brought the ships to London. Thus did the 'nation's toil pass lightly away,' cries the contemporary historian; and with the dispersion of the fleet the Danes were at hand, and again for three years the kingdom was cruelly ravaged, Hampshire suffering heavily with the southern, midland, and eastern counties; truce being purchased at £48,000 in 1012.[1]

We must cut short this tale of guilt, misery, and dissension. The winter of 1013 saw the unhappy Æthelred, a fugitive from Svein and his own people, at Southampton, whence he slunk off to the Isle of Wight and passed over to Normandy. He was recalled on the death of Svein, which occurred suddenly on February 3, 1014, but the Danish fleet had proclaimed Cnut, the son of Svein. The king returned in Lent, and Cnut retired before him. The elated English revenged themselves on the remnant of the Danes and on the people of Lindsey (Lincolnshire), who had been forced into treaty with them. Cnut, on his part, thinking England now lost, cut off the ears and noses of the brave and noble young men who had been delivered to his father as hostages, set them on shore at Sandwich, and made off to Denmark. Even now the English had reminders of the Danish yoke in a tax at the time imposed of £21,000 for Thorkell's army, the king's ally at Greenwich, bought over by Æthelred some time before.[2]

Thorkell himself was reconsidering his position: the result was, that leaving the bulk of his army behind, he sailed off to Denmark, gave his services to his old master's son, and brought that monarch back to England with a powerful fleet in the spring of 1015, and before the end of the year Cnut was master of Wessex.

On the death of Æthelred, 23rd April 1016, his brave son, Eadmund, became king. Cnut at this time was in Southampton, whither came, in obedience to his summons, the thanes and clergy—the Witan, the wise men—of Wessex, to abjure their allegiance to the house of Æthelred and swear it to the Dane: yet the solemnity was barely ended when, with a sudden turn of fortune, Wessex more joyfully received the intrepid Eadmund. It was only for a hasty moment. Within six months of his accession Eadmund was forced to divide his kingdom with the invader. To Cnut Mercia and Northumbria fell, the rest, including of course Wessex, remained to Eadmund; but

[1] Eng. Chron. sub ann. [2] Ibid.

immediately after this he was murdered (November 30, 1016), and the whole passed to Cnut.

The kingdom thus acquired was divided into four parts—Mercia, East Anglia, Northumbria, and Wessex; the three former being governed by lieutenants, but Wessex—the core of the whole—being reserved for Cnut himself. Under his strong rule the country rose from its ruin; and there can be no doubt that both Winchester and Southampton very greatly revived. To the favour of this monarch we have attributed the removal of the town to a better site.

It is very certain that the character of the king underwent a remarkable change after he became possessed of the English crown. Bloodthirsty and savage at first like his fathers, he became strong, wise, temperate, religious. His laws, his policy, his address to the people on his return from Rome—which, together with the future immunity to travellers through Gaul secured by his pilgrimage, is placed by Henry of Huntingdon second among the three great occurrences in his reign—bear witness to the change. However, our object is not to deal generally with his character or reign, but to introduce the *third* remarkable occurrence, which concerns us much, though without pledging ourselves to Henry's estimate of it.

The year is uncertain, the month, day, and hour alike unspecified, though, considering our mud shores, we presume the tide was nearly high, when King Cnut sat himself on the Southampton beach in a royal chair, while round him was gathered a large and brilliant court. What occurred may now be told in the words of the earliest extant narrator.

'Thou belongest to my rule, cried the monarch to the rising tide, and the land on which I sit is mine, nor has there been any one to resist with impunity my empire. I command thee therefore that thou rise not on my land, nor wet the garments or feet of thy lord. But the sea flowed on as usual, laving without reverence the king's feet and legs. Whereupon jumping back he exclaimed: Let all the inhabitants of the earth know that vain and trifling is the power of kings, and that none is worthy of the name of king but He whose nod the heaven, the earth, the sea obey by laws eternal.' [1] And ever after

[1] Henry of Huntingdon, under 1036 (Cnut died in 1035). There are two principal versions of the ancedote. That given above is the original, in which the king is assumed to be teaching somewhat dramatically those about him. The other version, which generally places the scene at Westminster, makes the king address the waves in the arrogance of his heart, thus robbing the incident of its shred of probability and its poetry.

It will be observed that Huntingdon does not venture upon the place of the occurrence, nor say where the crown was devoted. Winchester is supposed to have received the gift, and of course Southampton was the place. As to the this rebuke to flattery Cnut's royal crown might be seen on the brows of the crucifix in token of the king's humility. He died at Shaftesbury on November 11, 1035, and was buried at Winchester.

On the death of Cnut, Eadward (afterwards the Confessor), the son of Æthelred by Emma, hastened over from Barfleur to Southampton with forty ships, as a competitor for the crown. He met with no favour from his mother at Winchester, who was anxious to secure everything for Harthacnut, her son by Cnut, then absent in Denmark. Seeing this, Eadward in his vexation plundered the neighbourhood and returned the way he came,[1] while Harold (Harefoot), the bastard son of the late king by Ælfgifu, his concubine, the daughter of Ælfhelm, Earl of the Northumbrians, became acknowledged king. He died in March 1040, but his reign, like that of his successor Harthacnut, who died in June 1042 from excesses and deep drinking, requires no notice here.[2]

precise *spot*, there seems to have been no consent. Milner (in 1798) says, 'The memory of the identical spot is still pointed out at Bittern, in Northam harbour, by the tradition of the inhabitants' (i. 134). Englefield, writing a little after, would not accept this, and conjectured another site, and has himself become the *author* of a tradition. A still more modern *tradition* fixed it on the old beach line now destroyed by the construction of the docks, the memory of which has been kept up by Canute Road. But an hotel-keeper of late years yet more exactly discovered the spot, and to his authority we may just as well bow.

[1] Hardyng makes Ælfred, the other son, land at Southampton. But this is probably a confusion of the above narrative with the compromise of the Witenagemot between the claims of Harold and Harthacnut and the unfortunate expedition of the unhappy Ælfred to Sandwich, which ended in his barbarous murder, through the treachery of Earl Godwin, at the instigation of Harold. (See Lives of Ed. Conf. 37, Eng. Chron., sub 1036.)

[2] Before taking leave of the Danes, it may be well to describe, as far as possible, the old Danish vessel blown to pieces by Mr. Crawshay a few years ago, and which previously had been known as existing in the Hamble mud. It lay in the bed of the river, about three-fourths of a mile above Bursledon Bridge, and had evidently been burnt down to the water's edge. The vessel was 130 feet long and clinker built. The timbers were of very large size, and had attached to them planking in three thicknesses. In the timbers were round holes for wooden trunnions, some of which remained, and square iron clamps or rivets. (Compare the contemporary English expression, 'The Northmen departed in their *nailed* barks,' Chron., A.D. 937.) The planking was set to the timbers in cement, which was freely used in the trunnion holes and at all joints: the seams were caulked with a mossy fibre. The timbers were of oak. Within the last seventy years, the old figure-head, 'a lion with its paws erect'—as described to me—was standing outside a cottage, but was ultimately cut up for firewood. Some fragments of this old vessel are in the Hartley Museum.

In 1848 a vessel of large size and great antiquity was found imbedded in the mud at Southampton, and a drawing of it was sent to the Archæological Institute in March 1851. It was supposed by many to be Roman, but was afterwards described to me by an engineer who saw it as similar to the vessel at Hamble.

Domesday.

5. The little that can be gathered about the town during the reign of Eadward the Confessor, who now succeeded, will be found in the account of Domesday below. Southampton just appears in the rebellion of Earl Godwin, but there is nothing of moment to record.

The great survey of landed property made by order of the Conqueror, and called Domesday from the searching nature of its inquisition and the final authority with which it would speak,[1] was finished in 1086.

The following is the local account:—

'In the borough of Hantune the king has four score men less four in demesne who pay £7 in land-gable,[2] and paid the same in the time of King Eadward. Of these, twenty-seven pay 8d. each, two pay 12d. each, and the rest, fifty in number, pay six pence each.[3]

'These held land in the borough which had been made free of claims (quietam terram) in the time of King Eadward by the king:

'Odo[4] of Winchester; Anschil the priest; Chetel, Fulghel, [and] Tostil, sons of Elric, had sixteen acres of land; Gerin eighteen acres; Cheping had three houses free of tax, and now Ralph de Mortemer holds them; and Godwin four houses, these Bernard Pancevolt holds.

'After King William came into England, sixty-five French-born and thirty-one English-born were lodged in Hantone. These among them all paid £4 and 6d. for all customs.

'These underwritten have the custom of their houses in Hantone by grant of King William:

---

1 See Dialogus de Scaccario, i. 16.

2 Land-gable—gable, from gafol, a tax or tribute; Fr. gabelle.

3 There appears to be an error in the figures somewhere.

4 Most or all of these old tenants had other holdings in the county, some of them considerable property, of which they had been dispossessed at the Conquest, as in the case of Cheping, whose name frequently occurs in Domesday, and whose confiscated estates mostly fell, as here, to the powerful Norman, Ralph de Mortemer, a relative of King William on the mother's side, and one of his commanders. So also in the case of Godwin, who held several properties, in all of which he was succeeded, as here, by Bernard Pancevolt. The three 'houses' mentioned above are referred to in the entry about Chilworth, where they are called 'hayes in Hantone,' showing that there was enclosed ground around them: they were assessed at 18d. Besides the above, Bernard held three yard-lands at Hardley, which had been turned into forest. It appears from Domesday that some 140 hides (hide = about 100 to 120 acres) had been afforested between the time of Eadward the Confessor and that of the survey; the greater part of these additions being made, as here, on the borders of the ancient Ytene: this made up what was called the New Forest. There is no doubt of the destruction of many habitable places (see Ellis, Introd. to Domesday, i. 109; Hallam, Middle Ages, ii. 312; Morgan, Normans, 6; Lappenberg, Normans, 214).

'G.[1] the bishop [has the custom] of one house; the abbey of Cormeilles, one; the Count of Evreux, two; Ralph de Mortemer, two; Gilbert de Bretville, two; William son of Stur, two; Ralph de Todeni, one; Durand de Gloucester, two; Hugh de Port,[2] one; Hugh de Grentemaisnil,[3] two; the Count of Mortain,[4] five; Aiulf the chamberlain, five; Humphrey his brother, one; Osbern Gifart, one; Nigel[5] the physician, four; Richerius[6] de Andeli, four; Richard Pugnant,[7] one; Stephen[8] the steersman, two; Turstin[9] the chamberlain, two; Turstin the engineer, two; Anschital[10] the son of Osmund, three; Rainald Croc,[11] one.

'The Abbess of Wherwell[12] has a fishery and a small plot of land. Formerly they returned 100 pence, but now ten shillings.'

The burh or borough was the tún, grown in its dimensions, strengthened in its defences, augmented in its privileges, and recognised as a distinct unit, of as much account in its degree as the shire of which it was geographically a part, and according to the completeness of its organisation it became in the course of time free from shire jurisdiction in all respects. In the account before us from Domesday, the king has in the borough seventy-six tenants in demesne, who paid the same amount of gable as under the Confessor. These were the

1 No doubt Geoffrey de Moubray, Bishop of Coutances, who had been rewarded with many possessions in various parts of the country.

2 Sheriff of Hants in the time of William I. He held some fifty-five in Hants, besides property elsewhere.

3 Hugo de Grentmesnil, Earl of Leicester, was nephew of the Conqueror and owned most of the borough of Leicester. He had been intrusted (see Freeman, Norm. Conquest, iv. 74) with the government of Hampshire.

4 The Earl of Mortain held several lands in the county, besides a vast number of manors in all the south-west counties. He held also Pevensey, but his palace was at Bermondsey. He was half-brother to William I.

5 Nigel, the Conqueror's physician, held lands in Neteham hundred.

6 It has been suggested that he was a troubadour attached to the court (Woodward and Wilks, Hist., ii. 168).

7 Richard Pugniant held Letelie (site of *Netley* Abbey), in Mansbridge hundred. It was assessed at one hide, but in King Edward's time at three. There was a little church (ecclesiola) there, and besides the open land, a wood for forty hogs. It was worth an 100s.

8 Stephen the steersman was connected also with Warwick (Morgan, 207): he was no doubt Stephen Fitz Erard, the 'captain' of William's ship.

9 Turstin the chamberlain, and probably also treasurer, held Houghton, Somborne hundred, in succession to those who held for King Edward.

10 He also succeeded to land formerly held by Godwin at Houghton.

11 In the next column in Domesday this holder is called the *son* of Croc; his father may have been the huntsman of the New Forest. He held from the king a hide of land in Olvestune (Olaf's town—? Woolston) in Mansbridge hundred. Tovi held it before. He also had land in the Isle of Wight.

2 The Abbess of Wherwell was sister to Eadward the Confessor, and to her custody he committed his wife Eadgyth (see Lappenberg, ii. 250).

burgesses, the free inhabitant householders, fulfilling the duties of their position in scot and lot, taxation and service, sworn, enrolled, pledged.

Next we have a list of persons who had held land or houses in the borough, quieted of claims, in the time and by grant of King Eadward, and who perhaps so continued to hold under King William, with certain specified exceptions. Then we come to the settlements made by or in the time of King William: these tenants represent the increase of the town and of the royal revenue from it since the days of King Eadward. The preponderance of Normans will be observed: why they altogether paid so much less than the original tenants does not appear.

A long list follows of those who had the custom of their houses by a grant of King William. They were mostly great land-holders in the country, as a glance at the footnotes will show. Their houses may have been inhabited by persons who, being otherwise qualified, became burgesses by their residency. The phrase occurs in Domesday that such an one 'has' so many 'burgesses,' that is, possesses the property on which they reside. And these powerful landlords at Hantune may have 'possessed' burgesses though they were not such themselves—the burgesses being always the resident trading population, who subsequently came to have supreme authority and government in the towns owing to their enrolment in strong trading guilds; and when they had purchased the ferm of their towns, they became identical in almost every respect with what were afterwards known as corporations.[1]

Only a general inference as to the size and population of Hantune can be drawn from the Domesday account. There were many houses, if such they might be called, of the poorer classes of which no account could be taken, whose occupiers enjoyed few or no privileges. Still the borough appears diminutive when measured by other great towns: all that can be said is that it was now rising in consequence—the days of its suffering were over; and while the great majority of the cities and towns of England had fallen into grievous decay since the coming of the Normans, Southampton and the few ports leading to the Continent alone showed signs of prosperity. The growing importance of the place may be seen in the number of powerful barons and other wealthy folk who possessed houses or lands within its limit.

After Domesday the earliest historical notices of the town occur in connection with its ferm: we devote the next section to its history.

---

1 See Merewether and Stephens, Boroughs, pp. 201, 207, 221. So 'burgesses' may have possessed property in other places than those of their own settlement. Thus under the account of Romsey Abbey fourteen 'burgesses of Winchester' paid 25s.

## SECTION II.—*The Fee-Farm.*

1. The fee-farm rent was the composition or reserved rent paid to the king in right of his demesne and in lieu of ancient claims: it covered also petty customs and fines. The collection of this payment was sometimes in the hands of a vicecomes or præpositus, sheriff or reeve, sometimes in those of a wealthy townsman, or even of his wife or widow (instances will be seen below); and to those in charge of the farm the king's writs were constantly directed (as will be also seen) concerning his pecuniary requirements under many different heads.

Hanton.[1] Roger the son of Folcher renders account for the farm of Hanton, which he had in charge for the third part of a year.
In the treasury, £25, 2s.
In livery (wages) to the chaplain of the castle for last year, £1, 3s. 4d.; to the same for the present year, by writ, 9s. 8d.
In wages to the porter and watchman, 19s. 4d. 1155–5
In wages to John the controller[2] of accounts, 19s. 4d.
In transport service by writ of the king, £2, 7s. 6d.
And there remains of the king's farm for the third part of the year, £68, 8s. 10d.

In the following accounts alms are given from the royal revenue to the monks of Lire and Cormeilles, who already possessed houses in Southampton free of dues. In favour of the latter abbey a charter of Henry II. is preserved by inspeximus (dated 1281) of the Bishop of Lisieux,[3] in which the king confirms to them all their lands, churches, chapels, tithes, and possessions; and in Southampton he gives them a charge of £9, 5s., freeing the monks and men of their demesne from all customs. To Lire he gave a similar charge and favours. The Knights-Templars had only been introduced into England in the reign of Stephen, and the payment to them is new.

William Trentegeruns renders account for the farm of Hanton for half a year.
In the treasury —
In payments to the same William by writ of the king, £50.
In alms newly assigned to the Knights of the Temple, 13s. 4d.
In tithes assigned to the monks of Lire and Cormeilles, £18.
In wages to John the controller, £2, 1s. 6d.
In wages assigned to the chaplain, porter, and watchman, £3, 3s. 4d.
In works at the castle, by writ of the king, £7.
In transporting the king's treasure, by William Cummin, 17s.
For cages to transport the king's hawks and falcons, 12s. 6d.
In transport service, by writ of the king and queen, £10, 5s.
And there remains due to the king, £112 blank.[4]

[1] Hunter's Pipe Roll.

[2] Contrataliator. This John in later years is styled Contrarotulator. He controlled the accounts by keeping the counter-tallies.

[3] Madox, Formulare, p. 8.

[4] Blanched or tried silver. It was the mark of an ancient holding when a

Hanton. William Trentegeruns renders account for £112 of the old[1] farm of Hanton.

In the treasury, £12.

And in payments to himself and his wife, £100 blank. And he is quit.

And the same sheriff renders account of the new farm.

In payments to himself, the sheriff, and his wife, £242, 8s. blank.

(Payments to the Knights-Templars and abbeys of Lire and Cormeilles as before.)

Wages to the controller, £3, 0s. 10d.

Wages to the chaplain, porter, and watchman, £4, 11s. 4d.

Works on the castle bridge, £4, 14s. 4d.

Works on the chapel and baily bridge, £3, 12s. 4d.

Making a parapet (bretesche) on the same bridge, 10s.

In transport of the king, £14, 13s. 4d.

In transports by writ of the king, £7, 13s. 6d.

On the queen's board when she came from Normandy, £1, 7s. 2d.

And for unlading wine and flour, £1, 7s. 5d.

Turstin was the sheriff of Hants at this time, William, who is here rendering his account, being the appointed officer within the borough.

Hantune. William Trentegernuns (sic) renders account of the farm of Hanton.

(Payments to the Templars, abbeys of Lire and Cormeilles, and to the controller as before.)

To Wimarch, mother of Nicholas, land-tax during life, 3s.

Works on the castle bridge and chapel, £1, 11s. 4d.

The king's board at Brockeherst, by writ of the king, £16.

For carriage of the king's deer and catching them, £1, 19s. 6d.

Passage of the same, £3, 8s. 5d.

Carriage of the king's wine from Hantune to Winchester, 18s.

In passages by king's writ, £14, 16s. 6d.

And there remains due to the king, £237, 4s. blank.

1170-71. In the 17th Henry II., Richard de Limesey rendered account for £76, 6s. 11½d. from the old farm of Hanton, and for £200 blank or tried silver from the new farm. The alms were the same; the allowance for the chaplain, guard, and porter of Hanton was
1173-74. £3, 11s. In the 20th year, Robert de St. Lawrence renders account for £31, 16s. 4d. of the old farm and £200 of the new. He claims for the usual allowances, and in addition, for land given to the lepers of Southampton, £1, 3s. 2d.; for land also near Porteswoda, given to the canons of St. Denys by writ of the king, 7s. 2d.

---

farm had thus to be rendered, and not merely *numero*, by reckoning. Out of a certain quantity of silver, twenty shillings were melted down, and the quality of the rest was judged by this pound which had passed through the purging fires. It was said 'to burn' so many pennyworths, and a similar amount was charged to every other pound, the sheriff or reeve having to stand by the result (Dialogus de Scaccario, ed. Stubbs, p. 183, &c.)

[1] By the expression 'old' and 'new' farm is to be understood the residue of rent from the previous together with the amount for the current year. On a change of office, the sheriff or reeve under the term 'old farm' gives account of the balance with which his predecessor had left him to deal (Dialogus, p. 26).

The allowance for the lepers and canons of St. Denys will be observed.

In the 25th year, Cecilia, his wife, gives in the account for him. In the treasury was a balance of £73, 5s.[1] 1173-79.

The following return belongs to 1 Richard I. 1189-90.

Hanton. Gervase, reeve of Sudhanton, renders account of £456, 4s. 9d. blank of the old farm of Sudhanton, and of £200 blank of the new farm. In the Treasury nothing.

(Payments to Knights-Templars and the monks of Lire, the lepers of Southampton, and the canons of St. Denys, for land given them, as before.)

And in wages of the royal yacht or 'snake' (esnecca [2]) during six passages with treasure before the coming of our Lord King Richard into England, by writ of the king, £45.

And for hiring six ships for the use of the clerks of the treasurer and of the chamberlains, by the same brief, £12, 15s. 7d.

And in repairs of the royal yacht when she was sent to meet the king, £10, 5s. 4d., on king's writ, by testimony of Alan Trenchmere.

And in the passage of the Duke of Saxony, in payment of the esnecca and other five ships, by writ of the king, £19, 10s.

Also in three passages in smaller ships with treasure, by the same royal writ, £10, 10s. 2d.

Also in the passage of Geoffrey, Bishop of Ely, in two ships, by writ of the king, £5.

And in the passage of John de Montacute and of the messengers of the queen to her son, by writ, &c., £2.

And in the passage of the Bishop of Bayeux and the treasure with him, by writ, &c., £2, 10s.

For hiring one ship for the carriage of five hundred bacon hogs and forty weys (pensas) of cheese, which were sent into Normandy, by writ of the king, to supply his castles, £2, 19s.

And in short passages, by writs of the king, £2, 3s.

And also after Michaelmas this year, in payment of the esnecca when she crossed for the first time after the coronation of King Richard, by writ of the king, £7, 10s.

And for hiring a ship for the man and horse armour (ad harnasium) of the barons who crossed with the same treasure, by the same writ £2, 17s. 8d., &c.

In the same year, Galfrid the son of Azon rendered account for the old and new farm of the *shire*, and among other things charged for 1189-90.

[1] Exemplification of Town Accounts, from Exchequer Rolls, dated 10th April (1402), 3 H. IV., in possession of Corporation. Henry Bowet, Bishop of Bath and Wells, was treasurer. He had been consecrated November 20, 1401, and was translated to York, October 7, 1407.

[2] These swift royal yachts, esneccæ, or snakes, were continually crossing from this port and being allowed for. In 1166 (12 H. II.), wages when the king crossed over in Lent, £7, 10s; and in the passage of the King of Scotland, £7, 10s. by writ of the king; and in the passage of Sir Geoffrey, the king's son, in an esnecca and two other ships, £10. In 1176 (22 H. II.), wages of the esnecca when the king's daughter crossed over to go into Sicily, by writ, £7, 10s.; and wages of seven ships which crossed with her, £10, 12s.; and in 1184 (31 H. II.), wages to the esnecca when the Duke of Saxony and the queen crossed, by writ of Ranulph de Glanville, £7, 10s. (See Nicholas's Hist. of Royal Navy, i. 434.) The wages of the captain was 10d. a day (Dialogus, p. 184).

repairs to the houses within the tower[1] of Hantone, the royal castle and its precincts being no part of the town fortifications for which the borough was answerable.

In the 4th Richard I. (1192–93), William Briewere accounted for £106, 13s. 8d. of the farm of Hanton, and in the 10th year (1198–99), the sheriff of the *shire* accounted for the same amount from the town farm.[2]

In 1199 Hugo de Bosco, sheriff of Hants, offered King John twenty marks to hold the town to farm till the feast of St. Michael next after the coronation; whereupon it was ordered that if William Briewere desired to retain the town so long he should pay the twenty marks which Hugo had promised. Hugo apparently succeeded and was charged his twenty marks.[3]

Town purchases fee-farm, 1199.

2. We have now come to the memorable year in which the town purchased its fee-farm, obtaining it together with that of the port of Portsmouth, and all that belonged to the farm of Hanton in the time of King Henry, for the fine of £100, and the annual rent of £200, payable at the Exchequer each Michaelmas Day.[4] Thus in 5 John (1204), the *men* of Sudhantone—a common term for the burgesses—render account by the hands of Azo, who was perhaps Alderman, for the £200 of the farm of Sudhanton with Portesmue: in 9 John (1208) they did the same: in the 11th year (1210), they rendered for two years together, and claimed allowance for £5 each year for land at Portswood and Kingsland given by King Richard to the canons of St. Denys.[5] In the 17th John (1216), Richard de Leicester, who in and before 1199 had been controller of the town, as his ancestors were before him, but had in that year been ousted from his office by Robert Hardwin, who had fined for it with the king,[6] answered for the town's farm.

It seems probable that the guild-merchant may have negotiated the purchase of the fee-farm, and that those who accounted at the Exchequer in the town's behalf were the officials of the guild. The

[1] Et in reparandis domibus in Turri de Hantone vj$^{li}$. et xij$^{d}$. per breve Regis, et per visum Roberti contrataliatoris.

[2] Exemplification of Town Accounts from Exchequer Rolls.

[3] Rot. de Oblatis (Hard. 93); Rot. Cancellar., p. 254.

[4] See below under charters; also Madox, Excheq., i. 402. 'Burgenses de Hamton dant Domino Regi Cl. pro habenda Villa de Suhamton ad firmam in perpetuum pro CCl. per annum cum portu de Portu Mues, et omnibus aliis pertinentiis ad firmam Villæ de Hamton pertinentibus, unde eadem villa saisita fuit tempore Regis Henrici. Et habent cartam Domini Regis inde de prædictâ firmâ respondendâ ad festum S. Michaelis ad Scaccarium Domini Regis' (Oblat. 1 John, m. 19).

[5] Exemplification, &c.; see also Madox, Ex. i. 409.

[6] Abbrev. Plac. 1 John; Madox, Ex. i. 202.

same amount of fee-farm remained chargeable, with an increase to be presently mentioned, till the 22nd Henry VIII. (1530–31).

In the 2nd Henry III. (November 29, 1217) we find that the town had been taken into the king's hands, the Earl of Salisbury, who had previously received a grant of it, being required to withdraw his bailiffs: the farm was also ordered to be accounted for as usual at the Exchequer.[1] At this period the town, or *city*, as it is called by a slip, is said to have been wholly in the king's demesne, and those who had settlements in it held directly from the crown.[2]

Increase, 1276.

In the 4th Edward I. (1276) the Exchequer Roll records a pardon to the burgesses for certain transgressions—apparently the wounding a king's bailiff in the execution of his duty—on account of which the king had seized the town into his hands by the judgment of his court, and had restored it (May 22) to the townsmen, upon a fine, for the usual farm, but with an increment of forty marks (£26, 13s. 4d.),[3] a circumstance[4] referred to by an Act of 22nd Henry VIII. (1530–31), where it is also stated that the increment remained till the passing of that Act.

Accordingly, in the 5th Edward I. (1277) the farm is distinctly stated to be £200, together with the *new* increment of £26 and one mark (13s. 4d.), as contained in the preceding roll. So in the following years and reigns, after deducting the appointed alms the farm always produced £200, 19s. 8d.[5]

The apparent exceptions arise from the fact that the increment was not always included in the farm, and the whole was sometimes apparently spoken of in general terms. Thus in a lease of the customs granted by Peter de Lyons (no doubt the mayor) and twenty others to Robert le Mercer and seventeen others (Mich. 30 Edward I. 1302), the farm of the town is put at £200. The members belonging to the town of Southampton are said to be Portemue, Hamele, Linnentone, Scharprixe, Kyhaven, and Rumbridge;[6] and in the lawsuit with Lymington (17 Edward II. 1324), the mayor, bailiffs, and community

---

[1] Rot. Litt. Claus. sub dat.

[2] Testa de Nevill, p. 236 (time of Hen. III. and Ed. I.)

[3] Exemplification of Town Accounts, &c., also Pat. 4 Ed. I. m. 23 and m. 21; see also Rot. Parl. i. 58 a, &c., where, however, the increase is stated to be £20.

[4] In the contemporary Rolls just referred to, it is not stated that the increment was added on account of the transgression, but it may be a safe inference. The king's houses in the town were excepted from the general farm to the burgesses, and the king would dispose of them as he chose.

[5] Ibid.

[6] Original indenture of lease. The farm is put at the same amount in the 29 and 31 Edward III. (1301, 1304).

of Southampton say that they hold the town and port of the town from beyond Hurst to Langstone at the annual farm of £220.[1]

In the town books the amount of the farm is variously stated, but this arises from the payments having been generally made by instalments, which were constantly in arrears or only part paid up. Sometimes also the alms and liveries were included, sometimes the reverse. Thus in 1438 the sum of £225 was paid for the farm, the seneschal receiving 6s. 8d. for carrying it to London.[2] In 1441 the sum of £200 was paid; in 1447 the farm was correctly set forth in the charter to be 340 marks (£226, 13s. 4d.); about 1512 it appears as £218,[3] which will not tally with the petition and Act of 1530–31.

Abatements.

3. The burgesses were occasionally released from full payment on special grounds, such as the cost of the fortifications (see below), or on woeful representations of their condition. Thus the town being constantly, by its own representation, on the point of financial collapse, Edward IV. and Richard III., at the commencement of their reigns (1462 and 1484), remitted arrears of fee-farm, among other matters, in general pardons to the mayor and burgesses.[4] In the early years of the next century the borough seems to have been systematically two or three years behindhand in its payment.

Writs.

4. Before finishing the account of the farm, we may turn to some of the charges upon it. The practice of drawing by writ upon the royal dues has been noticed above, the sum advanced being placed to the town's credit at the Exchequer. Thus the bailiffs were frequently directed to advance money in gifts from the king or in payment to his soldiers, as in 1215, when, under the oversight of William Briewere, they were ordered to find money for the king's soldiers and archers who had come from Poitou to Winchester. Writs for repairs constantly occur:[5] thus in 1224 for the gutters of the king's chamber at Southampton. Among the more miscellaneous objects we have the carriage of a big fish from Portsmouth to Oxford (1224), the carriage for Geoffrey de Lucy of five cartloads of lead for work at the castles of Guernsey and Jersey (1226). Wine orders were very constant: thus they were ordered to purchase from the men of Savaric de Mauleon at South-

---

1 See Madox, F. B., 220–222.

2 Steward's books.

3 'Md. that the hole charge for the fee-ferme of the towne of S. amountith yerely unto the summe of ccxviij$^{li}$, whereof is paid yerely to the king's grace cliij$^{li}$: to the queen's grace yerely xlvj$^{li}$, to Shene yerely ix$^{li}$ vs., to Fodringay yerely viij$^{li}$ xvs., Summa totalis ccxviij$^{li}$.'—*Boke of Remembrances*, f. 1.

4 Bundle of pardons (Corp. Arch.)

5 See further under Bailiffs, Castle, Trade, &c.

ampton a quantity of wine for the use of the king's chamberlain and soldiers going to Poitou (1224).[1]

The payments to religious houses continued. The Master and College of St. Mary and All Saints at Fotheringay, founded in 1411 by Henry IV., succeeded to the £8, 15s. which had formerly been paid to Lire; and the priory of Jesus of Bethlehem at Shene, commenced by Henry V. in 1414, received the £9, 5s. formerly given to Cormeilles.[2] Alms.

The town has often been bestowed in dowry upon queens of England. It had been thus settled for life on Queen Eleanor, wife of Henry III. and mother of Edward I.; and in the 13th year of the latter monarch (1285) the burgesses were charged with various transgressions in withholding the royal dues from the king and queen, on account of which the town had been taken into the king's hands. Settlements on queens.

Queen Eleanor died in 1292, and on September 10, 1299, King Edward endowed at the church-door his second wife, Margaret of France, with the farm of the town, which was to yield her £201, 3s. 2d., besides the alms and allocations. He also gave her a long list of manors, castles, and towns, among which were the castle of Southampton, the manor and park of Lyndhurst, with the New Forest and the bailiwick and hundred of Redbridge: these last items were to bring in £150.

Queen Margaret died 14th February (11 Ed. II.) 1318,[3] and Isabella of France, wife of Edward II. and mother of Edward III., next enjoyed this £201, 3s. 2d.[4]

Joanna of Navarre, queen of Henry IV., had a jointure of 150 marks from the farm by patent dated 19th April (1 Hen. IV.) 1400: indentures between the queen and the town as to her payment also exist bearing date 12th November (1 Hen. VI.) 1422.[5] She died in 1437.

Among the provisions of dowry for Margaret of Anjou on her marriage with Henry VI. in May 1445 was the grant of £1000 per annum from the great and little customs of the town; and in 1454 (32 Hen. VI.) an annuity of £100 from the fee-farm was confirmed to her.[6]

---

1 Numerous such examples are to be found in the printed Close Rolls of John and Henry III.

2 Steward's books, 1485, 1457, &c.

3 Exemplification of Town Accounts from Excheq., &c., 11 Ed. II. Rot. Parl., i. 18, &c.; Rymer, ii. 854 b.

4 Abbrev. Rot. Orig., 14 Ed. III. (1340). See under Castle and Burning of Town.

5 Corp. Archives.

6 Rot. Parl., v. pp. 120, 133, 262.

Ten years later the usual annuity of £46 out of the farm was resumed by Act of Parliament (4 Ed. IV.) 1464,[1] and in 1466 the king granted it to Elizabeth, his queen.[2] Three years after the mayor had to borrow £7 of Robert Blewet to make up the allowance.[3] In 1471 her majesty received more than the usual grant, some arrears being included: three years after the exact sum was forwarded. In 1478 Thomas Stydolf, the queen's receiver-general, acknowledged to receiving the same,[4] the like amount being continued by grant of 5th March (1 Hen. VII.) 1486. The town made an effort to pay the queens with some regularity, even when it was lapsing into a chronic state of arrears about its farm. This is seen in the accounts of 1501, 1507, and other years.[5] In the reign of Henry VIII. similar payments were made; and in 1605 the same settlement was made on his queen by James I.[6]

Royal household.

But the chief charges on the fee-farm usually went in other directions; as, for instance, to the household. Thus a writ dated 10th December (1 Ed. IV.) 1461 directed the sheriff of the town to pay to Sir John Fogge, treasurer of the royal household, the sum of £133, 6s. 8d. from the farm.[7] These payments for the household varied considerably, and were subsequently made a matter of regulation by Parliament in 1450, when the sum of £26, 18s. 6d. was paid by the town, but in 1495 the sum of £154.[8] Then grants were made to great nobles for various purposes, as, *e.g.*, to Cardinal Beaufort, the king's uncle, in 1439 a grant of £10, 14s. 6d. per annum for the Hospital of St. Cross, Winchester. But passing to larger amounts:

To great nobles.

On December 14, 1461, only four days after the writ above cited for the treasurer of the household, an annuity of £154 from the farm was confirmed to Richard Nevill,[9] the 'stout Earl Warwick,' the greatest man in England. Payments to this nobleman continued till he fell at Barnet on Easter Day 1471, though not without the usual amount of confusion and delay. On one occasion (1469–70) the mayor himself had to ride up to London 'to rekyn $w^{t}$ the erle of Warwicke.' He 'was ther xij days, for the wheche xij days the costes comyth toe $L^{s}$ $vj^{d}$;' and in the following year an account was presented of money given and lent to the town in 'contentacion of the fee-ferme.' The account of 1461 shows the mayor, Robert Bagworth, intrusted with the payment of £20 from the farm to the Dowager-Countess of Shrewsbury, cousin of the Earl of Warwick.[10]

1 Rot. Parl., v. p. 518.
2 Liber Remembranc. H., Rot. Parl., v. 626.
3 Steward's books, 1470–71.
4 Steward's books.
5 Ibid.
6 Town Journal.
7 Lib. Remembranc. H., f. 32.
8 Rot. Parl., v. 174 b.; vi. 499 b.
9 Lib. Remembranc. H., ff. 32, 33.
10 Steward's books.

The next settlement, to the same amount (£154), was made upon William FitzAlan, Earl of Arundel. Payments to him occur frequently, in a bewildering amount of small instalments, till his death in 1487 (3 Hen. VII.) The town sometimes tendered a payment in wine, and occasionally the Earl would draw upon them for his friends, *e.g.*, for the Abbess of Amesbury a hogshead of wine, and similarly for many others. Sometimes his letters are pathetic as to his non-payment, always expressing the great moderation of his demands, but begging his 'right trusty and well-beloved friends and neighbours, the mayor and his brethren,' to bear in mind his great charges (Jan.–Nov. 1482). Two years later he specifies the charges, 'as well in setting forth to the sea our right entirely beloved son Sir John Arundel, Knt., by commandment of our sovereign lord the king, as in finding and sending certain great number of men diffensibly arrayed unto the king's highness, when we shall be by his grace commanded;' he concludes by requesting that they will forthwith 'send safely unto us our said duties without further delay' (April 1484).[1]

5. It will be gathered that the town was occasionally put to straits in producing its rent. It was frequently obliged to resort to loans and gifts from wealthy individuals. Thus, in Hilary term 1457, seventeen sums were advanced towards the fee-farm, making a total of £42, 6s. 8d.[2] In 1461 we find one of the chief burgesses thrown into the Fleet at the suit of John, Lord Wenlock, of the Privy Council, for the 'rerage' of the fee-farm; and on July 24, 'Symkyn Patrycke and John Gryme, by the commandment of the mayor and of all the worshipful burgesses of the town, rode to London to labour for the worship of the town and the welfare of Richard Gryme, the which was in the prison of the Fleet for the debt of the said town.' The sum of £20 was paid for his deliverance.[3] The case of this burgess illustrates one of the positions of Madox, that anciently a corporate community might be made answerable for the trespass or debt of particular members, and particular members for the community;[4] and the visit of the burgesses to Richard Gryme falls in with the Guild ordinances (No. 11) by which it was provided that any guildsman in

How the farm was raised.

[1] Steward's books and letters affixed.

[2] Steward's books.

[3] Steward's books, 1461; Lib. Remembranc. H., f. 25 b. Item, lent to Richard Gryme for his delyverans ayenst my lord Wanlok, xx[li].

[4] The instance given by Madox shows that the townsmen of Southampton (13 John) had got into their hands a large sum of the king's money which came from Ireland, when the two bailiffs, Roger Swein and William Anglicus, together with six principal men—Simon de St. Lawrence, Robert the Talliator, Denys Fortin, Walter Fleming, Roger Bonhait, and Thomas de Bulehus—were charged with the money, and found pledges to answer the king (F. B., p. 158).

prison, in whatever part of the kingdom, should be visited at the common expense, and his release procured if possible.[1]

The same year, John Walker, the sheriff, was summoned to the Exchequer, whither he rode at the town's cost for 20s., and was amerced in the sum of £3, 6s. 8d., which was rendered at the hands of John Ingoldsby, afterwards apparently one of the Barons of the Exchequer, who was repaid by the town.[2]

Reduction. 6. Returning now to the amount of the fee-farm: in 22 Henry VIII. (1530–31) a permanent remission of forty marks (£26, 13s. 4d.) was made to the burgesses on petition alleging their great expenses and the decay of trade.[3] But in 1533 the Corporation wrote to Cromwell urging again their great charges in the defence of the town against the sea and on the walls, begging that their arrears 'may be stalled,' that they might have a chance of paying in future; as yet they had derived no benefit from past favours. By the 28th Henry VIII. (1537) matters had got so much worse, that in January Thomas Lyster, the mayor, under fear of a process out of the Exchequer and the seizure of the town's liberties, had recourse to the merchant Nicolyne Dogra, called also Demagrine, who came to his temporary relief; and in October the following year the same merchant advanced £200 for the farm, receiving in security West Hall,[4] a locally noted tenement, which stood on the site of the present Grammar School. By the 3rd Edward VI. (1549) the sum of £1844, 1s. 6d. was owing to the Exchequer; of this total, the amount of £1044, 1s. 6d. was remitted in the following year (1550) upon the Corporation entering into a bond for £1000 to pay the remaining £800 at the rate of £100 per annum.[5]

Reduced to £50. 7. But in the 6th Edward VI. (1552) the important and permanent reduction was made that, under certain conditions, the rent should be but £50.[6] Still in September (3 Eliz.) 1561 we find the town indebted to many persons in various sums, and especially to John Caplen, who at the request of the Corporation undertook to receive and administer all sums that might be due to the town within the next two years, and therefrom (1) to pay the fee-farm, the officers' wages, and other ordinary charges; next (2) to satisfy the other creditors; and (3) the said John Caplen, 'of his good natuer and accustomed goodness is contente that his own dette shalbe laste payed.' No repairs were to be executed for the town or any money transactions negotiated without

[1] See Guild Ordinances given below. Richard Gryme returned home to enjoy the sweets of freedom in his garden in East Street—'on the south part of the said street within the gate'—for which he paid 12d. (1469); a few years after he appears as Lieutenant of Hampton (1474–75).

[2] Steward's books. [3] Stat. Realm, iii. 351, 352.

[4] Boke of Remembrances, ff. 37, 41 b.

[5] Bond (among bundle of pardons), Audit House. [6] See under Charters.

the cognisance of John Caplen.[1] Loans from the burgesses in payment of the fee-farm not uncommonly occur.

The above reduction to £50 was confirmed by the last governing charter, that of 27th June 1640 (16 Charles I.), on the same conditions.[2] These were, that the petty customs should not have amounted in any year to £200; that no ships called 'carracks of Genoa' or 'galleys of Venice' should have visited the port, and that a certificate should accordingly be sent each year to the Lords of the Treasury and the Barons of the Exchequer. Certificates of the amount were regularly sent, but in 1803 an Act of Parliament was passed (43 Geo. III., cap. 21) abolishing the payment of petty customs to the Corporation, and giving them instead one-fifth of the port dues to be received by Commissioners created under the Act. In consequence of this, on November 9, 1804, they transmitted to the Treasury and Exchequer a certificate reciting the Act and affirming the extinguishment of the petty customs. This certificate was rejected for want of stating the amount received in lieu of petty customs; and on 23d November another was forwarded by the Corporation estimating the sum set apart from wharfage, cranage, anchorage, groundage, storage, &c., at one-fourth of the sum paid them by the Commissioners, or one-twentieth of the Commissioners' net receipts.[3] The certificate is still prepared in the same way every year, and each 9th of November it is most humbly signified in the prescribed quarters that no ships called 'carracks of Genoa' or 'galleys of Venice' have arrived at the port. In this way £150 of the old fee-farm is formally got rid of: it remains to follow the reduced farm of £50.

Sold by Commonwealth.

It had been paid to the Crown from the time of Edward VI. to the death of Charles I. Under the Commonwealth it was sold, September 29, 1650, together with the fee-farm of the city of Hereford (£42), by the Commissioners appointed for selling the fee-farm rents of the late Crown of England under the Act of the then present Parliament, to Azariah Husband and his heirs for the sum of £785, 11s. 8d.[4] After the Restoration, this, with other Crown properties, was resumed; and on the 26th Charles II. (1674), the £50 fee-farm of the town of Southampton was sold to Sir Robert Holmes, who became the purchaser of several other rents at the same time; the following note occurring at the end of the list of properties conveyed in the 'Enrolment of Sale':—

Sold by Charles II.

[1] Boke of Remembrances, f. 90.

[2] Yet the Town Journal states that, October 3, 1656 (8 Charles II.—Commonwealth), Roger Pedley, the sheriff, demanded of the town £200 for the fee-farm, which he was commanded to levy by writ of Exchequer. There must have been some informality on the town's part.

[3] Journal, Nov. 9, 1804, &c.; Report on Municip. Corp., 1835.

[4] Counterpart deed of sale (Record Office).

'All which said several rents are discharged by an indenture of bargain and sale, dated the 31st Jany. in the 26th year of the reign of King Charles II., A.D. 1674–[75], for and in consideration of the sum of £9751 . 19 . 0 paid into the receipt of his Majesty's Exchequer, as by a tally dated 20th day of Oct. 1674 may appear. Because the same are sold and conveyed unto Sir Robert Holmes Knt. his heirs and assigns for ever, and so for their only use and behoof, and not upon any other trust or confident whatsoever.'[1]

The fee-farm next passed to John Garland, Esq., and his heirs, being sold and conveyed by the trustees for sale of the Crown fee-farm rents,[2] under indenture enrolled in Chancery, dated 5th December (33 Chas. II.) 1681. It was afterwards conveyed to Thomas Osborne, first Duke of Leeds, in whose family it remained till 1737, when it was sold by Thomas, Duke of Leeds, great-grandson of the above, to Ann, Countess of Salisbury, widow, for a consideration of £1500.

Hatfield Charity School.

The Countess of Salisbury had lately built, at her own costs, a schoolhouse and residence for the purposes of a 'charity school,' in which twenty female children of the parish of Hatfield should be taught to read and sew,—a provision which it was supposed would satisfy the needs of the parish; and she now purchased this fee-farm with a view to the endowment of the school, joining in a tripartite indenture, made December 10, 1737 (11 Geo. II.), with James, Earl of Salisbury, her eldest son, of the second part, and the Honourable William Cecil, her younger son, and Matthew Lamb, Esq. of Lincoln's Inn, of the third part, by which the site of the school premises, together with all the buildings erected on the ground, and this fee-farm for an endowment, were granted, bargained, and sold for nominal sums to the above persons of the third part, and their heirs, as trustees for the school. The buildings are described as fronting westward to the street leading through the town, and eastward to Hatfield Park. The trustees were directed to apply £30 per annum for the salary of the mistress, £10 for clothing the children, and the remaining £10 for the taxes that should be assessed on the fee-farm rent and on the premises, and towards repairs.[3] Such is the history of the old town rent to the present time, the circumstances of which have been entirely forgotten,[4] though the fact of a settlement on the charity school appears in the Journal of October 28, 1825, and again at the end of the petty customs certificate of Michaelmas 1836, thus: 'Ordered that the Treasurer of the Borough do pay to the Trustees of Hatfield's charity the sum of £40 . 2 . 0, the remainder of the fee-farm rent, land tax deducted.' A similar order occurs under November 24, 1837.

[1] Inrolment of Sale of Fee-farm Rents (Land Revenue Office).

[2] A link is evidently wanting, which I am unable at present to supply.

[3] Close Roll, 11 Geo. II. (1737), No. 16.

[4] See the Report of Municip. Corp. Commission, 1835, where it is stated that little or nothing is known on the matter.

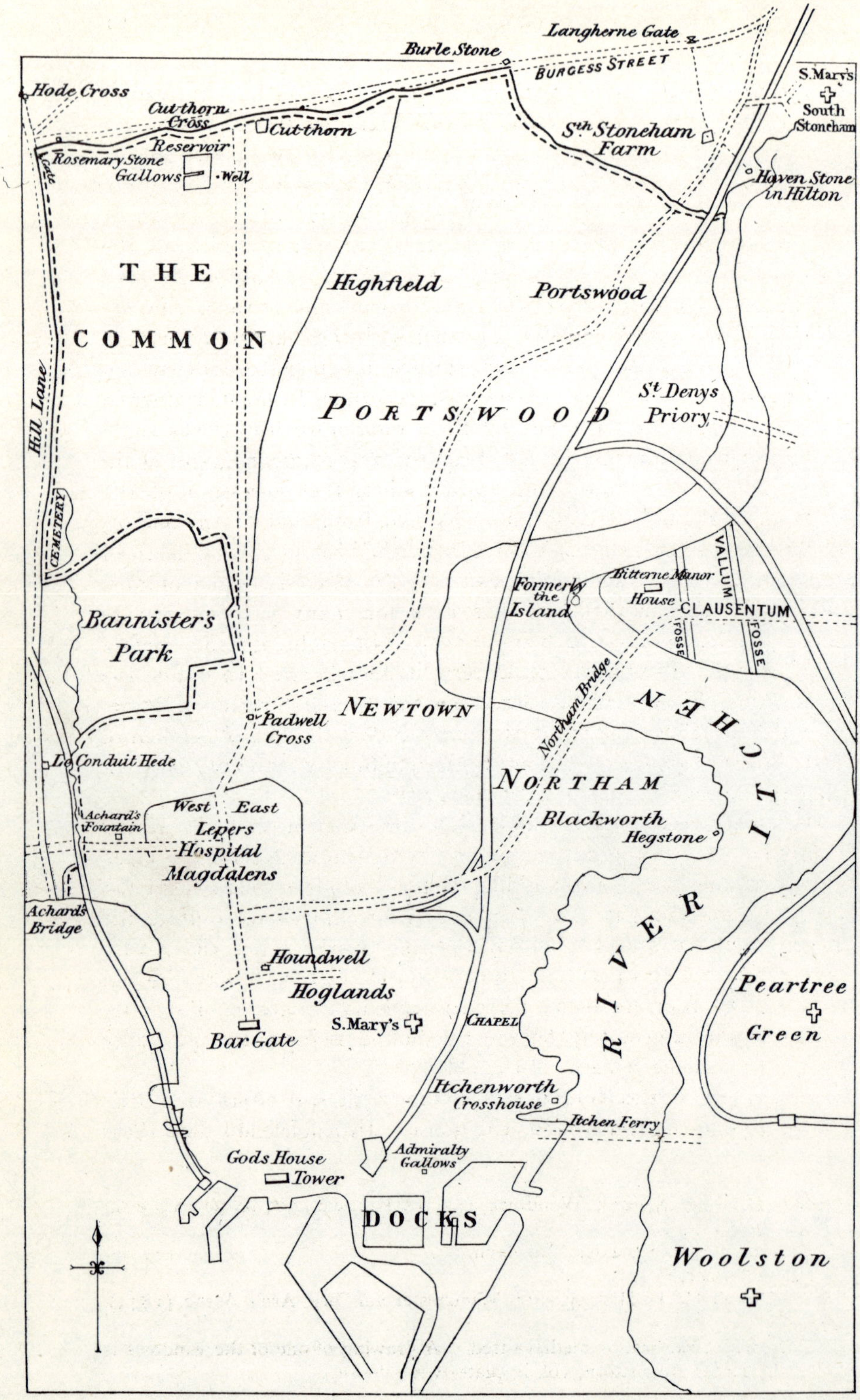

Langherne Gate
Burle Stone
BURGESS STREET
S. Mary's
South Stoneham
Hode Cross
Cut-thorn Cross
Cut-thorn
Reservoir
Sth Stoneham Farm
Rosemary Stone
Gallows
Well
Haven Stone in Hilton
THE COMMON
Highfield
Portswood
Hill Lane
PORTSWOOD
St Denys Priory
CEMETERY
Bitterne Manor House
Formerly the Island
VALLUM
CLAUSENTUM
FOSSE
FOSSE
Bannister's Park
Northam Bridge
NEWTOWN
Padwell Cross
Le Conduit Hede
NORTHAM
RIVER ITCHEN
West
East
Lepers Hospital
Magdalens
Achard's Fountain
Blackworth Hegstone
Achard's Bridge
Houndwell
Hoglands
Peartree Green
S. Mary's
CHAPEL
Bar Gate
Itchenworth Crosshouse
Itchen Ferry
Gods House Tower
Admiralty Gallows
DOCKS
Woolston

# CHAPTER III.

## *LOCAL AND DESCRIPTIVE.*

### SECTION I.

*Liberties or Precincts: Account of Boundaries and Encroachments.*

"THE present extensive[1] precinct was granted by King John, as is 1199.
"set forth below (but I never saw his grant); and in 38 Henry III. "it is described as under:—

"'This is the inquest taken by twenty four lawful men [here follow the 1254.
"'names of the jury] in the 38th year of King Henry, son of King John, at "'Shyrlegh before Sir Ernald de Bosco, at that time justice in eyre to the "'king's majesty, who say upon their oath that this is the bound and limit "'between the forest of Bere and the king's majesty's town of Suthampton: "'viz. From Achard's bridge (now Four-post bridge) as the way lies northward "'by the crosses to Cut-thorn, and from Cut-thorn to Burlestone, and from "'Burlestone to the water course of Furzewells as it goes down to the river "'Ytchen.[2] Within which bounds and limits of the liberties of the king's "'majesty's town of Suthampton the canons of S. Denys have and hold a "'certain wood called Portswood by a grant from Richard, formerly king of "'England, in free, full, and perpetual alms. And this wood is without the "'Regard and exempt from impeachment of waste. For which wood and the "'land called Kingsland the aforesaid king remitted one hundred shillings of "'his farm of the town of Suthampton.'

"The above boundary was confirmed,[3] 7 Edward IV., by Henry 1467.
"Bourchiere, Earl of Essex, justice in eyre. In his confirmation the "above inquest is recited verbatim.

---

[1] In 26 Henry II. (1180) William Briewere was made forester of the forest of Bere, with power to take any one transgressing therein between the 'bars' of Hampton and the gates of Winchester (Dugd. Bar., i. 700). Dr. Speed, who identifies the position of the 'bars' with that of the Bargate—which is by no means certain; the original Bargate was standing at the date of the above grant, and the 'bars' may have been at the entrance of the town's liberties—takes this appointment as an indication that the town precincts were not then as extensive as subsequently.

[2] Viz.: 'De ponte de Acardo sicut via extendit se per cruces versus Aquilonem usque Cuthorne, et a Cuttethorn usque ad Burlestone, et de Burlestone usque ad aqueductum de Fursewelle sicut descendit in Ychens.'—*Oak Book*, fol. 56.

[3] Liber Niger, fol. 108.

1488. "In 4 Henry VII. the precincts are described as under:[1]—

"'The perambulacon of the franchies of the toune of Suthampton graunted "'by King John[2] and confermed by mayny other noble kings his successours, "'and of late the bounds of the same franchies by vertue of a writte oute of the "'eschequier of the saide graunte, and remaynyng in the Audite house, sett "'oute by Thomas Overey as hereafter followith.

"'Item, first, fro Barred gate, the north gate of Southampton unto Acorn "'[otherwise Acard's] brig and crosse, west north west: and fro the Acorn "'brig and crosse unto the Hode crosse, north, thorough the village called Hill: "'and fro the Hode crosse to the Cutted-thorne crosse, suth suth est: and fro "'the Cutthed-thorne crosse to the Berell stone crosse, est, at Burger's strete "'ende, and so along Burger's strete and thorough Kinghern [otherwise Lang-"'herne] yate unto Haven stone in Hilton upponne the water side, est: and "'fro Haven stone along as the water lyeth unto Hegstone at Blackworth, "'suth: and fro Hegstone [latterly Millstone] as the water lyeth to Ichen-"'worth [*i.e.* by the cross house] suth; and fro Ichenworth as the water lyeth "'to the Mesyne due [Maison Dieu] yate of Suthampton, west.'"

It is difficult to reconcile what have become the modern municipal and parliamentary limits with those given in the documents above: a glance at the map will show what the differences are. It remains, then, to examine the old landmarks. The charters will not help us, as they only determine from time to time that the precincts are to be the same as usual, that is, no doubt, as described in the old inquisitions, which are no further explained.

Western boundary.

We take first the western boundary. "According to this boundary "the east side of the village of Hill should be within the jurisdiction "of the town. That point was disputed so early as 20 Henry VIII. "[1528–29], for in the steward's accounts for that year there is an "article charged for a fee[3] to counsel concerning that business, "but how it ended then I do not find. Some years after this right "was tried at Salisbury assize, and the Corporation, not having "exercised their jurisdiction there for many years, were cast upon "a non-user."

Unfortunately there is little to be added to this concise statement. Many years subsequently, namely, in 1571, the 'controversy' with Mr. Whitehead about the common, as also with Lady Dawtrey, was ordered to be tried at law, the nature of the trial being not quite

[1] Lib. Rememoranc. BB., f. 1 b.

[2] In the 'Boke of Remembrances,' last page, in a copy belonging to the reign of Henry VIII., the grant is said to have been made in 1 John (1199).

[3] 'Costs for the meeting of the Town's counsel and mistress Whitehede for the variance of our liberties in Hill lane.' The details of the dinner follow, over which the lady of the manor and the lawyer discussed the point; lastly comes, 'Item to master Wintershull for his labour hither v$^{s}$.' Several times before this, as in 1526–27, we find the town repairing 'the king's high way at Hill' (Steward's book; Temp. T. Overey, sub anno).

clear. But in the spring of 1596 a suit, apparently in point, was 'yet depending undecided in her Majesty's Court of Wards and Liveries' between Master Whitehead and the town. 'He seemeth to lay challenge,' say the court leet jury, 'unto all or the most part of the common pasture belonging to us and others the inhabitants, leading up within our liberties and perambulation towards Cut-thorn, as yet time out of memory ever enjoyed, held, and occupied by the inhabitants of Southampton without any lawful challenge or impeachment.' They therefore think it right to define again their liberties, which they do much in the form of 1488.

Four years after (1600) we find them presenting that 'the vanes at Hill bridge doe not stand as in times past. . . . We challenge our liberties on the east side of Hill street, and the inhabitants there ought to do their suit and service at our Law day, as we suppose, our perambulation considered and regarded which leadeth us hereunto.' The same presentment was made in the following year.

A few years later, namely, October 1608, a letter was ordered to be written to Sir Henry Whitehead 'in answer to his concerning the common and a hogshead of wine which he demandeth as due to him yearly for the Friar's head, which as yet to this [house's] memory was never paid;' but as early as 1478 there had been an agreement of some kind about the spring between the burgesses and Master Whitehead.[1]

In 1611 Hill is again stated to be within the liberties, and the old complaints about the vanes occur; also the jury present, as they have done before, the need of a 'court of survey' for viewing all the town's lands and writings, that they may not only know but enjoy their rights.

In 1651 a trial occurred in reference to Banister's[2] farm, the only notice of which in the town books, as far as observed, is the following, which is fragmentary:—

'Friday, March 19, 1651–52.—Whereas a suit was commenced and brought by Sir Edward Banister in the name of Richard Symes, tenant of Banister's farm, against James Needle and James Flower, collectors of the Parliament taxes in the ward of All Saints, within the town of Southampton, for taking a distress upon the land of the said farm for the assessments charges thereupon; and by order of the Court of Upper Bench at Westminster where the said suit was commenced, the trial of the said suit was ordered to be at New Sarum, in the county of Wilts, at the assizes there, and the point in issue was by that order to try whether Banister's farm were in the county of Hants or in the county of the said town: the town of Southampton in defence of the said suit and in maintenance of the ancient bounds of the said town and county did, among other

1 Steward's books.

2 Under December 1474 the sum of eight shillings was given to the town-clerk 'to pay unto Whytehede for the matter of Banestres Court.'

evidences, produce at the said assizes before the Lord Chief Justice Rolle these writings or evidences hereafter written, the true copies whereof are as follow:— Henricus Bourochier, comes Essexiæ et Justiciarius itinerans omnium forestarum, &c.'

The document is the confirmation of 1467–68 mentioned above; but no other 'writings or evidences' are given, nor is anything said as to the date or issue of the trial.[1]

It is certain, however, that the Corporation continued to lay claim to the largest boundary. Thus about the date of the above entry, namely, at the court leet in 1652, they present—

'That the metes, bowndes and precincts of this Towne and County are and ought to extend first from the Bargate . . . unto Hood Crosse, w$^{ch}$ standethe in the great comon w$^{t}$out the comon of Hampton, about [blank] paces from the corner of the hedge of the s$^{d}$ inclosed comon of Hampton w$^{h}$ waye from Acorn bridge to the aforesaid Hood crosse lyeth northward through a village caled Hill,' &c.

They complain at the same time that many great annoyances arising within the precincts cannot be inquired of, nor the penalties levied for the same, 'for want of an officer within this Towne antiently called the Lord Mayor of the Buckinges, wherefore wee desire that suche an officer be yearly choasen at the accustomed tyme accordinge to the antient custom of this Towne, and that the order belonginge to the s$^{d}$ office may, by the authorety of this Coorte, be revived and confirmed for tyme to com.'

The presentments of the court leet jury slightly vary with the opening of the next century. From about 1704 they present that the metes and bounds '*ought* to extend *through* a village called Hill,'—as if that line were being gradually abandoned,—and thence by the long route through Langherne gate and by the Haven Stone to the *Sandy* Gate of the town—a corruption, after various transformations, for the 'Maison Dieu Gate,' which having first appeared in the latter half of the seventeenth century, is perpetuated in the court leet books of the present day. But from the year 1713 the form '*through* the village' is dropped, and the boundary line is drawn 'northward *from* the village

1 Dr. Speed in his first book presented to the Corporation (p. 35) says:— "But these ancient bounds [those described above in the document 4 Henry "VII., 1488–89] are at present something reduced, for the Corporation having "neglected to exercise their jurisdiction at Hill for some time, and afterwards "attempting to recover it, were cast at Salisbury Assize upon a non-user; so "that the rivulet which runs from the common to Achard's bridge is now reckoned "the boundary.

"A.D. 1651.—There was a trial at Salisbury Assizes to determine whether "Bannister's farm was within the county of the town or no. *N.B.*—It was "determined in the negative."

called Hill.' In 1748 the name of Sidford is joined with that of Hill, and from that date to the present time the bounds have been formally presented each year as extending northward '*from* a village called Hill and Sidford.'

The annual perambulations, while they lasted, continued to be made along the brook, as if Bannister's Court were still within the liberties, and the freedom of that district from borough dues seems to have been regarded as a prescriptive immunity. The Commissioners of 1832 adopted the brook along its whole course as the boundary of the parliamentary borough in the map annexed to their Report,[1] and by the Boundary Act (2 & 3 Will. IV. cap. 64) the parliamentary borough and the district called the town and county of the town of Southampton were to be conterminous. On the other hand, the Municipal Corporation Commissioners in 1835 excluded the disputed district from the county or municipal borough, and the Boundary Commissioners of 1868 have affirmed the exclusion in the map affixed to their Report, and the line is so drawn in the beautiful maps of the Ordnance Survey. Thus the question of the western boundary now rests.

Boundary at north-west.

Passing to the north-west angle of the borough limits, we observe an ancient boundary stone standing, as the court leet books describe it, about a hundred paces to the north of the enclosed common. This is the Hode Cross mentioned in every description of the franchises as the stone to which the boundary line stretched northward from Acorn Bridge, and through which it passed S.S.E. to Cutthorn. There was, therefore, at this part, according to the ancient inquisitions, land which formerly belonged to the town outside the present municipal and parliamentary limits which are simply those of the enclosure. This part of the common seems to have been hedged and ditched in 1577, not altogether to the satisfaction of the court leet jury if it be referred to in the following extract, which gives a curious picture of the helpless way in which matters seem to have been overlooked. In 1579 they present—

'That whereas of late daies theare hathe bin a peece of our comon and heathe ditched and hedged and enclosid in and planted wi$^{th}$ willows under the name of a shadow for our cattel w$^{ch}$ have hitherto many yeres past prosperid verie well as the comon was beefore, wherefore we dessire yt may be pulled down agayne and levelid as before, for we doubt that in short time yt wilbe taken from the common to some particuler man's use, w$^{ch}$ weare lamentable and pitiefull and not sufferable; for as our auncestors of theire greate care and travell have provided that and like other many benefyts for us theire successors, so we thinck it o$^{r}$ dwetie in conscience to keep, uphold, and maintaine the same as we founde yt

[1] Boundary Report, 1832, p. 229.

for o[r] posteritie to come w[th]out diminishing eny part or parcel from yt, but rather to augment more to yt yf yt may be.'

Immediately they continue:—

'Also wee fynd that theare ys a great peice of our sayd comon and heathe leaft unclosed from the rest by Hoode crosse, for what purpose wee know not, but we doubt that in continuance of time yt will [be] quit lost, and so by littell and littel [we shall] loose and diminish oure Lyberties w[ch] we so long time have enjoyed w[ch] weare greate pitie.'

Similar presentments were made in other years, *e.g.*, in 1580, 1587, 1591, with the like warning of there being 'lefte unclosid of the common at Hoode crosse a great quantytie of grounde, w[ch] being left out in tyme to come may be lost yf good regard be not had thereof.' Jurisdiction over the larger boundary has always been claimed, as it is in words at the present day; but, for whatever reason, this portion of the ancient liberties has long been abandoned, and the boundary remains, as drawn by the Parliamentary Commissioners in 1832, along the enclosure, on the evidence of the latest perambulations.

North-east boundary.

At the north-eastern limits the ancient inquisitions and the court leet books describe the boundary line as passing the Burle or Borell Stone along Burgess Street to Langherne Gate, and thence to the Haven Stone. For some reason or other, the modern perambulations appear to have confined themselves to the shorter route by the Burle Stone, and along the stream there to the river Itchen; and in accordance with this the Commissioners of 1832 drew the boundary, in which they have been followed by those of 1868.

But beyond the evidence from the inquisitions, there is also that of the Corporation having exercised jurisdiction in time past as far as the Langherne Gate and Haven Stone line. Thus in 1488[1] repairs were done upon the four crosses of the franchise, upon Acorn Bridge, Langherne Gate, the Haven Stone, Hegstone, &c. In 1594 one Thomas Betts was fined £5 for removing the Haven Stone, which is described as a boundary. This was discovered 'in our last circuit riding,' so that at that period they took the longer route. The stone was to be replaced under a penalty of £20. In 1600 the court leet 'present the postes and vanes at Langhthorne gate, and lickwise at Havenstone by Hilton are sett to be amended and new cullored. Also the passage betwene the two postes nere Havenstone is so moyry as is not passable: wherefore we amerce Sir Michell Blunt, knyght, that holdeth Stonage furme in xij[d]. Be it comanded to him to cause the same mire and durt to be amended thesside the lawdaye next uppon paine of x[s].' In the next year, however, matters are not amended as far as the vanes and posts

[1] MS. temp. T. Overey, sub anno.

are concerned, for they 'are altogether decayed and the vanes taken down, whereof we crave redresse and reformation by order of the steward.' There also occurs another presentment of Sir Michael Blunt which seems to affect the district in question. After this no important notice of the north-eastern boundary has been met with till the present century. In the year 1819 the Alderman of Portswood reported[1] 'that the boundary stone called Haven stone, situate at Portswood, dividing the County of this Town from the County of Hants, had been taken away and converted by some persons' to the use of South Stoneham Mill. Strict inquiry was made, and as it proved that the stone had been removed by a servant without the knowledge of his employers, and that another had been placed in its stead, the matter was allowed to drop after ample apology. In the same year a new boundary stone, bearing the arms and monogram of the town, was placed at Langherne Gate, where it is now standing.

It seems probable that the ancient boundary line passed from Langherne Gate through South Stoneham farm, having struck and followed a little watercourse, which would thus be the 'water of Furzewell,' a name now unknown in the district. It would then cross the Portswood road some 250 yards north-east of the present boundary.

" In consequence of this boundary, including Portswood, the Prior " and Convent of St. Dionis, as lords of Portswood, agreed by an in- " denture, bearing date 20 Richard II. (1396), that the inhabitants of " Portswood should submit to the jurisdiction of the town, and should " attend the Town Court Leet, and should be rated with the town for " the king's supplies; their proportion to be for every fifteenth £1, 6s. 8d.[1] " The Corporation pay a rent of £4 a year to the owners of the manor " of South Stoneham, and it appears in the Journal that in the year " 1638 Mrs. Clarke, the owner at that time, produced to the Cor- " poration some deeds by which such a rent is granted payable out of " certain lands, tenements, and hereditaments in the town of South- " ampton and the liberties thereof, by the mayor, bailiffs, and burgesses " of Southampton. The Journal does not say on what account this " rent was granted, but it is supposed to be for riding through part of " the lands of that estate in the perambulation of their liberties. The " date of those deeds is 9 and 15 James I.

The Law-day.

" The ancient custom was to hold a Court Leet at the Cutted- " thorn, where a place was enclosed for that purpose, and all the " inhabitants were summoned to ride the bounds and attend the " court every year on the 3d Tuesday after Easter on the penalty

[1] Journal sub anno.

[2] Lib. Remembranciarum H., f. 115.

"of 1d. for every defaulter: a dinner[1] was provided there at the "expense of the Corporation. They came afterwards to hold their "court in town in the morning, and rode the bounds in the afternoon, "and at their return the sheriff gave a supper to the whole company; "but within a very few years this has been left off, and they hold "their court in town, and the Mayor and Sheriff, very poorly "attended, ride the bounds in a kind of private manner."

Present conclusion.

The county of the town of Southampton, as shown above, is almost certainly somewhat shrunk from its ancient dimensions, but it has at all events gained accuracy of definition: it is, in fact, identical with the borough, comprising an area of 1980 acres, and consisting of the parishes of All Saints, Holy Rood, St. Lawrence, St. John, St. Michael, so much of the parish of St. Mary as lies west of the Itchen, the tithing of Portswood in the parish of South Stoneham, and Southampton common, which is extra-parochial.

The district is separated from the rest of Hampshire for certain county purposes, though these of late years have again become diminished; but as it is all under the jurisdiction of the Corporation, the municipal institutions of the borough are, in fact, those by which the county is governed.

An account of the common lands will follow naturally on the foregoing.

## SECTION II.

### *The Common and Common Lands.*

The Common.

"What is now called Southampton Common was formerly part of "the manor of Shirley or Surlie, and 12 Henry III. or A.D. 1228

[1] "Expenses of the Law-day at Cutthorn, 14 Henry VII. (1499), Steward's books:"—

| | *s.* | *d.* | | *s.* | *d.* |
|---|---|---|---|---|---|
| A crope of beffe | 2 | 4 | Two gallons claret wyne | 1 | 4 |
| Four leggs of mutton | 1 | 0 | Orengys | 0 | 2 |
| Do. do. | 1 | 0 | Musterd and vineger | 0 | 2 |
| Three dos. of bred | 3 | 0 | Two hundred of wood | 1 | 4 |
| Half a barrell doble beer | 1 | 8 | A man to dresse the mette | 0 | 8 |
| Half a barrell fyne hyl beer | 1 | 0 | Two poor men to turn | 0 | 3 |
| Ten gallons peny ale | 0 | 10 | Two poor boys | 0 | 2 |
| Twelve chekens | 1 | 0 | A carte to Cut-thorn | 0 | 8 |
| Four pyggs | 2 | 0 | For whyt dysches | 0 | 8 |
| Two lambys | 2 | 0 | Making a both | 0 | 3 |
| Butter and eggs | 0 | 8 | Hyre of two garnysche off Wessell | 0 | 8 |
| Chese | 0 | 3 | The 12 men when they gafe ther verdyt | 2 | 0 |
| Salt | 0 | 1 | Two men beyring the two long plankes, and setting the two barrys | 0 | 4 |
| Half a bushel of flowre | 0 | 8 | | | |
| Half a pond of peper | 0 | 8 | | | |
| Saffryn, cloves, and mace | 0 | 4 | | | |
| Preuyns and raysyns | 0 | 8 | | | |

"a Fine of it was passed between the town of Southampton and "Nicholas de Surlie, lord of that manor, in which the bounds of it "are described:

"This is the final concord[1] made between the burgesses of Southampton, on "the one part, and Nicholas de Surlie, on the other part, in the houses of the "castle of our lord the king at Southampton on the vigil of Pentecost, in the "12th year of the reign of King Henry son of John, before Sir Thomas de "Muleton, Robert de Lexinton, Ralph Musard,[2] at that time justices in eyre, the "residents in the aforesaid houses of our lord the king, and many other of the "king's faithful men then present: Concerning the common pasture of the town "of Southampton lying on the north part of the lands of William Wolgar, John "Blancbully,[3] Amise Fortin, and of land which belonged to John Chopin, about "which contention had arisen between the parties: Namely that the aforesaid "Nicholas acknowledges the right of the Burgesses to the same pasture and quit-"claims for himself and his heirs for ever whatever right he had, or might have "had, in the aforesaid pasture, 'as the land stretches in length from the corner "'and ditch[4] of the aforesaid William Wolgar's land as far as Kotterorne[5] as "'the king's kingway coming from Achard's bridge leads from the corner and "'ditch of William Wolgar to the said thorn-bush of Kotterorne which is upon "'the highway; and also all the pasture in breadth within the highway that "'leads from the aforesaid thorn-bush of Kotterorne as far as the cross of "'Burlston which is on the great road between Hanton and Winton; and all "'the pasture as it stretches in length from the said cross of Burlston to the "'corner and ditch of the land which was John Chopin's as the great high-road "'leadeth that comes from Winton to Hanton; and all the pasture as it "'stretches in breadth from the corner and ditch (or fence) of the land which "'was John Chopin's to the corner and ditch (or fence) of the aforesaid "'William Wolgar. So that the whole pasture included between the said three "'highways, clear of the fences of the forenamed William Wolgar, John Blanc-"'bully, and Amise Fortin, and of the land which was John Chopin's, which "'was planted [*i.e.*, the pasture] with trees when this Fine [finalis concordia] "'was passed, shall remain to the said Burgesses, &c. And for this acknow-"'ledgement of their right, and the quitting claim to the said pasture, the said "'Burgesses paid to the said Nicholas ten marks of silver.'

"At the same time it was agreed that the cattle of neither party "should come upon the other's common, but that each should have a "free passage to and from their own common.

"A.D. 1549. It was declared that Northam has no right of "common. Rights.

"A.D. 1570. An order was made that no Portswood people should

[1] Liber Niger, f. 107.

[2] He had fined in £100 for leave to marry as he liked, 3 Ric. I. (1192). Most of the fine was relaxed. Madox, Excheq., ii. 224.

[3] John Blancbully had the King's great ship called the 'Queen' during his life at a rent of fifty marks a year, from the year 1232 (see Madox, Excheq., i. 509).

[4] Fossatum, more widely *fence*.

[5] So in the original. Dr. Speed, who has given this part of the document, has Kottethorne, Cutthorn being meant.

"put any cattle upon the common till Mr. Knight and Lady Dawtrey "show their right.

"About the same time several people of Portswood[1] and Hill paid "fines for trespasses of their cattle upon the common."

Rights of common belonged only to the inhabitant householders of the town. In 1580 a certain Peter Quate was fined for assuming these rights, 'and being a battchyller, and not keping howsse, ought not to kepe any cattal at all.'[2] The town books, especially in the sixteenth century, abound in regulations on turning out of cattle, and 'oppressors of the common'—that is, persons who turned out too many head, or otherwise unlawfully—were sharply dealt with.

Southampton common, which is exempted from building by Act of Parliament, remains substantially the same in extent as in the sixteenth century, but within its ample circuit many improvements have been made by roadmaking and planting. It comprises about 376 acres of lovely and varied forest scenery. Before leaving it we must mention three spots with very different associations.

Gallows.

The site of the gallows is covered by the reservoirs on the upper part of the common to the left of the Winchester Road. The last execution here was on July 27, 1785, in the shrievalty of Thomas Mears, Esq., the criminal being the late butler of Mrs. Bagenal, of 16 Above Bar, condemned for having burglariously entered her dwelling and stolen plate. He had been committed by the mayor (John Monckton, Esq.) and Thomas Guillaume, Esq., justices of the peace for the town and county, on February 28, and tried and convicted at the summer assizes held in the Guildhall, July 9, 1785.

Cutthorn.

Cutthorn was an enclosure near the north boundary of the common, and to the right of the Winchester Road, deriving its name from some famous 'cutted-thorn;' in ancient times it being common for manorial courts to be held in the open air round some remarkable tree—an oak, an apple, a thorn, as it might chance—a practice which recalls some most primitive associations. We speak of Cutthorn also elsewhere.

Cemetery.

Under the powers of 6 & 7 Vict. 1843 (July 4), the rights of common and all other rights were severed from fifteen acres of the common, and that portion vested in the mayor, aldermen, and burgesses for the purposes of a cemetery, to be divided according to the needs of the place into consecrated and unconsecrated ground.

[1] "There are several affidavits which prove the town's right to the common "exclusive of S. Denys (*i.e.*, Portswood): and also the copy of a lease by which "the town granted a part of the common to the lord of S. Denys for 60 years on "condition that he should fence it (Papers concerning Lady Dawtrey in Audit "House)."

[2] Court Leet Book, 1580.

The service for the dead in the consecrated ground was to be performed by the incumbent of the borough parish from which the deceased should be removed for interment; and in the case of persons not dying in any such parish, the duty of officiating devolved on the incumbents of the borough parishes in monthly rotation. The Act gave the Corporation power to borrow £7000 upon the fees, and provided for the addition of five acres when required. The ground selected, at the south-west corner of the common, was left as far as possible in its natural beauty: it was fenced, drained, further planted, and intersected with roads and paths as its purpose demanded. Three chapels were erected—one for the Church of England, in the Norman style, another for the Nonconformists, and a third for the Jews, both of Early English character; the curators' lodge and entrance gate being Perpendicular. The total cost of the cemetery, with preliminary expenses, was about £10,000. It was opened in 1846, when the church portion was consecrated by the Bishop of Winchester (Sumner). The additional five acres were enclosed and the part allotted to the church consecrated in 1863.

The cemetery is kept in beautiful order under the supervision of the Corporation.

**The Avenue.** The avenue, which connects the common with the town, commences at the fountain erected near the site of Lubery, afterwards Padwell Cross, so named from former owners of adjacent property, and subsequently, for a like reason, called John-a-Guernsey's Cross. The avenue was originally commenced at this spot in February 1744–45, and continued in 1750 and subsequent years. It is said that some of the trees were planted in commemoration of the battle of Culloden, which was fought on April 16, 1746. It has of late years been considerably extended.

The common and the avenue are extra-parochial, in consequence, possibly, of their having at a remote period belonged to the ancient forest of Bere. The land south of the common on each side of the avenue has, however, for centuries been included in the adjacent parishes.

## Section III.

*Other Common Lands: Saltmarsh—Old Controversies—Modern Transformations.*

Formerly there were other common lands of some extent. "In "1549 several persons made oath that they knew Mr. Baker's close, "Mr. Rigg's close, Mr. James's close, the two chantry closes, Hound- "well, Kingsland, Hogland, Maudelin two fields, Lobery mead, the "closes in S. Mary's lane, and where the Prior of S. Denys made his

" garden, common to the use of the cattle and beasts of the commons " of the town after the crop was taken away, and also the town ditches " common throughout the year.[1]

" The town ditches are leased out by the Corporation as part of the " waste; but how the town came to lose their right of common in " most of the other lands above mentioned I cannot learn. They have " it still in the same form in Houndwell, Hogland, and the two " Maudelin fields, but in none of the rest.

" There is another article of common belonging to the town, " namely, the field called God's house meadow, which is common from " Lammas to the Purification—to God's house the rest of the year; " and the Saltmarsh, which is common all the year."

Saltmarsh.

This Saltmarsh stretched round by the shore from God's House gate to Cross House and Chapel, and was surrounded by a bank thrown up as a protection from the sea, the repair of which was a constant source of feud, the Corporation maintaining that the commoners were bound to repair it in consequence of their exercise of common, and asserting that their own duties as to sea-banks were confined to such as were at the feet of the walls, and so part of the fortifications.

In order to maintain the banks they sometimes attempted a rate,[2] sometimes they let the crop of a portion of it, as to the porters in 1526; but efforts at enclosure, for whatever purpose, were constantly resisted. Ultimately, in 1681, the Corporation got a commission of sewers for this marsh; and the disputes continuing as of old, a renewal of the commission was talked of in 1753, to avoid which some private persons repaired the banks.

Trial of rights with God's House.

We turn to a more important controversy—one with God's House, brought to arbitration in 1503. It was the town's contention at that time that all the lands eastward of Orchard Lane and south of Crampe or Marsh Lane, together with a little marsh stretching from Cross House to the chapel of the Holy Trinity on the north, were properly common and belonged to the town by royal grant, but that in the first part of the fifteenth century the authorities of God's House had made serious encroachments and erected fences, which the mayor and community of the town had broken up in assertion of their rights, apparently about 1438. After this the land was said to have remained open till the mayoralty of John Walker in 1466 and the wardenship of John Pereson—he became warden about 1459—when the latter disseised the town of certain lands, a part of the great marsh or common, having bought over the mayor by a grant of some of the land in

[1] Liber Niger, f. 105. See also Court Leet Book for 1550.
[2] See extract at the end of this Section.

question, which he consented to hold from the Hospital. A few years after this, apparently about 1471, in the mayoralty of Robert Bluett, the mayor, burgesses, and commonalty again asserted their right by forcibly removing the fences; and the controversy continuing, Christopher Bainbrigge, who became warden of St. Julian's in 1495, preferred a petition to the king and council against the Corporation, upon which the matter was put to arbitration. The Hospital's case does not appear; but on the town's part a number of ancient inhabitants made oath on the 18th January 1503 (18 Hen. VII.) before John Edmund, Prior of Montsent, and Sir Robert Peck, Knt., of Baddesley, in support of the town's claim: there were a veteran named Richard Woodleff, 'aged 104 and more,' John Millbrook, aged 93, John Burges, Abbot of Letley (now Netley), aged 76, Thomas Gage, aged 86, and 'many others.'

The land in dispute was at this time partially divided into closes by hedge and ditch. Outside God's House gate and north of the present bowling-green, at that time unenclosed, the land south of East Street and between the town ditches and Orchard Lane, now thickly built over and crossed by Bell Street, Mount Street, Union Street, College Street, Bernard Street, Britton Street, containing also Brunswick Square, Charlotte Street, and many other small streets and courts, was then divided into three gardens or closes, of which that to the north belonged apparently to John Fleming, the middle one to Thomas Thomas, and that to the south, which joined what is now the bowling-green, to Christopher Ambrose. The two closes belonging respectively to Thomas and Ambrose were in dispute. Immediately to the east of these three gardens was a large close or field bounded on the north by Crampe or Marsh Lane, and on the east by the Saltmarsh. This was the land now included by Marsh Lane on the north, by Orchard Lane and Terminus Terrace on the west and east, and by Upper and Lower Queen's Terrace on the south, and containing Cross Street, Chandos Street, Winchester Terrace, Bridge Street, Oxford Street, Latimer Street, Threefield Lane, Queen Street, and several others. South of this enclosure was a little field or close lying to the north of the road leading from God's House gate towards Itchen Ferry, bounded on the west by Newtown or Orchard Lane, and adjoining the garden of Christopher Ambrose, and on the east running to the Saltmarsh: this land is now known as Porter's or God's House Meadow. The Saltmarsh was the whole stretch of land partly now built over by the railway terminus and adjacent streets, limited on the west by the before-named enclosures, on the south and east by the sea, and on the north by Crampe or Marsh Lane as far as Cross House at the ferry, near which was a portion of ground called the Little Marsh. Besides the above lands, certain rents arising from houses (specified) in the town were in dispute, amounting altogether to 47s. 2½d., to which the master, brethren, and sisters of God's House laid claim as theirs from ancient time.

The award. In the award, which was made by Mr. Justice Kingsmill and Mr. Richard Broke, gentleman, on the 28th October 1504 (20 Hen. VII.), the two gardens and the great field, as also the town rents, were adjudged to God's House for ever, together with the use of the smaller field (Porter's or God's House Meadow) from the Purification to Lammas each year, after which the meadow was to be common to the town: on the other hand, the whole of the Saltmarsh was adjudged to the town, to be common throughout the year. Releases between the parties were passed accordingly on 6th February 1505 (20 Hen. VII.) In that from Christopher Bainbrigge, warden of St. Julian's, to the Corporation, the great marsh is described as abutting on the highway which leads from God's House gate to Itchen Ferry towards the south and east, upon two closes or fields belonging to the warden of God's House towards the west, and upon a little lane (venellam) called Crampe Lane, and a certain small marsh lately belonging to the said warden but now to the Corporation, towards the north. The little marsh by Itchen Cross abutted on the great marsh towards the south, upon the Itchen Water towards the east, upon Crampe Lane and land belonging to the precentor of St. Mary's on the west, and a property belonging to the chapel of the Holy Trinity on the north.[1]

Bowling-green. The bowling-green should here be mentioned. The first probable reference to this paddock as a place of recreation which has been observed occurs under 1550, in which year a townsman, the lessee of the King's Orchard, was presented for keeping 'common playinge with bowles, tabylles and other unlawfull games agaynst the kinges statute.'

The King's Orchard, called in Elizabeth's time the 'Queen's,' was close to this spot.

The Act which prohibited 'inferior people' from playing at bowls and other games had been passed in 1541, and such persons were constantly being fined for infringing the statute. The bowling-green was, in short, as described in 1635, and has continued to be, a ground 'where many gentlemen, with the gentile merchants of this town, take their recreation.'

Orders about Saltmarsh. Before passing to modern transformations of the Saltmarsh, we may notice one or two past regulations. Refuse from the streets was frequently ordered to be strewn over Saltmarsh, whether as manure or for raising the level of hollow places. Brewers in 1567 were ordered

[1] See Corporation documents relating to Saltmarsh and God's House.

to dig no more clay in Saltmarsh for their bungs until they had carefully filled up all existing holes; wherever they dug they were to fill up. In 1576[1] and other years, offenders in this respect were heavily amerced, sometimes apparently for digging at all. Under the former year is an order about pasturage, which we give as a specimen of such regulations:—Saltmarsh was to be shut from Ladyday to May-day, then open till Houndwell should be rid of hay, after which Saltmarsh was to be closed and Houndwell and the Heath (the common) open till East and West Magdalen cornfields should be harvested. Then the cattle were to go into the Magdalens and Houndwell was to be closed; and the Magdalens being eaten bare, Saltmarsh was to be opened again till Houndwell and East and West Magdalens should be sufficiently grown.[2]

The modern development of the town depended very much on the way in which these common lands would be dealt with, occupying as they did a valuable and extensive zone round the ancient town. A railway had been under consideration as early as 1825, but the scheme for a railway and docks was not fairly afloat till 1830. In November that year the Corporation received a deputation from subscribers to the railway, and expressed their readiness to make arrangements with any respectable company that might be formed for the advancement of the port. Various other questions which had been mooted, such as the employment of the poor on the common lands, and the nature of the rights over such lands of those whose consent (under 1 & 2 Will. IV. c. 42) had first to be obtained, directed the further attention of the Corporation towards the common fields.[3] Meanwhile in February 1832 leave had been granted to the railway company to pass over the town mud-lands and marsh according to a plan exhibited; and in November 1833, preliminaries being completed for introducing the railway bill into Parliament, the Corporation again expressed their hearty concurrence and desire to co-operate in the scheme. The bill was passed in the following year. Rights looked into.

But the Marsh Improvement Act, 7 & 8 Vict. 1844 (July 4), completed the history of the common lands for the present. The various portions to be dealt with were the marsh, formerly the Saltmarsh, common all the year to the scot-and-lot paying inhabitants, and containing upwards of 16 acres, and the fields called East Magdalens or Marlands, containing about 22 acres, West Marland containing 16 acres, and Hoglands 11 acres, all which were common Marsh Improvement Act.

[1] Temp. Thomæ Overey, sub anno; Court Leet Books, ib.

[2] Court Leet Books, 1567.

[3] Journal, Feb. 18, 1831, March 28, 1831, Nov. 9, 1832, Oct. 32, 1834, Feb. 20, 1835, &c.

six months in the year. The marsh, though intersected by the railway and the Itchen Bridge Road, was imperfectly drained and liable to be flooded by the tide, and thus a constant source of nuisance to houses in the vicinity. This tract of ground, detached and forming no part of the common fields, was peculiarly eligible for building purposes, owing to its proximity to the railway terminus. Accordingly the Act gave power to the Corporation to let this portion on building leases, all rights of common being extinguished, and directed that the money arising from the improved estate should be employed in buying up a certain leasehold interest in East Marlands, behind Sussex Place and Northam Bridge Road, for £740, and in the purchase, at £250 per acre, of the fee-simple of all the common fields which were to be vested in the Corporation, and reserved henceforth for the benefit of the public. In the marsh a reservation was made of four acres, bounded by Marsh Lane on the north, Itchen Bridge Road on the south, the railway on the east, and the road from the terminus to Marsh Lane on the west, for a recreation ground. This portion is now utilised as a cattle-market, and occasionally as a fair-ground, under the authority given to the Corporation by the Act for the removal of Above Bar Fair. The Corporation received powers to drain and fill up the remnant of the abortive canal in Houndwell, to erect lodges for keepers, and otherwise to improve and manage the public lands for common use. The issue of the Act has been the formation of the public parks, which are not only a yearly increasing ornament to the town, but of essential service to a growing population rapidly surrounding them on all sides. It seems strange to have to record that the bill had been petitioned against by the vestries on account of the powers taken by the Corporation to enclose the marsh.

The Parks.

NOTE.—*The Agreement for the Inhabitants to repair the Banks at the Saltmarsh.*

After 1505.

'Be it knowen to all the Inhabytants and Comyns of this Towne of Suthampton, that the Meyre, Bailiffs, and Burgesses of the same be content and agreyd that the sayde Inhabytants and Burgesses shall have the Saltemershe Comyn in manner and form following, and upon such conditions as hereafter ensue.

'Fyrst, if the Inhabytants of the Towne of Suthampton wylbe content to bere ther parte of the Charge of 19l. 11s. 0, and odd money wch hath be spent upon the Saltmershe this last yer past, for making of the Groynys and other Charges for the defence of the Se agenst the same Mershe, and over and above that, to bere ther parte of the Charge that shall be yerely requyred, nedefull for the contynual kepyng and defendyng of the See oute of the sayde Mershe, that then they to have lyke Liberty and profyte of the sayde Mershe, as the sd. Meyr, Bailiffs and Burgesses shall have after the Rate.

'Or ells, Wher as the sayd Meyr, Bailiffs, and Burgesses have bene at grete and importunate Charges for the same Mershe (fyrst in the Lawe by Arbitrement, and otherwise, and allso) in the makyng of a Gutt or Sluce, and other charges, w$^{ch}$ the sayd Meyer, Bailiffs, and Burgesses have ryght wel and lovyngly consyder'd had be to grevous for the sayd Inhabytants to have borne, that notwithstanding, if the sayd Inhabytants wylbe content for ther part that six or eight of themselves, suche as the sayd Meyer, Bailiffs, and Burgesses shall name, wyl be bound by obligation to the sayd Meyer, Bailiffs, and Burg$^{s}$. and to ther Successors, that they and ther Successors from hensforth shall defend the See oute of the sayde Mershe, and every part thereof, and also when any of the sayd six or eight fortune to dissease, or that there be no mo left of them alyve but four, or three at the lest, then as many other of the sayd Inhabitants to be nue bound, in manner and form as is above sayde, and by the Nomination of the sayd Meyr, Bailiffs, and Burgesses and ther Successors, that then the sayd Meyr, Bailiffs, and Burgesses be content that then it lye opyn and be comyn for every man, as wel to the Inhabitants as Burgeysys.

'Or ells, To close it in, and lete it to ferme by the yer, till oon croppe be takyn thereof yerely, whyche croppe shall be spent upon the same, as shall be thought most nedefull, and after the sayd croppe be so taken, the sayd Mershe to be opyn and comyn, as wel to the sayd Inhabitants as to the Burgeysys.

'And notwithstanding the Premisses, if the sayd Inhabitants wyl be content at ther Cost and Charge to sufficiently nue make up the Banke from Itchyn Crosse to the Groynys, so that it may surely defend the See out of the sayd Mershe, and the same Banke so by the sayd Inhabitants at this oon tyme sufficyently made, yerely hereafter, when the sayd Banke shall nede Reparation, to bere ther parte of the same Reparation with the sayd Meyr, Bailiffs, and Burgeysys after the Rate; that then the sayd Mershe lye opyn and be comyn, as wel to the sayd Inhabitants, as to the sayd Meyr, Bailiffs, and Burgeysys.

'And the sayd Meyr, Bailiffs, and Burgeysys be content to discharge the sayd Inhabytants of paying of any penny of the said 19$^{l}$. 10$^{s}$. 0. and odd money, and of all other charges w$^{ch}$ the sayd Meyr, Bailiffs, and Burgeysys have bene at upon the nue making of the sayd Gutt, Sluce, and Bankes, so that hereafter all such Reparations as hereafter shall be nedefull, as wel upon the sayd Gutt and Sluce, as upon the sayd Banke, by the sayd Inhabitants so nue made, shall be borne at every tyme nedefull, as wel by the sayd Meyr, Bailiffs, and Burgeysys, as by sayd Inhabitants Rately.'

To this the inhabitants replied as under :—

'As to the Salte Mershe your pore Comyns sayn, oute of tyme of mynd hit hath ben an opyn Comyn, and occupyed for a Comyn wele, ease, and profett, for the Burges and Comyns of this Town, saff unto now late there was a Sute and Contraversy between the hooll body of this Town and theym of Gods-hous, for the defens of w$^{ch}$ Sutes and other labours, your pore Comyns for the Recovery of the same bare ther parte of the Charges and Cost everych of them Rately, after ther Degre, and more wold have don rather than to have lost it. And in lyke wyse your seyd pore Comyns will be ever ready to do for such a Comyn Wele if any other person or persons hereafter wold attempt any such Sutes, to theyr pore power and Degre, and over that will ever be ready to withstand all manner of persons with theyre bodyes and Goods that wold attempt to usurp upon any poynt or parcell of the Libertyes and Fraunchyses of this Town, besechyng and praying your honourable Masterships all, that the sayd Salte Mershe maybe as of auncyent tyme it hath ben, that is to say opyn Comyn still for all Burgessys and Comyns of this Town, without that it in any wyse shall be lette to ferme for any Rent yerely in no manner wyse, ne the fyrst Cropp taken of it in no yere to come, but it to stand full Comyn, as of old tyme it hath ben. Theise Premisses to be by your discretion considered, we humbly beseeche you to be good Masters to your pore Comyns.

'And your sayd pore Comyns sayn, as to pay any money farther for the makyng of the Slusse, Brigge, or Cutte makyng there, they prayn your Wissedoms in that matter to asses non of theym, for they intend to pay non, in no wyse. But this they seyn that if ever in tyme to com it shall happen any more farther defens or Reparation to be don all aboute the seyd Mershe, wheder it be grete Works or small, what fortune that hereafter shall fall, your seyd pore Comyns sey they will ever be redy to bere theyr Rately parte to theyr power and pore degrees, as our Masters the Burgessys of the Town shall do for the amendyng of the same Mershe, or the defens of it, and that so it may please your Mastershipps remembryng your pore Comyns are not as yet at a fordele in richesse, trustyng to God to encrese under your Mastershipps so ye be content with this theyr answer at this tyme. And so they shall pray to God for you.

'And Worshypfull Masters, if there be any poynte in this aunswere that doth or shold sounde to any greff or displeasure to you, or w[ch] nedeth amendement, so that it may conduce to a good and general Comyn Wele, lete be knowe your discrete mynds in Articles by wrytyng, and so we trust to accomplish your mynds for the universal Wele of you, Master Meyr, your Comburgessys, and all the Comyns who are your own pore Comyns.'

1517. As a curious picture of the times, the sequel to the foregoing agreement is given. The 'pore Comyns' could not bind their successors; and the banks needing repair, an order of the House was made, March 1517, for putting up half the marsh nearest the town, on which the butts stood, from the Purification to St. Peter's Day, with a view of meeting the expenses from the proceeds of the crop. On the Tuesday after this order, when the mayor (John Perchard) and his brethren were holding the king's law-day in the Town Hall, some three hundred of the commons, men and women, swarmed into the Saltmarsh, broke down fences and banks, then rushing in a mass to the Guildhall, made 'presumptuously and unlawfully a great shout,' to the annoyance of the court within. They then walked two and two with picks and shovels as far as Holy Rood Church and Cross, close to which was the mayor's house, where one of them had the audacity to cry, 'If Master Mayor have any more work for us, we be ready.' Then they went home. Such conduct could not be borne. On the Saturday following, Sir William Sandes, one of the King's Council, appeared on the scene with letters directed to the mayor for the immediate apprehension of the chief offenders. That night the ringleaders fled, but six *other* persons were seized, hurried up to London, and lodged in the Marshalsea. What became of the chief offenders does not appear, but eternal banishment was proclaimed against them unless they returned and submitted. Petitions were quickly got up in every parish for the unfortunate six: the banks, it was said, should be repaired, and no such outrage ever repeated, would the mayor and his brethren use their good offices towards these unhappy men? The authorities began to relent, and proclamation was made that all, whether men or women, who had taken part in breaking down, should now at once put up the banks. This done, the mayor and his brethren assured the commons of their good offices. A letter was written to my Lord Cardinal, Chancellor of England, showing his grace that the commons were very sorry 'for their sad unlawful deeds;' that they had repaired damages, and submitted themselves to such further correction as the mayor might think good. A letter was also written to my Lord of Winchester, begging him to write to the Lord Cardinal. In consequence of all this, the captives were delivered out of the Marshalsea on July 16, and were adjudged by the Lord Cardinal and the Council at their coming to Hampton to sit in the open stocks under the pillory; the mayor, the king's lieutenant, and his brethren were to take care to walk down the street that way, and the penitents were to say these words, 'Master Mayor, we have offended the king's grace and all you in making a great riot and unlawful assembly, contrary to the king's laws and the good rules of the town, whereof we acknowledge ourselves guilty, and beseech you and your brethren to be good masters unto us hereafter and to forgive us.' The whole program was faithfully carried out. The mayor, in the name of his brethren, accepted the apology, and assured the woe-begone figures under the pillory that no grudge should be borne against them. 'And therupponne [he] commaunded them owt of the stokkes, and hadd them to the Audite hous, and bound them by obligacon to be good aberyng ageynst the Kinges grace and the Mayor and his Brethryn hereafter, and so delyveryd them.'[1]

## SECTION IV.—*The Fortifications.*

The fortifications belong in part to the Norman period. Of this range of date are the core of the Bargate, with a portion of the present walls, some existing works below the castle, and domestic buildings in the line of the western wall, and forming part of its original circuit.

**Periods of construction.**

It will be convenient to refer to some of the probable dates of construction. The castle was in existence in 1153, as in that year it is mentioned in the terms of agreement between King Stephen and Prince Henry.[2]

In the 4th John (1202–3) costs to the amount of £25, 6s., under the supervision of Walter Foran and Robert Hardwin, were allowed for carrying timber to the castle to make there 'the king's houses,' for sinking a well in the castle, and for other repairs; and in that and in the following year the king allowed £100 each year out of the fee-farm towards the walling of the town.[3]

During the latter part of the reign of Henry III. two murages were granted, that is, liberty to collect tolls for a certain number of years, for the building or repair of the walls. The former of these, for ten years, was granted from November 30, 1260; the second, for five years, on November 12, 1270. A considerable number of tolls are scheduled on these grants.[4]

In 1321 (May 26) a murage was granted for three years from date,[5] after which a renewal was petitioned for.[6] By this time the flanking towers, to be mentioned presently, had been added to the Bargate. The quayages and barbican duty, granted from 1323 to 1346 (see Quays), should also be mentioned as having an immediate connection with the fortifications. To this period we venture to assign the arcade-work

1 Boke of Remembrances, ff. 11–14.

2 See below, last chapter; also above, pp. 29, 30.

3 Pipe Rolls, 4 and 5 John. 'King's houses' were also being made or repaired at Portsmouth.

4 Pat. 45 H. III. m. 22; 55 H. III. m. 28.

5 Pat. 14 Ed. II. p. 2, m. 8.

6 Rot. Parl. ii. 439.

Invasion. described below. The next efforts of construction were called forth by the invasion of the town in 1338, for which see below in the last chapter. It appears that, in spite of murages, the town was not entirely walled. The enemy are supposed to have landed at 'the gravel,' or in that immediate neighbourhood, and this weak quarter was now ordered to be strengthened. By the advice of his council, the king issued a mandate for the building of a stone wall as quickly as possible towards the sea,[1] Stephen de Bitterle being commissioned (March 30, 1339) to find all necessary timber, and governors were appointed with special view to the fortification of the town and the reassurance of the inhabitants. A writ in aid of the enclosure was issued in 1340.[2] In 1345 (May 20) a murage, at considerable length, was granted for six years;[3] and ten years later the burgesses received a further grant for ten years, in the usual form of a penny in the pound, a halfpenny in 10s., and a farthing in 5s., on all goods brought into or carried out of the town, whether by land or water, by their own burgesses or not, in aid of the walls. This was dated 28th June (29 Ed. III.) 1355.[4]

Further repairs were ordered in April 1369, and contributions were exacted from all persons according to their means, workmen being employed at the wages of the community.[5] Accordingly, in 1376 (50 Ed. III.) we find the poor commons and tenants praying the king to take the town into his hands and forgive them the farm for the last two years, which, together with £1000 besides, they have expended on the fortifications. They say that the town is but half inhabited owing to the above burdens, and that those who are left are preparing to go. They also ask for soldiers to defend the town and neighbourhood, being themselves unable to hold the place against the force which they hear is being prepared by the enemy.[6] They received no relief at the time, but there had evidently been a considerable outlay on the walls.

In the first year of Richard II., under the immediate apprehension

[1] Rot. Orig. 13 Ed. III., rot. 50. Compare also Sir H. Englefield's remarks on this wall as it stood in his time.

[2] Rot. Orig. 14 Ed. III. (Feb. 18).

[3] Pat. 19 Ed. III. p. 1, m. 12.

[4] The Corporation possess the exemplification of this grant, dated 10th February (39 Ed. III.) 1365, made at the request of the burgesses. See also Liber Niger, p. 109. The above grant of 1355, given at length by Dr. Speed, was erroneously supposed by him to have marked the commencement of the fortifications. In his version a misreading occurs which helped the above mistake. It has not been thought necessary to reproduce his chapter on the fortifications as a whole; any information from it will be specified, and where it appears it will be notified, as usual, by quotation marks.

[5] Pat. 43 Ed. III. p. 1, m. 23.

[6] Rot. Parl. ii. 346 b.

of invasion, the mayor and bailiffs were ordered to look to the walls and compel necessary contributions (December 8, 1377); and a few months later (April 9, 1378) provision was made for the reconstruction of the castle keep.[1] Sir John Arundel had been appointed governor in the preceding July. **Keep.**

In 1400 (1 H. IV.) a grant of £200 per annum—£100 out of the duty of wool in the port of the town and £100 out of the fee-farm for the first year, but after that entirely from the latter source—was made in aid of the fortifications, provided the inhabitants raised among themselves £100 each year for the like purpose. This £300 per annum was to be spent under the supervision of Richard Mawardyn, king's esquire, of the mayor, and the controller of the port.[2] By this time the beautiful octagonal projection had been added to the front of the Bargate. **Front of Bargate.**

Henry V., in the second year of his reign (1414), released 140 marks (£93, 6s. 8d.) from the fee-farm for ten years, with license to purchase lands in mortmain to the value of £100 in aid of the fortifications.[3] At this period possibly, or not long after, the spur-work and tower outside God's House gate were added. Under the act of resumption of 1482 (22 Ed. IV.) grants for repairs of the walls were especially saved to the town;[4] but at this very time we have a note of their miscarriage. Thus the steward's book of 1483 (rather 1484) contains an account of the town's suit 'ayeynste Roger Kelsale,[5] Elizabeth Sorell, and Thomas Nutson, as to the xl$^{li}$ the which was graunted to the reparacon of the walles by Kynge Edwarde for vij yeres: and they and Richard Wystard have take alowance of the same as for iiij yeris, and have not paid hit to the towne.'

In 1486 (November 9) license was given to export thirty sacks of wool free of custom, in aid of the maintenance of the walls, stathes, and quays of the port.[6]

"8 Henry VII. [1492–93].—The king granted £50 out of the fee-"farm toward the making of the new wall on the west side of the "town. Several private persons[7] contributed at this time, among "other the Lord Arundel, whose name was given to one of the towers "called 'Arundel tower' to this day. There was another tower called "'St. Denis Tower,' from whence it is probable that the canons of "that priory had contributed to the fortifications of the town."

[1] Pat. 1 R. II. p. 2, m. 7, and p. 6, m. 7.
[2] This document is printed in Madox, F. B., p. 290.
[3] Rot. Parl. iv. 53; Pat. 2 H. V. p. 3, m. 13.
[4] Ibid. vi. 201 a.
[5] See under Members of Parliament.
[6] Materials for Hist. of H. vii. (Rolls Series), ii. 38.
[7] See Steward's books, 1493.

In 1511 (February 7) the Corporation obtained license to export a hundred sacks of wool, free of custom, towards the repair of the town walls inundated by the sea.[1] It will be convenient now to take up Dr. Speed's narrative, which gives a good account of the precautions used against such damage.

Sea-banks.

"1 Mary [1553-54].—It is entered in the Journal that it was an "ancient custom for the lightermen of the town to bring yearly their "lighter-loads of stones to lie between the piles or town walls, and they "were ordered to go forthwith to the isle of Wight, either to Sandye "bay or the Nedelles, to load with chalk. 'And they shall have for "'every lighter of 20 ton a barrell of beer, and under 20 ton a verkyn "'of beer,' which agreement was made at the building of the south-"side next Catch-cold; and they are henceforth, upon warning given "by any officer of the town, to bring or cause to be brought, the "lighter of chalk or stone for the defence of the town walls, and to "discharge it in such a place as seemeth good to the town.

"1634.—The boatmen of Heath [Hythe] were ordered to bring "stones according to ancient custom.

"1683.—Heithe boatmen. Their ancient duty and service is to "bring every half year one boat or lighter-loading of stones and to "throw or put them against the town walls within the piles, or else to "pay 4d. every time they land any passenger or goods, to be levied by "the water-bailiff upon their cordage, sails, &c.[2] The meaning of all "this is that the sea-shore is piled all along at the bottom of the town "walls, and the stones were to be laid between those piles to save the "foundations of the walls from being washed away. There was for-"merly a horse ferry to Hythe which was under the government of "the magistrates of this town, and most probably the boatmen who "plied the ferry were the persons of whom this duty and service were "required. These piles thus filled up with stones are called Banks in "the Journals: thus 'A.D. 1609.—The bank under Arundel tower is "'ordered to be speedily amended.'"

Though the boatmen had to contribute the stones, the town originally put in the piles and kept them up: thus, in 1469 the town purchased 'a grove of wood' from the Abbot of Netley for 53s. 4d., in order to make piles by the seaside.[3]

"In all their general charters, since the town was fortified, the "charges and expense incurred by the town on the fortifications are "mentioned as the reason for granting them such extensive privileges; "and the general charter of Edward VI. does for this reason release

[1] Papers, &c., of H. viii. (Rolls Series), vol. i.
[2] "Journal."
[3] Steward's books.

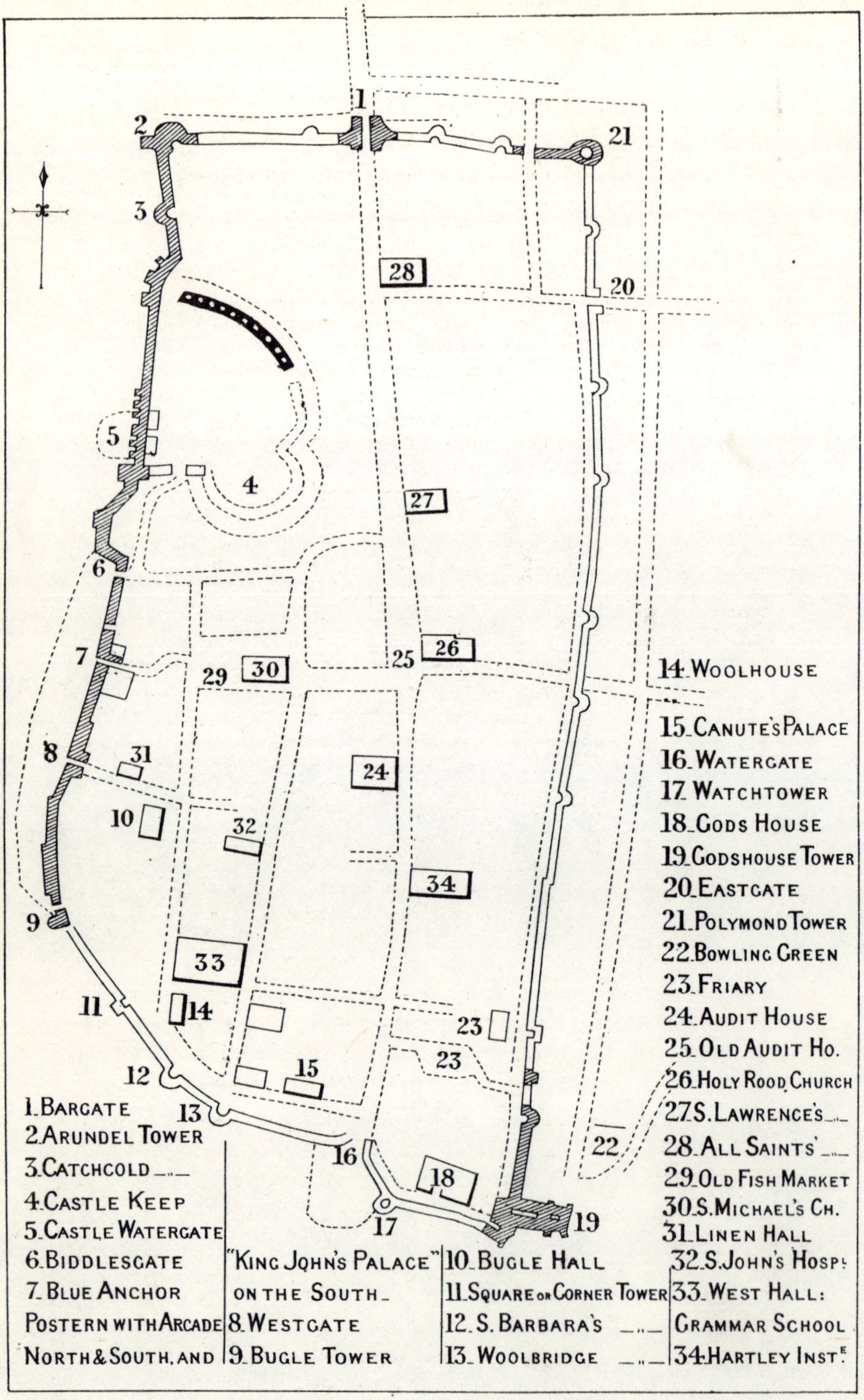
1. Bargate
2. Arundel Tower
3. Catchcold — " —
4. Castle Keep
5. Castle Watergate
6. Biddlesgate
7. Blue Anchor
Postern with Arcade
North & South, and
"King John's Palace"
on the South —
8. Westgate
9. Bugle Tower
10. Bugle Hall
11. Square or Corner Tower
12. S. Barbara's — " —
13. Woolbridge — " —
14. Woolhouse
15. Canute's Palace
16. Watergate
17. Watchtower
18. Gods House
19. Godshouse Tower
20. Eastgate
21. Polymond Tower
22. Bowling Green
23. Friary
24. Audit House
25. Old Audit Ho.
26. Holy Rood Church
27. S. Lawrence's — " —
28. All Saints' — " —
29. Old Fish Market
30. S. Michael's Ch.
31. Linen Hall
32. S. John's Hospl.
33. West Hall:
Grammar School
34. Hartley Instn.

"£150 a year of the fee-farm rent of the town on certain conditions "(as mentioned elsewhere). For the same reason one of their privi- "leges, viz., the forfeiture of all strangers' goods sold in the town by re- "tail or to strangers, was confirmed by Act of Parliament, 4 James I.; "and in the year 1719 Mr. Serjeant Pengelly gave his opinion that "the town's right in this matter was good; but upon a trial the town "was cast."[1]

Having noted above the chief periods of construction, we may now survey the fortifications, leaving to the end of this section the story of their decay.

### *The Walls.*

Medieval Southampton was defended by a lofty wall, some 25 to 30 feet in height, forming an irregular parallelogram, measuring on the north side about 217 yards, on the east 786, on the south side from east to west as far as the arch by the site of Bugle Tower within Madame Mäes's garden, about 435 yards, and from that point to the north-west angle of the town some 543 yards. The wall was strengthened at intervals all round by twenty-nine towers.[2]

**The Gates.** There were seven principal gates, four of which remain. These are North or Bar gate, God's House or South Castle gate, West gate, and the postern, now called Blue Anchor gate. Those which have disappeared were the East gate, Biddle's gate on the west, and the South or Water gate. In addition to these there was a Castle Water gate now walled up, and a postern near the Friary and God's House, the site of which is lost. The insertion a little to the north of West gate in front of Collis's Court is of old date, though not original: that called York gate in the north wall east of the Bargate is of the last century.

**Bargate.** The Bargate or north gate is a fine structure of various periods in two stages, the upper of which is occupied by the Guildhall, and the lower pierced by a principal or central archway, with a postern of modern construction on either side. Remains of the original Norman gate-house, also in two storeys, are to be seen under the central passage and above within the present Guildhall. Confining ourselves first to the north side of the Bar, we observe two half-round towers set well back, one on either side; these started boldly from the original gateway, and were additions to it in the Early Decorated period.[3] Subsequently to this addition and to the alterations on the south, that

**North side.**

1 "Journal."

2 Speed's Theatre of Great Britain, first published in 1596. He died in 1629.

3 See a paper by G. T. Clarke, Esq., F.S.A., on the 'Ancient Defences of Southampton,' in the Builder, December 28, 1872, and Archæol. Journal, vol. xxix.

beautiful projection was added on the north side, consisting of three sides of an octagon, which gives the gateway its distinctive character. This was probably in the reign of Richard II. On the front and broader face of this projection a narrow buttress well advanced flanks the central archway on either side, running up into a bold corbel table supporting large and handsome battlements carried round the building; there being on this north side five embrasures on the broad front of the octagon and two on each of the narrower faces, but the merlons on these are fallen away and should be replaced. Between these buttresses, on the north face, there are four machicolations in the battlements over the central archway, two to the east of the eastern buttress, and only one to the right of the western buttress, the width on one side being greater than on the other; the reason for this difference not being apparent. On each of the narrower faces of the projection there are three machicolations.

The central archway has been pared and cut away to make the opening as wide as possible. It may be divided longitudinally into three or four periods, according as the gate was altered as above described.

**Bargate posterns.**

The posterns are perforations of the flanking towers: that on the east was completed in February 1764; at each end were posts and a turnstile; and in March 1774 the Commissioners of Pavement had permission to construct a similar passage on the western side,[1] though prints of 1777 continue to show but one postern.

The posterns are open to the central roadway by two cross arches on each side, the two next the north being in part original. These latter, belonging to the Perpendicular work of the end of the fourteenth century, terminated by oillets or loopholes having view and command of the ditch on either side; but when the posterns were made these terminations were carved away, and the openings subsequently widened.

Underneath the gate the inner mouth of these loopholes, on either side, is observed to open from the wider of two arches composing an arcade in the wall of the roadway in advance of the Norman work; and within the narrower of the arches which adjoins the Norman pier part of the basement of the decorated tower flanking is seen to be framed with the old loopholes still defending the inner or Norman gate.

The cross or lateral arches to the south may have been insertions in the place of old recesses.

---

[1] Comp. Journals sub annis.

The upper stage of the gate between the buttresses is pierced by three narrow loopholes, that in the middle being crossed. These are partially restorations, for at one time two sash windows disfigured this face, while a picture of Queen Elizabeth,[1] set up about 1594, and subsequently the royal arms, placed there in the mayoralty of Alderman Steptoe in 1664, covered the central loop. This royal picture was sadly abused by a certain Michael Craddock, who was arraigned for his critical remarks and made to give £5 to the poor. The arms were the work of Walter Crocker, whose predecessor, Alexander Crocker, enjoyed European fame as a ship-carver. On July 1, 1664, the town agreed with Walter that—

Upper stage, north side.

'If he shall for all future tymes be of good and honest behaviour, and approve himself to be a compleate and sufficient workman in his profession, and at his own costes shall make, carve, and coulour, according to arte and approbacon, the Kings Majesties armes, and them set up (being of a sufficient proporcon) over Bargate in the place where Queen Elizabeth's picture formerly was fixed, and also give sufficient security to the Towne to save them harmlesse from his charge, that then he is to be admitted a free commoner to exercise his said arte in this Towne: But if he shall not fulfill all and singular the conditions above said, whereby he shall not be admitted as above said, then he shall have the said Kings armes to his own use and benefitt.'

These arms, by which Walter Crocker purchased his freedom, were removed in 1852. On the same stage there is a loophole in each of the narrower sides of the projection, also in part restorations in place of modern sash windows.

We may now examine what are called in the court leet books the 'monuments at Bargate.' First, there are the two lions [2] on lofty pedestals, one on each side of the buttresses flanking the central archway. These originally stood at the end of the bridge which crossed the ditch here, and struck terror into the mind of a certain traveller in 1635, who, speaking of the town as the 'neatest and completest in all these western parts,' describes his entering—

Monuments at Bargate.

'At the North gate thereof with no little fear, between the jaws of two ramping lions and two thundering warriors, Exipat, that fearful giant, on the one side, and brave Bevis of Southampton on the other, if above them had not been placed our late renowned virtuous Queen Elizabeth [see above] to daunt their courage and quell their fury, and to suffer peaceable passengers to have quiet and safe entrance.' [3]

The earliest observed notice of lions at the Bargate occurs in the court leet book of 1619, where is an order for their being varnished

[1] Boke of Remembrances, fol. 182, January 1594–95.

[2] See a very interesting paper on the 'Heraldry and Exterior Decorations of the Bar Gate,' by B. W. Greenfield, Esq., Barrister-at-law (Rayner, Southampton, 1875).

[3] See Duthy, p. 440.

to prevent them from rotting, the lions of that period being of wood; their representatives of the present day having been cast in lead in 1743, during the mayoralty of Richard Raymond, Esq., whose name is inscribed on their pedestals. They are said to have been the gift of William Lee, Esq., son of Lord Chief Justice Lee, who received the freedom of the borough in June that year.[1]

Until lately the panel paintings of Sir Bevis and his giant esquire Ascupart, referred to above, rested on the footing of the buttresses; Sir Bevis on the right hand, looking towards the Bar, with the date 1644 in the left-hand corner, probably that of the repainting; in the middle the letter M, the initial of the mayor that year; and in the right-hand corner the date 1319, possibly a conjecture as to the antiquity of the work replaced. The court leet books of 1635 and 1640 had presented these 'monuments' as much in decay. The paintings—constantly referred to in descriptions of Southampton, as by Samuel Pepys in 1662—have been touched up from time to time, but have now been removed into the townhall in preference to any further restoration—a matter rather to be regretted.

**Heraldry.** The heraldry of the Bargate has been elucidated for the first time correctly by Mr. Greenfield in the treatise already mentioned. The gate bears eleven shields on its northward projection, two in the spandrels of the archway, and nine in a frieze of sunken panels carried round the buttresses above the bold string-course which divides the building into two stages. Of these nine, there are one upon the face of each buttress, one in the space beyond each, and five between them. The escutcheons in the spandrels probably belong (not of course the blazonry) to the original construction, but those in the frieze may be insertions. Unhappily, the tinctures on all the shields are nearly obliterated: they should certainly be restored with judgment: meanwhile it may be well to describe them here.

We commence with the frieze. The shield to the east or extreme left bears the cross of St. George of England; that to the extreme right the cross of St. Andrew, for Scotland. In the middle of the frieze, over the apex of the arch, is the coat of Noel: *Or, fretty gules a canton ermine,* placed there in honour of two Noels, Viscounts Campden, father and son, successively Lords-Lieutenant of the county and town and county of Southampton: (1) Edward, who married Elizabeth, daughter of Thomas Wriothesley, Earl of Southampton, by whom, on the death of her father in 1667, he succeeded to the property of Titchfield, received the freedom of the borough in 1675,

[1] Mr. Greenfield thinks that they may have been the gift of one of the Leighs of Testwood near Totton, whose coat he finds on the Bargate (pp. 7, 25).

becoming in the next year Lord-Lieutenant, and M.P. for Hants in February 1678–79. Created Baron Noel of Titchfield in 1681 during his father's life, he was advanced to the Earldom of Gainsborough in December 1682, after his father's death in October that year. (2) Wriothesley Baptiste, son of the last, was appointed to the Lord-Lieutenancy when Viscount Campden, on his father's resignation in 1684. In May 1685 he was returned to Parliament for the county of Hants; in 1687 he resigned his Lieutenancy, and on the death of his father in 1689 succeeded to the Earldom.

The shield on the eastern buttress bears the arms of Pawlett: *Sable, three swords in pile point downwards, argent, pomels and hilts, or;* in honour, no doubt, of the first and second Dukes of Bolton. (1) Charles Pawlett, son of John, Marquis of Winchester, who from November 1643 to October 1645 held out his house at Basing for the king; as Lord St. John was elected M.P. for Hants to the Parliament of 1660 and 1661, and as Baron St. John of Basing became Lord-Lieutenant in 1667, holding that office till 1676, having received the freedom of Southampton in 1668. He had succeeded his father as Marquis in 1674, and was again appointed Lord-Lieutenant in April 1689, being created Duke of Bolton about the same time. (2) Charles, second Duke, upon the death of his father in 1699, had been returned for the shire in 1681, 1685, 1688, 1690, and 1695. In 1702 he became Lord-Lieutenant and Lord Warden of the New Forest; in 1708 governor of the Isle of Wight; and on the accession of George I. in 1714 he again received the Lord-Wardenry and Lord-Lieutenancy, with other appointments. He died in June 1722.

To the right of Pawlett is the shield of Tylney: *Argent, a chevron gules between three griffins' heads erased gules with beaks or.* Frederick Tylney, of Rotherwick, in the county of Southampton, Esquire, admitted burgess in 1676, and in August 1702 returned M.P. for the borough; in the following month he presented to the Corporation a large silver-gilt tankard. He again contested the borough, but unsuccessfully, at the general election in 1705. He died in 1725, at the age of eighty, having, among other charitable works, founded some scholarships at Oxford, augmented several benefices, and been a benefactor to the city of Winchester.

To the right of Tylney is De Cardonnel: *Argent, a chevron voided azure between three trefoils slipped vert.* Adam de Cardonnel, admitted a burgess in 1662, was in 1690 excused serving the office of Sheriff on account of his age. He was for some time collector of customs at this port, and dying in January 1710–11 at the age of ninety, was buried at God's House. His son, Adam de Cardonnel, secretary to the Duke of Marlborough, returned for the borough in seven Parliaments between January 1700–1 and November 1710, was, at the disgrace of Marlborough, expelled the House for corrupt practices in 1712. No doubt the arms were on the Bargate before this year. Adam de Cardonnel was a subscriber to the rebuilding of St. Mary's Church in 1711.

To the right of the escutcheon of Noel, already described, is that of Fleming: *Gules, a chevron between three owls argent.* The Flemings were for centuries connected with this town and neighbourhood (see under Mayors, Conduits, &c.) Thomas Fleming, Solicitor-General in 1594, knighted in 1601, Chief-Justice of the King's Bench in 1607, was Recorder of Southampton while Solicitor-General, and was returned for the borough to the Parliaments of October 1601 and March 1603–4. His eldest son, Thomas, knighted in 1608, sat for the borough in 1614 and 1620–21. Edward, great-grandson of the last, of North Stoneham, successfully contested the borough with Sir Charles Wyndham, knight, of Cranbury, in 1689, but subsequently was unseated. His son Richard, of North Stoneham, sat for the borough in 1710 and during twelve successive years. It was probably in his honour that the Fleming shield was placed on the Bargate.

The next shield on the right hand is attributed to the Leighs of Testwood: *Gules, a cross engrailed within a bordure engrailed argent.* Thomas Leigh, Esq., of Testwood, son of Sir John Leigh, Knt., who became possessed of Great Testwood through his marriage with Elizabeth, daughter and heir of Sir Thomas West, Knt., second son of Lord Delawarr, was admitted a burgess of Southampton in 1620. The same compliment is recorded of Philip and Edward Leigh of Testwood, Esqs., in 1659 and 1677.

The shield on the western buttress is that of Mill: *Per fesse argent and sable, a pale and three bears salient, two and one, counterchanged muzzled and chained or.* The escutcheon bears the Ulster badge, and doubtless belongs to Sir John Mill of Newton-Bury, in the parish of Eling, Hants, and of Camois Court, Sussex, Bart., so created December 31, 1619. He was the eldest son of Lewknor Mill, Esq., of Camois Court, by Cicely, daughter of John Crook, Esq., of Southampton (see under Mayors and M.P.s). Sir John Mill sat for the borough in the Parliaments of 1624 and two succeeding years. He died in May 1648, aged sixty-one years. The name of Mill is of constant occurrence on the burgess roll of the town.

In the left spandrel of the arch we have the shield of Wyndham: *Azure, a chevron between three lions' heads erased or.* Sir Charles Wyndham, Knt., who represented the town in Parliament from August 1679 to July 1698, was the son of Sir Edmond Wyndham, Knt., of Kentsford, Somerset, one of the first who, in 1641, appeared in arms for the king. Sir Charles married, in 1665, Jacoba, only child of Major-General James Young, formerly one of the gentlemen of the privy chamber to Charles I., and niece and heir to Dr. John Young, Dean of Winchester, Master of St. Cross and owner of the Cranbury estate. Sir Charles, who became tenant of the estate through his wife, resided at Cranbury for upwards of forty years, and dying there in 1706, was buried at Hursley. On the death of Lady Wyndham in 1720, the property was sold to John Conduit, Esq., who successfully contested the borough in 1734. On his decease in 1737, the Cranbury estate was purchased by Thomas Lee Dummer, Esq., through whose family it passed to that of Chamberlayne.

On the right spandrel is the shield of Newland: *Argent, on a chevron, the upper part terminating in a cross pattée, three besants.* Benjamin Newland, merchant, of London, knighted in August 1679, sat in Parliament for this borough from February 1678–79, when he was returned in company with Thomas Knollys, Esq., of Grove Place, till July 1698. He married Ann, daughter of Robert Richbell, merchant, of Southampton (see under Mayors and M.P.s). Sir Benjamin Newland was possessed of the estate of Drayton, in the parishes of Farlington, Widley, and Wymering, Hants, by purchase from Mary Richbell, his sister-in-law, in 1689.

**South side of Bargate.**

The south side of the Bargate presents a handsome but restored elevation, the basement showing the archways of the central roadway and of the posterns, with an entrance doorway both right and left. Beyond that to the right are further remains, and there are indications of work in advance on the east side of this door southward.

In the upper stage, upon a bold string-course, are the four windows of the townhall, restorations under Mr. Edward Roberts, F.S.A., each of two lights and filled with stained glass, the gift of Mr. Edward Lanham, a member of the Council in 1864–65, when the whole of this front was cleared from a surface of rough-cast; the sashes of the previous century were abolished, and hoods and corbels supplied to all the arches and windows. Resting upon the string-course, and between the middle windows, there is a niche, now occupied by a figure of George III. in Roman costume; and above this is a sun-dial. The whole front is surmounted by wide battlements on a somewhat lower level than those of the north, with six embrasures, the westernmost of which carries a watch-bell; the second and fifth merlons being pierced with crossed loopholes. The whole of this front is the result of enlargement or re-facing, probably in the early part of the fourteenth century. Its restoration, as mentioned above, was effected in the mayoralties of Aldermen Brinton and Bowman, and was greatly due to the energy of

Alderman, now Sir Frederick, Perkins, Knt. It was carried out by Mr. Poole, then borough surveyor.

Details of south side.

Taking now the outside details, the entrance doorway to the left communicates with the modern police-station and with a staircase admitting to the hall above; much of this is ancient work. The police-station is on the site of the old prison establishment at Bargate, which also occupied a third of the gate itself. Repairs of the Bargate prison and that of St. Michael's (of which more hereafter) are mentioned in the steward's book of 1441 and in subsequent years.

Prison.

In January 1553 (6 Ed. VI.) the house to the west of the Bargate—the site of the present police-station—was assigned as 'the counter' for debtors, the keeper receiving from each inmate sixpence for every meal and twopence for his bed.[1] The two departments of the prison establishment continued side by side; but in March 1774, when it was determined to carry a postern through the old prison, it was provided that a new gaol should be made in God's House Tower, the estimate for which was given at £140. Of this sum £100 was advanced by the Commissioners of Paving and £40 charged on the county.

Watch-bell.

The watch-bell in the embrasure was one of three or four bells at different stations in the town which answered one another in ringing the watches or sounding alarms. In 1579 the court leet complained that the watch-bell of the castle was not kept in order, and recommended that one should be set on Bargate at the west end of the hall, and that the bells should properly answer one another, 'for that yt is a comfortable hearing.' The present bell has the inscription and date, 'In God is my hope. R.B. 1605.'

Niche.

The niche is probably coeval with this face of the gate, but we do not know how it was originally filled. In the mayoralty of John Thornburgh, in 1705, it was ordered that a statue of her Majesty Queen Anne be erected over the Bargate facing English (High) Street, and that a sun-dial be placed over the statue. The above date and mayor's initials are still to be seen on the dial. It measured out for the Queen below little more than a hundred years, for in 1809 her memorial was dismounted and relegated to a niche in the Guildhall, where it may still be seen, and the present statue of George III., imitated from that of the Emperor Hadrian in the British Museum, was placed in its stead. It was the gift of John Henry Petty, second Marquis of Lansdowne, who, presenting it to the Corporation, described the figure as 'bearing no mean resemblance to his Majesty.' The statue was placed in the niche, where the Marquis had desired it might stand, on September 12, 1809.

[1] Boke of Remembrances, fol. 66.

The door of the eastern staircase bears the shield of the town arms in facsimile of that placed there in the mayoralty of John Ayres in 1725. Ascending, we enter the Guildhall, an apartment constructed within the shell of the gate, projection, and flanking towers in 1852, under Mr. W. J. Elliott of Southampton, measuring 52 feet long by 40 feet in the broadest part, and fitted up as a court of justice; the grand jury room, which had been in the northward projection, having been at this time thrown into the hall, and a new room carried out to the west for the accommodation of the grand jury. In this new room the weekly petty sessions of the borough are held. Before the alteration, the justices' seat, with a picture of Solomon's judgment above it, was placed at the west end of the long and narrow hall. The picture may still be seen in the adjoining room. The following entry concerns it:— Guildhall.

'May 7, 1725.—John Ayres, Esq., Mayor.—Ordered that Mr. Mayor have a new King's arms painted in the Town hall, and the picture of Solomon's judgment refreshed and repaired and Bevis and Ascapart's pictures painted anew, and all the carpenter's work relating thereto for 4 guineas and a half, at which price the said Mr. Mayor has undertaken to procure the whole to be done, and the same to be borne at the county charge.'

Immediately to the right of the hall as we enter is the niche containing the statue of Queen Anne. Beyond this is a plain round-headed arch belonging to the original Norman gate-house. Within the flankings and projection are the usual arrangements of a court of justice. On the western side is the entrance from the old side tower staircase. It now connects the hall with the police premises below, and may for centuries have served a similar purpose. Beyond this again, and facing the entrance to the hall, are the doors into the apartment constructed in 1852. On the south side are the four pointed windows of Decorated aspect filled with stained glass (see above), descriptive of the history of the borough, as represented by the shields and devices of some of its early benefactors.

It is possible that the alterations to the gate on the south side in the first half of the fourteenth century may have been carried out to provide a fixed Guildhall; or there may have been no such hall till after the octagonal front was projected. In the earlier history of the gate, the space required for working the portcullises and drawbridge would have left little room for civic purposes; but after the addition on the north side the regulation of the defences may have been confined within the projection, and thus ample room left for the hall. No Guildhall here before fourteenth century.

The ordinances of the Guild-merchant (see below) make no reference to a Guildhall. The Guild meetings were held at different places (ord. 4); the community assembled for the business 'in a place provided,' as if perhaps for each occasion (ord. 32); the common chest, with the treasure and muniments, was kept in the chief alderman's (*i.e.*, the mayor's) house, or in that of the seneschal (ord. 35); in much later times it was ordered to be kept in the Guildhall or Audit-house.

In the steward's book of 1441, under the heading 'Bargatte,' the first observed notice occurs of a 'town hall' in repairs to the lead of its roof: mention is also made of a new key for the 'tresory dore in the hall.' A few years after (1468) we find the hall made a receptacle for guns in an account of the distribution of artillery among the various towers of the fortifications. 'Fyrst, in ye Guyld halle over ye Bargate j gonne of Bras chawmbred of hymself. Item, in the same place ij gonnes and v chawmbres w$^{t}$ treselz to ye sam. Item, in the sam plas ij gonnes w$^{t}$owght chambres. The wheche ij gonnes lay in ij towrs the wheche beth next to ye seyd Bargate estward to seynt Denys towr.'

Westward course of walls.

We now follow the westward course of the walls. At about 100 feet from the gate is the site of a half-round tower, which in 1468 seems to have carried 'ij gonnes w$^{t}$ ij chawmbres.' A few yards beyond this, the wall, destroyed to this point in 1854, is traced behind the houses on its way to Arundel Tower, a drum now in ruins, at the north-west angle of the walls, 22 feet in diameter and from 50 to 60 feet high. In 1490–91 an account of repairs gives the following names: from the 'Corner tower next Hille to Cacchecold tower and about the walles to Bridelles gate,'[1] Corner tower being that which was afterwards called Arundel.[2] The court leet books of 1587 and following years presented 'Corner tower on north side Catchcold' as greatly damaged by the sea, which washed the west wall from this point to the re-entering angle south of the castle. After many dolorous presentments of this tower and of the walls in its vicinity, of the necessity of the banks under the tower being mended to prevent its falling, together with one or two announcements about 1627 that the wall without Arundel Tower—*has* fallen down,' the House (*i.e.*, the Town Council) authorised certain freemasons named to rebuild the corner of the wall and repair the buttress. The wall was to measure in length 40 feet, to be 12 feet high, 4 feet in thickness at the base and 3 at top.

Arundel tower.

[1] MS. Temp. T. Overey, sub anno.

[2] It is not possible to identify all the towers round the walls, though very many names occur in the town books. Some were called after their lessees, for the towers were generally leased out by the Corporation whether to private individuals or for purposes of trade. In 1517 one of the towers was let to Master Dr. Fawne, Rector of All Saints, at twelvepence a year, 'as long as it shall please the said doctor to occupy it, except in time of war.' Similarly we have Overey's and Brodock's Towers, Shoemakers' and Coopers' Towers, and the same tower may from time to time have gone under different names.

The masons were to receive £24, and enter into a bond for the security of their work for ten years.[1] This was in 1651. But the court leet continued to present the tower itself, till in 1658 the word *fiat* is written in the margin, as if no more delay could be hazarded. But it does not appear that very much was done. The level within the walls here is some 30 feet or more above that of the road or beach below.

**Catchcold.** About 130 feet southward from the north-west angle is 'Catchcold,' which gave its name to a plot of ground from Arundel Tower to the old castle enceinte.[2] From 'Catchcold (*i.e.*, the tower) to Bidelsgate the walls are much decayed' in 1587. In 1615, Arundel, St. Denys at the north-east angle of the town, all the west towers, and 'Catchcoald' were to be looked to for various reasons, and great stones were to be laid at the foot of the latter to act as breakwaters. Catchcold, which, with the adjacent curtain for some feet, Mr. Clarke considers to be a Perpendicular addition to what seems to be a Decorated wall, is a fine half-round tower, about 20 feet in diameter and 30 in height, with bold machicolations at the level of the connecting wall. A path from the castle chapel, common time out of mind to the town's people, led into Catchcold, and from thence to Bargate.[3]

**Albion Steps.** South of Catchcold a flight of steps, built against the face of the wall in 1853, ascends from the western shore road some 30 feet to a point nearly 100 feet from the tower. From thence the wall, in substance Norman, runs obliquely south-west some 60 feet to a rectangular buttress heading a salient, the angles of which are crossed with low pointed arches pierced as garde-robes. About 20 feet to the south of this, the north wall of the castle baily struck the town wall, the abutment of a plain rectangular buttress supporting the junction.

**Town and castle wall.** The walls, probably of Norman date and about 38 feet high, now continue southward some 370 feet, being common both to the town and castle, as far as the remains of a tower at the south-west angle of the castle baily. Somewhat more than half-way the bonding in the face of the curtain is broken for about 15 feet perpendicular in two lines, giving something the appearance of a coped buttress cut back flush with the wall. In a straight line with this, foundations as of a strong wall have been discovered in the rear, curiously coinciding with a line of wall drawn in Speed's (1596) plan, though too much reliance must not be placed on him, as he totally omits the north ballium wall, unless this line be blundered for it. Close south of this broken bond there commences a series of six rectangular buttresses of various dimensions and at slightly different intervals, the first three being additions upon the Norman wall, the rest perhaps original, though all have been

1 Journal. 2 Terrier of 1634. 3 C. L. Book, 1579.

partially renewed. The fourth of these buttresses, about 13 feet broad, bears on its face two slight traces of broken bonding. Sir Henry Englefield described it as having a doorcase in it, high above the foot of the wall, which, he conjectured, was the water gate of the castle. This buttress divides a portion of the wall which is very interesting. Immediately to its north is a vaulted chamber, lying north and south, 55 feet 3 inches long by 19 feet 6 inches wide and 25 feet in height, the only indication of which from without is a narrow pointed window like a large loophole. On entering through this aperture the floor is discovered to be on a higher level than the ground outside; the roof is a perfect wagon, the ribs of which, now ruthlessly cut away, sprang from Norman corbels, which have mostly disappeared—a dilapidation which occurred about 1775. A doorway leading outward to sea exists in the wall to the north of the loop, but is completely masked, no trace of it being observed from outside. The communication from the vault to the surface above, some 30 feet higher than its floor, is not apparent: movable steps were no doubt used for its water gate. To the south of this vault, and cut off from it externally by the wide buttress mentioned before, the wall exists in two stages for about 32 feet as far as the sixth and last buttress. It is divided horizontally by a plain string, above which are indications of two round-headed windows, and below two narrow apertures similar to that before described. There must have been chambers in this part of the wall beneath the modern 'Castle Gardens.' Outside this part of the castle wall there was probably in ancient times something of a quay. In the Close Rolls of John and Henry III. we frequently read of the 'Castle Quay,' as if it actually belonged to the castle,[1] which West Quay, separated by a portion of the town, never did. The occurrence of these chambers would seem independently to suggest that there must have been a quay or landing-place beneath them. This point will be further touched when we come to the 'King's houses.' About 20 feet from this double-staged wall are the remains of the tower at the south-west angle of the baily.

Vaulted chambers and Castle Quay.

*The Castle.*

The castle wall, which we will now follow, turned nearly due east, portions of it still existing behind the houses on the south of Castle Gardens. At about 110 feet from the south-west angle it crossed Castle Lane (south). Here was the south gate of the baily, demolished about 1770. Beyond this the wall continued eastward some 40 feet

Castle baily wall.

[1] The 'Castle Quay' does not seem to have been repaired by the townsfolk. The Sheriff of the county was occasionally, as in 1218, ordered to repair it with the king's cellars in the castle.

till it struck the lofty mound of the keep, deeply intrenched and boldly scarped, round which it described three parts of a circle for about 400 feet, the hill's diameter being 200; it then started off obliquely with a north-eastern inclination for about 60 feet, then in a north-westerly for another 85 feet, crossing at this point Castle Lane (north), where was the principal gate of the castle, destroyed also in the last century, though a fragment may still be seen on the north of the lane. Beyond this the wall made a curve to the north-west till it struck the curtain, as above described, south of Catchcold. A considerable and curious portion of this enceinte remains, the foundations of which, on square piers and rounded arches, were sunk some 15 feet into the ground. The wall is described as having stood 'on the top of a high bank with a deep ditch at its foot,'[1] but towards the end of the last century the surface was lowered considerably, and the foundations of the baily wall, denuded of earth, have since exhibited an abnormal and extensive arcade of fourteen or more perfect arches, some of them slightly pointed, at a height of about 12 feet above the present level, the span of the arches averaging 9 feet and the piers about 7 feet square. This foundation carried a battlemented wall, some of the ashlar of which may still be detected.[2]

The keep, of which nothing now remains, was probably a bold shell of masonry with a chemise or encircling wall about it. It stood upon the southern front of the lofty semicircular area, proudly dominating the town, and forming part of the enceinte of the castle fortifications, according to the usual arrangement. We have no earlier account of it than that of its rebuilding under Sir John Arundel, when a patent, dated April 9, 1378, directed Henry Marmesfeld, John Pyperyng, and Richard Baillyf to procure the erection as quickly as possible of a certain tower on the 'old castell hill' with two gates, a mantelet, and barbican of stone, that is, an encircling wall about it with an outwork before the gate.[3] Material was to be procured and carriage provided at the king's cost, the charges for which would be met immediately; and all necessary stonemasons, carpenters, or other workmen

**The keep.**

**Rebuilt.**

[1] Buller's Englefield, p. 47.

[2] In 1856 this interesting work was threatened with destruction, together with other remains of walls and towers. However, a meeting convened in January by the mayor (Mr. S. Payne), supported by Mr. Kell, Mr. Stebbing, Mr. Brannon, Mr. Falvey, and others, determined to address the Town Council on the subject. In consequence of this movement the borough continues to possess some of the most singular and interesting architectural remains in the kingdom. See Journal of Brit. Arch. Assoc. xii. 207.

[3] Super quendam montem vocatum 'oldcastellhill' quandam turrim de petrâ et calce, et duas portas in eâdem turri, et unum mantelettum cum quodam barbicano de petrâ et calce circa dictam turrim, &c. (Pat. 1 R. ii. p. 6. m. 7).

were to be taken from the counties of Somerset, Dorset, Wilts, Southampton, Oxon, Berks, Surrey, and Sussex, and kept at the works as long as needful at the king's wages.

Leland in 1546 says of it: 'The glorie of the castelle is in the dungeon [keep], that is both larg, fair, and very stronge, both by worke and the site of it.'[1] Speed, writing at the end of the same century, describes it as 'most beautiful, in forme circular, and wall within wall; the foundation upon a hill so topped that it cannot be ascended but by stairs.'[2] In 1599 Hortensio Spinola, in his report on the southern ports, described the castle of Southampton as being strong, with sixty pieces of artillery and 100 soldiers.[3] Yet in 1618 the keep was ruinous:[4] in 1635 the traveller quoted in a former page speaks of it as an 'old ruinated castle, on a high mounted hill, environed with a round strong wall.'

Chapel.

Within the baily was the chapel of the castle, and apparently towards the north-west of the enclosure, for we find it occasionally reckoned in the beat of the town watch. Thus about 1504, when provision was made to receive the king's grace (Henry VII.), four aldermen with their 'vynteners' or inferior officers were assigned to see the town in good order, their wards being thus set, starting from the castle southward, and so going round the walls. The first, from the castle wall to the site of the old wool-bridge; from that to the Friar's tower and garret; from thence to the Eastgate; and thence to the chapel in the castle.[5] This chapel, dedicated to St. George, had an endowment by royal letters of £10 per annum on the customs of the town. Among the chaplains were Friar John Bury;[6] Sir John Chewe,[7] September 20, 1485; Thomas Vasse, August 2, 1508; Robert Tawley, December 23, 1572; John Clerk,[8] on death of last, 1526; he was there ten years later. A chantry was founded here by Edward IV. in 1478, and in 1553 Nicholas Hill, incumbent of the chantry, received a pension of £6.

Baily.

It would appear that some dismantling of the baily had taken place at the close of the fifteenth century, when the 'castle wall' is said to have been pulled down,[9] and by 1550 the 'Castle Green' had become a place where rubbish might or might not be shot; in 1591 it had been

---

1 Itinerary, iii. 107.
2 Theatre of Great Britain, reprint 1650, p. 13.
3 Cal. State Papers.
4 See below, where also other details.
5 Lib. Remembranc. i. f. 14, 27.
6 Dec. 13, 1483. Pat. 1 R. III. p. 1, m. 25 (1).
7 Rot. Parl. vi. 377 a.
8 Papers of Hen. VIII. sub dat., and Valor. Eccl.
9 After the last passage given from Dr. Speed he continues: '13 Hen. VII. [1498–99].—The castle wall was pulled down.' The remainder of his chapter is given below.

for some years let to the butchers by Captain Parkinson—no doubt the governor—and the court leet jury presented that the 'sheep have spoiled the hill'—that is, the hill of the keep—'most ruinously;' they beg that no more sheep or cattle be allowed there; they also state that the windows and gates of the castle tower lie open to all the inhabitants, whereof they desire reformation. This letting of the herbage was further presented as a grievance in 1594, on the score that Captain Parkinson had ten years previously granted it to the town for the term of his life; it seems also that right of passage through the castle to the archery butts had been questioned by the tenant.

**The butts.** These butts, at one time called the great butts, though it is difficult to see how a proper range could have been secured, were on the east side of the Castle Green, because the St. Laurence people were constantly being presented for throwing refuse from their back-doors by the castle butts.[1] The ditch at this part may therefore have been filled up, or the butts may have been in the ditch, a not unlikely position if length could have been found. It is also possible that the range may not have been long, as in 1587 these butts were pronounced 'meetest for the younger people.'

The castle was the seat of military government and defence in the Middle Ages. It was also in the castle that the king's justices itinerant held their court.[2]

**Notices.** The following notices concern the early governors, their duties, or the castle itself.

**Constables.** In February 1205 (6 John) Robert de Cantilupe was custos of the town. In the same year the constable was ordered by writ to deliver to Brian de l'Isle a tun of wine from the royal store. In the next year he was ordered to restore wine detained from a burgess of Rochelle, and to release a ship which he had seized in error, it appearing under certificate of the mayor of Rochelle that the vessel belonged to that port.

In April 1206 (7 John) he was charged with the duty, in common with Walter Fortin and William de Langetot, of seizing for the king's use ships at Southampton and neighbouring ports. The vessels were to be capable of carrying eight horses each at least, and were to be assembled at Portsmouth by Whitsun Eve. They were to be provided with bridges and hurdles for the landing and protection of the animals. The names of the owners were to be enrolled, as also how many mariners were in each ship and how many horses each could carry. Vessels happening to be laden were at once to discharge their cargoes; owners who hesitated were to be taken for enemies.

---

1 Court Leet books, 1574, 1577, 1579, &c.

2 See document above, p. 49.

The next year the constable received from William Briewere, the king's forester, under writ from Winchester, twenty rafters from the royal wood of 'Knutes wude' for the repair of the king's hall at Southampton.

In 1213 (14 John) WILLIAM BRIEWERE received the county of Southampton, with the custody of Southampton Castle, during the king's pleasure.[1]

ADAM DE PORT was governor[2] in 1213.

In 1215 (16 John) two trusty messengers, Thomas de Erdington and Henry de Ver, were dispatched from the king to WILLIAM DE ST. JOHN (son of the last), constable of Southampton Castle, with instructions which the king had been unwilling to commit to writing. The constable was to expect other messengers the following day, meanwhile he was to receive as certain what he would hear from those now sent, or from Thomas alone if the other could not be present, concerning the safe custody of the royal castles and person. A similar visit was directed to various other officials in different places.

A few years later (1222, 7 H. III.) the needs of Southampton Castle had to yield to those of Winchester; and the bailiffs of William Briewere were directed to deliver to the mayor of Winchester, for the repairs of the castle there, the sixty beams from 'Cnichte wude' which the Prior of the Hospital had given the king for the repairs of Southampton Castle.

A portion of the castle at least was dilapidated in 1246 (30 H. III.), and the townspeople were fined 270 marks for withdrawing several duties belonging to the castle, and for selling timber, lead, and stone from that now demolished building.[3]

On June 17, 1273 (2 Ed. I.), the custody of the town was committed to ADAM DE WINTON[4] during the king's pleasure.

In 1330–31 (4 Ed. III.) the custody of Southampton and Christchurch castles was granted to THOMAS DE WEST (afterwards Lord la Warre), with other holdings, at a rent of £435. In the next year the custody of these castles, together with the manor and park of Lyndhurst, and the new forest, the hundred of Redbridge, and forty shillings rent paid by the abbot and convent of Reading, and other perquisites, were renewed to him for life at the annual rent of £130, the sum generally maintained.[5]

In October 1338 the 'French' invasion occurred (see below, last

---

[1] The above are from printed Patent and Close Rolls.

[2] So Dugdale Bar. i. 463, but his reference (Pat. 15 John, p. i. m. 9) appears to be faulty: the appointment is not on the Roll.

[3] Madox, Exchq. i. 568.

[4] Fines Rolls, 2 Ed. I., m. 19.

[5] Rot. Orig. Abbrev.

chapter), immediately after which the town was seized into the king's hands, in active censure on the mayor, bailiffs, and burgesses, who had fled before the enemy. It was then[1] committed to JOHN DE SCURES and THOMAS CONDRAY, to hold during pleasure, on October 12. The commission (as are the following documents) is tested by Edward, afterwards the Black Prince, who had himself been left guardian of England in his father's absence at the ripe age of nine years. On November 10 JOHN DE PALTON and JOHN DE BOKLAND[2] were commissioned in the same terms; and on November 13th, among other steps taken, John de Hampton, Walter de Estcote, and others, were commissioned to inquire into the loss of the king's wools by fire; how much, and of what quality, had been left after the enemy had retired.[3]

Under one influence or other the mayor and bailiffs recovered heart, and humbly begged for the restoration of their town and liberties; receiving them back on March 15, 1339, apparently on no harder terms than that they should do their duty in future, and hold the town vigorously against the foe;[4] and orders occur to John de Flete, clerk, keeper of the arms in the Tower of London, to send forthwith all kinds of weapons for the use of the town.[5]

EDMUND DE LA BECHE, RICHARD DE PEULE, and STEPHEN DE BITTERLE were appointed chief guardians, for the safe custody of the town, with a certain number of men at arms, on April 12, 1339, and on the same day Philip de Thame, Prior of the Knights Hospitallers in England, was desired to send thirty men-at-arms as an auxiliary, to remain in the town, or at St. Denys's Priory, or close at hand, in readiness against any foreign attack.[6] Robert atte Barre was the king's receiver and victualler to the troops at Southampton, May 12; Nicholas atte Magdalene being appointed to the same office, June 11.

THOMAS BEAUCHAMP, Earl of Warwick, was next made constable or chief guardian; his commission, running in the name of the Black Prince, is dated Kennington, July 13, 1339 (13 Ed. III.)[7] The guardianship was committed to him from the Monday (July 26) after the Feast of St. James for a quarter of a year. He was to have with him a hundred men-at-arms, their quality specified, fifty being of his own men. He had power to muster the men-at-arms of the Prior of the Hospitallers, and those of Berkshire, and others who should be sent to aid in keeping the town. The inhabitants had in considerable

---

[1] Rot. Orig., 12 Ed. III., rot. 15. [2] Ibid., rot. 17.
[3] Ibid., rot. 30. [4] Ibid., 13 Ed. III., rot. 4. [5] Ibid., rot. 29, 38.
[6] Rot. Alemanniæ, 13 Ed. III., m. 8, m. 11.
[7] The original document was purchased at a public sale in London in 1849 by R. Laishley, Esq., then mayor, and presented to the Corporation. It hangs in the Council-chamber. See also Rot. Alemanniæ, 13 Ed. III., m. 6.

numbers deserted the place, and the Earl was enjoined to compel the return of the fugitives, on pain of forfeiture of their goods; while £50 in silver were granted towards repairs. The Earl accordingly at once issued a proclamation on the day he received this indenture. By the roll of Nicholas atte Magdalene, he appears to have entered the town with his retinue of fifty men-at-arms and fifty archers on July 25, and to have remained till August 25th.[1]

On August 29, four days after the retirement of the Earl, Brother PHILIP DE THAME, Prior of the Hospital of St. John of Jerusalem, superior of the Knights-Hospitallers in England, was appointed guardian with similar powers; and on September 15 a further effort was made by royal proclamations and threats to induce the return of the burgesses and inhabitants.[2]

On November 3 the same year (1339) STEPHEN DE BITTERLE and WILLIAM DE WESTON, sergeants-at-arms, were appointed chief guardians to superintend the men-at-arms and archers of the counties of Berks and Wilts, assigned for the defence of the town.[3]

In the same regnal year (13 Ed. III.) Sir RICHARD TALBOT received the guardianship, with fifty men-at-arms and one hundred archers, at the king's wages, to be paid him in advance. He was himself to receive a guerdon of £100, and £100 in part payment of an old debt, and was enjoined to see the town fortified at the expense of the inhabitants, with help from the king if necessary. The Bishop of Winchester, the Prior of St. Swithin, and the Abbot of Hyde, were desired to arm their men in the manors nearest to Southampton, and to be ready to enter and defend the town if required. And further, two pinnaces, one belonging to Millbrook, another to Roger Normaund,[4] were assigned to wait on the commands of Mons. Richard in the port of the town. He was to take order about the fugitive burgesses. Commission at the same time was given to Stephen de Bitterlye and William de Weston, sergeants-at-arms, to take timber and other commodities from owners, at a certain price, for the safety of the town. All the arms in the place, of whatever kind,[5] were to be delivered by list to the guardian, and a writ of attendance was directed to the Sheriff of the county requiring him to provide Mons. Richard with all necessary supplies.[6]

---

[1] An order was also issued on the day of the Earl's appointment (July 10) to the Sheriff of the county to make proclamation and compel the return of the people, on pain of confiscation of their goods.

[2] Rot. Alemanniæ, 13 Ed. III., m. 5 and m. 4.

[3] Ibid., m. 1. [4] See under M.P.s.

[5] Item qe les espringalx, engyns, arblastes, actines, launces, payneys, blasouns, targes, purkernels, fer, plum, esteantz en la dite vile, &c.

[6] Rot. Parl. ii. 108 *b*.

After this, on July 4, 1342, the PRIOR OF ST. SWITHIN, Winchester, and the ABBOT OF HYDE were in commission as guardians against foreign enemies.[1]

JOHN DE BEAUCHAMP of Warwick received the custody of the castle, &c., for good service[2] in 33 Ed. III. (1359–60).

HENRY PEVEREL was appointed guardian[3] April 10, 1360, and desired to repair the fortifications, which were in much need of it: within two years he died seized of lands and tenements in the town of Southampton, as well as, among other possessions, the manor of Lyndhurst, and holdings in Mansbridge and Peniton, and of Middleton and Chilworth manors.

RICHARD PEMBRIDGE[4] succeeded (35 Ed. III. 1361–62), receiving the custody of the castle for life, with that of the manor and park of Lyndhurst, the keepership of the New Forest and of the hundred of Redbridge, together with the forty shillings rent from a tenement in the forest paid by the Abbot of Reading, at the annual rent of £130. He was to have the burden of repairs, but in the next year the king, as a mark of affection, remitted for his life £40 and forty marks from the rent.[5]

On June 12, 1369 (43 Ed. III.), HUGO DE ESTCOTE[6] was appointed captain, with full powers of arresting all rebels against the king or the government of the town; his attention was also called to all regrators, artisans, or workmen, who should offend against the several statutes respecting them. No time was specified for the duration of his office. The captaincy of the castle or town, and the custody, wardenry, or guardianship were not always identical appointments.

ALMARIC DE ST. AMAND[7] was appointed guardian on August 13 the same year, and by letters of that date, directed to the keepers of the peace and arrayers of men-at-arms in the county of Wilts, &c., order was given for 100 men-at-arms and 200 archers to be sent to Southampton. Two days after (August 15) Almaric was confirmed as captain and guardian, always to be ready to resist the king's enemies from France.

In the next year, August 22, 1370 (44 Ed. III.), HUGO DE ESTOTE, Knt., and JOHN PULMOUND, mayor,[8] were appointed to array all men sound in body in the town and suburbs for defence 'against our French enemies, who have often invaded and burnt towns on the coast:'

---

[1] Pat. 16 Ed. III., p. 2, m. 34.
[2] Rot. Orig. Abbrev., p. 255.
[3] Pat. 34 Ed. III., p. 1, m. 21.
[4] Pat. 35 Ed. III., p. 3, m. 25.
[5] Rot. Orig. Abbrev., p. 258.
[6] Pat. 43 Ed. III., p. 2, m. 44.
[7] Ibid., m. 23. At the same time men-at-arms and archers were ordered for Portsmouth. Warin de l'Isle was captain and custos there.
[8] Pat. 44 Ed. III., p. 2, m. 5, a tergo.

men too feeble to serve were to find substitutes. Under the same year payment of £2 occurs to John Tipet,[1] valet of the king's chamber, lately sent into Hants, Wilts, Berks, and Oxon, to collect and train archers, and bring them to Southampton to be ready against invasion.

In the 46 Edward III. (1372–73), JOHN DE FOXLE[2] received for life the custody of the castle, with the other emoluments as in the case of Pembridge, but at the full rent of £130, from which his executors were cleared Michaelmas 1382,[3] the grant being renewed in the fiftieth and fifty-first years.

The next year (1 R. II. 1377) was one of singular trial and glory to the town, under the guardianship of Sir JOHN DE ARUNDEL,[4] who was appointed on July 9th, to have with him 100 men-at-arms and 100 archers, who were to be gathered from any quarter and retained at the king's pay. We have already mentioned the works at the castle under this governor.

IVO FITZ-WARYN was governor of the town 1 Henry IV. (1399).[5]

EDWARD, EARL OF RUTLAND, who appears to have held the honours which went with the castle of Southampton in the latter years of Richard II., had been restored to those emoluments, and was holding the castle of Southampton towards the close (1411) of the reign of Henry IV.[6]

In 1414 RICHARD SPICER, Esq., with forty archers, was appointed for the safe keeping of the king's carracks, ships, and vessels in the port, for a quarter of a year, against invasion.

In the next year (1415) JOHN POPHAM was constable of the castle, and to his custody Richard, Earl of Cambridge, Henry, Lord le Scrope of Masham, and Sir Thomas Grey were committed on charge of high treason, for which they were executed.[7]

Possibly HUMPHREY, DUKE OF GLOUCESTER, murdered February 28, 1447 (25 H. VI.), was constable of the castle, as he died seized of the lordships which went with it.

JOHN HOTON was constable, with the honours and emoluments next below described, in the time of Richard III. (1483–85).

Sir JOHN CHEYNE, Knt., received the appointment March 3, 1486 (1 H. VII.), with the wages of £10 per annum out of the customs of the port; he was also made constable of Christchurch Castle, steward

[1] Issue Roll, sub anno.
[2] Rot. Orig. Abbrev. for 46 and 51 Ed. III., and Pat. 50 Ed. III., p. 2, m. 27.
[3] Memorand. Rolls, Mich. record, 6 R. II. rot. 24.
[4] Pat. 1 R. II., p. 1, m. 20. See further, under date, in last chapter.
[5] Pat. 1 H. IV., p. 5, m. 23.
[6] Memorand. Rolls, Mich. record, 13 H. IV. rot. 5.
[7] Rot. Parl. iv. 66. See further below, last chapter.

of the lordships and manors of Christchurch, Ringwood, and Hunton, keeper of the New Forest, with custody of the manor, and wages of fourpence a day out of the customs. Other stewardships were granted him at the same time.[1]

In the latter part of this reign THOMAS THOMAS was constable; he was excepted from the general pardon in the first year of Henry VIII. (April 30, 1509), but received it a month later (May 30). He died shortly after.

Sir WILLIAM SANDIS, Knt. was appointed, vice the last, on January 10, 1510, at the salary of £10. This patent being invalid, the office was regranted him April 9, 1512.[2]

In 32 Henry VIII. (1540) Sir THOMAS WRIOTHESLEY, Knt., afterwards Earl of Southampton, was made constable of the castle.[3]

In the latter quarter of this century CAPTAIN PARKINSON (see above) was in command. He seems to have been no great friend to the town, especially if a petition refers to him, bearing date about 1599, in which the mayor, &c., appeal to the Council for redress against James Parkinson, captain of Calshot Castle, who detained ships at the castle under pretence of castle dues, and forbade them going up to the town, 'to the ruin of its trade and custom.'

In 1616 Sir ROBERT LAND was captain at twopence per day; but the castle was falling more and more into a neglected and ruinous condition.

In 1618 the ruined castle, its site and ditches, passed by a grant of King James I. (July 16) in consideration of a sum of £2078, 0s. 1¼d., to Sir James Ouchterlony and Richard Garnard, citizen and clothworker of London, who in the next month (August 10) consigned their interest to William Osey, of Basingstoke, who in his turn made it over to George Gollop, of the town and county of Southampton, merchant, on July 10, 1619 (17 James I.) In 1636 (14th March—11 Charles I.) George Gollop obtained the royal grant[4] of the castle and its ditches to himself and heirs at the yearly rent of thirteen shillings and fourpence. The property remained in the Gollop family some few years. Under 1650 we find Peter Gollop in possession, and on October 11 that year he gave permission to Major Peter Murford, commandant of the town, to take such stones from the castle as he might think needful for the repair of the fortifications.[5]

Site granted away.

Subsequently to this "the site became parcelled out to several "people who have built houses and made gardens upon the ground;

[1] Materials for Hist. of Hen. VII., i. 344.
[2] Brewer's letters, &c., of Hen. VIII., under dates.
[3] Dugd. Bar., ii. 383.
[4] Pat. 11 Charles I., pt. 8.
[5] Journal, October 11, 1650.

"and the ditch of it is converted into gardens to some houses in the "town that lay round it. The hill on which the castle stood remains, "and has a summer-house upon it built with the materials of the old "castle: this was formerly a windmill. There is enough of the walls "left to shew the compass of it; and within its precincts some arched "vaults have been found in digging the foundation of houses, &c., "which some people fancy were private ways to other parts of the "town, but I take them to have been magazines and storehouses for "the use of the castle. There is one in a garden adjoining to the town "wall."

Subsequently to Dr. Speed's death in 1781 the castle hill was purchased from Mr. Watson in 1804 by Lord Wycombe, afterwards (May 7, 1805) Marquis of Lansdowne—elected burgess August 21, 1805—who resided near Peartree Green. On his coming into the family estates he laid out large sums of money on the castle hill, and by degrees erected an extensive castellated mansion of brick and stucco, which appears to have contained within it some remnant of the old fortress. On his death, November 15, 1809, his successor and half-brother, whose great delight was in driving about with four foresters not much bigger than Newfoundland dogs, eventually sold the mansion for valuable building material. It was put up for sale July 1816, together with the freehold site of the castle, having a frontage towards the river of 277 feet.[1] The mansion was taken down in 1818, when the mound was lowered;[2] and in 1823–24 Zion Chapel (now Zion Hall) was erected, and opened June 9, 1824—Rev. J. Crabbe, minister—on the site of the Norman keep.

The walls resumed.

We may now return to the town walls. Starting from the south-west angle of the baily, we immediately leave the high level of the castle platform and cross what was the mouth of the ditch. The wall, which is here low and fragmentary, now runs south-west, at an angle of about 18 degrees, to a tower heading the salient, at a distance of some 100 feet from the baily, into the remains of which one of the small houses in Lansdowne Place is built. It then runs southward for about 80 feet, where we should expect another tower, and re-enters sharply to the east, so as to cover Biddle's gate, which was set some 50 feet back.

Biddle's gate.

This gate, variously called West gate next the castle, and even Castle gate, and ultimately Biddle's gate, is described as having been

1 Hants Telegraph, June 24, 1816.

2 In 1822 a silver penny of Offa was found at the castle keep with the name of the moneyer, BANHARD, in two lines. It is preserved in the Hartley Institute.

'merely an arch in the wall,' 'a low gate with a pointed arch, over which are the brackets of two machicolations.[1]

Biddle's gate appears to have been a favourite place for depositing refuse, although one of the chief inlets to the town. In 1511 his Majesty was expected that way, hence, though a poor man had already been set to make 'clene the doyng hyll at the Bedelles yatte,' receiving twelvepence for his pay, so great an event deserved an extra scrub. 'Item, paid for the reddyng of the Bedelles yatt at the Kynges comyng, iiij.'[2] In short, our ancestors were not over-nice. Suffice it to say, that sewers, drains, and other conveniences did not receive the attention which civilised life now exacts. Latrines placed near the gates—there was one by Biddle's gate—serving for the mass of the townspeople, were constantly requiring attention, which not being paid—a catastrophe of common occurrence—the indignant court leet jury had frequently to complain of the state of the walls and streets as rendered 'corrupt, verie filthie, and noyssom to passe by.' Let us leave this quickly.

Ancient quay.

We are now upon the ancient quay of the town. From the north-west angle of the fortifications the sea washed the foot of the wall as far as the turning in to Biddle's gate till within the last thirty years; for the handsome roadway beneath the western wall is of recent construction, having been due chiefly to the exertions of the late Rev. T. L. Shapcott, a former vicar of St. Michael's. The ancient quay on which we are supposed to be standing was of considerable extent. Speed's map (1596) makes the shore extend to Bugle Tower, the remains of which are just beyond the house of Madame Maës. If this be taken as accurate, a length for the whole shore of about 700 feet is given. What was distinctively called West Quay was projected some distance into the sea like a broad pier opposite West gate. Much of this land frontage deserves special attention.

Town wall.

Immediately below the site of Biddle's gate an arcade commences, which is believed to be perfectly singular and unlike anything in England;[3] it stretches for some 260 feet southward. Beyond this the wall passes behind houses for some 120 feet, coming occasionally into view, till we arrive at the opening into Collis's Court, where to the left we observe the picturesque fragment of a tower, three sides of an octagon, the front being carried up from a broad and bold rectangular buttress, which has its hollow angles crossed by arches to support the other sides. Fifty feet farther is West gate, beyond which the wall

[1] Buller's Englefield, p. 16.

[2] Steward's books, sub annis.

[3] On this construction see Viollet-le-Duc's "Walls of Avignon" (Military Architecture, ed. Parker, p. 149, &c.)

passes within the garden of Madame Maës's premises for some 230 feet to the remains of Bugle Tower.

Towers destroyed.

This line of defence was strengthened by several towers, three[1] of which at least were in the arcade; for on April 7th, 1775, Mr. Martin of the Long Rooms, who catered for the rank and fashion of the place, obtained leave to take down parts of three round towers on the West Quay opposite his own houses; and on June 2d further permission to remove the top of the wall over 'Beidles gate,' which appeared to be dangerous. It must be remembered that when a 'highly genteel and polite society' came flocking to Mr. Martin's rooms, the only approaches were through Biddle's and West gates. Mr. Martin, moreover, helped to attract and retain the visitors; thus the Corporation did not hesitate when it became a question whether Mr. Martin or the towers should go.

Pilgrim's Pit Tower.

The first of these destroyed towers was probably 'Pilgrim's Pit' Tower, close to Biddle's gate, deriving its name, as did the gate itself sometimes, and a garden there, and the immediate vicinity, from what was called the 'Pilgrim's Pit'—probably some famous *well*, which I cannot help connecting with the pilgrimages to St. Thomas of Canterbury. In 1348, Agnes le Horder bequeaths a tenement in the parish of St. Michael, in the street called 'Pilegrimes putte.' The name 'Pylgrymes put' occurs in an inquisition taken at Southampton in 1367. In 1441 we read of the 'west gate next the castle called pylgrymys pyt.' In 1468 we hear of the 'towr at pylgryms pyt,' which carried 'j gonne w$^t$ iij chawmbres.'[2]

The second tower may be placed in front of the fourth arch of the arcade, where we observe broken work aloft and two rectangular piers, each four feet wide, which do not bond with the arcade work, but run up to the top of the wall with straight joints, the width of the arch between them being 6 feet 4 inches.

For the site of the third tower we must pass on to the broad pier, with a modern house-door in it, next beyond the ninth arch. Now, this very broad pier, with the adjoining flat arch of 18 feet and the pier beyond, has been partially rebuilt. But looking attentively at it, we find that it is really made up of two rectangular piers, each four feet wide, with a flat arch of 6 feet 4 inches between. The identity of measurement will be noticed with that of the arch above mentioned. Such was the arrangement in Englefield's time; but to accommodate a house in the rear the wall has been brought forward from

1 Speed's map (1596) gives three towers between Biddle's and Blue Anchor gate: Dr. Speed's plan gives two, one half drum, the other square: Milne's Survey (1791) shows two half drums.

2 Steward's books, sub annis.

between the piers flush with their outer face, thus reducing the whole in effect to one breadth of wall space of over 14 feet, and completely altering the original features, though high above the modern doorway unmistakable signs of broken vaulting are left. The piers also are unconformable with the arcade. Of this now filled-up arch, with that of 18 feet adjoining and the pier beyond, Englefield says: 'These two arches and their three piers, together with another similar narrow arch and its thick piers [the one above described], seem as if they had belonged to a building which projected beyond the present front of the wall; for the face of the small arch is rough, as if broken off.' At the beginning of this century, moreover, there appear to have been no signs of crenellation over these rectangular works, as if they were unfinished at the top, while there was an embrasure over every pier of the arcade. It is impossible to say what may have been the character of the building in front of the two last-mentioned arches; but we may with great probability place here our third tower.

The fact that the arcade was originally fitted to or furnished with towers has not, I believe, been noticed; and it is singular that Sir H. Englefield should not have mentioned this destruction, which had only occurred some twenty-five years before he wrote.

We may now turn to the arcade. It runs south from Biddle's gate, as we have stated, for about 260 feet, and is composed of the walls, four feet thick and thirty high, of Norman buildings of domestic and mercantile character, together with a fronting or masque of piers and arches of a more or less pointed character, applied against the former for additional strength. The work at the rear of the arcade is pure Norman, belonging apparently to the middle or early part of the twelfth century. Numerous door and window spaces may still be traced in this older work, several of which have been cut across or partially blocked by the arcading. The Arcade.

The arches of the arcade are nineteen in number, or rather now we must say eighteen, since No. 10 has been filled in, as before explained. They are of various span, but the average is a trifle under eleven feet. The piers on which they are turned have a footing of eighteen inches above the ground, with a total height to the spring of the arches of about twelve feet, a breadth of 2 feet 2 inches, and a depth of 3 feet 3 inches from the more ancient wall. To this wall the piers are joined through their entire height, but between the arches which spring from them and the wall behind a wide chase is left, something like the groove for a portcullis, only having an average breadth of 1 foot 8 inches. The front work or masque raised upon these arches is bonded at unequal distances to the wall behind, at the parapet level, with long stones, which from below give the effect, as they served the purpose, of machicolations completely screened from view. An ample rampart walk was thus afforded with a strong breastwork in front, cleft by a somewhat narrow embrasure over every pier.

Details of Arcade.

Commencing at Biddle's gate, the first of the series of arches differs from the others in being sharply pointed. Within this first bay, which is only 5 feet 3 inches in width, and extending into the second, Englefield describes a low semicircular arch, now hidden behind the modern plinth. The second and third bays are each eleven feet broad; the second containing a semicircular archway, which was filled up when this defence was made, and was pierced with a loophole still to be seen on the inner side of the wall; similar loops being also observable at breast-height in other parts of this defence. The third archway, blank in Englefield's time, now contains a modern doorway leading into a court beyond. There may also have been an opening above. We now come to one of the rectangular-looking works before mentioned, against which the arcading rests on both sides, and which is, therefore, probably more ancient than the arcade. It consists of two piers, each four feet broad, with a flat arch of 6 feet 4 inches between. Within this archway to the left was a low Norman doorway. Arch No. 5 is 9 feet 3 inches in breadth: in the wall behind it there may be seen the trace of a small loop. The sixth, seventh, eighth, and ninth arches are each eleven feet broad. No. 6 has a semicircular arch in the wall behind it to the left; No. 7, a segment-headed door and a Decorated niche; No. 8, two ancient pointed doorways, that to the right half hidden by the next pier; that to the left probably opened in lieu of it, and now again in use as the entrance to a house in the rear; No. 9, a blank wall, but now pierced by a carpenter's Gothic window belonging to the house behind. This brings us to the other rectangular work, presenting a breadth of pier or wall surface of over fourteen feet, as already described, and showing the remains of broken vaulting high above the modern street door. Next is the rebuilt flat arch of eighteen feet, and the pier of six feet beyond, also rebuilt, forming the remainder of the same rectangular work. The wall behind the broad arch is blank and bears traces of plaster on its surface. The arcade work commences again with the eleventh arch, that and the three next arches being each eleven feet wide. It contains behind it, according to Sir H. Englefield, a rough pointed arch, which may be concealed behind the plinth. Within No. 12 is the wide opening into Blue Anchor Court, over which, just within, is the date of this insertion, 1644, in the mayoralty of Thomas Mason. No. 13 may have had a couple of openings above; No. 14 contains one small loop. The fifteenth arch, 11 feet 9 inches wide, has within it the ancient postern, now called Blue Anchor, but formerly Lord's Lane gate, and still more anciently Postern gate. This gate has been much cut away to obtain width, but the grooves of its portcullis remain in the head of the arch. No. 16 has within it on the ground-floor a large semicircular arch, the old entrance from the twelfth-century house behind to the quay or beach. In the second stage a plain double light Norman window existed in Englefield's time, but has since been improved into a common wooden loft door. This archway is 11 feet 4 inches wide. Nos. 17 and 18 are each twelve feet wide. The wall behind No. 17 contains on the right one half of a lofty segment-headed opening cut off by the right pier, and on the left a segmental insertion of smaller proportions, possibly substituted for the other when the arcade was built. Above this latter opening is a good two-light Norman window with a loop to the right. No. 18, the last now in the arcade, has within it the wide modern opening of rough doors leading into the remains of the above twelfth-century house called King John's Palace. Over this till late years there existed another two-light Norman window, similar to the last, though partly cut off by the arcade; but all traces of this are now gone, and the wall is much patched about with brickwork. The arcading was continued farther south, but there are no means of judging how far. Blue Anchor postern.

In estimating the probable date of this construction, attention must be given to the character of the arcade, the style of the work displaced by it, and any documentary evidence which may bear on the matter. It is submitted that no trace exists in the arcade itself of Norman or even transitional character, and that there is nothing to negative its being of Edwardian origin. But special regard must be had to the character of the work against which it is built. Thus, turning to the foregoing description, we observe the piers of the arcade blocking up and cutting across, not only Norman windows of the date of King Stephen, but also a pointed archway (No. 8) and a segment (No. 17). These and probably more instances point to a much later age. General documentary evidence from murages and quayages indicates a great activity along this quarter in the Edwardian period; more money was spent on the walls at that time than before or after. Whether or not in connection with the arcade, but certainly with the quay-work about this part, the burgesses had about 1326 constructed a wooden barbican towards the sea, which they subsequently constructed of stone, obtaining a 'barbican duty' for some years in consequence (see under Quays). Upon the whole, we venture to ascribe this partial conversion of Norman mercantile buildings for purposes of defence, the looping the wall, and the erection of the arcade, to the period marked out above—the earlier part of the fourteenth century. Date of Arcade.

Buildings in the rear.

Of the buildings in the rear, whose front openings we have described, some of the houses (*e.g.*, that in arch No. 1) would seem to have had vaults below; in other cases the openings indicate floors on a different level. Immediately joining Biddle's gate there was an ancient building, into the remains of which the present Castle-house has been built. The first openings of the arcade were probably connected with this building. But there are two houses, separated by the postern gate, well known to students of ancient domestic architecture, which should be described here.

Norman houses.

The more important of these houses is that to the south, occupying the space immediately behind the last three bays of the arcade. Its internal measurements are on the south side 44 feet, on the east 41 feet, on the west along the town wall 35 feet, and on the north along Blue Anchor Lane 43 feet. The principal part of it is now a mere shell, the roof and ancient woodwork not having been replaced, but a portion of the second floor immediately to the rear of the west wall has been kept up. The house was in two stages throughout, the chief rooms being on the second floor. In the north wall of this storey are the remains of a handsome Norman fireplace[1] in a fairly preserved state, with a perfect shaft in each jamb, and a chimney carried to the top of the building. On this floor were the only windows of the house, five in number, one being a mere loop and four of two lights each, all of which looked to the front or town-wall side, except one double window on the north, which faced the lane and the Norman house opposite. The double windows were divided into their two lights by a shaft with cap and base, except in the case of one (in archway 16), now gone, which seems to have been formed simply by the grouping of two small apertures. On the inside the windows are contained within round-headed recesses, having a bold round bead on their inner edge. On the same floor are the remains of an intramural passage which started from the middle of the east side and was carried to the south wall, where light was admitted by a small aperture, and then westward within the south side. It communicated with the town wall. Part of this fell away in 1866. On the ground-floor are two Norman doorways, one above mentioned under arch 16. Against the south wall and not bonded into it are two low piers, projecting some five feet, upon which arches have been turned, probably for cellar or stable accommodation. There are no traces of a staircase, which was probably therefore of wood and within the building. We have already

[1] Mr. J. K. Dymond, who has lately paid some attention to this building, has observed four courses of Roman bricks in the fireplace, not in the position of firebricks, but higher up, and, as he conjectures, for the sake of ornament and variety of colour.

described the west exterior when speaking of the last three bays of the arcade. The north exterior in Blue Anchor Lane contains on the basement a Norman doorway, and farther on a later insertion. On the second stage are the chimney shaft, projecting from the wall like a flat Norman buttress and carried on a table of four corbels; and to the right of this, a two-lighted window divided by a shaft with cap and base, the weather having been excluded by wooden shutters.

The house on the north of the lane was smaller, and owing to its having been constantly inhabited, and for some generations as an inn or lodging-house, it has preserved fewer original features. Its external measurements are, from west to east 45 feet, with a total depth from north to south of about 20 feet. It preserves in front the original Norman doorway, and in the rear some ancient work may be detected from Blue Anchor Court.

The tradition which makes these houses, or the larger of them, to be King John's Palace is of recent origin,[1] and may be traced to Mr. Duthy, whose interesting posthumous work appeared in 1839; other local names have been given from the conjectures of Sir Henry Englefield. There is no doubt, however, that John was frequently at Southampton, and that he had here a 'king's house' or 'houses' separate from the castle platform, though not necessarily for his own dwelling purposes. 'King's houses' also existed in Winchester, Portsmouth, and many other places.

Where and what were the king's houses?

Under 1189 and 1201, and other years, we have notices of the 'king's houses' in the 'tower' or 'castle' of Hampton; and the hall spoken of before, for the repair of which rafters from Knutswood were supplied (9 John), may have been in the castle, also the king's gaol (7 H. III.); so also the king's court, for which a door was to be made without delay (8 H. III.) Walter de Karron was keeper of the 'king's houses' at twopence a day in 1224, and Richard the Poor, Bishop of Sarum, the keeper also of Winchester and Porchester castles, in 1225. But the following entries relate either to houses which must have been distinct from any buildings on the lofty castle platform, or to a quay with which they were connected. In 1214 (16 John) the bailiffs of Southampton were directed to repair 'the quay of the castle;' and in the following year 'our chamber, and our cellar of our castle, and likewise the quay of the same castle.' In 1218 (2 H. III.) the sheriff (county) is ordered to repair 'the cellar of our castle for the storing of our prisage wines, and likewise the quay of the same castle.' In August 1221 (5 H. III.), and in the year following, the king directed the bailiffs of Southampton

[1] But the tradition of King John's pond is much older. The pond, destroyed a few years ago, is mentioned by that name in the Court Leet Book of 1670.

to repair 'our quay before our houses,' and, in November 1222, to repair without delay 'our quay during the winter, lest owing to that quay any damage occur to our houses at Southampton;' and at a fitter season they were to carry out the work more perfectly. In 1225, too, writs direct the bailiffs to cause repairs 'upon our houses at Southampton, and on our quay there;' and to repair the quay, 'that no loss occur to us on account of our houses through neglect of such repairs.'[1]

The house or houses here spoken of were certainly not much above high-water mark, and stood by or upon a quay connected apparently with the castle. Why should not the king's storehouses have been partly identical with the old castle vault and the chambers adjoining, the quay being a landing-place attached to the castle immediately below those chambers? The 'king's houses' may have been little more than offices connected with the storage department and the reception of royal dues in kind, over which it was needful to place a highly responsible official to look to the king's 'rights.' Such places may have been specially required for purposes of business connected with an ever-moving court; and some of them may have actually been erected on the quay, and of less substantial character than castle walls. Certainly there appears no reason why the monarch should have resided in Blue Anchor Lane, or elsewhere, when he had at his command the ample space of the Norman fortress.[2]

West gate. We have already described the walls as far as West gate. This is a plain rectangular work, flush with the wall in front and without buttresses, 23 feet broad and 30 deep. It is in three stages,[3] the lowest of which is pierced by a roadway 10 feet wide, covered by a low pointed vaulting, and formerly kept by a heavy doorway set back towards the middle of the vaulting, having a couple of portcullises to defend it on the side away from the town; while immediately on the inside there is a wide chase, 18 inches broad, which suggests some arrangement for preventing the door being forced. The flanks and headway of this central doorcase have as usual been much cut and pared for the sake of width, and its original features can hardly be detected. In the vaulting between the two portcullis grooves may be observed nine apertures, three along the crown line, and three in the haunch on each side, for the purpose of worrying a foe from above: they are about six inches square at the mouth, but diminish upwards. The gate defences were worked from the second stage, above which is a third, surmounted by

[1] See printed Close Rolls, under dates.

[2] So late as Queen Elizabeth, royalty dates missives 'from our tower of Southampton.' See last chapter below.

[3] The tower over West gate was constantly called, and let as, the Pigeon House. In 1642 the rent was 13s. 4d. (Steward's books).

a crenellation of two embrasures, front and back, and of three on each side, the whole being capped by a plain roof. On the town side a stairway, immediately to the left and adjoining the tower, leads to the rampart walk on the walls.

This gateway has stood fairly well through many vicissitudes. An early notice of paving occurs in connection with it in 1441.[1] 'Payd þe x daye of Marche to Emond Pavyer . . . for pawynge of þe West hethe ȝate, viij$^{s}$. Item, payd þe x daye of Marche for xviij lodys of stonys fro þe Watyrȝate to þe West hethe ȝate to þe seyd pavynge, 1$^{s}$. viij$^{d}$.' One of the last notices of this gate occurs in the Journal for February 15, 1744–45, when its portcullis was ordered to be removed as a 'nuisanse, and of no manner of use.'

From West gate the curtain stretches for about 230 feet, with a south-west inclination slightly convex, having a broad rectangular bastion of no great depth on its front, as far as the early eighteenth-century house of Madame Maës, beyond which there appears a lofty arch something similar to those of the arcade, connected with a tower of which some vestiges remain. Immediately in the rear of this wall, starting almost from West gate, is a curious fifteenth-century timber house on a stone basement, built against the town wall, but preserving the rampart walk throughout its length, along which defenders might pass without interfering with the house or houses, the 'walk' being entered from the side of West gate, as mentioned above. A similar arrangement was observed in other parts of the town. The length of this building, originally divided into two principal chambers, is about sixty feet; its width, exclusive of the rampart walk, about twenty feet; the roof is extremely good.

To the south of the tower and behind the wall is a plot of ground formerly called the 'Spanish burial-ground.'

The tower just spoken of was probably that called 'Bugle Tower'— 'the tower beneath Bull Hall Garden'[2]—Bull or Bugle Hall being just above it on the east. The ancient shore or quay seems to have come as far south as the tower, and there to have stopped. Bugle Tower.

From this point the wall still exists in ruins, or is to be traced, running south-east by east for 300 feet, as far as the remains of a square tower—probably that called Square or Corner Tower in the books[3]— at the entrance to Cuckoo Lane, adjoining the modern Bugle Hall. Square or Corner Tower.

On the face of the wall, a little short of 'Square Tower,' are to be seen the arms of the town under a Tudor moulding, together with several huge gunstones worked into the wall, in memory, as some have

[1] Steward's books. [2] Court Leet Books, 1571, and Muster Books.
[3] Ibid., 1625, and ditto.

supposed, of the direful French invasion of a previous century, when the town was burned. The foe are believed to have landed in this quarter, which was formerly called the 'Gravel.' The arms may perhaps mark the rebuilding of this portion of the defences in the sixteenth century.

From Square Tower the wall passed the ends of Bugle Street and French Street, and joined the Water-gate, which crossed the High or English Street. This portion of the wall was removed in consequence of quay extension improvements by the Harbour Commissioners under the Act of 1803, but a portion of it appears again in front of Castle Hotel, near where it joined the Water-gate. In its convex sweep of about 600 feet from Corner Tower there were two towers—St. Barbara's and Woolbridge—the latter 'the round tower at the corner of Woolhouse;'[1] which building, judging from the direction of the watch patrols of the sixteenth century, in which it is mentioned, must have been in this locality, and may have been the ancient store at the south-east corner of French Street, near the present mouth of Porter's Lane, which, at one time called Le Cheyne,[2] was afterwards called sometimes Wool Street, and may have had more than one building in it devoted to the trade (see next paragraph).

St. Barbara and Woolbridge Towers.

Porter's Lane.

This lane formerly ran behind the wall at the ends of Bugle Street and French Street, having been much more extensive than at present, and forming the connection between the streets at the south end of the town. Commencing at its ancient mouth is a fine old building at the south-east corner of Bugle Street, a memorial of the town's mercantile grandeur in the Middle Ages, presenting the appearance of an ancient hall of remarkably solid construction: it has a Spanish chestnut roof, and curious cylindrical buttresses along the street. Its length is about 80 feet, breadth 40 feet. This building was certainly called the 'wey-hous' and 'wolhous' in the middle of the fourteenth century.[3] It is now usually known, from its more recent occupation, as the 'Spanish prison.'

Immediately on the north of this building was an ancient lane. Adjoining it on the east, and all along the southern quay, are traces of handsome stores of considerable importance. At the south-east angle of French Street is the ancient store which may have been called the 'Wool House' in the sixteenth century—it was certainly close to this spot; or 'Canute's Palace,' which adjoined this store, may have been the 'Wool House.'

---

[1] Court Leet Books, 1625; Lib. Rem. H. f. 14, 17; Muster Books, &c.

[2] Part of this was probably the holding of John Slegh—a void piece of ground called La Chayne, worth 3s. 4d.—granted him for good conduct in 1382 (Pat. 5 R. II. p. 1, m. 12).

[3] Deeds of R. Mascall, 1365, R. Bechefounte, 1388 (Westhall docs.), &c.

'Canute's Palace,' so known since the publication of Sir H. Englefield's 'Walk,' is an interesting relic of a late twelfth century house which has been gradually destroyed, and will, it must be feared, be swept away under modern improvements. Sir Henry Englefield has accurately described this building as it existed in his time.[1] Its front extended 111 feet, being probably the whole of the original frontage: the height to the top of the wall was seventeen feet, the ground may have risen some two feet. The building is in two storeys, a string-course ten feet from the ground runs below the upper windows. Formerly there were two ancient archways in the basement; above, in the middle, were the two large Norman windows, something of which still remain, and which appear to have formed part of a composition of three; on the right of these windows were remains of two other Norman two-light windows, more or less perfect; on the left hand were two others symmetrically placed, and beyond these a single-light opening. The thickness of the front wall is 2 feet 9 inches; the back wall appears to have run about 16 feet 8 inches in the rear, so that the whole interior, having no traces of partition walls in stone, represented two long galleries, one upon the other, of about 105 by 16 feet 8 inches. The wide central windows are dropped two feet below the string-course, and probably came down to the floor. Sir Henry Englefield erroneously conjectured that this interesting building might have been Canute's Palace, and from his time the tradition obtained that it was such. It may have been a building for commercial no less than residential purposes, possibly forming part of a larger plan; and the wide and low windows, before which there could have been originally no town wall, may have been designed on a plan of convenience for taking in stores. 'Canute's Palace.'

Before 1833 about thirty feet of the front from the west angle had been destroyed to make way for a mean house; since then further dilapidations have occurred.

The Water-gate crossed the High Street a few feet to the rear of the ancient machicolations still to be observed on the front of Castle Hotel and slightly to the north of the present entrance to Winkle Street. Thus that street would have been left without the gate had not the wall struck boldly out to sea south-east by south from the east side of the gate to a lofty round tower—Watch Tower—on the sea-line at the distance of about 110 feet, now marked by the bow window of the Sun Hotel, which stands on its basement. On its west side the gate was recessed and protected by the rounded curtain or flanking tower, while on the east its approaches were completely covered, as Water-gate. Watch Tower.

[1] Archæologia, xiv. 84–89.

was also a considerable part of the quay, by this salient wall of 110 feet. The original entrance to Winkle Street from the High Street was by a narrow passage, the mouth of which opened a little due east of the gate; thus the street or alley very much followed the bend of the wall;[1] and in old times its mouth in the High Street was crossed by the archway of the ancient custom-house, or of a house adjoining. We know from the Steward's book of 1468 and other sources that the "kynges custum hows dore' was 'by þe Water gate,' and 'j gret gonne upon wheles' stood before it.

Winkle Street.

Custom-house.

The above arrangement of walls and gate was at length found inconvenient. The Water-gate blocked the bottom of the High Street, and there was no communication whatever with the quay except through that gate. The sea washed the town walls on each side of the quay; and the only way from the platform, that is, from the land side on the east, was through Godhouse gate and Winkle Street, with its bend northward. In 1789 a postern was ordered to be made at Water-gate to increase the accommodation; and it may have been carried through the rounded curtain or flanking tower on the west side. But this additional help was insufficient; and shortly after a breach was made in the wall on the other side, adjoining and immediately to the south of the gate, a house which had been built against the wall being removed for the purpose of connecting the quay more directly with Godshouse gate and the platform beyond. This breach is represented by the present entrance into Winkle Street, after the opening of which the disposition of the houses on the north became slightly altered, and the former narrow mouth of the street built over. The loss of the abutment of the above wall and house (in August 1800) shook the gate; some of its machicolations fell, and the structure remained an object of desolation till it was removed in 1804, with some ancient buildings attached to it. Among these were part of the curtain on the west, and the ancient custom-house on the east flanking of the gate.

Water-gate Postern.

Water-gate was a wide and deep structure, with a low pointed arch and the usual defences to its opening. Above was a boldly projecting parapet with seven machicolations: all the windows in the second stage faced the High Street.

This gate, like the Bar, was formerly adorned with lions and the royal arms. Thus, in May 1501, 'Hew Carpenter' was paid for 'iij peces of tymber for the lyons at the Water-gate, v.': other payments occur about these lions. Also 'payd to John Stayner and his

Water-gate.

[1] Winkle, sometimes from Vinkel, a corner (suggestion of Mr. Ferguson in 'Northmen in Cumberland'), see Notes and Queries, 6th series, vol. v. p. 476. In the present case, probably a more commonplace derivation may serve.

felow for makyng of the armys at the Water-gate, xiij$^{s}$ iiij$^{d}$.'[1] Under April 1609 we find this entry: 'Ordered that the king's majesty's armes shalbe sett upp in a frame uppon the Water-gate in the outer side thereof towards the sea betwene the two lyons.'[2] There were a couple of large brackets supported on corbels, one over each haunch of the arch, for what purpose does not appear. A print of 1784 shows a modern pediment, crowned and flanked with pinnacles rising out of the roof of the gate just behind the corbel table; it seems to have been furnished with a sun-dial.

This gate probably was not erected much before the reign of Richard II. It is mentioned in a patent[3] of the first year of that king; but it was still called the 'New gate'—novam portam vocatam Water-gate—in a patent of the twentieth year.[4] It seems indeed to have been left incomplete, since the roofing-in of the tower over Water-gate—or 'Flood-gate,' as it was also called—formed part of the stipulation in a lease of that tower, with one contiguous on the west, granted by the mayor and community to William Ravenston, burgess, for the term of twenty years from Michaelmas 1403. He was to render all services due to the capital lords of the fee, and render to the mayor one red rose each St. John Baptist's Day.[5]

Oddly enough we find the whole work in a weak and ruinous condition a few years later; and William Soper, a wealthy and patriotic burgess, possibly the builder of the ships 'Holy Ghost' and 'Grace Dieu' in 1414, or his immediate descendant, having put the towers in repair at his own heavy cost, received a lease of the premises from September 1439 for the term of a hundred and twenty years, at the annual tribute, as before, of one red rose on the Nativity of St. John Baptist. The premises are thus described. The lessee was to hold, from the Watch-bell station[6] to the east of the gate, the Gate Tower itself with its western flanking, and a void plot of ground beyond as far as the first stone-way leading up to the ramparts on the west. This was in a line with the south side of the present Porter's Lane. In

1 Steward's Book, 1501.

2 Journal.

3 A void place by 'le Water-gate' had been granted to John Slegh in 1377 (Pat. 1 R. II. pt. 6. m. 16).

4 Quit-claim from W. Brugis and Gilbert Harry, chaplains, to Walter Nicoll and Elena his wife of a cellar and bakehouse 'in venella jacente inter novam portam vocatam Water-gate et portam lanarum;' the premises were thus in Porter's Lane. Date Oct. 21 (1396), 20 R. II. (among Corporation documents).

5 Lease dated August 1403 (4 H. IV.)

6 A quodam gradu et loco ubi jam pendet le Watchebelle ex parte orientali, &c. There was a watch-tower on the town walls over God's House Conduit in this position—just to the east of Watergate—in 1615, 1618, 1670, &c. (See Court Leet Books.)

addition to this, on the east side of the gate, he obtained an equally important grant of the void plot of ground or street between Water-gate on the west and the house of a certain John Bacon on the east. He had permission to build over this space afresh, provided he left between the said John Bacon's house and his newly to be erected edifice a certain highroad (via regalis), 13 feet broad, with a headway of at least 16 feet below the solars or upper chambers, which he might construct over it. This was, no doubt, the original mouth into Winkle Street. The above dimensions were specified to ensure proper room for the passing of carts and men-at-arms and their serving-men with lances and arms. The premises thus demised extended southward towards the town wall, and the lessee was to be furnished with the key of a wicket made in the great gate, outside of which he probably possessed some sheds. William Soper covenanted for himself and his successors to repair and maintain the towers and all buildings erected or to be erected on the premises, and in time of war to defend the same with their own arms and at their proper costs. The Corporation had the right of re-entry if the buildings fell out of repair, and so remained for a whole year.[1] It does not appear when Soper's tenancy actually ended, but John Ingoldsby, the recorder, surrendered a lease of the towers at Water-gate in May 1477 (17 Ed. IV.)[2] A somewhat similar grant of the Water-gate Tower and 'mansion' adjoining was made in the mayoralty of John Walssh, in April 1496, to Richard Palshid, who obtained licence to erect a solar or solars between the Gate Tower and the Custom-house, leaving a space below for the lading and unlading of carts, &c., so as to be no hindrance to the business of the town.[3] He had also a 'skelyng' or shed by the gate just outside the walls. Palshid was to bear all the burdens of war and defence, and enjoy his premises for eighty-four years at an annual rent of twelve pence.[4] He was holding the property in 1509,[5] the town-clerk at that period being Richard Palshid, perhaps the same person. A hundred years later (September 1609), the lease of the 'house over the Water-gate,' which he had held from Robert Knaplock, was renewed for forty years to James Courtney in his own name; but no topographical marks occur.

Winkle Street.

From Watch Tower below Water-gate, the wall, some vestiges of which still remain, passed eastward with a southerly inclination for about 250 feet, when it touched the south flanking of God's House

1 Lease and counterpart (one of these is exhibited at the Hartley Institution). For the will of W. Soper, see Lib. Niger, fol. 54.

2 Deed in Audit House.

3 Quoddam solarium sive quædam solaria in alto et nôn in basso edificanda.

4 Indenture in Lib. Niger, fol. 67.

5 Steward's Books.

gate, thus forming the south-east corner of the town, the gate itself standing east and west. This portion of the wall did not exist at the end of the thirteenth century, as we have proof that the south side of the quadrangle of God's House was exposed to the sea.[1]

God's House gate and spur-work.

In order to describe God's House gate and the adjacent work at right angles with it, we will take our stand on the platform or quay, which gives one of the most striking views the town affords. The gatehouse is a plain oblong structure in two stages, 23 feet deep and 30 feet broad, with its south end projecting as an obtuse angle beyond the line of the south wall. A lofty vaulted roadway, 10 feet wide, pierced through it, communicates with Winkle Street; and no other ancient opening occurs on the basement, which was used as a dungeon. This roadway is divided longitudinally in the middle by the heavy arch of a doorcase, now much cut away. Its front was defended by a portcullis, between the chase of which and the central doorway the vault is supported by two massive cross ribs; while in the rear of the central arch three ribs of slighter proportions carry the vaulting on rather a higher level. The appearance of this gateway from below is decidedly handsome. The second stage is lighted by three single windows, with one in each face of the angular projection—probably enlargements from loops—and one in the rear looking up Winkle Street. The whole is capped by a plain roof with eaves.

The position of the gateway passage at the extreme right was partly governed by the necessities of the town wall, which abutted on the opposite side within. It must also be noticed that the gatehouse was in existence before the erection of the handsome gallery and tower to our right, which have in effect thrust the old entrance into a corner. These latter buildings belong to the close of the fourteenth or beginning of the fifteenth century, while the gatehouse may be placed a hundred years earlier. The object of the addition was to secure a more extensive flank defence for the gate and completely cover its approach, which along the length of the new building was a shore-way of no more than 30 feet wide. The tower also was constructed to protect the sluices of the ditch, while a large additional accommodation was afforded by the whole for troops and stores.

Details of spur-work and tower.

This handsome work projects at right angles with the gate about 85 feet from its north flank. The building connecting the gate with the tower is about 55 feet in length by 30 feet in depth, and is in two floors, the lower of which had no apertures on this side, but the upper is adorned by a loop or oillet next the gatehouse, and by three good flat-headed two-light Perpendicular windows. A coped parapet sur-

[1] See under 'God's House.'

mounts the front. The tower—called sometimes 'God's House Tower,' from its proximity to that house—is a finely proportioned structure of three stages with bold corner buttresses, those at the open corners being diagonal, divided into stages, and finally setting off at the parapet line. The upper storeys are furnished with flat-headed two-light windows, one in each open side; and the whole is crowned by a large and strong battlement work, having only one embrasure, very widely splayed on every side, designed for fire-artillery. A staircase turret on a squinch between the wall and left-hand buttress leads out of the top storey to the flat roof and parapet. Beneath the basement is an arched space, through which the canal projected at the beginning of this century was to have passed, the sluices of the original ditch having been in the same position. The south front of the tower has been sadly mutilated by the partial defacement of the original windows and the insertion of various openings to accommodate its comparatively recent use as the town prison. Yet it is in a better condition now than a few years ago. The sheds and buildings at its foot on the south and east sides, in connection with its former occupation, having been cleared away, it stands out in something of its pristine dignity.

The earliest mention of this tower which I have found is in the account of military stores [1] in 1468, when, among other things, we find in 'Goddes hows towr j broken gonne. Item in þe sam towr ij holl gonnes and j serpentyne. Item in þe sam towr x chawmbres for gonnes and serpentynes. Also in þe sam towr a gret spruce cheste w[t] xix chawmbres longyng to þe Orgons after specifyed. Item in þe sam chest j baner steyned vp on lynyne cloth w[t] þe kynges armes and oder. Item in þe same towre iij hold pollaxis. Item in þe sam towr . . . iij qrtes of barell gonne powder. Item in þe sam towr gonne stones of dyvers sorts.'

Mill-house. Close by the tower was the 'Mill-house,' which I am unable to identify, unless indeed the connecting building between the tower and gate were so called, or it were in the angle of the town wall overlooking the ditch to the rear of this spur-work, and protected by it. At all events, it occurs in the account of the defences between God's House Tower and the tower next to it in the east wall. The Mill-house was on the curtain, as apparently guns might be ranged from it: 'Item paid to labores that sette owte the gonnes of the Mille-house, iiij[d].' [2] It was also a receptacle for military stores: 'Item in the same hows j gret brokyn chawmbre þ[t] servedd for a gonne callyd Thomas w[t] þe Berd [beard], the wheche seyd gonne called Thomas w[t] þe Berd, new bownd and pencylled, as in þis sam bok shew[t], w[t] ij holle chawm-

[1] Steward's Books, 1468. [2] Ibid., 1469.

bres to þe sam, w[t] viij gonne stones and viij tampons to þe same were delyuered by Master Andrew James, leftenaunt, þe xxx day of May An° viij R. E. iiij to my lord Scales by endenture, as y onderstond. Item in the towr next Goddes hows towr in þe est party ij gonnes. Item in Gebon Cornmongers towr ij gonnes w[t] chawmbres. Item in Mechell Lukes towre ij gonnes w[t] vj chawmbres.' These were the first three towers up the east side.

In connection with the preceding may be placed the following: 'Item rec[d] of Syr John Walker for ij howses, þ[t] is the Longhouse afore Goddyshowsse w[t] a skelyng and a gardyn w[t] the stabelys beside *the Mylle*, paying yerly to the Toune and he to repayre hit . . vi[s]. viij[d].'[1] The Longhouse with its stable and loft before God's House is frequently mentioned,[2] and is probably to be identified with the Perpendicular building whose remains we see opposite God's House, with the town wall behind it. Longhouse.

Leland describes the tower or South Castle as a 'castelet welle ordinauncid to bete that quarter of the haven.' This was in 1546. No subsequent notes of interest have been found about it.

The circumstances have been already related under which the old tower became the town gaol in 1775. It was but ill adapted for the purpose, and the condition of the borough gaols became a subject of frequent complaint within a few years. The establishment at the South Castle embraced a gaol for felons and debtors and a Bridewell, the gaoler in each case being one of the sergeants-at-mace, who by ancient custom received the prisons to eke out their salaries. Town gaol.

The Bridewell was over the gate, and had been settled here since 1707. The keeper's salary was £2 in addition to his payment of £15 as sergeant-at-mace. There was a surgeon, but no chaplain. Prisoners were allowed the usual sixpence a day, and a bushell of coals weekly among them all. The premises—subsequently they embraced Solent Cottage and Platform House—consisted in 1810 of three rooms, a dayroom about 15 feet square, and two bedrooms each 12 feet by 9 feet. There was also a room in the keeper's house for those who paid four shillings per week. The borough allowed a crib bedstead, straw-in-ticking bed, two blankets and rug for each. There was no courtyard, nor any employment for the prisoners, nor a proper division between the sexes.

The debtors' prison was in the tower. The gaoler received no salary, but was paid by fees, these being: entrance, four shillings;

---

1 Steward's Books, 1486.

2 *e.g.*, Steward's Books, 1469, 1493. In 1474 the Longhouse was let in two tenements under the arrangement of Ric. Gryme, the lieutenant: the part towards the west at forty shillings, that towards the east at thirty shillings per annum.

discharge, two shillings of first action; ten shillings the second, and every other action; and two shillings to the turnkey. A surgeon was sent by the mayor when wanted. The allowance to paupers was sixpence a day, and a bushell of coals per week served for the whole prison. The wards consisted of two rooms, with glazed windows and fireplaces, 16 feet by 12 feet each, to which the Corporation allowed a bedstead with woollen mattress, two blankets and a rug. The room at the top of the tower was furnished by the keeper, for which he charged two shillings and sixpence per week. There was a small courtyard (46 feet by 36 feet) attached; it was well supplied with water, not paved, and ducks and fowls were kept in it.

The felons' gaol was within the gallery, between the tower and the gatehouse. The gaoler, who at the beginning of this century was also a tailor, received a salary of £20, in addition to £15 as sergeant, but he had no fees. There was no chaplain, nor was divine service ever performed; there was, however, a surgeon. The allowances were sixpence a day each, and one fire for all, a bushel of coals being apportioned for the week. A narrow slip, 34 feet by 7 feet, immediately behind the front wall, was the only courtyard; it was furnished with a stone sink and a pump, frequently without water, especially in summer. There were four small rooms for prisoners, each about 11 feet square, with iron grated and glazed windows and fireplaces. Each of these had a bedstead with straw-ticking bed, two blankets, and a rug; but there was no proper separation of men and women. The entrance to the prison was through a small square door inserted in the wall, and now again filled up, immediately to the left of the recent store opening. Over the door was painted, 'Pray remember the poor prisoners' box.'[1]

With the increase of population the evils of the old gaol were intensified. The Commissioners of 1835 reported its condition as very bad; and at this time the population of the borough had risen to nearly 20,000. It was finally abandoned upon the erection of a new and spacious gaol in 1854–55; but this has been closed under the operation of the Prisons Act, 1877. Upon the removal of the gaol, the South Castle remained vacant, until the gatehouse and gallery were again brought into requisition, at the end of 1875 and in the year following, for permanent storage accommodation. The business of the town was so rapidly increasing that all available space was needed. In consequence of which, the old buildings were cleared of every vestige of their former occupation with the exception of the tower. When gutted, the basement of the gallery was seen to have been covered with a groined

Spur-work and tower turned into stores.

[1] Imperial and County Register for 1810; Gentleman's Magazine, October 1810.

vault; at the west end a newel staircase, now removed, communicated with the floor above, and with the chamber over the gateway by means of a mural stairway branching from it, which latter portion still remains. Out of this chamber another passage, through its north-east angle, constructed in the thickness of the wall, and betraying some sign of itself across the hollow angle outside, still admits into the long gallery, lighted by its three perpendicular windows, over the formerly vaulted basement. When clearing the buildings, occasion was taken to restore carefully the south and east fronts, every external feature of the original being preserved. Two doorways were, however, inserted, one of large dimensions in the basement of the gallery, and a smaller in the south-east face of the gateway flank. It is to be hoped that when the time comes the handsome tower may be well treated: it wants but to have its prison windows abolished and the old lights fully opened out.

Statue of Prince Consort.

Before passing on, we may remark the statue in terra cotta of the late Prince Consort, presented to the town by Sir Frederick Perkins in 1877. It does not appear to advantage in this position, while the venerable tower and adjacent buildings owe nothing to its presence.

East wall.

From the north-west corner of the spur-work just described the wall is seen above the houses in front of it as far as a half-round tower, 23 feet in diameter, at the distance of 160 feet, into which a small house has been built. Farther on, at a distance of about 90 feet, are the remains of a small rectangular tower, 22 feet broad; and at another distance of about 90 feet is the root of a second rectangular tower, 30 feet broad. These two last were conjectured by Sir H. Englefield, probably erroneously, to have been added in the time of Edward VI.;[1] Mr. Clarke considers them much older, and perhaps bearing out this view we have an entry of the towers 'by the Friars' being let for two shillings in 1509: these rectangular towers being just behind the Friary.[2] Nothing remains of the other towers as far as East gate, so that no means exist of comparing their relative age. But it may be observed that while Leland (1546) says 'there be vj fair tourres in the walle betwixt the Est gate and the South gate,' the Muster Book of 1544 enumerates seven, and possibly omits one as too small for special defence. Speed's map (1596) gives eight, in which number both Englefield and Dr. Speed[3] agree, six[4] being circular and two square. The wall is traceable along much of this line. Leland says of East gate

[1] Buller's Englefield, p. 9.

[2] Steward's Books.

[3] On his plan.

[4] One of these, of which I have a drawing, crossed the pavement of the modern Bridge Street on the south side, where Back-of-the-Walls runs into it. Another tower 'behind the Star' often occurs in the books.

Eastgate. that it is 'stronge, but nothing so large as the Barre-gate.' It was a heavy structure, with flanking towers projecting boldly into the ditch. Grose's drawing, taken in 1772, seems to suggest that the front part of the gate had been thrown out beyond its flankings, something after the manner of the Bargate. Its front was defended by four rows of loops, two in each row, one above the other: the mouth of its entrance being kept by a portcullis, behind which was a heavy door. The east front had prominent diagonal buttresses setting off at the corbel table, on which, in place of battlements, were large embrasures for fire-artillery, one in each of the three fronts. In 1670 the ancient bridge before the gate was pulled down and rebuilt of one arch eight feet wide, with stone taken from the castle. The mason found all other materials and received £8. In 1775 leave was granted to the Commissioners of Pavement to take down Eastgate, on paying £16 to the Corporation. There was a chapel over Eastgate dedicated to St. Mary. Agnes le Horder[1] left a bequest to it in 1348. In 1641 we find the chapel let to Alderman Exton, together with a tenement and garden close by. It had apparently for many years been desecrated, and let as a warehouse.[2] Between Eastgate and the north-east corner of the town there was one small tower, as we know from the Muster Books, Leland, and Speed (1596); but it must have disappeared in Englefield's time, as he does not mention it. Its site is shown on the Ordnance Survey as just south of the East Street Brewery; it may have been the tower called 'Little Tower' in the Journal of March 3, 1775.

St. Denys's or Polymond Tower. At the north-east corner of the walls stand the remains of St. Denys's Tower, or Polymond's, as it is styled in the Muster Book of 1544. It was a drum, 28 feet in diameter, in three stages; and in November 1828 leave was granted to remove the two upper storeys, and in the following month the whole. However, there are considerable remains to this day. Leland speaks of it as very fair and strong; Englefield describes it as having been a high round tower, which seemed to have been built with embrasures for cannon. In 1468 it was furnished with 'j gonne w[t] owght chawmbres.' Afterwards heavy guns were provided for this tower. In 1654 it had fallen into great decay; one great gun on the top of the tower had a rotten carriage, 'and the whole loft on which the said gun standeth is rotten, and in great danger of a sudden fall. Allso there is another great gun on the rampier by the said tower nere buried in the ground, which we desire may be carried to the tower'—*i.e.*, God's House Tower. From the position of this last gun we may perhaps gather that there was a work in front of St. Denys's Tower.

---

[1] Addit. 15, 314, pp. 85, 86. [2] Steward's Books, 1641-42.

Turning westward towards Bargate, much of the wall remains behind the houses; there are also the remnants of two half-round towers, which we have noticed before, the former of these, distant 160 feet from St. Denys's Tower, having a diameter of 16 feet; the latter about 120 feet farther, with a diameter of 22 feet. Another distance of about 120 feet brings us again to the Bargate.

From the Muster Book of 1544 we learn certain other details of the walls, together with the names, number, and position of the towers.

1544. Loops or crenels manned.

From Catchcold to West-gate there were 79 loopholes in the wall; to each of these men were assigned, the town being then divided into eight parts for the purpose of defence, a certain specified district (see under 'Watch and Ward') being assigned for the safeguard of each piece of wall. From West gate to St. Barbara's Tower were 59 loopholes; from St. Barbara's to God's House Tower were 56 loops; then on to the Friar's Garret or Tower, next beneath the Friars, 53 loops; then to the tower behind Holy Rood Church, 52 loops; thence to the East gate, 49 loops; from East gate to Bargate, including what were over East gate, there were 53 loops; from Bargate to Catchcold, including 22 over the gate, there were 64 loops. It is evident that, at all events, over the gates, if not entirely so, the crenels or embrasures in the battlements are meant in the above enumeration.

Towers manned.

From an assignment for the defence of the towers made by the mayor and his brethren at the same date we gather the following names and curious particulars.

Arundel Tower and one little tower towards Bargate were assigned to the shoemakers, curriers, cobblers, and saddlers. Bargate Tower with one little tower towards Polymond's was held by the town; the next small tower and Polymonds were assigned to William Knight and John Capleyn. The next little tower towards East gate, and the East gate Tower itself, were intrusted to the goldsmiths, blacksmiths, lockiers, pewterers, and tinkers. Next come seven towers enumerated from East gate to God's House Tower. The first five were known by the names of the citizens opposite whose gardens they stood; the sixth was over against the Friars; the seventh was next to God's House Tower: for the keeping of these no appointment had as yet been made. God's House Tower, the Watch Tower, and Water-gate Tower were kept by the town. The tower by the Wool-house was given to the mercers and grocers; that 'callyd now St. Barbara's Towre and the Corner Towre next to Beaulieu Selde' were assigned to the brewers and bakers. The tower behind Bull Hall was given to the coopers; West gate to Mr. Baker; the tower behind Thomas Marsh's house to the vintners, mariners, and lightermen; that against Mr. Huttoft's to the weavers, fullers, and cappers; and the tower next 'Bedille's gate' to the butchers, fishers, and chandlers.

Decay of walls and towers.

Having completed our survey of the walls,[1] we may finish the story of their decay. The keeping in repair a mile and an eighth, or more, of walls and towers had been a burden for centuries, and, to do the townfolk justice, they had never disguised their grief. They seem to have taken revenge on the walls and towers as soon as the necessity for such protection was relaxed. In 1550 Mr. Mylles, who may have been the recorder, wanting to cart some chalk into his premises, calmly opened a passage through the town wall, and stuffed the hole with clay and stone, 'which,' say the leet jury, 'we thincke ys not sufficient; whrefore we require yt to be made w[t] lyme and stone as the rest of the walle ys for the safegard of the same.'

Back of the walls.

It was of course essential in a fortified town to have a clear and passable way at the rear of the walls. On the east or more remote side of the town this seems to have been a frequent difficulty from one cause or other. The gardens of the High Street (many of them) ran down to the Back-of-the-Walls; and by custom the inhabitants on the east side of the town were bound to keep that passage properly gravelled. This they not seldom neglected. A complaint to this effect occurs in 1566. But a few years later we find this roadway choked with houses, and in 1596 the court leet wake as from a dream, and make the following extraordinary presentment:—

> 'We present that all the small Towers behinde the east side of the towne howses within the Towne walls are all converted into dwellinge howses of verie poore people w[ch] is like to growe into great inconvenience as well for endamageringe the Towne by harbouringe of lewde persons therein as impayringe the walles in that they have all of them made great wholes through the walles for their lights, whereof we pray redresse.'[2]

Walls generally.

In 1606 the mayor was desired to see to the repairs of the walls, and to charge the expense in his accounts. In 1650 a certificate of their decay was sealed and directed to the barons of the Exchequer. During the spring and summer of 1667, under apprehension from the Dutch, the fortifications of Southampton, with those of Portsmouth, Calshot, and the Isle of Wight, were put in order under the eye of the Lord Gerard. By April 9 the fortifications of the town and dock of Southampton were going on at great pace, three companies of foot being wholly engaged on the work.[3] In 1676 the portcullises were still in working order but beginning to be disregarded, as about that time

[1] A further notice of the walls and towers will be found under 'Watch and Ward.'

[2] Court Leet Books.

[3] Calendar State Papers under date.

raids seem to have been made on the sheers and ropes by which they were worked: they were ordered however to be restored. After serious complaints to the Government in 1683 and 1702 on the state of the fortifications and their burden upon the inhabitants, with little relief in answer, the Corporation directed that the walls should be repaired 'where there is a necessity in the most frugal manner,' under the inspection of Mr. Mayor. But in 1764, the enlargement of Water-gate quay being on hand, the crumbling parapets of the town walls were largely utilised for this purpose; and in the same year such of the gates (that is, the *doors* of the gates) as were a nuisance were ordered to be removed. Dr. Speed, writing about 1770, continues—with the omission of a short paragraph—from where we left him off, "the walls are still "standing all round the town, but are in a very ruinous condition; "only those on the south and west sides, which lie next the sea, are "kept in such repair as to prevent damage from the sea." It was a practical joke of the period to shut the town gates at unheard-of times, and in 1786 an order was issued for securing the gates to prevent this improper sporting of the town's oak.

We have already mentioned some serious destructions in 1775, about which period the Corporation seem to have made no special favour of permitting the removal of portions of wall or towers. But in 1791, in contemplation, we must suppose, of a more radical excision of the old defences, they presented a memorial to the Treasury for leave to take down some parts of the town walls which had become ruinous, and to convert the material.[1] Subsequently to this nearly the whole of the south wall, together with the Water-gate, was removed under the powers of 43 G. III. c. 21 (1803) by the commissioners there appointed for the improvement of the harbour.

The Ditches.

Leland (1546) describes the town ditch as being double on the whole of the north side, and on the east nearly as far as South or God's House gate; it was well supplied with water through its course. The tide was admitted on the south, but this was probably not the case on the north, where the natural elevation of the ground was so much greater. This portion of the ditch may have received drainage from the town: thus in 1478 a hole was made in the wall above Bargate to let the water into the ditch 'by commandment of Master Grym beyng leutenaunt.' Speed's map (1596) shows that the whole of the ditch to the west of the Bar and as far as the first tower to the east had been filled in. This half of the north ditch, being probably unconnected with the tide, had a greater tendency to become choked, and the in-

[1] Journal sub annis.

habitants of above Bar were constantly throwing their refuse into it, in spite of penalties of five shillings on this nuisance and the presentment (1579) that 'allso yt wer very necessary that a torne pycke were ther made to avoyd yt.'[1] Even on the east side of the Bar a portion of the ditch had been filled up, kine being kept there, 'which rubbeth down the butts.' All this part, on both sides of the bridge, we find permanently filled in by Speed's time (1596). This ground, as having belonged to the ditch, was considered a part of the town waste. The portion to the left of the Bar was for some time previous to 1777 known as the Rope Walk, but at that date its name became changed into Orchard Street.[2]

Orchard Street.

Archery Butts.

To the right of the Bargate, and immediately adjoining the plot filled up, which extended to the first tower, stood the archery butts on the bank between the ditches, approached by a bridge from the north.[3] They are mentioned in 1485,[4] and constantly afterwards. The existence of these butts on the bank in the middle will help us, failing direct evidence, as to the width of the ditch. Considering the room which our ancestors must have required for their favourite and indeed commanded pastime, we can hardly place the counterscarp of the moat nearer than the south side of Hanover Buildings, that is, at about 100 or 120 feet. Notices of Bargate Bridge do not help us as to the breadth of the ditch. The roadway of Hanover Buildings marks the ancient road which led round by the moat.

Moat neglected.

In reference to the east and north-east sides, the leet jury present, in 1571 and 1573, that it were

> 'Needefull that the sluse at Godes house weare opened wheareby the water might have his course and recourse into the towne dyches from the sea, and out of the said dyches into the sea againe, for by the meanes of the stoppinge thereof the town dyches are drye and growen almost to pasture ground.'

There was water enough, however, for the 'cucking stool' for scolds in 1579.[5]

Lease of the town ditches.

It had been the practice from early times to let the town ditches. In 1482–83, the rent of that between Bargate and East gate was two shillings; between that and God's House, three shillings and fourpence. The renting of the ditches went on, like the leasing out of the towers,[6]

[1] Court Leet Books.

[2] Journal, April 1777. There was a roper above Bar, if not on this spot, in 1698–99 (All Saints Reg.) In the latter part of last century a rope-walk existed to the north of Hanover Buildings.

[3] In 1618 Thomas Lee was presented for not making (*i.e.*, perhaps remaking) a bridge across the ditch to the town butts.

[4] Steward's Books.

[5] Court Leet Books.

[6] Steward's Books, 1482–83, 1485, 1493, &c.

only interrupted at critical periods. In 1625 they were leased, with all their fishing, pasturage, banks, islands, &c., to Mr. Edward Exton for forty years, at a fine of £5 and a yearly rent of six shillings and eightpence;[1] but under October 1648 we find Mr. Exton excused his rent in consequence of the ditches having been used for defence and of no profit to him. In 1687 the ditches were leased to William Crop for a fine of £24 and a yearly rent as above of six and eightpence.

Traces of the north ditch exist behind the houses on the south of Hanover Buildings, but on the east side it is to be distinguished through its whole course, the back of the walls marking the immediate rear of the ancient fortifications, and the ditches or canal[2] walk the counterscarp of the old town moat.

The platform dates from the end of the thirteenth century, if we are right in considering a quay made by the Prior of God's House near his close to be identical with it;[3] but its enlargement may have occurred soon after the introduction of fire-artillery. It was without God's House gate, opposite the bowling-green, but its ancient form and size have now become obliterated under handsome modern extensions. There was formerly a 'bulwark' somewhat to the rear of the platform and immediately at the foot of the bowling-green. In 1457, under the terror of French invasion—it was seven years after the loss of Normandy, and the year in which Sandwich was burnt—there was some activity along the shore-line between God's House gate and Itchen Cross, where in the last century, in the fashionable period of Southampton's history, was a lovely and far-famed drive, with its row of elms at the side. Some of the accounts of this year may relate to work on the platform. Perhaps also to the same neighbourhood may be referred an entry in 1469 of a fee to William Tempull, master of the king's ordnance, for observing 'the making of bulwarks.'[4] By 1559 the 'bulwarks' over against God's House had fallen into bad repair, and were to be put in order by the Provost of God's House. A little later (1577) the sea-banks beneath the bulwarks demanded attention, as also the 'bulwark' and the weather-house by the ferry; this latter being Cross House,[5] and the 'bulwark' just spoken of probably the defensive work referred to by Dr. Speed as a 'wooden fort' in his sentence on the platform and ditch: "A.D. 1647 the platform was built and repaired. "There is a broad ditch all round the town on the land side; and on "the shore opposite to the mouth of the river Itchen was a wooden fort,

The Platform.

Outwork.

[1] Lease.

[2] So called from the unfinished canal brought through it in 1795.

[3] See under 'God's House.'

[4] Steward's Books.

[5] Court Leet Books.

"the piles of which remain still." Under the above notice (Feb. 1647–48) it was ordered that the platform without God's House gate 'be built and repaired with stonework four feet thick, and a range of stones set against the bulwark over against the bowling-green;'[1] Thomas Mason and Peter Clungeon, who had both filled the civic chair, being appointed to overlook the work. The platform was furnished with great guns, which constantly seemed to want new carriages. Later on, in 1761 and 1769, the old guns were ordered to be sold and a peaceful saluting battery formed. But some improvement was desired in 1835, when the mayor applied to the Board of Ordnance for some 'cannons to place on the platform to fire on joyful occasions,' and received from Portsmouth the six nine-pounders which are still in their places. Besides these there is an ancient culverine, made by order of Henry VIII., as its inscription states; and there are some relics of the siege of Sebastopol presented by the War Office in 1857.

Cross House.

The 'Weather House,' or Cross House, mentioned under 1577 in connection with 'the bulwark' or wooden fort close by, bears within it the town's escutcheon and rebus with the initials of Peter Clungeon, mayor, and the date 1634, that of its restoration under this mayoralty, after its tottering condition had been presented for many years.[2] It stands at the ancient landing-place, and being formed of two intersecting walls covered with a conical roof, was 'profitable,' as the court leet remark in 1596, 'not only for those who wait for the boat, but for a shelter against rain.' A tradition, which is older than 1719,[3] assigns its erection to the bequest of an old lady in the seventeenth century, who caught her death of cold while waiting for the ferryboat; but tradition has failed to put the lady far back enough. Cross House most probably represents, or is the basement of, the old boundary cross at Itchenworth—so the spit or landing-place on which it stands was called; and if so, it possesses considerable antiquity. As a 'weather house' it was old in 1577, and wanted serious repairs. It is frequently mentioned in the town books.[4] In 1813 there was a question of removing it to some other spot, and it is supposed to have been in danger since. In 1835 the town were said always to have repaired it; since then, however, it has been put in order by private liberality, at least on one occasion. We trust it will be suffered to remain; a very fractional expenditure now and then will preserve this curious little building for centuries.

[1] Journal. [2] See Court Leet Books for 1615, 1633, &c.

[3] The tradition is mentioned in Addit. 14, 296, a collection of notes on Hampshire of that date.

[4] *e.g.*, Court Leet Books, 1667; Journal, 1695, &c.

At this spot, the ancient landing-place as well as a boundary point of the borough, the ferrymen of the Itchen did homage to the mayor and corporation at the stated perambulation of the town, engaging to carry over the burgesses and their families free of charge, in return for the permission to land passengers on the town side of the river.

In 1767 the ferrymen having refused free passage to a burgess, the town clerk reported to the proprietors of the ferry—Thomas Dummer, Esq., and James Mylles, Esq.—the conduct of their tenants, who, on October 20, urged no doubt by the proprietors, appeared and made their submission, acknowledging that their right of landing passengers depended on their service of carrying the burgesses and their families free of toll.

This state of things went on till the establishment of the new ferry.[1]

## Section V.—*The Quays.*

There was a 'Castle Quay' (see p. 74) in the early part of the thirteenth century distinct from that of the western shore; but this latter quay, whenever constructed, was the centre of life and trade in mediæval Southampton. A quayage in the usual form was made in aid of repairs to this quay for one year in 17 Edward II. (1323); and two years later a similar grant for seven years was obtained, the letters, dated Lichfield, 18th March 1326 (19 Ed. II.), reciting that the burgesses had begun to construct the quay and enclosures of the town by royal mandate, but after serious outlay were not able to finish without such relief.[2] In the following year (18th March, 1 Ed. III., 1327) they obtained from the new monarch what was really a confirmation of the former quayage for six years.[3] West Quay.

In connection with these works on the quay, the townsmen had constructed a wooden barbican as a defence towards the water, and for greater security against foreign invasion had commenced rebuilding it in stone. On this plea they further obtained (10 Ed. III., 1336) a grant of a penny in the pound on all merchandise for five years, and on the expiration of that term (1341) secured a renewal for a similar period.[4] In 1339, a controversy about the payment of this barbican duty, which had arisen with the men of Winchester, was terminated (February 26) by a release to them from this impost for five years.[5] Barbican.

---

1 From the Journals. See further under 'Admiralty' and 'Itchen Ferry Bridge.'

2 Pat. 17 Ed. II. p. 1, m. 9.; 19 Ed. II. p. 2, m. 17.

3 Pat. 1 Ed. III. p. 1, m. 5.

4 Pat. 15 Ed. III. p. 1, m. 39.

5 Indenture among Corp. Archives.

In 1502 the quay from Biddle's gate for some distance was let to John Dewtrey, 'to occupy with mylstonys, canestone, sclattis, colys, &c.', other burgesses having right to use any part they might choose to pay for.[1] Leland calls this a 'large key for shippes;' a few years later (1569) it occurs in the books as 'galley key.'[2]

"This quay was lengthened in 1576.

"A.D. 1583, a decree[3] was sent down under the Exchequer seal, "signed by several officers of the customs, certifying that West Quay "and Water-gate Quay are the only quays to this port.

West and Water-gate Quays.

"In 32 Chas. II. (1680), the lawful quays of Southampton, a head "port, were thus by commission returned into the Exchequer:—

"South Quay or Water-gate has one pair of stone stairs at the south end, and "two other pair on the east side. It measures about 223 feet in length from the "Water-gate and town wall to the head of the said quay; and in breadth, by "the said gate and wall, about 190 feet, and only about 63 feet at the head.

"West Quay measures about 225 feet in length from the West gate to the "head of the quay, and in breadth, near the said gate and wall, about 58 feet, "but at the head of the said quay not more than 37 feet."[4]

In the middle of the last century, West Quay served for the Channel Islands trade, which was very considerable, and the Guernsey and Jersey vessels always anchored off it.

Water-gate Quay.

Judging from a patent of 12 Ed. IV. (1411), it would seem that South or Water-gate Quay was then new. The patent sets forth that the burgesses, with the assistance of Thomas Mydlington, one of their number, had constructed at great cost a certain bank called a 'wharf,' with a crane upon it, at 'la Watergate,' in aid of the fortification and merchandise of the place, and for receiving custom, and that they had incurred the indignation of many who had been accustomed to evade or purloin the dues: the king, therefore, desired the work might be maintained henceforth, and authorised such toll from all parties using the wharf or crane as was levied in London, or at other ports where such accommodation (ripa et crana) existed.[5]

In 1441 the town books mention this wharf and crane: in 1457 the quay was 'paved' with gravel, and at the same time a 'gret gone' was laid upon it.[6] Other notices occur in 1468 and 1470; at the same time mention is made of an 'East Key,' which must mean the same, unless, as is possible, the platform be intended.

---

[1] Lib. Rememb. H. sub anno. [2] Court Leet Book. [3] Journal.

[4] Guide to Merchants, or Modern Practice of Court of Exchequer, 1730, p. 105.

[5] Pat. 12 H. IV. m. 18 (March 26). [6] Steward's Books.

"In 1525 the new quay at Water-gate was piled, and the next year "it was paved and gravelled." Leland describes it as a 'faire square key forcid withe Piles into the Haven water for shipps to resort to.' Speed (1596) speaks of both quays as being 'stately.' "In 1613 this "quay was lengthened sixty feet," and the town being at this expense, petitioned the king, without sucess, for five hundred trees from the New Forest for their walls and quays. In 1724 Mr. John Grove proposed to enlarge the quay by adding two circular piers according to a plan produced by him. The Corporation gave their approval, recommending him to raise subscriptions, and promising £200 on the completion of the works. The encouragement seemed insufficient, and nothing resulted.[1] However in due course an enlargement came. "In 1765 "South quay or Water-gate was again lengthened forty yards"—to gain six feet in depth—"towards the expense of which the two members of "Parliament for the town, Hans Stanley, Esq., and Henry Dawkins, "Esq., contributed £558 each; and this is the present state of that "quay which is the principal one. The Corporation paid £450 out of "their common stock."

Harbour Board.

The great improvement of this quay dates from the commencement of the present century under the Pier and Harbour Commission, called into being and empowered by the 43 Geo. III. cap. 21 (1803), subsequently to which the Acts of 50 Geo. III. cap. 168 (1810), and 9 Vict. (June 18, 1846), were passed, each amending the former.

The Royal Pier, of which more hereafter, was erected under the 1 and 2 Will. IV. cap. 1 (1831), the powers of which were extended by 1 and 2 Vict. cap. 63 (1838).

The Harbour Board was reconstituted and all the above Acts were consolidated in 1863, subsequently to which (1877) a further Act was obtained. Under the powers thus given very extensive additions have been made from time to time; the quay was extended from the Royal Pier eastward for about 300 yards along the south side of the town, while opposite the end of the High Street the town pier was projected for some 150 yards at right angles with the quay, forming a part of it. Still eastward a farther considerable extension of the quay has been made of late, completely absorbing the old platform, the whole forming an ample space for the ever-increasing traffic, and a handsome approach to the town.

The general duties of the Harbour Board are the regulation of the shipping in the roads and harbour, the marking out, maintaining, and lighting channels, &c., much as in the old Act of 1803, an analysis of which is given under "Modern Trade."

[1] Journal sub annis.

## SECTION VI.—*Conduits and Waterworks.*

Grant to Friars, 1290.

Nicholas de Barbeflet or de Shirlee, on June 16, 1290 (18 Ed. I.), obtained licence to grant, and the Friars Minor of Southampton to receive, and to enclose with a stone wall, the fountain of Calwell or Colwell, in the manor of Shirley, and thence to take the water underground beyond the land of the said Nicholas to Achard's Bridge, and from that bridge by the king's highway to their church in the town of Southampton.[1]

The Friars carried out their work as soon as they could; and 'le Conduit hede' at Hill, or Friars' Conduit at Spring Hill House, still remains as a monument of their industry. It was made over by the Town Council a few years ago to the Rev. J. L. Carrick, the owner of the surrounding property, by whom it has been cleaned out and put in order. It is an interesting structure, in three vaulted chambers, the outermost of which was evidently an addition to keep the whole under lock and key. Next to this, through a short passage, is an inner vault, originally used as the water-head; then at a sharp angle a low tunnel, about 10 feet long, 2 feet 9 inches broad, and 5 feet high, leads to the third chamber, about 6 feet in diameter, in which the water rises. There is still a good supply, though it has been shortened by the cutting of the main sewer down Hill Lane. From 'le Conduit hede' the Friars took their water by a large leaden pipe to the neighbourhood of Achard's Bridge, where they built the water-house, remains of which still exist close to St. Peter's Church. Into this water was subsequently conveyed from Lobery Mead — the modern Grosvenor Square and Polygon—where the remains of a small ancient stone conduit—called Lobery, and by corruption Lubberly, or middle conduit—existed some short time ago. There was also a 'little conduit,' the modern remains of which in brick are still to be seen above Achard's fountain in Goswell or Waterhouse Lane.[2]

Friars grant water to town, 1311.

The Friars granted the use of their water to the town on the Feast of the Purification, 1310–11 (4 Ed. II.), out of their singular reverence to Henry, Archdeacon of Dorset, and their good-will to the community of the town of Southampton, in the presence of Henry de Lacy, Earl of Lincoln, at that time the King's Lieutenant,[3] and John Sandale, the King's Treasurer;[4] allowing the burgesses to carry one pipe, with a

[1] Pat. 18 Ed. I. m. 24. See also 'Friars Minor,' below.

[2] Court Leet Books, 1670 and 1652; Steward's Books, 1493, 1474, 1461.

[3] Appointed Regent, September 1310, during the King's absence against the Scots.

[4] Afterwards (1316) Bishop of Winchester; appointed Treasurer, July 1310.

key, from the cistern of their lavatory to English Street through the Friary wall; the burgesses also erecting at their own cost outside the wall of the Friary a cistern to receive the water, and providing for the waste to be conveyed back into the cloisters of the Friary.[1]

"In process of time the pipes ran to decay, and the Friars were not "rich enough to put them in repair: so one of the burgesses having left "a legacy towards the repair of them, the Friars conveyed all their right "and title to the conduit head, pipes, &c., to the mayor and corporation "by the following grant:"[2]—

To all the faithful in Christ, &c., Robert Horewoode, warden of the Order of Friars Minor of the town of Southampton, and the convent there: Whereas our conduit-head at Hill, together with the system of leaden pipes from it, has fallen into decay, we, on the requisition of John Flemyng and Thomas Winterbone, executors of the will of John Bennett, late a burgess of Southampton, grant the same, for the good of his soul, to John Mascall, mayor, and to the community of Southampton: the executors engaging to erect a conduit opposite Holy Rood Church, and to bring the whole of the water thither through leaden pipes newly made at their expense, though partly with the old materials, and at this conduit to fit two pipes of equal capacity, one to discharge into a cistern for the use of the mayor and community, the other to be carried, also at the expense of the executors, to the old place for the supply of the Friars within their cemetery wall. The date of this patent is Southampton, October 3 (8 Hen. V.) 1420.

'Le conduit hede' conveyed to town, 1420.

In 1515 (7 Hen. VIII.) John Flemynge, of the town of Southampton, Esq., in a deed of gift dated June 1st, sets forth that—

Whereas the mayor, bailiffs, and burgesses possess a waterhouse in Goswell Lane, into which water is conveyed from a water-head in Lobery Mead belonging to him, he conveys to the mayor, &c., the head in Lobery Mead and the watercourse, with permission of entrance for repairs, as well in Lobery Mead as elsewhere between the said spring and the head in Goswell Lane. His seal of arms being unknown to many, the deed is attested by a notary public in presence of the right honourable and prudent men, John Dawtrey, Esq., and Richard Palshyd, collectors of customs in the town and port of Southampton, Nicholas Cowarte, Richard Hyll, and John Husee, gentlemen, with many others.

Lobery conduit conveyed, 1515.

By indenture of agreement with the Corporation (Aug. 21, 1515), the same John Flemynge obtained leave to put a

'Sosprey, otherwise called a small pipe of lead made with a stop,' into the main pipe of the conduit 'at the south-west corner of All Hallows Church unto the said church wall, and there to issue out at a cock of brass to be made staunch' at the cost of the said John Flemynge; to be used at all times between All Hallows Tide and the beginning of August, provided there were sufficient water at the other conduits. He undertook to enclose the place; and the warden of the Friars (now Observants)—'because the conduit first moved and came by the said Friars'

[1] Lib. Rememb. H. f. 113 b.

[2] Ibid., ff. 114, 115. The document, transcribed at length by Dr. Speed, is only given in substance above.

—and the mayor of the town were to have keys, with power to stop the water if the other conduits gave out, and to close the sosprey permanently if it were proved detrimental to the other supplies.[1]

Pedley's proposal, 1594.

Many years after this a certain Roger Pedley of Southampton, yeoman, undertook to bring a stream of water, four feet broad and two feet deep, to the Bargate, and thence a stream into the town, one foot broad and one deep; or, failing this, to use the existing springs and bring water into a conduit-house to be erected at the east end of St. Michael's Church, whence water should flow for all, day and night. In consideration of this the Corporation leased to him, 26th June (37 Eliz.) 1594—

All their banks, ponds, and ditches round the town walls, together with their garden plot on the south side of the George, on part of which lately stood a pound, and a strip of waste along the highway leading from the town towards the common, for the term of 160 years at forty shillings annual rent. Leave was given him to petition the Queen in the name of the Corporation for power to bring water from any stream within ten miles of the town for the said work through any man's ground; it being arranged that any grant or privilege coming to the Corporation in consequence of such petition should be reconveyed by the town to Pedley, &c., for 160 years at the yearly rent of twelve pence. (It does not appear that he made such petition.) Pedley was to have the monopoly of water supply, and to keep his system in repair for 160 years, nor suffer his stream to overflow: for the purpose of scouring the channel at needful times he might divert the water through Gosling Lane, and make a conduit at the end of it. He was forbidden to avail himself of any water then in use or damage the old conduits; and failing any *bonâ fide* carrying out of his plan within seven years from the date of lease, the indenture was to be void.[2]

"A.D. 1617.—The sons of the above Roger Pedley surrendered this "lease into the hands of the Corporation, who granted a new one to "Arthur Baker for sixty years. A.D. 1620.—The rent was reduced from "twenty shillings to three shillings and fourpence. A.D. 1675.—The "house where the leaden cistern stood at St. Michael's was taken down.[3] "From all which it is plain that the scheme did not succeed;" and the town continued to be supplied from the old Friars' head; the repairs to the water system being provided for by rate on the inhabitants from time to time.[4] "They went on in this manner very well till about the "year 1738, when some captious people refused to pay the rate and "raised such a mutinous uproar in the town, that the Corporation

[1] The two last documents, from papers in the Audit House, given at length by Dr. Speed, are here considerably abridged.

[2] Boke of Remembrances, f. 184. Dr. Speed has given this document in full; it is here very much abridged.

[3] "Journal."

[4] Dr. Speed refers to the 'Boke of the Condyte Money, 1536,' in which the names of the inhabitants are set down with a certain sum against each.

"thought fit to waive this their undoubted right and joined with the "mutineers in a petition[1] for an Act of Parliament,[2] by which the "whole property and management of the town waterworks are vested "in commissioners, of whom the mayor, recorder, and six senior bur-"gesses are always to be eight, and twenty-four others are to be chosen "yearly out of the several parishes as other parish officers are chosen. "The consequence of this is that the town is now supplied with the "same water just as it was before at five times the expense. Town applies to Parliament, 1739.

"Besides this conveyance of water to the town, there are in a com-"mon field called Houndwell Field two springs, from which the water "is conveyed into a water-house in the same field. What the original "use of this house was I nowhere find; but 6 Henry VII. (1490) a 'new "well' was made here, and 'a watering place for hors and a washing "place for women.' There is another conduit of which I find no "mention anywhere. It stands near the Hospital of God's House, and "as the master of that hospital brought the water to the convent of "the Friars,[3] it is very probable that he at the same time continued "it to the neighbourhood of his own hospital." Houndwell. God's House conduit.

The water system of the town is described in the Act of 6 and 7 Will. IV. cap. 96 (1836), for maintaining the public conduits and other waterworks, and for providing an additional supply—as commencing from several springs and conduit heads, and a conduit head and adjacent pump—Achard's—at some distance from the town, from whence the water was distributed to four public conduits in the High Street, known as All Saints, Holy Rood, Friary, and God's House conduits, and also to Houndwell water-house in the Houndwell common meadow. Of the two water sources at Houndwell, that to the south was supposed to be of great efficacy in diseases of the eye, and was constantly resorted to in the last century for its peculiar properties. Water system before 1836.

On the removal of these conduits the town was supplied by upwards of forty public fountains or conduits erected from time to time in convenient places; but with the increasing population a larger supply was demanded. The old Act of 1747 was amended by 43 Geo. III. cap. 32 (1803), and that again by 50 Geo. III. cap. 20 (1810). Waterworks on the common had been constructed under the old Acts, but in 1830 the Commissioners obtained from the Corporation a grant of an acre and a half of land for an additional reservoir to be formed at

[1] Journal, Nov. 3, 1738; Nov. 6 and 30, 1739.

[2] 20 Geo. II. cap. 15, 1747: An Act for repairing, improving, and maintaining the public conduits and other waterworks to the town of Southampton. Stat. at Large, vol. xix. p. 45.

[3] See "Register of the Convent."

the north of that already existing, in order to bring water from Wood Mill and thus augment the supply gathered from the common.

The Act above mentioned of 1836 repealed all the former, and gave increased powers to the commissioners, the mayor, recorder, aldermen, and councillors, together with twenty-six elected inhabitants; and shortly afterwards the artesian well on the common was projected. From July 1838 to February 1851 the excavations on this well were carried on—the total cost of the work being about £20,000, and a total depth of 1317 feet was reached. Of this, by means of iron cylinders and brickwork, 464 feet were sunk through the tertiary beds; the diameter at the top of the shaft being 13 feet, diminishing to 7 feet at the lower part. The beds passed through consisted of 2 feet of soil, 74 feet lower Bagshot beds of sand and clay in alternations, 304 feet of London clay, consisting of sandy clay with seams of water-bearing sand, and pebble beds towards the top, 84 feet of plastic clay, with the usual bed of greensand at the base. The chalk was reached at a depth of 464 feet, where the masonry was terminated. The seven-foot shaft was continued 99 feet in the chalk. A boring was then made with a 7½-inch augur to a further depth of 754 feet, making a total of 853 feet in the chalk and 1317 from the surface. The chalk contained flints all but the last 10 feet, which contained veins of clay and were very cloggy. At this point the boring was stopped, the results not being considered sufficiently promising.

Great well on the common.

Most of the water of the well appeared to come from the chalk. Previously to 1842, when the boring commenced, 20,000 gallons per day were raised; in 1844, after considerable progress had been made in boring, this increased to 50,000 gallons, and finally, in September 1851, to 130,000 gallons.

The question of this well was before the Geological Section of the British Association at Southampton in 1846, and again at the meeting of the Association in August 1882, when the recommencement of the boring was contemplated, an opinion being elicited to the effect that the experiment would be well worth trial, either by driving out horizontally in the chalk to intercept water fissures, or by continuing the boring to the upper greensand, and if necessary through the gault to the lower greensand.[1] Accordingly, on October 14, 1882, after further consideration, the Town Council resolved on a contract for the completion of the work, the results of which are looked forward to with the utmost interest.

Returning to the works under the Act of 1836, two wells were sunk

[1] Paper of Messrs. Shore & Westlake, read before the British Association, August 1882; report of discussion in local papers, &c.

at Northam, one at a cost of £2932, 16s. 6d., the other £357, 7s. 8d.; the reservoirs and mains cost £2084, 10s.

In 1850 another Act (13 and 14 Vict., July 15) was obtained, under which, and the Public Health Acts of 1848 and 1850, new works were commenced. A supply of water was obtained from near Mansbridge, beyond Wood Mill, in the valley of the Itchen, about a couple of miles to the east of the new waterworks. Here a reservoir and engine-houses for pumping were constructed, and two new reservoirs adjoining each other formed on the common near its northern limit, capable of holding together about 5,000,000 gallons. More recent Acts.

In addition to these, the town is supplied from three older reservoirs to the south, which in the aggregate are of equal capacity with the more recent. Thus a copious distribution is secured through every street and court.

## SECTION VII.—*Pavement, Lighting, and Watching.*

A pavage, or toll in aid of paving, had been granted to Southampton as early as the 8 Richard II. (1384).[1] The following entries occur under 1457: 'To the pavyer for payyng of iij teyse[2] and an halfe in the myddylle of the stret be Robert Belhows [the Seneschal's] dore, and for ij pottes of sand ij$^{s}$. x$^{d}$. Item, to the pavyer of London for pavyng of xij teyse of pavement taking viij$^{d}$. for a teyse x$^{s}$. viij$^{d}$.' There must have been some extras. Under 1441 we have several accounts of paving stones being provided.[3] 1384.

In 1477 (17 Ed. IV.) the following Paving Act was passed:— Act 1477.

'To the right wise and discrete Comons in this present Parlement assembled, humble besechen unto youre Wisdoms the Maire, Shirrefs, and Bailiffs of the Towne of Suthampton that where the said Towne is full febly paved and full perilous and jeopardouse to ride or goo theryn and in especiall in the High Streetȝ of the said Towne, that is to seie froo the Barre yate to the Watergate and other ij Streetes there gretly occupied withe Cariage and for faute of paving there, divers youre Lieges and other Straungers thider resorting have been oftentymes gretly hurte and in perill of their Lives, and the said Mair, Shirefs, and Baillifs have no Londes nor Tenementes, Rentes nor other yerly revenuȝ in Comōn wherby they may make and repare the pavements in the same Towne requisiteȝ.'

It was ordered in consequence that owners of property, on notice from the mayor, sheriff, and bailiffs, should be compelled to pave at their own charges before their doors as far as the middle of the street,

[1] Pat. 8 R. II. m. 31.

[2] A fathom. The tese in London was (29 Ed. I., 1300–1) stated to be 7½ feet in length, and 'one foot of St. Paul' in breadth (see Liber Albus, i. 279; Liber Custum. i. 100).

[3] Steward's Books.

and on their failing to do so within a quarter of a year after such notice, it became lawful for the mayor, &c., to pave and levy costs by distress. Tenants on being distrained for what the landlords should pay might stop the amount out of their rents, or recover by action of debt in the court of the town.[1]

In pursuance of this Act it was ordered (December 1482) that—

Town paviour.

'A paviour be ordeyned to dwell in a house of the towne, price of xiij^s^. iiij^d^., rent free, and to have yerely a gowne to this intent that he shall with a sargent of the same towne doo serche the pavement of the said towne, and also to pave in all places nedefull withyn the said towne and doo all thyng that longeth to that office, takyng his wages for his labor as it is used for a Tese: provided alway that the stone and all maner thyng to the said pavement belongyng be ordeyned by hym or theym afore wose house the pavement shall bee noyouse or nedefull of reparacon.'[2]

The town paviour remained an institution, the price of his work varying. In 1509 he was paid for 'paving 154½ toyses, from the beginning of Bargate to the Barrs without the gate, every tees vj^d^.' In 1579 a paviour appointed for life covenants to pave the streets and lanes at 1½d. a yard, and not more; but if employed for private paving in courts or enclosures, he may charge according to agreement.[3]

The pavement continued to be regulated by the Act of 1477 till November 1769, when a new paving scheme was matured; and on 12th December the town seal was affixed to a petition to Parliament for a bill embodying the recommendations of committees of the Corporation and of the original promoters of the scheme; and on February 24, 1770, to a further petition for including lighting and watching: all of which was carried into effect by the 10 Geo. III. cap. 25, 1770.

Lighting.

Little occurs on the ancient lighting of the town.

Watching.

On the watch there is more to be said. The Statute of Winchester (13 Ed. I., 1285) provided that the gates of walled towns should be closed from sunset to sunrise; that no one should lodge in the town or suburbs from nine in the evening till day unless his host would be responsible for him; that the bailiffs of towns should every week, or at least every fifteen days, make strict inquiry concerning all inmates. The towns were to be kept, as in time past, by watches proportioned to the number of the population. Strangers might be arrested on suspicion, or the hue-and-cry raised after them. These regulations, which did little more than enforce old traditions, were comparatively

---

[1] Dr. Speed has this Act; it is printed in the Rolls of Parliament, and is here given in abstract. In the same year provision was made for paving Canterbury, Taunton, Cirencester, and other places.

[2] Liber Niger, fol. 1 b.

[3] Boke of Remembrances, fol. 136 b.

fresh at the date of the copy of the guild ordinances given below (see Nos. 46 to 51).

The division of the town into wards for the sake of order is no doubt immemorial. There were five wards at the time of the ordinances, each with its organisation; afterwards there were four, which appear to have been subdivided on special occasions or emergencies. About 1504, four wards are described, each with its alderman and his 'vynteners'—inferior officers literally having charge of twenty. A little later the town was divided into eight, and even ten parts, very accurately described, each with its warden. About 1521 the watch was ordered to be nightly kept, and strict search made once a week by every alderman through his ward. The wards were:—(1.) St. Michael's and St. John's parishes; (2.) Holy Rood; (3.) St. Lawrence's; and (4.) All Saints: four or five vinteners and a sergeant being assigned to each alderman. Closely on this there follows an order for six 'new watchings' within the town; two were to keep the walls, the other four to go about the streets, and 'ofttimes to walk up to the Castle Hill, and there to have a good prospect of the sea' and every quarter of the town, to guard against fire and surprise.[1] In 1544 there were four wards set, and later in the same year eight; and in 1570 (12 Eliz.) we find the town similarly divided into eight parts, and furnished with eight principal wardens, the mayor and his brethren being desired by the lord-lieutenant to see that all the able men within the liberties, amounting in the whole to 439, were supplied with armour and weapons, and that none left the town or liberties without permission. But in the following July, all the householders were turned into special constables, and were desired to have in their shops, or other places next the street, 'holbertes or clobbes contynually standing, to be at all tymes redye to assist Mr. Maior.'[2] Judging from the court leet books, we might suppose that Dogberry and his crew had taken charge of the borough watch a little later; for under 1577 it is complained that only 'weak and poor men' are set to do the work: henceforward the householders were themselves to perform their lot, or provide sufficient deputies. They were warned of their turn, beat, and hours by the sergeants, who also reported to Mr. Mayor each morning the names of the watchers through the previous hours, so that no man might be charged with this duty on successive nights.

Wards.

A little later, the total male population for the purposes of muster, between the ages of sixteen and sixty, being 495, we find 421 able-bodied men armed with calivers, pikes, bows, and bills. In 1583 there

Muster Rolls.

[1] Boke of Remembrances, ff. 21 b. 22.

[2] Muster Book, 1544; Boke of Remembrances, ff. 108 b, 113.

were 439 able-bodied men all named, householders and others; the women finding substitutes. The summary of weapons was as follows:—Corselets, 34; morion heads (conical skull-caps), 45; hand-guns, 16; jacks (jerkins), 6; bows, 71; sheaves of arrows, 86; halberts, 37; bills, 195; pikes, 23; swords, 41; daggers, 38; coriars (cuirasses), 13; alman-rivetes (light armour), 31; hagbashes (heavy hand-guns), 28; shirts of mail, 1; skulls, 12; steel caps, 2. The total number of males in 1589 was 600, able-bodied 505. In this year Walter Lambert was captain, and William Abere, gent., muster-master appointed by the lord-lieutenant of the shire. There were two lieutenants, two ensigns, four serjeants, two drummers, one fife, and one clerk. The names and kinds of arms were enumerated as usual under the wards. Some possessed their own arms, some found arms for others; some householders provided two or even three men.[1] Ecclesiastics bore their part. Under 1621, in answer to Privy Council letters directed to the Archbishop of Canterbury, Bishop Andrewes, with the advice of his chancellor, Sir Thomas Ridley, issued a mandate for the provision of horse, arms, and other furniture required from every benefice. The parsonage of St. Mary was called upon for one light horse, no more being required from the Dean of Winchester or the college. The vicarages of Holy Rood and St. Michael were to furnish one 'muscat' each; the parsonage of All Saints the same. St. Lawrence and St. John, under sequestration at this time for the non-payment of dues, were passed over.[2]

Watch and ward.

Returning to the more special watch and ward of the town in the troublous times of January 1642, four householders, severally armed with musket and sword, and stocked with powder, bullets, and lighted match, watched each night in their own persons, or if validly hindered, found sufficient deputies, in the suburb above Bar and in East Street; and six householders within the walls 'in the most convenient places for discovery.' In the daytime two sufficed for the watch above Bar. Persons were warned of their turn in the usual way, those for night ward being required to appear before the mayor at eight o'clock in the evening to receive their charge, and at six o'clock in the morning they were relieved by the day watch. This order, to remain in force till Mr. Mayor and the justices should arrange otherwise, was not to supersede 'the former ancient watch.' Every Sunday, during the time of divine service, the gates of the town were kept shut, with the exception of the wickets at Bargate and Water-gate.

[1] Muster Books. See also Journal, September 12, 1612, and July 16, 1628.

[2] Extracts from the Registers of Bishop Andrewes and others belonging to Jesus Chapel, Peartree Green.

In 1656 the vestry of St. Lawrence furnished soldiers for keeping watch and ward, employing one or two at a time constantly, in accordance with a custom of ancient time in every town or parish.[1]

Under the national scare arising out of the impostures of Oates, the town dreaded being surprised or set on fire in November 1678. The watch was accordingly ordered to be trebled, and twelve persons were warned for this purpose, half of whom at least were to be provided with firearms. Later on we gather from the minutes of St. Lawrence's parish that the public arrangements for the nightly watch were considered insufficient; at least in 1731, when the vestry agreed to maintain a watchman out of the poor-rate for their parish, and applied to the justices for relief from contributing to the public watch.

The Corporation petitioned in 1739 for an Act to regulate the watch as well as maintain the waterworks, but nothing seems to have been effected as to watching till 1770.

Condition of streets and sanitary arrangements.

The earliest regulations on the condition of the streets and of sanitation are contained in the ordinances of the Guild (see Nos. 42, 43). In spite of these, the town was often very filthy, though the court leet did not fail to draw attention to the matter without respect of persons. 'Mr. Maire kepith a sowe in his backsyde,'—so runs a plain-spoken presentment of 1550,—'whiche is brought in and oute contrary to the ordenaunce of the towne: wherfore be yt comanded to hym and all other that they kepe no hoges within the towne to the anoyaunce of theire neighbours upon payne that every of them that so shall kepe any swyne to forfyte for every xv daies he shall so offende, xx$^{d}$.' Kine were not to be milked or fed in the streets; slaughter-houses were not allowed within the walls; slops were never to be thrown into the streets; refuse-heaps would not be tolerated; ditches, culverts, bunneys were to be kept clear. Yet from the earliest steward's accounts (1441) the town books abound in violations of these wholesome rules, and the court leet has not seldom to fly at the highest game. The 'Proffeste of God's house' was presented in 1559 for neglecting a sanitary duty; dung mixons were constantly found about the streets and lanes, and even before the church doors. 'There is a greate heape of soyle and roobidge befor Mr. Mayor his garden in the Easte Street' (1576). At another time the alderman of Portswood was presented for 'haveing severall loades of dunge within Rockstone gate w$^{ch}$ hee is pleased to calle his priviledge, but we amerce him ij$^{s}$. vj$^{d}$.'

We learn through the court leet book of 1675, from a back reference to books of more than a century previous, that by ancient custom

[1] Churchwarden's Accounts; also Instructions from Privy Council as to Musters.

Scavage-money.

of the town scavage-money for the payment of scavengers (in the modern sense) was a duty payable by every housekeeper of the town, and was formerly collected by two persons in each ward appointed by the court leet jury, who not only collected the money, but directed the scavengers in their work. The money was always delivered to the steward.

Surveyors of highways.

In the seventeenth century there were twelve surveyors of the highways, two for each of the following wards or divisions:—Holy Rood, St. Lawrence, All Saints without the Bar, St. Michael and St. John, All Saints within the Bar, Bag-row and East Street.

Town chimney-sweeper.

The chimney-sweeper to the town was a new official in 1654; he was regularly sworn into his office, to the effect that he would be ready at every call to sweep any number of chimneys at the rate of fourpence apiece; and to secure the residence and due attention of so useful a functionary, every householder was to pay him one penny per annum, 'as is used in many other cytyes and townes, called by y^e name of a smoake peny.'[1]

Precautions against fire.

For provision against fire, hooks or crooks and ladders were always kept in readiness in the market-place,[2] and in 1675 'engines' besides the crooks. No local orders have been met with as to the construction of roofs or walls; but as a provision against fire, no one was permitted (1657) to keep hay or other combustible matter in any loft or room, near a dwelling-house within the town; and in 1684, during the dry season, tubs of water were required to be kept standing day and night at every housekeeper's door.

Act of 1770.

We may now join the threads of our narrative at the Act of 1770 (10 Geo. III. cap. 25), 'for the better paving, repairing, and cleansing the streets and other public passages in the several parishes and wards of St. Michael, St. John, Holy Rood, St. Lawrence, All Saints within the Bar, All Saints without the Bar, and East Street and Bag-row within the town and liberties of Southampton; and for preventing nuisances and annoyances therein; and for widening and rendering the same more commodious; and for lighting and watching the said streets and public passages.' In dealing with the Bar gate and walls, we have noticed some of the earlier work of the commissioners under this Act. In 1810 further powers were obtained under another local Act (50 Geo. III. cap. 169); and by the Municipal Corporations Act, 1835, and continued in 1882, the watching was placed under a committee of the Corporation, to be from time to time elected.

---

[1] Court Leet Books, 1640, 1675, 1654.

[2] Journal, 1618; Court Leet Book, 1615.

In 1838 the widening of Bridge Street,[1] which with the increasing traffic had become both inconvenient and dangerous as a thoroughfare, and many other alterations in the streets and roads, were taken in hand by the Improvement Commissioners; but it was soon found advisable to obtain further powers to meet the growing necessities of the town. A committee was appointed in September 1843 to consider the expediency of obtaining an Act to amend and enlarge the Paving and Lighting Acts.[2] In 1770, when the first Act was passed, the population could not have exceeded 6000; in 1811, after the passing of the second, it was but 9617; in 1841 it was 27,774; and a couple of years later it was upwards of 30,000. Extensive suburbs had sprung up, which had never been contemplated under the old Acts, and were not reached by their provisions; the need of an Improvement Act adapted to the enlarged circumstances had therefore become urgent. A comparison of the property rated to the poor with that liable to rates under the Acts gave the following results:—Rateable value to paving, &c., £44,329; rateable value to poor-rates, £96,088, leaving a difference of property to the extent of £51,759 not rated to paving. In 1844 the desired Act (7 & 8 Vict., 1844, July 19) was passed for 'paving, lighting, draining, cleansing, and otherwise improving the town, and for removing and preventing nuisances and annoyances therein.' The existing Acts were repealed, together with so much of the 13 Geo. III. cap. 50 as related to the repairs of highways, &c. Finally, the powers of the old Improvement and Waterworks Commissioners ceased upon the application of the Public Health Act, 1848, to Southampton.

The Corporation became the Local Board of Health, and are now in this respect known as the Urban Sanitary Authority.

## Section VIII.

### *Audit-House and Markets—Municipal Buildings.*

In the early part of the fourteenth century the church of St. Cross or Holy Rood was removed from the middle of the High Street to its present position farther back, after which the Audit-house was erected on the ancient site of the church. Notices of it occur in 1457, 1471, and other years. Leland (1549), describing the features of the High Street, says, 'There ys a fair house buildid yn the midle of this streat for accomptes to be made yn.' The accounts were frequently made palatable with rare good wine and jollification. Had the antiquary turned over the steward's books, he would have come across

Old Audit-house.

[1] Report of Improvement Committee, December 5, 1838.

[2] Report of Committee, September 29, 1843.

entries like the following:—'This hys the expensse of y[e] mayer and hys bretheryn in the Audyt-hows atte etyng of the bukke that my lord of Arendell giff the vj day of September' (1473). The fabric was, as usual, in two stages, the lower being available for market or shops.[1]

"The market for butter, eggs, &c., was originally kept in the High "Street opposite St. Lawrence's Church; the fish-market in St. Michael's "Square, and the butchers' shambles at the dead wall of the Friary."

Poultry-market.

In reference to the former, many inhabitants and strangers having represented to the Corporation that there was no shelter at St. Lawrence's Cross against the rain and tempest, 'which often happened on market-days,' whereby victuals, buyers, and sellers were the worse, it was agreed (March 1570, 12 Eliz.) to erect a convenient and comely market at the south end of the Audit-house, which was carried out by June, and to abandon the old site at the cross.[2] The intended removal gave offence to some few, and attempts were made to stop it after the election of the new mayor, Reynold Howse; upon which the Corporation exhibited a lengthy document to the Queen's Council, setting forth the reasons which had induced them to make the change; the old place had been found too small, was uncovered, and the chatter of the market-folk annoyed the worshippers in the church close by; every formality had been complied with; only a few interested persons of no weight had made objection, and to such the order and governance of the town did not belong.[3]

Fish-market.

The fish-market in St. Michael's Square had an erection over it; in 1457 a portion of this was let as the 'Cloth-house' for twenty shillings a year;[4] in 1525 the 'loft' over the fish-market was let to the warden of the bakers for twenty years at twenty shillings a year[5]—fish odour disagreeing with neither cloth or bread. This market was slightly peripatetic. Some time before 1603 it was at the poultry cross or market in the High Street, and was in that year ordered back to the Square; in 1615 it was again sent into the High Street above the Audit-house near the Bullring, where it remained till the erection of the new Audit-house. "A.D. 1698.—The Corporation built butchers' "shambles at the Market-house."[6]

In the latter half of the eighteenth century the old Audit-house did not strike visitors with the same admiration with which it had affected

[1] In the Steward's Book of 1457 'void places' under the 'town hall' are let. This must refer to the Audit-house, as under the 'town' or 'guild' hall at Bargate there could have been no such accommodation.

[2] Boke of Remembrances, f. 104 b.

[3] Lib. Rememor. BB., ff. 45, 46.

[4] Steward's Books.

[5] Boke of Remembrances, f. 26 b.

[6] Court Leet Books and Journals.

the great antiquary upwards of two centuries before. It had been patched up from time to time, and extensive improvements were made in 1763; but the inevitable fact had to be faced that the building was no longer fit for the town, and modern requirements demanded that it should be improved off the face of the High Street. Old Audit-house condemned.

In 1771 a new site, considered then fairly central, consisting of the house and garden of Mr. Alderman Purbeck, about 230 feet long and between 40 and 50 feet broad, was purchased by the Corporation for £1305, and the first stone of the present Audit-house was laid on September 27, 1771, in presence of Edward Noble, Esq., mayor. The architect was Mr. John Crunden, of Bolton Street, Piccadilly. His work was much admired, and it was quite on a level with buildings of the kind in other large towns. The outlay was over £7000. The façade towards the street, of Portland stone and in the Doric style, can hardly be described in the terms usual at the time. But the building is a handsome edifice in two stages, the lower of which was till lately open and used as a market; above were the council chamber (as at present), the office of the town-clerk, that of the borough treasurer, and the various other municipal offices, which also of later years occupied a house adjoining to the south, now rebuilt in the recent improvements, and adapted to the general plan. The council chamber has a good interior. Several fine pictures adorn its walls, some the gift of the late G. F. Pitt, Esq., in 1831, who also in the same year presented to the town his collection of books for a free library, which, together with fifty-three volumes presented by the Record Commission in 1834, are now incorporated in the library of the Hartley Institute. A sword of state—a medieval two-handed weapon—drawn in time of war, and the old colours of the Southampton Volunteers, occupy corners of the apartment. The council chamber was intended no less as a hall for meetings and banquets than for the business of the council, the existing clerk's room, lately the town-clerk's apartment, serving at first for the business of the Corporation. New one built.

The Audit-house was opened on October 5, 1773, but for purposes of marketing many old-fashioned folk, as usual, refused to take kindly to the changed locality, and so much trouble seemed likely to arise that the Corporation thought of applying for an Act to establish and regulate the new market. However, with the aid of the recorder, matters were settled in a less costly fashion, proclamation being made, October 22, 1774, notifying the removal of all the markets, with the exception of those for corn and grain, to the new site.[1] The markets Removal of markets.

[1] On November 25, 1788, an atrocious attempt was made to burn the premises by means of combustibles placed under the butchers' shambles in Market Lane.

removed are specified as those for butter, eggs, and poultry; for butchers' meat; for herbs, fruit, and garden stuff; and also for fish and other provisions, which had till then been kept in and about the late market or Audit-house and near the Dolphin and Nag's Head Inns.

In 1816, more room being required, the green-market again took possession of the High Street, under authority of the Commissioners of Pavement, till a better place should be provided. In September 1822 an additional green-market was established, by proclamation, in a building provided in the Ditches adjoining the new butchers' market, which had been opened in April 1821, near the bridge crossing the canal at the bottom of Bridge Street. This range of buildings, erected by private venture, and situated opposite the Wheatsheaf Inn, was called St. George's Market. The green-market was thus disposed of; but yet another and a last sweep was needed for the High Street, the pigs being still in front of Holy Rood Church on the ancient site. These the Commissioners of Pavement successfully attacked in August 1832, and by the aid of the Corporation they were finally driven into St. George's Market before the end of the year.

St. George's Market.

High Street cleared.

As has been stated, the Audit-house of 1771 has now been considerably enlarged, and convenience has been secured, though the general result can hardly be said to be worthy of the town. It was the best that could be done on the present site. The architect was Mr. James Lemon, C.E.; the outlay something over £3000. On the ground floor are arranged the offices of the borough surveyor, medical officer of health, inspector of nuisances, borough engineer, and inspector of weights and measures. In the basement is the muniment room. On the upper floor are the council chamber and anteroom, the committee room, mayor's parlour, town-clerk's offices, those of the borough treasurer and clerk of accounts, &c.

It may be anticipated that this arrangement, however commodious, will give place before many years are over to a more suitable and dignified building.

The corner-stone of the additional buildings was laid by J. B. Thomas, Esq., then mayor, on October 22, 1879, and a year from that date—namely, on Wednesday, October 20, 1880—the whole of the improvements had been finished, and were formally opened by the mayor, W. H. Rogers, Esq.

## Section IX.—*The Hartley Institute.*

Those whose recollection of Southampton can carry them some few years back will remember the three dreary-looking red-brick houses with narrow casements, dating apparently from the early part of the last century, in one of which Henry Robinson Hartley formerly resided, as his father had before him. But the houses had been closely shut up for many years, and the few old elm-trees in front could not redeem this spot from being a most melancholy eyesore to the otherwise beautiful High Street.

Henry Robinson Hartley came into a good fortune, just after he had attained his legal full age, on the death of his father in April 1800. Henry Hartley, the father, descended from an old family of gentry in the Craven district, had come from the North and settled in Southampton as a wine importer, the great local trade of the time; his uncle, Mr. George Robinson, having preceded him about 1744. Mr. Robinson became sheriff of the town in 1751 and mayor in 1762 and 1773; and Henry Hartley obtained the mayoralty in 1775.

Soon after coming into his property, the subject of this notice shut up his house and left the town; nor did he ever return to reside in Southampton, visiting the place only so occasionally and privately that he was known by sight to few. He was supposed to have taken an aversion to the town; yet when he died at Calais, aged seventy-two, on May 24, 1850, it was found that by will bearing date August 13, 1843, he, then residing at Newington in Surrey, after making certain bequests to relatives and servants, had given the whole residue of his personal estate to the mayor and Corporation of his native town, upon trust, to employ the proceeds in such a manner as might best promote the study and advancement of the sciences of natural history, astronomy, antiquities, and classical and Oriental literature in the town of Southampton; such as by forming a public library, botanic gardens, observatory, and collections of objects in connection with the above sciences, in the parish of Holy Rood.

The property amounted to £103,887; but the will being disputed, and a long and expensive Chancery suit ensuing, the Corporation, after paying some £35,000 taxed costs and compromising with some of the claimants, realised at length, in 1858, no more than the sum of £42,525. Having thus far, at such heavy cost, vindicated the will, the Corporation sought the advice of the town as to the form the bequest should assume; and in November the same year the general opinion was pronounced in favour of a scheme not very unlike what has been carried out. Accordingly in 1859 an order of the Court of Chancery was made establishing the present Hartley Institute on the above general lines. It was arranged that the sum of £15,000 should be laid out on the site and buildings; and as the three houses above spoken of, the leasehold interest of which Mr. Hartley had owned, offered a favourable site, the spot connected personally with Mr. Hartley was selected; and the

Corporation having acquired by gift from Queen's College, Oxford, the freehold of the houses, added to the estate some Corporation land at the back, made the most of the money that had fallen to them, and began to build. The foundation-stone was laid by Lord Palmerston in 1860, and the Institute was formally opened by him, October 15, 1862, Dr. Bond having been appointed curator.

The building is a handsome Palladian structure in three storeys, with a façade of about 74 feet to the High Street. A triple entrance, with caryatides, opens into a spacious hall supported by columns and adorned with statuary, out of which runs a wide corridor leading to the lecture theatre, art galleries, secondary staircases, &c. To the left of the main entrance is the apartment of the Southampton Chamber of Commerce, beyond which are lavatories. On the right of the entrance are the council and the executive officer's rooms. The main staircase is to the left hand of the entrance to the corridor. Beyond this and to the left of the corridor is the museum—which may eventually be turned into the library on a further building scheme—50 feet long, and having two galleries entered from the main staircase. The theatre, at the end of the corridor, fitted with large orchestral and two side galleries, is about 64 feet long by 58 broad, and calculated for 1000 persons. Beyond the theatre and at the sides are art galleries and lecture rooms. On the first storey, main entrance, are a handsome reading-room, 70 feet long, and a library adjoining. On the upper storey the chemical department is arranged. The buildings have cost about £20,000. The library at the Institution comprises three or four different collections, among which is the Pitt Library (spoken of below), and contains over 20,000 volumes. In the Institution are located a school of art in connection with South Kensington, occupying a suite of rooms specially built for the purpose; a school of science and engineering, occupying a similar set of buildings; a junior medical school; a department of general literature; and large chemical and physical laboratories. There is a staff of lecturers and teachers attached to the Institution. The fees for day students vary from £15 to £24 per annum, and there are evening classes during the winter months, which are open to artisans and others at small fees. The students have gained many distinctions and appointments in various Government services, including the public works and telegraphic departments of India, the Woolwich and line examinations, the Control departments, &c., and have won many open scholarships and similar distinctions at the universities, the Royal School of Mines, and elsewhere; and during the year 1881–82, 340 students, day and evening, attended the classes.[1]

[1] Mr. Shore's Guide.

The Institution is governed by a council, which consists of the mayor, nine members of the town council, and six who are not members of the town council. The executive officer is Thomas W. Shore, Esq., F.G.S., F.C.S., under whose care the work of the Institution is being largely developed.

## SECTION X.—*The Ordnance Survey Office.*

At the beginning of the century the Government erected on a site of about two acres of land near the entrance to the Avenue some cavalry barracks, with all the usual appliances. In 1816 the use of these buildings was converted into a military asylum for boys, serving as a branch of the Royal Military Asylum at Chelsea. It was superintended by a commandant, chaplain, adjutant, surgeon, and other necessary officers; and at one time contained from three to four hundred boys, who were well fed and taught, and patronised by great folk from time to time. In May 1823 they were all removed to Chelsea, and the asylum was used for female children. These, like the boys, were to be orphans of both parents, or daughters of fathers who were serving in the regular army abroad, the mothers being dead: they were clothed, fed, and taught, and put to service. About 1840 these children were also removed to Chelsea, and the destination of the buildings and site became for a third time altered.

The Ordnance Survey Office was established at Southampton on this old site, and partly in the old premises, in 1841. In 1855 an extensive new wing was added, and in 1873 the old main building was pulled down. The whole of the premises have now been remodelled and greatly enlarged.

This office is the headquarters of the Ordnance Survey of the United Kingdom, the work of which is carried on by four companies of the Royal Engineers, in addition to a staff of upwards of 2000 civilians. Of this force, about 500 are employed here; consisting of all the necessary artists, clerks, and mechanics, under a director, assisted by an executive officer and officers in charge of departments.

A full account of the work of this department was presented by Major-General Cooke, C.B., R.E., at the visit of the British Association in August 1881.

There is an observatory on the premises, the register of which commences with the year 1855: the observations are constantly published in the local papers.

From this office parties of the Royal Engineers were sent on the survey of Jerusalem and Sinai, which has had such interesting results.

# CHAPTER IV.

## *MUNICIPAL.*

### SECTION I.—*The Guild Merchant.*

THE Guild Merchant having been the nurse of the town's corporation and the original guardian of its liberties, it seems right to put in the front such account of the Guild as we are able to give. This will be best done by exhibiting its ordinances at length, of which, however, and of the versions extant, some account must be also given.

Version. 1. The earliest version of the ordinances of the Guild Merchant is to be found in an ancient and curious volume, which is one of the most interesting of the town records. It is a small quarto on vellum, bound in oak covers, one being much longer than the other, and having a square hole in the lower part to put the hand through while using the volume. On the outside are a couple of merchants' marks.[1]

The ordinances commence at the top of folio 10, and are written continuously without any break to the fifth line of folio 20, the heading of each being in rubric. The handwriting is apparently that of the first part of the fourteenth century. Prefixed to the ordinances, on folio 9, is the guildsman's or burgess's oath, in which mention is made of a mayor, a title which does not occur in the ordinances themselves. The oath, which is in rubric and in a larger hand than the rest, appears to be of the same age. The ordinances are of various dates, some of them probably belonging to the earliest period of the Guild The translation of this oldest version is given below.[2]

2. The next is a version called the 'Paxbread.' It is a free translation from the Anglo-Norman ordinances, with certain omissions, made by W. Overey, town-clerk, 1473. It commences:—'Heare after folo

---

[1] This book was noticed by the late Mr. Thomas Wright in Winchester volume, Brit. Archæol. Assoc., 1846, where also is a drawing of the covers by Mr. Fairholt. A table of contents is to be found in the Record Commissioners' Report, 1834.

[2] Dr. Speed transcribed the text and gave a translation, which has been consulted in that given below. The Anglo-Norman text, here excluded from want of space, was edited by Sir Edward Smirke, but without translation, and is to be found printed in the Archæological Journal, vol. xvi. 1859, pp. 283–296.

[w]ithe the contynue of a boke named the paxbreade . . . [be]inge the olde rules and ordinaun[ces] of the good t[own] of Suthampton made by greate [deli]beracon b[y] the awncyent fathers in time passed [for] the utilitie and comon welthe as well f[or th]e burgeasses and bretheren of the gilde as of a[ll the] dwellers and inhabitantes within the franchis and liberties of the saide towne: the which auncient fathers made the saide booke of olde tyme in Frenche tonge, and the first sadd and good rule to be had and settled amounge them, and so for to conteyne in the same unto the worldes end: and seth by William Overey, sonne and heire unto William Overey sometyme mayer of the saide towne, translated out of Frenche into Englishe, he beinge burgesse succeedinge his saide father's burgeswicke by inheritaunce, and by free election afterwarde chosen clerke and made shreve of the said towne the yere of grace M^l^cccclxxiij [12 Ed. IV.] the xv daye of September: which translacion so made was fully compiled and finished the saide yere by the saide William Owrey the yonger, and after by him geuen and presented unto the maior at that time being and to his bretheren, burgesses of the saide gilde, with all the inhabitantes of the same, the yere of grace M^l^cccclxxviij (1478).' The town copy now existing is not the original, but was written after the beginning of the reign of Henry VIII.

No account is hazarded of the name 'Paxbread'[1] by which the ordinances had come to be known.[2]

Overey's work contains:—1. The burgesses' oath, substantially the same as that printed below;[3] 2. Translation of the French ordinances; 3. The oaths of all the officers of the town. (1.) The mayor's oath is a more ancient form of that given below; in it occurs 'ye shall see to be donne all the pointes of the paxbreade, and of ij bookes called the booke of certentes of office, and of a booke [of] casualties late ordayned

1 Constant references occur to chapters in the 'Paxbread,' *e.g.*, in 1522 James Pryvett was 'discharged from the liberty of the guild' for making a fray on one of the burgesses with a dagger, 'contrary to the lawdable custom of the town, as in the 13th chapter of paxbread doth appear' (Burgess Book).

2 Nor can I explain the following extraordinary entry:—

'Paxbrede: M[d] that John a Side solemply sworne uppon a booke the xvij yere of Kynge Harry the vij[th] the xvij[th] day of March [1502], hath confessed that he hath the copy of the paxbrede of this Towne which he hadd of Thomas Stanwey, sumtyme servaunt to Jamys Meryke; over that he is sworne to se the same copy delyvered, the same self copy: and also he is sworne that he nor othir person for hym shall take any copy of the same. And the vij day of March a° Regis H. vij xviij°, according to the othe aboue wretyn he hath brought in the same booke, and it was brent before hym' (Lib. Remembranc. H. f. 8).

3 See the oaths printed under the offices.

for the welthe of this town by Thomas Overay[1] then mayor' [1488–90], &c.; (2.) Oath of the four aldermen; (3.) Of the sheriff; (4.) Of the recorder or town-clerk; (5.) Of the bailiff of the courts; (6.) the water-bailey and of the broker; (7.) Of the water-bailey and his clerk; (8.) Of the steward; (9.) Of the four sergeants; (10.) Of the crowners; (11.) Of the constables; (12.) Of the bidelles; (13.) Of a prisoner when liberated.

3. The third version occurs in the second part of the volume last mentioned. It contains the following oaths:—1. Of the burgesses; 2. Of the commoners; 3. The mayor; 4. The four aldermen and justices; 5. Constables of staple; 6. Recorder or town-clerk; 7. Sheriff; 8. Bailiff; 9. Coroner; 10. Constable; 11. Petty customer; 12. The four discreets of the market; 13. The four sergeants; 14. The receiver of customs; 15. Brokers between merchants; 16. Cloth-measurers; 17. The steward; 18. Measurers of salt and corn; 19. Teller of leather; 20. Alderman of Portswood; 21. The bidelles. The ordinances which follow are considerably modernised and enlarged,[2] and are the same as in No. 5 (below).

4. The fourth version in the order of time is found in the 'Burgess Book' of 1496. It presents the same list of oaths as the last, and contains in the margin some additions which appear in the later texts. Opposite the commoner's oath a note about the Protector is obliterated. After the ordinances, which have nearly assumed their most modern shape, comes a new batch of oaths. That of the recorder was new, and 'the right wo. Mr. Thomas Fleminge, her Majesty's Sollicitor General, was, the vij daye of April 1601,' sworn upon it; then the oath of non-burgesses, written after 4 Jas. I., subsequently altered to serve for the Protector, and again altered; the oath of the justices; of the assistants or common councillors; and of the gauger.

5. A version[3] written in the time of Charles I., from which a few footnotes are given below. It contains the same oaths as version 3,

[1] The ordinances of Thomas Overey consist of thirty-two articles of minute regulation for the town officers, and for enforcing the points of the Paxbread and for trade rule. 'Thees been the remedies provided and ordeyned by Thomas Overy, mere, &c., for divers grevous compleyntis, &c. And if these said remedyes, provisions, and ordinaunces shuld not be put in execucion and contynue, hit shuld be to thutter distruccion of this seid gode towne, the whiche God defende.' They were passed by the Common Assembly, July 1, 1491 (Lib. Remembranc. BB., ff. 5, 6–9). Article 20 provides that the old ordinances granted to various crafts should be still observed. Article 24, strangers coming to the town were to be assigned by the mayor, 'to be hosted and lodged with sufficient burgesses dwelling within the same town.'

[2] It had been intended to give a collation of these books, but space has failed utterly.

[3] This book was in the possession of Dr. Speed.

with the additions of version 4. The ordinances are considerably modernised (as in version 3), the word 'burgess' always appearing instead of 'guildsman.' The following are the chief additions:— Ordinance 17. Forbidding innkeepers to receive the merchandise of strangers into their houses; 63. Forbidding the purchase of articles on shipboard under the Isle of Wight, except through a broker; 64. An order about the watch, about 1521; 65, 71, 72, 73. Orders about beer-brewers (c. 1550); 66. The town steward to put in sureties; 67. Butchers above Bar not to retail meat there, but to sell at the Friar's gate with the other butchers; 68. The measure of Newfoundland fish; 69. Prohibiting the sale of salt by water measure; 70. Payment for the use of the crane for great timber, and 79 for millstones; 74. Regulation for butchers; 75. Cows not to be milked in the town; 76. Beer-brewers not to have iron-bound carts; 77. Masty dogs not to run about the streets; 78. Regulating shoemakers and cobblers; 80. Tin dealers to carry their tin to the tin-house and pay the porters.

6. The book of 'oaths of office' now in use. It was commenced by Richard Stanley, town-clerk, 1648–53. The ordinances in this copy present many slight variations from those in the last, but are substantially the same. Ordinance 69 is omitted. There are these additions:— 80. None to be sworn burgesses but such as are free of the Corporation by birth or service, without consent of the majority of the Corporation; 81. No one to be chosen mayor, sheriff, or bailiff who has not been high steward; 82. Costs of Admiralty courts at Leape, Lymington, and Keyhaven limited to £8, and at Hamble to forty shillings; 83. Officers in the customs are to have no government in the town; 84. No burgess who has not been resident a year and a day is to have any voice in the election of mayor, &c., unless he be the recorder, or has been a burgess of parliament for the town; 85. Order of precedence among the burgesses; 86. Strangers' goods to be weighed at the king's beam; 87. Apprentices of burgesses and franchisers, term to be for seven years at least, according to the statute;[1] enrolment to be made within six months in the Audit-house book; 88. No one to set up a shop without licence unless he has been apprenticed in the town for seven years; 89. No craftsmen dwelling in the town or franchise to take into employ any men-servants other than denizens and those bound apprentice; 90. The manner of surveying the town lands, &c. 'Item, that the mayor and aldermen of the wardes shall make true . . .' here three leaves are cut out, and so Mr. Stanley's ordinances come to an end. There is little variation in the oaths of this collection. A marginal note against the burgesses' oath states that by order of

[1] See 5 Eliz. c. 4, s. 24 (1562–63), and 7 Jas. I. c. 3, s. 2 (1609–10).

Common Council, February 1769, the clause about apprentices is to be omitted. Under the mayor's oath a later hand gives directions as to his swearing, and how he is to be invested with the tippet by the recorder and the late mayor or next senior alderman.

We now turn to the significance of what we find. We have before us the history of the borough constitution, as far as it is contained in these ordinances, from about 1300 to the period when the Corporation had assumed that shape in which the Municipal Reform Act found it in September 1835.

Guild ordinances regulate the town.

The first thing to remark is that the old ordinances profess to regulate both the Guild Merchant and the town. It is evident, therefore, that at the period of the earliest laws the borough government had merged its identity in that of the Guild.

Officers.

The alderman (Ordinance 1) was the usual title of the head of a guild; the seneschal or steward, chaplain, echevins, and usher were officers also of the Guild; but some of them had at this period functions which were clearly beyond those of the original Guild Merchant. This latter was an association for the protection and promotion of trade of whatever kind; hence, after it had assumed full governing power in the towns—for the history of one town is that of many—we find it in connection with the various craft guilds, approving their ordinances, receiving money considerations from them, and supervising in many ways. To this guild character of the governing body the general power of trade regulation belonged, as also that of the appointment of burgesses and their succession by inheritance.

At the period of these French ordinances (c. 1300), which, be it remembered, certainly represent a much older date, nothing remained beyond the sign or tradition of the two jurisdictions having been separate, so completely had the Guild dominated over the old borough idea. But whenever the Guild became settled as the supreme authority—and it may have been from its first existence by charter (probably in the time of Henry I.)—there entered at that period an element of restriction alien from the more ancient government of the towns. The privileges of the borough communities were shared by all the free, that is, unservile town-dwellers who bore their part in the public burdens; but with the Guild the privileges became restricted to the few, and a system of local administration arose which fills us with amazement in reading medieval or much more recent history. Yet, in a larger view, the exclusiveness of the guild system was a necessary step towards the freedom of the country; for it is observed[1] that the vindication of class privileges is one of the most effective ways of securing public

[1] Stubbs, Constit. Hist., iii. 562.

liberty so long as public liberty is under the general oppression of tyranny.

The alderman or chief alderman of the town—*i.e.*, the alderman (originally) of the Guild Merchant, as distinguished from those of the wards—is the head of the Guild and of the town (Ord. 53). With him are joined two bailiffs (27, 29, 32, &c.), and twelve sworn men of the town from the class of prodeshommes or 'discreets,' and called so themselves *par excellence* (18, 27, 29, 32, 44). They were afterwards styled the 'twelve assistants.' These twelve discreets were to be elected each year by the whole community, the two bailiffs being elected the same day from the same class of prodeshommes (32). Besides these officers, there were four sworn men discreets of the market (31), and twelve aldermen of wards, who had the view of frankpledge in their wards, and controlled the police and sanitary regulations of the town (37, 38, 45, 46, &c.) The seneschal or steward acted as treasurer under the direction of the chief alderman (8, 35), and the four 'skavyns' (1, 2, 3, &c.)—as the word was usually written and pronounced—probably served him in a subordinate capacity. The usher gave warning of town meetings, and was perhaps the mouthpiece of the Guild in proclamations.

Alderman. Bailiffs. Twelve discreets. Discreets of market. Aldermen of wards. Steward. Echevins. Usher.

The Guild did not always meet in the same place (4, 32), perhaps in this respect preserving the old tradition of the Guild Merchant, which was not even confined to town-dwellers. The Guild meeting was to be held twice[1] in the year—the Sunday next after St. John Baptist's Day (June 24) and that after St. Hilary, January 13 (1). There is no mention of a guildhall.

Meetings. No hall mentioned.

Passing now from the officials to the general town community, the most important personage is the guildsman or *burgess*, for the burgess no longer means the free resident householder, paying his scot and bearing lot, sworn and enrolled in the court of the borough. The word has obtained a more restricted meaning, which became bound to it only the more tightly till in the Act of 1835 it was liberated and restored to something more like its original. The guildsman or burgess was a member of the body which held the government of the town; he had the fullest municipal rights, and the first enjoyment of every privilege; his place in the Guild had either been inherited or purchased by fine (9, 10, &c.), on his satisfying otherwise the necessary requirements, one of which was residence; for the Guild Merchant having been now long time strictly localised, it had adopted the old tradition, so far, of

The guildsman.

[1] These were solemn no less than festive gatherings. At them the ordinances were carefully read over and explained. Thomas Overey's ordinances make this clear.

town-dwelling being essential to the exercise of town functions and the enjoyment of town privileges. The only exception to this requirement was in the case of those whom the Guild delighted to honour or whose favour it hoped to secure by the compliment of honorary membership (57): the guildsman could not give away or barter his place (10).

The franchiser.

After the guildsman comes the man of the franchise (12, 13, 14, &c.), that is, the dweller within the liberties of the town who bore his part in duties and taxation, and who was admitted to trade by the enabling and essential permission of the Guild. A guildsman might lose his place in the Guild, or even forfeit his franchise (12, 65, &c.); and the franchiser might of course be deprived of his rights, when he would be counted as a stranger (75, &c.)

Deprival of condition.

The stranger.

The stranger or foreigner was not necessarily, or indeed generally, a foreign subject, but one who did not live within the town liberties: such a person was made to understand that his frequenting the markets and his very presence within the town were matters of sufferance (23, &c.)

'Men of the town.'

Ordinance 30 shows us how to interpret 'man of the town;' it is evidently a comprehensive term including both the guildsman and the franchiser. So the expression 'ordinances of the guild and of the town' (44, 45) refers to the one code which regulates the whole community, and does not imply two bodies, one having reference to commerce, the other to local government, though the phrase may preserve the tradition of separate jurisdiction. This hint of a former state of affairs is perhaps more distinctly involved in No. 53.

It was in comparatively recent times that the name of Guild was finally given up. At the period of the French ordinances it was prominent, and so continued for a couple of centuries or more. The entries in the 'Burgess Book' of 1496 record admissions 'into the gilde' or into 'the libertie of the gilde.' One or other of these forms occurs without a variation till the admission of Bishop Horne in 1562, whose name is the last thus entered. After this there is a marked change in the style. The next and most of the subsequent admissions are 'to be one of the burgesses,' or, in the latest times till 1835, 'admitted and sworn a burgess.' Still in 1597 we find an admission 'to be one of the burgesses and guilde;' and the same or similar form of 'guild and burgess' occurs not unfrequently till 1704; after which the name does not appear in documents, and only remains in the word guildhall.

Following upon the distinction between 'the guildsman' and 'man of the franchise,' the latter enjoying special liberties from the Guild without all the privileges of the guildsman, we find in the volume called 'List of Burgesses from 1697' an 'admission of freemen,' towards the end, the first entry being dated October 5, 1694. These were admissions of tradesmen to trade in the town, and of townsmen

Freemen.

to succeed to freedom on completion of their apprenticeship, the latter being admitted gratis. The forms are 'admitted and sworn a freeman of this town to use the trade of,' &c., 'having served an apprenticeship within the town, is admitted and sworn a freeman of the town to use the trade of,' &c. The list is not quite chronological, and a meagre enrolment compared with the list of burgesses. It may not have been complete. The last entry seems to belong to 1796.

## THE ORDINANCES OF THE GUILD MERCHANT.

1. *How the alderman, seneschal, chaplain, echevins, and usher shall be elected.*—First, let there be elected and established for the Guild Merchant an alderman,[1] a seneschal, a chaplain, four echevins,[2] and an usher. And be it known that the alderman shall receive from every one entering into the Guild fourpence, the seneschal twopence, the chaplain twopence, and the usher one penny. And the Guild shall be held twice in the year, that is to say, on the Sunday next after St. John Baptist's Day, and the Sunday next after St. Hilary.

2. *During the time of the Guild none shall come among them except through the alderman.*—And during the Guild no one belonging to it shall introduce any stranger except by order of the alderman or seneschal. And the alderman shall have a sergeant[3] to serve before him, the seneschal another sergeant, and the two echevins a sergeant, and the other two echevins a sergeant, and the chaplain shall have his clerk.

3. *What the alderman shall have each night as long as the Guild shall be held.*—And during the Guild the alderman shall have each night of its session two gallons of wine and two candles, and the seneschal the same; and the four eschevins and the chaplain, each of them one gallon of wine and one candle; and the usher, one gallon of wine.

4. *What the lepers shall have during the Guild.*—And during the Guild the lepers (les meseaus) of La Maudaleyne shall have of the alms of the Guild two cesters[4] of ale; and the sick of God's House and St. Julien, two cesters of ale; and the Friar's minor, two of ale and one of wine; and four cesters of ale shall be given to the poor where the Guild shall be held (la ou la gilde serra).

5. *No guildsman shall go forth from the town during the session of the Guild.*

[1] The mayor of the town continued very commonly to be called 'the alderman' in deeds and other documents till towards the middle of the fourteenth century.

[2] Eskevyns. The following, from 'English Guilds,' Early Eng. Text Soc., 1870, will be of use:—'An aldirman, wyse and wittye, able and konyng to reulen and gouern þe company . . . and four skeuaynes, trost men and trewe, for to kepyn and reseyuen þe goodes and þe katel [chattels] of þe gilde' (p. 46).

[3] A servyer devaunt ly. It probably means to execute orders: compare the Winchester 'Usages' (English Guilds, p. 350); 'Also fowre seriauntes sholde be in þe town y-swore, ȝerdes [maces] berynge, for to don þe hestes of þe mayre and of þe baylyues.'

[4] Cesters. Dr. Speed takes it for setier or septier, which he makes a liquid measure of eight pints or one gallon.

—And while the Guild is sitting, no member of it shall go forth from the town for business without the leave of the seneschal. If any one does so, he shall be fined two shillings, and pay them.

6. *How two guildsmen shall visit the sick of the Guild, and what each approved man*[1] (*prodeshome*) *shall have.*—And during the Guild if any guildsman be out of the town, so that he did not know when the Guild would take place, he shall have a gallon of wine, if his servants come for it; and if a guildsman be ill and in the town, wine shall be taken to him, two loaves and a gallon of wine, and one dish of cooked food;[2] and two of the approved men (prodeshomes) of the Guild shall go to visit him and look to his condition.

7. *When a guildsman dies,*[3] *those who are of the Guild busy themselves, likewise all who are of the Guild and in the town shall be at the service of the dead.*—[Words repeated] and guildsmen shall carry the body, and bring it to the place of sepulture. And he who will not do this shall pay, on his oath, two shillings to give to the poor. And those of the ward where the dead man shall be shall find a man to watch with the body the night that the dead person shall lie in his house. And so long as the service of the dead shall last, that is to say, the vigil and the mass, there shall burn four wax tapers of the Guild, each taper of two pounds or more, until the body be buried. And these four tapers shall remain in the keeping of the seneschal.

8. *The seneschal shall keep the rolls and the treasure of the guild under seal.*—[Words repeated] of the alderman of the Guild.

9. *How the next heir of a deceased guildsman shall have the seat of his father.*—And when a guildsman dies, his eldest-born son or his next heir shall have the seat of his father, or of his uncle if his father was not a guildsman, but of no other relation, and shall give nothing for his seat. But no husband (baron) by reason of his wife can have a seat in the Guild, nor demand it by any right of his wife's ancestors.

10. *No one has the right or power of* [*selling or*] *giving away his seat in the Guild.*—[Substance repeated] and the son of a guildsman, other than his eldest, shall be admitted to the Guild on payment of ten shillings, and shall take the oath.

11. *If a guildsman be in prison in any place in England.*[4]—[Words repeated] during a time of peace, the alderman with the seneschal and one of the echevins shall go at the cost of the Guild to procure (porchacer) his deliverance.

---

[1] Prodeshomes. An understood and restricted class of the men of better standing, from whom the officials were chosen (see Gloss. to Lib. Custumarum, p. 753). This word is always rendered by 'discreets' in the more modern English versions of these ordinances.

[2] Mes de la cusyne. 'A messe of the kichene' (Overey).

[3] This ordinance is omitted in Overey's version, 1473; but its equivalent appears as cap. 2 in later versions, where the mayor and his brethren are charged with this duty under two shillings' penalty.

[4] Modern version (No. 5), 'By reason of the affairs of the town.'

12. *If any [guildsman] strike another with his fist, and be thereof attainted, he shall lose his guildship until.*—[Words repeated] he has purchased it again for ten shillings, and shall take the oath like a new member. And if a guildsman strike another with a stick or a knife, or any other weapon of whatever kind, he shall lose his guildship and his franchise, and shall be held a stranger until he be reconciled to the good men of the Guild and have made recompense to the person whom he has injured, and be fined to the Guild twenty shillings, which shall not be remitted.

13. *If any stranger strike a guildsman, and be of the franchise, or offend.*—[Substance repeated] and be reasonably attainted, he shall lose his franchise and go to prison for a day and a night.

14. *If any one who is neither of the Guild nor of the franchise strike a guildsman.*—[Substance repeated] and be thereof reasonably attainted, he shall be imprisoned two days and two nights, if the offence be [not] such as to deserve graver punishment.[1]

15. *If a guildsman revile or asperse another guildsman and complaint be made of it.*—[Words repeated] to the alderman, and he be reasonably attainted thereof, he shall pay two shillings fine to the Guild; and if he cannot pay he shall lose his guildship.

16. *That no one of the franchise, or any other, come to speak or do evil against a guildsman; and if he do this and be attainted.*—[Substance repeated] before the alderman, he shall give a fine of five shillings or lose the franchise.

17. *And no one shall come to the council of the guildsmen unless he be a guildsman.*—[Sentence repeated.]

18. *If any one of the guild forfeit his guildship by any act or trespass, and be excluded.*—[Words repeated] by the alderman, seneschal, echevins, and the twelve sworn[2] men of the town, and would have it again, he shall do all afresh, just as one who had never been of the Guild, and shall make amends for his trespass at the discretion of the alderman and the discreets (prodeshomes) aforesaid. And if any one of the Guild or of the franchise sue another out of the town, by writ or without writ, he shall lose the guildship and the franchise on proof thereof.

19. *No one shall buy anything [in the town of Suthamtone] to sell again in the same town, except he be a guildsman.*—[Words repeated] or of the franchise. And if any one do so and be attainted thereof, all that he has so bought shall be forfeited to the king. And no one shall be quit of custom unless he have made it clear that he is of the Guild or of the franchise, and this from year to year.

20. *No one shall buy honey, seim,[3] salt herrings, oil, millstones,[4] or hides,*

[1] 'Si le trespas est tiel que il pende plus graunt punysement.' Smirke suggests that a negative has been omitted. The modern laws (No. 5) have 'and to have greater punishment according to his trespass.'

[2] See under Ord. 27.

[3] Fat, lard, &c., or fish-oil (see Ord. 75).

[4] So the modern versions: the word is *moeles.* In Ord. 71 occurs *tourn de moeles*, a pair of millstones.

*except a guildsman.*—[Words repeated] nor keep a tavern for wine, or sell cloth by retail, except on market or fair day, nor keep above five quarters of corn in his granary to sell by retail, if he be not a guildsman; and whoever shall do this and be attainted shall forfeit all to the king.

21. *Of ordering division (de partie maunder) in merchandise between guildsman and guildsman before.*—No one of the Guild shall be partner or joint dealer in any of the foresaid merchandises with any person who is not of the Guild, by any manner of coverture, art, contrivance, collusion, or any other manner. And whosoever shall do this and be attainted, the goods so bought shall be forfeited to the king, and the guildsman shall lose his guildship.

22. *If any guildsman fall into poverty and have not wherewith to live.*—[Words repeated] and cannot work or provide for himself, he shall have one mark from the Guild to relieve his condition when the Guild shall be held. No one of the Guild or franchise shall avow another's goods[1] for his own, by which the custom of the town may be injured. And if any one do so, and he be attainted, he shall lose the guildship and the franchise, and the merchandise so avowed shall be forfeited to the king.

23. *And no denizen or stranger shall [bargain for] or buy merchandise [coming into the town] before a burgess.*—[Repeated] of the Guild Merchant, so long as the guildsman is present and desires to bargain for or buy those goods; and if any do, and be attainted, all that he has bought shall be forfeited to the king.

24. *How a guildsman[2] shall have a share in (departira) the merchandise, which another guildsman buys.*—And any one of the Guild Merchant shall share (deit partir) in all merchandise which another guildsman or any other person shall buy, if he comes and demands part, and is on the spot where the merchandise is bought, so that he satisfy the seller and give security for his own part (quy il soit en seur del seon). But no man who is not of the Guild can or ought to claim share with a guildsman against his will.

25. *The customs[3] and all other matters shall be paid without delay.*—And if any guildsman or other of the town refuse a part as aforesaid to a guildsman, he shall neither buy nor sell in the town that year except victuals.

26. *If a merchant of the town buy wine or corn and do not custom.*—And if any merchant of the town buy wine or corn, so that all the risk be on the buyer,

---

[1] Evidently two ordinances run into one. As bearing on the latter part and on Ord. 30, compare an order, January 6, 1563–64, complaining that the town had suffered from strangers cellaring their goods within the town, and then, by colour of their freedom elsewhere, or by sufferance of the townspeople, or by the townsmen themselves, selling their goods to other strangers, without duty paid, as freely as if they were burgesses or freemen of the town. Therefore, no burgess or other inhabitant was to sell the goods of any not enfranchised, after it was cellared, to any but burgesses or freemen (Boke of Remembrances, f. 94).

[2] This and the following ordinances are omitted by Overey down to Ord. 30, which is with him cap. 23.

[3] The connection between rubric and chapter here is not apparent.

he shall pay no custom for those goods; but if any part of the risk be on the seller, he shall pay.

27. [No rubric.]—It is provided that the chief alderman of the town, with the bailiffs and the twelve sworn men,[1] shall be watchful over the merchants, as well strangers as denizens, as often as shall be required, to see that they have sufficient security[2] for their debts and of the recognisance of their debtors; and the day of the recognisance shall be enrolled before them, so that if that day be not kept on the showing of the creditor, the debtor shall be immediately distrained, according to his recognisance, in his lands or chattels, to make satisfaction according to the usage of the town without any pleading, so that the townsmen shall not suffer by default of payment of their debtors aforesaid.

28. *And if a guildsman will not suffer himself to be distrained for debt, or [being distrained shall break through, or make removal, or] break the king's lock, and be [thereof] attainted.*—[Substance repeated] he shall lose his guildship until he has bought it again for twenty shillings, and this each time that he offends in such manner. And he shall not at all be the less distrained (et ja le meyrȝ ne seit distreint) until he has made satisfaction for the debt he owes; and if he will not submit to justice as aforesaid and be thereof attainted, he shall go to prison for a day and a night like one who is against the peace; and if he will not submit to justice, let the matter be laid before the king and his council in manner aforesaid.

29. *For the assise of bread and ale, let it be held rightfully in all points.*—And the chief alderman, and the twelve sworn men, or the bailiffs, each month, or at least four times a year, [shall take care] that the assize of bread and ale be well kept in all points according to the price of corn.

30. *That no man of the town sell merchandise of a merchant [stranger] bought under pretence.*—[Substance repeated] whereby the merchandise would be sold for more than the merchant could have sold it by his own hand, and so the town's people would lose their profit; but the merchants who bring their goods for sale shall sell them by their own hand. And he who shall do this, and be thereof attainted, shall lose his guildship, if he be a guildsman, and if he be of the franchise, he shall lose his franchise until he has made amends to the town for his offence.

31. *That the market for fish and meat and poultry*[3] *be held in all points.*—And every year, on the Morrow of St. Michael, shall be chosen two discreets who shall be sworn to take care that the statutes made concerning the fish-market be

---

1 The existence of these 'twelve sworn men' (and in Ord. 18, 29, &c.) is explained by Ord. 32. They were the 'assistants of the mayor' in the modern laws. The Winchester 'Usages' require that the mayor's council shall consist of four-and-twenty sworn men 'of þe meste gode men and of þe wyseste of þe town, for to treulyche helpe, and counseyle þ forsaid meyr, to saue and susteyne þe fraunchyse,' &c.

2 See charter 40 H. III. No. 1 (1256).

3 The word is written *peletrine*, *peletrie*, which would mean *peltry*, woolfels, sheep-skins with wool; but the context seems to require poletrie, *poultry*; and the modern laws have so taken it.

observed in all points, and they shall have the several points in writing. In like manner there shall be two discreets elected and sworn to take care that the statutes concerning meat and poultry be observed in all points. And these four sworn men shall take care that the statutes concerning bread brought to market from out of town be well observed : and if any do otherwise, notice shall be given to the chief alderman and the bailiffs.

32. *How twelve discreets shall be elected to maintain the king's peace, and how bailiffs, sergeants, &c.*—Every year, on the Morrow of St. Michael, shall be elected by the whole community of the town assembled in a place provided, to consider the estate and treat of the common business of the town—and then shall be elected by the whole community, twelve discreets to execute the king's commands, together with the bailiffs, and to keep the peace and protect the franchise, and to do and keep justice to all persons, as well poor as rich, denizens or strangers, all that year ; and to this they shall be sworn in the form provided. And these twelve discreets shall choose the same day two discreets from among themselves and the other profitable and knowing men to be bailiffs for the ensuing year, who shall take care that the customs be well paid : and they shall receive their bailiwicks on the Morrow of St. Michael's, as has been customary. And this shall be done from year to year ; so that the bailiffs shall be removed every year, and the twelve aforesaid if occasion be. The same shall be done with regard to the clerk and sergeants as to making and removing them.

33. *That no bailiff give respite or take pledge for the custom, nor lend [give credit for] the custom.*—[Words repeated] due on anything that is to be carried out of town ; and if he do so, and be thereof attainted, the bailiff shall pay double the sum for which he gave credit ; and the bailiff shall be responsible for everything that is customable on entry into the town, so that the town be no loser by his default, if he would not answer for it by paying double.

34. *Every entry of a ship and of customable goods [and every export from the town] by sea shall be enrolled.*—[Substance repeated] so that at the end of a week the exports of the town may be known ; and the chest of the customs shall never be opened but in presence of the chief alderman and the twelve sworn men, or six at the least ; and then that amount of export [the custom] shall be enrolled in a double roll, so that the chief alderman shall have one roll and the bailiffs the other, and that amount shall be put into the common chest ; so that nothing shall be taken out or spent but in presence of the aforesaid alderman and sworn men.

35. *That the common chest be in the house of the [chief] alderman or of the seneschal.*—[Repeated] and the three keys of it should be lodged with three discreets of the aforesaid twelve sworn men, or with three of the echevins, who shall loyally take care of the common seal, and the charters, and the treasure of the town, and the standards, and other muniments of the town ; and no letter shall be sealed with the common seal nor any charter taken out of the common chest but in the presence of six or twelve sworn men, and of the alderman and seneschal ; and no body shall sell by any kind of measure or weight that is not sealed, under forfeiture of two shillings.

36. *This is ordained that the bailiffs shall have nothing from any article*

*which belongs to the custom as of forfeiture.*—[Substance repeated] or from the entering of corn, or for weighing; nor shall they have anything except amercements, and presents, and firewood, that is to say, one [billet from every][1] cart of firewood from each carter who brings firewood to town for sale, and then the carter shall have one penny for his wood.

37. *Those who have committed offence against the alderman shall be amerced at the award of the discreets;* and any one who is of the town and may have to be amerced for any offence shall have his amercement taxed according to the offence, and by award of the alderman of the ward of which he is.

38. *Those who are summoned to the court of the king or to the assembly.*—[Repeated] to hear and execute the king's commands, or for the common business of the community of the town, and come not at the summons, and the summons be witnessed to by a sworn sergeant, shall be amerced as often as they shall offend in this sort, whoever they be, poor or rich, at the discretion of the alderman of their ward, and the fine shall be immediately levied [to the use] of the town.

39. *That no man harbour hay, oats, or other corn, after that these goods are brought for sale.*—[Repeated] into the market: if any one does, and he be thereof attainted, he shall lose all that he has so harboured.

40. *That no hired house which a merchant stranger has hired harbour another's goods.*—No merchant stranger who has hired a house or cellar in the town may or can harbour any merchandise not his own in that house or cellar, by any manner of pretext, by which the rents of houses belonging to the burgesses of the town would be lessened; and whoever shall do this, and be reasonably attainted, shall be heavily fined at the discretion of the town and according to the offence.

41. *That no butcher or cook sell other than nice-looking and clean food under pain.*—No butcher or cook shall sell to any man other than wholesome and clean provisions, and well cooked: if any do, and he be thereof attainted, he shall be put in the pillory for an hour of the day, or give two shillings to the town for the offence.

42. *That no butcher or cook throw into the street any filth or other matter.*—[Repeated] whereby the town or the street may become more dirty, filthy, or corrupt; and if any one do this and be attainted, he shall pay a fine of twelve pence for every such offence in the manner aforesaid.

43. *That no man have before his house muck or dung, or pigs going about.*—No man shall have any pigs going about in the street, nor have before his door or in the street muck or dung beyond two nights; and if any one has, let whoever will take it away; and he who shall have acted contrary to this statute shall be grievously fined.

[1] Overey has 'shides of wood,' *i.e.*, *billets*. Version No. 5, 'A shide of wood to the use of him that keepeth the Bargate, that is, to wit, of every cartfull of wood that cometh to the town to be sold one shide of wood, except such as be free.'

44. *How the twelve sworn men shall be attentive in all points to the bailiffs of the town.*—The twelve sworn discreets shall swear that they will be helpful and advising to the bailiffs of the town in all points to provide for the king's commands and to do justice indifferently, as well to poor as to rich, and to support the bailiffs in all places according to right and the franchises and usages of the town; and they shall be at every court, and shall come at the summons of the bailiffs as often as they shall be summoned for hearing the king's commands or for giving judgment in court; and they shall keep secret and hold the counsel of the town, and shall cause to be observed the statutes of the Guild and of the town, uniformly with the chief alderman, the seneschal, and the echevins.

45. *Of that which the aldermen and guardians of the streets of the town of Suthamtone, &c.*—The aldermen, guardians of the streets of the town, shall swear loyally to keep the king's peace, and to cause to be enrolled the names of all who are in their ward, and once in every month at least shall go round to see that the points and ordinances made for their ward be well kept; and if they find anything in their ward that is against the ordinances of the Guild and of the town, they shall give notice of it to the chief alderman and the bailiffs of the town, and they shall not fail of this if they would enjoy the franchise of the town.

46. *Of two aldermen who shall keep the peace within the boundaries.*—It is provided, by common consent of the town, that from the North gate to the East gate, and to the corner which belonged to Richard[1] de la Prise and the capital messuage which belonged to John de la Bolehusse, on both sides of the street, with all the parish of our Lady in East Street, there shall be two aldermen elected as guardians to take care that the peace be well kept within the boundaries aforesaid, and they shall cause to be enrolled the names of all who are dwelling in their ward, and they shall be bound in good security to keep the king's peace, and their sureties shall be enrolled; and they shall take care that no person stay in their ward beyond one night without giving such security as before is said, if he desires to remain in the town, that the town may receive no hurt or damage through him. And the two aldermen shall once in eight days, or in fifteen days at least, go round their ward to see that nothing be done contrary to the form aforesaid within their ward. And if there be any offender in the ward who will not submit to be attached, the sworn sergeants of the town and the aldermen [of the ward], or the whole of their ward, shall go with all their power and follow the malefactor until he be taken; and if the aldermen do not this, the town will cast the blame on them (la vile se prendra a eus).[2]

47. *Concerning the watches of the town, let them be wisely appointed and*

---

[1] In a deed of John de Bynedon (mayor in 1286) mention is made of the house which *belonged* to R. de la Prise, and in which Philip de la Prise afterwards lived. The date of the deed is July 1299 (Madox, Form., p. 382). "The corner "of R. de la Prise is the corner of the Butcher Row which leads into French "Street. See Ord. 49."

[2] Overey has 'all the ward shall go with their full power and sue the malefactors till they be taken; and if the alderman will not do so, the town shall lay the charge to the said alderman.'

*kept in all particulars in their.*—And the aldermen shall take care that the watches of the town be well kept and prudently managed in their ward.

48. *From the corner which belonged to Richard de la Prise unto New-town, two aldermen in all.*—From the corner which belonged to Richard de la Prise, and the capital messuage (great house, chief mys) which belonged to John de la Bolehouse, and unto the sea, together with Newtown Street,[1] there shall be two aldermen in the form aforesaid.

49. *For French Street to the sea two aldermen as is aforesaid.*—For all French Street, that is to say, from the corner which belonged to Richard de la Prise and Henry Brya on the other side, and on both sides of the street to the sea, there shall be two aldermen as is aforesaid.

50. *For Symenelstrete to the castle there shall be two aldermen.* — For Simnel Street with the fish-market, and the whole of Bull Street with all Wesheuthe (West Quay) to the castle, there shall be three aldermen as is before provided.

51. *Outside North-gate to Lubriestrete there shall be three aldermen.*—Outside Northgate, on both sides of the street, with Fuleflode,[2] with the Strand and Lubriestrete,[2] there shall be three aldermen in the form aforesaid.

52. *That no fisherman sell fish which has come in a ship or great boat without the alderman.*—No fisherman for the future that brings fish to the town in a ship or great boat shall unload or sell his fish before he has the bailiff's leave; and he that does so, and is attainted, shall be grievously punished. And this must be understood to extend to salted fish. The same is ordained for all other merchandise.

53. *That the alderman be chief*[3] (*cheveteyn*) *of the town and of the Guild in* [*the*] *town* (*i.e., of the town*).—The alderman is chief of the town and of the Guild, and should principally be at pains and careful to maintain the franchise, and the statutes of the Guild and of the town; and shall have the first voice in all elections and in all matters that concern the town and the Guild.

54. *And if the bailiff, or other official of the town, offend and do not right.*—[Substance repeated] or if the bailiff of the town do not justice to denizens and to strangers according to his oath, about which complaint be made, or if without complaint the matter be notoriously and publicly known, the alderman shall call together the seneschal, the echevins, and the sworn men of the town, and they shall correct such offence, and do justice [lacking] by default of the bailiff.

55. *The community may be assembled for business as often as necessary.*—[Sub-

[1] "Orchard Lane was formerly called Niewetone Lane and Niewetone Street."

[2] "There are several orchards and gardens next the shore behind the George "Inn which had probably houses belonging to them; if so, this place may be "the Full-flood mentioned. Lubrie Street seems to have some reference to "Lobery Mead at the north end of the town, and was probably the upper part "of the street without the gate which leads to that mead, and is supposed to "have had more houses in it formerly than at present."

[3] Later version (No. 5), 'The mayor shall be the principal officer of the town according to the grant, and shall be so reputed and taken, as he hath been time out of mind,' &c.

stance repeated] by the seneschal, either to execute the king's commands, or for extraordinary cause, or for the common business of the town.

56. *In case of contention [arising] between burgesses in [the] town.*—[Repeated] and complaint being made, those between whom the contention and strife have arisen shall be sent for, and he who shall have committed the offence shall be obliged quickly to make amends before the discreets, so that good peace and unity may be kept among the discreets of the town. And if any one be refractory and will not be ruled, he shall be dealt with according to the ordinances of the town.

57. *If any one, [not] an inhabitant in the town, be by the favour of the discreets there admitted.*—[Repeated] into the Guild, his heir cannot in his father's right enjoy any benefit of that favour of the Guild.

58. *If two men of the Guild bear witness [on oath] to an offence committed against the statutes.*—[Repeated] and contrary to the franchise of the town, their testimony shall stand and be believed ; and if those who so bear witness be reasonably attainted of having borne witness falsely, those who have uttered such testimony shall lose the guildship, according to the ordinances.

59. *No broker shall bring any merchant, denizen or stranger.*—[Repeated] to buy any goods if the purchaser be not a sufficient man, and both willing and able fully to pay and satisfy the seller, under pain aforesaid.

60. *No broker shall store the merchandise of strange folk or their goods.*—[Repeated] on the penalty aforesaid ; and brokers are bound by their oath to inform the alderman if a stranger buys and sells again within the town.

61. *[If] any one [of the town] buys a ship-load.*—[Repeated] of wine or corn in the gross, and a burgess of the town desires to have a tun of wine or two or three quarters of corn for his own use, he shall have it at the price for which it was bought any time while the purchased goods remain in the seller's hands.

62. *If any one of the town buy wine or other customable merchandise.*—[Repeated] between Hurst and Langston, he shall pay the custom and prisage, if the goods be purchased of a man liable to pay.

63. *No one shall [go out[1] to meet a ship bringing wine] or other merchandise coming to the town in order to [buy] anything.*— [Substance repeated] before the ship be arrived and come to anquor for unlading ; and if any one does so, and be attainted, the merchandise which he shall have bought shall be forfeited to the king.

64. *Let no one sell any fresh fish, either in the market or street, but the man who has caught it in the sea.*—It is provided by common consent (par comon conseil) of the Guild that no one shall sell any fresh fish either in the market or street, but the person who has caught it in the water, or shall have bought it without Calchesores (Calshot). And those who bring fish in a boat shall bring it all into

[1] 'Also no regratour ne go owt of towne for to engrosy þe chaffare, vpon payne for to be fourty-dayes in þe kynges prysone' (Winchester Usages). 'And that they forstalle no ffyssh by the wey, ner none other vittelle comynge to the market of the cite, from eny straunge contrey, or fro the see' (Worcester Ord.)

the market at once; and if they conceal any part of the fish in their boat, they shall lose all; and if [the fisherman] delivers any part of the fish for sale by another than himself, he shall lose all; and if any huxter-woman bring fish to sell it again, she shall lose all.

65. *No one shall buy fish before sunrise or after sunset.*—[Repeated] and if any one do so, and be thereof attainted, if he be a guildsman he shall lose his guildship, and if he be of the franchise, he shall lose his franchise and suffer imprisonment a day and a night.

66. *No one from Millbrook or elsewhere shall bring fish [from] beyond [into ?] the town of Suthamtone.*[1]—[Substance repeated] without asking leave or without paying custom; and whoever does so, and is thereof attainted, the merchandise so brought in shall be forfeited to the king.

67. *No butcher or other person shall sell the hide upon a beast elsewhere than in the town.*—[Repeated] and no one shall dress hides or dry skins if he be not a guildsman. The same is to be observed of the hides of horses, pigs, and other hides, and fresh skins of sheep, wethers, and goats.

68. *Every person who brings bread in a cart to sell shall sell that bread by [his own] hand.*[2]—[Repeated] and by no other, and if any [of such] bread be found in the hand of other, it shall be lost.

69. *No guildsman shall go on the water to meet fish coming to the town in order to buy it, and [if] any one does so.*—[Substance repeated] and buys it before the ship has arrived and come to anquor, he shall lose his guildship. And if any other who is not a guildsman be attainted of going to meet fish and buying it before the ship has arrived and is at anquor, if he be of the franchise he shall go to prison a day and a night; and if a stranger who is not of the franchise does so, he shall lose all that he has bought.

70. *No regrator of kids, lambs, birds, geese, capons, and hens.*—[Repeated] chicken, or other kind of victual of cheese, fresh butter, eggs, shall buy any kind of victuals to sell again before the hour of prime[3] sounds, nor before the discreets of the town and other free men of the country have bought their eatables. And no regrator shall go out of the town to meet any victuals coming to town to buy such; and he who does so, and is thereof attainted, shall lose what he shall have thus bought.

71. *It is provided concerning the porters of Suthamtone that they shall take.*—[Repeated] 1½d. for lodging a cask of wine in cellars upon the sea-shore, and from the shore in English Street to the lane that was Walter le Fleme[n]g's, and in French Street to the house where John de Wyte used to live, and from Westhithe

[1] Overey has 'shall bring fish *unto* the town,' which is no doubt the meaning. The words are: 'Nul ne meyne (in the body of the law ameyne) peisson outre la vile de Hamtone.'

[2] This odd law was perhaps to ensure the baker being traced should his bread be bad; for the same reason he was to put his mark on each loaf (see Winchester Usages, Eng. Guilds, p. 355, and comp. Stat. de Pistoribus (c. 1266), which orders the baker's mark on different kinds of bread.

[3] That is, six o'clock A.M.

to the cellars which belonged to Sampson del Puytȝ (of the well), and to the king's castle, and to the capital messuage[1] of the Lady Cleremond (Dame Cleremonde), where she used to live. Also for carrying a tun of wine on rope slings (poleins) or hand-barrows (lotels) from the shore aforesaid to the church of St. Cross or St. Michael's, three pence; and beyond those churches whenever they carry a cask of wine to any other place in the town, four pence, &c. . . . And the porters aforesaid shall do business for the burgesses of Hamtone before that of any stranger in all points; and if they do not, and offend in any point against the statutes aforesaid, they shall be imprisoned for a day and a night without bail, and shall not bear the office of porters for a year and a day.

72. *There shall be no broker in the town of Suthamtone without being appointed by the discreets.*—[Repeated] and being sworn thereto at the office of the brokers in the form provided, and finding good security to keep loyally his oath aforesaid, &c.

73. *If any man perform the office of a broker without having been sworn to it.*—[Repeated] no merchant, denizen or stranger, shall be obliged to pay him anything, and he shall be forbidden the office, and he shall not intermeddle with it by any means without leave of the alderman and the discreets of the town on pain of imprisonment. And the brokers shall endeavour in all kinds of merchandise, to the best of their power and on their oath, to advance the interests of the burgesses of the town in all manner of purchases and sales before all other merchants, in such manner that the profit of the burgesses of the town be made before any strange merchant is provided with goods; and they shall not show, or cause to be shown, or give notice to any strange merchant, of any kind of merchandise before the burgesses of the town are provided with it, and have refused or purchased [from] it.

74. *No sworn broker shall be both merchant and broker.*—[Repeated] nor keep a tavern for wine, nor trade at all on his own account, nor go share or be partner with any other merchant in any kind of merchandise; and if any do so, and be thereof attainted, he shall lose his broker's place.

75. *No burgess or other person shall buy or sell fundrible of seim.*—[Substance repeated] which is called 'blobbe;' it is also ordered that 'of every barrell the head shall be smitten out at the low-water mark when the clear sayme shall be drawn, and that the bottom be broke out because of corruption and divers other damages that might come of it;'[2] and if a guildsman does this, and any guilds-

[1] This house, formerly belonging to the Prior of Runceval, by gift of William, Earl of Pembroke, in the time of Henry III., had been made over by the Prior and Convent to the Lady Claremund at a rent of forty shillings a year, and after her death William of Gloucester and Richard, his brother, had entered as her heirs (Inquis. 8 Ed. I. 1279–80). The date of this part of the ordinance is therefore probably early in the reign of Edward I.

[2] This rendering is from Version No. 5. The words are: 'e que de chescún tonel seit feru hors le funȝ sus le grant mer de la mer, et ny passe pas la floudmark, quant le cleŕ seim serra hors tret, qil ne seit effonce pour corrupcion et́ pour autre gref damage que en porra avenir en la.' Dr. Speed takes *seim* to be train or fish oil; *funȝ* (which he reads *fiunȝ*) "to be a corruption from fonce: "*foncer* signifies to head a cask; *defoncer* and *effoncer*, to beat out the head."

man of the Guild bear witness to it, he shall lose the guildship; and if one of the franchise does it, he shall lose the franchise and be counted a stranger; and if any other person does so, he shall go to prison a day and a night, and find sureties who shall engage to make amends for his trespass at the award of the alderman, the echevins, the seneschal, and the sworn men.

76. *That guildsmen shall come at the hour of prime the morrow after the Guild begins.*—[Substance repeated] and he who comes not shall be fined six pence, and pay immediately; and if a guildsman comes not to the assembly in the morning, and is in the town, he shall be fined two shillings, and pay without remission.

77. *Salt herrings (com arange sale y vient).*—It is provided by common consent of the Guild that salt herrings coming to the port of Suthamton, by whomsoever brought, shall be sold in every ship at the highest price at first, according as they intend to make their profit, so that after the first price is set neither the master of the ship nor their hosts [1] (ne lour hostȝ) shall increase the price above the first sale; and whosoever does this, and thereof is attainted, all that increased price shall be forfeited to the common profit of the town without contradiction.

Such are the old Guild ordinances, which are clearly of various dates. Some of them are probably declarations of the immemorial constitution of the Guild Merchant; others are additions at a later period. The law, or rather usage, more or less consistent with the general law of the land, says Smirke, sanctioned very large and arbitrary powers of local legislation in such fraternities and other corporate bodies; powers exercised for purposes often mischievous, generally selfish, and sometimes at variance with common right. It was not until 1436–37 that this practice was restrained and put under control by statute 15 Henry IV. cap. 6, which compelled the registration of charters, &c., and the approval of ordinances; still further extended by 19 Henry VII. cap. 7 (1503–4), concerning private and unlawful statutes.

Some comparison with the charters, a brief abstract of which follows, might possibly be instituted with a view to date; at the same time, it must be borne in mind that charters were frequently nothing else than confirmations of privileges and customs which had really been used long, very long, before the concession of such charters.

[1] That is, the owners of the fish.

## Section II.—*The Charters.*

A notice[1] of the town charters from Henry II. to Charles I., whether known through the originals or by inspeximus, is contained in the present section.

1154 1189. 1. The first is that of Henry II., known by inspeximus of several kings:—

Henry, King of England, Duke of Normandy and Aquitaine, and Earl of Anjou, to his reeves and ministers of Hamton, greeting: I ordain that my men of Hanton shall have and hold their guild and all their liberties and customs, by land
1100–1135. and by sea, in as good, peaceable, just, free, quiet, and honourable a manner as they had the same better, more freely, and quietly in the time of King Henry, my grandfather; and let no one upon this do them any injury or insult. Witness, Richard de Humet, Constable, Joceline de Bailiol, at Winchester.

1189. 2. Charter of Richard I. (known by inspeximus), granting the burgesses freedom 'from toll, passage, and pontage, both by land and water, both in fairs and markets, and from all mercantile custom (de omni seculari consuetudine) in all parts of the king's dominions, both on this and the other side of the sea.' Warwick, Sept. 28 (1 R. I.)

1199 (June 26). 3. King John repeated his brother's grant: as the oldest extant charter in the hands of the town, the text is given in full:—

'Johannes, Dei gratiâ, Rex Angliæ, dominus Hiberniæ, dux Normanniæ et Aquitaniæ, comes Andegaviæ, archiepiscopis, episcopis, abbatibus, comitibus baronibus, justiciariis, vicecomitibus, præpositis, et omnibus ballivis, et fidelibus suis, salutem: Volumus et firmiter præcipimus et hâc præsenti cartâ confirmamus quod Burgenses nostri de Suhampton sint quieti de theloneo et passagio et pontagio, tam in terris quam in aquis, tam in feiris quam in mercatis, et de omni seculari consuetudine, per omnes terras nostras citra mare et ultra, et per omnem potestatem nostram, et prohibemus ne quis eos super hoc disturbet, aut injuram ullam, molestiam, aut gravamen faciat, super forisfacturam nostram in hiis quæ ad nostram pertinent potestatem. Testibus, W. Rothomagensi archiepiscopo, E. Eliensi episcopo, Willelmo Marescallo comite de Penbroke, Willelmo filio Radulfi senescallo Normanniæ, Gavin de Glapion, Rogero constabulario Cestriæ. Datum per manum H. Cantiæ archiepiscopi cancellarii nostri apud r[upem] Andel[iaci][2] xxvj die Junii anno regni nostri primo.'

1199 (June 29). 4. Three days later, as is known by inspeximus, he granted to the burgesses 'the town of Suthampton to farm for ever, with the port of Portesmues, with all the appurtenances, liberties, and free customs, and all other things which belonged to the farm of the said town in the time of King Henry our father, to hold to farm of us and our heirs for

[1] Dr. Speed has a lengthy abstract of most of the charters in Latin and English. Space forbids more than the substitution of the following notice.

[2] The scribe of the 'Book of Charters' misread this word, and has supplied over the fracture in the original charter the word 'Aurmall.' This Dr. Speed has followed in his version. The real place was no doubt the Chateau Gaillard in the Andelys.

ever, paying for it yearly into our exchequer on the Feast of St. Michael £200 sterling. Wherefore we will, &c., that the foresaid burgesses shall have and hold the aforesaid town, with the aforesaid port of Portesmues, &c., for that farm. Aurivall, 29th June (1 John).

5. A confirmation by Henry III. (original) of the town at fee-farm, 1227. together with the port of Portsmues. Date May 3 (11 Henry III.)

6. Charter of freedom from toll, as 1 Ric. I., &c. Dated as last, 1227. May 3 (11 Hen. III.)[1]

7. Charter (original) of freedom from the power of the Cinque Ports. 1252. The barons of the Cinque Ports are enjoined to take no cark in the port of Southampton and Portsmouth, nor execute attachment, or do them injury contrary to their liberties and customs: 'if ye do otherwise, we shall not dissemble our displeasure, but shall levy the penalty on you and your goods with severity.' Westm., 14th May (36 H. III.)

8. Charter (original) of freedom from arrest in their persons or 1256. goods for any debt for which the burgesses are not either sureties or principal debtors, unless it shall happen that the debtors be of their body and have wherewithal to satisfy their debts in whole or in part, and that the burgesses fail of doing justice to the creditors of the said debtors. Bristol, 14th July (40 H. III.)[2]

9. Charter (known by inspeximus) granting or confirming a 1256. town court and the election of coroners: prohibition to sheriffs of county, &c., to interfere. Burgesses not to be impleaded out of their borough for any tenements or chattels within the liberties. Dated as last, Bristol, 14th July (40 H. III.)[3]

10. Charter of Edward II.[4] (known by inspeximus) confirming 1317.

---

[1] Charter Rolls, 11 H. III., p. 1, m. 7.

[2] Dr. Speed explains this charter by a reference to the ordinances of the Guild Merchant, where (Ord. 27) the Guild are required to look into the goodness of the security offered for debts—as in statute merchant—and he suggests that some person who had lost money by a debtor whose security had been allowed by the Guild had sued the Guild for the debt, and that this charter was granted to prevent such suits in future. The Municipal Corporations Commissioners (1835) suggest that the charter might have reference to a custom which seems to have once prevailed, by which a Corporation, a member of which had a claim on a member of another Corporation, seized the goods of any freeman of the latter found within the jurisdiction of the former 'in Withernam,' until the Corporation to which the debtor belonged, or the debtor himself, made satisfaction.

[3] By writ of November 11, 1226, the same king had prohibited the holding of any court of pleas outside the town of Southampton and against its liberties, touching tenements in the town, otherwise than courts used to be held there in the times of Henry II., Richard I., and John: any such causes were to be removed from the county to the town, to be terminated there, as had been accustomed (Close Roll).

[4] Dr. Speed observes that there must have been a charter of Edward I., since he finds (Seymour's Survey of London, ii. 154) that the town was seized into the king's hands, 18 Ed. I., for wounding a king's bailiff while serving a

former charters, and granting freedom from murages and pavages in all parts of the kingdom. Westm., 28th March (10 Ed. II.)

1327. 11. Charter of 1 Edward III. (known by exemplification of Westm., 14 Ed. III. April 4, 1340, on account of the original being burnt) granting immunity from loss of privilege on account of non-use; confirming 40 H. III. Burgesses not to sue or be sued out of the borough; not to be put with strangers or strangers with them on juries about land, &c.; such juries to be held in the borough by the burgesses themselves. Freedom from quayage in all parts of the kingdom. Westm., 28th March (1 Ed. III.)

1383. 12. Charter of Richard II. (original) inspecting and confirming former charters, but making no new grant. Westm., 5th Nov. (7 R. II.)

1401. 13. Charter of Henry IV. (known by inspeximus and Rot. Chart. 2 H. IV. p. 1, No. 7) confirming former charters. Granting town court, cognisance of pleas, real, personal, and mixed, as well those held by assize or certification as of all others whatsoever concerning lands, &c., in the town and liberties, by land or sea: to be held in the Guildhall (Guyhalda). Confirmation of court leet. Grant of goods of felons [1] from among the landholders or residents within the town and liberties. Grant of fines on trespasses, and on purprestures by land or water. Grant of all wastes. Appointment of justices (see below under 'Courts'); county justices not to interfere. Assize of bread, beer, and other victuals; assay of weights and measures; and the exercise of all duties belonging to the office of clerk of the market. Westm., 29th Jan. (2 H. IV.)[2]

1414. 14. Charter of confirmation by Henry V. (known by inspeximus and Rot. Chart. 2 H. V. p. 2, No. 8),[3] with provision for immunity against non-use. Westm., 30th Dec. (2 H. V.)

---

writ, after which the farm was increased by £20. This seems to be the circumstance detailed in Rot. Parl. i. 58 a, where no date is given; but is it not the same as that referred to in the patent of 4 Edward I.? See above, p. 33.

[1] Dr. Speed refers to the case of Peter James (Madox, F. B. p. 208), who when late mayor in the first part of the reign of Henry VI., "was sued in the "Court of Exchequer for £20, the value of the goods of an inhabitant of the town "convicted for felony, which he had seized. He pleaded this charter of 2 H. "IV., confirmed by 2 H. V. and 4 H. VI. But the court notwithstanding ad-"judged that he should be charged to the king with the said £20. The felon "was indeed convicted out of the town, but the charter 2 H. IV. directs that "the mayor, &c., shall have the felon's goods 'ubicunque justicia de eo fieri "debeat,' wherever he shall be convicted. Perhaps the felony was committed "out of the town, which might alter the case."

[2] Two grants are extant, dated respectively February 13 and February 12 (2 H. IV.), for the purchase of £100 a year, and for acquiring lands to that amount.

[3] The Corporation possesses an exemplification of charters, dated 4th October (4 H. IV.) 1416.

15. Charter of confirmation by Henry VI. (original), made by consent of Parliament, 1 H. VI., but dated Westm., 24th October (4 H. VI.) 1425.

16. Charter of incorporation, 23 Henry VI., sets forth as usual the heavy charges of the town from its being liable to the attacks of enemies and from its large fee-farm: in consequence the town is now 'INCORPORATED for ever of one mayor, two bailiffs, and burgesses, to be one community perpetual, incorporate in word and deed, by the name of the MAYOR, BAILIFFS, AND BURGESSES;' to be fit in law to prosecute all pleas, &c., to acquire and hold lands, &c. Provision for the election of mayor and bailiffs on the Friday before St. Matthew's Day each year, and in case of death, deposition, &c., within fifteen days after such vacancy. Mayor to be escheator, and no other to interfere. Right of imprisonment. Grant for further ease of the town, 'and of the port of Portsmouth, which port is within the liberty of the said town of Southampton,' that they shall be exempt for ever from obedience to the constable, marshal, or admiral of England, or the steward, and marshal, or clerk of the market, who shall by no means enter the town to hold pleas, or hold pleas out of the town concerning matters within the same. The mayor, &c., to be clerk of the market. Strangers prohibited from buying of, or selling to, strangers. Grant of staple, and election of mayor and two constables of the staple on the Friday before the Feast of St. Matthew each year, with proviso as above in case of death, &c. Election permitted of brokers, packers, porters, carriers, &c., as in times past. May have goods of outlaws and persons attainted within the town and its liberties. Freed from king's purveyors. Westm., 29th July (23 H. VI.)[1] 1445. Portsmouth.

17. Charter of 25 Henry VI. (original) creating the county. The merchants and mariners of the town being incommoded by the sheriff of the county serving writs on them, this charter grants, in consideration of the premises, and of the heavy fee-farm of 340 marks (£226, 13s. 4d.), 'that our said town, with the port and precinct thereof, and the port of Portsmouth,[2] which is now called the town of Southampton and its precincts, shall be one entire COUNTY, incorporated in word and deed, separate and distinct from the county of 1447. Portsmouth.

[1] A writ is extant for not molesting the mayor, &c., and of fines granted by charter, dated 3d February (20 H. VI.) 1442.

[2] On the margin of this charter is written in a later hand, with recollections of old controversies with Portsmouth: 'Note, how farre the countie of the town of Suthampton doth strech;' and just below, 'The porte of Portismouthe is parte of the countye and of the towne of Suthampton.' The above charter provides towards its close that 'no prejudice, under pretence of this our grant, shall accrue to the bailiffs, &c., of Portesmuth with regard to any privileges granted to or used by them in times past.'

Southampton for ever,' and shall be called 'OUR COUNTY OF THE TOWN OF SOUTHAMPTON.' Sheriff to be chosen each year on the Friday before St. Matthew's Day, and certified by the mayor to the barons of the Exchequer: in case of death, &c., a new one to be chosen within ten days and certified as above. The sheriff to hold a county court (see under 'Courts'). Burgesses not to be made assessors or collectors of taxes out of the town. Westm., 9th March (25 H. VI.)

1451. 18. Charter of 30 Henry VI. in confirmation of former grants (original). And further, mayor to have authority to perform all acts which belong to the offices of steward and marshal of the household and admiral of England within the town and precincts. Westm., 12th Sept. (30 H. VI.)

1452. In the following year, notwithstanding charters, a dispute having occurred with the justices of the county, a writ was issued from the king to John de Wyncestre and his colleagues, the justices appointed to hear and determine concerning the offences of workmen and dyers in the county of Southampton, setting forth a complaint of the burgesses that whereas they had always enjoyed, and ought to have, the power of assize of bread and beer, and the fines and amercements of shoemakers, clothiers, dyers, and other artisans, as also of butchers, fishmongers, salt merchants, regrators, and other victuallers, in aid of their fee-farm of £200 per annum, the justices were intending to levy such fines on pretence of their commission: the justices were hereby warned that the contention of the burgesses had been maintained in the Parliament at Westminster; they were therefore commanded not to molest the burgesses, but permit them to have all those fines, as in times past, in aid of their farm. Westm., 12th Oct. (31 H. VI.)[1]

1461. 19. Charter of Edward IV. (original). In consideration of the expenses of the mayor, &c., in the frequent defence of the town, which is one of the most ancient in the kingdom, and has frequently shown its loyalty to former kings, and 'particularly very lately to ourselves,' former charters are confirmed and additional privileges stated to be given. Appointment or confirmation of town court, pie powder court, justices' court, court leet (see under 'Courts'). Exemption from serving on juries, &c., out of the town. Resistance authorised against the king's officers, clerk of the market, or admiral attempting to carry out any act of their office within the town or precincts. Westm., 16th Dec. (1 Ed. IV.)[2]

---

[1] Oak Book. Dr. Speed has given the document *in extenso.* It is here very considerably abridged.

[2] The cost of this charter is thus given in the Steward's Book :—'Payd for confyrmacyon of our newe Schartter by the honde of Richard Aysche, viiij$^{li.}$ ix$^{s.}$ Also

20. Charter of confirmation[1] (known by Inspeximus) of chart. 1468.
23 H. VI. 'late king in fact but not by right:' no additional grant. Date 12th June (8 Ed. IV).

21. Ratification (known by inspeximus) of charter 1 Ed. IV. 1480.
Westm., 20th August (20 Ed. IV.)

22. Charter of Richard III. (original) confirming Edward IV.'s con- 1484.
firmation of former charters. Westm., 10th Dec. (2 R. III.)

23. Charter of Henry VII. (known by inspeximus of 2 Henry VIII.) No date appears.[2]

24. Charter of confirmation by Henry VIII. (original). Westm., 1510.
2d Oct. (2 Hen. VIII.)

25. Charter reciting and confirming (original) that of 8 Ed. IV. 1514.
Date Westm., 23d Nov. (6 H. VIII.)

26. Charter of Edward VI. (known by following exemplification)[3] 1552.
regulating and limiting the payment of the fee-farm thus:—When the petty customs in any year shall amount to £200, or when any ships called carracks of Genoa or galleys of Venice shall come to the port to ship or unship cargo, the full fee-farm of £200 is to be paid; but when the petty customs fall below £200, and when no such ships make their appearance, the farm is to be but £50, rendered at the Exchequer on the Feast of St. Michael the Archangel. And the king remits arrears in consideration of the burdens borne by the mayor, &c., and of the present poverty, decay, and ruinous condition of the town and inhabitants; as well on account of the repairs of the walls and forts called 'bullwerkes,' now in a ruinous state and demanding attention, as also on account of the town being a frontier lying on the sea-coast towards Normandy, France, and other southern parts, and thus properly situated to oppose foreign enemies, which the mayors, &c., have been always ready to do and will do in future. And the charter directs that they shall certify to the barons of the Exchequer at least before the fifteenth day after the Feast of St. Michael what the petty

---

payd for the fyne of the same by Rychard Aysche xl$^{s.}$ and for the lace xx$^{d.}$ Allso payd for the wrytyng of the same Schartter liij$^{s.}$ iiij$^{d.}$: also for enrolling of the same Schartter xl$^{s}$. Summa iiij$^{li.}$ xiij$^{s.}$ iiij$^{d.}$ Also payd to a manne for to seke up dyverse of owre old Schartterys by Rychard Aysche x$^{s.}$'

[1] The Steward's Book of 1469 records a fine on a man for suing another out of the franchise.

[2] In 1501 (16 H. VII.) the bailiffs of the sheriff of the county (Hants) were imprisoned for arresting a man within the town liberties. 'Item [received] of the Shryf of Hamptonshire, John Philpot, for bycause his servaunts and baylifs entered within oure ffranchise to arest a man, and were putt in prison, and so remayned tyll the sayd Shryf came to this towne in propria persona and entreatid the Towne, and for a knowlege of a fyne gave to the Towne x$^{s.}$' (MS. Temp. T. Overey, sub ann.)

[3] The charter is enrolled, Pat. 6 Ed. VI. p. 6. m. 3, &c.

customs have been, and whether such ships have or have not come to the port; and failing this, the whole £200 fee-farm shall be rendered. Dated 4th April (6 Ed. VI.)

1553. 27. Exemplification of the foregoing (original), the town having been charged with the full amount for the previous year, from which they obtained release. Westm., 27th April (7 Ed. VI.)

28. Charter of Philip and Mary[1] (known by inspeximus of 14th James I.): no date appears.

29. Charter of Elizabeth (known as above): no date appears.

1616. 30. Charter of confirmation (original). Date, 15th June (14 James I.)

1640. 31. The last governing charter,[2] of 16 Charles I. (original). The heads are as follows:—The incorporation as in 23 H. VI.; election of officers; in case of refusal to serve, others to be elected within twenty days after the Feast of St. Matthew; appointment of recorder, by that name for the first time; mayor given a casting vote in elections; deposition of mayor provided for by recorder, aldermen, and common council; deposition of aldermen and bailiffs; new officers to be chosen; mayor to be escheator as in 23 H. VI.; appointment of coroner as in 40 H. III.; the precincts ordered to be the same as before, and town granted to farm for ever, together with the port of Portsmouth; limitation and release of the fee-farm as in 6 Ed. VI.; rate of petty customs to remain as before; the town made a county, with sheriff and county court, as in 25 H. VI.; a staple appointed, &c., as in 23 H. VI.; appointment of brokers, porters, &c., as in same; mayor, &c., to have cognisance of pleas as in 2 H. IV., and hold courts as in 1 Ed. IV.; to be clerk of the market as in 23 H. VI.; to have assize of bread, &c., as in 2 H. IV.; appointment of justices (see under 'Courts'); provision for removal; confirmation of court leet; fines, &c., in aid of fee-farm, as in 2 H. IV.; not to be put on juries outside town, as in 1 Ed. IV., nor made assessors, &c., as in 25 H. VI., nor constables, &c., out of the town; to be free of toll, passage, &c., as in 1 R. I.; not to be impleaded out of the borough as in 40 H. III.; not to be put on juries with strangers or strangers with them, as in 1 Ed. III.; freed from murage and pavage as in 10 Ed. II., and from quayage as in 1 Ed. III.; to hold lands, &c., as in 23 H. VI., but not to exceed the amount of £100 a year; mayor to execute office of steward, marshal, and of

---

1 In this reign the Corporation received grants on the importation of sweet wines, which were afterwards confirmed by Acts of Parliament (see under 'Trade').

2 The cost of this charter was £219, 17s. (Journal, 1641, f. 308). It appears to have been read in the House in English for the first time on September 2, 1640; after reading, it was put into the great chest with the English paper copy. This last seems to have disappeared.

admiral, as in 30 H. VI.; appointment of court of admiralty (see under 'Courts'); foreign bought and sold as in 23 H. VI.; confirmation of gauging and weighing; freedom from prisage all over the kingdom as by Act of Parl. 23 H. VIII.; appointment of common council to consist of mayor, recorder, aldermen, bailiffs, and sheriff, and all who have held those offices, for ever, to assist the mayor, with power to make statutes, bye-laws, &c.; appointment of a court of orphans; appointment of town-clerk or common clerk of the town, who shall be clerk of the peace and sessions, and have fees; four sergeants-at-mace; fines for refusal to take office in the town; powers of Corporation to tax the inhabitants; piccage and stallage to be paid by strangers; one or more prisons to be kept in the town; a corn-market to be held every Thursday; mayor, &c., to take tolls. No person who has been mayor obliged to bear arms in person. For the benefit of sailors and fishermen, and the bettering of navigable streams, mayor, &c., may cleanse all creeks and rivers leading to the town, or within the liberties where the tide flows, and take the soil for their own use. The town having incurred a quo warranto in the Court of Exchequer, brought against them in Trinity term, May 29,[1] 1635, for the exercise of divers liberties, privileges, &c., without any warrant or royal grant; and having answered nothing in bar or abatement of the information, through Martin Boothby, their attorney, judgment went against them, as follows: 'That all and every one of the said liberties, franchises, and privileges set forth in the said information should be from that time taken and seized into our hands, and in our hands should remain, and be quite extinguished and taken away; and that the said mayor, bailiffs, and burgesses should be distrained to make fine with us for their use and usurpation upon us of the said liberties, privileges, and franchises.'[2] By the present charter all penal consequences of this judgment were remitted, together with all trespasses, contempts, and misbehaviour of the mayor, bailiffs, and burgesses, and confirmation was granted of all liberties, privileges, &c., contained in any Act of Parliament, letters patent, or charters not specially altered by these presents. Westm., 27th June (16 Charles I.)

Soon after the Restoration, namely, in May 1661 (13 Car. II.), the House considered the desirability of renewing the last charter or pro- Question of renewal of charter.

[1] Q. R. Mem. Rolls, Trin. 11 Car. I. No. 37.

[2] Dr. Speed conjectures that this quo warranto may have been brought against the town for their having neglected to certify to the Exchequer the amount of petty customs in that year, no account of which appears; and he suggests that the omission may have been designed with a view to their application for a new charter.

curing a fresh one[1]: a question which from this time periodically exercised the Corporation.

Towards the end of the reign (Nov. 7, 1683, 35 Car. II.), a committee, consisting of the mayor, Dr. Speed, and others, was appointed to examine again the affairs of the town in relation to their charter. In Trinity term that year, June 1683, the franchises and liberties of the City of London had been seized into the king's hands as forfeited on a quo warranto in the King's Bench, and the boroughs were made to feel that their privileges granted or acquired of old time would be subject to revision by the crown; accordingly they were invited to surrender their charters with a view to renewal on what, it was represented, would be favourable terms; the object of the crown being to obtain a direct hold over all municipal elections. On November 23d the committee wrote, through Sir Benjamin Newland, one of the M.P.s for the borough, to Sir Lionel Jenkins, the principal Secretary of State, excusing themselves on the score of poverty for not immediately surrendering their charter.

As a Corporation they had ever been anxious to show their loyalty, but now to their sorrow could only look on and approve of their neighbours' deeds, who had laid their charters at his Majesty's feet. At a Common Council held on the 7th they had agreed to this step, but on examining the charges consequent on such action, they found themselves wholly unable to proceed. True, Southampton had been a rich place heretofore, but a series of misfortunes had brought it low. The late rebellion had robbed the Chamber of all public money; the plague had consumed their inhabitants, of whom no less than seventeen hundred had died; the Dutchmen[2] had spoiled them of nearly all their ships; and lately the Act of Prohibition[3] had rendered their looms useless, and families hitherto prosperous were now added to the public burden. Added to this the revenues of the town were incredibly sunk; the sweet wine duty, which had formerly brought them £200 per annum, now scarcely yielded £6, and the Corporation had difficulty in meeting their liabilities, as also in paying the great rent[4] to the king of £67, and keeping up the walls and defences, bulwarks, quays, and sea-banks, the cost of which the king's progenitors had been so mindful of that they had remitted £150 of the old rent when the trade of the port was far greater and the other burdens were less. Finally, since they were unable to defray the cost of a surrender, they begged his honour 'soe to represent their condition to his most sacred Majesty that the true cause of their tardiness in delivering up their charter may be known to be the want of money, not of loyalty.'

---

[1] Journal, May 8.

[2] This was probably in 1667, when the Dutch forced their way up the Thames and did much damage along the south coast. But the injury from them to the Southampton trade was not of course confined to one year.

[3] Reference is perhaps to 29 and 30 Car. II. cap. 1, sec. 70, &c.

[4] The fee-farm does not seem, however, to have been paid directly to the crown at the date of this letter (see under 'Fee-Farm').

Meanwhile the Council determined, in case his Majesty still desired a surrender, not to wait for a quo warranto, but to yield at once and get a new charter on the best terms they could. On December 13th, Dr. Owen Wynne, secretary to Sir Lionel Jenkins, replied to the Council:—

That Sir Lionel had moved his Majesty to renew their charter gratis; that the king had been 'pleased to declare, That the town of Southampton being now a town and county, the necessity of trying there all causes arising within the town is a great trouble to the judges and a grievance to the people: That his Majesty is of opinion that that franchise of being a county being surrendered among others, it should be united to the body of Hantshire: That all other liberties, excepting that of being a town and county, should be saved and restored.' On such terms his Majesty would consent to their having a new charter for nothing, if they could not come up to half fees, the rate at which other poor Corporations had renewed.

The House agreed to the king's terms; on September 8, 1684, the instrument was sealed surrendering their charter, with all their lands, tenements, patents, and grants, and the petition for a new one signed; and on November 25 letters of attorney under the town seal empowered Dr. Speed, Owen Wynne, Esq., and James Crosse, or any one of them, to act on the town's behalf in obtaining the new charter. The king's death occurred on the following February and the matter fell through.

*The House agrees to extinguishment.*

James II. following the policy of the preceding king in regard to the Corporations, a quo warranto dated November 28 (3 Jas. II.), 1687, was issued against the town, calling upon the mayor and bailiffs to appear at Westminster and answer for their liberties, privileges, and franchises. This document was exhibited to the mayor by the under-sheriff, Richard Good, just half an hour before noon at the Council meeting on January 23, 1687–88. Thrown into consternation by this hostile move, which however could not have been unexpected, the Council sought the aid of the recorder, and took care to dispatch a messenger that night. On February 9 they wrote the Attorney-General, that having been served with a quo warranto, they had resolved to make no defence, but humbly submit the charter to his Majesty's mercy; they said that nothing but their poverty had hindered the renewal of their franchises before, which had been promised by his late Majesty on very gracious terms; and at the present time poverty alone hindered their action, since they could not meet the necessary charges; they begged that their suffering judgment to pass by default might not be interpreted unfavourably; they had been advised to that course as most submissive to the king, least troublesome to the Attorney-General, and easiest for themselves. Towards the end of the year it was understood that the quo warranto would not be pressed; and on November

*Quo Warranto.*

*They submit.*

5, 1688, the recorder was desired to employ some one 'to see that a noli prosequi be entered upon the quo warranto brought against the town,' and for this the Corporation were ready to disburse.

September 1688.

Meanwhile "a new charter" had actually been prepared, and, according to Dr. Speed, "was sent to Southampton and lodged, as "tradition says, in some private hands among the dissenters, in order "to be produced at a proper time; but as the attempt [of the king to "repeal the Test Act failed] it was stifled and cancelled. It is now in "the hands of the Corporation."

Proposed charter of James II.

The following are the heads of the intended charter of James II. (original):—The ancient franchises of the town having, for various abuses, been seized into the king's hands by a judgment on a quo warranto, a new charter is granted on petition of the inhabitants as follows:—The town and precincts to be a distinct county. The mayor, &c., may hold lands, sue and be sued; may have a common seal and change it at pleasure. A Common Council, to consist of mayor, recorder, thirteen[1] aldermen, and twelve burgesses, one supervisor of the customs, and one common clerk. Mayor to be chosen from the aldermen, who are to be continued as before. Common Council may make laws, &c. The mayor, recorder, four senior aldermen, and four burgesses, to be justices. Three justices (the mayor and recorder or deputy being two) may take cognisance of trespasses, &c., but not of crimes involving loss of life or limb without special commission. Mayor may have a deputy from among the aldermen. On death or removal of any officer, another to be chosen in manner used during the previous seven years. Lawful for the king, by order, and under seal of Privy Council, to remove any officer or burgess. Lawful, within twenty days of such removal, or death, on royal letters mandatory, to choose, admit, and swear any one or more, on the nomination of the king, into the vacant places; and however small the number attending, after proper notice lawful for them to elect such person or persons named in the letters mandatory. Elections contrary to the tenor of these presents void. Dispensation to all officers and burgesses from taking the oath of the king's supremacy, and the oath of allegiance, and the oath in the Act of Parliament 'for regulating Corporations' (13 Car. II.), and from receiving the sacrament of the Lord's Supper, and from subscription in the Act 25 Car. II. 'against Popish recusants, &c.' No recorder or common clerk to be admitted to office without royal approbation under seal. Corporation may possess manors, &c., under £100 a year. After the perfecting of this charter new securities to be given for their debts.

---

[1] "The charter recites the names of the thirteen new aldermen and the "twelve new burgesses, and many of them were dissenters."

Confirmation of all ancient privileges not altered by these presents. Dated 15th September (4 James II.)

The rectification of the old charter in some particulars long continued a question, and the Corporation occasionally went to some expense in the matter. On September 6, 1723, a petition for a new charter was agreed to by a majority of the House and received the town seal; a confirmation of all former grants was requested, together with such additional franchises as the king might see fit. Nothing, however, came of this action, and the charter of 16 Charles I. (1640) continued in force till the Municipal Corporations Act (5 and 6 Will. IV. cap. 76), 1835.

Further questions of renewal.

## Section III.—*Municipal Offices.*

At the commencement of the thirteenth century we find Southampton governed by the king's bailiffs, two or three in number. To these officers the king directed his writs on every conceivable occasion; about repairs to the king's houses, his cellars, highway, his gaol; about his farm, or sending the royal alms from it to the proper quarters, or making advances from it on the king's behalf; about royal licences given to particular persons to trade in Southampton; about sending ships on the royal errands, or preparing men and horses to accompany the king; about arresting ships in the port during the king's will, or the chattels and bodies of men; about paying the king's debts, or carrying his wine about the country, making his good will known to foreign merchants, and giving them permission to come to the port of Southampton; about murages and other reliefs to the town. At this early period there was also a constable of Southampton, who probably was the military governor (see under 'Castle').[1] But it is equally clear that early in the same century an officer styled the mayor was frequently at the head of affairs.

### *Of the Mayor.*

1. There was certainly a 'mayor' about 1217, and Benedict Ace ruled in that capacity at least from 1237 to 1249. At the end of this long tenure of office, whether or not in reflection on its late possessor, the burgesses obtained by royal patent (22d October 1249) the curious grant that neither they nor their successors should at any time be governed by a mayor.[2] 1217.

[1] In 1199 (10 Ric. I.) the men of Southampton were tallaged by Hubert, Archbishop of Canterbury, Chief Justicier, at fifty marks for the retaining of serjeants (see Madox, Excheq., i. 705).

[2] Pat. 33 H. III. m. 2. Rex omnibus, &c., salutem. Sciatis quod con-

Election.

The election of the mayor, as also of the two bailiffs, no doubt in accordance with ancient precedent, was ordered by the charter of formal incorporation, July 1445 (23 H. VI.), to take place each year on the Friday before the Feast of St. Matthew. The electors were the burgesses. However, in a patent fifteen years later (December 1460), we find that the method of election was in reality much more restricted. By a custom, there reported to have existed from time immemorial, the outgoing mayor, on the Friday before St. Matthew's Day, in the presence of the bailiffs and burgesses in the Guildhall, nominated two burgesses, one of whom was to be chosen as his successor by the assembly.[1] In spite, however, of this nomination, the mayor himself might be re-elected. The following incident drew forth the patent:—In 1460 Richard Gryme, the outgoing mayor, had made choice of Nicholas Holmehegge and Walter Fetplace, and had submitted them, according to ancient custom, to the assembly for an election to the mayoralty for the ensuing year, when certain burgesses—Andrew James, Thomas Payn, John Payn, jun., and Walter Bargate, with the assistance of Robert Bagworth, the sheriff, and Walter Aylward—protested against the old manner of election in the following energetic fashion: A set of riotous and badly disposed persons, to the number of a hundred or more, collected together by influence of the above, rushed to the Guildhall, and with daggers drawn and menacing cries broke in upon the assembly, interrupted the proceedings, caused Robert Bagworth to be elected, and bringing him in triumph on their shoulders, placed him in the chief magistrate's seat as mayor. The patent called forth by these turbulent proceedings pronounced the old custom of election to be good, and directed it to be observed as heretofore, and a mayor to be chosen accordingly. We are not informed what immediately transpired, but the popular voice so far prevailed that Robert Bagworth became mayor for the ensuing year, and Walter Aylward was sheriff.[2]

Private nomination.

The above custom was at some time or other varied for a practice which Dr. Speed knew and thus describes:—"There is one part of the "ceremony relating to the election of the mayor which is founded "wholly upon custom, being mentioned in no charter. It is called "the 'private nomination.' The form of it is this: On the Friday "before the Feast of St. Bartholomew [August 24] the mayor and "aldermen meet in the Audit-house, and put two aldermen and two

cessimus Burgensibus nostris de Suhampton quod ipsi et eorum hæredes aliquo tempore non habeant majorem in prædicta villa nostra de Suhampton. In cujus, &c. Westm., Oct. 22.

1 That is, the court, 'Ad curiam "assemble" vulgariter nuncupatam' (1413), 'at the assemble holden in the Guyhald' (1482).

2 Pat. (Dec. 1, 1460) 39 H. VI. m. 13.

"junior burgesses upon nomination for mayor, or they put any four "burgesses;[1] and on the morning of the day of election, the Friday "before St. Matthew [September 21], the same persons meet together "and strike off two of those four; the remaining two are proposed to all "the burgesses for one of them to be elected mayor by balloting." It was usual, however, before this was done, for the outgoing mayor to let it be known which of the two names it was desired should stand. The ballot which followed was generally a matter of form. "Of what "antiquity this private nomination is I cannot find; the proceedings "of it are enrolled. It is mentioned in the mayor's accounts as a "thing of course in 19 Elizabeth 1587; and I have seen the rolls of it "as far back as 1615. Notwithstanding which, it appears by the "Journal that in 1617 two of the burgesses at the election of the "mayor openly in the Town-hall opposed the ancient custom of the "private nomination, but being called before the Common Council "for the same, they submitted. In 1724 the burgesses again opposed "it, when Chief Justice Eyre, who had been recorder of the town "twenty years, and had quitted that office the year before, was present, "and declared that the custom was good in law, and that it ought to "be kept up.[2] When any burgess is put upon election for mayor, he "is continued three years, if not chosen before the expiration of that "time; and after being rejected three times, he is laid by till his turn "comes round again."

The above custom of private nomination was continued till the passing of the Municipal Corporations Reform Act of 1835, under which, according to a uniform rule provided therein for all boroughs, and extended by the Act of 1882, the mayors are elected by the Council each 9th November from among the aldermen or councillors, or persons qualified to be such, so that previously to election the mayor need not have been a member of the Corporation.

The duties and importance[3] of the office of mayor grew with the Dignity of the office.

[1] It seems to have been usual previously to the Municipal Corporations Reform Act (1835) to place in nomination the two senior aldermen who had not served the office of mayor twice, and the two senior burgesses who had served as sheriff but not as mayor.

[2] In 1759 it was ordered, on account of some laxity in apparel, that the aldermen should attend at the private nominations in their scarlet gowns, and that the mace and oar should be borne before the mayor on his way to and from the Audit-house; that the town-clerk should also attend in his gown (Journal, August 17).

[3] It need hardly be said that affronts to the mayor were heavily visited. As a specimen the following appraisement for 'unfittyng wordes to y$^{e}$ meyer be a borges' may be noted:—'Item [received] of Jamys Grace for a fyne for gevyng unfitting wurdes vnto me the sayde meyre the tyme of my meyraltie, and after agreed yn the Audite howse for iiij$^{li}$. xiij$^{s}$. iiij$^{d}$.'

privileges of the town. Besides his former judicial and administrative functions, the mayor by the charter of formal incorporation (23 Hen. VI.) was made king's escheator; and the town was exempted from obedience to any constable, marshal, or admiral of England, or to the steward and marshal or clerk of the royal household, who were to hold no pleas within the town or liberties, or within the port of Portsmouth, which was included in the town's jurisdiction; but the mayor himself was to be clerk of the market; and the town being at this time made a staple, and permission given to choose each year a mayor and two constables of the staple on the Friday before St. Matthew's Day, the chief officer of the town in point of fact became the mayor of the staple, with all the necessary attributes of that office, and the bailiffs were the constables.

By charter 25 Henry VI. (March 1447), the town with its liberties and port was made a county, power being consequently given to elect a sheriff, to be certified by the mayor to the barons of the Exchequer. Five years later (30 Hen. VI.) the authority and office of steward and marshal of the household and admiral of England within the town, liberties, and port of the town and county, were conferred upon the mayor.

In charter 1 Edward IV. (1461) the presidency of the mayor over the various courts is set forth. The charter of 16 Charles I. (June 1640)—the governing charter till 1835—re-granted in particular every privilege which had before been enjoyed, with certain variations and additions. In the grant of admiralty an appeal was given to the Lord High Admiral of England. The mayor was made gauger and weigher of goods at the king's standard. By the same charter the Common Council, with the mayor at its head, was newly defined; a court of orphans was instituted; and the dignity of the mayor's office was consulted by the permission that no person who had filled the chair should be obliged to bear arms in person, but might always be permitted to find a suitable deputy. Previously to 1835 the mayor was always appointed one of the four aldermen of wards, and one of the auditors of accounts; he was also appointed aulnagar, that is, measurer or superintendent over the assize of cloth, one of the keepers of the town keys and of the great chest, and one of the supervisors of land: these offices were entirely nominal. Since the Act of 1835 the duties of the mayoralty have been laid down for all boroughs, and need not be here detailed. Among various official acts which the mayor has been called upon to perform was that of the solemnisation, or rather legalising, of marriages during the Commonwealth period—a duty placed upon him in common with other magistrates by Cromwell's Act, dated 24th August 1653, which prescribed that banns of matrimony should be published in the nearest market on three several days, and that the ceremony should be performed by a justice of the peace, whilst a registrar was appointed in every parish for the purposes of registration. Thus we find in the church registers, from the above date till the Restoration, marriages constantly performed by the mayors, Horne, Pitt, Clungeon, Scale, Capelin; also by the mayor of Winchester, and by various other justices of the peace, not only of the town and neighbourhood, but of Salisbury and other places. Among the town burgesses whom we find thus most frequently employed appear to be Peter Le Gay, Thomas Cornelius, Christopher Walleston, Robert Wroth, Joseph De la Motte.

Allowances.

Formerly, like the members of Parliament, the mayors received remuneration. Under 1481 we find £10 per annum assigned to the mayor of old custom. In 1505 John Fleming, mayor, was ordered to receive the same, provided that no mayor in future had anything to do with the town's money. In 1617 the allowance, which had been £20 since 1578, was increased to £50, and in 1623, on account of the town's indebtedness, reduced to £30, viz., £20, the older sum, and £10 instead of the privilege of making a burgess. In 1726 the allowance of £20 was taken away: it is stated to have been originally granted when the town had £500 at interest, and might be restored when the Corporation should have £400 at interest: this occurred later. Dr. Speed says of his time: "The perquisites of the mayor's "office are very small, depending chiefly on the will of the Common "Council, who have sometimes ordered a sum of money for the "mayor's table, never exceeding £50, generally much less. At other "times they have ordered some articles of the public money of the "Corporation to be given to the mayor, which last is continued still, "but it amounts to no great matter. The mayor has likewise the "liberty of making one burgess in his year, and the price for admis-"sion is the mayor's perquisite: but all these things depend on the "will of the burgesses, who have frequently altered them. The mayor "has besides some port dues, but they are trifling." In 1802, instead of the dues on corn and coals, then discontinued, the mayor was allowed twenty-five guineas per annum. In the depression of 1830 all dinners, perquisites, and even the daily newspaper hitherto taken in for the mayor, were stopped.

Instances of the mayor creating burgesses are numerous. In 1501 (17 Hen. VII.) he was permitted to make a burgess by way of wiping off a debt of £10 owed him by the town. In 1534 (26 Hen. VIII.) Anthony Guidotti, merchant, of Florence, afterwards knighted for his services to the state, April 1550, was made mayor's burgess, but was crossed out, together with Giles Hashert, by Mr. Baker, mayor, because they were strangers, and had been made burgesses by Mr. Huttoft without the consent of his brethren, contrary to the order of the town.[1]

The mayor has no perquisites at the present day, but it would be lawful for him to receive such remuneration as the Council might think fit.

Deposition.

"Though the form of deposing the mayor be directed by the "charter (16 Charles I.), yet there is no instance of it being done by "the Corporation without the intervention of superior power. In 2 "Edward IV. (1463) a mayor was deposed by the king's mandamus. "But since the charter of Charles I. the only instances are that A.D. "1665 William Higgins, mayor, and some others, were expelled the "Corporation by order of Cromwell and his Council." The avoidance of the office is provided for in certain cases under the present law.

Refusing to serve.

"The fine for refusing to serve the office of mayor has usually been "£100, which has been commonly given to the person chosen in the "place of the recusant. In 1643 Richard Cornelius for £100 was "excused from ever serving the office of mayor or any other office, but "still kept his place in the Corporation."

In earlier centuries the burdens of municipal office, like those of parliamentary representation, were not unfrequently avoided. In November 1414 (2 Hen. V.) Thomas Armorer, who had filled the office of bailiff for many years, appeared before the mayor, aldermen, bailiffs, and others of the *prodes-hommes* assembled in congregation, and produced letters patent of the late king (December 1412) granting him freedom from serving any corporate office for the rest of his life.[2]

The fine for not serving is placed at £100 by the Acts of 1835 and 1882.

"*The Mayor's Oath.*

Oath or declaration.

"You shall well and truly serve the King our Sovereign Lord, and his heirs "and successors, in the office of the Mayoralty of this town: and the same town "shall surely guide and keep to the behalf our Sovereign Lord the King, his heirs "and successors: and the King's profit shall do and maintain that belongeth "unto you; and the right of our said Sovereign Lord and all that to the crown "appertaineth in the said town you shall lawfully keep and save: you shall "not assent to any hurt or concealment against the town, but all good orders of "the said town to the uttermost of your power you shall maintain. And where "you know any of the King's right, be it in lands, in rents, in franchises, or in suits, "concealed or withdrawn, you shall cause it to be revealed. And if you cannot

1 Burgesses' Book. Guidotti died December 2, 1555. His house at Hampton is noted by Leland as remarkably fine. In the subsequent decay of the town under Elizabeth it had fallen into sad disrepair, and proclamation was made, March 1569, at the house 'late called my lady Guidotte's' by the mayor, under stat. 32 Hen. VIII. (1540), cap. 18.

2 Liber Niger, f. 23 b.

"do it, you shall show it the King's Majesty, or them of his most honourable "Council, the which shall certainly show it to our said Sovereign Lord. And that "lawfully and rightfully you shall intreat the King's liege people within your "liberties, and that you shall do right to all men, as well to strangers as to "Englishmen, to poor and to rich, in that belongeth to you for to do. And that "neither for riches, for reward, for gift, for promise, for favour, ne for hatred, you "shall no wrong do to any man, nor none shall suffer to be done, as far as you "may, or to your power. And that you shall put good guard and rule upon the "assise of bread, and wine, ale, and other victuals, measures and weights, within "the said town, making due and ready search, and execution of all defaults : you "shall all good and laudable orders of the town see to be observed and kept in all "points, and this to follow accordingly : and all other things appending or apper-"taining unto the mayor of the said town to do, or to be done, you shall well and "truly do to the uttermost of your power. So help you God by this Book."

The ancient oaths of mayor, &c., are no longer taken as oaths, but as solemn declarations. They were continued to be used until the passing of the Promissory Oaths Act, 1868. The declaration on acceptance of office prescribed by the Act of 1882 is the same as under that of 1835. The mayor is now invested with the chain of office, the gift of Bercher Baril, Esq., at Christmas, 1792, as anciently with the tippet; he also receives, 'that he may always have money in his pocket,' the £5 of ancient coins given under the will of Andrew Meares of Millbrook shortly before 1658. The coins are preserved in the Audit-house.

## *List of Mayors, Bailiffs, and Sheriffs.*

There hangs in the Audit-house a list of the mayors, &c., of the town, commencing with 1237—a beautiful specimen of calligraphy, in which the town seals of the various periods are accurately drawn: this list was substituted on 19th December 1828 for earlier and less correct tables, which commenced with 1445, and have now disappeared.

The authorities for a list of mayors among the town archives are chiefly, for the period before 1444, a very considerable number of separate deeds of different kinds, and enrolments in Liber Niger; from September 1444 to 1619 the succession of all the town officers is regularly entered in Liber Remembranciarum H., ff. 37 to 84 b, and from f. 90 to 102 b. From the last date onward the entries occur in the various town journals

In the following list the Audit-house tables have been always kept in view, any additions or rectifications of reading being specified; minute variations in spelling the same name are not noticed. Entries marked * are additions to the Audit-house tables.

| Year of Taking Office. | Mayors. | Bailiffs. |
|---|---|---|
| 1205 (7 John) | ... | *William de St. Lawrence, *Thomas de Bussuse.[1] |
| 1209 (11 John) | ... | *Goce.[2] |
| 1212 (13 John) | ... | *Roger Swein, *William Anglicus.[3] |
| *c.* 1217 (1 H. III.) | *A *mayor* mentioned.[4] | |
| 1222 (6 H. III.) | ... | *Ralph Isembart, *Michael le Fleming.[5] |
| *c.* 1235 (19 H. III.) | ... | *Walter Fortin, *John de la Bulehuse, *Robert Monachus.[6] |
| 1237 (21 H. III.) | Benedict, the son of Azon. | Walter le Fleming. |
| 1247 (31 H. III.) | Benedict, son of Azon. | Walter le Flameng, William Fortin. |
| 1248 (32 H. III.) | Benedict, son of Azon. | Walter le Flameng, *Thomas Blundus, *Matthew Gese.[7] |
| 1260 (44 H. III.) | ... | *Roger Noel, *John Fortin.[8] |
| 1262 (46 H. III.) | ... | Thomas de Andever, Ralph the Little. |
| 1270 (54 H. III.) | Simon de la Bolehuge. | Thomas le Blunde, Robert le Mercier. |
| 1284 (12 E. I.) | Robert le Mercier. | William Beanbel. |
| 1286 (14 E. I.) | John de Bynedon. | Henry le Fleming, James Isambert. |
| 1288 (16 E. I.) | Robert le Mercier. | John de Puteo, Adam le Hordyer. |
| 1290 (18 E. I.) | ... | *Robert le Barbur, *Robert le Mercer, *Peter de Lyons.[9] |
| 1291 (19 E. I.) | Robert le Barbyr. | John de Puteo. |
| (?) | *Robert le Mercier.[10] | *Thomas le Blunde, *John de Borgoyne. |
| 1294 (22 E. I.) | Thomas le Blunde. | Peter de Lyons. |
| 1295 (23 E. I.) | Robert le Mercier. | Nigel[11] de la Wilderne, John de Bourgoyne. |
| (?) | *Robert le Barbour.[12] | *Peter de Lyons, *John de Vaus. |
| 1298 (26 E. I.) | Robert le Barbyr. | John de Schyerlye, John Holebury. |
| (?) | *Peter de Lyons.[13] | *John de Holebury, *William Bassingrom. |
| 1300 (28 E. I.) | John de Schyerlye. | William Bassingrom, Walter Forst. |
| (?) | *Peter de Lyons.[14] | |
| 1303 (31 E. I.) | Adam le Horder. | William Fugehel, *Robert le Horder.[15] |

1 Printed Close Rolls. 2 God's House Computus. 3 Madox, F. B., 158.

4 'The *mayor* and men of Southampton to Peter, Bishop of Winchester, and Hubert de Burgh, justiciar, &c.' Letters, time of H. III. (Rolls Series).

5 Printed Close Rolls. 6 Deed of Prior Richard, Addit. 15, 314, f. 71 b.

7 Madox, Form., p. 379. Tables put Blunde and Gese under 1249.

8 Abbrev. Plac., 44 and 45 H. III. 9 Rot. Parl.

10 Deed of Richerius Tresaut. A note of interrogation means that the actual year is uncertain, though the persons were in office close to the period at which they are placed. 11 Tables, Michael.

12 Deed of Henry le Lung. 13 Deed of Prior Richard of St. Denys.

14 Lease of Customs. 15 West Hall Deeds.

| Year of Taking Office. | Mayors. | Bailiffs. |
|---|---|---|
| (?) | ... | *Thomas Stone, *Nigel de la Wilderne.[1] |
| (?) | *Robert le Mercer.[2] | *Philip or John de Puteo, *Henry de Lymm. |
| 1311 (5 E. II.) | John de Scherley. | William Fugehel, William Basingrom, jun. |
| 1313 (7 E. II.) | Hugo Sampson. | John de Vaus, Nicholas[3] de Mondenard. |
| (?) | *Thomas de Binedon.[4] | *Nicholas de Lyonns, Hugo Sampson. |
| 1315 (9 E. II.) | Henry de Lym.[5] | John de Vaus, William Fugehel. |
| 1316 (10 E. II.) | Thomas de Bynedon.[6] | Richard de Sutton, John de Vaus. |
| 1317 (11 E. II.) | Richard de Barefluet. | Robert Waryn, William Bassingrom. |
| 1318 (12 E. II.) | Hugo Sampson. | Richard Forst, John Stacy. |
| 1319 (13 E. II.) | John le Flemynge. | John Balmayr [Balvayr ?], Richard Bagge. |
| 1320 (14 E. II.) | Henry de Lym. | John de Ronde, Nicholas Sampson. |
| 1321 (15 E. II.) | Richard Forst. | John le Barbyr, John de Vaus. |
| 1323 (17 E. II.) | Hugo Sampson. | John le Barbyr, Richard de Suttone. |
| 1324 (18 E. II.) | Thomas de Bynedon. | John le Barbour, Richard de Sutton. |
| 1326 (20 E. II.) | Walter de Brakkelye. | Robert de la Barre, Thomas de Nutshulling. |
| 1328 (2 E. III.) | Roger Norman. | Robert de la Barre. |
| 1329 (3 E. III.) | Henry de Lym. | John Barbour, Nicholas de Mondenard. |
| 1330 (4 E. III.) | Roger Norman. | Nicholas de Mordenard, Robert atte Barre. |
| 1331 (5 E. III.) | Thomas de Bynedon. | Henry le Flemynge, Nicholas de Mondenard. |
| 1332 (6 E. III.) | Nicholas de Mondenard. | Robert de la Barre, Thomas de Nushellynge. |
| 1333 (7 E. III.) | Hugo Sampson. | Robert de la Barre, Thomas de Nushellynge. |
| 1334 (8 E. III.) | Lawrence de Mees. | Nicholas Sampson, Robert atte Barre. |
| 1336 (10 E. III.) | Thomas de Bynedon. | Robert de la Barre, Walter de Brakkeleye. |
| 1339 (13 E. III.) | John Forst. | Nicholas Lony, Walter de Brakkele. |
| 1340 (14 E. III.) | Thomas del Marche. | Adam Inweys, Robert de Colyngburne. |
| 1341 (15 E. III.) | John Forst. | Nicholas Sampson, jun. |

[1] West Hall Deeds. [2] Deed of Le Mercer and West Hall Deeds.
[3] Tables, Michael. [4] Deed of W. Bassingrom. [5] Tables, Lynn.
[6] These were in office in February 1317 (10 E. II., deed of Matilda Basingrom), so that they were elected in September 1316, not in 1317 as Tables; for similar reason the dates are varied from those in the Tables by one year very frequently till 1370.

| Year of Taking Office. | Mayors. | Bailiffs. |
|---|---|---|
| 1342 (16 E. III.) | Richard Imberd. | William de Baddeby. |
| 1343 (17 E. III.) | Nicholas Lony.[1] | Robert de Colyngburne. |
| 1344 (18 E. III.) | Henry le Flemynge. | John le Clerk. |
| 1345 (19 E. III.) | John Fysmarke. | Robert de Colyngburne. |
| 1346 (20 E. III.) | Richard Comyn. | Robert de Colyngburne. |
| 1347 (21 E. III.) | Richard Elmele. | Adam Inweys. |
| 1348 (22 E. III.) | John Forst. | John Wytegode. |
| 1350 (24 E. III.) | *Thomas le Clerk.[2] | *John Haynes. |
| 1354 (28 E. III.) | John le Clerk. | Thomas de Abyndon. |
| 1357 (31 E. III.) | *Adam Inweys.[3] | *Henry Staunford. |
| 1358 (32 E. III.) | Adam Inweys. | John Jardyn, Henry Staunford. |
| 1359 (33 E. III.) | Adam Inweys. | John Custumer. |
| 1361 (35 E. III.) | John Wytegode. | Henry Staunford. |
| 1362 (36 E. III.) | John le Clerk. | Henry Staunford. |
| 1363 (37 E. III.) | John le Clerk. | Henry Staunford. |
| 1365 (39 E. III.) | John Polymond. | William Malmeshull. |
| 1366 (40 E. III.) | William Bacon. | Edward Dieugard. |
| 1367 (41 E. III.) | *John Wytegode.[4] | *Nicholas Langestoke. |
| 1368 (42 E. III.) | Edward Dieugard. | Roger Mascal, *John Scarlett.[5] |
| 1369 (43 E. III.) | John Polymond. | William Malmeshull. |
| 1370 (44 E. III) | ... | Nicholas Sherwynde. |
| 1371 (45 E. III.) | Radulph Tailleur.[6] | *William Malmeshull.[7] |
| 1372 (46 E. III.) | Robert Bechesfounte. | William Malmeshull. |
| 1373 (47 E. III.) | William Bacon, jun. | William Malmeshull. |
| 1374 (48 E. III.) | Nicholas Langstocke. | John Swofham. |
| 1375 (49 E. III.) | William Bacon. | |
| 1376 (50 E. III.) | ... | William Malmeshull. |
| 1377 (1 R. II.) | William Malmeshull. | Richard Mey. |
| 1378 (2 R. II.) | William Malmeshull. | Richard Mey. |
| 1379 (3 R. II.) | Nicholas Langstocke. | William Walderne. |
| 1380 (4 R. II.) | John Polymond. | John Swofham. |
| 1381 (5 R. II.) | John Polymond. | John Flete. |
| 1382 (6 R. II.) | John Polymond. | John Swofham. |
| 1383 (7 R. II.) | William Walderne. | William Bowyer. |
| 1384 (8 R. II.) | John Polymond. | John Flete. |
| 1385 (9 R. II.) | John Polymond. | John Flete. |
| 1387 (11 R. II.) | William Mapel. | John Appelby. |
| 1388 (12 R. II.) | William Mapel. | |
| 1390 (14 R. II.) | William Maple. | John Flete. |
| 1391 (15 R. II.) | John Polymond. | John Flete. |
| 1392 (16 R. II.) | John Polymond. | John Flete. |
| 1393 (17 R. II.) | Walter Long. | John Penkeston. |
| 1394 (18 R. II.) | Nicholas[8] Langestocke. | John Flete. |
| 1395 (19 R. II.) | John Flete. | John Botiller. |
| 1396 (20 R. II.) | William Mapel. | John Penkeston. |
| 1397 (21 R. II.) | John Flete. | Richard Bradewey. |

[1] Tables, Richard; name is Nicholas in Deeds.

[2] Oak Book. [3] Deed. [4] Deed. [5] Deed of W. of Wykeham.

[6] Left on authority of Audit-house Tables. Ralph Tailleur was certainly one of the four 'Scavins' in March 1372 (46 E. III.), having doubtless been elected in September 1371, so that this entry is doubtful.

[7] Deed of John le Clerke. [8] Tables, Michael.

| Year of Taking Office. | Mayors. | Bailiffs. |
|---|---|---|
| 1398 (22 R. II.) | William Overey.[1] | Richard Bradewey, *John Botiller. |
| 1399 (23 R. II.) | William Ravenston.[2] | Thomas Wellis. |
| 1400 (1 H. IV.) | John Botiller. | John Cosyn, John Derynge. |
| 1401 (2 H. IV.) | Thomas Middelyngton. | Henry Holewey, William Nicholl. |
| 1402 (3 H. IV.) | Thomas Middelyngton. | Henry Holewey, John Barflet.[3] |
| 1403 (4 H. IV.) | Thomas Middelyngton. | John Cosyn, John Beneyt. |
| 1404 (5 H. IV.) | Henry Holwey. | John Cosyn, Thomas Armorer. |
| 1405 (6 H. IV.) | Richard Bradewey. | John Cosyn, John Mascall. |
| 1406 (7 H. IV.) | William Overey. | John Cosyn, Thomas Armorer. |
| 1407 (8 H. IV.) | Walter Longe. | William Nicholl, Thomas Armorer. |
| 1409 (10 H. IV.) | John Beneyt. | John Mascall, Thomas Armorer. |
| 1410 (11 H. IV.) | Henry Holwey. | William Bredlep, Thomas Armorer. |
| 1411 (12 H. IV.) | William Nicoll. | John Maschall, Thomas Armorer. |
| 1412 (13 H. IV.) | Henry Holwey. | John Renaud, Thomas Armorer. |
| 1413 (1 H. V.) | John Beneyt. | Thomas Regald, Thomas Armorer. |
| 1414 (2 H. V.) | John Mascall. | Walter Fettiplace, Thomas Armorer. |
| 1415 (3 H. V.) | John Renawd. | Thomas Regald, Robert Danyell. |
| 1416 (4 H. V.) | William Soper. | Peter James, Robert Danyell. |
| 1417 (5 H. V.) | William Nicoll. | Peter James, Robert Danyell. |
| 1418 (6 H. V.) | John Benet. | Thomas Regald, Robert Danyell. |
| 1419 (7 H. V.) | Walter Fettiplace. | John Selder, Benedict Wychefort. |
| 1420 (8 H. V.) | John Mascall. | Thomas Frelond, Benedict Wycheford. |
| 1421 (9 H. V.) | John Mascall. | Thomas Frelond, Benedict Wycheford. |
| 1422 (1 H. VI.) | *William Nicoll.[4] | *Thomas Frelond, *Benedict Wychefort. |
| 1423 (2 H. VI.) | Thomas Belle. | John Selder, Benedict Wychfort. |
| 1424 (3 H. VI.) | William Soper. | Henry Bacon, John Emory. |
| 1425 (4 H. VI.) | Thomas Frelond. | Thomas Wynterborne, Adam Merysh. |
| 1426 (5 H. VI.) | Walter Fetplace. | John Estewell, Robert Floryse. |
| 1427 (6 H. VI.) | William Nicholl. | John Selder, Robert Floryse. |
| 1428 (7 H. VI.) | Peter Jamys. | John Emory, Robert Floryse. |
| 1430 (9 H. VI.) | Thomas Belle. | John Emory, Benedict Wychefort. |
| 1431 (10 H. VI.) | Thomas Belle. | John Emery, Benedict Wychfort. |
| 1432 (11 H. VI.) | Walter Fetplace. | Ralph Chamberleyn, Robert Hovyngham. |
| 1433 (12 H. VI.) | John Emery. | Robert Aylward, Robert Hovyngham. |
| 1435 (14 H. VI.) | Peter James. | Adam Mersh (or Bochier),[5] Robert Floryse. |
| 1436 (15 H. VI.) | Robert Aylward. | Peter Payn, Robert Floryse. |
| 1437 (16 H. VI.) | (?) William Nycoll. | |
| 1438 (17 H. VI.) | William Marche.[6] | John Bedyll, James Thyrletharappe. |
| 1439 (18 H. VI.) | Walter Fetplace. | William Flecher, James Thyrletharappe. |

[1] Was in office September 10, 1399, therefore elected previous year (Deed).
[2] Prob. in office this year; Tables, 1398.
[3] Tables, Basset.
[4] Deed, July 1423.
[5] Deeds of J. Boteler and J. Barnabas.
[6] Deed of W. Soper.

| Year of Taking Office. | Mayors. | Bailiffs. |
| --- | --- | --- |
| 1441 (20 H. VI.) | Robert Aylward. | John Bedell,[1] Nicholas Holmhegge. |
| 1442 (21 H. VI.) | Robert Aylward. | John Budell, Nicholas Holmhegge. |
| 1443 (22 H. VI.) | Walter Fetplace. | Gabriel Corbet. |
| 1444 (23 H. VI.) | Walter Fetplace. | |
| 1445 (24 H. VI.) | John Flemang.[2] | *John Cadese, *Andrew James. |
| 1446 (25 H. VI.) | John Flemmynge. | |

By charter of March 9, 1447 (25 Henry VI.), the town was erected into a county, and permitted to choose a sheriff on May 1, 1447. After this date the names of the sheriffs are entered on this list, and the bailiffs are omitted.

| Year of Taking Office. | Mayors. | Sheriffs. |
| --- | --- | --- |
| 1447 (26 H. VI.) | Peter James. | Henry Bruyn. |
| 1448 (27 H. VI.) | John Wylliams. | |
| 1449 (28 H. VI.) | Robert Aylward. | Andrew James. |
| 1450 (29 H. VI.) | John Payne. | William Harbelton. |
| 1451 (30 H. VI.) | John Payne. | Simon Patryk. |
| 1452 (31 H. VI.) | Andrew Jamys. | Thomas Payne. |
| 1453 (32 H. VI.) | Robert Aylward. | Gabriel Corbet. |
| 1454 (33 H. VI.) | Nicholas Holmehegg. | John Dunne. |
| 1455 (34 H. VI.) | John Wylliams. | Walter Clerk. |
| 1456 (35 H. VI.) | John Wylliams. | Walter Fettplace. |
| 1457 (36 H. VI.) | Walter Clerk. | William Nedham. |
| 1458 (37 H. VI.) | Walter Clerk. | Richard Gryme. |
| 1459 (38 H. VI.) | Richard Gryme. | Robert Bagworth. |
| 1460 (39 H. VI.) | Robert Bagworth. | Walter Aylward. |
| 1461 (1 E. IV.) | John Dunne.[3] | John Walker. |
| 1462 (2 E. IV.) | John Payne, deposed by order of king, May 13, 1463, and Walter Fettiplace elected May 20. | Gilbert Cornemonger. |
| 1463 (3 E. IV.) | Walter Fettiplace. | Michael Luke. |
| 1464 (4 E. IV.) | Walter Fettiplace. | William Nedham. |
| 1465 (5 E. IV.) | Gilbert Cornemonger. | Richard Asshe. |
| 1466 (6 E. IV.) | John Walker. | Vincent Pittelesden. |
| 1467 (7 E. IV.) | John Walker. | Robert Bluet. |
| 1468 (8 E. IV.) | Robert Bagworth. | John Burghbrigge (or Pourbike).[4] |
| 1469 (9 E. IV.) | John William. | Thomas Reynolds. |
| 1470 (10 E. IV.) | John William. | John Spryng. |
| 1471 (11 E. IV.) | Robert Bluet. | Thomas Avan. |
| 1472 (12 E. IV.) | Thomas Payne. | William Ovray. |
| 1473 (13 E. IV.) | John Walker. | Geoffrey Moumbray. |
| 1474 (14 E. IV.) | William Ovray | Vincent Tehy. |
| 1475 (15 E. IV.) | Robert Bagworth. | William Gunter. |
| 1476 (16 E. IV.) | Thomas Raynold | William Burgbrigge. |
| 1477 (17 E. IV.) | William Gunter. | John Shropshire. |

[1] Tables, Bridell.
[2] Deed of R. Rodende.
[3] Tables, Donne.
[4] Deed of Joanna Tylby.

| Year of Taking Office. | Mayors. | Sheriffs. |
|---|---|---|
| 1478 (18 E. IV.) | John Ludlowe. | Lewis Eynes.[1] |
| 1479 (19 E. IV.) | John Shropshire. | John Spryng. |
| 1480 (20 E. IV.) | Thomas Avan. | Thomas Smyth. |
| 1481 (21 E. IV.) | Lewis Eynes.[1] | Walter William. |
| 1482 (22 E. IV.) | Walter Wylliam. | David White. |
| 1483 (1 R. III.) | Walter Wylliam,[2] fled after his re-election, and took sanctuary, and John Walker,[2] was elected 29th Sept. (1 R. III.) | Christopher Ambrose. |
| 1484 (2 R. III.) | Vincent Tehy. | Richard Harewode.[3] |
| 1485 (1 H. VII.) | William Gunter. | William Perchard. |
| 1486 (2 H. VII.) | Christopher Ambrose. | Thomas Dymmok. |
| 1487 (3 H. VII.) | Lewis Aynes.[1] | Thomas Overey. |
| 1488 (4 H. VII.) | Thomas Overey. | William Hekley. |
| 1489 (5 H. VII.) | Thomas Overey. | Massias Salmon. |
| 1490 (6 H. VII.) | Thomas Overey. | Reginald Chamber. |
| 1491 (7 H. VII.) | Thomas Dymock. | John Gildon. |
| 1492 (8 H. VII.) | Thomas Dymock. | John Godfray. |
| 1493 (9 H. VII.) | William Gunter. | John Walsh. |
| 1494 (10 H. VII.) | Masse Salmon and John Walsh.[3] | Peter Spryng. |
| 1495 (11 H. VII.) | John Walsh. | William Justise. |
| 1496 (12 H. VII.) | John Godfrey. | John Ward. |
| 1497 (13 H. VII.) | Christopher Ambrose. | James Maryk. |
| 1498 (14 H. VII.) | Vincent They. | Robert Busshoppe. |
| 1499 (15 H. VII.) | Peter Spryng. | John Flemyng. |
| 1500 (16 H. VII.) | Robert Busshoppe. | John Bawdwyne. |
| 1501 (17 H. VII.) | William Justice. | Ralph Calton. |
| 1502 (18 H. VII.) | Thomas Dymmok. | Robert Yonge. |
| 1503 (19 H. VII.) | John Flemyng. | John Goughe. |
| 1504 (20 H. VII.) | John Fleming. | Robert Wright. |
| 1505 (21 H. VII.) | John Godfrey. | Nicholas Cowart. |
| 1506 (22 H. VII.) | John Baudewyne. | Richard Hylle. |
| 1507 (23 H. VII.) | Robert Bisshoppe. | Peter Stonerd. |
| 1508 (24 H. VII.) | Robert Bisshoppe. | John Favour. |
| 1509 (1 H. VIII.) | Nicholas Cowert. | John Grygge. |
| 1510 (2 H. VIII.) | Nicholas Cowart. | William Chalk. |
| 1511 (3 H. VIII.) | Richard Hylle. | John Husee. |
| 1512 (4 H. VIII.) | Peter Stoneherd. | John Percherd. |
| 1513 (5 H. VIII.) | John Bawedwyne, died Feb. 15, 1514, and John Favour elected. | William Westmylle. |
| 1514 (6 H. VIII.) | William Chalke. | Thomas Lyestarr. |
| 1515 (7 H. VIII.) | William Chalke. | Robert Milles. |
| 1516 (8 H. VIII.) | John Parchard. | Nicholas Dey. |
| 1517 (9 H. VIII.) | Thomas Lyster. | Gilbert Mountegue. |
| 1518 (10 H. VIII.) | Nicholas Dey. | Walter Baker. |

[1] Tables, Laurence Gynes. [2] See under M.P.'s; Tables, John Walter.
[3] Tables, Harew. [4] Lib. Remembranc. H.

| Year of Taking Office. | Mayors. | Sheriffs. |
|---|---|---|
| 1519 (11 H. VIII.) | Richard Hyll. | Sampson Thomas. |
| 1520 (12 H. VIII.) | Richard Hyll. | Thomas Huse. |
| 1521 (13 H. VIII.) | Gilbert Mountegue. | Henry Huttoft. |
| 1522 (14 H. VIII.) | Walter Baker. | Henry Waterman. |
| 1523 (15 H. VIII.) | Sampson Thomas. | William Jamys. |
| 1524 (16 H. VIII.) | John Perchard. | John Ichyn. |
| 1525 (17 H. VIII.) | Henry Huttoft. | Peter Westbroke. |
| 1526 (18 H. VIII.) | Thomas Hussey. | Richard Caplyne. |
| 1527 (19 H. VIII.) | Thomas Lyster. | Thomas Huttoft. |
| 1528 (20 H. VIII.) | Nicholas Dey. | John Piers. |
| 1529 (21 H. VIII.) | Henry Waterman. | John Walshe. |
| 1530 (22 H. VIII.) | Walter Baker. | Edward Mercaunt. |
| 1531 (23 H. VIII.) | Walter Baker. | Roger Thomas. |
| 1532 (24 H. VIII.) | Richard Capleyn. | Nicholas Berell. |
| 1533 (25 H. VIII.) | John Perchard. | James Groce. |
| 1534 (26 H. VIII.) | Henry Huttoft. | Robert Millett. |
| 1535 (27 H. VIII.) | Sampson Thomas. | James Stonerd. |
| 1536 (28 H. VIII.) | Thomas Lyster. | Roger Thomas. |
| 1537 (29 H. VIII.) | Thomas Husse. | Edward Markant. |
| 1538 (30 H. VIII.) | Nicholas Dey. | William Barwell.[1] |
| 1539 (31 H. VIII.) | Peter Westbroke. | Thomas Rigges. |
| 1540 (32 H. VIII.) | Peter Westbroke, died. Nicholas Burwell.[2] | Thomas Berry. |
| 1541 (33 H. VIII.) | Walter Baker. | Thomas Fasshon. |
| 1542 (34 H. VIII.) | Thomas Rygges. | Edmund Bysshoppe. |
| 1543 (35 H. VIII.) | Richard Capleyne. | John Vaughon. |
| 1544 (36 H. VIII.) | Thomas Lyster. | Stephen Omedeux. |
| 1545 (37 H. VIII.) | Thomas Fasshon. | Thomas Beckingham. |
| 1546 (38 H. VIII.) | James Stonerd. | Robert Renegar. |
| 1547 (1 E. VI.) | Thomas Beckingham. | Thomas Welles. |
| 1548 (2 E. VI.) | Edmund Bisshopp. | Thomas Godard. |
| 1549 (3 E. VI.) | Thomas Ridgis. | Richard Butler. |
| 1550 (4 E. VI.) | Thomas Godarde. | John Caplen. |
| 1551 (5 E. VI.) | Richard Butler. | John Fletcher. |
| 1552 (6 E. VI.) | John Caplyne. | John Staveley. |
| 1553 (1 Mary) | John Capelyn. | George Vincent. |
| 1554 (1 & 2 P. & M.) | John Stavely. | Richard Hawkyns. |
| 1555 (2 & 3 P. & M.) | John Flecher. | Edward Willmott. |
| 1556 (3 & 4 P. & M.) | Richard Hawkins. | John Gregory. |
| 1557 (4 & 5 P. & M.) | George Vincent. | Nicholas Capelyn. |
| 1558 (5 & 6 P. & M.) | John Gregory. | William Staveley. |
| 1559 (1 Eliz.) | Edward Willmott. | Thomas Mill. |
| 1560 (2 Eliz.) | Nicholas Capelyn. | Henry Russell. |
| 1561 (3 Eliz.) | William Stavely. | Thomas Edmundes. |
| 1562 (4 Eliz.) | Henry Russell. | John Brodoke. |
| 1563 (5 Eliz.) | Richard Buttler. | John Marche. |
| 1564 (6 Eliz.) | Richard Butler. | William Capelin. |
| 1565 (7 Eliz.) | John Brodocke. | Reginald Howse. |
| 1566 (8 Eliz.) | Robert Eyer.[3] | John Awnde, died in July 1567;[4] Thomas Edmundes elected. |

[1] Tables, Berell.

[2] Roll of Mayors.

[3] Tables, Ayre.

[4] Lib. Rem. H.

| Year of Taking Office. | Mayors. | Sheriffs. |
|---|---|---|
| 1567 (9 Eliz.) | John Marche. | William Jefferys. |
| 1568 (10 Eliz.) | John Croke. | Lawrence Grosse, died March 2, 1569;[1] John Knight, elected March 7. |
| 1569 (11 Eliz.) | Richard Godderd. | Thomas Terner.[2] |
| 1570 (12 Eliz.) | Reginald Housse. | Thomas Shuxborowe. |
| 1571 (13 Eliz.) | John Knight. | Thomas Dingley. |
| 1572 (14 Eliz.) | William Jefferys, died December 29;[3] William Capelin elected January 2. | John Jackson. |
| 1573 (15 Eliz.) | Thomas Shuxboro. | John Aylls. |
| 1574 (16 Eliz.) | Thomas Dingeley. | Hugh Durvall. |
| 1575 (17 Eliz.) | Robert Knaplock. | Barnard Courtemell. |
| 1576 (18 Eliz.) | John Aylls. | John Favor. |
| 1577 (19 Eliz.) | Nicholas Caplin. | Robert Moore. |
| 1578 (20 Eliz.) | John Jackson. | Richard Biston. |
| 1579 (21 Eliz.) | Bernard Cortmill. | William Barwicke. |
| 1580 (22 Eliz.) | William Staveley. | Richard Goddard. |
| 1581 (23 Eliz.) | Richard Biston. | Peter Janverin. |
| 1582 (24 Eliz.) | William Barwicke. | John Erington. |
| 1583 (25 Eliz.) | Richard Goddard. | John Ballicar. |
| 1584 (26 Eliz.) | John Crooke. | Andrew Studley. |
| 1585 (27 Eliz.) | John Erington. | Robert Russell. |
| 1586 (28 Eliz.) | Andrew Studley. | Paulle Elliott.[4] |
| 1587 (29 Eliz.) | Andrew Studley. | Peter Stoner. |
| 1588 (30 Eliz.) | John Bullackre. | Thomas Goddard.[5] |
| 1589 (31 Eliz.) | Peter Stoner, died January; John Knight, elected January 12.[6] | Alexander Paynton. |
| 1590 (32 Eliz.) | John Jackson. | John Exton. |
| 1591 (33 Eliz.) | Thomas Holmes. | John Hopton. |
| 1592 (34 Eliz.) | Alexander Payneton. | John Caplin. |
| 1593 (35 Eliz.) | John Hopton. | Robert Crosse,[7] died March 13, 1594; *Thomas Fashin, elected March 28. |
| 1594 (36 Eliz.) | John Exton. | Lawrence Grosse. |
| 1595 (37 Eliz.) | Paul Ellyott. | John Jeffrye. |
| 1596 (38 Eliz.) | William Wallop. | John Gregorie. |
| 1597 (39 Eliz.) | Richard Beiston. | Thomas Lambert. |
| 1598 (40 Eliz.) | John Jeffrye. | John Mayjor. |
| 1599 (41 Eliz.) | Thomas Lambert. | Richard Cornellis. |
| 1600 (42 Eliz.) | John Mayjor. | John Greene. |
| 1601 (43 Eliz.) | Richard Cornellius. | Thomas Sherewood. |
| 1602 (44 Eliz.) | Edmund Aspden. | William Nevie. |
| 1603 (1 Jas. I.) | Thomas Sherwood. | Robert Chambers. |
| 1604 (2 Jas. I.) | William Nevey. | John Cornishe. |
| 1605 (3 Jas. I.) | Robert Chambers. | Edward Barlow. |

[1] Lib. Rem. H. [2] Tables, Toiner. [3] Lib. Rem. H.
[4] An under-sheriff was appointed this year, and from 1594 was appointed regularly.
[5] Tables, John Mayjor. [6] Lib. Rem. H. [7] Ibid.

| Year of Taking Office. | Mayors. | Sheriffs. |
|---|---|---|
| 1606 (4 Jas. I.) | John Cornishe. | John Longe. |
| 1607 (5 Jas. I.) | Edward Barlow. | Philip Toldervey. |
| 1608 (6 Jas. I.) | John Longe. | Thomas Bedford. |
| 1609 (7 Jas. I.) | Philip Toldervey. | William Marrinell. |
| 1610 (8 Jas. I.) | William Wallop. | Christopher Cornellius. |
| 1611 (9 Jas. I.) | Thomas Bedford. | Henry Carpenter. |
| 1612 (10 Jas. I.) | William Nevey. | Arthur Baker. |
| 1613 (11 Jas. I.) | Edward Richardes. | John Mayjor. |
| 1614 (12 Jas. I.) | Arthur Baker. | William Merryett. |
| 1615 (13 Jas. I.) | John Mayjor. | George Gollop. |
| 1616 (14 Jas. I.) | John Longe. | Richard Dalbie. |
| 1617 (15 Jas. I.) | William Merryeth. | Henry Caplin, sen. |
| 1618 (16 Jas. I.) | Lawrence Prowse. | Charles Darvall. |
| 1619 (17 Jas. I.) | Edward Richardes. | Peter Priaulx. |
| 1620 (18 Jas. I.) | Richard Dalbie. | Edward Exton. |
| 1621 (19 Jas. I.) | George Gollop. | *John Elzey.[1] |
| 1622 (20 Jas. I.) | Peter Priaulx. | Nicholas Pescod. |
| 1623 (21 Jas. I.) | Edward Exton. | Francis Knowles. |
| 1624 (22 Jas. I.) | John Elzey.[2] | Thomas Combes. |
| 1625 (1 Chas. I.) | Nicholas Pescod. | John Clungeon. |
| 1626 (2 Chas. I.) | Francis Knowles. | Nathaniel Mills. |
| 1627 (3 Chas. I.) | Thomas Combe. | Charles Darvall. |
| 1628 (4 Chas. I.) | John Clungeon. | Peter Seale. |
| 1629 (5 Chas. I.) | Nathaniel Mill. | Thomas Mason. |
| 1630 (6 Chas. I.) | Peter Seale. | Peter Clungeon. |
| 1631 (7 Chas. I.) | Thomas Mason. | John Guillam. |
| 1632 (8 Chas. I.) | George Gallop. | John Rigges. |
| 1633 (9 Chas. I.) | Peter Clungeon. | Barrish Daniell. |
| 1634 (10 Chas. I.) | John Guillam. | Robert Wroth.[3] |
| 1635 (11 Chas. I.) | Peter Pryaulx. | Henry Bracebridge. |
| 1636 (12 Chas. I.) | Edward Exton. | Humphrey Ryman. |
| 1637 (13 Chas. I.) | Arthur Bromfeild. | Joseph Mason. |
| 1638 (14 Chas. I.) | Robert Wroth.[3] | Edward Tatenell.[4] |
| 1639 (15 Chas. I.) | Henry Bracebridge. | Richard Cornelius. |
| 1640 (16 Chas. I.) | Nicholas Pescod. | Henry Pitt. |
| 1641 (17 Chas. I.) | Humphrey Ryman. | Peter Legay. |
| 1642 (18 Chas. I.) | Peter Seale. | John Benger. |
| 1643 (19 Chas. I.) | Thomas Mason. | John Benger.[5] |
| 1644 (20 Chas. I.) | Henry Pitt. | John Benger. |
| 1645 (21 Chas. I.) | William Stanley. | Christopher Walleston. |
| 1646 (22 Chas. I.) | Peter Clungeon. | James Capelin.* |
| 1647 (23 Chas. I.) | Peter Legay. | Thomas Cornelius. |
| 1648 (24 Chas. I.) | James Capelin. | William Horne. |
| 1649 (1 Chas. II.) | Christopher Walleston. | Nicholas Capelin. |
| 1650 (2 Chas. II.) | Robert Wroth.[3] | William Higgens. |
| 1651 (3 Chas. II.) | Joseph Delamott. | James Clungeon. |
| 1652 (4 Chas. II.) | Thomas Cornelius. | Henry Ward. |
| 1653 (5 Chas. II.) | William Horne. | Edward Marsh. |

[1] Roll of Mayors. [2] Tables, Eben.
[3] Tables, Wieth. [4] Tables, Tatenes.
[5] Roll of Mayors; Tables, Nathan: Bachelor.

| Year of Taking Office. | Mayors. | Sheriffs. |
|---|---|---|
| 1654 (6 Chas. II.) | William Higgens. | Edward Downer. |
| | Both mayor and sheriff deposed by order of Cromwell, August 15, 1655, and William Horne and Edward Marsh elected August 22, for the rest of the year. | |
| 1655 (7 Chas. II.) | Henry Pitt. | Charles Smith. |
| 1656 (8 Chas. II.) | James Clungeon. | Nicholas Clement. |
| 1657 (9 Chas. II.) | Peter Seale. | William Pinhorne. |
| 1658 (10 Chas. II.) | Nicholas Clement. | Jacob Legay. |
| 1659 (11 Chas. II.) | James Capelin. | John Steptoe. |
| 1660 (12 Chas. II.) | Edward Downer. | Arthur Bracebridge. |
| 1661 (13 Chas. II.) | William Stanley. | John Tayler. |
| 1662 (14 Chas. II.) | Robert Richbell. | Kingston Friar. |
| 1663 (15 Chas. II.) | John Steptoe. | Jacob Ward. |
| 1664 (16 Chas. II.) | Thomas Cornelius. | John Parsons. |
| 1665 (17 Chas. II.) | Arthur Bracebridge. | Edward Richards. |
| 1666 (18 Chas. II.) | James Clungeon. | Richard White. |
| 1667 (19 Chas. II.) | William Horne. | William Walleston. |
| 1668 (20 Chas. II.) | Kingston Fryar. | John St. Barbe. |
| 1669 (21 Chas. II.) | John Winder. | Nicholas Stanley, jun. |
| 1670 (22 Chas. II.) | Robert Richbell. | John Loving. |
| 1671 (23 Chas. II.) | Richard White. | John Rowte. |
| 1672 (24 Chas. II.) | William Stanley, jun. | Alexander Hill. |
| 1673 (25 Chas. II.) | Jacob Ward. | Christopher Smith. |
| 1674 (26 Chas. II.) | Thomas Farr. | James Crosse. |
| 1675 (27 Chas. II.) | William Walliston. | Henry Norbonne. |
| 1676 (28 Chas. II.) | James Crosse. | John Rawlings. |
| 1677 (29 Chas. II.) | Alexander Hill. | Elias Degruche. |
| 1678 (30 Chas. II.) | John Rowte. | Richard Godfrey. |
| 1679 (31 Chas. II.) | Edward Downer. | George Shergold, died.<br>James Mellish, elected. |
| 1680 (32 Chas. II.) | Christopher Smith. | Thomas Cornelius. |
| 1681 (33 Chas. II.) | John Speed, M.D. | Alexander Alchorne. |
| 1682 (34 Chas. II.) | Elias Degruchey. | William Lyne. |
| 1683 (35 Chas. II.) | James Mellish. | John Smith. |
| 1684 (36 Chas. II.) | Thomas Cornelius. | Robert Vernon. |
| 1685 (1 Jas. II.) | William Bulkeley. | Edward Elwes. |
| 1686 (2 Jas. II.) | Alexander Alchorne. | Cornelius Macham. |
| 1687 (3 Jas. II.) | Richard White.[1] | William Crop. |
| 1688 (4 Jas. II.) | William Lyne. | Peter Bulkeley. |
| 1689 (1 Wm. & My.) | John Smith. | William Pocock.[2] |
| 1690 (2 Wm. & My.) | John Thornburgh. | Jonathan Ingles. |
| 1691 (3 Wm. & My.) | James Crosse. | Thomas Everhard. |

1 Continued in office over the year. On Wednesday, October 24, 1688, the king's proclamation for restoring Corporations was read; and October 26 the private nomination was ordered for the new election. Friday, November 9, the election of the mayor was ordered to be on the Friday following; but his successor, who was mayor *elect* on Friday, November 23, did not come into office till December 5, 1688.

2 On refusal of Robert Culliford, who was fined £25.

| Year of Taking Office. | Mayors. | Sheriffs. |
|---|---|---|
| 1692 (4 Wm. & My.) | Edward Elwes,[1] died February 26, 1693. Christopher Smith. | David Widdall. |
| 1693 (5 Wm. & My.) | Robert Vernon. | Thomas Bracebridge. |
| 1694 (6 Wm. & My.) | John Speed, M.D. | Thomas Rice. |
| 1695 (7 Wm. III.) | Cornelius Macham. | John Winter. |
| 1696 (8 Wm. III.) | William Cropp, M.D. | Aaron de Veuile. |
| 1697 (9 Wm. III.) | Elias Degruchey. | Daniel Veal. |
| 1698 (10 Wm. III.) | Peter Bulkeley. | Richard White. |
| 1699 (11 Wm. III.) | Jonathan Ingles. | Jacob Ward. |
| 1700 (12 Wm. III.) | James Mellish. | Charles Smith. |
| 1701 (13 Wm. III.) | Thomas Cornelius. | Samuel Downes. |
| 1702 (1 Anne) | Thomas Bracebridge. | William Godfrey. |
| 1703 (2 Anne) | Thomas Rice. | Andrew Webb. |
| 1704 (3 Anne) | John Thornburgh. | Richard Smith. |
| 1705 (4 Anne) | Aaron de Veulle. | Thomas Macham. |
| 1706 (5 Anne) | Richard White. | Francis Gardiner. |
| 1707 (6 Anne) | Arthur Atherley. | John Grove. |
| 1708 (7 Anne) | Charles Smith. | Edmund Moody. |
| 1709 (8 Anne) | William Godfrey. | Roger Andrews. |
| 1710 (9 Anne) | Andrew Webb. | Earlesman Richey. |
| 1711 (10 Anne) | Thomas Cornelius. | William Smith. |
| 1712 (11 Anne) | Francis Gardiner. | Thomas Ingles. |
| 1713 (12 Anne) | John Thornburgh. | George Bussell. |
| 1714 (1 Geo. I.) | John Grove. | William Cornelius. |
| 1715 (2 Geo. I.) | Richard White. | John Ayres. |
| 1716 (3 Geo. I.) | Edmund Moody. | Francis Cabot. |
| 1717 (4 Geo. I.) | Arthur Atherley. | Thomas Wells. |
| 1718 (5 Geo. I.) | Charles Smith. | Francis Andrews. |
| 1719 (6 Geo. I.) | Thomas Ingles. | Leonard Cropp. |
| 1720 (7 Geo. I.) | William Godfrey. | William Reade. |
| 1721 (8 Geo. I.) | William Cornelius. | Charles Reade. |
| 1722 (9 Geo. I.) | Thomas Cornelius,[2] died June 1, 1723. Roger Andrew, elected June 12. | Richard Raymund. |
| 1723 (10 Geo. I.) | Francis Gardiner. | Arthur Bracebridge. |
| 1724 (11 Geo. I.) | John Ayres. | Richard Taunton. |
| 1725 (12 Geo. I.) | Francis Cabot. | Robert Vernon. |
| 1726 (13 Geo. I.) | John Grove. | William White. |
| 1727 (1 Geo. II.) | Leonard Cropp. | Richard Atherley. |
| 1728 (2 Geo. II.) | Thomas Ingles. | Robert Sadleir. |
| 1729 (3 Geo. II.) | William Reade. | Richard Purbeck. |
| 1730 (4 Geo. II.) | Roger Andrews. | Thomas Cornelius. |
| 1731 (5 Geo. II.) | George Shergold. | George Barton. |
| 1732 (6 Geo. II.) | Richard Raymond. | Robert Ballard. |
| 1733 (7 Geo. II.) | Arthur Bracebridge. | Francis Cabot, jun. |
| 1734 (8 Geo. II.) | Richard Taunton. | Joseph Ward. |
| 1735 (9 Geo. II.) | William White. | Arthur Atherley, jun. |
| 1736 (10 Geo. II.) | Richard Atherley. | John Herring. |

[1] Journal.

[2] Journal.

| Year of Taking Office. | Mayors. | Sheriffs. |
|---|---|---|
| 1737 (11 Geo. II.) | Leonard Cropp. | Richard Serle. |
| 1738 (12 Geo. II.) | William Freeman. | William Knight. |
| 1739 (13 Geo. II.) | Robert Sadleir. | George Hammond. |
| 1740 (14 Geo. II.) | Richard Purbeck. | Leonard Cropp, jun. |
| 1741 (15 Geo. II.) | Robert Ballard. | John Wheeler. |
| 1742 (16 Geo. II.) | Richard Raymond. | William Purbeck. |
| 1743 (17 Geo. II.) | Richard Taunton. | Edmund Moody. |
| 1744 (18 Geo. II.) | Arthur Atherley. | William Lowder. |
| 1745 (19 Geo. II.) | William White. | Richard Searle. |
| 1746 (20 Geo. II.) | William Knight. | Edmund Ludlow. |
| 1747 (21 Geo. II.) | Richard Atherley. | John Langford. |
| 1748 (22 Geo. II.) | Robert Sadleir. | Samuel Saunders. |
| 1749 (23 Geo. II.) | Richard Purbeck. | Thomas Hasker. |
| 1750 (24 Geo. II.) | Robert Ballard. | Richard Vernon Sadleir. |
| 1751 (25 Geo. II.) | Leonard Cropp. | George Robinson. |
| 1752 (26 Geo. II.) | William Purbeck. | Josiah Smith. |
| 1753 (27 Geo. II.) | Edmund Moody. | Richard Ayres. |
| 1754 (28 Geo. II.) | Arthur Atherley. | Peter Spinks. |
| 1755 (29 Geo. II.) | George West, Captain. | Thomas Guillaume. |
| 1756 (30 Geo. II.) | William Knight. | Thomas Guillaume. |
| 1757 (31 Geo. II.) | Richard Serle. | Gideon Tabuteau. |
| 1758 (32 Geo. II.) | Edmund Ludlow. | John Bridger. |
| 1759 (33 Geo. II.) | William Freeman. | Edward Noble. |
| 1760 (34 Geo. II.) | Richard Vernon Sadleir. | Samuel Miller. |
| 1761 (1 Geo. III.) | Leonard Cropp. | John Monkton, M.D. |
| 1762 (2 Geo. III.) | George Robinson. | Thomas Abraham. |
| 1763 (3 Geo. III.) | William Purbeck. | George Miller. |
| 1764 (4 Geo. III.) | Edmund Moody. | William Jolliffe. |
| 1765 (5 Geo. III.) | Henry Hartley. | Arthur Hammond. |
| 1766 (6 Geo. III.) | Richard Serle. | Robert Ballard. |
| 1767 (7 Geo. III.) | Thomas Guillaume. | William Seward. |
| 1768 (8 Geo. III.) | Edmund Ludlow. | John Brysault. |
| 1769 (9 Geo. III.) | John Bridger. | Clement Hilgrove. |
| 1770 (10 Geo. III.) | Edward Noble. | Thomas Mears. |
| 1771 (11 Geo. III.) | Richard Vernon Sadleir. | Richard Vernon Moody |
| 1772 (12 Geo. III.) | Samuel Miller, jun. | Arthur Atherley. |
| 1773 (13 Geo. III.) | George Robinson. | John Mullins. |
| 1774 (14 Geo. III.) | John Monkton, M.D. | Henry Ward. |
| 1775 (15 Geo. III.) | Henry Hartley. | William Bulkeley. |
| 1776 (16 Geo. III.) | Robert Ballard, jun. | Samuel Blount. |
| 1777 (17 Geo. III.) | Samuel Figgal Reade. | Thomas Guillaume. |
| 1778 (18 Geo. III.) | Clement Hilgrove. | Edward Noble. |
| 1779 (19 Geo. III.) | Thomas Guillaume. | John Monkton. |
| 1780 (20 Geo. III.) | Thomas Mears. | Arthur Atherley. |
| 1781 (21 Geo. III.) | Edward Noble. | Robert Ballard. |
| 1782 (22 Geo. III.) | Richard Vernon Moody. | Clement Hilgrove. |
| 1783 (23 Geo. III.) | Arthur Atherley. | Samuel Blount. |
| 1784 (24 Geo. III.) | John Monkton. | Thomas Mears. |
| 1785 (25 Geo. III.) | John Mullins. | Clement Hilgrove. |
| 1786 (26 Geo. III.) | Robert Ballard. | Richard Vernon Moody. |
| 1787 (27 Geo. III.) | Samuel Figgal Reade. | Thomas Durell. |
| 1788 (28 Geo. III.) | Thomas Mears. | Sir Yelverton Peyton, Bart. |
| 1789 (29 Geo. III.) | Clement Hilgrove. | William Smith. |

| Year of Taking Office. | Mayors. | Sheriffs. |
|---|---|---|
| 1790 (30 Geo. III.) | Thomas Durell. | John Butler Harrison. |
| 1791 (31 Geo. III.) | Sir Yelverton Peyton, Bart. | Sir John Collins, Knight, Captain. |
| 1792 (32 Geo. III.) | William Smith. | James D'Auvergne, General. |
| 1793 (33 Geo. III.) | John Mullins. | Bercher Barill. |
| 1794 (34 Geo. III.) | John Butler Harrison. | Alexander Scott, Admiral. |
| 1795 (35 Geo. III.) | James D'Auvergne, General. | Nathaniel Heywood, Colonel. |
| 1796 (36 Geo. III.) | Alexander Scott, Admiral. | Frederick Breton. |
| 1797 (37 Geo. III.) | Arthur Atherley. | Richard Light. |
| 1798 (38 Geo. III.) | Thomas Durell. | Joseph Bishop. |
| 1799 (39 Geo. III.) | Sir Yelverton Peyton, Bart. | Valentine Fitzhugh. |
| 1800 (40 Geo. III.) | Nathaniel Heywood, Colonel. | Philip Seward. |
| 1801 (41 Geo. III.) | Frederick Breton. | William Lomer. |
| 1802 (42 Geo. III.) | Alexander Scott, Admiral. | William Smith. |
| 1803 (43 Geo. III.) | Frederick Breton. | Samuel Silver Taylor. |
| 1804 (44 Geo. III.) | Thomas Durell. | John Rowcliffe. |
| 1805 (45 Geo. III.) | William Smith. | Andrew Williams. |
| 1806 (46 Geo. III.) | Samuel Silver Taylor. | William Tinling. |
| 1807 (47 Geo. III.) | John Rowcliffe. | William Lintott. |
| 1808 (48 Geo. III.) | Sir Yelverton Peyton, Bart. | John Brice. |
| 1809 (49 Geo. III.) | William Lintott. | William Edward Jolliffe. |
| 1810 (50 Geo. III.) | Samuel Silver Taylor. | Richard Eldridge. |
| 1811 (51 Geo. III.) | John Butler Harrison. | George Atherley. |
| 1812 (52 Geo. III.) | William Edward Jolliffe. | Walter Raleigh Smith. |
| 1813 (53 Geo. III.) | John Rowcliffe. | Thomas Vavasour Durell. |
| 1814 (54 Geo. III.) | Richard Eldridge. | Stephen Lintott. |
| 1815 (55 Geo. III.) | William Lintott. | John Sadleir Moody. |
| 1816 (56 Geo. III.) | George Atherley. | John Rushworth Keele. |
| 1817 (57 Geo. III.) | William Edward Jolliffe. | Stephen Lintott. |
| 1818 (58 Geo. III.) | Walter Raleigh Smith. | Samuel Le Feuvre. |
| 1819 (59 Geo. III). | Richard Eldridge. | John Jolliffe. |
| 1820 (1 Geo. IV.) | Stephen Lintott. | Joseph Lomer. |
| 1821 (2 Geo. IV.) | George Atherley. | Wilson Lomer. |
| 1822 (3 Geo. IV.) | John Rushworth Keele. | James Bovill. |
| 1823 (4 Geo. IV.) | Richard Eldridge. | Philip Carteret Fall. |
| 1824 (5 Geo. IV.) | Stephen Lintott. | William Oke. |
| 1825 (6 Geo. IV.) | Samuel Le Feuvre. | Richard D. Pritchard. |
| 1826 (7 Geo. IV.) | John Jolliffe. | Martin Maddison. |
| 1827 (8 Geo. IV.) | Joseph Lomer. | Stephen Judd. |
| 1828 (9 Geo. IV.) | James Bovill. | William Le Feuvre. |
| 1829 (10 Geo. IV.) | Philip Carteret Fall. | Peter Rainier. |
| 1830 (1 Wm. IV.) | John Rushworth Keele. | Peter Breton. |
| 1831 (2 Wm. IV.) | William Oke. | William Ward. |
| 1832 (3 Wm. IV.) | John Jolliffe. | John Rushworth Keele. |
| 1833 (4 Wm. IV.) | Stephen Judd. | Joseph Lomer. |
| 1834 (5 Wm. IV.) | William James Le Feuvre. | James Bovill. |
| 1835 (6 Wm. IV.) | William James Le Feuvre. | James Bovill. |
| 1836 (6 Wm. IV.) | Peter Breton, from January 1 to November 9. | George Hunt. |

| Year of Taking Office. | Mayors. | Sheriffs. |
|---|---|---|
| 1836 (7 Wm. IV.) | Charles Du Cane. | Samuel Silver Taylor. |
| 1837 (1 Vict.) | Joseph Lobb. | Thomas Griffith. |
| 1838 (2 Vict.) | Joseph Bernard. | William Hooke Steere. |
| 1839 (3 Vict.) | Peter Breton. | John Hole. |
| 1840 (4 Vict.) | Joseph Lobb. | Joseph Rankin Stebbing. |
| 1841 (5 Vict.) | Peter Dickson. | Abraham Abraham. |
| 1842 (6 Vict.) | Edward Mayes. | Henry Fricker. |
| 1843 (7 Vict.) | George Henderson. | Richard Coles. |
| 1844 (8 Vict.) | Thomas Griffith. | Joseph Ball. |
| 1845 (9 Vict.) | Joseph Lobb. | John Aslatt. |
| 1846 (10 Vict.) | William James Le Feuvre. | Henry Brett. |
| 1847 (11 Vict.) | Daniel Brooks. | Joseph Lankester. |
| 1848 (12 Vict.) | George Laishley. | Richard Andrews. |
| 1849 (13 Vict.) | Richard Andrews. | John Traffells Tucker. |
| 1850 (14 Vict.) | Richard Andrews. | Sampson Payne. |
| 1851 (15 Vict.) | Richard Andrews. | James Blatch. |
| 1852 (16 Vict.) | Joseph Lankester. | William Aldridge. |
| 1853 (17 Vict.) | John Traffells Tucker. | Richard Coles. |
| 1854 (18 Vict.) | Sampson Payne. | James Caldecott Sharp. |
| 1855 (19 Vict.) | Sampson Payne. | John White. |
| 1856 (19 Vict.) | John Traffells Tucker, appointed deputy-mayor May 10; Sampson Payne, died May 22; Richard Andrews, elected May 31. | |
| 1856 (20 Vict.) | Richard Andrews, resigned December 22; John White, elected December 26. | Ebenezer Williams. |
| 1857 (21 Vict.) | John White. | John Richard King. |
| 1858 (22 Vict.) | Edward Palk. | Charles Copeland. |
| 1859 (23 Vict.) | Frederick Perkins. | James Ricketts Weston. |
| 1860 (24 Vict.) | Richard Coles. | John Carter. |
| 1861 (25 Vict.) | Frederick Perkins. | Thomas Bowman. |
| 1862 (26 Vict.) | Frederick Perkins. | George Simon Brinton. |
| 1863 (27 Vict.) | George Simon Brinton. | David Davis. |
| 1864 (28 Vict.) | Thomas Bowman. | Samuel Michael Emanuel. |
| 1865 (29 Vict.) | Samuel Michael Emanuel. | Rolles Driver. |
| 1866 (30 Vict.) | Samuel Michael Emanuel. | Charles Bromley, died July 4, 1867; Thomas Bowman, elected October 7. |
| 1867 (31 Vict.) | Joseph Rankin Stebbing. | William Furber. |
| 1868 (32 Vict.) | Joseph Rankin Stebbing, paid fine for not accepting office; Frederick Perkins, elected Nov. 20. | Edward Mayes. |
| 1869 (33 Vict.) | Frederick Perkins. | George Dunlop. |
| 1870 (34 Vict.) | Thomas Pibble Payne. | Arthur Andrews. |
| 1871 (35 Vict.) | Henry Joseph Buchan. | Robert Jennings. |
| 1872 (36 Vict.) | William Hickman. | Edwin Jones, resigned November 10, 1873. |

| Year of Taking Office. | Mayors. | Sheriffs. |
|---|---|---|
| 1873 (37 Vict.) | Edwin Jones. | William Gamlen. |
| 1874 (38 Vict.) | George Mason Passenger. | Stephen Seward Pearce. |
| 1875 (39 Vict.) | Edwin Jones. | William Henry Rogers, resigned November 9, 1876. |
| 1876 (40 Vict.) | Henry Abraham. | John Emilius Le Feuvre. |
| 1877 (41 Vict.) | Alfred Leighton M'Calmont. | George Thomas Harper. |
| 1878 (42 Vict.) | John Blount Thomas. | Rolles Driver. |
| 1879 (43 Vict.) | William Henry Rogers. | Edward Bance. |
| 1880 (44 Vict.) | John Henry Cooksey. | James Seward Pearce. |
| 1881 (45 Vict.) | William Henry Davis. | John Davis Barford. |
| 1882 (46 Vict.) | William Henry Davis. | John Miller. |

### *Of the Recorder.*

2. "It is probable that they always had the assistance of a lawyer "in their business, by whatever title they called him: perhaps the same "person executed the offices of recorder and town-clerk before their "charters distinguished those offices. The 'person skilled in the law,' "appointed in a judicial capacity by the charter 1 Edward IV. [see "under 'Courts'], was certainly a recorder in the same sense as we now "use the term, though not called by that name; but the office appears "by that charter to have been annual.

Deposition.

"Though the deposition or removal of the recorder be supposed "and implied in the charter (16 Car. I.), yet the manner of doing it is "not directed. However, it has been done, for [Dec. 5] 1651, Mr. "Hildesly wrote to the Corporation to choose a new recorder, which "being communicated to Mr. Levingston, the then recorder, he agreed "to it, and John Lisle, Lord Commissioner, was chosen; but "[Dec. 9] 1658, Mr. Levingston brought a writ of restitution from "the Upper Bench, and the next year he was restored in obedience "to that writ, and John Lisle quitted.

"In 1703 the recordership was declared void by the absence of "Roger Mompesson, Esq., and his not attending to the town business.

"The recorder was formerly expected to reside in the town, and "Mr. Penruddoke signed a promise in the Journal always to reside here "in the vacation."

Emoluments.

In 1457 the recorder's wages were £5 per annum; he had also, as was usual, his livery gown at Christmas, made of five yards of 'musterdyvelyg' at 3s. 4d. the yard. This continued to be his payment for a considerable period.

"In 1649 it was ordered that the recorder be allowed £20 a year for "his house-rent, so long as he should live in the town. In 1688 it was "determined that his fee should be £5 a year. But there are frequent "instances mentioned in the Journals of presents of wine being made "to the recorders on account of their trouble in attending the law-

"suits of the town. They formerly had constantly a new year's gift "sent them of sugar, spice, wine, or olives."

*The Oath of the Recorder.*

"You shall be faithful and true to our Sovereign Lord the King of England "and his heirs, Kings or Queens of England. You shall minister common right "after the common law of England, and the laudable customs of this town, to "every person that shall duly require the same, as well to poor as to rich. You "shall also true counsel give unto the Mayor and his brethren to your power, and "their counsel you shall well and truly keep, and not be absent from them at such "places and times as you should personally give your attendance without the "licence of the Mayor, or that you be otherwise reasonably occasioned. And "as well all these things as all other things that to your office of Recorder of this "town shall or doth belong, as near as you can, you shall truly do and execute. "So help you God." Oath.

The duties of the recorder are now regulated under the consolidating Act of 1882.

*List of Recorders.*

Occupants.

"John Ingoldesby held the office in 23 Hen. VI. 1444."

Richard Palshid, in 22 Hen. VII. 1507 (see under 'Town-Clerk').

"John Mille, in 37 Hen. VIII., 1547 (Leland's 'Itinerary').

"Thomas Mylle, in 7 Ed. VI. 1553.

"James Brande," in 2 & 3 Ph. & Mary, 1555.

"Mr. Hooper, in 12 Eliz., 1569.

"John Penruddoke, in 14 Eliz., 1571."

Thomas Fleming[1] (afterwards Knight), Solicitor-General, in 43 Eliz., 1601; resigned December 1603.

"Robert [William[1]] Brock," on resignation of last, 1 Jas. I., 1603.

"Thomas Clerke,[2] in 9 Jas. I., 1611.

"Henry Sherfield, in 15 Jas. I.," 1617–18; elected January 30; sworn February 16.

"Robert Mason, in 9 Chas. I., 1633; Recorder of Winchester; soon after of London.

"Thomas Levingston, in 10 Chas. I., 1635," on death of Mason, by recommendation of King Charles; resigned (see above) December 1651.

"John Lisle, Lord Commissioner," December 20, 1651; sworn and admitted September 16, 1652; resigned April 1, 1659.

"Thomas Levingston," restored April 6, 1659, in obedience to writ of Richard Cromwell, dated November 29, 1658.

"Roger Gollop," elected September 29, 1662 (14 Car. II.)

"Giles Eyre, of Brickworth, 33 Chas. II., 1681," elected May 6, on death of last; admitted and sworn August 16, same year.

"John Wyndham, 2 Wm. & Mary, 1690," elected October 4, *vice* Sir Giles Eyre resigned; sworn October 10.

"Thomas Wyndham, of Lincoln's Inn, 8 Wm. & Mary, 1696," elected July 6, *vice* last resigned; admitted and sworn July 13.

"Roger Mompesson, of Lincoln's Inn, 10 Wm. & Mary, 1698," on death of last; admitted and sworn May 9.

---

[1] See Burgesses' Book.

[2] Dr. Speed has Cheeke.

"Robert Eyre, of Lincoln's Inn (afterwards Chief-Justice)," 2 Anne, 1703, on dismissal of last; elected June 14; sworn September 3, same year.

"Robert Eyre, son of the former, on his father's resignation, 9 Geo. I.," 1723, elected July 26, *vice* Sir Robert Eyre, resigned.

"William Eyre, serjeant-at-law, 16 Geo. II.," 1742, elected October 22, *vice* Honourable Robert Eyre, resigned; sworn the same day; also sworn J.P. and Common Council-man.

"Cranley Thomas Kerby," 5 Geo. III., 1765, elected and sworn September 6; died June 7, 1800.

Charles Hilgrove Hammond, barrister-at-law, elected September 12; sworn recorder and J.P. September 18, 1800; resigned October 25, 1830.

Peregrine Bingham, of the Middle Temple, barrister-at-law, elected November 5; sworn December 10, 1830.

Alexander James Edmund Cockburn, of the Middle Temple, barrister-at-law, elected July 26, 1840; afterwards Lord Chief-Justice.

Edmund Smirke, afterwards knight, succeeded Sir Alexander Cockburn, August 13, 1846.

William Major Cooke, succeeded Mr. Smirke, October 19, 1860.

Montagu Beere, appointed in succession to last, July 7, 1862.

Thomas Gunner, in succession to Mr. Beere, October 31, 1870; died March 3, 1883.

Alfred Henry Say Stonehouse-Vigor, late recorder of Penzance, took the oath and made the declaration prescribed, April 11, 1883.

## *Of the Town-Clerk.*

Town-clerks and their office.

3. "There is little said of the town-clerk in the ancient books of "the town, but in one of them (1570) he is called clerk of the records "of the town, which seems to be expressive of his office, the recorder "being keeper of the records."

It will be convenient to give an account of the office under such notices as occur of its occupants.

In 1315 (9 Ed. II.) William Fowell received a bushel of wheat from God's House for professional assistance.[1]

John le Barbur (15 Ed. II., 1321) received a quarter of wheat under similar circumstances.[1]

John Fysch, held office in 1365 (39 Ed. III.)[2]

John Giles (1457, 36 Hen. VI.) has 'five yerds of musterdyvelyg' for his gown. The wages of the town-clerk, as of the recorder, were £5 per annum, with a varying sum for paper and parchment and ink.[3]

Watkyn or Water Latham (9 Ed. IV., 1469), on May 22d he rode with the king to Chichester on town business.

---

1 God's House Computus, under years.

2 Deed of Roger Mascall.

3 Steward's Books. The following particulars, unless otherwise specified, are derived from the Steward's Books and Journals under dates.

William Overey, chosen September 15, 1473 (12 Ed. IV.), also sheriff; he was the translater of the Paxbread (see p. 132).

William West (1 Hen. VII., 1486), wages for one quarter of a year, twenty-five shillings.

William Erneley (1 Hen. VII., 1486), wages for three quarters of a year, £3, 15s.; he continued in office at least till 1501.

Richard Palshed, December 1502 (18 Hen. VII.), also styled recorder.

John Mylles (4 Hen. VIII., 1512–13), see under 'Recorder.'

John Knight, resigned in March 1562–63, recommending as his successor Robert Knaplock.

Robert Knaplock (5 Eliz., 1563).

Richard Waterton, town-clerk, appointed, September 1568, to act as under-sheriff till Mr. Turner, who had been elected high sheriff, returned from beyond seas.

Thomas Lark, clerk to the Honourable Sir Francis Walsingham,[1] Knight, elected (26 Eliz., 1584) to succeed as town-clerk on the death of Waterton, an event then expected.

John Friar, notary public and clerk of the records, town-clerk (43 Eliz., 1601), was holding office in December 1608.

Richard Pidgeon was in office January 1609–10 (7 Jas. I.)

Edward Phillater (13 Jas. I., 1615), then town-clerk, complaining of oysters being dredged within the haven by fishermen of Weston and others, obtains the monopoly of all the oyster-beds, on the understanding that he is to serve the town with good oysters at two pence the hundred at most, to keep the haven in good order, and to bring in five hundred oysters for the mayor's annual fish dinner.

"In 1639 (14 Chas. I.) Mr. Pittis was chosen on condition that "he pay £40 a year to the town as long as he enjoys the place, and "shall not go forth of the town without the mayor's licence. Ordered "likewise that the town-clerk be new chosen and new sworn every "year. In (September) 1646 notice was given to the town-clerk to "void his place, it being held only during pleasure."

Richard Stanley, elected July 8, 1648 (24 Chas. I.) The recorder having claimed £5 for coming to Southampton to the election, was refused by the House on the ground that his salary of £5 per annum was to cover expenses.

Mr. Nutley, 1653 (5 Chas. II.), refused a deputy in May 1654; and, June 5, "voted to be discharged for not attending in person "upon the duty of his office. [The above order was revoked and] notice "was given him, August 10, to attend in person, and reside in town by

[1] Compare Merewether and Stephens' History of Boroughs, pp. xlvi., 1346.

"September 15;" but in December William Hancock was deputy, and so remained till the election of a new town-clerk.

Francis Coles, elected January 19, 1657–58, with the consent, though without the presence, of Commissioner Lisle, the recorder; the late town-clerk (Nutley) being unable to reside in the town owing to his great business. He was sworn and admitted January 22.

Allan Lockhart, March 1659–60 (12 Chas. II.); he resigned October 15, 1660, completing his resignation November 12, and recommending his successor.

Henry Clifford, of Lincoln's Inn, November 12, 1660. Of late years the office had been in an unsettled state.

"In 1668–69 (20 Chas. II.) Mr. Ferdinand Knapton was chosen "[January 15] town-clerk, on condition that he should accept such "terms as the Corporation would offer him. When he heard these he "refused to accept them, and his election was declared void. He brought "a mandamus [May 9, 1699] for his admission, but without effect."

Mr. Pocock was elected January 22, 1668–69 (20 Chas. II.); admitted and sworn July 3. In March 1673–74 he was required to resign, "because his other business took him off from his attendance on the "affairs of the Corporation."

"In 1699 (11 Will. III.), ordered that Mr. William Pocock do show "cause why he should not be removed from his office for non-attendance "at the town courts and for not entering the records, and for setting the "mayor's name without his leave to the return of a writ of error. I do "not find what the issue of this was. In 1699 a letter was sent to Mr. "Swanton, clerk of assize, asserting the town's right for their town-"clerk to officiate in the commission of oyer and terminer as clerk, "without the clerk of assize. This was probably a special commission "for the town, which was customary at that time; but now (since "1725) the town is put into the Western Circuit when they have any "assize business, and one of the judges comes hither, and of course "brings the clerk of assize with him.

"In 1701 (13 Will. III.) Mr. Richard Beel was chosen [September "20], on the death of last, on condition of residing in the town with "his whole family," requiring no salary, and not absenting himself above nine or ten days each term.

"John Knapton, appointed" July 9, 1707 (6 Anne), to act till Michaelmas; elected town-clerk September 30, 1708, proposing to execute the office gratis, only receiving the usual perquisites, and to collect the rents, &c., leaving his reward to the discretion of the Corporation. "In 1718, Mr. Knapton being in a declining state of health, "Mr. John Godfrey, his clerk, was admitted as deputy [June 20], and "was sworn to keep the secrets of the Common Council."

"In 1729-30 [January 1], 2 Geo. II., John Godfrey was chosen on " Mr. Knapton's death; to have no salary, nor to practise in the town " court as attorney, directly or indirectly. Mr. Godfrey grew very " infirm the latter part of his term, and Samuel Figgal Reade was " admitted to be his deputy."

"In 1767 (7 Geo. III.) Charles Le Gay was chosen [February 2], " on death of last.

"In 1774 (14 Geo. III.) William Daman was chosen [March 5], " on death of Le Gay," and sworn April 5, 1774.

Thomas Ridding, on death of last, chosen March 27, 1787; sworn April 20, 1787; appointed steward of court leet, April 3, 1789.

William Curry, appointed March 13, 1804, on the death of last; sworn March 23 the same year.

Thomas Ridding, May 7, 1810, on the death of Curry, elected and sworn before the recorder, May 12; steward of the court leet, May 29, 1810. Mr. Ridding guided the Corporation through the critical period which preceded the Municipal Corporation Reform Act of 1835, receiving a special vote of thanks, December that year; he resigned August 1838.

Charles Edward Deacon, of the town and county of Southampton, attorney-at-law, was appointed August 16, 1838.

Richard Seward Pearce, of the town and county of Southampton, solicitor, on resignation of last, appointed July 6, 1870.

Previously to the Act of 1835, the town-clerk was appointed by the mayor, recorder, aldermen, and Common Council; and under that Act (as by the present, 1882) by the Council, that is, the mayor, aldermen, and councillors, to hold during pleasure, but he must not be himself a member of the Council.

" *The Oath of the Town-Clerk.*

"You shall be faithful and true to the King of England and his heirs, Kings " and Queens of England; you shall see that true records are kept, and due " processes made between party and party, and true judgments in their suits to be " given, as nigh as you can, in the Mayor and Bailiffs' behalf. If ye be required, " ye shall minister common right after the common law of England and the " laudable customs of this town to every person that here will sue, as well poor as " rich. And also true counsel you shall give to the Mayor and his brethren to " your power, and their counsel shall well and truly keep: and not be absent " from them at such places and times, without licence of the Mayor, or otherwise " reasonably occasioned, as you should usually give your attendance. And all " other things that to your office belongeth, as near as you can, you shall do. So " help you God."

No declaration is now required by law of the town-clerk.

*Of the Burgesses.*

Qualifications and admission.

The burgesses were originally the free resident householders, enrolled in the borough court, and bearing their part in the public burdens both as to taxation and duties. But from an early period irregularities occurred in their appointment *ab extra*. Thus, among many instances, in 1303 royal letters patent granted the right of burgesses at Southampton to John de London of Bordeaux, and in 1312 extended them to his wife Blanche, and their sons and daughters in every particular.[1]

"The charter gives so little direction relating to the burgesses that "most things relating to them depend upon practice and bye-laws or "orders in their Journals, and regard chiefly their election and dis-"franchisement.

1. "And first of their election. The eldest son of a burgess has a right "to succeed his father; see 'Laws of the Guild' (Ord. 9), where this "is extended to the next heir." Such eldest son or next heir was sometimes admitted in his father's or uncle's lifetime, when however he paid a fine, which was often remitted; other sons of a guildsman were admitted on payment of a fine of ten shillings, which was also frequently excused (Ord. 10).

Residence.

Residence was required of burgesses, who forfeited their position if absent from the town for a year and a day, though sometimes this requirement was dispensed with. In December 1485 (1 Hen. VII.) Robert Reynold was admitted on condition of dwelling within the town. In 1508 (24 Hen. VII.) F. Baudewyne was admitted 'because he did promise himself to inhabit within the towne.' In 1510 (2 Hen. VIII.) Nic. Seggewike was 'disgrated' because he was not dwelling within the town within a year and a day after summons, according to the custom of the town. Others were 'discharged from the Guild' because they were 'no inhabiters' or 'not dwelling within' the town; sometimes such were readmitted on a fine, presumably upon their becoming resident. In 1579 (21 Eliz.) a burgess, 'according to the ancient custom of this town,' was 'disgraded for that he hath been dwelling out of the said town about twelve months and a day.'

Admission on special reasons.

Admissions to burgess-ship were granted frequently for special reasons.

In 1508 (23 Hen. VII.) Harvey Hayward had also part of his fine remitted 'for that he shall dwell within the town and be a helper as he may,' that is, with ships and boats. In 1509 (1 Hen. VIII.) Richard Kene was admitted by common consent, but with sad reflection on the good people about—'because he is an honest man and good of name.'

[1] Pat. 31 Ed. I. m. 44; 6 Ed. II. p. 1, m. 12; 18 Ed. II. p. 2, m. 17.

John Orpit, Vicar of St. Michael's, was admitted into the Guild, 1510 (2 Hen. VIII.), by common assent, 'because he hath always been a helper of the town.' At the same time John Wilcok, D.D., Vicar of Holy Rood, was admitted. In 1520 (July, 12 Hen. VIII.), John Millet, of the Isle of Wight, was admitted on his promising to reside in the town, and victualling the town with his fish. In 35 Hen. VIII. (1543) a couple of barber-surgeons were admitted free, on the understanding that they were to be 'ready at the commandment of the mayor and burgesses and their successors, to exercise their craft or science when need shall require without excess taking for the same.' A certain William Bowyer, gentleman, was admitted gratis in August 1557, because he had 'married an alderman's wife' and was altogether well thought of in the town. The admission to burgess-ship was exercised in an arbitrary fashion. In 1545 it was agreed by a majority of the aldermen and burgesses that no more Guernsey and Jersey men should be admitted without a distinct vote. On this and some other points the court leet jury of 1550 were peremptory: 'And yf ye refuse this to do, we will ye stryke all our names owt of y bookes, and so comyt all the charges of the towne into y[r] handes. We speake not this for nothinge, but for theire occupyinge and craft wilbe the decaye of our occupyinge.'

It seems that a few years later the making of burgesses 'for friendship' had become too common, and was said to have lowered the office in public estimation; hence, in 1561 (3 Eliz., September 15), it was ordered that the fine for burgess-ship should be £10, 'except prentices, or such that be men of honour and worship, that shall so request for their pleasure, for no gain of the petty customs, and men's children which ought of right to inherit their father's room, according to the Paxbread.'

The practice having obtained of admitting 'gentlemen and others' into the 'fellowship of freemen or burgesses,' without their being obliged to undertake the offices of constable, steward, or bailiff, but enabled at once to advance to the dignity of sheriff and so of mayor, the court leet in 1600 presented this grievance and prayed a remedy. Gentlemen burgesses objected to.

Half a century later the town offices could scarcely be filled for lack of burgesses. In 1652 the court leet presented that the jury of that court had, by ancient custom, consisted of burgesses only, descending in order from the high sheriff, who should be foreman, but that for want of a sufficient number of burgesses, not only was that service in danger of being neglected, but the other offices of the town, which should devolve on burgesses alone. They prayed, therefore, 'that men able and capable of the office of burgess-ship be elected,' and fined on their refusing to serve. Lack of burgesses, 1652.

A similar complaint of lack of burgesses was made by the town

1660. council after the Restoration. It was therefore ordered (September 12, 1660), that all such resident inhabitants within the town as the mayor and Common Council should think fit to nominate gratis as serving burgesses within the next six months should accept the position under a penalty of £20.[1]

When and where to be admitted.

In January 1675–76 it was ordered that residents and traders living elsewhere should only be admitted as burgesses on a Friday, the usual meeting day of the Common Council, and only in the Audit-house, in presence of the council after due notice; but any noble or gentle man desiring to be made a burgess might be admitted any time in a House summoned for the purpose. A similar order was repeated subsequently.

In 1707 it was "ordered that no person shall be sworn a burgess "until he shall first be proposed to the Common Council duly summoned "and assembled, and the whole community be called on to give their "consent; and any persons chosen contrary to this order, their election "to be deemed void. A.D. 1730, the charters being silent concerning "the election of burgesses, it is ordered unanimously that only the "Common Council have a right to vote, and that every burgess be pro-"posed at the Common Council six days at least before his election, or "his election to be void. But a nobleman may be sworn at a common "council without such notice if nine at least be present. This order is "observed still [*i.e.*, *c.* 1770].

And by whom.

Dismissal.

(2.) "Disfranchisement, in its largest sense, signifies being deprived "of the freedom of the town, which was formerly attended to here with "as much punctuality as it continues to be in the City of London; but "at present it is understood to mean only being disburgessed or ex-"pelled the Corporation."

For assault.

In 1495 (11 H. VII.) Griffyn Alcocke, who had been admitted freely as the eldest son of his deceased father, was 'disgrated' for assault on Jermain Griffith, whom 'he did streke with his fiste.' Those who had been disgrated were frequently readmitted on payment of a fine. Offences against the peace by fist, sword, or dagger, as laid down in the Paxbread, were constantly visited with expulsion.

Protesting against Corporation law.

"A.D. 1558 [May 30, 4 and 5 Phil. and Mary], two burgesses were "expelled the Corporation for publishing a protestation against the "mayor and aldermen taxing the town without calling the rest of the "burgesses.

"A.D. 1565, a burgess was disfranchised for saying that the "Corporation made laws against reason and conscience; another for "colouring strangers' goods (see Laws of the Guild, Ord. 30).

[1] In 1689 Thomas Bernard, grocer, was fined £50 for refusing to be sworn a burgess.

"A.D. 1570, a burgess was disfranchised for calling another bur- "gess a knave (see Laws, Ord. 15). Abuse.

"A.D. 1574 [16 Eliz.], Giles Sharpe was disfranchised for non- "payment of the queen's butlerage, commonly called Prisage," and bringing a quo warranto on the town.[1] Leading town into trouble.

"A.D. 1602, Andrew Studley, alderman, was turned out of the "Corporation, but not out of his freedom of the town. The articles "against him were falsifying the Corporation's books of accounts in "various instances for his own advantage, embezzling the public money, "and taking a bribe to procure a lease at a small fine. Falsification.

"A.D. 1610, Henry Capelin was disburgessed for refusing to pay "£4 banquet-money at his admission. *N.B.*—He afterwards paid it, "and was admitted. Hostility to good cheer.

"A.D. 1659, several burgesses were expelled by Cromwell, who, in "1662, were restored by the Commissioners for regulating Corporations, "and some others were then expelled. Of these last, James Capelin[2] "was the chief; but as these were not acts of the Corporation, they "are not to be placed to their account." Cromwell.

"A.D. 1662, a burgess was disfranchised for entering strangers' "goods at the custom-house in his own name.[3] He brought a writ of "mandamus to be readmitted, but the writ was returned *re infectâ*. "At length he agreed to a reference, and in 1681 notice was given to "the collector of the customs that he still continued disenfranchised, "that the collector might recover the arrears of prisage that were due "from him. Evasion.

"A.D. 1676, Thomas Farr, alderman, was excluded from the Common "Council for embezzling the Corporation's effects when he was mayor. Dishonesty.

"Expulsions have not been practised for many years back."

*Other Orders concerning Burgesses.*

"Ordered [1559, 2 Eliz.] that all burgesses from the sheriff "inclusively upwards shall provide and use one right honest gown of "crimson or scarlet cloth on certain days under the penalty of £10." By a minute of August 4, 1569, "the aldermen's wives are also "ordered to wear scarlet on the same days under the same penalty," according to old custom; and their husbands were desired to see that the gowns be provided and worn. Aldermen whose wives did not possess such gowns were to be fined £10, and those whose State and apparel.

[1] See under 'Prisage.'

[2] See "Minute of the Proceedings against Capelin," below in last chapter, date 1662.

[3] "Perhaps this is what is meant above (A.D. 1565) by colouring strangers' "goods, rather than the circumstance mentioned in the Laws of the Guild."

wives, though possessing, did not wear them were to be mulcted ten shillings each day. All the gowns were to be ready against the coming of the queen, under pain of £10; and the ladies were to wear with their scarlet gowns 'frentche whoddes' (French hoods).

"A.D. 1588. The fine for not having a scarlet gown was set at "£5, for not wearing it at ten shillings.

"A.D. 1593. A sheriff was fined for not wearing scarlet on Easter "Day, but was forgiven on his submission.

"A.D. 1616. Mr. George Gollop, having been sheriff, was fined "£10 for not having a scarlet gown, and others were admonished to "provide them. Half this fine was remitted, the other half was paid.

"A.D. 1613. Ordered that the burgesses and their wives shall be "placed in all public assemblies and churches according to their degrees, "by one of the serjeants appointed to that office.

"A.D. 1637. Ordered that the burgesses shall attend Mr. Mayor "on all days of meeting, or upon summons, on pain of twelve pence. "The days of assembly are the Friday before St. Matthew's Day, "Michaelmas Day, the Friday after Michaelmas Day, and Saturday "following, Christmas Day, Easter Day, Trinity Eve, Quarter sessions, "Gaol delivery, and at the coming of the king." It had been presented in 1594 as a discredit for burgesses to go to the Law Day at Cutthorn on foot, and they were desired to attend Mr. Mayor on horseback as heretofore, on pain of two shillings and sixpence, and in like manner to accompany him in the circuit round the liberties. None were to be absent without leave.

Feasting encouraged.

In June 1753 it was ordered that burgesses on being sworn into office should make their entertainments separately, but this order, provocative of good cheer, acted prejudicially on the Corporation. Within the last preceding years a considerable number of clergy and gentry had been admitted; and the expense of the feasting became an objection to the honour of burgess-ship; moderation in such entertain-

Restrained.

ments was therefore urged (September 11, 1767). Sheriffs were advised to ride the bounds in the forenoon and to give no repast but at Cutthorn, and the Audit-room was placed at the disposal of the sheriff and bailiffs for the feasts at Trinity Fair. In 1775 (September 26) new regulations were made on this subject. The entertainments usually given by the senior and junior bailiffs on the second and third court days after their election were discontinued, and after 1777 the feast given by the sheriff at Cutthorn was no longer to be provided by that officer, but in lieu thereof the mayor was authorised to charge five guineas in his annual accounts, afterwards (1778) increased to ten guineas, in order to furnish what was necessary at the same place. In future, also, the entertainments usually provided by the bailiffs and sheriff at Trinity Fair were to be discontinued, and the mayor was empowered to prepare instead a modest refreshment at the public expense. These regulations, it was hoped, would ease future burgesses, the allowance to the mayor was therefore reduced to twenty guineas; the stipend of fifty guineas being continued to the existing members of the Common Council during their mayoralties in consideration of past expenses. By a further regulation (September 29, 1783), it was ordered that every new serving burgess should, on his admission to the Corporation, deposit fifty guineas in the chest by way of composition for the expenses of entertainments formerly given by the bailiffs and sheriff, in return for which the Corporation undertook to indemnify such serving burgess for all usual entertainments, and also to pay the costs of his *quietus* at the expiration of his shrievalty, and moreover to allow him out of the chest during his mayoralty the old allowance of fifty guineas notwithstanding the former resolution. This payment of fifty guineas by incoming burgesses was informally dropped about 1795, and was so permitted by minute of May 30, 1800.

From one cause or other the scarcity of burgesses to fill the town offices was experienced again, 1788, the Corporation making a spirited appeal to the gentlemen of the grand jury at quarter sessions (October) with a view of recruiting their ranks. The appeal met with remarkable success; it is here given in abstract.

Lack of burgesses again, 1788.

The Corporation, seeing such a respectable grand jury, could not but hope that 'the arm of the magistrate might be strengthened' by their support in checking the increasing licentiousness of the people. 'The spirit of discord and delusion had gone forth,' and was 'operating with the worst effect on the minds of men who, instead of a conscientious submission to established laws and customs, vainly sought for advantage by opposition to all order and authority, affecting to revile the power under which they dwelt safely.' The complicated wickedness of the 'inferior class of inhabitants,' the shameless indecencies and blasphemies,[1] were such as 'all the watchfulness of the magistracy would not be able to prevent or punish without the concurrence of those of superior rank.' The Corporation then go on to show their origin, and defend their existence. Southampton enjoyed singular privileges, and might boast of grants superior to those of most other towns; and 'while the current of its customs and privileges flowed unmolested by turbulent and seditious men, it was esteemed a secure, peaceful, and desirable residency for people of all denominations.' What gain could malevolent men obtain by a dissolution of the present Corporation? There must be (1.) 'disorder, violence, and rapine

Appeal of Corporation.

[1] Compare Massy, History of George III., vol. ii. p. 64.

till some new establishment could be formed, and new powers given to another set of men, who, under a different name, would still be a corporate body intrusted with the execution of law, but without conferring on the public any of the benefits of the present charter.' Then they (2.) specify the immense benefit of the admiralty jurisdiction, which could only come by charter. But for this, 'murder and robbery might be committed with impunity by villains who, escaping to the water,' might defy 'the shortened arm of justice.' Or supposing for a moment (3.) that 'the present Corporation, wearied out by unprovoked indignities,' were 'induced to retire and resign their charter,' was it likely that 'such resignation would or could be accepted at the loss of certain sums annually paid to Government, and to certain grantees under the crown, all issuing from the petty customs, that averred grievance which some pretended arose from the corporators?' The payment of such would be exacted with a heavier hand through revenue officers. Then (4.) how could the town walls, quays, and market-places be kept up? Again, (5.) 'should the barrier which now separates us from the county at large be thrown down, the town courts, the courts both criminal and civil, must in consequence be removed to Winchester, and every individual inhabitant of this place would be liable to serve on juries six times yearly, besides occasional special juries, at an expense of both time and money at least a hundred times greater than arises to them while we thus happily enjoy a state of peculiar jurisdiction.' Let then 'men of virtue and abilities' rally round the Corporation and assume 'a participation of those powers and privileges which unworthy men are anxious to attain to. Diminished in numbers, we have lost nothing of that spirit which should ever accompany authority, and by which we are enabled to bear the burden of quick returning offices, and to despise the unjust reproach of being tenacious of our rights. If, animated by the same spirit, you accede to our wishes, that burden will become light, and that reproach will be heard no more.' Having disposed of certain possible objections to their proposal, the Corporation declares that if nothing comes of it, 'you and others who may survive must submit to see the honour of magistracy debased in the hands of men destitute of every qualification for so important a charge.'

Answer.

Forthwith two knights and eleven esquires signified their intention of joining the Corporation, and others quickly (October 17) followed; and on November 3 there were elected as serving burgesses:—Sir John Collins, Sir Richard King, General D'Auvergne, George Rogers, Benjamin Caldwell, John Stewart, M.D., Philip Dumaresque, William Sotheby, Alexander Irwine, Samuel Rollestone, Burcher Barrell, Noah Le Crass, Colonel Heywood, Alexander Scott, Thomas Dixon, John Harrison, George Vincent, Alexander St. Barbe, Frederick Britton,

Thomas South, George Bastide, James Ayscough, Esquires. It does not appear that the town after this suffered from a lack of serving burgesses.

" *The Burgesses' Oath.*

" You shall swear by the contents of this book that you shall from henceforth be " faithful and true to our Sovereign Lord the King, and to his heirs and successors. " Obeisant and obedient you shall be to the Mayor and other officers of this town. " The franchises, customs, and ordinances thereof you shall well maintain to your " power, and keep harmless in that you may. You shall contribute to all manner " of charges within the town, as summons, watches, wards, contributions, taxes, " tallages, lot and scot, and all other charges, bearing your part thereof as a Bur- " gess ought to do. You shall not colour or bear the name of any foreigner's or " stranger's goods, whereby the King or town may lose any custom, brokage, or " advantage. You shall know no foreigner or stranger to buy or sell any mer- " chandise with any foreigner or stranger within this town and the franchises " thereof, but you shall warn the Mayor for the time being, or his deputy, of the " same. You shall sue or implead no inhabitant of this town out of this town " without the special licence of the Mayor or his assistants, or the more part of " them, for the time being. You shall take no apprentice for less term than seven " years, within the first year whereof you shall cause him to be enrolled; and at " his term's end you shall consent and procure him to be set up, as much as in you " lyeth, in this town, if he have well and truly served you. You shall know no " gathering of people, conventicles, or conspiracies made against the King's peace " or the ordinances of this town, but you shall warn the Mayor thereof, and let " them to your power. The counsel of the said town you shall faithfully keep, and " attend the Mayor, for the time being, at all sessions and other assemblies usual, " not being lawfully occasioned to the contrary. All these things you shall well " and truly perform and keep. So help you God and the contents of this " book."

*Honorary Burgesses.*

" They have likewise honorary burgesses; they call them out-bur- " gesses, because they are mostly gentlemen who do not live in the " town. But they sometimes pay this compliment to gentlemen that " are inhabitants. They are sworn, and their oath is called—

" ' The oath of such gentlemen as are admitted to the freedom of a burgess of " ' the town, and not altogether subject to such taxes, tallages, lot and scot, and " ' other attendances as other the common burgesses who pay fine for their freedom " ' are liable to.

" ' Ye shall be faithful and true to our sovereign lord the king, and his heirs " ' and lawful successors; and the franchises and customs and ordinances of this " ' town of Southampton you shall maintain and keep harmless in that you may " ' to your power. So help you God.'

" These honorary burgesses have a right to vote in the election of " a mayor and of members of Parliament; and in matters of general " concern to the town it has always been usual to call a meeting of all " the burgesses that are in the town; but these honorary ones cannot " be present at the deliberations of a Common Council."

The following notices concern honorary burgesses:—In 1490 (6 Hen. VII.) my Lord of Winchester was 'made burgess' free of charge, 'but of his gentilnes he pardoned us for the same the fyne of the pavelyne[1] and all other costes longing to the same with the homage for that yere.' The Abbot of Beaulieu and others were also admitted. In 1514 (6 Hen. VIII.) Thomas Skevington (or Pace), Bishop of Bangor and Abbot of Beaulieu, was admitted 'into the liberties of the gilde of the town' by free gift. He was a donor of some of the town plate. These are among the earliest instances observed; that of 1490 is the first of the creation of honorary burgesses. There can be little doubt, however, that if the records had remained perfect we should have been supplied with earlier cases, the creation of such burgesses being provided for in the oldest copy of the Ordinances extant—that of c. 1300 (see Ord. 57). Space forbids our dwelling on the very copious entries of honorary burgesses.[2] From the end of the seventeenth century the roll of burgesses consists very largely of non-townsmen and generally of men of position.[3] The entries from this latter period (1697) bear each a two-shilling stamp; a century later the stamp increases to four shillings; in 1806 to £1; in 1808 to £2; in 1815 to £3.

It was resolved (January 30, 1829) that each Common Councilman who had attended during the last twelve months should be allowed to nominate an honorary burgess; but in October 1831 it was decided that no resident within the united parishes of the town should be eligible for nomination; the rule being waived in favour of G. F. Pitt, Esq., the donor to the Corporation of his library, who was elected December 23. The last admission to the burgess-ship bears date June
Act of 1835. 1, 1835. With the passing of the Municipal Corporation Reform Act (September 9, 1835) the admission to burgess-ship by gift or purchase became illegal (sect. 3).

Within the ten years immediately preceding that Act fifty-three burgesses had been elected, forty-seven *honorary* and six *serving*; there being in the Corporation just previously to passing the Act twenty resident or serving burgesses and about one hundred and sixty non-resident, chiefly honorary. The former exclusive privileges of trading enjoyed by burgesses had long since ceased. Before the passing of the first Pier Act in 1803, they were exempted from wharfage dues; but on the application for that Act it was agreed that the burgesses should give up this right of exemption, and the Corporation that of petty customs, receiving in exchange[4] a portion of the dues levied under the Act.

---

1 See below under 'Courts.'
2 Entry of Burgesses from 1496 to 1704.
3 Admission of Burgesses from 1697 to 1835.
4 See page 39.

The burgesses latterly had no privilege excepting that, whether resident or not, they, equally with the inhabitants paying scot and lot, were electors of members of Parliament for the town.

Act of 1882.

Under the present law, the universal qualification for enrolment as a burgess is that of being a male of full age, who, on the 15th of July in any year, is, and has been during the whole of the then last preceding twelve months, in occupation, joint or several, of any house, warehouse, counting-house, shop, or other building (in this Act referred to as qualifying property) in the borough, and has during the whole of those twelve months resided in the borough or within seven miles thereof, and has been rated in respect of the qualifying property to all poor-rates made during those twelve months for the parish wherein the property is situated; and has on or before the 20th of the same July paid all such rates, including borough rates (if any), as have become payable by him in respect of the qualifying property up to the then last preceding 5th of January. Disqualifications for enrolment are being an alien, or having been in receipt of union or parochial relief or other alms within the twelve months aforesaid, or being disentitled under any Act of Parliament.

Town Council.

The burgess roll is prepared each year by the town-clerk according to the several provisions of the Act; it is published as directed and printed for sale. The burgesses elect the town-councillors on November 1, who must fulfil conditions beyond those of an ordinary burgess; and on March 1, or on another day with the approval of the Local Government Board, they elect the auditors and assessors from among persons qualified to be councillors.

## *Burgesses of Parliament.*

The authority for the names in the following list, except in the few cases otherwise specified, is the parliamentary return to the order of March 1, 1878, which has, in the former part, greatly amended all previous compilations. The dates are those of the actual meeting of Parliament.

| | | | |
|---|---|---|---|
| 1295. 23 Ed. I. Nov. 13. | Peter de Lyons.[1]<br>John de la Barre. | 1300–1. 29 Ed. I. Jan. 20 (Lincoln). | No return made by the bailiffs.[2] |
| 1298. 26 Ed. I. May 25 (York). | John Flemeng.<br>William Fowel. | 1302. 30 Ed. I. Oct. 14. | John de Shirlie.<br>William Fughel. |

1 The returning officers were the bailiffs, other burgesses being bound as manucaptors or bailsmen for the appearance of the elected members at the appointed day and place. The members were *bonâ fide* burgesses of the town: this continued till the time of James I., after which the form of previous election to burgess-ship was always followed. It was attempted to restore the old custom in April 1625, and select only inhabitants.

2 Such entries mean that the town shirked the duty and expense of making a return: a negligence which seems to have been provided against by stat. 23 Hen. VI. c. 14.

| | |
|---|---|
| 1304–5. 33 Ed. I. Feb. 28. | No return. |
| 1306. 34 Ed. I. May 30. | John le Flemyng. |
| 1306–7. 35 Ed. I. Jan. 20 (Carlisle). | Bartholomew le Engleis. Nigel de la Wylderne. |
| 1307. 1 Ed. II. Oct. 13 (Northampton). | No return. |
| 1309. 2 Ed. II. April 27. | No return. |
| 1311. 5 Ed. II. Aug. 8. | No return. |
| 1311. Nov. 12. | John de Shirle. Henry de Lym. |
| 1312–13. 6 Ed. II. March 18. | William Bassingrom. William Foghel. |
| 1313. 7 Ed. II. Sept. 23. | Henry de Lym.[1] John le Flemyng. |
| 1314–15. 8 Ed. II. Jan. 20 | Henry de Lym.[2] John le Flemyng. |
| 1318. 12 Ed. II. Oct. 20 (York). | John Clerk. Richard Wegge. |
| 1319. 12 Ed. II. May 6 (York). | Richard de Sutton. Henry Forster. |
| 1321. 15 Ed. II. July 15. | No return.[3] |
| 1322. 15 Ed. II. May 2 (York). | John de Ronde. John Forst. |
| 1322. 16 Ed. II. Nov. 14 (York). | John Jurdan. William Broun. |
| 1323–24. 17 Ed. II. Feb. 23. | Henry de Lym. Robert de la Barre. |
| 1326–27. 20 Ed. II. Jan. 7. | John le Flemyng, sen. John le Barber.[4] |
| 1327. 1 Ed. III. Sept. 15 (Lincoln). | Nicholas de Staunford. John Forst. |
| 1327–28. 2 Ed. III. Feb. 7 (York). | John Ronde. John de Vans. |
| 1328. 2 Ed. III. April 24 (Northampton). | Roger Normaund. Henry de Lym. |
| 1328–29. 3 Ed. III. Feb. 9. | Henry Burry. Henry le Flemyng. |
| 1329–30. 4 Ed. III. March 11 (Winchester). | John le Flemyng. Andrew Haywode. |
| 1331–32. 6 Ed. III. March 16. | Roger Normaund. Thomas de Bynedon. |
| 1332. 6 Ed. III. Sept. 9. | Roger Normaund. |
| 1332–33. 6 Ed. III. Jan. 20 (York). | John de Weston. R(ichard) le Clerke. |
| 1333–34. 8 Ed. III. Feb. 21 (York). | Laurence de Mees.[5] |
| 1334. 8 Ed. III. Sept. 19. | Henry Flemyng. Laurence de Mees. |
| 1335. 9 Ed. III. May 26 (York). | Hugo Sampson. Roger atte Hurne. |
| 1335–36. 10 Ed. III. March 11. | Henry Flemyng. Roger atte Hurne. |
| 1337. 11 Ed. III. Sept. 26. | No return. |
| 1337–38. 12 Ed. III. Feb. 3. | Henry le Flemyng. Robert atte Barre. |
| 1338. 12 Ed. III. July 26 (Northampton). | No return. |
| 1338–9. 13 Ed. III. Feb. 3. | Roger Normaund. Thomas de la Marche. |
| 1340. 14 Ed. III. March 29. | Nicholas Lonye.[6] Adam Ineys. |
| 1341. 15 Ed. III. April 23. | Nicholas Lonye. Richard Imberd. |
| 1343. 17 Ed. III. April 28. | Nicholas Lonye. Adam Inweys. |

[1] Writ for their expenses was issued from the return day to November 15 at two shillings each per day, tested November 18 (Parliamentary Writs, II. cclvi.) In the early days, and through the Middle Ages, the town paid the burgesses; in later times the burgesses paid the town.

[2] Writ of expenses, tested at York, December 9, 1318 (Ibid.)

[3] Writ was returned to John de Ronde, bailiff of the liberties of the town, but he gave no answer to the sheriff (Ibid.)

[4] Writ of expenses at two shillings per day for each, tested at Westminster, March 9, 1327 (Prynne, p. 83).

[5] See Prynne, Fourth Part of Brief Register. Writ for expenses of Laurence de Mees was issued for twenty shillings for ten days.

[6] It was a frequent practice to summon specialists for consultation with the Council or Parliament on matters touching the king's honour and the safety of merchandise, to whom the same

| | |
|---|---|
| 1344. 18 Ed. III. June 7. | No return. |
| 1346. 20 Ed. III. Sept. 11. | John Wygayn.<br>Ralph Beauflour. |
| 1347-48. 21 Ed. III. Jan. 14. | John Fismark.<br>Richard Imberd. |
| 1348. 22 Ed. III. March 31. | John de Worgan.<br>Thomas de Abyndon. |
| 1350-51. 25 Ed. III. Feb. 9. | John le Clerk.<br>John Fismark. |
| 1352. 26 Ed. III. Aug. 16. | Henry Stanford. |
| 1353. 27 Ed. III. Sept. 23. | No return found. |
| 1355. 29 Ed. III. Nov. 23. | John le Clerk.<br>Thomas de Abyndon. |
| 1357-58. 32 Ed. III. Feb. 5. | John le Clerk.<br>John Wytegod. |
| 1360. 34 Ed. III. May 15. | John Jardyn.<br>William Warewyk. |
| 1360-61. 34 Ed. III. Jan. 24. | John Clerk.<br>John Jardin. |
| 1362. 36 Ed. III. Oct. 13. | John Wytegod.[1]<br>Thomas de Kyngton. |
| 1363. 37 Ed. III. Oct. 6. | John le Clerk.<br>John Wytegod. |
| 1364-65. 38 Ed. III. Jan. 20. | John le Clerk.<br>John Polymond. |
| 1368. 42 Ed. III. May 1. | John Wytgod.<br>Ralph Taillour. |
| 1369. 43 Ed. III. June 3. | No return. |
| 1371. 45 Ed. III. June 8 (Winchester). | William Bacoun. |
| 1372. 46 Ed. III. Nov. 3. | John Clerk.<br>Richard Mey. |
| 1373. 47 Ed. III. Nov. 21. | John Clerk.<br>John Polymond. |
| 1376-77. 51 Ed. III. Jan. 27. | Richard Mey.<br>William Malmeshull. |
| 1378. 2 R. II. Oct. 20 (Gloucester). | William Bole.<br>Philip Cake. |
| 1379-80. 3 R. II. Jan. 16. | John Polymound.<br>William Bacon, of St. Michael's. |
| 1381. 5 R. II. Nov. 3. | John Polymond.<br>William Bacon. |
| 1382. 5 R. II. May 7. | John Polymond.<br>William Bacon, sen. |
| 1382. 6 R. II. Oct. 6. | John Polymond.<br>John Flete. |
| 1382-83. 6 R. II. Feb. 23. | Richard Meye.<br>William Bowyare. |
| 1384. 7 R. II. April 29 (Salisbury). | John Polymond.<br>John Flete. |
| 1384. 8 R. II. Nov. 12. | John Polymond.<br>Richard Mey. |
| 1385. 9 R. II. Oct. 20. | John Emmory.<br>William Bole. |
| 1386. 10 R. II. Oct. 1. | John Pengeston.<br>Roger Mascall. |
| 1387-88. 11 R. II. Feb. 3. | William Mapel.<br>John Scarlet. |
| 1388. 12 R. II. Sept. 9 (Cambridge). | Nicholas Sherwynd.<br>John Bygard. |
| 1389-90. 13 R. II. Jan. 17. | William Mapel.<br>Thomas Appelby. |
| 1391. 15 R. II. Nov. 3. | William Mapel.<br>Thomas Appelby. |
| 1392-93. 16 R. II. Jan. 20 (Winchester). | William Mapel.<br>Thomas Appelby. |
| 1393-94. 17 R. II. Jan. 27. | John Pengeston.<br>Thomas Appelby. |
| 1394-95. 18 R. II. Jan. 27. | Thomas Appelby.<br>Thomas Marleburgh. |
| 1396-97. 20 R. II. Jan. 22. | Thomas Appulby.<br>John Deryng. |
| 1397. 21 R. II. Sept. 17. | Walter Lange.<br>John Deryng. |
| 1397-98. Jan. 27. (Shrewsbury). | Parl. continued. |
| 1399. 1 H. IV. Oct. 6. | Thomas Middelton.<br>Richard Bradeway. |

allowances were made as to members of Parliament. Thus in this Parliament three or four owners of ships and merchants having been summoned from Southampton, expenses for forty-four days (£4, 8s.) were allowed by writ to (Hugo or Nic.) Sampson, who appeared for the town (Prynne Fourth Part, &c., pp. 186, 188).

[1] John Wytegod appears to have lent £100 to Edward III. some little time after this, having repayment in July 1370 (Pell Issue Roll, 9th July, 44 Ed. III.)

| | |
|---|---|
| 1402. 3 H. IV. Sept. 15. | Thomas Midlyngton. Thomas Marlebergh. |
| 1405–6. 7 H. IV. Feb. 15 (Coventry). | Walter Lange. John Penkeston. |
| 1411. 13 H. IV. Nov. 3. | John Shypton. Thomas Marleburgh. |
| 1413. 1 H. V. May 14. | Thomas Armorer. William Sopere. |
| 1413–14. 2 H. V. Jan. 29 (Leicester). | Thomas Armorer. Thomas Marleburgh. |
| 1414. 2 H. V. Nov. 19. | William Sopere. Thomas Marleburgh. |
| 1415. 3 H. V. Oct. 21. | Thomas Marleburgh. Benedict Wycche-ford. |
| 1419. 7 H. V. Oct. 16. | William Sopere. William Chamber-leyne. |
| 1420. 8 H. V. Dec. 2. | William Sopere. William Chaumber-leyn. |
| 1421. 9 H. V. May 2. | Thomas Marleburgh. Richard Thornes. |
| 1421. 9 H. V. Dec. 1. | William Soper. John Mascall. |
| 1422. 1 H. VI. Nov. 9. | John Mascall. Thomas Marleburgh. |
| 1425. 3 H. VI. April 30. | William Sopere. Richard Thornys. |
| 1425–26. 4 H. VI. Feb. 18 (Leicester). | William Overey. Thomas Marleburgh. |
| 1427. 6 H. VI. Oct. 13. | Peter Jamys. William Chaumber-layn. |
| 1429. 8 H. VI. Sept. 22. | William Soper. William Chamber-leyn. |
| 1430–31. 9 H. VI. Jan. 12. | William Soper. William Chamber-leyn. |
| 1432. 10 H. VI. May 12. | William Soper. William Chaumber-leyn. |
| 1433. 11 H. VI. July 8. | William Soper. William Chaumber-leyn. |
| 1435. 14 H. VI. Oct. 10. | William Chamber-leyn. John Payn. |
| 1436–37. 15 H. VI. Jan. 21. | William Marche. John Kirkeby. |
| 1441–42. 20 H. VI. Jan. 25. | William Soper. William Chamber-layn. |
| 1446–47. 25 H. VI. Feb. 10 (Bury St. Edmunds). | William Stone. John Payn. |
| 1448–49. 27 H. VI. Feb. 12. | William Soper. William Stone. |
| 1449. 28 H. VI. Nov. 6. | John Flemang. William Stone. |
| 1450. 29 H. VI. Nov. 6. | John Payn. Nicholas Holme-hegge. |
| 1452–53. 31 H. VI. Mar. 6 (Reading). | Andrew Jamys. Thomas Chamber-leyn. |
| 1455. 33 H. VI. July 9. | John William.[1] Walter Clerk.[2] |
| 1461. 1 Ed. IV. Nov. 4. | Richard Aysche.[3] Andrew Jamys. |
| 1472. 12 Ed. IV. Oct. 6. | Robert Bluet.[4] Walter Fetplace. |
| 1477–78. 17 Ed. IV. Jan. 16. | John Walker. Roger Kelsale. |
| 1482–83. 22 Ed. IV. Jan. 20. | Thomas Reynold. Roger Kelsale.[5] |

1 Received forty shillings in part payment of his Parliament wages on April 3d, during his mayoralty ; knighted in 1456.

2 In the next book of accounts we find payment to Walter Clerk 'for his parlement wages holde at Westm. the xxxiij yere of Henry the Sexte for cxix dayes in parte of payment of his parlement wages x$^{li}$ xix$^{s}$.'—*i.e.*, he received the half of two shillings a day (Steward's Book, 1457).

3 'Item payd by the honddes of Rychard Aysche for the parlement wages for the sayd Rychard and Anddrew Jamys for lix dayys, for the day iiij$^{s}$, the fyrst yere of Kyng Edward the iiij$^{st}$. sm xj$^{li}$ xvis.'—that is, two shillings a day each (Steward's Book, 1461–62).

4 Prynne.

5 Roger Kelsale was attainted (11 R. III. 1483–84) with Walter Williams, Sir William Overey, J. Fessant, &c. ; a reversal of this attainder being granted 1 Hen. VII. (1485). Rot. Parl. vi. 246, 273.

| | |
|---|---|
| 1483–84. 1 R. III. Jan. 23. | John Shropshire.[1] John Walker. |
| 1485. 1 H. VII. Nov. 7. | Thomas Reynold.[2] Thomas Overey. |
| 1487. 3 H. VII. Nov. 9. | Sampson Norton.[3] |
| 1495. 11 H. VII. Oct. 14. | Thomas Thomas. John Dawtrey.[3] |
| 1503–4. 19 H. VII. Jan. 25. | John Flemynge.[3] |
| 1523. 14 H. VIII. April 15 (Black Friars). | Nicholas Dey.[4] John Mille. |
| 1529. 21 H. VIII. Nov. 3 (London). | Nicholas Dey. John Milles. |
| 1541–42. 33 H. VIII. Jan. 16. | Christopher Stowe.[5] John Glynne. |
| 1547. 1 Ed. VI. Nov. 4. | John, prob. James, Stonard.[5] |
| 1552–53. 7 Ed. VI. Mar. 1. | James Stonard, Alderman. |
| 1553. 1 Mary. Oct. 5. | Sir Francis Flemyng. Thomas Mille. |
| 1554. 1 Mary. April 2. | Richard Buttler, Merchant. James Brende, Gentleman. |
| 1554. 1 & 2 P. & M. Nov. 12. | James Brenne, Gentleman. James Stoner, Merchant. |
| 1555. 2 & 3 P. & M. Oct. 21. | James Brande, Recorder of Southampton. Thomas Fasshyn, Merchant. |
| 1557–58. 4 & 5 P. & M. Jan. 20. | John Staveley, Gentleman. James Brande, Gentleman. |
| 1558–59. 1 Eliz. Jan. 23. | Thomas Bekingham, Merchant. Edward Willmott, Merchant. |
| 1562–63. 5 Eliz. Jan. 11. | John Caplyn, Gentleman. James Brande, Gentleman. |
| 1571. 13 Eliz. April 2. | Edward Horsey, Esq.[6] John Crook, Gentleman. |
| 1572. 14 Eliz. May 8. | Sir Henry Walloppe, Knight.[7] Nicholas Capelin, Gentleman.[8] |
| 1584. 27 Eliz. Nov. 23. | Thomas Dyggs, Esq.[9] Thomas Goddard, Gentleman. |
| 1586. 28 Eliz. Oct. 15. | John Penruddock, Esq. William Thorley, Gentleman. |

1 Shropshire and Walker received the usual wages, January 21; John Walker received pardon, with the rest of the burgesses, for all offences, &c., June 1, 1484. This was in answer to a supplication to the king from the mayor (Walker), 3d December (1 R. III.) 1483, defending the town's privileges through John Shropshire, Walter Latham, &c. (Steward's Book).

2 These two burgesses seem to have been paid (£7, 13s. 4d.) January 23, 1486 (1 H. VII.) They left the Friday before St. Leonard's Day (November 6), and returned the morrow after St. Luce's [Lucy's] Day (December 13) (Lib. Remembr. H. 152 b, 155).

3 So Dr. Speed in his brief list.

4 These burgesses seem to have been members at this time (Lib. Rem. H. 88), as they certainly were in the next Parliament (see Parl. Returns, 1878).

5 Willis's Notitia Parliamentaria.

6 Ibid. Edward Horsey, captain and constable of Carisbrook Castle, and governor of the Isle of Wight from 1565 to 158 ; knighted December 1577.

7 Fulk Greville, Esq., sat part of the three sessions for Wallop abroad in the queen's service (Beatson, Reg. of Parl. i. 457).

8 Towards the parliamentary charges of Nicholas Capelin, £10 (see Temp. T. Overey, 1580).

9 October 23, 1584, the nomination of one of the burgesses was given to the Earl of Leicester on his request. Thomas Goddard was the town's nominee; both were to bear their own charges, and neither receive anything from the town (Boke of Remembrances, sub ann.)

| | |
|---|---|
| 1588–89. 31 Eliz. Feb. 4. | Thomas Wilkes, Esq.<br>Richard Goddard, Gentleman. |
| 1592–93. 35 Eliz. Feb. 19. | Sir Thomas Wilkes, Knight.<br>Thomas Heton, Esq. |
| 1597. 39 Eliz. Oct. 24. | William Wallop, Esq.<br>Francis Bacon, Esq. |
| 1601. 43 Eliz. Oct. 27. | Thomas Fleminge of Stoneham, Esq., Solicitor - General, Recorder of Southampton.<br>Thomas Lambert, Esq. |
| 1603–4. 1 Jas. I. March 19. | Sir Thomas Fleminge, Knt., Solicitor-General.<br>Sir John Jeffrey, Knt. |
| 1614. 12 Jas. I. April 5. | Sir Thomas Fleminge, Knt. (son of the above).<br>Henry Sherfeild. |
| 1620–21. 18 Jas. I. Jan. 16. | Sir Thomas Flemynge, Knight, of Southampton.<br>Henry Sherfeilde, Esq., Recorder of Southampton. |
| 1623–24. 21 Jas. I. Feb. 12. | Sir John Mill, Bart., of Southampton.<br>Henry Sherfielde, Esq., Recorder of Southampton.<br>Thomas Bonde, Esq.,[1] *vice* Sherfield, elected for Salisbury. |
| 1625. 1 Chas. I. May 17. | Sir John Mill, Bart.<br>George Gollop, Alderman, of Stanbridge and Southampton. |
| 1625–26. 1 Chas. I. Feb. 6. | Sir John Mill, Bart.<br>George Gollop, Alderman. |
| 1627–28. 3 Chas. I. March 17. | John Mayjor,[2] Alderman.<br>George Gollop, Alderman. |
| 1640. 16 Chas. I. April 13. | Sir John Mill, Bart.<br>Thomas Livingstonne, Esq., Recorder of Southampton. |
| 1640. 16 Chas. I. Nov. 3. | George Gollop,[3] Alderman.<br>Edward Exton, Alderman. |
| 1654. (Protector's). Sept. 3. | John Lisle, Esq., one of the Lords Commissioners of the Great Seal, and Recorder of Southampton. |
| 1656. (Protector's). Sept. 17. | John Lisle, Esq. |
| 1658–59. (R. Cromw.) Jan. 27. | Thomas Knollys,[4] Esq., of Grove Place, Nursling.<br>Roger Gallop, Esq., of Stanbridge. |
| 1660. 12 Chas. II. April 25. | William Stanley, Esq.<br>Robert Richbell, Esq. |
| 1661. 13 Chas. II. May 8. | Sir Richard Ford, Knight,[5] Alderman, of London.<br>William Legg, Esq. |
| 1678–79. 31 Chas. II. March 6. | Thomas Knollis, Esq., Merchant.[6]<br>Benjamin Newland, Merchant, of London. |

[1] On March 1, 1623–24, the Corporation wrote to Sir John Mill and to Mr. Recorder (Sherfield) for their assistance in obtaining a new election (Journal).

[2] See under 'Mayors.'

[3] On death of Gollop, town agreed (December 2, 1650) to petition for a continuance of their ancient privilege of having two burgesses of Parliament, and for a writ to choose a new one.

[4] Election was at the Guildhall, Monday, January 10, between the hours of nine and eleven. The burgesses had to assemble at the Audit-house by eight o'clock (Journal, January 7, 1658–59).

[5] These two members had been invited by the Corporation to accept burgess-ships with a view to their representing the town, and were elected respectively in April and March 1661; Colonel William Legge was Lord of the Bedchamber to Charles I. and Charles II.

[6] On the voting (February 5) Knollys had 34 and Newland 41 votes of the burgesses of the town who were the electors (Journal, February 7, 1678–79). Knollys had sat in the Parliament of 1658–59; during the present he died, and was buried in Westminster Abbey, June 3.

| | |
|---|---|
| 1679. 31 Chas. II. Oct. 17. | Sir Charles Wyndham, Knight, of Cranbury, near Winchester.<br>Sir Benjamin Newland, Knight. |
| 1680–81. 33 Chas. II. March 21. | The same. |
| 1685. 1 Jas. II. May 19. | The same. |
| 1688–89. (Interregnum.) Jan. 22. | Sir Benjamin Newland, Knight, of London.<br>Richard Brett, Esq., of Marwell, co. Southampton.<br>Edward Fleming, Esq.[1] (*vice* Brett, deceased), Nov. 25, 1689.<br>Sir Charles Wyndham, Knight, the same day (*vice* Fleming, or rather *vice* Brett). |
| 1689–90. 2 W. & M. March 20. | The same. |
| 1695. 7 W. III. Nov. 22. | The same. |
| 1698. 10 W. III. Aug. 24. | Sir Benjamin Newland, Knight.<br>John Smith, Esq.<br>Roger Mompesson, Esq., Recorder of Southampton (*vice* Newland, deceased, Dec. 27, 1699). |
| 1700–1. 12 W. III. Feb. 6. | Roger Mompesson, Esq., Recorder of Southampton.<br>Mitford Crowe, Merchant. |
| 1701. 13 W. III. Dec. 30. | Adam de Cardonnel, jun., Esq.<br>Mitford Crowe, Esq. |
| 1702. 1 Anne. Aug. 20. | Frederick Tilney, Esq.<br>Adam de Cardonnel, jun., Esq. |
| 1705. 4 Anne. Oct. 25. | Henry Viscount Woodstock.<br>Adam de Cardonnel, jun., Esq. |
| 1708. 7 Anne. Nov. 18. | Viscount Woodstock.<br>Simeon Steuart, Esq. (*vice* Lord Woodstock, who elected to serve for the county).<br>Adam de Cardonnel, jun., Esq. |
| 1710. 9 Anne. Nov. 25. | Adam de Cardonnel,[2] Esq.<br>Roger Harris, Esq. (*vice* Cardonnel, expelled).<br>Richard Fleming, Esq. |
| 1713–14. 12 Anne. Feb. 18. | Richard Fleming, Esq.<br>Roger Harris, Esq. |
| 1714–15. 1 Geo. I. March 21. | Thomas Lewis,[3] Esq., of Soberton, Hants.<br>Richard Fleming, Esq. |
| 1722. 9 Geo. I. Oct. 9. | Thomas Lewis, Esq.<br>Thomas Missing,[4] Esq., of Stubbington. |

[1] The new writ was ordered November 2. Edward Fleming was elected by the mayor, bailiffs, and *select* burgesses, but petitioned against by Sir Charles Wyndham; when the House decided (December 31, 1689) that the right of election was with the burgesses and inhabitants paying scot and lot; and Wyndham was declared elected. On this most righteous decision, or no doubt having it in view, Dr. Speed says, "About this time the scot and lot people claimed a right to vote, which "made the election of M.P.'s no longer a Corporation affair; and therefore the names of the "members are not entered in the Corporation books after this time." His very scanty list, which commences with 1441–42, ends with 1685.

[2] Secretary to the Duke of Marlborough; expelled the House for receiving an annual gratuity of 500 gold ducats from contractors for bread and bread waggons for the army; new writ ordered February 26, 1711–12.

[3] Presented the town with £200, which the Corporation (August 10, 1722) agreed should go to their old standing debts. They proposed further to meet every year in the Audit-house on the anniversary of Mr. Lewis's birthday to keep it in a suitable manner in memory of his gift (Journal).

[4] Proveditor-General for Gibraltar and Port Mahon.

| | |
|---|---|
| 1727–28. 1 Geo. II. Jan. 7. | Robert Eyre,[1] Esq.<br>Anthony Henley, Esq.<br>William Heathcote,[2] Esq. (*vice* Eyre). |
| 1734. 8 Geo. II. June 13. | Sir William Heathcote, Bart.<br>Anthony Henley, Esq.<br>John Conduit, Esq., of Cranbury (*vice* Henley, on petition, April 1735).<br>Thomas Lee Dummer, Esq. (*vice* Conduit, deceased).[3] |
| 1741. 15 Geo. II. Dec. 4. | Peter Delmé,[4] Esq.<br>Edward Gibbon, Esq. |
| 1747. 21 Geo. II. Nov. 10. | Anthony Langley Swymmer, Esq.<br>Peter Delmé, Esq. |
| 1754. 27 Geo. II. May 31. | Anthony Langley Swymmer, Esq.<br>Hans Stanley,[5] Esq., of Paultons.<br>Henry Dawkins, Esq., of Dunston, Berks (*vice* Swymmer, deceased; new writ March 24, 1760). |
| 1761. 2 Geo. III. Nov. 3. | Henry Dawkins, Esq.[6]<br>Hans Stanley, Esq., appointed Governor of Isle of Wight, 1765; Cofferer of H. M. Household, 1766; new writ ordered, re-elected. |
| 1768. 8 Geo. III. May 10. | Henry Viscount Palmerston, Baron Temple, of Mount Temple.<br>Right Hon. Hans Stanley, appointed Governor of Isle of Wight; new writ May 16, 1770; re-elected. |
| 1774. 15 Geo. III. Nov. 29. | John Fleming, Esq., of Stoneham Park (Tory).<br>Right Hon. Hans Stanley (T.), appointed Cofferer, &c.; new writ Nov. 1, 1776; re-elected; died; new writ Jan. 24, 1780.<br>John Fuller, Esq., of Rosehill, co. Sussex (T.), *vice* Stanley, deceased. |
| 1780. 21 Geo. III. Oct. 31. | John Fuller, Esq., of Rosehill, Sussex.<br>Hans Sloane, Esq. of South Stoneham (T.) |
| 1784. 24 Geo. III. May 18. | John Fleming, Esq.<br>James Amyatt, Esq., of Freemantle (T.) |
| 1790. 31 Geo. III. Nov. 25. | James Amyatt, Esq.<br>Henry Martin, Esq., (T.), of Stratford-place, London, Capt. R.N., Controller of Navy, created Bart. July |

[1] Made Commissioner of Excise; new writ ordered May 14, 1729.

[2] In September 1729 Mr. Heathcote presented the Corporation with 700 guineas for the public good—£200 for repairing the sea-banks, £105 towards an organ for Holy Rood, £230 towards fire-engines and waterworks' debt, and £200 for the use of the chamber, which they appropriated in a specified way. In August 1732 Mr. Heathcote proposed to bring water into the town; leave was given him to open ground for the purpose, and thanks returned for his liberality (Journal).

[3] John Conduit, Master of the Mint, died May 23, 1737; new writ ordered June 1, 1737.

[4] In May 1742 Mr. Delmé presented the town with £500 (Journal). Edward Gibbon was father of the historian. This election was caused by the sudden creation of 170 new freemen in the Tory interest (Gibbon, Autobiog., p. 18).

[5] Made a Commissioner of the Admiralty; new writ ordered December 1, 1757; re-elected.

[6] These members gave between them £1116 towards lengthening the quay, May 1764. Mr. Dawkins was a great donor of turtles.

| | |
|---|---|
| | 28, 1791; died; new writ August 19, 1794.<br>George Henry Rose, Esq. (T.), of Cuffnalls, co. Southampton, *vice* Martin. |
| 1796. 36 Geo. III. Sept. 27. | George Henry Rose, Esq.<br>James Amyatt, Esq. |
| 1802. 43 Geo. III. Nov. 16. | James Amyatt, Esq.<br>George Henry Rose, Esq., of Lower Brook Street, London. |
| 1806. 47 Geo. III. Dec. 15. | Arthur Atherley, Esq., jun. (W.)<br>George Henry Rose, Esq., of Mudeford, Christ Church. |
| 1807. 47 Geo. III. June 22. | George Henry Rose, Esq., of Muddiford.<br>Josias Jackson, Esq., (W.), of Bellevue, co. Southampton. |
| 1812. 53 Geo. III. Nov. 24. | Arthur Atherley, jun., Esq. (W.), of Welbeck, Marylebone, co. Middlesex.<br>George Henry Rose, Esq., appointed Clerk of Parliament; new writ March 1818.<br>William Chamberlayne, Esq. (W.), of Weston Grove, *vice* Rose. |
| 1819. 59 Geo. III. Jan. 14. | William Chamberlayne, Esq.<br>Sir William Campion De Crespigny, of Kingsrew, Fawley Bart. (W.) |
| 1820. 1 Geo. IV. April 27. | Sir W. C. De Crespigny, Bart.<br>William Chamberlayne, Esq. |
| 1826. 7 Geo. IV. Nov. 14. | William Chamberlayne, Esq.<br>Abel Rous Dottin, Esq. (T.), of Bugle Hall, Southampton.<br>James Barlow Hoy, Esq., of Midenbury (T.), *vice* W. Chamberlayne,[1] who died Dec. 10, 1829. |
| 1830. 1 Wm. IV. Oct. 26. | Abel Rous Dottin, Esq.<br>James Barlow Hoy, Esq. |
| 1831. 1 Wm. IV. June 14. | Arthur Atherley, Esq. (L.), of Arundel, co. Sussex.<br>John Storey Penleaze, Esq. (L.), of Bossington, co. Southampton. |
| 1833. 3 Wm. IV. Jan. 29. | Arthur Atherley, Esq.<br>James Barlow Hoy, Esq., unseated on petition, April 1833.<br>John Storey Penleaze, Esq., *vice* Hoy. |
| 1835. 5 Wm. IV. Feb. 19. | James Barlow Hoy, Esq. (C.)<br>Abel Rous Dottin, Esq. (C.) |
| 1837. 1 Vict. Oct. 15. | Abel Rous Dottin, Esq.<br>Viscount Duncan, (L.) |
| 1841. 5 Vict. Aug. 19. | Lord Bruce (T.), of Broomhall, Fifeshire.<br>Charles Cecil Martyn, Esq. (T.), of Whitehall Gardens. On petition these elections declared void. Aug. 1842 new elections *vice* above.<br>Humphrey St. John |

[1] At nomination on January 7, 1830, at Guildhall, show of hands in favour of Mr. Hoy, but poll demanded on behalf of John Storey Penleaze. The voting lasted five days, final numbers being Hoy, 437; Penleaze, 174; majority for Hoy, 263.

| | |
|---|---|
| | Mildmay, Esq. (T.), of Berkeley Square, London.<br>George William Hope, Esq. (T.), of Curzon Street, London. |
| 1847. 11 Vict. Nov. 18. | Alex. James Edmund Cockburn, Esq., Q.C. (L.), of Wakehurst Place, co. Sussex.<br>Brodie M'Gie Wilcox, Esq. (L.), of Dorset Square, London.<br>Cockburn re-elected after appointment as Solicitor-General, July 17, 1850.<br>Sir A. J. E. Cockburn, Knight, re-elected after appointment as Attorney-General, April 2, 1851. |
| 1852. 16 Vict. Nov. 4. | Brodie M'Gie Wilcox, Esq.<br>Sir A. J. E. Cockburn, Knight, appointed Chief-Justice of Common Pleas, November 21, 1856.<br>Thomas Matthias Weguelin, Esq. (L.), of Goldings, Hertford, February 1857, *vice* Cockburn. |
| 1857. 20 Vict. April 30. | Brodie M'Gie Wilcox, Esq., of Portman Square.<br>Thomas Matthias Weguelin, Esq. |
| 1859. 22 Vict. May 31. | William Digby Seymour, Esq. (L.C.), of the Inner Temple.<br>Brodie M'Gie Wilcox, Esq., died November 6, 1862.<br>William Anderson Rose, Esq. (C.), of the Mansion-house, London (December 8, 1862) *vice* Wilcox. |
| 1866. 29 Vict. Feb. 2. | Right Hon. Russell Gurney, Q.C. (C.)<br>George Moffatt, Esq. (L.) |
| 1868. 32 Vict. Dec. 10. | Russell Gurney, Q.C.<br>Peter Merrik Hoare, Esq. (C.) |
| 1874. 37 Vict. March 5. | Sir Frederick Perkins, Knight (L.)<br>Right Hon. Russell Gurney, Q.C., died May 31, 1878.<br>Alfred Giles, Esq. (C.), of Cosford, Godalming, *vice* Gurney. |
| 1880. 43 Vict. April 29. | Alfred Park Butt, Q.C. (L.)<br>Henry Lee, Esq. (L.), of Sedgley Park, Manchester. |
| 1883. 46 Vict. | Alfred Giles, Esq. (C.), elected April 6, *vice* Butt, elevated to the Judgship of the Admiralty Court. |

*Aldermen.*

Little has been said of the dignities of aldermen and sheriff. The earliest mention of aldermen occurs in the Ordinances of the Guild Merchant, when the 'chief alderman,' who was no doubt the mayor, and the twelve aldermen of wards, are mentioned; the office of these latter seems to have been chiefly that of police and sanitary regulation. The first charter which refers to aldermen is that of 2 Hen. IV. (1401), in which power was given or confirmed to elect four aldermen from among the burgesses for the purposes therein stated. The last governing charter (16 Chas. I. 1640) speaks of six aldermen, but probably the number was indefinite, and nothing is said as to their election or creation. Previously to the Act of 1835 the aldermen were those who had served the mayoralty, and they became such at the expiration of their office without any election; their number at the passing of the Act was nineteen, including the mayor. The aldermen are now ten in number, as arranged by the above Act, one-half of whom go out of office every third year, but may be re-elected. They hold office for six years, and are chosen from the councillors or persons qualified to be such; the councillors themselves requiring a certain property qualification, holding office for three years, and one-third going out of office each year.

### *Sheriff.*

The grant of a sheriff, to be chosen from among the burgesses, was made by charter of 25 Hen. VI. (1447). For the occupants of the office see above.

Before the Act of 1835 the sheriff was elected by the mayor and burgesses from the burgesses. He was invested with the powers of a county sheriff; he attended at the assizes when held for the town and county of the town, and at the sessions, for both of which he summoned the juries. He held a county court when necessary, and executed writs from the superior court, which were directed to him immediately. He was not connected in any way with the civil court of pleas. His principal duties were performed by an under-sheriff.[1] He is now appointed immediately after the mayor each 9th of November, with the powers of a county sheriff, which indeed he is, continued to him.

### *Of the Bailiffs.*

"Though the serving of offices be the charter qualification for "membership in the Common Council (see charter 16 Chas. I.), yet "some have been admitted on their paying fines for office. As the "office of bailiff is the first, and consequently the introductory one to "the Common Council, I shall give a few instances relating to that "office and the sheriff's, which were sometimes excused together.

"A.D. 1696. Mr. Richard White was excused from serving the "office of water-bailiff for a fine of £10; and in 1697 excused from "that of senior bailiff for £7, and was sworn of the Common Council. "*N.B.*—The junior bailiff is water-bailiff, the senior, bailiff of the court.

"A.D. 1726. Mr. William Freeman was excused from serving

[1] Report of Commissioners, 1835.

" the offices of bailiff and sheriff for a fine of £30; and if it be the " recorder's opinion that he is a member of the Common Council by " fining, to pay £5 more. *N.B.*—He was a member of the Common " Council.. The fines of composition for offices have been very different " at different times, and some have been excused without any fine " at all; so that the whole appears to depend upon the will of the " Common Council.[1]

" It has been usual [of later years] to choose the bailiffs out of the " younger burgesses who have not served that office before. But in " 13 Eliz. 1571, it is recorded that Richard Goddard, though an alder- " man, was chosen one of the bailiffs, for certain reasons them moving."[2] In 1587 it was ordered that the senior alderman of the town should henceforth be the chief bailiff of the court of the town of Southampton, and that the younger bailiff of the same court should preside at Trinity Fair, and be at the charges thereof.[3]

Until the Act of 1835 the bailiffs were, jointly with the mayor, judges of the civil court of pleas; and with the mayor were also the returning officers at the election of members of Parliament.

### *Of the Steward and Treasurer.*

Steward.

" The office of steward has been laid aside for some years; when " it was in use, the steward received and paid all, except some few " articles that belonged to the mayor's office, and both the mayor and " the steward delivered in books of their accounts every year. There " are many of these books in the Audit-house;" they range from 1441 to 1699, and are among the most interesting sources of local history. " But some of their stewards having proved very deficient, they came to " a resolution to hold an audit half-yearly for the receipt of their rents, " and to appoint a treasurer, and to settle their accounts every quarter."

The court leet had demanded a general audit of the town accounts in 1652, as the fines and amercements for many years past had either not been levied, or not carried to the town's account. Several stewards and other officers had made no return of the annual rents and profits, as they were bound to do; it was therefore desired that these various officers should bring their accounts to be examined by the auditors, and in the margin is written *fiat*, which was usual when it was intended that a presentment should really have some effect.

Treasurer.

The office of treasurer succeeded to that of steward. Under the

[1] Dr. Speed after this instances a considerable number of fines taken in lieu of accepting the various offices; these compositions, as he observes, are to be distinguished from the amercements for refusing office.

[2] " Book H., f. 61."

[3] Boke of Remembrances, f. 153.

present law the treasurer, whose office it is to keep the accounts of the borough, is appointed by the Council, and holds office during pleasure. He cannot be a member of the Town Council.

*Other Officers.*

"There are some other officers appointed from among the towns-
"men who are not burgesses; as four discreets of the market." These were anciently chosen on the Morrow of St. Michael, two to superintend the meat-market and two the fish-market; and all four were to see that the statutes concerning the sale of bread were observed (Guild Ord. 31).

"Discreets of the market."

"I do not find this office mentioned in any charter.

"The form of their oath will show their business:—

"'Ye shall well and truly serve in your office of Discreets of the Market. Ye
"'shall see that they sell good victual and wholesome for man's body, both in fish
"'and flesh, and be indifferent between buyer and seller; and that the fish-market
"'begin according to Mr. Mayor's proclamation. And all other things that to
"'your office belongeth ye shall well and truly execute. So help you God,' &c.

"They still continue [*c.* 1770] to burn unwholesome victuals."

Four discreets of the market are now appointed from the borough police, but they have no duties to perform.

"As Portswood is within the liberties of the town, they every
"year choose an officer of that tithing, who is called Alderman of Ports-
"wood. His business is that of a head-borough or constable, and he
"is sworn into his office in the town court."

"Alderman of Portswood."

The earliest observed notice of this officer occurs under 1469, when he pays over to the steward on the law-day 'for divers alewytes xxij^d.;' similarly in 1488. In 1507 'alewytes for the yere xiij^d.;' in 1512 he pays sixteen pence for two years. The alderman is still appointed every year in pursuance of ancient usage, but he has no duties to discharge.

"The serjeants, besides their duty of attendance upon the mayor
"and Corporation, are sworn officers to execute all attachments, arrests,
"&c., within the town and its precincts."

"Serjeants."

Before the Act of 1835 two of them were gaolers, one of the debtors', the other of the felons' prison; the third collected the tolls of the poultry and vegetable market, and the fourth was water-bailiff.

The four serjeants-at-mace were formerly elected by the 'twelve men at the common assembly in the Guildhall,' and could only be removed by the same power (1548);[1] in the next century they were commonly called 'biddels' (beadles). Towards the end of it (1675),

[1] Boke of Remembrances, f. 53.

Isaac Watts, the father of the hymnologist, on refusing to renounce the covenant and take the oaths on being appointed 'bidell,' was adjudged to have refused the office and fined £3. On being chosen again 'bidell' for the ward of St. Michael and St. John, he was freed from the office for seven years at a fine of forty shillings; chosen to the office of constable, October 1, 1703, he was excused on payment of five guineas, but was not to be let off again under double that amount.[1]

There are now but two serjeants-at-mace, who, with the town-crier, are attendants upon the Corporation and Justices.

"Porters." "By charter 23 Hen. VI. (p. 155) they are empowered to appoint "brokers,[2] packers,[3] porters, and carriers, as they had been used to "do before that charter. The brokers and packers are now out "of date, but the porters are, and always have been,[4] united into a "kind of prescriptive company, under the direction of the Corpora-"tion. They have a common stock of horses, carriages, &c., and their "pay is collected by a common steward and divided among them. "Their number is limited to seven besides their steward." The same number had been prescribed in 1501 and subsequent years. Under 1547 we have a notice of the working of the company. They found sureties to pay the town their rent. The accounts were made up every Saturday night before the master, who divided to each his share. They were to provide four able horses to serve the merchants with, each horse to be worth at least twenty-six and eightpence.[5]

"They buy and sell their places; but must be admitted, and may be "turned out, by the Common Council, who also appoint the rates of "the carriage,[6] which is at present for every pipe of wine 6d., for

[1] Journals.

[2] By order of 1520, neither merchant strangers nor burgesses were permitted to bargain with ships arriving under Wight or in Hampton Water, and to pay ready money, by which means coin would be carried out of the realm, contrary to the king's laws and hurtful to the town's custom, but they were to employ brokers, and the payments were to be made within the town (Boke of Remembrances, f. 18 b.)

[3] In 1469 the packers paid for 'the ferme of the pekkyng,' £5, 6s. 8d. In 1482 they paid £6 (Steward's Books). In 1518 one paid to the town for his place twenty-six shillings and eightpence, and 'to dwell in a new house according to the order of the town.'

[4] Probably they were already associated when, in Close Roll, 4th June (9 Hen. III.) 1225, the king directed the bailiffs of Southampton to pay them for cellaring one hundred casks of wine. 'Præcipimus vobis quod habere faciatis *beremannis* Suhamptoniæ id quod habere debent pro C doliis vini portandis et ponendis in celariis nostris de Suht. super canteras, et computabitur vobis ad Scaccarium.' But in another account shortly before we read of 'hiring' porters.

[5] Book of Rememb. H., f. 87 b. In 1469, like the packers, they rendered account for the 'ferm' or rent of their porterwyke (Steward's Book).

[6] "See Laws of the Guild, No. 71."

"every hogshead 3d., to any part of the town within the walls; and "they are answerable for any accident that may happen till the cask "is safe upon its stand in the cellar." The porters of course had a strict monopoly.[1]

"Besides these there is a set of inferior porters called bearers, "because their proper business is to carry such things as may be borne "on men's backs, as corn, coals, &c. These, too, were always under "the Corporation's direction, and were formed into a company. "Bearers."

"No bearers have been appointed by the Corporation for many "years; and as all restrictions of this kind are now discountenanced, "everybody carries that will. But the credit of the porters and the "moderate price at which they carry, together with the circumstance "of their being obliged to stand to all accidents that may happen in "the carriage, are sufficient inducements to most people to give them "the preference."

Previously to the Act of 1835 the following offices, not mentioned in charters, were held in the Corporation:— Officials unmentioned.

Aldermen of the wards (see p. 208), four in number; beadles of the wards, fourteen, and extra beadles indefinite; constables, two; auditors of accounts, indefinite; weigher of wool, one, whose duties, once important, had become nominal; aulnager, one; measurers of corn and of coal, indefinite; scavenger, one; keepers of the keys of the gates, four: these were always the mayor, the late mayor, and two senior resident aldermen; besides these there were originally regularly appointed warders of the gates; keepers of the keys of booths, two: these were supposed to have reference to booths erected at the fair held above Bar; keepers of the keys of the great chest (where the minutes were kept), three: these were the mayor and bailiffs, but the mayor really kept the keys; crier, one, who attended quarter-sessions, kept the weights and scales, and keys of the market gates, and was paid for crying by those who employed him; supervisors of land, mayor and aldermen indefinite in number: they had, however, no duties as such, the property of the Corporation being entirely managed by the Common Council; water-bailiff, one, whose functions in early times seem to have been responsible, but who latterly was in general one of the serjeants-at-mace: he used to attend the mayor when performing any duty in the capacity of admiral. His functions of late years had been to attend the

[1] It appears that the porters sometimes acted as scavengers. In 1667 they were presented for not having carried away a mixon over against the French church (Court Leet Book). In 1526 they seem to have paid twenty shillings for their 'ferm,' and to have received half the penalties for casting dung in the streets, provided they acted as informers and presented the offenders (Boke of Rememb., f. 27).

officer of the court of pleas of the town with the silver oar, the badge of the town's admiralty, when it had been his duty to make arrests on the water within low-water mark; sand-walkers, indefinite: these formerly watched for waifs and wrecks, and their appointment, which was made under seal, had been during the French war an object of desire as a protection against impressment.[1] There were latterly between twenty and thirty; wardens of Sendy's gift, two.

Besides the above there were anciently—

Gunner. The town gunner, an official who appears in the earliest consecutive town records. In the Steward's Book of 1457 are some interesting

His work. entries concerning the gunner and his work. His wages were sixpence a day; his office to superintend the making of gunpowder and the handling and repair of the guns. In the year above mentioned the French fleet, which subsequently burnt Sandwich, stood before the town, and preparations for defence had to be made. Among the items occur—

> Payd to John Branne, gonner, for iiij days, ij$^{s.}$
>
> Item for hys ij men to help hym to make gone powdere for iiij dayes, iij$^{s.}$ iiij$^{d.}$
>
> Item to a laborere ij dayes to bete coles for the gonepowder, viij$^{d.}$
>
> Item payd to John of Chamber for iiij dayes to helpe the gonner to make gonepowder, xx$^{d.}$

Then follow accounts for labour on the ordnance for four days, and on the bulwarks:—

> Item payd for a voyd hoggeshed to put in gonepowder, vj$^{d.}$
>
> Item payd for ij quarters of charcole for fyre to make gone powdere, xij$^{d.}$ (also for 'coles' for the same purpose).
>
> Item for ij sevys for to syfte gonnepowder withall, xij$^{d.}$
>
> Then again wages to John Branne, the gunner, and 'to the sayd John for a reward for brennyng of his clothys, xij$^{d.}$'
>
> Item payd for vj whyt lethere bagges to put gonnepowdere in, xiiij$^{d.}$
>
> Item payd to Angell Aldebrand for ij quarter of saltpeter for to make gonnepowder withall, xxx$^{s.}$ iiij$^{d.}$
>
> Item payd to my master the meyre for halfe C brymeston for gone powder, ix$^{s.}$ iij$^{d.}$

Then payments for laying the guns:—

> Item payd to Symken for iij partes of a day to help to ley the gret gonne upon the key, iij$^{d.}$
>
> Item payd to John Myles, carpenter, for his laboure ij dayes and an halfe upon the gret gonne, xij$^{d.}$
>
> Robert Carpenter was also paid for work during thirteen days 'in stokking of

[1] In 1804 a certain sand-walker belonging to the admiralty jurisdiction of the Corporation having been impressed, representation was made by the mayor as admiral of the port to the admiral commanding at Portsmouth, stating the facts of the case and requesting the discharge of the official. The claim was immediately allowed (Journal, May 10, 1804).

gonnes' and laying guns in the new wall, &c. His wages were sixpence a day, and those of his man fivepence.

Item payd to John Gonner thatt cam fro Sandwyche for hys labor by the commandment of my master the meyr, xiij$^{d.}$

The gunner was protected, as was usual, with hoardings and shutters: His cover.

Item payd for nayles to nayle the bordes to kevere the gonner withall, iij$^{d.}$

His station was probably at God's House Tower, and the first affray was by candlelight.

Item payd for v$^{li.}$ of candellus that were wasted in Godes hows towre and in the bolewerke, that nyght the furst affray was, v$^{d.}$ The affray.

In relation to the above incident numerous entries occur of hasty repairs to the walls, gates, and quays, and of stopping the 'ways up to the walls,' there being abundant quay space outside the town, from which there were many communications (see p. 85). Men had been also sent in opposite directions to learn news of the fleet:—

Item payd to Richard Assche (see p. 156) for a man to ryde to Portysmothe to bryng redyng [sailing] tydynges owt of Normandy of the Frenshmen, xij$^{d.}$

Item payd to Will. Taylour for hys labour and costes to ryde to Lepe to inqwere tydynges of the Frenshmen, xj$^{d.}$

Help had been also invoked from other towns, and the soldiers had to be entertained:—

Item payd to Davy Berebrewer for a pyp of bere that was dronke at the Barreyeate when the furst affray was of the Frenshemen, vj$^{s.}$ viij$^{d.}$ Soldiers refreshed.

Item payd to Richard Smythe for drynkyng potts that were bowght of hym when the sowdyers of Salysbery dyned in the Frerre [Friary], ix$^{d.}$

Item payd to John Ball for bred that was ete at the Baryeate when the sowdyers were here, vj$^{d.}$

Item to John Forest for wyn yevan to Thomas Hampton and other gentylmen when sowdyers were here, ij$^{d.}$

Item payd to Edward Cateyn for a pyp of wyn that was bowght when the sowdyers come to town of Salysbery and of other places, liij$^{s.}$ iiij$^{d.}$

In 1512 (4 Hen. VIII.) a townsman offered his services as gunner at the yearly salary of twenty-six shillings and eightpence and a gown. He was to receive twopence for the making of every gun-stone, and sevenpence a day 'when he workyth yn makinge of gon-powder,' and fourpence a day for every man so employed by him. A few years later he was ordered to serve the town in peace and in war at ten shillings per annum, having also an allowance of four yards of cloth at three shillings and fourpence per yard for his livery. In 1657 the town drummer and the town gunner each received as annual wages thirteen shillings and fourpence.

The town carpenter is frequently mentioned; he paid for his place, and had a livery. Carpenter.

Of the town paviour, scavenger, and chimney-sweep we have already spoken (see pp. 120, 124).

The town brickmaker with his kiln on the common is referred to in

Brick-maker. the court leet books of 1575 and elsewhere. In 1623 the price given him for bricks was nine shillings and sixpence per thousand; a few years later it was set at ten shillings. In 1704 the assize of bricks, according to ancient custom, was said to be 10 inches in length, 4¾ in breadth, and 2½ in thickness.

Cowherd. This officer, who also resided on the heath—the 'Cowherds' is still known—seems to have looked after all the common lands, and had the general superintendence of the cattle there turned out. In 1570 he made an affidavit, which reads most improbably, that the late Sir Francis Dawtrey had tried to bribe him to allow his cattle to go on the common.[1] In the next year we find him at his duties in the Saltmarsh. It was the law that all men and boys above the age of seven years should practise the art of shooting; but the cattle in the Saltmarsh being found a great nuisance, the 'coward' was ordered[2] to keep his beasts on Sundays and holidays out of the shooting-places. These were in the Saltmarsh, Houndwell, the Ditches, Castlegreen, and elsewhere.

Besides the cowherd there were four overseers and twelve drovers of the common.[3]

Carrier. The common carrier might also be considered as a town official. He had a distinct monopoly. In 1593, during the season of plague (July), then daily increasing, the common carrier between the town and London was kept outside, nor permitted to enter the gates of Southampton with his cart and baggage, or by his servants, on any pretence whatever. The carrier compounded with the town for his place, and carried merchandise at a certain tariff fixed by the town. In 1602 his fine was £10. Some years later (1637), his trade falling off from fear of infection, he was allowed to increase his charges.

Foot-post. Besides the carrier there was a foot-post between the town and London, who wore a silver badge with the town arms, and had a monopoly. He usually started on Monday or Tuesday.[4]

Minstrels. The town minstrels.—At one time the town appears to have possessed a body of musicians, who received regular wages and a livery. In 1433 they appear to have been but three in number.[5] But independently of these, strolling bodies of minstrels, under the name and protection of some great lord or important town, constantly received the town's wages and gratuities for their enlivening performances. Thus the king's and queen's minstrels, those of the Earl of Arundel, of my Lord Cardinal, and innumerable others, are of constant occurrence in

[1] Boke of Remembrances, f. 106 b. [2] Court Leet Books, 1571.

[3] Court Leet Books, 1640, 1675.

[4] In 1637 a certain person was restrained from going to London on the Monday and Tuesday to the hindrance of the foot-post.

[5] Steward's Books, 1433-34.

the town accounts, with their rates of payment. By a warrant of Privy Council (1593) players had been forbidden to give their entertainments within the city of London or seven miles of it, in consequence of the late sickness, from the fear of infection arising from a concourse of people; but outside that distance, and in other cities and towns, they were at liberty to exercise their skill, and were advised to do so, that they might keep in readiness for her Majesty's pleasure whenever she should call for them. Accordingly an order (May 6, 1593) informed the town that a famous company just arrived would play at convenient times, hours of divine service excepted.[1] The craft of minstrelsy was, however, becoming discredited. The Act against beggars and vagabonds (14 Eliz. 1572) had included among the proscribed 'common players in enterludes, and minstrels not belonging to any baron of this realm;' and a final blow was probably received under the 39 Eliz. 1597, cap. 4, which repeated the former enactment. In 1623 we find the town musicians asking for their liveries, which they received with a broad hint to ask no more, but take what was given them. A few years later silver badges with the town arms were distributed to the musicians by the mayor.

**Players.**

As kindred to musicians, a notice may be given of stage-players. The utmost indulgence was given to scenic performances. It seems to have been the custom to permit the use of the townhall for this purpose; but in 1624 the practice was forbidden, owing to the disorder in which the hall was constantly thrown; the table, benches, and forms there set for holding the king's courts being 'by these means broken and spoiled,' and when the mayor and officers came for the administration of justice, especially in pie-poudre courts, which were liable to be held without much notice, the court was constantly found in an unseemly and unsavoury condition.

**Guild or mayor's priest.**

The ancient Guild Merchant not only regulated the trade and the civil government of the town, but preserved a certain religious and eleemosynary character, and had its chaplain with definite duties and an understood position and allowances.[2] Subsequently the chaplains, who appear to have been appointed permanently, received a fixed stipend of £3, 6s. 8d. per annum, with a gown and hood, worth generally about thirteen shillings and fourpence, consisting of four yards of cloth at three shillings and fourpence. Thus in 1457 Sir William[3] was Guild-priest at the above amount. In 1478 Sir Harry the same. Occasionally the mayor's priest was employed on confidential duties. It appears that during a visit of King Edward IV. to the town in 1481,

[1] Liber Notationum, 1593. [2] See Guild Ordinances, Nos. 1, 2, 3.
[3] Steward's Books.

some knave stole a cruise belonging to the royal silver. Apparently the thief was suspected to be in the royal retinue, for the king having moved on to Winchester, Sir David was desired to ride to Hyde Abbey, where probably the king was lodged, to inquire into the matter, taking with him a bottle of Malmesey worth sixpence as a present to the Abbot. On 16th July Sir David again rode to Winchester 'to make examynacion for one that toke the crusse,' and, possibly as a result of his diplomacy, the thief was detected, for a little after John Smith, the tailor, received twenty-four shillings and eightpence as a reward for riding to London with the king's silver, by the advice of the mayor and his brethren.[1] In 1486 Sir Richard received pay as Guild-priest. In other years the livery and wages are mentioned, but not the men. In 1501 and 1509 Sir William, who was also Holmehegg or Holmage chanter, was Guild-priest. Sir Hector held both offices in 1543, and the price of cloth must have risen, since his gown and tippet cost six shillings per yard.[2]

After this signs of the old office disappear from the town books. In the following century it was the custom for the Corporation to pay forty shillings as a present to the rector or vicar of the parish in which the mayor for the time being happened to reside, as a gratuity for the performance of such offices as might still be required; and possibly the parish priest was thus considered Guild or mayor's chaplain. In September 1638 the steward was ordered to pay the above sum 'to Mr. Edmundson, minister of Holy Rood, the minister of the parish wherein the mayor dwelleth, as it is accustomed, as a gift and gratuity from the town. The money was brought to the assembly, and Mr. Edmundson was sent for to the House to receive it here, as the ministers heretofore have done, and did receive it as a favour and courtesy from this House in all thankful acknowledgment.'[3]

No later entry has been observed in reference to the mayor's or Guild chaplain till the present century, when in January 1805 we find his salary arranged at £5, 5s. per annum. In December 1820 the resignation of that office by the Rev. Thomas Mears is recorded after a service of twenty-five years. On his death in 1835 the Corporation subscribed twenty guineas to his monument, partly in consequence of his having been so long their chaplain.[4] Since that time it has generally been, and still is, the custom for the mayor to choose the rector or vicar of the parish in which he resides to act as chaplain during his year of the mayoralty. The office is of course purely honorary.

[1] Steward's Books, 1481–82.
[2] Steward's Books under dates; also Liber Rememb. B.B., fol. ii. for 1491.
[3] Journal, September 1638.
[4] Journal, December 15, 1820; May 4, 1835.

## SECTION IV.—*The Staple.*

"There is no mention of a staple in this town before the charter "23 Henry VI., but they always practised statute merchant,[1] and "many of the laws of the Guild[2] are formed upon that plan. Their "book of records on this subject, used even after they had a staple "under the above charter, is still called 'the book of statutes mer-"chant.' They did here, as in other places, transact all money "matters this way, though the persons concerned, or the business, had "no relation to merchandise or trade properly so called. A few in-"stances will show this:—

"In the reign of James I., Thomas Fleming, Knt., of North Stoneham, was "bound to Andrew Munday of Nutshaling, by statute merchant in £3000.

"William Lisle, Knt., of Wootton, in the Isle of Wight, to John Foyle of the "Middle Temple, was bound by statute merchant in £1000. It appears by the "defeasances that these were for lands sold by statute merchant.

"Philip Leigh of Testwood bound to Mary Leigh of Testwood, £8000.

"Thomas Mompesson of the Close, Sarum, bound to Eleanor Hodges, "£3000.

"Sir John Mill bound to Sir John Clobery, £1000.

"A.D. 1654, Thomas Dummer of Chicknell, in the parish of North Stone-"ham, in the county of Southampton, yeoman, was bound to John Comfort of "Portsmouth, in the county of Southampton, merchant, by statute merchant, in "£600. This was discharged A.D. 1662.

"A.D. 1658, the Right Hon. Heneage, Earl of Winchelsea, was bound by "statute merchant to Mary Russell, widow, daughter to John, Lord Viscount "Scudamore, in £16,000.

"The latest statute in this book is dated A.D. 1689. They all run "'pro merchandisis in hac stapulâ emptis'—for merchandise bought "in this staple—though the transactions had nothing to do with mer-"chandise. The Corporation still continue to elect officers of the "staple every year, who are sworn into their offices: the mayor taking "the oath of Mayor of the Staple, besides the oath of mayor as a "civil magistrate."[3]

## SECTION V.—*Of Exemption from Prisage.*

Prisage of wines—subsequently called the 'butlerage'—was an ancient duty under which the king claimed out of every ship laden

[1] Dr. Speed, in a portion of his notice of the staple, not printed here, discusses the difference between statute staple and statute merchant, the former being only a statute merchant executed before the officers of the staple. This he instances by a staple recogisance in his hands, in which William Esteney, co. Southampton, Esquire, was bound to Thomas Colrithe in a hundred marks sterling for goods bought of him in the staple of Westminster (May 25, 1416). This was really to secure Colrithe in the possession of an estate, a deed being annexed reciting the recogisance, and declaring that it shall be void if Colrithe is maintained in quiet possession.

[2] "See Law 27."

[3] The last vestige of the above was swept away in 1835.

with wines containing twenty tuns or more, two tuns of wine, one before, the other behind the mast, at his price, which was twenty shillings for each tun.

"The payment of this duty was remitted to the burgesses of this town "first by a charter, 10 Henry VIII.—which charter does not appear— "and afterwards by an Act of Parliament, 22 Henry VIII. (1530–31). "But as one tun of red wine a year out of the prisage of this port had "before this remission been granted to each of the following Abbeys, "Beaulieu, Titchfield, Lettely or Netley, Waverley, and St. Denys, for "the celebration of mass, these five tuns are exempted in the Act. "Upon the dissolution of abbeys these five tuns, being the goods of "the Church, returned into the king's hands; but they were not regu- "larly paid, which neglect brought on a quo warranto 5 [16 ?] Eliza- "beth; and in 1608 one Mr. Birchmere, who was prisage-master, "or farmer of the prisage, sued the town for arrears of these five tuns "of abbey prisage. The town was cast, and paid 500 marks. After "which the king, upon their petition, granted them a perpetual "exemption from paying these five tuns of prisage for the future;" with remission of all arrears from 4th February (27 Hen. VIII.) 1536 to the date of the patent, February 6 (6 Jas. I.), 1609.

"This payment of 500 marks was a great blow to them, and as " [this excepted butlerage] was a duty that should have been paid by "the burgesses, it was agreed by the consent of all that an order "should be made to lay such a tax upon all wines imported by bur- "gesses as the mayor and his brethren should think fit.

"An order was accordingly made the same year (1608) that 2s. "per tun on all wines bought for the use of burgesses, or bought "by burgesses of foreigners, be paid, in consideration of the charge "which the Corporation had been at in paying the arrears of the five "tuns of abbey prisage, and procuring a charter of discharge from "that duty for the future. This order to continue for one year." The impost was in reality paid several years, and was disputed in 1620, when reference was made to the recorder, under whose award it was probably stopped. It was revived in the next century; and in 1708 the collector of customs was desired to receive two shillings per tun from the burgesses in lieu of prisage, which was said to be after old custom. It is evident that the reason of the payment had been forgotten; after a few years it was finally dropped.[1]

"They have had some trials at law on this exemption from prisage, "but their right has always been supported when their proceedings "have been regular."

[1] Abridged from Dr. Speed.

## SECTION VI.—*Of the Admiralty Jurisdiction.*

The charter of King John granted the town of Southampton to the burgesses at farm, together with the port of Portsmouth, and all the appurtenances, liberties, and customs which belonged in former times to the farm of the town. It seems probable that some maritime jurisdiction was perpetuated from ancient days under this grant, and accordingly we find the town assuming very extensive rights before the formal grant of admiralty by the charter 30 Hen. VI. (1451). In 1239 (see under 'Petty Customs') their rights within the *port* of Portsmouth were acknowledged. In 1285 the burgesses destroyed as hurtful to navigation a weir which had been constructed at Cadlands by the Abbot of Titchfield. The Abbot brought his action, but was cast, the jury finding that no weir had existed within memory, but that formerly there were piles in the water as if there had anciently been some such construction, which they were inclined to think had been destroyed on account of its injury to the shipping.[1] In 1302 (see 'Petty Customs') we find the burgesses giving a lease of the customs over a wide extent which was clearly identical with the port. "In a trial, 17 "Edward II. (1324), with Lymington about the petty customs it is "set forth that from Hurst to Langston is within the port of South- "ampton. *Ancient rights.*

"The admiralty jurisdiction was first granted by charter 30 Henry "VI. (1451); the extent of it was to be extremities of the ancient "port"—that is to say, from Langston on the east, including the port of Portsmouth, and from Hurst on the west, including Lymington, together with all tidal harbours, rivers, creeks, &c., within the boundary line.[2] *1451.*

According to the settlement of the bounds of the port of Southampton as returned into the Exchequer in the 32 Chas. II. (Mich. term) 1680, the line on the west was drawn from Christ Church Head, thence south-east to the Needles, then eastward in a supposed straight course to the west end of the Brambles, thence to Hill Head on the mainland at the mouth of the Southampton Water, and so up the *Port limits.*

---

[1] Abbrev. Plac. Mich. 13–14 Ed. I.

[2] The grant (July 14, 1628) to Mary Wandesford, wife of Sir George Wandesford, and daughter of Robert Pamplin, late yeoman of his Majesty's robes, and to her sister Margaret, wife of William Wandesford, and their heirs, of all the mudlands between high and low water mark in the haven of Southampton, and other specified parts of Hampshire, with power to 'inn' or enclose them, gave great offence to the town's people as an infringement of their admiralty; and on September 26, 1636, Dame Mary Wandesford petitioned the Privy Council for redress against certain of the burgesses for disturbance of her enclosures. Commissioners were appointed, who met at the Dolphin, and summoned the defendants before them (October 14), but they failed to appear.

stream of Redbridge, including all bays, channels, roads, bars, strands, harbours, &c. On the east the limits were curtailed, as Portsmouth was excluded; though in the settlement of that port, as returned into the Court of Exchequer at the same time, it is described as 'a member of the port of Southampton,' as is also the port of Cowes.[1]

Exercise of powers.

"In consequence of their grant they exercised every branch of "admiralty power: they had in the town an admiralty court and "prison, they claimed all wrecks, took cognisance of fishing in the "water within their precincts, which they suffered none to do but such "fishermen as were licensed by them. And as by the admiralty law "it is sea everywhere to the first bridge, they claimed a right to exercise "that power as far as Redbridge on the river Test, and as far as Wood "Mill on the river Itchen.

"There are many instances in the Journals of their exercising full "power on all the water within their district. Thus:"—

In 1474 a man was paid for going to Langston along the coast to "look after wrecks belonging to the town's admiralty; in 1499 a mast "was brought as a wreck from the Isle of Wight; in 1502 a man was "fined for dragging oysters;" in 1569 the men of Keyhaven were presented for 'perking yells at all times'—pricking eels at unlawful seasons. "In 1610 Sir Thomas West of Testwood prosecuted some "licensed fishermen for fishing below Redbridge. The House advised "them to use Sir Thomas well, and no doubt he would withdraw his "action, which they supposed to be grounded on their fishing with "unlawful nets, and not in opposition to the town's right. The "action was withdrawn. In 1611 owners of boats were ordered to "bring oysters to the quay for the marshal of the admiralty to lay "them in convenient places in the harbour, according to ancient cus"tom. In 1632 the Corporation granted a warrant to the fishermen "of Itchen to take away guns from all persons shooting at fowl upon "the sea within their admiralty. In 1642 they gave a grant for fish"ing in Itchen ferry river; in 1649 their right of fishing there was "disputed; and the same year Mr. Peter Clungeon surrendered his "lease for fishing and fowling in the Itchen ferry river. So it appears "that they were cast in the dispute." In 1658 the court leet presented that the fishing between Southampton and Redbridge had been usurped by Mr. Thomas Knowles and others, to the hurt of the place.

Itchen Ferry.

"In 1613 it was ordered that the burgesses and their servants "should pay nothing for their passage over Itchen ferry; and the

[1] Modern Practice of Exchequer (1730), pp. 40, 95, 105; also below, 'Courts.' In 1432 the customer at Southampton was desired to appoint deputies at Lymington, Newport, and Portsmouth (Rot. Parl. iv. 417).

"ferrymen were presented for taking money of them.[1] About the "same time it was ordered that the fishermen of Itchen ferry should "lay gravel on the shore on the town side of the ferry. But these "matters relating to the ferry seem rather to depend on their having "the liberty to land their passengers on the town side than on the "admiralty jurisdiction.

"The passage to Hythe was formerly a ferry, and the Corporation "once applied for a charter for it; on which Sir Christopher Parkins, "one of the king's Masters of Requests, sent to them for information "concerning this matter. Their answer was, that by virtue of their "admiralty jurisdiction they had always settled the price of the pas- "sage as follows: for a man and a horse 3d., for a single man 1d., "market people ½d., a cow 3d., 20 sheep 6d. But nothing came of "this, and that ferry has been dropped many years.[2] Hythe Ferry.

"A.D. 1684, some of Cowes were prosecuted for a riot within the "town's admiralty.[3]

"The same year an accident happened which put an end to their "usual exertion of their admiralty jurisdiction. The case was as "under:—[4]

"A Dutch ship, laden with wines, had been by stress of weather "stranded on Calshot Spit, which is within the admiralty of South- "ampton. When the mayor heard of it he hired a vessel, and taking "with him some of the burgesses and some of the custom-house "officers, went down to save what he could for the owners; his com- "pany, besides mariners and labourers, being about ten persons. "When he came down, he found that one Robert Wetherick had "seized the ship and cargo as a wreck for Sir Robert Holmes, gover- "nor of the Isle of Wight, as admiral of that part of the coast. Upon "the mayor's declaring the place to be within the admiralty of "Southampton, Wetherick went away to get, as he said, further "orders from Sir Robert Holmes, and the mayor set his people to "work to save the wines by hoisting them out of the wreck into a galliot "hoy which he had provided for that purpose. The next day, while "they were at work, Wetherick returned with several others, and "again seized the wines, declaring that he did it by order of Sir Robert "Holmes. However, after two or three hours' interruption, there "being some danger of the wines being spoiled, they suffered the men

1 Captain Smith, the builder afterwards of Jesus Chapel, Peartree Green, had the ferry at this time, and had 'oftentimes willed the passengers aforesaid [*i.e.*, the ferrymen] to take nothing of the burgesses' (Journal, August 6, 1613).

2 It is now a regular steam-ferry.

3 See above, p. 221, as to extent of port at this period.

4 "Brief of the case in my hands."

"of Southampton to go on, as well as themselves, and when the "galliot hoy was full, the mayor and his company sailed with her "for Southampton, in order to bring the said wines to the king's "custom-house there, being upwards of ninety hogsheads. But when "they came about half way up the river, Wetherick and his company, "about twenty, who had pursued them, entered their ship armed with "guns and drawn swords, by the command, as they said, of Sir Robert "Holmes, and did cut and beat several persons on board the said hoy, "and threaten to kill the persons thereupon if they did not depart, "and also the master of the hoy if he did not sail back to Cowes with "the wines. On which the mayor and his company gave up the "point. But Sir Robert Holmes afterwards lodged a complaint "against them at the Council Board,[1] where a determination was "given against the Corporation.

"This check put a stop to the career of their 'admiralty jurisdic-"tion,' though they exercised it afterwards in some points, as:—

"Journal." "A.D. 1687, they granted a deputation to the men of Hythe to "collect a duty on vessels to repair the causeway there, being within "the town's admiralty.

"It appears that in 1707 they had some dispute with the Duke of "Bolton on the town's admiralty, but the matter does not seem to have "been decided. In 1708 it was ordered that a proper person should be "sent by Mr. Mayor to a court of admiralty to be held at Portsmouth "by the Duke of Bolton, with a letter to his grace's judge advocate, "and a protestation declaring the town's rights. It appears likewise "that in 1709 some steps were taken towards an attempt to recover "the admiralty jurisdiction, but the affair was dropped.

"Within the memory of some persons now [1770] living they have "given licenses to fishermen, and have gone once a year to fish them-"selves as high as Redbridge and Woodmill; but these have been "long left off, and they have now scarce any remains of their ad-"miralty except their silver oar, and their going sometimes a kind of "circuit to keep admiralty court at Lymington and some others places, "where they sometimes got some small matters of wrecks. But this "is in general looked on as a mere formality, and is reckoned to be a "jaunt of pleasure rather than of business."

Admiralty rights were finally extinguished in 1835.

Southampton is now the head-port for Christchurch, Lymington, Keyhaven, Beaulieu, Hamble, and Redbridge; its custom-house is

[1] The mayor was summoned to attend the King and Council on January 29, 1684–85, to prove the right of admiralty and the bounds thereof, then questioned by Sir Robert Holmes, vice-admiral of Hants. The House ordered the records to be searched and the case legally got up (Journal, January 21, 1684–85).

mentioned below under 'Docks.' The harbour of Southampton commences at Hill Head, the boundary between the port of Southampton and Portsmouth, and stretches across in a right line to a point just below Calshot Castle.

### SECTION VII.—*Petty Customs.*

The petty customs were the duties on merchandise payable to the town, as determined by tables kept by the Corporation, from all places within the limits of the port. These places were vaguely described in the early charters, but are set forth in a lease of the customs, 30 Ed. I. (1302), from Peter de Lyons, no doubt the mayor, and twenty-one others, to Robert le Mercer and seven others, in which the members of the town demised under the lease, and for which the fee-farm of £200 per annum was rendered, are said to be Portemue, Hamele (Hamble), Linnentone, Scharprixe (on the east side of the Lymington river, south of Walhampton), Kyhaven, and Rumbrygge.[1] Within the lease were included the rent of the land-gable, and all profits of amercements, forfeitures of bakers and other.

Contentions with Portsmouth, 1239.

Disputes on the petty customs were of early and frequent occurrence: first, in regard to Portsmouth. The charter of John (June 29, 1199) had granted to the burgesses of Southampton the perpetual farm of their town, together with the port of Portsmues, and all customs and privileges which belonged to the farm of the town of Southampton in the time of Henry II. On plea of this grant the burgesses claimed jurisdiction not only in the port, but in the town of Portsmouth; a claim brought to issue in 1239 (24 Hen. III.), when the burgesses of Southampton having sued those of Portsmouth for damages on the ground of their having taken certain customs, fines, &c., within the port of Portsmouth, a concord was arranged, by which the burgesses of Portsmouth renounced claim to customs, &c., arising *within the port* of Portsmouth, and acknowledged the right of Southampton, and those of Southampton gave up claim to any rights *outside* the limits of the same port; and to avoid future disputes it was agreed, with the royal licence, that henceforth all amercements and profits from strangers, both in the town and in the waters of the port, should be equally divided between the burgesses of Portsmouth and those of Southampton, and that each party should have a bailiff of its own appointed to hear and hold pleas in the town of Portsmouth, who should proceed by jury, and make oath to each other faithfully to divide and adjudge all profits equally between the two towns; the king's rights to great sea-fish and his other profits of the sea being preserved. It was further

[1] Indenture in Corporation Archives.

provided that all pleas of the crown happening within the *port* of Portsmouth should be presented to the king and his justices by the coroners and bailiff of Southampton, but that all arising within the *town* of Portsmouth should be presented by the burgesses of Portsmouth and their bailiff. On these conditions the burgesses of Southampton remitted to those of Portsmouth all the damages set forth in their plea, the latter paying five marks of silver for this remission.[1] Dated November 21 (24 Hen. III.), 1239.

The port of Portsmouth continued to be a member of the liberties of the town of Southampton according to the charters of the latter; as, for instance, in those of greatest importance, in the 23 and 25 Hen. VI., and in the last governing charter of 1640 (16 Chas. I.) It so remained as a more or less acknowledged fact[2] till the changes of 1835.

Lymington, 1324.

The earliest extant dispute with Lymington on the petty customs was in 17 Ed. II., when Geoffrey Scurlag, the mayor, William Culhout, and eighteen others, 'men' of the town of Lymington, were attached to answer to the king and to the mayor, bailiffs, and other men of the community of the town of Southampton in a plea of trespass, in taking tolls at Lymington, which belonged to the farm of Southampton. The burgesses of Southampton represented that they held their town and port, extending from beyond Hurst to Langstone, of the king at a fee-farm of £220 per annum; that on that account certain customs of all merchandises within those limits belonged to them, except in the cases of such merchants as were free by royal charter; they therefore prayed damages to the amount of £500 from the men of Lymington for the invasion of their rights by taking customs of salt, corn, barley, and oats, cloth, wax, and other wares, and for assaulting Walter de Depeden, the king's customer, who was agent for the town of Southampton at Lymington. In defence it was denied that Lymington was within the port, the assault on the customer was also denied. The jury, however, found that all the water between Hurst and Langstone was of the port and within the precinct of the port of the town of Southampton; that the king's progenitors, all the while they held the said town of Southampton in their own hands, had received the whole custom arising from wares and merchandise brought by ship, as well at Lymington and Southampton or elsewhere, before they demised the said town to the mayor and community; that the said mayor and community ever since they had held the town at ferm had in like manner received the same; that Lymington was within the bounds and precincts of the port of Southampton; that the custom

[1] Oak Book. Dr. Speed has this document in full.

[2] See above under 'Admiralty,' and below under 'Admiralty Court.'

of goods and wares brought by ship to Lymington belonged of right to Southampton, and had hitherto been enjoyed by the mayor and community of Southampton. Damages were given against Lymington to the amount of £200, while it was found that Walter de Depeden had not been beaten.[1]

"Similar fate has often attended Lymington on this subject. But "A.D. 1730 the people of that place had the address to get their cause "moved from the courts above to the courts of assize, where a jury "from their own neighbourhood gave a verdict in their favour. And "here I think the matter has rested ever since with regard to Lymington. The Corporation have had many controversies on this subject, "but I learn from a late conversation with some of their members "that they have of late years found the course of the law so averse to "their claim that they at present confine themselves merely to the "port of the town."

About 1730 the borough of Lymington petitioned Sir Robert Walpole, first Lord of the Treasury, that as their harbour was situated twenty-five miles from the port of Southampton, of which it was a creek, it might for the convenience of merchants be made a member of that port. Accordingly the Government established a custom-house at Lymington, subordinated to the port of Southampton, which is continued to the present day.

Constant feuds arose in the medieval towns on the payment of toll and custom, as was inevitable from the practice of granting immunity by royal charter from such payments, or from some of them, to the inhabitants of various cities and boroughs or other bodies; a list of the towns free of dues in Southampton will be found at the end of this section.

In 1239 a controversy with Marlborough about toll extorted by the 'good men' of Southampton contrary to the privileges of Marlborough was settled (June 17) by an arrangement that each should be free in the other's town.[2] Marlborough, 1239.

Again, in 1260, the bailiffs of Southampton, Roger Noel and John Fortin, were attached to answer the burgesses of Bristol for a similar infringement of privilege, the men of Bristol claiming freedom from toll, passage, and other customs throughout England, Normandy, and Wales under a charter of Henry II. The case was not decided on its merits; the bailiffs alleging in reply and producing in court the charter of the then present king, Henry III., which exempted them from being impleaded out of the borough.[3] Bristol, 1260.

A few years later a controversy about tolls occurred with Netley

1 Madox, F. B., p. 220.
2 Corp. Document (enrolled chart. 23 Hen. III. m. 3).
3 Abbrev. Plac. Mich. 44 and 45 Hen. III.

Netley Abbey, 1288.

Abbey, which had been founded in 1239. In 1288 the bailiffs of the town had distrained certain 'men' of the Abbot for payment of toll, whereupon the Abbot brought his action against the bailiffs, Robert le Barbur, Robert le Mercer, and Peter de Lyons, in 1290, pleading that by charter of Henry III. and confirmation of the present king, his predecessors and himself, the Abbots of Netley, and their 'men' of Soteshal, Walonfolling, Hun, and Totington, had been made free of toll throughout the kingdom. Adjustment was made in 1290 by freeing the Abbot and his men from toll on goods bought and sold for their necessities, as food, clothing, and the like, but binding it on them, notwithstanding their charter, if they went into the market like common merchants.[1]

Bishop of Winchester, 1312.

The bishops of Winchester claimed freedom for their 'men' from paying toll or custom at all times within the borough of Southampton; and in 1312 Bishop Woodlock proceeded against the town in consequence of the bailiffs having demanded toll and stallage from one of his men, whose goods they had also distrained on his refusing to pay. Judgment went against the town.[2]

New Sarum, 1329.

In the 2 Ed. III. (1329) a suit between the city of New Sarum and the town of Southampton concerning certain tolls and customs levied at Southampton from the citizens of New Sarum was brought to concord in the following shape: that the inhabitants of New Sarum should for ever be free from all toll, murage, pavage, quayage, pontage, &c., in the town of Southampton, and within the port and liberties of the same; but in consideration of the mayor and community of Southampton holding the town in fee-farm, the citizens of New Sarum agreed to pay the usual custom on the several articles there and then specified in the agreement.[3]

Coventry, 1456.

In 1456 (34 Hen. VI.) an agreement between the towns of Southampton and Coventry arranged that the merchants of neither place should pay toll to the other.[4]

As a matter of revenue, in later centuries the petty customs were let to Nathaniel Mills in 1632 for five years at £135 per annum; in 1645 to William Higgins and James Clungeon, together with cranage, wharfage, gauging, weighing, and hallage of linen cloth, hostelage, and anchorage of ships, keelage of boats, &c., and the loft over the tin-house called the linen-hall, as also the cellar called the weigh-house, together with all beam rights, scales, &c., for five years at £132 per annum. Scheduled to the lease is an inventory of the weights belonging to the town. In 1654 the same were leased to John Bachelor for

---

1 Rot. Parl. vol. i. p. 20.

2 Oak Book.

3 Oak Book. Dr. Speed has this document.

4 Document (Penes Corp.)

three years at £135; in 1658 they were let for £100; in 1659 for £85; in 1661 to Nicholas Caplin at £110; in 1723 to John Grove for ten years at £30, he paying, however, the fee-farm of £50 per annum.[1] Later in the century they produced £150 a year.

"The burgesses pay no petty customs, and a burgess entering the "goods of a person not a burgess to defraud the Corporation of the "petty customs, is punished with disfranchisement. In 1700 it was "ordered that if a foreigner—that is, a person not a burgess—bring "goods to the port, and an inhabiting burgess buy them and enter "them in his own name, that burgess shall pay the petty customs."

The petty customs were abolished in 1803 (see page 39).

---

The following list of free towns is taken from 'The book of rates of the toll, brocage, pontage, petty custom, and all other duties due, belonging, or appertaining unto the mayor, bailiffs, and burgesses of the town of Southampton . . . according to the ancient custom of the said town time out of mind.'

At the end of a long list of duties[2] arranged alphabetically occurs the following note: 'The tenants of the Duke of Lancaster renewed their charter the xxij of November in the third year of Queen Elizabeth, in which charters are

Kings Somborne,
Romsey,
Stockbridge,

and the manor of Hartley and members of the same are free of prestations, theolony, pannage, lastage, tallage, carriage, passage, package, and terrage.'

'Hereafter follow the names of such towns and places as are free; and if any other claim to be free, let their charters be seen, by what kings, and in what year they were made free.

Andever, for all the company of freemen.
Alresford, free.
All the tenants of St. Swithun's, free.
All the burgesses of Winchester.
All the honours of England.
Bristow.
Broughton.
Bishopstoake.
Brember.
Brightport.
Basingstoake.
Burford.
Beaverly.
Bath.
Bedford.
Co[l]chester.
Canterbury.
Coventry.
Chichester.
Dartmouth.
Downton.
Dyndbeth.
Exeter.
Eastiverley.
Glocester.
Guildford.
Gomesester.
Heartford, East.
Hillstone.
Haverford.
Harwich.
Hull.

---

1 Leases.

2 Given by Dr. Speed in his Appendix, but omitted here from want of room.

Honours of Wallingford.
Hoverton.
Ipswitch.
Kings Sumborne.
Kibolis Evanton.
London.
Lancaster.
Lockerley.
Little Sumborne.
Lyme.
My Lord of Winchester's tenants.
My Lord of Hyde for his house.
Marleborough.
Norwich.
Nottingham.
Newcastle-upon-Tyne.
New Colledge.
Oxford.
Overton.
Portsmouth.
Plymouth.
Reading.
Torksey.
Twyford.
Shrovesbury.
St. Cross.
Salisbury—half custom.
South Howton.
Scarborough.
Stafford.
Vyes.
Weekham.
Wells.
Worcester.
Weymouth.
Walton.
Wallingford.
Witch.
Wymborne.
Winchester College.
Yarmouth.
York.'

Then follows 'The rate of brocage and pontage,' and an attestation to the correctness of the copy of the foregoing by Thomas Mason, mayor, and others, dated 2d August, 20 Car. I., 1644.

## SECTION VIII.—*Fairs.*

"These are not mentioned in any of the general charters, but all "depend on particular grants.

### *Trinity Fair.*

Trinity or Chapel Fair, 1496.

"Henry, by the grace of God King of England and France, Lord of Ireland, "to all to whom these presents shall come, greeting : Know ye that, for the devo- "tion which we bear to the holy and glorious Virgin, Mother of God, and for the "love which we have and long time have had for our town of Southampton, "considering that by a confluence of our subjects and others the said town "may be greatly improved and advanced in wealth and prosperity, and in order "that a greater confluence of people may be made there in future, we have, of "our special grace and mere motion, granted to our beloved in Christ the Mayor, "Aldermen, Sheriff, Bailiffs, Burgesses, and community of the said Town of "Southampton, and their successors, as also to William Gefferey, hermit of the "Chapel of the Holy Trinity and the blessed Mary aforesaid, a Fair and Market to "be held every year at and about the said Chapel of the Holy and Undivided "Trinity, near the said town of Southampton, on the Feast of the Holy Trinity "and for three days immediately following after the said Feast, in which Chapel "the said glorious Virgin is very frequently honoured by the faithful in Christ.

Trinity Sunday and three following days.

"To have and to hold the said Fair and Market, with free ingress and egress "for all our subjects coming thither to trade. To hold the said Fair by the "aforesaid Mayor, &c., and their successors, and also by the aforesaid William "Gefferey, hermit, on the said Feast and three days as is aforesaid, during our "pleasure. In testimony whereof we have made these our letters patent :

"Witness myself at Westminster 19th July, the eleventh year of our "reign.[1]

"The remains of the chapel here mentioned were standing a few "years ago on the spot where the miller's house is now built.

"The fair is kept by the head bailiff of the town, who presides "in it as chief magistrate, and half the profits of the fair are paid to "the owner of the site of the chapel.

"The Journal for the year [Aug. 28] 1646 makes mention of a "charter[2] of 2 Henry IV. (1400) and another of 2 Richard III. (1484) "for holding this fair, but no such charters appear." It is, however, tolerably certain that the above is but a grant of confirmation; the town charter of 1 Edward IV. (1461) contains a confirmation of a court of pie-poudre, which proves the existence of some fair possessed by the town.

*Three Other Fairs.*

"Elizabeth, &c., to all, &c. Know ye that for the improvement of our town "of Southampton and its condition, and for the public good of the said town, "we have given and granted to the Mayor, Bailiffs, and Burgesses of the town "of Southampton, and their successors for ever, that they and their successors "shall for the future for ever have and hold every year within the said town and "its precincts three Fairs or Markets: namely, one on the Tuesday next before "the Sunday commonly called Shrove Sunday, to last that whole Tuesday and "the two days next following. And one other on St. Mark's Day, to last that "whole day and the two days next following. And a third on the Tuesday next "after the Feast of St. Andrew the Apostle, to last all that day and also for the "two days next following. Together with a court of Pie-poudre to be held there "during the time of the said Fairs, and each of them, with all the liberties, free "customs, tolls, tallages, piccages, fines, amercements, and all other profits, com- "modities, and emoluments whatsoever belonging or appertaining to such Fairs "or Markets, and to the court of Pie-poudre, or from such Fairs, &c., arising. "Yet so that these Fairs and Markets, or any one of them, shall be no prejudice to "other Fairs and Markets in the neighbourhood, &c. In testimony whereof, "&c.: Witness the Queen at Westminster, 22d Jan^y the 42^d year of our "reign (1600)."[3]

Tuesday before Shrove Sunday and two days. April 25 and two days. Tuesday after November 30 and two days.

The mill-house (see above)—that is, the building formerly so used—still retains a vestige of the ancient chapel or hermitage, which was of some honour in times gone by for pilgrimages and otherwise. Here in the 'Chapel of our Lady of Grace,' in August 1510, King Henry VIII. made his offering of six shillings and eightpence. The chapel stood

Trinity or Chapel Fair continued.

[1] Dr. Speed rightly concluded that this patent must belong to Henry VII. or Henry VIII. from its mention of a sheriff, there being none in 11 Henry VI. The original grant is preserved in the Hartley Institute; it is found enrolled Pat. 11 Henry VII. p. 2, m. 10 (12).

[2] The Court Leet Book of 1603 makes a similar reference to a charter of Henry VI.

[3] Pat. 42 Eliz. Part 25 (1600).

much exposed to the river, which was considerably broader at its mouth in ancient times than at present; and the bailiff's permanent booth, erected near the chapel for the purposes of the fair, was constantly needing protection from the waves. In the neighbourhood of the chapel was a backwater or pool, still in part remaining, with the saltmarsh beyond. From St. Mary's litton, or churchyard, a causeway led to the hermitage called the 'causey of our Lady of Grace,'[1] now Chapel Road; and strange as it may seem, this paved and gravelled highway was often broken upon by the sea,[2] and within living memory has been washed over by the tide nearly as far as the railway bridge. On the other side, the chapel or hermitage was connected with Itchen Cross (Cross-house) by another causey still remaining. The fair was held round the chapel according to the charter, and occasionally some of the stalls would encroach within; a practice censured by the court leet of 1603, who found that by the charter (see note above) 'standings' within the chapel were not warranted. They therefore warned an offender to set up no more stalls inside, 'unlesse' indeed 'he shall first compounde w^th^ the town for their good will herein.' The chapel had probably long ceased to be used as such; in 1563 (July 6) Thomas Gardiner petitioned for leave to purchase 'the free chapel of St. Mary de Graces,' late of the possessions of St. Denys's Priory.

Chapel Fair.

The opening of the fair was a matter of ceremony and of expense, owing to certain attendant 'solemnities,' which possibly were of a festive character; and in 1600 it was ordered that the bare 'substance' only should be retained, namely, the proclamation of opening, the presence of the watch, and last, not least, the bailiff with his pie-poudre court, the whole body of the burgesses being bound to attend Mr. Mayor to the proclamation. At this the privileges of the fair were set forth, and ready justice was promised to every man without fail; the sentence concluded thus:—

> 'This presente Fear to begginne the Trinitie eve at none, and so to contynew and endure unto Wensdaye at night. Therefore now at none begyn in Godes name and the Kinges, and God sende every man good lucke and this Fear good continuaunce: and God save the Kinge and all his well willers. Amen.'[3]

And ceremonies.

The fair was opened by the mayor and Corporation till comparatively lately. After the proclamation a pole was raised, on the top of which was fixed a large glove, or gloved open-hand, still existing. The senior bailiff then took possession of the fair as chief magistrate for the time within its precincts, and president of its court, a guard of halber-

[1] Steward's Book, 1509, &c. At one period adjoining the south side of this road was a croft called St. Andrew's Croft (Add. 15, 314. f. 42).

[2] Court Leet Book, 1577, &c.

[3] Paxbread vol. 1478.

diers being appointed to keep the peace by day and to watch by night. On the Wednesday at noon the glove and pole were taken down by order of the mayor, with which ceremony all was over. The bailiff entertained the Corporation in his booth at the opening and during the continuance of the fair, and unfortunates who dreaded another kind of bailiff enjoyed immunity from arrest within its precincts. The glories of the opening day began to fade very sensibly about 1840, and within the last few years have become finally extinguished. The fair itself, reduced to one day, is now held in the cattle ground near the railway. It had long ceased to be of value to the Corporation, and its advantage to the general public was questionable. In 1751 the profits of the borough from Trinity Fair were leased out for seven years at a guinea and a half per annum, and in 1744 those from St. Mark's Fair were demised for three years at two guineas each year.

The patent of 42 Elizabeth (1600) concerning Shrovetide, St. Mark's, and St. Andrew's Fairs was also a confirmation, and not an original grant, at least as regards the two former, for the court leet called attention to them in 1596. They might have wanted a spur. Powers were sought in the Northam Bridge Act, 36 Geo. III. 1796, for putting an end to St. Mark's or Above Bar Fair, held on the 6th and 7th May, and in 1875 it was abolished. The two other fairs, never very flourishing, were in existence at the beginning of the century, but had disappeared before 1834.

**Above Bar Fair.**

**Two others.**

## SECTION IX.—*The Courts of the Town and County of the Town.*

### *Court Leet.*

The court leet, commonly called the Law-day, as being the ordinary tribunal, the most ancient local criminal court here as everywhere else, was held before the mayor, aldermen, and discreets of the town on Hock Tuesday, *i.e.*, on the third Tuesday after Easter Day, most anciently at Cutthorn, but afterwards frequently in the Guildhall, the town-clerk being of later times steward and judge of the court, the sheriff foreman of the jury; the latter being summoned originally from the burgesses alone, but more recently with greater latitude.

**Third Tuesday after Easter.**

The office of the court leet was to inquire regularly and periodically into the proper condition of watercourses, roads, paths, and ditches; to guard against all manner of encroachments upon the public rights, whether by unlawful enclosure or otherwise; to preserve landmarks, to keep watch and ward in the town, and overlook the common lands, adjusting the rights over them, and restraining in any

**Duties.**

case their excessive exercise, as in the pasturage of cattle; to guard against the adulteration of food, to inspect weights and measures, to look in general to the morals of the people, and to find a remedy for each social ill and inconvenience. More than this, it took cognisance of grosser crimes of assault, arson, burglary, larceny, manslaughter, murder, treason, and every felony at common law. These offences were presented by the leet jury as indictors, and action was taken accordingly. But for the greater number of matters brought before the leet the remedy was summary by amercement or fine.

In ancient time one most important function of the court leet was taking the pledges of freemen, who, all above the age of twelve years, with certain exceptions, were bound to be sworn and enrolled. A laxity in this practice prevailed, however, early in the seventeenth century. Under 1615 we find the complaint 'that many young men and youths have been dwelling here a year and a day and have not been sworn to the king's obedience as they ought, the town-clerk to have care thereof.' But in the margin of the court leet book it is justly objected, probably by the inculpated official himself, 'The jury ought to inquire of this and make presentment upon their oath, and not to refer it to the steward of the court.' From this period backwardness of enrolment in the court books was not uncommonly presented.

Court Leet Books.

The court leet books are extant from 1550 to the present day, with here and there a gap of a more or less serious extent. After the middle of the eighteenth century they become of little interest, and are at the present time mere repetitions of the presentment as to the metes and bounds of the town, made year after year at the formal meeting of the court.

Considerable use has been already made of these books in the present work. Entries relating to trade regulation will also be found below. The following notices may be added in this place:—

Apparel.

Under 1576 we find some curious regulations as to apparel; and first for the ladies:—

'Dyvers women in this towne doo not weare whyte cappes but hattes, contrarie to the statute, as yt may appeare by the churchewardens theire presentments every week.'

The names of the offenders follow. But on the whole subject of attire the jury delivered themselves in the following grave fashion:—

'The apparell in tymes past used comenlie to be worne by the maiors, aldermen, shreffes, and baylifes, and there wyves within the Towne of Suthampton, particularly followethe confessyd by Mr. John Gregory, alderman, and William Maister, the Towne Stewarde, eyther of them of thage of lxxv. at the lest.

*Apparell of the Maior and Aldermen.*—A gowne of skarlett furryd w$^{t}$ martirnes[1] or foynes[2] for the wynter, and faced with satten damaske or uther the lyke silke being blacke or russett collar for the summer.

A tippett of velvett worne upon the same gowne.

A gowne of vyolett in grayne[3] faced or furred w$^{t}$ the like furres and the like silke, and other gownes of fyne clothe garded withe velvet and faced with silke.

A jackett or coote of velvett, damaske satten, chamlett or wustede w$^{t}$ a welt or garde of velvett.

A dublett sleved w$^{t}$ velvett, satten damaske, or suche like silke with buttons of sylver.

Hosse of fine puke[4] or skarlett w$^{t}$ garters of silke.

Crest cappes withe broade silke lase about them.

Short gownes of fyne clothe.

Hattes of velvet and silke throme.[5]

Ringes of gold of dyvers waightes, some of more and some of lesse waight.

*The apparrell of the Meres and Aldermen's Wiefes.*—Trayne gownes of skarlett furred and lyned, w$^{t}$ gray amys[6] w$^{t}$ broade weltes[7] of velvett.

Trayne gownes of violett in grayne furred and lyned w$^{t}$ gray amyss w$^{t}$ broade weltes of velvett.

Gownes of murrey[8] in grayne or other fyne clothe w$^{t}$ purfulls[9] or gardes[9] of velvett blacke or lawne, and cuffes of velvett at handes.

Kyrtills[10] of damaske satten chamlett and worsted withe iij weltes of velvett upon them.

Peticotes of scarlett and other fine redd w$^{t}$ a belt of redd velvett.

*For the attyer of there heddes.*—Bonettes of velvett, mynever cappis, atyer of fyne lawne, hattes of silke throme, crest cappis and rownde cappes of velvett.

Partlettes[11] for there neckes of velvett w$^{t}$ buttens of golde enamyled and partlettes of lawne.

Girdelles of sylver and gylte called harnes gerdelles sett w$^{t}$ stone and perle and other goldsmythes worke enamyled, tache[12] hookes of sylver and gold ena miled and sett w$^{t}$ stone and perle, and the lace of goldsmythes worke, gyrdells of silke imbossed w$^{t}$ silver, greate pynes[13] of silver and gold enamiled, purses of velvett and silke.

About there necke a chayne of golde and dothe (sic) were braslettes and ringes, some of more waight and some of lesser waight.

A gowne of crymson in grayne furred w$^{t}$ fytche[14] or fased w$^{t}$ Saint Thomas worsted or satten of Sypris.

*The apparrell of the Shreves and Bayliefes.*—A gowne of violett in grayne furred and faced, the like furre and silke.

Other gownes furred with badger, foxe, and lame.[15]

Jackettes or coates of satten chamlett or worsted garded with velvett.

Dublettes[16] of satten or wosted.

Hattes of sylke throme.

Hosse of fyne clothe playne.

Girdills and garters of silke.

---

1 Fur of the martin.
2 Polecat's skin fur.
3 *I.e.*, the foundation of it.
4 Puce, which is explained as *flea*-coloured.
5 A coarse material.
6 Amice, covering for the head and shoulders.
7 Turning down of material, hem or edging.
8 Dark red colour.
9 Trimmings or facings.
10 Jackets.
11 Ruffs for the neck.
12 Tache, a clasp.
13 Pins.
14 Polecat.
15 Lamb.
16 Doublet, close-fitting vest.

*Shreves and Bayliffes Wieves.*—Clothe gownes of crymsen in grayne, some lyned, with gray amys, and some w$^t$ silke for the somer, w$^t$ purfulls and gardes of velvett and cuffes of velvett.

Other clothe gownes purfelyd w$^t$ velvett and lyned w$^t$ wosted: kyrtills of chamlett wested and suche lyke w$^t$ weltes of velvett on them. Partlettes of velvett w$^t$ buttons and clapsis of gold enamiled and partlettes of lawne. Gyrdells of silver and gilte called harnes gyrdells and other goldsmythes worke enamyled, tache hankes [1] of sylver and gold enamyled, greate pynnes of sylver, purses of velvett and other silke. Chaynes, brastlettes, and ringes of gold of dyvers waightes, some of more and some of less waight.

Thomas Beckingham, late of the towne of Suthampton, alderman, for truthe declarethe that all thinges before said in these thre severall descriptions before going towching the auncient apparrell of the maior, shreve, and bayliffes and there wifes, and every of them, is of a truthe, and have byn tyme out of mynde used to be by them woren, for that he is of the age of lxv yeres, or thereabouts, and hathe byn a dweller and trader to the said towne of Suthampton by the space of xlv yeres, and hymselfe hath been maior and borne all the offices forsaid, and by reason therof he and his wief hathe worne the same.

The names of the jurors immediately follow.

Under the next year (1577) several presentments were made of infringement of the statute of apparel, with the particulars of each offence, *e.g.*, Walter Earl wears guards of velvet on his hose; John Delisle's wife has a petticoat guarded with velvet; Martin Howes a gown of Norwich worsted with a broad 'byllyment' lace of silk, and his wife a hat of taffety lined with velvet. Other wives erred in a similar way; John Mills's wife had a cap of velvet and guards in her gown, &c.

Witchcraft.

During the sitting of the court in 1579 a complaint of witchcraft was made against a certain Widow Walker, whereupon the leet jury prescribed the following test:—

'We dessire y$^r$ worships to examine hir before you, and to permyt five or six honest matrons to se hir strippidd to thend to se wheather she have eny bludie marke on hir bodie w$^{ch}$ is a comon token to know all witches by, and so either to stop the mouthes of the people or els to proceade farder at y$^r$ worships pleasure.'

Divine service.

Attendance at divine service was noticed by the court leet. Under 1580, 'we present that touching divine service we cannot find any that any ways do offend, Stephen Barton's mother and Martin Bowes's wife only excepted, which often we have presented.' Eleven years later (1591) the carelessness of many in this respect was presented who 'all the wike longe cometh not to the churche and especially on the Saboth daye.' The churchwardens are required to search all ale-houses, &c., 'on the Saboath dayes.'

In 1600 and several following years all was found well touching divine service, as likewise concerning treasons, murders, felonies.

[1] Clasp handles.

The law of fencing between neighbour and neighbour we find perpetually laid down in the books. The local custom was for the south to fence the north and the east the west, and toward the highway every one was required to make his own fence. Fencing.

In 1587 the places of punishment are presented as out of repair contrary to the statute, viz., the pillory, the stocks above Bar, and those in East Street. About this period every householder was to have his club ready in his house against a fray. Pillory.

In 1594 the town was suffering under a plethora of 'inmates and under-tenants, as well strangers as others, which still increaseth, by which the town is not only impoverished greatly, but also in great danger of infection, hurt by fire, and such like inconveniences.' A similar complaint was made in 1603 against greedy landlords, who, to the great destruction of the town, had admitted too many under-tenants. They were now warned only to admit substantial lodgers who could pay their town and parish charges, otherwise the landlords would have to pay. A few years later landlords were ordered to put in pledges for their tenants (1611, 1618, &c.) Over-crowding.

The foregoing are in themselves but meagre extracts from these interesting books. It must be borne in mind, however, that the court leet records have been freely used in all parts of the present work.

The court leet has been for many years practically obsolete, but might be revived. Its power was exercised in 1802 against certain encroachments on the manorial property of the Corporation in the waste mud-lands to the north of Chapel Mill, made by persons under the authority of the bishop's steward. Notices were served on the persons so building and encroaching, and on May 11 they were granted leases under the Corporation. Court Leet obsolete.

Again in 1819 some action was taken as to the north-eastern boundary of the county of the town.

In 1846 it was suggested by the late town-clerk that a perambulation of the liberties over their widest possible extent should be held, with a view to settling the question about the boundaries through an action for trespass. The circuit never came off.

### *The Town Court.*

The common court of the town, as it was usually called, a civil court of pleas of ancient date (charters 40 Hen. III. 1256, 2 Hen. IV. 1401), was ordered by charter of 1 Edward IV. (1461) to be held in the Guildhall (Guihalda) before the mayor and bailiffs, on the Tuesday in each week on personal pleas, and on pleas of lands and tenements on the Tuesday once in a fortnight.

Several town court books are extant, the earliest bearing date

22 Ed. IV., 1482; but Liber Niger contains some more ancient records of the court.

Before the passing of the Municipal Corporation Act, 1835, the common court of the town was held on the Tuesday in every week for the first three weeks after the election of each new mayor, and on every alternate Tuesday afterwards.

*County Court.*

When in 25 Henry VI. (1447) the town and liberties became erected into a county separate and distinct for ever from the county of Southampton or Hampshire, the grant of a sheriff and his court were naturally involved. The county or sheriff's court was ordered to be held every year from month to month on a Monday, and all business which might lawfully be brought before county courts was to be transacted in it.

Present courts.

The court here fell into abeyance with the general decline of business in county courts. It had no relation to the modern county court. This is held, under the modern Acts, at the courthouse in Castle Square; the quarter and petty sessions for the borough and the petty sessions for the county being held in the Guildhall, the ancient place of justice.

*Court of Quarter-Sessions.*

The form of the justiciary court of the town has varied at different times. Under the ordinances of the Guild Merchant (Ord. 32) there were to be elected by the whole community twelve discreets, who, with the two bailiffs, were empowered to execute the king's commands, to keep the peace, protect the franchise, and maintain right between man and man. By charter 2 Henry IV. (1401) power was given to elect out of their own body four aldermen, three or two of whom, together with the mayor, and with four, three, or two of the more honest and discreet persons of the community, to be chosen yearly by the mayor and community, should exercise the office and authority of justices of the peace in as full and ample manner as the justices of the county hitherto, but were not to proceed in felonies without a special commission.

The charter 1 Ed. IV. (1461) ordered that a person skilled in the law,[1] to be chosen the Friday before St. Matthew's Day, should be added to the court of justices, which was otherwise composed of the mayor,

[1] Master Harvey seems to have been standing counsel to the town from about 1469 to 1471. In 1478 Watkin Ford appears to have been the same. From about 1493 to 1513 Master William Frost was the 'lerned counsell of the town,' and received for his annual fee twenty shillings. In 1528 Master Wintershull held the position. (Steward's Books.)

four aldermen, and four other burgesses of the more honest and discreet persons—the prudent, approved, *probi homines* or *prodeshommes*, here and above, and so constantly, recognised as a distinct and well-known class. The charter of 1640 made the mayor, the Bishop of Winchester, the recorder, and ex-mayor, together with five aldermen and two of the more discreet burgesses to be the court, the mayor and recorder being always of the quorum; but previously to the Act of 1835 it was not the practice for the bishop or for the burgess-justices to attend. The court had cognisance of all offences triable at county quarter-sessions, and also of capital felonies, but seldom exercised jurisdiction in these latter, removing them where possible to the assizes of the county of Hants, or in case of such removal being barred, whether by the prisoner or the prosecutor, petition was sent to the Home Office or to the judges of the Western Circuit for a commission of assize made out for the county of the town.

A very large number of the sessions books, rolls, and papers are extant from about the year 1588.

### *Court of Orphans.*

The charter of 16 Charles I. gave power to the mayor, recorder, aldermen, bailiffs, and sheriff, to hold a court of orphans for the town and county, with authority over their persons and goods, as in the case of the Lord Mayor and aldermen in the city of London. The court had become obsolete by the middle of the last century.

Though granted apparently for the first time by the above charter, the principle on which the court rested had been anciently recognised, and belonged to the very idea and nature of a guild. In 1562 silver plate belonging to children under age was delivered to the mayor and burgesses to hold in their behalf. John Staveley, by his will in the same year, among other bequests, gave a piece of plate to the town, beseeching 'the maior and his brethren to be as fathers' to his children.[1] Idea inherent in Guild.

### *Court of Admiralty.*

The admiralty jurisdiction, with the court incident thereto, was granted by charters[2] of Henry VI., in which power was given to the mayor to exercise all the functions of admiral of England within the town and port of Southampton, the interference by the admiral of England within those limits being prohibited. The charter of 16 Chas. I. 1640, confirming and revising previous grants, enjoined that the court

[1] Lib. Nig., fol. 99; Boke of Remembrances, fol. 93.

[2] See charters 23 Hen. VI. 1445, 30 Hen. VI. 1451, also 1 Ed. IV. 1461. See above under 'Admiralty Jurisdiction.'

should be held in the Guildhall or other place within the liberties—it was frequently held 'uppon the Watergate'—as often as need should require, and should be composed of the mayor, recorder, and four aldermen, or any three of them, the mayor or recorder being one, calling to their aid when necessary a civil lawyer for their better information. Cognisance was given of all pleas and plaints personal which belonged to the Admiralty, and of all actions of contract if the parties or their goods were attached within the liberties, with the same power of execution as that possessed by the admiralty court of England. Authority, of course, was given to choose all officers of the court, such as registrars, notaries, attorneys, scribes, proctors, marshals, servants, &c. An appeal was allowed to the Lord High Admiral, who was by himself or by his deputy permitted to hold court within the town or its precincts, and to perform all necessary functions of the admiralty, but only, as it seems, on appeal. There appears, however, to have been anciently some acknowledgment due from the town to the superior court;[1] thus under 1526–27 occurs an entry,[2] 'Paid to Mr. Odell, my lorde admyralles deputie, for the allowaunce of the admyraltie of our towne vnder his brodd seale, xxvj^s. viij^d.'

The first in the regular series of admiralty records now existing bears date 14th July 1493 (8 Hen. VII.), when courts were held (1.) at Keyhaven, in the accustomed place on the sea-shore, before Thomas Dymock, mayor and admiral of the port, John Walssh, burgess, George Cockys, steward of the town, W. Erneley, town and admiralty clerk, and others. By the oath of the jury all was reported well, and two men of Keyhaven were sworn to administer and execute in the mayor's name all duties belonging to the admiralty there. (2.) At Lepe, on July 15. The jury was composed of men representing Hythe, Lepe, Pennehall (Pennington?), Ower, Exbury, Hardley, and Cadlands. Two persons were sworn, as above, to carry out the mayor's duties in his behalf. The jury presented that a monk and certain servants of the Abbot of Beaulieu had, contrary to the king's peace, rescued a Portuguese bark which had been seized in behalf of the mayor. Minor presentments followed. (3.) At Hamul-on-the-Rice (Hamble), on September 24, in the accustomed place on the sea-shore, the jury representing Hamullryse (Hamble), Shotshale (Satchell), Bussilden (Bursledon), and Letley (Netley). Among other matters, it was presented that 'when Barlyes bott of the Isle of Wyght was drownyd therein was drowned a prest' and certain others, who were buried at

1 A gallon of wine or other gratuity was also occasionally presented to my Lord Admiral. (See Steward's Book, 1493.)

2 MS. Temp. Thomæ Overey sub data.

Netley, and that the Abbot had retained £3, 6s. 8d. which the priest had in his purse. Other presentments followed about the removal of timber, keeping the channels clear, &c.

The number of jurors at these courts varied very greatly. At a court at Hamull Rice (Hamble), on 27th April 1508 (23 Hen. VII.), the jury consisted of no less than thirty-six persons, two from Itchen, three from Letley, seven from Hamull Rice, three from Botley, two from Warisaysshe (Warsash), eight from Shotshame (Satchell), eleven from Brisselden (Bursledon), which may represent the comparative importance of those places at the time.

From the early part of the seventeenth century the courts seem to have been held at irregular periods. In 1615 the court leet presented that no admiralty sessions had been held since the last mayoralty of Mr. Wallop (1610), and urged that a court should be summoned, 'lest time, the devourer of all things,[1] and the omittance of the priviledge' caused its loss. Presentments similar in character were made in 1629, 1630, 1705, 1706, 1721, and no doubt in other years. In 1707 and 1708 courts were apparently held at Lymington, the Southampton Corporation asking leave to erect their booth on Lymington quay, and in the latter year to carry their oar erect through the borough.[2] On September 10, 1756, the admiralty circuit, which had been then for a long time intermitted, was ordered to 'be gone' by the Corporation, and the recorder was to be paid a 'handsome gratuity if he attend.' His attendance having been promised, the mayor was desired to entertain him and the aldermen at dinner on the first day (September 20), an allowance of three guineas being voted for the purpose, the same as at a sessions dinner. Before the meeting of the court, the Corporation of Lymington objected (September 18) to a booth being set up on their quay for the purpose without their leave having been first obtained, which they alleged had been usual. The Corporation of Southampton replied that they could find no such precedent, but consented to ask leave; and accordingly erected their booth and marched with their trumpeter and silver oar through the borough of Lymington. The records of these courts are the last entered in the books. They were held: (1.) At Southampton, in the Guildhall, on Monday, September 20, 1756 (30 Geo. II.), before George West, Esq., mayor, W. Eyre, Esq., recorder, John Godfrey, town-clerk and registrar of the court, and five proctors, the water-bailiff, and four marshals. The sand-walkers, who

[1] This language and sentiment, though not altogether uncommon, may have been delivered by a certain N. Fuljambe, possibly deputy town-clerk, who in another place draws out and signs a list of Sir Thomas White's legacies, 'lest time, the devourer of all things, should hinder the remembrance of them.'

[2] King's Lymington, p. 106.

were but six in number, were not present, but were ordered to attend at Lepe. The jurors, fifteen in all, represented Southampton, Millbrook, Redbridge, Totton, Eling, Marchwood, Dibden, Hythe, Itchen. The boundaries of the admiralty jurisdiction were presented as extending 'from the bridges of Eling and Redbridge down the Southampton Water, and from Botley Bridge down Hamble river into the Southampton Water, thence down to Calshott Castle, and from thence half-seas over to the Isle of Wight from the Iron Hand, which was time out of mind set up at Keyhaven, and down the creek there to Hurst, and thence to Langston Point near Portsmouth, including all the waters, creeks, shores, and maritime places within Hurst and Langston as far up as the first bridges.' Various presentments were made, and fines levied on two sand-walkers for fishing contrary to their duties and the Act of Parliament in that case made. It was desired, also, to put in force the statutes against unlawful nets. The right of fishing and of licensing fishermen was presented as belonging to the Corporation. (2.) At Lymington, on September 21, the jurors, twenty in number, representing Lymington, Woodside, Keyhaven, Milford, Boldre, Pennington. (3.) At Lepe, on September 22, the jurors, who numbered twenty-two, were from Ashlet, Ower, Hardley, Lepe, Tilbury, Exbury, Stanswood, Stone, Holbury, Hythe. (4.) At Hamble, on Thursday, September 23, the jurors, eighteen in number, being from Hamble, Weston, Netley, Bursledon, Helhead, Swanwick, Warsash, and Brunage. The presentments at the various courts were all of the same character.

It had been intended to hold an admiralty circuit in 1798, before which year no court had been held for some time, and it was feared the omission might prove injurious to the rights of the Corporation. However the town resources were exhausted by various contributions on national emergencies, subscriptions for the troops and fleet, relieving the families of the killed, and other enlarged benefactions; it was therefore resolved that—

'The intended and necessary circuit through the said admiralty jurisdiction be further suspended until the Corporation purse shall be so replenished as to admit of so expensive a mode of asserting so valuable a prerogative.'

The opportunity never seems to have occurred, and the last vestige of the old jurisdiction was the continued appointment of sand-walkers. All rights of admiralty were finally extinguished by the Municipal Corporation Act, 1835.

### *Pie-Powder Court.*

A court of pie-powder with the usual objects and powers was held from ancient time during the fairs of the town. It was regulated by charter[1] 1 Ed. IV. (1461), and confirmed by that of 16 Chas. I. (1640).

*Pavilion Court (Winchester).*

This court, though not belonging to the town of Southampton, but to the Bishop of Winchester, and held as a pie-powder court of special authority on St. Giles's Hill, Winchester, during the celebrated St. Giles's Fair, has yet left so many traces on the town books that it should be here mentioned. The fair itself, which originated in a grant of William the Conqueror to Bishop Walkelin, lasted at first one day. This was extended by William Rufus to three days, by Henry I. to eight, by Stephen to fourteen, and by Henry III. to sixteen days. During the continuance of the fair no business could be done in the city, or in Southampton, or within seven leagues of the hill all round; and collectors were appointed at Southampton and on the roads leading to the city to gather the appointed duties on merchandise brought to the fair. These profits went to the See of Winchester, though various foundations also enjoyed certain benefits from them. St. Giles's Fair.

Controversies with Southampton arising from the fair were not infrequent. In 1250 the bailiffs and burgesses had agreed with Adomar (Ethelmar), elect of Winchester, concerning restrictions of their commerce during the fair;[2] but in 1260 the bailiffs complained that they had been unlawfully hindered in their tronage and pesage on pretence of the fair by Gerard le Grue, afterwards (1267) sheriff of Hants, but then seneschal of the bishop. They took nothing by their suit.[3] Five years later (1265) they proceeded against the bishop, John de Exon, for stopping their traffic during the fair, on the ground that they had charter rights for trading at all times.[4] In the end, the monopoly of the fair was affirmed.

The pavilion court of the fair, so called for being held in a tent, was presided over by certain justiciars, called judges of the pavilion, who were authorised by letters patent, probably confirmatory, of Richard II. and Edward IV., to have cognisance of pleas and other matters during the fair, and to receive and keep for the same period the keys, and assume the custody, of the city. The mayor delivered up his powers accordingly for the time being on the eve of each St. Giles's Day. Court.

It appears that a fine was paid by the town of Southampton to the pavilion court every year.

1 The action of pie-powder courts was confined to each fair or market, both as to duration and limits, by statute 17 Ed. IV. cap. 2. Before that statute these courts had assumed a more extensive jurisdiction.

2 Chart. 39 Hen. III. m. 5; also Reg. Pontiss., ff. 201, 202.

3 Abbrev. Plac., 44 Hen. III.

4 Ibid., 49 Hen. III.

Fines.

Under 1457, 'Item to my lord Byschop [Waynflete] of Wynchester, for the fyne of the pavylon delyverd to Water Clerke, xx$^{s.}$'

Under 1478 the fine for the pavilion at St. Giles's Fair was 26s. 8d.

Under 1488—

For the paulyn : also payd to Christopher Ambros[e] the xxvj day of August for a potte of gryn gynger weyng viii$^{li.}$ the whyche was presentyd to my lord [1] of Wenchester . . . viij$^{s.}$

Allso for a potte of sowkett weyng ix$^{li.}$ presentyd to the sayde lord . . . iiij$^{s.}$ vj$^{d.}$

Allso for ij pottes to put y$^{e}$ genger and sowkett yn, xij$^{d.}$

Allso payd to Mr. Vensent for vj lovys off soaker weyng xxij$^{li.}$ [at $5\frac{1}{2}$d.], x$^{s.}$ j$^{d.}$

Allso payd for pakthede for to torse ye sayd gere, ob. [$\frac{1}{2}$d.]

The hire of five horses for the mayor at delivering the present was 20d., and a man was paid 8d. for carrying it.

Allso payd to ye kepar of the park of Waltam for the convaying off Mr. Mayor and his felyshepp frydyng (sic) to Waltam, for the brege was broke in y$^{e}$ lane, iiij$^{d.}$

Also paid to my lord's porter, 12$^{d.}$; for horse meat at Waltham, 6$^{d.}$; for beer for the men, 5$^{d.}$; and to the passengers [ferrymen] of the Itchen, 4$^{d.}$

Sept. 2, to Christopher Ambrose and two others riding to Waltham to my lord for pawlyn, 8$^{d.}$ and 12$^{d.}$

Sept. 3, paid for the costs of Mr. Customar Christopher Ambrose, Mr. Vensent, and Thomas Demok w$^{t}$ other burges the nomer [number] of xiiij horse for to ryde to Wenchester to mete w$^{t}$ my lord for to mak our fyne for y$^{e}$ pavlyn, for meet and drynk, ij$^{s.}$ iiij$^{d.}$

Allso pay[d] ye daye aforesayd for owr fyne of the paulyn, xxvj$^{s.}$ viij$^{d.}$

Under 1493—

Costes and expenses of the Powlyn tyme : *le Paulyn*, xij pounde of comfettes gyffe to my lord [2] of Wynchestre, price the pounde viij$^{d.}$ (packed in two boxes), x poundes and iij quarters of sokatte at vj$^{d.}$ the pounde, with six pots for the same.

Then came green ginger and pots, sugar, thirty-three pounds of 'caprys' and a barrel for them, and a barrel of muscadel.

To the yemen of my Lord of Wynchester in reward, xx$^{d.}$; payd to the clerkes and queresters of my Lord's chapelle in gifte, xx$^{d.}$ Item gyff to the porter there, xij$^{d.}$

Various other expenses attending upon their journey and the carriage of these gifts occur. Then further—

Payd to a man that rode to Waltham to knowe when the bysshop wold be at home, for him and his hors, ix$^{d.}$

Item payd for the beryng in of the barrell of wyne before my lord and bryngyng home of the panyers, iij$^{d.}$

Item payd for ij skynnys of whyte ledder to bynd the pottes of socate and grene gynger, vj$^{d.}$

Item payd to Robert Wryght for ryding to the Paulyn court, and for hors hire, xvj$^{d.}$

Item for Mr. Mayer, Mr. Overey, Mr. Dautre, and Maister Countroller rode to my lorde agayne to knowe the ffyne of the Paulyn, in expenses and hors hyre, viij$^{s.}$ viij$^{d.}$

---

1 Peter Courtenay. 2 Thomas Langton.

Item payd for a tun of reade wyne gyvyn to my said lord for a ffyne of the Paulyn, iiij$^{li.}$

*Nota*, and yet in the bysshoppes bookes is set but xl$^{s.}$ because it shalbe no precedente in tyme to come.

That is to say, the fine, for some reason or other, was much higher than usual, and its being repeated at that figure in future years was guarded against in this fashion.

Under 1501 the bishop received for the Paulyn, for three years ending Michaelmas 1500, two butts of malvesey, price £4, 13s. 4d. the butt, the total being £9, 6s. 8d., and the fine therefore per year about £3, 2s. 2½d.

But the fair and the court were no longer in their medieval glory.

## SECTION X.—*The Seals, Arms, Coinage, and Sir Bevois.*

1. There have been several official seals of the town, most of which bear the characteristic one-masted ship, the earlier having a steerage oar, a rudder appearing towards the middle of the fourteenth century; these seals generally show a star and crescent on the mainsail of the vessel or elsewhere. A new obverse to the latest town seal was presented, as acknowledged August 23, 1587, by Richard Etuer, late of Hampton, fishmonger of London. It bears a magnificent three-masted ship in full sail, with the newly given town arms on the mainsail; the older obverse was a one-masted vessel, no ship in England having had more than one mast till about 1514; on the forecastle were two men blowing with trumpets. The legend on the newer obverse is 'Sigillum commune villæ Southamtoniæ.' The original reverse, still in use, bears in a central canopied niche a figure of the Virgin and Child; within a niche on either side is a figure in adoring attitude; the legend is 'Mater Virgo Dei tu miserere nobis.' Casts of these and of various other official seals are to be seen in the Hartley Museum. Seals.

2. The arms of the town were granted by patent of August 4 (17 Eliz.), 1575; they are thus described:—'Per fesse, argent and gules, three roses counterchanged of the field; with crest and supporters, namely, upon the helme on a wreath, silver and gules, on a mount vert, a castell of gold; out of the castell, a quene in her imperial majestie, holding in the right hand the sword of justice, in the left the balance of equitie, mantelled, gules; dobled silver.' The supporters: out of two ships, proper, upon the sea, standing in the fore part of the ships, two lions rampant, gold. The patent states that the town had borne arms since its incorporation by Henry VI. Arms.

3. The regalia of the town require engraving for their explanation even more than the seals. The more ancient maces are exhibited in the Regalia.

Hartley Museum. The making of one of them is detailed in the Steward's Book of 1482–83. The silver oar of the admiralty, a cherished badge, has been mentioned elsewhere.

Coinage.

4. Among the borough and tradesmen's money tokens issued in the latter half of the seventeenth and in the eighteenth centuries, the following may be noted:—Halfpenny size, 'Cornelius Macham, his halfpenny;' on the other side, 'in Southampton 1667,' with the grocers' arms. 'William Jolliffe of' (grocers' arms); on other side, 'Southampton 1666, W^I.' 'George Freeman at ye white' (figure of *horse* in middle); on other side, 'in Southampton, 1668, his half-penny.' 'Henry Norborne in Southa^n his half-penny, 1668;' on other side, trade arms and initials H. N. A. After this the Corporation, by order of November 26, 1669, required all tradesmen to recall their halfpence and farthings by the 1st January next coming, it being arranged that the mayor should send for £20 worth of halfpence and farthings to be stamped on one side with the town arms, and on the other with 'The Corporation of Southampton,' and distribute them to the shopkeepers for the benefit of the poor of the Corporation. Proclamation was accordingly made December 3, 1669.[1] Halfpence and farthings of the above description are met with of this and subsequent dates. They were all called in August 28, 1672, in obedience to a royal proclamation of August 16.[2]

Late in the next century the following device was adopted:—A helmed head in profile, underneath 'S^r Bevois, Southampton, halfpenny;' on other side, 'Brewery and Block Manufactory United Company 1790;' edge, 'Payable at the office of W. Taylor, R. V. Moody and Co.' Other issues of this company differ slightly from the above; among these are the helmed head in profile, 'S^r Bevois, Southampton;' on the reverse, a rose and crown on a shield, 'Promissory halfpenny 1791;' edge, 'Payable' (as before). On another the helmed head, 'S^r Bevois, Southampton, halfpenny;' other side, 'Success to the Brewery and Block Manufactory 1791;' edge, 'Payable' (as before). A head in profile without a helmet, 'S^r Bevois, Southampton,' as above. They issued also farthings with the same devices and legends, date 1790. Of the farthing size of older date are 'Henry Miller in' (grocers' arms); other side, 'Southampton 1664;' in centre, 'H^M M.' 'Jacob Ward of' (other side) 'Southampton;' in the middle, 'W.' 'Richard Cornelius;' in middle, 'R.C.;' on other side, 'in Southampton 1660;' in middle a tun. Of mite size, 'William Jollife of' (grocers' arms) 'Southampton;' in centre 'W.I.' No date.

5. "I should be thought guilty of an unpardonable omission if I

---

[1] Journal, November 26, 1669; May 6, 1670, &c.

[2] Journal, August 28 and September 13.

"should pass over our champion Bevis or Bevois without some notice, "though, I confess, I know very little of him.

"Mr. Camden, speaking of the Earls of Southampton, says that "about the coming in of the Normans one Bogo or Beavoyse (Beavo- "tius), a Saxon, had this title, who, at the battle of Cardiff in Wales, "engaged the Normans. . . . Mr. Speed also calls him Bogo, and "gives him arms in the map of Hampshire; but neither he nor Mr. "Camden quote any authority for the existence of such a man. The "story told of him here is, that he fought with a giant named Ascapart "on the sea-shore near the town, and that Ascapart struck at him with "his club, but missing his blow, the club stuck fast in the mud, and "that while he was pulling to get it out, Bevis despatched him with "his sword." But according to the metrical romance the giant, vanquished in the fight, becomes Sir Bevois's treacherous esquire.[1]

Sir Bevois or Bevis.

[1] The metrical romance of Sir Bevois of Hampton appears to be of French origin, and to have taken shape under the minstrels of the Crusades, or soon after that period. It was first printed in Venice in Italian so early as 1489; it also appeared early in French, and was first printed in England by Pynson in quarto—'Sir Beuys of Southampton: The son of Guy Erle of Southampton'—no date. Many subsequent editions have appeared, but the versions are not identical. Extracts are given by Ellis; the romance was also printed by the Maitland Club in 1838.

# CHAPTER V.

## *THE TRADE OF THE TOWN.*

### SECTION I.—*General.*

THE prosperity of the port commenced with the Norman Conquest, and probably continued unabated till the loss of the French possessions in 1451–53. At the opening of this period (see p. 26) we find a preponderance of Normans settled in the town, and the constant transit between this port and Normandy must have tended to the wealth and importance of the place.

In the account of fifteenths rendered by William de Wrotham, Archdeacon of Taunton, for the fifteen months commencing July 20, 1204, and ending November 30, 1205, issuing from thirty-five ports, and amounting in the whole to £4958, 7s. 3½d., the fifteenths of merchants at the port of London amounted to £836, 12s. 10d., Boston, £780, 15s. 3d., Southampton, £712, 3s. 7d.[1]

Wine. The wine trade was settled here early. With the acquisition of the French provinces through the marriage of Henry II. (May 1152) with Eleanor of Poitou, daughter of William, Duke of Aquitaine, a considerable traffic was commenced with Bordeaux, in which this port shared very largely. The early Close Rolls[2] abound in writs to the bailiffs concerning the wine trade generally, or the king's wines, whether prisage or otherwise, or those of the wealthy folk whose concerns must have kept the port alive. Wine was the principal import; but beer, if we may put it in the same company, was at least an occasional export. Thus in June 1225 (9 Hen. III.) the bailiffs were directed to permit the exportation of beer in the case of a merchant of Flanders, notwithstanding a previous order against the exportation of grain or other victual to foreign parts. Merchants and wealthy men frequently treated directly with royalty as to their dues and permissions; hence many of the surviving writs.

Coeval with this early period are many of the vaults and cellars in

---

[1] Madox, Excheq., i. 772.

[2] A mass of these notices from the printed Close Rolls may be seen in Woodward and Wilks's History of Hampshire, pp. 174–204.

the older parts of the town. In this connection may be mentioned the ancient groined apartment of somewhat later date, now used as a bonded cellar, on the north side of Simnel Street, exactly opposite the mouth of Pepper Alley. This is the most ancient quarter of the town, and it is possible that in the substructures of the houses there may exist many remains yet undescribed. Old vaults.

The wool trade, which makes its first impress on the statute book in the reign of Edward I., obtains some of its earliest notices in Southampton from arrangements made for just weight. The custody of the tron, or weighing beam, was a long time in the family of the Earl of Warwick; and from a suit in 1275, and judgment the following year, it appears that a certain tenement in the town belonging to the Earl was held by service of weighing all goods in Southampton; Stephen le Neyre, with his brothers and sisters, being in occupation at that time, as their ancestors had been before them, presumably with the charge of carrying out this duty.[1] In spite of supervision, complaints were made in 1290 by Spanish merchants to Edward I. of deception in the auncel weight in our town. By this method of weighing, abolished by statute in 1351–52, the beam was balanced on the hand; the merchants reasonably prayed a safer method.[2] Wool.

In 1299 Nicholas de Barbeflet (see p. 114), burgess of Southampton, obtained by royal grant the tronage and pesage of wools for export from Southampton for six years at the yearly rent of forty shillings,[3] and in 1302 John Piacle, king's messenger, received the custody of the pesage for his long service, and for the tidings he brought the king of the birth of his son Edward.[4] In 1312 the custody of the sixth and seventh parts of the pesage was committed to William Mauncel of Minchin Hampton, and in 1316 a grant of the pesage which had belonged to Guy de Beauchamp, late Earl of Warwick, who had died in August 1315, at the annual rent of forty shillings.[5] Just previously to this (1314), by some abuse the standard weight intrusted to the burgesses had got into the hands of aliens, and the authorities of the Exchequer were commanded to see this righted.[6]

In 1327 Geoffry Hogheles was made collector of wool customs in the port of Southampton and along the coast as far as Weymouth; in the next year Hugo Sampson was added to the collectorship, John de Vienne taking his place in the following. Later in the same year John de Vallibus was appointed. Hogheles held the collectorship in

[1] Abbrev. Plac., Mich. 3 and 4, and 4 and 5 Ed. I.
[2] Rot. Parl., i. 47 b.
[3] Rot. Orig. Abbrev., 28 Ed. I.
[4] Ibid., 10 Ed. II.
[5] Ibid., 6 and 10 Ed. II.
[6] Rot. Parl., i. 332.

1330; in the next year Hogheles and Sampson together, and five years later (1336) Richard de Moundelard and Laurence de Mees.

The Beauchamp family retained their old office. In 1369 Thomas, Earl of Warwick, died, seised, among other possessions, of two messuages in Southampton and the office of pesage there. The same occurred in 1401 with Earl Thomas, son of the last; so of Earl Richard in 1439, and of Henry, Duke of Warwick, in June 1445. In October 1485 the office of 'peyser' was granted, during the minority of Edward, Earl of Warwick, to Thomas Troys, clerk of the works within the manor and park of Clarendon, Wilts, under Edward IV. and Henry VII.; the office of weigher in the parish of St. John being granted during the same minority to John Skydmore, in succession to Richard Aylesby. In 1509 Anthony Legh, chief clerk of the kitchen, was made weigher at the king's common beam *vice* the son of John Baptist Grymold.[1]

The office of pesage in the town was the more important in the Middle Ages since by an ordinance of Edward II. in 1320 Southampton was one of the ports from which alone wool could be shipped, the others being Weymouth, Boston, Yarmouth, Hull, Lynn, Ipswich, and Newcastle; while by the ordinance of the staples in 1353, which fixed the staples for wools, leather, woolfells, and lead at Newcastle, York, Lincoln, Norwich, Westminster, Canterbury, Chichester, Winchester, Exeter, and Bristol, to one of which places all such commodities were to be brought in the first instance to be weighed and sealed by the mayor of the staple, the port of Southampton was appointed for the shipping and weighing a second time of all that came from Winchester.

Venetian trade.

The earliest notice of the Venetian trade is connected with an affray between the patrons, merchants, masters, and mariners of five Venetian galleys and the town's people. Blood was shed and property destroyed, the Venetians rendering themselves liable for felony and homicide. As, however, it was far from politic to press the quarrel with these wealth-bearing strangers, the mayor and community, by desire of Edward II., proclaimed an immunity in April 1323, in consideration of a certain money compensation.[2]

"This port received great advantages from the following Act of "Parliament," which gave facilities to Genoese and Venetian merchants:—

1378. " 'Also it is ordained and agreed that all merchants of Genoa, Venice, Cata-
" ' lonia, Arragon, and of other kingdoms, lands, and countries lying westward,

[1] See Inquis. Post-Mortem under dates; Rot. Parl., vi. 366; Materials for History of Henry VII., and Brewer's Letters (Rolls Series).

[2] Cal. State Papers (Venetian).

" 'being at peace with our Lord the King, who will bring to Hampton, or any " 'other place within the realm, carracks, ships, gallies, or any other vessels, " 'laden or unladen, may freely sell their merchandise there to whom they " 'please, in the manner before mentioned, and may there reload their said " 'vessels with wool, hides, woolfells, lead, tin, and other staple commodities, " 'and may freely carry them to their own countries westward, paying at the " 'port where they load all manner of customs, subsidies, and other duties of " 'Calais, in the same manner as they would pay if they carried the same goods " 'to the staple at Calais, provided they give sufficient security that they will " 'carry them from thence westward, and not to any other place eastward than " 'to the staple at Calais, if haply they have a mind to go thither, on pain of " 'the forfeiture appointed aforetime.'[1]

"At that time the Genoese and Venetians carried on all the Levant " trade, and when they were excused from going up the Channel to " Calais, which shortened their voyage, they all came to Southampton, " which made this town the centre of all the Levant trade of the king- " dom. And so it continued to be till the exportation of wool was " prohibited in Henry VIII.'s time, which put a stop to the Levanters, " as wool was the commodity they chiefly wanted.[2]

"However, the Journals take notice of some few Venetian ships " being here after this time; as in 4 and 5 Phil. and Mary (1557-58) " and 11 Elizabeth (1569)—'John Crooke, mayor, a Venetian ship " 'here, £50.'

"The above circumstance is the reason that the ships of Venice and " Genoa are mentioned in the charters." From the date of the above encouragement for some hundred and fifty years the ships came almost with the constancy of the returning seasons, the regularity of their visits being broken before the middle of the sixteenth century.

The number of galleys commissioned each season by the Doge was from three to five. The decree of the senate was usually in much the same terms, specifying the course of the voyage, the duration of stay at each place, the number, duties, and pay of the officers[3] and men. The ships were generally here about sixty days, their coming being awaited with the greatest interest (see below, last chapter). The detention of the galleys on one pretext or other by order of our kings was often a source of annoyance and loss, and occasionally gave rise to correspondence.

Merchant vessels here, as in other ports, were constantly taken up

[1] 2 Rich. II. stat. 1, cap. 3 (1378). Dr. Speed has this Act, which is printed in Statutes of the Realm, ii. 8. The Act was confirmed 1 Hen. IV. (1399); see Rot. Parl., iii. 429.

[2] Dr. Speed probably refers to Acts 22 Hen. VIII. (1530-31), cap. 1, and 37 Hen. VIII. (1545), cap. 15.

[3] In 1439 a decree of the senate permitted the captain of the Flanders galleys to go ashore every day to hear mass, whether at Sandwich or Southampton.

Hindrances from shipping detentions.

on all kinds of service, the bailiffs being directed to furnish the vessels. Then at one time they are ordered to arrest all ships in port, together with the foreign merchants; at another, to release some and detain the rest. Occasionally, in their zeal to carry out the orders of the crown, they made mistakes and laid hands on the wrong men or ships. In 1217 they had to release some citizens of Dublin; and in the same year were attached to answer for the seizure of a Gascon ship laden with 140 tuns of the king's wine and with cloth belonging to the queen's wardrobe. Damages were laid at £700, but the bailiffs pleading error, got off with a fine of sixty marks of silver to Queen Eleanor.[1]

Again, in connection with a late proclamation against suffering men or horses to leave the port, the 'mayor' and men of Southampton were subjected to an inquiry in the same year (1 Hen. III. 1217) about some horses detained by them, belonging, as it now appeared, to Sir Richard Scarcaville, custos of the honour of Windsor. It seems from their letter to Peter des Roches, Bishop of Winchester, and Hubert de Burgh, justiciar, that on the day when Louis of France opened his siege of Winchester (June 1216, 18 John), a certain clerk came to the port with nine horses and two servants, representing himself as 'the man of the Lord Fulk de Breauté,'[2] to whom also the horses were said to belong; as, however, the clerk produced no royal license for shipment, or proof of ownership of the horses, they were detained till he should put himself right. Simon de St. Lawrence kept one horse valued at five marks; Richard de Leicester another valued at a hundred shillings; Thomas de Bulehuse (now dead) another worth five marks; Mikarly de Ambly one worth twenty shillings; Roger de Tonellario one worth ten shillings; Hosbert Petithome kept one, and three the clerk took with him. The sequel does not appear, but the story brings before us some old burgesses—of whom elsewhere—and for whom a merciful consideration was here asked.[3]

Hindrances from war.

The warlike peparations of our monarchs acted as a frequent hindrance to trade. Thus, in view of the expedition to France (1225), the bailiffs were ordered to arrest all the large ships in port, and send them to Portsmouth for service, but to permit fishing vessels[4] of or below

[1] Abbrev. Plac., Innocents' Day, 2 Hen. III.

[2] Fulk or Falkes de Breauté was at this time, with Savaric de Mauleon, in command of the king's southern army (see Dudg. Bar., i. 743, &c.; Stubbs, ii. 11, 12, &c.)

[3] Letters, time of Hen. III. (Rolls Series).

[4] In 1223, in consequence of an order for arresting and sending ships to Portsmouth, the bailiffs had seized even fishing-boats, and had got into trouble with some owners from Romsey, whose boats had been impressed. A writ was obtained for delivering the boats on condition of their being ready when called upon to do the king service.

twelve oars to go their way. In 1304 Edward I. granted to Philip the Fair, king of France, for his expedition against the Flemings, twenty ships, to be picked out from the best and largest of those of Southampton and the other southern ports, each ship to be manned with at least forty stout men and well found.

In 1306 (35 Ed. I.) all exports having been forbidden, the burgesses and good men of Southampton petitioned successfully that, as they lived by their ships and merchandise, they might be exempted and suffered to go with their ships to Gascony, and not elsewhere, for wines, on such security as the king and council might require.[1]

From piracy.

Early in this century we read of serious piracies on the Southampton wine trade, and of the reprisals and protests made in consequence; the trade from Bordeaux and Bayonne had suffered heavily.

A little later (1336, 10 Ed. III.) the collectors of customs were ordered to permit two ships of Roger Norman and Thomas de Bynedon to take a freight of thirty sarplars of wool to Gascony, notwithstanding that the king had ordered all ships and mariners to be impressed, and had forbidden any to go to those parts, except in large fleets, on account of the 'aliens' hovering about. In the next year (1337) similar permission was given to merchants of the Society of the Alberti of Florence to ship into Gascony seventy sacks of wool.[2]

General prominence.

In 1345 a return of all ships which served the king in the French war gives another relative view of the importance of Southampton. The whole fleet was divided into the north and the south. The south fleet was gathered from fifty ports or maritime towns from the mouth of the Thames along the south and west coasts, including Wales. The total number of ships in this fleet was 493, the mariners were 9030. Of these, 25 were king's ships manned by 409 mariners; London sent 25 ships and 662 mariners; Southampton 21 ships and 576 mariners. Some of the results seem surprising to us now; the little village of Hamble, near Southampton, and of course within its maritime jurisdiction, sent 7 ships and 117 mariners; Hook, 11 ships and 208 men; Portsmouth sent but 5 ships and 96 men; while Toway sent no less than 47 and 770 mariners; Dartmouth, 32 ships; Plymouth, 26; Bristol, 22; Lymington, 9 ships and 159 mariners; Poole, 4 ships and 94 men; the Isle of Wight, 13 ships and 220 men.[3]

Jealousy.

Under 1379 an instance of jealousy is recorded on the part of the merchants of London. It appears that a rich Genoa merchant had sought permission of the king to occupy the castle lately built, or rather

[1] Rot. Parl., i. 193. [2] Abbrev. Rot. Orig., 11 Ed. III.

[3] Bree's Cursory Survey, 336, 342. Bree gives also at length the case of Sir Nicholas D'Amory's prize, which was gone into by a Southampton jury under order of Council, pp. 231, 235.

rebuilt, at Southampton for the better security of his merchandise, holding out a promise of bringing untold wealth to the king and kingdom, while he undertook to make Southampton superior to all the ports of Western Europe. These great designs so inflamed the merchants of London that they procured his assassination one evening near his house.[1]

The year 1381 seems to have been specially prosperous to Southampton from the Venetian trade.[2]

Convenience for Norman traffic

It appears that in 1394 (17 Rich. II.) the merchants of the western counties—Hants, Wilts, Somerset, Dorset, and Berks—who found Calais a most inconvenient staple, petitioned that they might have the privileges conceded to the merchants of Genoa, Venice, Catalonia, and Arragon, and use Southampton as their port for Normandy, without carrying their wools to Calais, receiving also Norman goods at Southampton. However no relief came: 'Let them repair to Calais as is appointed,' was the reply.[3]

In 1402 (4 Hen. IV.) it was conceded to the Genoese that their goods might be unladen at Southampton and conveyed thence to London by land, conditionally on the merchants showing their goods and paying all dues before the customers of Southampton, and thus being released from paying scavage or toll on the 'showage' or opening of imported goods in London.[4]

Sale of ships.

Southampton also was made a centre when, in 1422, William Sopur, John Foxholes, clerk, and Nicholas Banister of Southampton, were empowered to sell certain ships for the king's benefit before the end of the next Parliament, proclamations of the coming sale being ordered in London, Bristol, Hull, Lynn, Yarmouth, and Plymouth, that persons desirous of becoming purchasers might repair at once to Southampton.[5]

Loans.

In 1436 (14th Feb., 14 Hen. VI.) loans were regulated by order of council in aid of the expedition into France[6] under the Duke of York in the April following. Southampton was put at 200 marks; possibly 100 was the actual amount of loan, as also in the case of Winchester.[7]

---

[1] Walsingham, i. 407; Stow, sub ann. 1379 and 1380.

[2] Walsingham, i. 450.

[3] Rot. Parl., iii. 322.

[4] Ibid., iii. 491, 520.

[5] Bree, 273.

[6] A few years after we have a curious notice of one of the captives in these wars. On March 8, 1450 (28 Hen. VI.), John Melton, who had done good service, but had been made prisoner with the Lord Gaucourt, and had now left two children in pledge, was permitted to trade from Southampton to France till the middle of the following May in a balinger called the 'Thomas of Hampton,' of 22 tons or under, with ten mariners and one page, in order to complete his ransom (Wars of English, i. 514).

[7] Ord. of Privy Council, iv. 319.

In 1451 alum was brought to our port in large quantities by the Genoese.[1] Alum.

At this period Southampton was also a great emporium for tin, and in 1453 (31 Hen. VI.) the king arrested it all for the public service. An urgent letter from the king and council (August 14) addressed to the mayor, Andrew James, and others—John Ewerly, Thomas Osbern, Symken Edward, Lawrence Moyen—gives them power to weigh and sell the tin lately arrested in the town by the king's command, and to send the produce in all haste to the Treasury, towards the cost of the army to be sent into Guienne in the approaching September under the Earl of Shrewsbury. Tin that could not be sold was to be sent to London; and those who had claims on tin sold were to be referred to the council at Westminster.[2] Tin.

In 1454 (32 Hen. VI.) a loan was ordered to be levied in the various ports to the amount of £1000 for keeping the sea and securing trade. London was set at £300, Bristol £150, Hampton £100, Norwich and Yarmouth together £100, the ports occurring in this order. Of the rest, none was put at more than £50.[3]

In the next year (1455) from a petition of the Commons we learn that Italian merchant strangers had been accustomed to ride about the country spying out the nakedness of the land, and with their ready money buying up at first hand wools and woollen cloth from such indigent people as were content to sell at great loss; they had also begun to manufacture, owing to which the price of woollen cloth had fallen. They were therefore restrained from buying wool, woolfells, cloth, or tin excepting in the markets of London, Hampton, or Sandwich.[4] In the following year the town seems to have become the resort of several wealthy Italians. Italian merchants.

In 1464 (4 Ed. IV.) Southampton was one of the ports from which, in common with Poole, Chichester, Sandwich, London, Ipswich, Boston, Hull, and Lynn, wools, woolfells, shorlings and morlings—that is, shorn sheep-skins and wool from the dead sheep—might be exported to the staple at Calais.[5] Export for wools.

In 1492 (June 24, 7 Hen. VII.), a staple of metals was erected at Southampton by royal proclamation, it being averred that mines of gold, silver, tin, copper, lead, and other metals remained unworked in England; in consequence of this the king had licensed an incorporation of a mayor and fellowship of merchants of the staple of metals at Southampton, for the purpose of working mines and uttering metals at reasonable prices. No metals were henceforth to be exported but at Staple of metals.

[1] Rot. Parl., v. 214, 216. [2] Ord. of Privy Council, vi. 156.
[3] Rot. Parl., v. 245. [4] Ibid., v. 334. [5] Ibid., v. 563.

one of the staples; nor was the melting of tin ore permitted to any who were not of the guild.[1]

A considerable section might be written on the assignments made from time to time on the customs of Southampton. Only one or two instances can be given.

Assignment on customs.

In 1417 (5 Hen. V.) the Bishop of Winchester (Beaufort), then chancellor, had lent to the victor of Agincourt the sum of £14,000 on security of the customs of wool, hides, wine, and all other merchandise in the port of Southampton and its dependencies; and the amount was not a third repaid when, in 1421 (9 Hen. V.), he advanced another £14,000 on the same security.[2] These heavy loans and assignments in repayment on the customs of Southampton were woven into the accusations against Beaufort made by Humphrey, Duke of Gloucester, in 1440. Hampton is represented to the king as being 'the best port in your royaume;' the cardinal, with his customers there, was not only the largest wool merchant in the kingdom, but more than probably was carrying on a trade directly prejudicial to the king's interest.[3]

Again, in February 1433 (11 Hen. VI.), the customs were pledged to the feoffees of the Duchy of Lancaster from the Easter of that year, to the amount of £6028, 13s. 7½d. for money borrowed by Henry V.;[4] and two years later (Feb. 1435, 13 Hen. VI.) the feoffees made another advance on a further assignment of the customs of the port of Southampton.[5] In 1451 a preferential payment of £20,000 was assigned on the subsidies of London and Southampton for the defence of the realm. Assignments for the royal household and in grants to officials and others cannot be specified.

During the first half of the reign of Henry VIII. there seems to have been a brisk traffic from Southampton, as well as from London and Bristol, with the Mediterranean and Levant. From hence were exported woollen cloth, calf-skins, &c., the chief imports being silk, camlets, rhubarb, malmsey, muscadel, and other wines; oil, cotton, wool, Turkey carpets, galls, and Indian spices.

Falling off of trade.

At the same time during this period the townsmen were bitterly complaining of the falling off of trade. In November 1528 the Bishop of Bangor, writing to Wolsey, and telling him of the joy in Hampton at his elevation to Winchester, by which he had become Earl of the former town, speaks of the hopes entertained from him by the towns-

1 See Letters of Rich. III. and Hen. VII. (Rolls Series).

2 Rot. Parl., iv. 111, 132.

3 Wars of English (Rolls Series), ii. 440. On the above accusation, however, see Prof. Stubbs, Constit. Hist., iii. 91.

4 Rot. Parl., 437, 463; Ord. Privy Council, iv. 141, 143.

5 Ord. Privy Council, iv. 290.

folk who had now small resort of shipping. In 1533 we have the complaint that the galleys and carracks do not come as they used.

Under 1551 we have a notice of some sixty ships laden with wool for the Netherlands sailing from this port; but the period of decay had set in.

At this time (1551) the expediency of establishing a free mart in England for the merchandise of cloth and tin was debated, and a paper on the subject was left in the handwriting of Edward VI. **Proposal for free mart.**

The experiment was first to be tried at Southampton, as a convenient resort for the merchants of Spain, Brittany, Gascony, Lombardy, Genoa, Normandy, and Italy, especially at that time, when circumstances were likely to 'decay the marts of Antwerp and Frankfort;' Southampton being also a better port than Antwerp. In the event of success at this port, the scheme was to be extended to Hull, which would serve for Prussia, Denmark, Sweden, and Norway.

Free mart was to be kept at Southampton for five weeks each year, commencing after Whitsuntide, so as not to interfere with St. James's Fair, Bristol, or Bartholomew Fair in London: freedom from arrest was ensured in coming and going, except in cases of treason, murder, or felony: no goods were to be shipped during the fair from any other place along the coast from Essex to South Wales: Southampton was to enjoy a strict monopoly during that period, no bargaining of wares being allowed elsewhere throughout the shires of Hants, Wilts, Surrey, Kent, or Dorset: a special pie-powder court was to be erected: agreement was to be made with the merchants of the staple not to hinder the mart by their liberties: fresh advantages were to be given to the Southampton people, who might also have a loan of money, if such could be spared: a good look-out would be kept by the king's ships at sea. **Details.**

After this, 'the discommodities and lets' to the mart are ranged under eight heads, with an answer to each. It might be said that 'strangers lack access hither by land,' but *enemies* would lack the same—an advantage not applying to the Flemish city: if the ill-working of our English cloths were objected, Parliament was about to take that in hand; yet even now the Flemings sought English manufacture: if it were urged that there was too much English cloth already in the Flemish market, the cloth might be bought up with English money and conveyed to Southampton for retail during the mart. The great merchants, it was true, had their dwellings at Antwerp, but they could enjoy no peace or safety there; they came from Bruges, where they were first settled, to Antwerp for English commodities, and now they would come to Southampton. As to the 'poverty and littleness of the town of Southampton,' room enough would be found for the strangers, who would meet there not only the town's people, but foreigners, Spaniards, Germans, Italians, Flemings, Venetians, Danes, &c., who would all trade together; and the merchants of London, Bristol, and of other places would certainly be found at Southampton during the mart.[1] Nothing came of this scheme.

Grants of Queen Mary.

"In order to recover a foreign trade to the town," continuing Dr. Speed from where we last left off (p. 251), "Queen Mary being pleased "with her reception when she met Philip of Spain, who landed here, "gave the Corporation a grant that all malmseys and sweet wines "growing in the islands of Candy and Retimo, or within any part of "the Levant, imported into England either by denizens or strangers, "should be landed only at the port of Southampton, on pain of "forfeiting 20s. for every butt, one moiety to her Majesty, the other "to the town.[2] This grant was confirmed by Act of Parliament, 5 "Eliz. 1563, but was limited to importations made by strangers; "which being only a temporary Act, it was made perpetual by "another, 13 Eliz. 1571." The privilege was worth some 200 marks a year.[3]

Town loss through Turkey Company.

"The grant is still in force [1770], but the establishment[4] of the "Turkey Company [in 1605], who have a grant of an exclusive right "to the Levant trade, and A.D. 1615 procured [April 17] a royal "proclamation to be issued to prohibit the importation of sweet wines "by foreigners, quite deprived the town of the benefit of it. The town "had many controversies on the subject, and [August 1615] petitioned "the king for redress." The matter was referred by the council to Secretary Lake, the Chancellor of the Exchequer, Master of the Rolls, and Attorney-General, who ordered the town to withhold their suit for a time owing to the troubles in Turkey. After waiting eighteen months they petitioned again, and their case was referred to Secretary Naunton, Sir Fulk Greville (afterwards Lord Brooke), then Chancellor of the Exchequer, Sir Julius Cæsar, the Master of the Rolls, and the Attorney-General, who pronounced for the petitioners: "on which the "Turkey Company were ordered to make some recompense to the "town; but they never did. The recompense desired by the town "was the liberty to import currants from the Levant." In 1618 the

[1] Burnet's Collectanea, vol. ii. pt. ii. pp. 115–120.

[2] Pat. 1 and 2 Phil. and Mary, part x. (August 9, 1554); Pat. 4 and 5 Phil. and Mary, part v. (June 17, 1558).

[3] "The Corporation usually farmed out this duty, sometimes for £200 a "year, as they set forth in a petition concerning the surrender of their charter in "1683. In 29 Eliz. 1587 the Earl of Leicester paid for it £133, 6s. 8d.; in "31 Eliz. 1589 the Earl of Essex paid 200 marks."

[4] Two temporary companies had been granted by patents of Elizabeth respectively in 1581 and 1593.

town had asked a compensation of £100, while the Company would only offer £50. By April 1624 the Corporation put their losses at over £1000, but eventually got nothing.

"In 1635 it was determined by a decree of the Exchequer that "Malaga wines were within the town's grant; and in 1723, upon "examination of the above decree, it was found that all the ports of "Spain within the straits were equally within the town's grant, and "that natives importing in foreign bottoms were to pay the duty. But "there is now [*i.e.*, *c.* 1770] so little wine imported in foreign bottoms "that it comes to nothing. The sweet wine duty produces now about "£20 a year, which is mostly, if not all, paid by Jews in London."

Decay of port and town. Alleged causes.

There is little doubt that the settlement of foreign refugees in 1567 did something for trade, though the town was loth to own it (see under 'French Church'). Under 1582 we find among the alleged causes of decay the haunting of pirates,[1] the numerous shipwrecks, and past abuse of prosperity; evidently the finger could not be put on the disease, but a suggestion is made of two free marts in the year, the payment of half customs, or a monopoly of the trade with Spain and Portugal. In 1587 (April) Leicester writing to Walsingham says that Bristol, Hampton, and others of the best towns are fast falling to decay; something must be done to revive trade, while great credit was due to the clothiers, who often kept the people at work to their own loss. In the year of the Armada (1588) the mayor writing to the council (April) says they are unable to furnish the two ships and pinnace required on account of the decay of trade and their heavy charges; moreover above a hundred and ten mariners had been pressed in the town for her Majesty's ships, so that there would not be enough found to man the vessels. Portsmouth was also said to be in a ruinous and weak condition.[2]

Merchant concerns at this time.

Belonging to the unprosperous reign of Elizabeth there remain among the town records several merchants' agreements with the owners of vessels, the greater number of which were of very small tonnage. Under 1576 mention is made of the 'Hope,' 'Gabriel,' 'Trinitie,' 'Mayflower,' 'Dove,' of Hampton, the owners of which devised them for one 'viage' to certain persons who were to pay the crews and other expenses; and most merchants seem to have declined the responsibility of a whole vessel. Thus the 'Mayflower,' 28 tons, was let out:—

[1] Piracy was and had been a constant evil. In 1550 there was a great take of pirates by the royal ships in the neighbourhood; some were executed and hung in chains at the admiralty gallows here, others distributed to other places 'for a terror and example.'

[2] There are several documents of Lord Howard of Effingham of this period, 1588, among the Corporation papers.

'John Cotton, m[r] of the Mayfflower, burthen of xxviij tonnes or thereabouts, hath demised unto Nicholas Capelin five tonnes, Thomas Buck six tonnes, John Hooper seven tonnes, of Suthampton, merchantes, for one viage from hence to Burdeux, ther to tarrie xvj dayes, to unlade and also to relade, &c., and from thence to Suthampton, fraights for every tonne xxxj[s]. th'one halfe at the right discharge and th'other halfe within tenne dayes after at the porte of Suthampton foresaid. The merchants to pay all the duties, the m[r] and five men.'[1]

Piracies.

A few months later occur several notices about piracies, and proceedings accordingly. In 1619 the port was required to raise £300 towards the suppression of this curse; but the mayor wrote to the council that with difficulty they had managed £150, and could not possibly do more. In 1622 the Corporation protest again 'their burdens are excessive; they have contributed £300 towards the fleet sent against the Algerines, have lent £140 for the Palatinate wars, and contributed towards the French Protestants; they have lost much by their trade, so greatly depending on France.'

Shipping in the port.

About 1572 there were fifty-three ships in the port of Southampton—the same number as at Bristol—a low figure as compared with some other places. There was one ship of 200 tons, one of 80 tons, one of 60, two of 50, one of 40, two of 35, six of 30, four of 25, ten of 20, four of 18, eight of 15, two of 12, four of 10, six of 5, and one of 6 tons.

In 1598 we find Southampton reckoned among the decayed towns, such as Newcastle, Hull, Boston, Lynn, northwards; and Poole, Weymouth, Bristol, and Chester, west and southwards.[2]

Other accounts.

Camden (1586–90) and Speed (1596) at the close of the sixteenth century speak nevertheless of Southampton as still rich and beautiful, famous for the variety and neatness of its buildings, and as being the resort of merchants. It is certain, however, that the town had before this passed the zenith of its prosperity, and had begun to decline. The Act of 22 Henry VIII. (1531) before quoted (p. 38) had described the foreign trade of the town as lamentably fallen off; and a previous statute of 1523 (14 and 15 Henry VIII.) 'for the haven and port of Southampton' had recited and made perpetual one of 11 Henry VII. (1495) cap. 5, wherein the following melancholy account is found; the statute deals with wears and engines unlawfully placed in the Southampton water:—

Decay of port and town.

'Before this tyme' it 'hath been the grettest haven, succour, and receite as well for marchauntes and shippes of this realme of England as of carrykis, galeyes and other shippes, and marchauntes of other regions and countries ther aryving and resorting, to the profite of oure Sovereign Lord the King, the great encrease of the marchauntes of this lond, and the comen wele and comforte of all the countrey therto adjoynyng, the which is now lately greatly decayed, and is

[1] Liber Notationum, sub ann.

[2] Cal. State Papers.

like shortly more to decaie by reason and occasion of divers and many weares and other engynes for fisshing ther made, levyed, fixed and had bitween a certeyn place in the said haven called Calshord and another place in þe seid haven called Redbrigge,' by reason of which 'within fewe yeres no ship of greate burden shall mowe come or arive in the seid Haven without due and hasty remedy be purveied in this behalfe.'

We have already mentioned some of the remedies attempted for the decay of trade at this port under Edward VI., Mary, and Elizabeth. Under James I. the Corporation obtained an Act of Parliament[1] (4 James I. c. 10, 1606–7) for confirmation of some parts of the charter granted in the 23 Henry VI. (1445) and for relief of the town, in which the privilege of exclusive trading in the town was maintained for its own freemen, exception being made in favour of the barons or burgesses of the Cinque Ports. We now resume and finish Dr. Speed's chapter, with the omission of two or three sentences:—

"After this the trade of the town was principally with France and "Spain; for which reason they opposed the establishment of a com-"pany of Spanish merchants in the city of London. Dr. Speed resumed.

"A.D. 1636. An additional duty was laid upon bay-salt, and this "town petitioned to be exempted from it because most of the shipping "belonging to the town was employed in the Newfoundland fishery; "and they were exempted in consequence of a certificate from the "customers that the town was in the division of the western ports "which were to be excused.

"A.D. 1656. The town petitioned the Parliament to be made a free "port, setting forth that it was the only port in England for the Levant "trade. This matter of making the town a free port has often been "talked of.[2] After the Restoration they had a great trade here for "French wines, which lasted till the high duties laid upon those wines "very much lessened the demand for them, which drove our merchants "into the Portugal trade, and they are now very deservedly remarkable "for the goodness of their port wines. Besides this, they have had a "Norway trade for timber, but they now deal chiefly with Russia for "timber and hemp.

"The Guernsey and Jersey trade mostly centres here, and they have "a pretty good share of coasting and coal trade.

"All the Cornish tin was once brought to Southampton, and the Tin.

[1] Dr. Speed has given the Act in full in his Appendix. It is printed in Statutes of the Realm, vol. iv. p. 1148. An exemplification of these privileges as to buying and selling, dated Westminster, 24th July (1607), 5 James I., with the great seal attached, is shown in the Hartley Museum.

[2] In 1754 the Corporation abolished their petty customs on African and American goods for twenty-one years, and offered any foreign merchant composition on reasonable terms.

"warehouse where it was kept is still called the Tin-house. There was "besides an office for the receipt of the duties upon tin, which is the "great house next to Holy Rood Church. When this method of "bringing the tin hither began, or how long it lasted, I do not find; "but the Tin-house is mentioned in some of the ancient laws of the "town, and 29 Henry VIII. (1537–38) the Journal says a burgess was "made with a view of bringing the tin trade to the town. But they "must have had it long before this, for 31 Henry VI. (1453) the king "arrested all the tin in Southampton, and sold it to his own present "use.[1] The office above mentioned was built about 5 Edward VI. (Jan-"uary, 1551–52)."

General notices resumed.

To return to the general history. None of the specifics of the period were of avail to stay the gradual decline. Yet it is not to be supposed that the townsfolk succumbed to fate without many an effort. The Journal of November 2, 1666, attempts in the following way to relieve the local depression:—

Efforts at restoring trade.

'Whereas it hath pleased God by a late distructive fire to consume the greatest parte of the City of London, whereby many persons of quality have lost their habitacons in that place, and there being in the Towne of Southampton (heretofore a place of very considerable trade, which by reason of the late civill warrs and mortality there is now depressed and gone) many very good houses with convenient cellars and warehouses, which now stand void and unimployed, wee the Mayor, Bayliffs, and Burgesses, out of tender respect to those sufferers before mentioned doe hereby publish and declare that if any of them that are merchants and men of credit and reputation shall think fitt to settle themselves upon the accompt of trade within the said towne, they shall for some small acknowledgment be admitted into the Corporation there, and be made as free to all intents and purposes as any member thereof. And this offer to continue for the space of twelve months after the date hereof and noe longer.'

The result does not appear. In the following century (1761) the Corporation made a similar offer, inviting 'merchants of credit and substance' to settle in the town, and offering (June 19) burgess-ships *gratis* to such as should come to reside, or should establish mercantile houses in the town.

All this bears out the picture of Bishop Gibson (1695–1722), who describes the greater part of the trade as lost and the great houses of the merchants as 'dropping to the ground.'[2] The local poem of the same period by Dr. Speed, printed as an appendix to Batt-upon-Batt, mourns to the same effect:—

. . . 'Hampton, in the days of yore,
The lawful pride of all the southern shore,

[1] "Cottoni Posthuma, p. 184."
[2] Defoe (1726), Letters, ii. 80, 81, and Stukeley (1723) give similar accounts.

With all advantages of Nature graced,
Betwixt the arms of fair Antona placed;
Guarded by forests both on land and sea
From storms, and man, the ruder enemy.'

Yet all is now changed—it is not an easy poem to quote from, and a little will suffice:—

'For age, who like a bloodhound glory traces,
And destroys towns as well as handsome faces,
Hath made thee poor and dull like other places.
. . . . . . . .
Whither are all thy winged lovers flown,
The mighty carracks and great gallion,
With all that numerous train which did resort
In marine coaches to thy crowded port?
They cease their courtship now, and only own
Thou hast been once a rich and handsome town.'

Newfound-land trade.

It appears that before the middle of the eighteenth century the Newfoundland fish trade, which had been chiefly located in this port, had migrated to Poole.

Channel Island trade.

The Guernsey and Jersey trade, which seems to have moved to this town from Poole[1] about 1515,[2] was in the middle of the last century, as stated above, in a flourishing condition; and wool was exported in large quantities from Southampton to the Channel Islands for the manufacture of worsted stockings, which were sent to England for sale. A brisk wine trade was carried on, together with much smuggling.

Shipbuild-ing.

A few years later it seemed as if the old spirit for building war ships in these waters were revived. The great building period was, no doubt, the reign of Henry V. Here he built his famous ships the 'Holy Ghost' and 'Grace Dieu,'[3] the former by William Soper in 1414, the latter by Robert Berd, clerk, surveyor, in 1417, each ship costing about £500; and in July 1418 the Bishop of Bangor was sent down from London to consecrate the latter, receiving £5 for his expenses.[4] These ships were adorned with the royal devices, swans and antelopes, and with the royal motto. In November 1594, from a list of ships built in

[1] Poole had been formally constituted a port in place of Melcombe, then decayed, in January 1433–34, on the lines of Southampton (Rot. Parl., iv. 445), as Melcombe had been (Ibid., iii. 70), and now again by order of the Treasury the custom-house at Poole has been closed, June 30, 1883, and that port placed under the collector at Weymouth.

[2] Boke of Remembrances, f. 16.

[3] The old 'Grace Dieu' probably came to an end in 1460. When in January that year some of the Earl of Warwick's men from Calais surprised Lord Rivers in bed and cut out his ships from Sandwich, the 'Grace Dieu' could not 'be had awey because she was broke in the botome' (English Chron., Camd. Soc., p. 85).

[4] Devon's Issue Rolls.

the several ports from the year 1581, amounting in all to forty-six, we find twenty-five built in London, seven in Bristol, two in Southampton, nine in the western ports, and one each in Ipswich, Hull, and Liverpool, with the royal allowance of five shillings a ton towards each.[1] But now in March 1782 the 'Mediator,' 44 guns, was launched at Northam; on the stocks were the 'Regulus,' 44, and 'Stately,' 64; the 'Saturn,' 74, was about to be laid down; she was launched in 1786. About the same period (April 1781) the 'Agamemnon,' 64, was launched from Buckler's hard on the Beaulieu river; in 1789 the 'Illustrious,' 74, from the same yard, making the twenty-first ship of the line built there by Mr. Adams; and in 1791 the 'Beaulieu,' 40, and in 1793 the 'Santa Margaritta,' 56, were added to the number.[2] No ships of war are now built at Southampton; at the same time vessels are launched in our river (see below) which would have astonished our forefathers, whether of the period of the snakes, cogs, and busses of Henry II., or of the dromons of Henry V., or of the gallant three-deckers of our more immediate ancestors.

## SECTION II.—*Trade Regulations.*

The following trade regulations in Southampton are gathered from the town books:—

Bakers' corporation.

The *bakers*, like most of the trades, were gathered into a corporation, with a common hall, admitting into their number by fine; and, like all the other trade corporations, they had relation to, and were supervised by, the town.[3]

In 1519 (11 Hen. VIII.) the bakers complained that the profits of baking biscuit for ships was engrossed by certain of their craft by subtle means, to the prejudice of the rest; for reformation whereof it was agreed before the mayor and his brethren, with the assent of all the bakers, that in future—

> 'Every baker shall bryng his porcion of biscatt into the hall over the market-place, and there to be sold by the mastres of the craft indifferently, so that every man shall have his porcion, and that no man take uppon hym to do contrary to this agrement uppon peyne to lose for every tyme x$^{s.}$; therof vj$^{s.}$ viij$^{d.}$ to the towne's use, and iij$^{s.}$ iiij$^{d.}$ to the light of Seynt Clement, and for the seconde defawte . . . to lese the libertie of there corporacon for ever.'[4]

The bakers had always to report to the town on the stock of grain they had ready for the supply of the public;[5] the same applies to the brewers.[6]

---

[1] Cal. State Papers.
[2] Local Newspapers.
[3] In 1441 all the bakers were fined.
[4] Boke of Remembrances, fol. 18.
[5] Ibid., fol. 26 b.
[6] Ibid., fol. 30.

In 1546 (38 Hen. VIII.) half a mark was received of the bakers for 'sealing their corporation,'[1] and the same for that of the brewers. Under 1584 the fine for admission into the corporation of bakers was fixed at twenty-six shillings and eightpence, half of which went to the town, and half to the corporation of bakers.[2]

One kind of bread.

In 1596 (March 25), in view of the scarcity of corn and the different kinds of bread then made, namely, white, wheaten, and household, it was thought convenient:—

'That only one kind of bread be made, which should be made of the wheat or other corn wholely as it comes from the mill without sifting or otherwise handling the same, either by taking the flour, the bran, or gurdgeons from the same, and in no case to make white or wheaten called raunged[3] bread, but one only sort of waye bread or household leavened bread, the same to be good and wholesome for man's body, and not corrupted (as by the statute in this behalf made).'[4]

Assize.

In 1644 the assize of bread was fixed at thirty-two shillings the quarter or four shillings the bushel; the year before it was thirty shillings the quarter or three shillings and ninepence the bushel.[5]

On February 20, 1663, a 'mutiny' occurred among the poor in consequence of the scarcity of bread, upon which Mr. Mayor summoned all the bakers and millers of the town to the council-house, and in presence of the justices and assistants offered them good wheat till harvest next at four shillings and sixpence the bushel, provided they would receive it in eight or ten days. And that they might not pretend want of money, he offered to give time for the payment, and to lend a storehouse *gratis* to hold forty or fifty quarters. On this the bakers and millers engaged not to sell wheat or meal above four shillings and sixpence the bushel till June 24th, and bread four shillings and sixpence.

Barber-surgery.

*Barbers.*—The fine for barber-craft, which embraced common surgery, was divided as usual between the town and the corporation of the craft. In 1512 (Feb. 9) Joanna, late wife of a barber, came before the mayor and agreed to the fine of twenty-six shillings and eightpence for setting up barber-craft, one moiety to go to the town, the other to the craft:—

'Whereunto the said barbours of there frowerd mynde wold not aggre. And because the barbours be bounde by there corporacon to do no thyng which shalbe prejudicall to the towne, therefore it is put to there choyse, whether *they* will pay to the towne the said 13s. 4d. for the towne's part, and *she* not to occupy the craft, or elles she to pay it, and occupy the craft.'[6]

The town at any rate should not to lose its fine.

1 Temp. T. Overey, sub ann.
2 Boke of Remembrances, fol. 141 b.
3 Raunged, ranged or sifted.
4 Ibid., fol. 195.
5 Journal, sub ann.
6 Liber Remembranc. H., f. 180.

1577. Paid Richard Davis, the barbour, the xvij$^{th}$ of August in parte paim$^{t}$ for healing Mother Chriscians legge of the almes house, x$^{s.}$[1]

Under 1638 (Dec. 14) we find the holder of an episcopal license in trouble. Martin Peale, a barber (surgeon), having been amerced by the leet jury, not only refused to pay, but

'Demeaned himself in a most insolent and contemptuous manner to the House, slighting and vilifying the magistrates and theire favour in granting him a freedome to use his trade here, saying that hee was not admitted a freeman by the Towne but by the Bishop, and that hee was told another tale when hee was with the Bishop. And being reproved by the House for his unmannerly language, said that hee had noe respect for this House and never got 6$^{d.}$ by the House; which proud and peremptorie language of soe meane a fellow in this place is not to bee indured. It is therefore this day ordered that he finde sureties for his appearance at the next sessions of the peace there to answer,' &c.[2]

Trimming.

The following entry concerns barber-craft in the modern sense. In 1608 the barbers complained of the infringement by one of their number of the orders made and subscribed in a past mayoralty; in consequence of which the offender paid two shillings and sixpence to the poor, and it was ordered (Dec. 9), and agreed to by the barbers, that none of them should henceforth trim any person upon the 'Saboth daye,' unless in the case of gentlemen strangers who should be in the town, or who should resort to it and desire to be trimmed at such otherwise forbidden time.[3]

Wholesale and retail.

*Brewers.*—In 1488 the fine for beer-brewing for the whole year for three persons was ten shillings each. In 1531 (23 Hen. VIII.), for the avoidance of gambling and idleness in the town, 'by reason that every other howse is a bruer or tapper,' it was agreed that 'a certen of bruers bothe of ale and bere' should be appointed 'to serve substancyally the said town, and also a certen yn every warde to be tappers of the same, fynding suretie that no nyght wacche ne unlawful games shalbe usid within there howses.' The brewers were to serve their customers in the gross, and not to tap beer for them in their houses, on the principle 'that one may lyve by another.' The tappers were the retail dealers or innkeepers.[4]

The following entries are worth noting:—

1552 (Nov. 6). Brewers were forbidden to receive their wood and fagots in carts or wains, but only by water in boats, upon pain, &c.; but they might have what was meant for their own consumption brought like other people.[5]

1562. Brewers were prohibited the use of iron bands on their cart wheels, 'for that it is thought to be a great annoyance to the town

[1] Temp. T. Overey, sub ann.
[2] Journal, Dec. 14, 1638.
[3] Journal, sub data.
[4] Boke of Remembrances, fol. 29.
[5] Ibid., fol. 64.

in breaking the pavement, which hath been, and is daily, chargeable to the inhabitants, upon pain,' &c.[1] The shaking up of the beer was also a grievance. In 1577 this inconvenience was charged to the use of iron-bound carts. Such a cart not only caused

'Decay' to the pavement, but it 'causeth the beer to work up in such sort that the barrels seem to be full when they are brought, but when they are settled they lack some a gallon of beer, some more, to the enriching of the brewers but the hindrance of the town.'

Two years after this the court leet presented, as they had often done before—

'That the bruers cartes arre bounde with iron, contrary to the comaundement to them geven, wherefore they are to be amerced, for that yt is not only a greate decayeing of the pavement of this towne, but also the cause of the spurging of theire beere so that their barrels can not come full to theire customers.'[2]

It was the practice, however, to bring round 'filling beer' to make up deficiencies, a rule sometimes overlooked by the brewers. But in 1579 the following curious regulation was made for the purpose of securing good measure: 'That in consideration the brewers shall not be hereafter constrained to bring "fylling beer" about to their customers,' they are to allow them twenty-one barrels for twenty, and at the same time are to see their barrels sent out full.[3] Clay from the Saltmarsh was used instead of bungs, and the jury were constantly bidding the brewers fill up the holes as they dug from time to time, or dig no more.[4] Filling beer.

The following regulations occur :—

In 1553 a certain person was admitted into the corporation of beer-brewers, and licensed (with another of the same corporation) to serve with beer Jersey, Guernsey, and Alderney.[5] Licensing.

In 1553 no beer-brewer was permitted, as before, to sell otherwise than in gross, and not by retail as by the pot or gallon, nor was he to 'occupye any typpling,' *i.e.*, keep a public-house. Nor was any brewer to sell the best beer above two shillings the barrel, or to make any 'dobyll dobyll bere,' upon pain, &c. The best sort of beer or ale was to be sold at a halfpenny a quart.[6]

In 1557 the prohibition against the extra strong beer remained, and was repeated in subsequent years. Good beer[7] was to be twenty-two pence the barrel,[8] single beer fourteen pence, and three halfpence beer not above eighteen pence the barrel.

1 Boke of Remembrances, fol. 92 b.
2 Court Leet Books, 1577, 1579.
3 Boke of Remembrances, fol. 135 b.
4 Court Leet Books, 1567, &c.
5 Boke of Remembrances, fol. 65.
6 Ibid., fol. 70.
7 Ibid., fol. 77.
8 In 1570 it was to be 20d.

In 1596 the prohibition of double beer being repeated, an order was made to brew 'one sorte of verie good and wholesome ordinarie beere' at two shillings and sixpence the barrel and not above.[1] But at the end of the year a beer-brewer, who appears to have been bailiff as well as a burgess of the town, was called to the Audit-house on a charge of brewing double beer, and on his contumacy was 'disgraded of his burgess-ship,' and finally 'committed to the Counter for his presumption and obstinacy.'[2]

Whether heads were stronger by the end of Elizabeth's reign, or for other cause, 'doble' beer[3] was permitted to be brewed in 1601 at three shillings and fourpence the barrel, and single at one shilling and eightpence. The price of double beer in 1606 was the same as above, but the ordinary was two shillings the barrel. It was further ordered that there were to be but 'six brewers within the town,' who should 'sell their ale a full quart within doors and three pints without doors.'[4] The assize was, of course, regulated by the price of malt and hops; and in January 1607–8, malt being two shillings the bushel and hops £8 the hundred, it was ordered[5] that double beer should be sold at four shillings the barrel, and the ordinary at two shillings. In 1643 the brewers were sent for to the House, and 'warned to brew theire strong beere not above eight shillings the humberton, and theire small beere not above [blank] the humberton,' and not to brew at any other rates at their peril.[6]

In 1702 the leet jury presented that the ancient custom of the town was to sell beer and ale by the hooped quarts, and they desired the justices when they granted licenses to insist upon this measure being observed.

In 1713 the jury state that 'the beer hogshead ought to contain sixty-three gallons, according to the ancient custom of the town, as proved at the assize at Winchester, March 4, 1655, in a suit commenced by W. Knight, brewer, of this town, for the burning of several casks, upon the jury's presentment that year, as may be seen in the leet book for 1654.' The ancient gauge for humbers was forty-two gallons, being the sixth part of a tun, and a barrel was by the statutes thirty-six gallons.

Where to sell meat.

*Butchers.*—In 1457 the rent for stalls at the Friar's Gate was four shillings each per annum, but a stall taken by the day was charged at one penny. In 1548 the butchers above Bar were forbidden to sell flesh in their shops by retail, but were to carry their meat to the

1 Boke of Remembrances, fol. 187 b.
2 Ibid., fol. 194 b.
3 Ibid., fol. 208.
4 Journal, 1606 (March 27).
5 Ibid., 1607 (January 27).
6 Ibid., December 9, 1643.

market at Friar's Gate, where also all foreign[1] butchers were to keep their market.[2] As to the price of meat in 1549, from May 20 to sixteen days before midsummer the butchers were ordered to sell good beef and veal at three halfpence per pound, and mutton at twopence, on pain, &c.[3] Not only was the price set, but frequently the hours of sale. In 1571 the butchers at Friar's Gate were prohibited from selling after one o'clock P.M., on pain of three shillings and fourpence for each offence: two wardens of the butchers were at the same time appointed to superintend all sales and matters of business.[4] In 1579 the butchers were forbidden to have slaughter-houses within the walls, a piece of sanitary regulation which deserves to be noted. In October 1593, certain irregularities having occurred, two wardens of the occupation were appointed for the year, who, by virtue of their office, were empowered to search every butcher's shop to see that his victuals were good and wholesome for man's body and not corrupt.[5] The appointment of wardens occurs under other years: their office was always of a similar kind.

**Bull-baiting.**

Bull-baiting was practised not only for amusement but with a notion that it made the meat more wholesome. In February 1496 John Johnson was fined two loads of fagots, to be laid at the butts behind the west quay, for killing a bull not baited.[6] Similar entries occur in the sixteenth and seventeenth centuries. The bull-ring was in the upper part of the High Street.

The following presentment occurs in 1633:—

**Blowing up veal.**

'That the butchers have often been warned not to beat their calves or prick their meat, and yet they do so beat and prick their veal, whereby the wind entereth, so the flesh swelleth with bubbles, as it were blown, which is unwholesome for man's body, for which they are amersed 10s. a piece.'

And in 1675 the jury presented—

'The dangerous practice of butchers in blowing up their veal, which may occasion infection; as we are credibly informed is done by most of the butchers.'[7]

In 1518 the butchers, chandlers, and glovers came before the mayor in the Audit-house, and the former bound themselves to the mayor and his brethren that they would not sell 'ther shepis vellis but oonly to the glovers of this towne;' the glovers agreeing to give to the butchers from Easter to shearing-time for every dozen eight shillings, from shearing to

[1] By no means foreigners in the modern sense.
[2] Boke of Remembrances, fol. 52 b.
[3] Ibid., fol. 55.
[4] Ibid., fol. 112.
[5] Ibid., fol. 176.
[6] Liber Remembranc. H., fol. 12.
[7] Court Leet Book. An order at Winchester occurs under 1565, in which butchers are warned against blowing or unlawfully stuffing their veal.

All-hallows-tide, two shillings and fourpence a dozen, and from All-hallows to Shrove-tide, five shillings a dozen;[1] nor were the butchers to sell tallow to any but the chandlers of the town.

*Cappers.*—In 1502 the fine on admission to the craft of cap-making was six shillings and eightpence to the town, and the same amount to the master of the craft.[2]

*Chandlers.*—In 1507 two chandlers sufficed for the town, who bound themselves in the sum of three marks 'to serve the towne of candylles of talow from hensfforthe for one farthing the pound.' In the next year three chandlers entered into a similar engagement.[3] The price rose in the course of a few years. In 1518 the price given to the butchers for tallow being six shillings per hundredweight, the chandlers were ordered to produce their candles at a penny a pound from Whitsuntide to Michaelmas, and from Michaelmas to Whitsuntide at a penny for the quarter pound, provided they were made with cotton, otherwise at a penny the pound. Huxters were debarred from retailing candles except at the above price.[4]

Prices.

In August 1519 the curates of the town complained—

Bad wax.

'That by meanes of makyng of false wex by wex-chaundelers yn myxyng rosyn and turpyntall w[t] the same yn tapors and candilles, not only the images, vestments, and awter clothes be gretely hurtid, but also it is a grete deceyte to the byers and very noyeous to all parisshoners beinge yn the chirches at the Dyvyne Servys. For reformacon wherof the said Meyre w[t] the advise of his brethryn called before hym yn the Audite hous . . . [the] wex chaundelers, that from hensfurth none of them shall myxe any rosyn or turpyntell w[t] wex yn makyng of tapors or candilles, &c., but to make all clene wex w[t] white matche, and not to use black torche weke, &c. And every of them to sett there marke uppon the tapors uppon peyn to forfeit all wex so myxed, and imprisonment vj dais and vj nyghts for the fyrst defawte, and for the seconde defawte to sitt oppynly yn the stokkes iij markett dais, and for the iij[d] defawte to be banysshed the towne.'[5]

Town chandlers.

In October 1548 certain tallow-chandlers engaged to furnish poor as well as rich with candles for the following year at three halfpence per pound, the butchers being obliged to furnish the tallow at eight shillings per hundredweight.[6] Similar arrangements were made a little later,[7] and the above remained the price of candles for some time.[8] In 1571 chandlers were appointed for the different wards;[9] in 1576 two seem to have sufficed as formerly in the town.[10] These were appointed for twenty-one years from Lady Day 1576; one was to serve the parishes

1 Liber Remembranc. H., 9 Hen. VIII.
2 Liber Remembranc. H., fol. 6 b.
3 Ibid., fol. ult. b.
4 Ibid., 9 Hen. VIII.
5 Boke of Remembrances, fol. 17.
6 Ibid., fol. 52.
7 Ibid., fol. 54.
8 Ibid., fol. 68 (1553).
9 Ibid., fol. 112.
10 Ibid., fol. 133.

of Holy Rood, St. Michael, and St. John, and the other to serve All-Saints, St. Mary's, Bag-row, and East Street; the tallow of the butchers was to be divided equally between them.

In the reign of Elizabeth, the most depressed period for the town, one chandler sufficed for all the local business;[1] and towards the end of the reign (1598), under the tight hand of the Corporation, we find this unfortunate monopolist, 'the town chandler,' complaining of his inability to serve the town as he ought, *i.e.*, at the price fixed; he was accordingly dismissed, and another chandler appointed.[2] In 1609 the price of tallow candles seems to have been fourpence the pound.

*Cloth-workers.*—In June 1504 the wardens of the shearmen (cloth-workers), with all their company, complained before the mayor and his brethren of wrongs done them by divers galleymen 'in takkyng[3] and foldyng certain clothes and kersies' contrary to their liberty; when it was agreed that 'merchant strangers and Basariotts' having servants of their own that could 'fold [and] takk such clothes and kersies' might use their servants' skill for their own goods, but not otherwise. It was also agreed that the shearmen should take for the 'takkyng and foldyng' for every kersey a halfpenny.[4] Complaints.

Under 1518 we have two batches of shearmen, eight in one, and ten in the other, there being two wardens to each batch.[5]

In 1554 'northeren men,' coming to the town with cloth to be sold, were declared 'free and frank of custom coming in at the Bargate for all such cloth as they bring upon horse and pay hallage.'[6]

In 1608 the shearmen complained of their office being usurped by certain who were now made to pay the town and the shearmen for their privilege. In March the following year (1608–9), the cloth-workers, clothiers, and serge-makers (French and English), were summoned to the House, and received orders to admit no more new-comers into their trade without leave. The same decree was issued to the shearmen-tuckers (fullers). These latter were desired (August) to bring their articles and orders to be confirmed and established; the articles which were agreed to are not recorded.

In 1618 the cloth-workers of Southampton and Winchester petitioned that the late unusual exportation of wool might be prohibited as damaging to the cloth trade, and reducing 3000 of their poor to distress.[7]

In September 1629 it appearing that the cloth-workers had omitted to read annually in public among themselves the articles of their

[1] Liber Remembranc. (1560), fol. 196 b.

[2] Boke of Remembrances, fol. 198 b.

[3] Dressing.

[4] Liber Remembranc. H., 19 Hen. VII.

[5] Ibid., fol. 191.

[6] Boke of Remembrances, fol. 72.

[7] Cal. State Papers.

corporation, they were fined £5: on paying which they were assured of the town's assistance in future against strangers and new-comers, according to the purport of their corporation.

The stock of the company had to be certified from time to time to the town. On October 14, 1670, the cloth-workers certified to having chosen their two wardens, and to the value of their stock being £19, 8s. 6d. The serge-makers also certified, but to the effect that they had no stock whatever.

In the court leet book of 1666 occurs a presentment of thirty-two clothiers, embracing some important names, and commencing with Joseph Delamot, alderman, for forcing their spinners 'to take goods for their work' [*i.e.*, instead of cash], 'whereby the poor were much wronged, being contrary to the statute, for all which they were amerced severally as followeth.' Yet no fine appears to have been exacted.

*Cobblers.*—Early in the sixteenth century the cobblers were fined for giving work in their occupation to certain men contrary to the rules of the corporation.[1] In 1576 they were presented as a body, 'for that they do usse to mende and cobble mens shewen w^t^ naughtie flittinge lether.'[2] Trade infringements were involved in the following entry:—Under 1578, 'received of a shoemaker for making a fault against the cobblers.'[3] In May 1633 the shoemakers complained of a certain cobbler for making new shoes. On inquiry it appeared to the House that both sides were in fault, viz., 'the said Foye for making new shoes,' and the shoemakers for mending 'old shoes.' Thereupon it was ordered that if either party offended, the shoemakers in mending old, or Foye in making new shoes, a forfeit of five shillings to the town would follow.[4]

Coopers' petition.

*Coopers.*—The enrolment of charter granted to the Society of Coopers in the time of Christopher Ambrose, dated December 6, 1486, recites their petition:—

> 'To the right honorable and right gracious syrs the meyre, aldermen, wisemen, and other good burgesses of the towne of Suthampton, mekely besechith the poore maisters artificers of the occupacon and crafte of cowpers within the same towne. That whereas the same artificers from daye to daye have bene, and yet are, contributours after theyr symple power unto the grete charges, taxes, taggages, and watches that have [been levied] upon the ayde reparacon and defens of the same towne, and have not wherof to lyve, ne to maynteyne theyr symple countenaunce and estate.'

They have had fair times in the past, owing to the resort partly of many foreigners and strangers—

> 'But of late ther have commen and resorted as well cowpers of aliens as

1 Liber Remembranc. H., f. 140 b.
2 Court Leet Book.
3 MS. Temp. T. Overey, sub anno.
4 Journal.

of dyvers nacions, as of other Englisshe straungiers which never were prentices of the seid occupacion and crafte of cowpers within the seid towne, and there have occupied the seid occupation and crafte of cowpers in howses, shoppes, and chambers within the seid towne as largely and as frely without impeticon or any fyne makyng unto the meyre, &c., unto the gretest damage, distruccon, and empoverysshement of the seid maisters artificers.'

They pray that no cooper be allowed to set up unless he—

'Have made fyne and gree with the mayre for the tyme being and with the maisters of the seid occupacon and crafte.'

The penalties of imprisonment and fine of one hundred shillings were added, the latter to be levied by the mayor's command and equally divided between the town and the coopers.[1] A few days after this (Dec. 12), the steward received a fine from the master-coopers in consideration of a livery granted to them by the mayor and his brethren, of thirteen shillings and fourpence, together with six shillings and eightpence, the fee for the town seal being affixed to the grant.[2] At about the same period the coopers were paid eightpence for tunning a tun of wine bought for the king on the occasion of his visit.[3]

Admission into the corporation of coopers was heavier than that of the other trades. In 1608, £4 was paid, and, on the usual plan, one half of the admission fine went to the town, the other to the society.[4]

In 1657 (April 17) the coopers' charter was again confirmed with the town seal.[4]

*Corvesers, Cordwainers, i.e., Shoemakers.*—The earliest notice observed occurs in 1488, when the town steward acknowledged receipt from the masters of the corveser craft (April 19) for the town's part of what they had gathered from the galleymen.[5] In the early part of the seventeenth century the entrance to the craft was a payment sometimes of thirty-five shillings to the town and thirty-five to the shoemakers' corporation.[6] In 1713 leave was granted[7] to the company of cordwainers to prosecute certain persons for using the trade of a cordwainer contrary to their privileges. Shoemakers.

*Dancing-School.*—Thomas Grymes having set up such an establishment, is ordered (Dec. 1608) to give it up, and settle himself otherwise or depart the town.[8]

*Fish-Sellers.*—In February 1550 seven fishmongers were appointed to serve the town for the whole year 'with good and wholesome fish,

1 Liber Niger, fol. 60.
2 Liber Remembranc. H., f. 170 b.
3 Steward's Book, 1486.
4 Journal.
5 Liber Remembranc. H., 3 Hen. VII.
6 Journal.
7 Ibid., July 10.
8 Journal.

well watered from time to time.'[1] Frequent orders occur about seasoning and watering fish at the proper times.

*Glovers.*—The white tanyers (tanners), otherwise called glovers, were prohibited from purchasing lamb-skins killed within the town, the skinners having to purchase and live thereby, and sell to the glovers at a reasonable price.[2] By an order of 1518 it had been provided that the glovers when they got their skins were to be careful to sell the wool only to dwellers in the town, upon pain, &c.[3]

In January 1644–45, the glovers complaining against certain newcomers for not 'confining themselves to journey-work, but privately working for themselves,' these latter were banished from the town.[4]

*Hackney-men.*—In 1558 certain 'horse-hirers' were appointed for the town with two wardens. The hire of a horse was fixed at eightpence for the first day, afterwards at sixpence. The time set for a journey from Southampton to London or Bristol was seven days, and the charge for a horse was to be six shillings, with sixpence extra for every extra day. Two days were assigned for a journey to Salisbury, and the hire of a horse was put at sixteen-pence, and sixpence for every day after.[5] Fines were paid to the town by the hackney-men for their privileges, which were protected as usual. A few years later (1577), the journey to London or Bristol was set at eight days,[6] the price being fixed at six shillings and eightpence, with not above one shilling and fourpence for each extra day. The journey to Sarum was still charged one shilling and fourpence.

A copy of a letter from Hampton Court, dated January 30, 1592–93, directs posting stations to be made between the Court, Portsmouth, and Southampton, in order that intelligence may be had the quicker from Normandy and Brittany, where the queen's forces were 'employed for the help of the king of France against his subjects.' The court being at Hampton, the stations were to be at Kingston-on-Thames, Guilford, Farnham, Alton, East Meon, Portsmouth, Southampton; the distances and charges for the horses being laid down.[7]

*Lacemaker.*—In 1608 one of this unthriving trade petitioned for the monopoly of 'gathering old goods in this town;' but his suit was

[1] Boke of Remembrances, fol. 58.

[2] Ibid., fol. 22, b, Nov. 1523.

[3] Liber Remembranc. H., 9 Hen. VIII.

[4] Journal. Glovers could yet pity glovers, and subscribed (1577) towards one who had been locked up four days in the Bargate for lack of a passport.

[5] Boke of Remembrances, fol. 77 b.

[6] So in 1609 a certain person released from the Bargate receives a passport to London, eight days being allowed for the journey (Journal, Aug. 1609).

[7] Boke of Remembrances, fol. towards end.

disallowed, as the matter was lawful for any one who carried himself honestly.[1]

*Linen Hall.*—In May 1553, 'considering that heretofore of long time, for lack of good oversight,' the merchants resorting to the town with linen cloth had, contrary to good order, after unlading their goods, stowed them away in various hostelries and houses, 'the town having both lofts and warehouses meet for the same,' which stand void by reason of the greediness of those who have more regard to their private gain and lucre than to the advancement and wealth of the town, it was ordered that the Linen Hall be used under severe penalties.[2] Notices of this hall occur from time to time.

*Mercers.*—In February 1486 (1 Hen. VII.) the steward received a fine of twelve pence from a man of Havant, a mercer, for that he went with his fardell up and down the town of Southampton hawking, contrary to the privilege of the mercers' craft.[3] Admission to the craft was, as usual, by consent of, and fine to, the town and the company or corporation of mercers within the town.

*Sergemakers, Sergeweavers, and Woolcombers.*—A company of these trades was formed in 1609 under the authority of the town, entrance to the trade being fixed at a fine of £5, divided equally between the town and the company. Apprenticeship was for seven years, enrolment being ordered as usual in the town books. New-comers of the same trade were not to be admitted into the town unless they brought a certificate of having been apprenticed here or elsewhere for seven years.[4] Previously to this arrangement sergeweavers appear to have been admitted on their giving security to the town for their sufficiency and good behaviour.[5]

In 1616 articles and orders concerning the above trades received the town seal;[6] but in February 1619–20 the above corporation of sergemakers, sergeweavers, and woolcombers dissolved by consent of all parties.[7] They had not thriven on the town's articles.

A corporation of the same trades was formed anew in 1657, their charter being sealed on July 24; the terms do not appear.[8] Shortly after this (1663), the town being in want of a woolcombmaker to supply the necessities of the woolcombers, Peter Purkis, whose patronymic is known in Hampshire story, humbly petitioned to be made a freeman of the town and to use the said craft. This was allowed, provided he should pay to the mayor fifty shillings by May 6.[9]

[1] Journal, fol. 65 b.
[2] Boke of Remembrances, fol. 68.
[3] Liber Remembranc. H., 1 Hen. VII.
[4] Journal, July 20.
[5] Ibid., Feb. 1608.
[6] Ibid., Dec. 1616.
[7] Ibid., Jan. 28, Feb. 4.
[8] Ibid., July 24, 1657.
[9] Ibid., March 6, 1662–63.

*Silkworkers.*—See under 'French Church.'

*Surgeon.*—In 1644–45 (Jan. 10) William Phillips, chirurgeon, was allowed to come with his family into the town and practise physic, but to go at a month's notice if desired.

In 1656 (Nov. 14) Dr. Johnson was ordered to bring a sufficient certificate from the parish where he last lived in London of his marriage and the time he lived there. On May 5, 1667, he received £5 from the mayor as a gratuity, beyond what he had been already paid, for his great attention during the plague.[1]

*Tailors.*—Under 1470 the fines of the tailor craft are entered at length, two pages of tailors occurring, together with their payments: the town and the masters of the tailoring art dividing the fines. The usual fine was thirteen shillings and fourpence.[2]

Individuals sometimes abjured their freedom. Thus, on August 18, 1474, in the presence of the mayor and his brethren and the masters of the occupation of tailors, with many more of the same trade, Cornelius Clerke 'released up his freedom and liberty of the said occupation,' desiring to depart from the town and go with a carrack, swearing on a book to do so, and never to do the same occupation within the town. The fifteen shillings which he had paid as his fine to the town and craft were, at his request, refunded.[3]

Tailors' petition.

Very similar in substance to the coopers' petition given above was that of the tailors in 1474–75, before William Overey, the mayor, aldermen, prudhommes, and other good burgesses of the town. They spoke of their support towards the great charges of the town for its repair and defence, and being unable to maintain their poor estate, they begged relief against strange tailors coming to the port in carracks, galleys, and ships of Spain, Portugal, Germany, Flanders, &c., and setting up their craft contrary to former and proper custom, without fine made to the town, to the destruction and impoverishment of the master-tailors and others of the same craft. The authorities were prayed to order that no alien tailor be suffered to keep shop, house, or chamber within the town or franchises of the same for the purpose of their work, except they first made fine and agreement with the masters of the craft, upon pain of imprisonment for the first offence, and for the second to be fined one hundred shillings, to be divided equally between the town and the master-tailors. For the concessions granted on this petition the tailors gave the town one hundred shillings sterling.[4]

Beneath the above enrolment is a further proviso, bearing date October 11 (15 Hen. VII.) 1499, to the effect that it should not be

[1] Journal, under dates.
[2] Liber Remembranc. H., fol. 36.
[3] Ibid., fol. 26.
[4] Liber Niger, fol. 13.

lawful for any man, whether burgess or commoner, to take either as journeyman or apprentice any other than an English subject, on pain of losing his freedom: nor was any foreign subject to be admitted to set up a shop for tailor's craft on any fine whatever.

The doings of the galley-tailors had always to be watched. In 1498 the names of six offenders remain on the books: 'These aforeseid tailors ben sworne uppon a boke affore Vyncent Tehy, then maire of Suthampton, that they shall not cutte nor make no manere garnaments of ony nacyon but of there owne nacyon upponne payne of gravouse punyshement.'[1]

In 1608, the corporations of the tailors and the blacksmiths having petitioned against certain who had set up trade without being free of the town or their corporations, were empowered to go with a serjeant and shut down the shop windows of the intruders. The coopers and cobblers made similar complaints shortly afterwards, and had the same remedy.

In November 1610 the freedom of the company of tailors was purchased at fifteen shillings and twenty shillings, the fine being divided as usual.

In September 1616 the company seems to have been placed on a new footing. In consequence of— Rearrangement of company.

'Divers persons, foreigners, and not free men,' who had come to the town and were exercising their craft, the tailors were in sad plight and likely to fall from bad to worse; they therefore petitioned with success: 1. That there may be a settled company and fellowship of the said craft and mystery of tailors established. 2. That they may yearly elect on the Friday before Michaelmas two men to be wardens or overseers of the company, to have the management and care of money, for which they must render account in the Audit-house before the mayor, &c., to such persons as shall next succeed them in their office. 3. Persons refusing to serve when elected to be fined thirteen shillings and fourpence, half to the town and half to the company. 4. Apprentices to be taken for seven years, &c. 5. Who should be enrolled in the Audit-house by the town-clerk in a book kept for the purpose, under pain of six shillings and eightpence, half to the town, half to the company. After this follow several other items at great length, dealing with apprentices, journeymen, foreigners, &c.[2]

On a petition of the tailors (May 17, 1644), certain offending strangers, who had kept open shop, had fourteen days given them to finish work in hand, after which they were to work journey-work or depart the town.[3]

*Tipplers* (*tavern-keepers*).—Cleanliness was sometimes lacking; a certain Guernsey man drinking (1569) in an alehouse in the town having been nearly poisoned owing to the dirty habit of publicans in

[1] Liber Remembranc. H. fol. 4 b.

[2] For all the above see Journal under years.

[3] Journal.

not washing out their pots, 'for voyding the daunger thereof we request that order may be taken that no innkeeper, tavener, or ale-house keeper do sell wyne, berre, or alle, but that ther pottes be wasshed, that men that byeth the same maye se the same drawen, and the pottes wasshed to avoyd the inconveniences that maye growe thereby.'[1]

Drunkards posted up.

In 1581 (August 10) the tipplers were forbidden to receive into their houses any of the common drunkards of the town, the names of many of whom are given.

Alehouses in excess repressed.

In 1601 the inordinate number of alehouses was presented,[2] a grievance which prevailed over the whole country.

On March 3 (1 Jas. I.), 1604, a circular letter from his Majesty was addressed to the mayor and justices concerning the excessive 'number of alehouses, victualling and tippling houses within this our realme, and of the great abuse in granting licenses for the same, and in setting them up and putting them down at pleasure,' without due regard to the number or quality of the persons licensed. His Majesty, with the advice of his Privy Council, takes order for reformation in this behalf, and—

'Finding that by the law and statutes of this our realm the keeping of alehouses and victualling houses is none of those trades which it is free and lawful for any subject to set up and exercise, but inhibited to all save such as are thereto licensed, which ought to be no more than a number competent for the receipt of travellers, and for supply of wants to poor people not able to provide for any quantity of victuals for themselves (which are the true, ancient, and natural use of these houses), and with this also that they be not made the receptacle of drunkards, felons, and loose and idle persons: we do hereby will and command you, the mayor and justices, &c., strictly to observe and put in use the directions hereunto annexed.'

These were:—1. Concerning the *number* of such houses necessary, the fitness of the persons to be licensed, and the revision of licenses granted before this time, that unfit persons might be rejected. 2. Publicans were to be licensed and allowed at the general quarter sessions. 3. Articles of good order were to be conceived by the justices for observance by innkeepers, and the justices were to see them observed. 4. Alehouse-keepers were bound by recognisance not to permit unlawful games, and to bring their licenses for inspection and reconsideration at the sessions twelvemonth wherein such license was granted. 5. The names of all persons licensed were to be registered, and a report on their conduct to be certified by the justices to his Majesty's Privy Council.[3]

Under 1608 a publican was 'disallowed to tipple any more' (*i.e.*, keep public-house), on account of his having kept 'dicing, carding, and many other unlawful games in his house,' which was presented by the 'biddels' of the ward of All Saints: other similar instances occur. In

[1] Court Leet Book. [2] Ibid.

[3] Journal. In the Parliament which commenced March 19 the same year, an 'Act to restrain the inordinate haunting and tippling in alehouses' was passed, 1 Jas. I. cap. 9.

1618, eleven persons were presented for keeping alehouses without license, so that the law had not been closely administered.[1] However, matters were reformed, and in February 1623 the mayor reported that he had obeyed the orders in suppressing unnecessary alehouses, and moderating the strength of the ale brewed.

*Tobacco-cutters.*—In 1644 a certain John Cannon, a foreigner of the Devizes, was sent for to the House, April 12, and warned to bring in two sufficient sureties by that day week to save the town harmless, or else depart; he was also warned to forbear cutting tobacco in the town at his peril. Still he went on cutting, and (May 17) on complaint of the tobacco-cutters, free commoners of the town, order was made that he 'presume not (after hee hath cutt about 80 lb. w^ch^ hee hath in his house) to cutt any more tobacco for himself or any others within the towne and the libertyes thereof at his perill.'[2]

*Vintners.*—In 1613 they were ordered to sell their Gascony wine at not more than sixpence a quart; subsequently (1633) white and red claret were included in a similar order. In February 1631–32 the vintners being summoned to the House to receive from the authorities the price of wine, made no appearance; whereupon Mr. Mayor, with the consent of his brethren, proceeded to publish the order for them.

*Wool.*—A 'sisterhood' of *twelve* women, two of them being wardens, of good and honest demeanour, existed in the sixteenth century as a company for the packing and covering of wool, their duties being 'to serve the merchants in the occupation of covering of pokes [pockets] or balous [bales].' They were sworn, and the regulations of their work are given at length.[3] The employment of women in this capacity is said to have been of long continuance.

In 1554 certain irregularities as to the attendance of the 'sisters' were adjudicated on. No one absent from her duties for more than three months was to be permitted to return to the 'sisterhood' without the mayor's license.

The following order also occurs:—

'Item, yt is ordered by the sayde maior and his bretherne that all suche as shalbe nomynated and appoynted to be of the systeryd shall make a brekefaste at their entrye for a knowledge, and shal bestowe at the least xx$^{d.}$ or ij$^{s.}$, or more as they lyste.'

The names of the *thirteen* are given, two being wardens.[4]

---

1 Journal.

2 Ibid., see also Cal. State Papers, Nov. 17, 1629.

3 Lib. Rememor. BB., fol. 26 b.

4 Ibid., fol. 28.

## Section III.—*Modern Trade.*

Some account of the Railway and Docks is a natural introduction to any notice of the modern trade of the town.

London and Southampton railway.

The formation of a Railway to London was thought of so far back as 1825, and the question was revived in earnest in 1830, when, on November 22, the Corporation received a deputation from the subscribers to the intended railway and docks, and in consequence passed a resolution affirming their willingness to treat with that committee, or with any respectable company that might be formed having in view the extension of the port.

On July 22, 1831, a resolution of the Southampton and London Railway Company was communicated by their chairman, Colonel Henderson, to the Town Council, empowering the directors to appoint the mayor an *ex-officio* director during his year of office and the year following. This arrangement was accepted by the Corporation, who expressed their sense of the public value of a railroad from London to Southampton; an opinion which they reaffirmed by a lengthy resolution of November 16, 1833.

The enabling Act having received the royal assent in July 1834, and the Corporation seal affixed to the conveyance of the needful land on October 30, 1835, the works were commenced in March 1836. By 12th May 1838 the line was opened from London to Woking Common, a distance of twenty-three miles, the trial trip being made that day, and accomplished in forty-five minutes. In May 1839 the line was completed from Southampton to Winchester, and from London to Basingstoke, the intervening space of eighteen miles being performed by coach. In the same month in the following year (1840) the whole line was in operation.

The Docks.

43 Geo. III cap. 21, 1803.

We may now turn to the Docks. These were contemplated under the Act 43 George III. cap. 21 (1803), 'for abolishing certain dues called petty customs, &c., and for making convenient docks,' &c., Mr. Rennie, the celebrated engineer, having reported favourably on their construction. The preamble of the above Act sets forth the antiquity of the port, which was capable of being rendered more commodious by the construction of docks and pier and the improvement of quays and wharfs. The Corporation had been entitled to 'petty customs' on exports and imports, which rights they were willing to relinquish on compensation being given.

The improvement sought to be carried out would involve considerable outlay, the cost of which should be defrayed by the trade of the port. Commissioners for all purposes under the Act were appointed as follows:—The mayor, recorder, common council-men, and their successors, with ten specific commissioners. Powers were given for making channels in the water by placing booms; making bye-laws for the shipping in the harbour; entering into contracts for building docks, piers, warehouses, &c.; all such erections being vested in the commissioners. The petty customs were in future to be received by them, monies arising from such duties being applied as follows:—1. The payment of one-fifth to the mayor and common council for the time being, as compensation for the purposes of the town. 2. To the building and repairing of the said piers, docks, warehouses, &c., and for keeping the channel marked out.

Accordingly the Corporation has received from the port account one-fifth of the dues collected, one-third of the fifth being taken in lieu of petty customs, and the other two-thirds in lieu of anchorage, groundage, wharfage, and storage.

The Act gave the commissioners power to remove the walls and gates of the town, which were in the way of the needful improvements (see p. 94).

The above Act was altered and amended by the 50 Geo. III. cap. 168 (June 9, 1810), as to the appointment and qualification of commissioners and as to the rates chargeable under the Act; but the formation of the docks was still in abeyance owing to the demand on capital by the improvements already being carried out (see p. 113). 50 Geo. III. cap. 168, 1810.

It was not till 1836 that the Dock Company was incorporated by Act of Parliament, the construction of docks being commenced in 1838 with a capital of £1,000,000, since increased to £1,500,000, of which £1,154,711 have been used (1882), leaving the balance for further works. Something over two hundred acres of mudland were originally purchased from the Corporation for £5000 for the purpose of the docks: a portion of this land still remains unenclosed.

The first stone of the docks was laid with full masonic honours on Friday, October 12, 1838, by Admiral Sir Lucius Curtis, Knt. and Bart., of Gatcombe House, assisted by the chairman (Joseph Liggins, Esq.) and directors of the Southampton Dock Company, in the presence of the mayor and Corporation and a distinguished assembly. The engineer was Mr. Francis Giles, the present member of Parliament.

The great tidal dock was commenced in October 1839, and completed at a cost of about £140,000. It was the largest in England, containing a surface of 16 acres of water, 18 feet deep at low water spring tides, entrance 150 feet wide, the average rise of tide being 13 feet; it was opened on August 29, 1842, the 'Liverpool' and the 'Tagus' entering it, the former with passengers and cargo on board from Gibraltar, the latter with the directors. The inner or close dock, then in progress, was not opened till 1851; it encloses 10 acres of water, and is 28 feet deep.

The first graving or dry dock was formally opened on 11th July 1846, having been about fourteen months under construction, at a cost of about £60,000. Another was opened in the following year. The entrance gates of these docks are respectively 66 and 51 feet in width, and the length of their floors 400 and 251 feet, with a depth of water over blocks of 21 feet and 15 feet. A third graving dock was finished in 1854. It is 80 feet wide, 500 feet in length, with a depth of 25 feet over blocks. The fourth has an entrance directly from the Itchen. It is 56 feet wide, 450 long, and 25 feet in depth over blocks.

The docks are fitted with all necessary appurtenances; there are numerous cranes, and three sets of powerful sheers worked by steam, for lifting masts, boilers, and heavy machinery up to 100 tons weight.

It is intended to construct another dock of 37 acres with a minimum depth of 26 feet at low water; and already the extension quay, 1720 feet in length with 20 feet of water at low tide, is completed and in constant use on its river side.

These docks having deep water, with the natural advantage of practically four hours of continuous high water, afford every convenience for the largest steam-ships; and being themselves within a sheltered, landlocked harbour, offer great immunity from risk and accidents. Cargoes of every description are landed and warehoused, or forwarded by railway with great expedition, there existing from the dock quays and warehouses perfect and rapid railway communication to all parts of the metropolis, the coalfields, and manufacturing districts. Additional railway facilities are about to be added by the construction of new lines directly connecting Southampton with the Midland and Great Western Railways. The Dock Company's own lines of railway, 10 miles in length, worked by their own locomotives, run on all the quays and into and alongside each warehouse, being connected at several points with the London and South-Western Railway. Trucks pass direct between the docks and every railway in the kingdom.

There are extensive bonded and free warehouses adjacent to the dock quays, and large vaults under the warehouses.

For the grain trade there are large and convenient warehouses fitted with improved machinery, with deep-water berths alongside, whereat grain-laden vessels of the largest tonnage may lie afloat and discharge.

By order of Privy Council there is a defined 'foreign animals wharf,' where animals landed must be slaughtered within fourteen days. By the same authority there is a 'foreign animals quarantine station;' animals landed there must be intended for purposes of exhibition or other exceptional purpose. There is also under order of Council a 'foreign animals reshipment station;' animals landed thereat must be intended for reshipment to a foreign country. Southampton is the only port which provides for the quarantine of foreign animals. Animals not subject to slaughter or quarantine are landed at approved places within the docks.

Within the area of the docks, eastward of its main entrance, is a large sugar-refinery, constructed by the Dock Company, and leased to Messrs. Garton, Hill, & Co. Here are made both refined sugar and 'saccharum' for brewing. Adjacent to the saccharum works is the extensive boiler and engine factory of the Royal Mail Steam-Packet Company, also constructed by the Dock Company. Here are all the appliances for the repairs of machinery and the construction of boilers for the fleet of this company, comprising twenty-five ships. On the western side of the close dock is a large coal depôt, built by the Dock Company, and leased to Messrs. W. Hill & Co.

Custom-house. Mercantile Marine office.

On the dock estate are the custom-house, Board of Trade, and dock offices, all substantial modern buildings, also erected by the Company. The Dock Company have also two sets of complete workshops, one for general repairs, the other for repairs of locomotives and pumping engines.

Embarkations.

The capabilities of the docks were demonstrated in the early days of last August (1882) by the unprecedented departure of troops. The transport department of the Admiralty dispatched hence to Egypt eleven large steam-ships, their aggregate tonnage being 37,352 tons—ten of these vessels having been ordered here from other ports, Southampton being selected as the port of embarkation. In one day five of the ships were dispatched, their united lengths being one-third of a mile. These conveyed, besides stores and war materials, some 1200 men and 850 horses, all of which arrived on the morning of the departure of the ships. The eleven transports took in all 175 officers, 3264 non-commissioned officers and men, and 2002 horses, three batteries of artillery, Royal Engineers' vehicles, and sundry equipments.

Visit of her Majesty.

On Wednesday, the 9th of August, her Majesty the Queen, accompanied by their Royal Highnesses the Princess Beatrice and Duchess of Connaught, their Royal Highnesses the Prince and Princess of Wales, with their sons and daughters, His Royal Highness the Duke of Cambridge, together with a number of distinguished naval and military officers, visited the docks and inspected the various transports, the Queen going on board one of the largest.

Ship-building trade.

The establishment of docks at Southampton gave a fresh impetus to all shipbuilding industries. At Northam on the Itchen, above the docks at Northam, there is the old and prosperous firm of Messrs. Day, Summers, & Co., where many of the largest mail steam-ships and other vessels have been built and engined. This firm manufactures large quantities of machinery for various places in England and abroad, and also for foreign Governments. Nearly all dockyards at home and abroad now use Day & Summers' steam-sheers, which have been made for lifting weights up to 150 tons. There is also the wooden shipbuilding yard of Mr. John Ransom, who has a fleet of sailing vessels of his own construction engaged in the foreign trade. And, not to mention further concerns of a smaller character, in 1876 the shipbuilding business was much extended by the establishment of the iron shipbuilding and engine works of Messrs. Oswald, Mordaunt, & Co. Since their arrival at Southampton this firm had launched, previously to August 1882, twenty-four sailing vessels, with an aggregate tonnage of about 40,920; and fifteen steamers, with an aggregate tonnage of 23,763. At the same date eleven ships were in construction with an approximate gross tonnage of 26,707 in the aggregate. A very large trade is now being carried on in their yard.

Growth of trade from docks and railway.

The modern prosperity of Southampton may be said to have been sketched out in the Act of 1803, which contemplated docks and other improvements; its actual growth as a prominent seaport and trading centre followed quickly upon the carrying out of these essential works. A Parliamentary return[1] of January 1847 shows how the trade had rapidly increased since railway and dock facilities had been given, and that in 1845 the port had stood fifth among the ports of the kingdom in respect to the number of ships outward and inward during that year, their tonnage, and the declared value of their exports. The number of ships, outward and inward, was 1435, their aggregate tonnage 300,134, while the declared value of the exports of British and Irish produce was £1,475,000, inferior only in amount to London, Liverpool, Hull, and Glasgow.

In 1846 the exports had risen to £2,996,275, and the number of ships belonging to the port was 230, with a tonnage of about 14,000.

In 1880 Southampton stood fourth among the English ports in regard to the total numbers of sailing ships and of steam-ships entering such ports; the numbers of such ships having been for 1879—

| | Number of Sailing Ships. | Number of Steam-Ships. |
|---|---|---|
| London, | 34,434 | 11,315 |
| Liverpool, | 6,012 | 7,804 |
| Bristol, | 5,523 | 3,362 |
| Southampton, | 2,744 | 2,125 |
| Hull, | 1,613 | 2,371 |

[1] Evidence in the House of Commons, 1882, on Didcot, Newbury, and Southampton Railway Bill.

In regard to the tonnage of the above ships, Hull stands 1,199,005 and Southampton 919,107, so that Southampton was after Hull in tonnage, but before in numbers. In the same list it is also before Bristol as to tonnage, which stands at 650,050 for the two classes of ships.

In the next year (1880) 3637 sailing vessels and 5011 steam-ships entered the port; and 3398 sailing vessels and 4993 steam-ships left.

In 1881, 3311 sailing and 5323 steam vessels entered, and 3101 sailing and 5245 steam vessels cleared.

In 1880 Southampton also stood third among the ports of England in regard to the tonnage of vessels (steam and sail) which cleared from and entered the various ports. The numbers were :—

| Ports. | Tonnage of Ships Cleared. | Tonnage of Ships Entered. |
|---|---|---|
| London, | 6,024,937 | 10,454,171 |
| Liverpool, | 7,215,137 | 7,245,227 |
| Southampton, | 2,006,436 | 2,027,270 |

In 1880 this port stood fifth among the English ports in regard to the tonnage of vessels belonging to the various ports, the total tonnage of Southampton vessels being 69,308; and it stood sixth in regard to the actual number of vessels belonging to the ports, the number belonging to Southampton (steam and sail) being 323 vessels.

The value of the total exports and imports at Southampton for the five years ending 1880 was as follows :—

| | Exports. | Imports. |
|---|---|---|
| 1876 | £8,229,850 | £9,198,924 |
| 1877 | £8,665,078 | £9,055,179 |
| 1878 | £8,335,808 | £9,191,027 |
| 1879 | £8,904,622 | £7,756,773 |
| 1880 | £9,306,326 | £9,205,183 |

Southampton stood fourth among English ports in regard to the value of its exports and imports, the value being for 1880 :—

| | |
|---|---|
| London, | £194,043,836 |
| Liverpool, | £191,489,838 |
| Hull, | £38,735,272 |
| Southampton, | £18,511,509 |

The following table[1] shows the tonnage of ships entering and clearing from Southampton :—

[1] Statement of Dock Company, presented to the British Association, August 1882, and information of Philip Hedger, Esq., Secretary and Superintendent.

*Tonnage (Register) of Ships for the Years* 1875, 1880, 1881, 1882.

| INWARD TONNAGE OF SHIPS. | | | | | | | |
|---|---|---|---|---|---|---|---|
| Year. | Foreign. | | Coasting. | | | | Total. |
| | | | With Cargo. | | In Ballast or Carrying Passengers. | | |
| | Sail. | Steam. | Sail. | Steam. | Sail. | Steam. | |
| 1875 | 54,952 | 996,013 | 102,349 | 369,673 | 26,735 | 146,524 | 1,696,246 |
| 1880 | 52,168 | 1,182,733 | 110,273 | 412,198 | 28,724 | 230,982 | 2,017,118 |
| 1881 | 37,620 | 1,187,889 | 107,847 | 475,094 | 29,898 | 251,526 | 2,098,874 |
| 1882 | 45,995 | 1,183,849 | 103,373 | 389,601 | 32,111 | 273,732 | 2,028,661 |
| OUTWARD TONNAGE OF SHIPS. | | | | | | | |
| 1875 | 38,499 | 1,006,124 | 65,665 | 286,469 | 74,741 | 226,437 | 1,697,935 |
| 1880 | 43,298 | 1,116,029 | 62,670 | 386,033 | 84,508 | 319,844 | 2,012,382 |
| 1881 | 29,833 | 1,138,651 | 60,023 | 411,525 | 94,161 | 359,873 | 2,088,066 |
| 1882 | 35,390 | 1,163,228 | 67,370 | 317,138 | 86,026 | 359,990 | 2,029,142 |

Total, 1875 . . 3,394,181 tons register.
,, 1880 . . 4,029,500 ,, ,,
,, 1881 . . 4,177,940 ,, ,,
,, 1882 . . 4,057,803 ,, ,,

*Statement showing Tonnage (Register) of Vessels entering at various Ports in* 1882.

| Port. | Foreign. | | | Coasting. | | | | | | | Total Foreign and Coasting. |
|---|---|---|---|---|---|---|---|---|---|---|---|
| | | | | Cargoes. | | | Ballast and Carrying Passengers. | | | Total. | |
| | Sail. | Steam. | Total. | Sail. | Steam. | Total. | Sail. | Steam. | Total. | | |
| Bristol . . . | 181,215 | 320,873 | 502,088 | 204,014 | 455,853 | 659,867 | 14,474 | 15,890 | 30,364 | 690,231 | 1,192,319 |
| Cardiff . . . | 770,208 | 1,381,543 | 2,151,751 | 160,507 | 148,955 | 309,462 | 531,323 | 1,442,757 | 1,974,080 | 2,283,542 | 4,435,293 |
| Hull . . . . | 355,292 | 1,268,143 | 1,623,435 | 54,131 | 198,698 | 252,829 | 10,931 | 37,837 | 48,768 | 301,597 | 1,925,032 |
| Liverpool . . | 1,502,430 | 3,662,781 | 5,165,211 | 316,690 | 1,933,006 | 2,249,696 | 150,783 | 285,713 | 436,496 | 2,686,192 | 7,851,403 |
| London . . . | 1,731,343 | 4,398,684 | 6,130,027 | 1,437,738 | 2,853,739 | 4,291,477 | 170,470 | 94,088 | 264,558 | 4,556,035 | 10,686,062 |
| Southampton . | 45,995 | 1,183,849 | 1,229,844 | 103,373 | 389,601 | 492,974 | 32,111 | 273,732 | 305,843 | 798,817 | 2,028,661 |
| Sunderland . | 178,835 | 524,453 | 703,288 | 93,695 | 32,713 | 126,408 | 519,348 | 1,254,617 | 1,773,965 | 1,900,373 | 2,603,661 |
| Swansea . . | 263,306 | 342,279 | 605,585 | 189,666 | 123,460 | 313,126 | 163,285 | 315,022 | 478,307 | 791,433 | 1,397,018 |
| Tyne Ports . | 614,968 | 2,093,385 | 2,708,353 | 419,252 | 308,331 | 727,583 | 438,950 | 2,210,575 | 2,649,525 | 3,377,108 | 6,085,461 |

*Statement showing Tonnage (Register) of Vessels clearing from various Ports in 1882.*

| PORT. | FOREIGN. | | | COASTING. | | | | | | | Total Foreign and Coasting. |
|---|---|---|---|---|---|---|---|---|---|---|---|
| | | | | Cargoes. | | | Ballast and Carrying Passengers. | | | Total. | |
| | Sail. | Steam. | Total. | Sail. | Steam. | Total. | Sail. | Steam. | Total. | | |
| Bristol . . . | 78,410 | 112,015 | 190,425 | 89,578 | 386,770 | 476,348 | 213,155 | 306,908 | 520,063 | 996,411 | 1,186,836 |
| Cardiff . . . | 1,213,887 | 2,686,183 | 3,900,070 | 314,497 | 368,619 | 683,116 | 14,952 | 43,802 | 58,754 | 741,870 | 4,641,940 |
| Hull . . . . | 290,300 | 1,090,352 | 1,380,652 | 58,943 | 182,329 | 241,272 | 58,010 | 235,502 | 293,512 | 534,784 | 1,915,436 |
| Liverpool . . | 1,507,193 | 3,375,685 | 4,882,878 | 271,778 | 1,489,825 | 1,761,603 | 195,098 | 711,369 | 906,467 | 2,668,070 | 7,550,948 |
| London . . . | 1,485,265 | 3,160,386 | 4,645,651 | 551,001 | 924,318 | 1,475,319 | no | record | ... | 1,475,319 | 6,120,970 |
| Southampton . | 35,390 | 1,163,228 | 1,198,618 | 67,370 | 317,138 | 384,508 | 86,026 | 359,990 | 446,016 | 830,524 | 2,029,142 |
| Sunderland . | 195,949 | 677,355 | 873,284 | 562,170 | 1,065,233 | 1,627,403 | 11,385 | 104,023 | 115,408 | 1,742,811 | 2,616,095 |
| Swansea . . | 328,916 | 489,560 | 818,476 | 259,636 | 261,786 | 521,422 | 11,094 | 39,678 | 50,772 | 572,194 | 1,390,670 |
| Tyne Ports . | 917,700 | 3,081,295 | 3,998,995 | 446,644 | 1,600,157 | 2,046,801 | 140,191 | 174,256 | 314,447 | 2,361,248 | 6,360,243 |

*Statement showing Total Tonnage (Register) in and out at various Ports in 1882.*

| | Tons. |
|---|---|
| London, . . . . . . . . | 16,807,032 |
| Liverpool, . . . . . . . . | 15,402,351 |
| Tyne Ports, . . . . . . . . | 12,445,704 |
| Cardiff, . . . . . . . . | 9,077,233 |
| Sunderland, . . . . . . . . | 5,219,756 |
| Southampton, . . . . . . . . | 4,057,803 |
| Hull, . . . . . . . . | 3,840,468 |
| Swansea, . . . . . . . . | 2,787,688 |
| Bristol, . . . . . . . . | 2,379,155 |

It will be seen that the above returns, communicated by J. E. Le Feuvre, Esq., place the port sixth in the kingdom.

The principal exports of Southampton for the year 1880 were as follows:—

| | |
|---|---|
| Apparel, . . . . . . . | £589,270 in value. |
| Arms and ammunition, . . . | £11,771 ,, |
| Beer and ale, . . . . . | 16,594 barrels. |
| Candles of all sorts, . . . . | 807,300 lbs. |
| Cotton yarn, . . . . . | 2,910,000 lbs. |
| Bags and sacks, empty, . . . | 69,396 dozens. |
| Cotton manufactured piece goods, . | 322,477,100 yards. |
| Hosiery and small wares, . . . | £209,081 in value. |
| Earthen and china ware, . . . | £22,377 ,, |
| Haberdashery and millinery, . . | £437,081 ,, |
| Hardware and cutlery, . . . | £164,142 ,, |
| Hats of all sorts, . . . . | 64,151 dozens. |
| Leather, wrought, . . . . | £396,246 in value. |
| Linen piece goods, . . . . | 4,664,300 yards. |

| | |
|---|---|
| Jute manufactures, . . . . | 5,582,500 yards. |
| Machinery and millwork, . . . | £259,393 in value. |
| Metals— | |
| Copper, wrought and unwrought, . | 13,793 cwts. |
| Iron, of all kinds, . . . . . | 11,453 tons. |
| Painters' colours, . . . . | £21,279 in value. |
| Paper, except hangings, . . . | 13,391 cwts. |
| Silk, manufactured and mixed, . . | £86,401 in value. |
| Telegraphic wires and appliances, . | £7248 in value. |
| Woollen and worsted yarn, . . . . | 12,900 lbs. |
| Woollen and manufactured cloth of all kinds, | 631,600 yards. |
| Worsted and mixed stuffs, . . . | 2,802,500 ,, |
| Flannels, carpets, &c., . . . | 1,557,600 ,, |
| Hosiery of other sorts, . . . | £101,822 in value. |

The principal imports[1] of Southampton for the year 1880 were as follows :—

| | |
|---|---|
| Animals, live cattle, &c., . . . | 14,347 in number. |
| Brandy, proof gallons, . . . | 14,357 galls. |
| Butter, . . . . . . . | 361,702 cwts. |
| Cheese, . . . . . . . | 19,606 ,, |
| Cocoa, . . . . . . . | 193,844 lbs. |
| Coffee, . . . . . . . | 106,072 cwts. |
| Wheat, . . . . . . . | 438,921 ,, |
| Barley, . . . . . . . | 386,833 ,, |
| Oats, . . . . . . . | 182,009 ,, |
| Maize, . . . . . . . | 105,463 ,, |
| Dyes, indigo, . . . . . . | 13,430 ,, |
| Eggs, great hundreds, . . . | 1,176,052. |
| Fruit, raw and unemptied, . . . | 113,650 bushels. |
| Hides, raw, . . . . . . | 25,907 cwts. |
| Hides, tanned, . . . . . . | 41,746 lbs. |
| Potatoes, . . . . . . . | 476,937 cwts. |
| Seeds, clover, grass, . . . . . | 20,810 ,, |
| Silk, raw, . . . . . . . . | 77,670 lbs. |
| Silk, manufactured, . . . . . | £18,007 in value. |
| Skins (sheep), number, . . . . | 733,790. |
| Sugar, unrefined, . . . . . | 84,207 cwts. |
| Sugar, refined, . . . . . . | 41,114 ,, |
| Timber, sawn and split, . . . . | 36,271 loads. |
| Tobacco, unmanufactured, . . . | 13,565 lbs. |
| Tobacco, manufactured, . . . | 133,108 ,, |
| Wine, . . . . . . . . | 206,414 galls. |
| Wool, . . . . . . . . | 21,069,190 lbs. |

Notice of Peninsular and Oriental Steam Company.

It would be impossible to omit all mention of the *Peninsular and Oriental Steam Navigation Company*, once and for so many years intimately associated with the prosperity of Southampton, though now all connection has been severed, and the port has recovered the blow. This Company secured a contract with Government, under competition, for carrying the eastward mails, and obtained a royal charter in

[1] Kindly supplied, with foregoing column, by T. W. Shore, Esq.

1840; it commenced with a capital of a million sterling, and power to increase the same to a million and a half, under condition of its opening an improved communication between England and India within two years.[1] The company at first selected Falmouth for landing its mails; but having met with several inconveniences in connection with that port, it made Southampton its head-quarters on the completion of the docks, in spite of a recommendation from the Treasury that Dartmouth should be selected, as had been appointed in the case of the Royal Mail Company and the West India mails. However, in each case the manifest convenience of Southampton, with its docks and railway directly in short communication with the metropolis, prevailed, and in 1842 both companies started their vessels from this port; and in August 1843 Southampton was confirmed as the port of landing and embarking the mails carried respectively by the Peninsular and Oriental and the West India Companies.

Chief steam companies in connection with port.

The chief companies in present connection with the port are as follows:—

*Royal Mail Steam-Packet Company*, incorporated by royal charter in 1840; entered on its first contract that year to carry mails to the whole of the British possessions in the West Indies and North America, with the colonies of France, Spain, Holland, Denmark, Mexico, and the Spanish main. The powerful ships provided by the company commenced their passages in January 1842, being surveyed at Southampton, and starting from that port. After a time the original routes were modified. The company's magnificent fleet of steamships is divided into two lines:—(1.) The West India line, carrying mails to the West Indies, Mexico, Central America, the North and South Pacific ports, &c.; and (2.) the Brazil and River Plate line for Vigo, Lisbon, Pernambuco, Rio de Janeiro, Monte Video, Buenos Ayres, &c.

*The Union Steam-Ship Company*, formed in 1853 as the Union Steam Collier Company, its name having been altered and registered as at present in 1856. This company is of Southampton origin, and was originally intended by its promoters for the coal trade; but on the outbreak of the Crimean war, the Peninsular and Oriental Company having withdrawn their vessels from Constantinople in consequence of their whole fleet being required for postal and war services, the directors of this company altered their original project, and having first run their vessels between Southampton, Constantinople, and Smyrna, chartered them in the British and French transport service. In 1857 a five years' contract was entered into with the Government for a monthly mail service to the Cape of Good Hope: in 1858 St. Helena

[1] Guide to Southampton, by Mr. C. J. Phillips.

and Ascension were added; afterwards Natal. Then the service was extended to Mauritius, to Algoa Bay, to Point de Galle, and to Zanzibar. The ships call at Plymouth on the outward voyage to the Cape.

*The London and South-Western Steam-Packet Company* is also of Southampton growth. Its vessels carry the Channel Island mails, and run also between this port and Cherbourg, St. Malo, Granville, Havre, and Honfleur. The fleet numbers eighteen vessels.

*Messrs. G. T. Harper & Co., Limited, Steam-Ships.*—There are five steam-ships belonging to this company, their tonnage being 6000.

*The Southampton, Isle of Wight, and South of England Royal Mail Steam-Packet Company, Limited.*—The vessels of this company, nine in number, ply constantly each day between Southampton, the Isle of Wight, and Portsmouth.

*The Southampton Steam-Towing Company* have three vessels in constant work.

Ships calling at port.

The following companies' ships call at this port:—

*The North German Lloyd Steam-Packet Company.*—Boston and New York, New Orleans and Baltimore lines.

*Liverpool, Brazil, and River Plate Company.*—This company's ships call here homeward bound from the Brazils to land cargo, passengers, and specie.

*The Netherlands Steam-Ship Company.*—The vessels of this company sail from Southampton every fortnight for Java, &c.

*Rotterdam Lloyd Steam-Ships,* carrying mails, sail from Rotterdam for Java *via* Southampton and the Suez Canal, calling at Penang, Batavia, Samarang, and Sourabaya.

*British and Irish Steam-Packet Company, Limited.*—The steamers of this company sail for Plymouth, Falmouth, and Dublin; also for Portsmouth and London.

*City of Cork Steam-Packet Company.*—The vessels of this company call here from Cork and sail for Cork *via* London.

*Clyde Shipping Company.*—This company's steamers leave Southampton for Waterford and Glasgow, and for Belfast and Glasgow, calling at Plymouth each voyage.[1]

*Rotterdam and Southampton Line.*—Ships arrive every Monday, sailing thence for Liverpool.

The steamers of the *Liverpool, Bristol, and London Steam-Packet Company,* and of the *London and Liverpool Steam-Ship Company,* arrive here every week, calling also at Falmouth and Plymouth.

[1] For preceding notices of the steam-ship companies, see the Guide of Mr. Shore, executive officer of the Hartley Institute.

Extensive *timber, grain,* and *coal* trades are also carried on.

The following companies are in connection with the trade of the town:— Companies in connection with trade of town.

*The Southampton and Itchen Bridge Company.*—It had been intended originally to build a permanent bridge over the river Itchen at the place of the original ferry; and early in 1834 the permission of the Corporation was sought for making a road across the marsh to the proposed bridge, for which a bill was in preparation for the ensuing Parliament. The Corporation, however, fearing damage to the navigation of the river to Chapel and Northam, refused their consent. A bill for a floating bridge was, however, introduced forthwith, to several clauses of which the Corporation took exception. The Itchen Bridge road was at once carried out; and the 'Southampton and Itchen Bridge and Roads Company' obtained their first Act in 1834, and their second in 1851. Their first bridge began to ply in 1836, and was supplemented by a service of boats. The bridges have been renewed on improved construction from time to time. Two large bridges are always now running, simultaneously leaving each side of the river, so as to avoid detention; the boats being only occasionally called into requisition. The bridges run on guiding chains.

*The Hythe Pier and Hythe and Southampton Ferry Company, Limited.*—The modern steam-ferry was started by private enterprise and a company afterwards formed. This company now owns the Hythe pier, recently built, and has power to purchase the ferry steamers.

*The Southampton Tramways Company* owns upwards of six miles of tramway through the main arteries of the town and immediate suburbs. It was incorporated in 1878.

*The Free Cobden Bridge,* opened June 27, 1883, across the Itchen, about a mile above Northam Bridge, gives another entrance into the town through St. Denys.

On the *Northam Bridge,* see pp. 3, 12.

*The Didcot, Newbury, and Southampton Junction Railway* will give a direct communication with the Midland Counties, Liverpool, and the North by its junction with the Great Western Railway at Didcot; and by its junction at Aldermaston will create a new and direct through line *via* Reading to and from London, Winchester, and Southampton. This railway is incorporated under four separate Acts of Parliament, passed in 1873, 1876, 1880, and 1882, the Acts providing that the undertaking shall be divided into three separate sections, called respectively the 'Newbury,' 'Southern,' and 'Southampton' sections. The 'Newbury section,' from Didcot to Newbury, was opened for traffic on April 12, 1882; the 'Southern section,' from Newbury to Burghclere, is under construction; and a special Act for the 'South- Didcot, Newbury, and Southampton Railway.

ampton section' having passed a committee of the House of Commons on May 15, 1882, and of the Lords on July 13, and the required capital being quickly subscribed, it is anticipated that the whole line will be completed in the course of 1884. The 'Southampton section' joins the 'Southern section' at Burghclere, and passes southward by Whitchurch, forming a junction with the main line of the London and South-Western Railway to Salisbury, Exeter, Plymouth, and the West; from Whitchurch it runs to Winchester, thence through Twyford, Allbrook, Chilworth, and Shirley to Southampton. Here the company will be assisted by arrangements with the Southampton Harbour Board and the Corporation, having obtained from the latter, free of cost, a grant of thirty acres of the mudland on the western shore for the purposes of their stations, &c. The company undertake to construct a new railway pier at Southampton, in connection with the line, for the accommodation of the passenger service to and from the port; in addition to which they will have the right to the joint use of the existing Royal Pier, access to which will be provided from the new pier. The happiest results to the port are anticipated from the completion of these works. The London and South-Western Company are at the same time largely developing their system.

Bridge of London and S.-W. Railway Company.

We may mention here also, as by no means unconnected with traffic, the magnificent *bridge* lately built by the London and South-Western Railway Company, spanning their line over the level crossings, and having two handsome limbs of approach from the town side and one from the Itchen Bridge road. This work, carried out by Messrs. Joseph Bull & Sons at a cost of some £42,000, is a prominent feature in this quarter of the town. It was opened publicly by the Mayor and Corporation shortly before the visit of the British Association.

# CHAPTER VI.

## CHARITIES.

### Section I.—*The Alms-Houses.*

Butler's Alms-houses.

In the year 1564, Richard Butler, in the first year of his second mayoralty, aided partly by charitable contributions, erected two alms-houses for sick people or persons sick of the plague on a plot of ground at the north side of St. Mary's Churchyard, left to the town by Thomas Lyster, sometime mayor (1536); and about the time of their erection,[1] Lawrence Sendy, burgess, gave £20 in trust to the Corporation for an allowance of forty shillings a year to the sick infected poor at the alms-house, if any there were; if not, to any other poor of the town.[2]

Ancient Alms-houses in East Street.

"There were other [five ancient and decayed] alms-houses in East "Street, of which I have met with no account. The site of these "last was very lately granted away by the Corporation to a person "[Isaac Malortie, Esq.] who has built some [three] dwelling-houses "there, which he calls York Buildings: the houses fronting the "[East] street stand upon the alms-house ground. The condition of "this grant was that he should build other alms-houses, which he did "on part of the ground belonging to those at St. Mary's"—a rent of forty shillings per annum for the old site in East Street being also secured by the Corporation for the benefit of the inmates.

Malortie's houses.

The new houses built by Malortie, five in number, thus added to the former two, were taken possession of by the Corporation in October 1768. Nos. 1 and 2 were allotted to the poor of Holy-rood, Nos. 3 and 5 to All Saints', and No. 4 to St. Lawrence's, according to the order in which the old houses had been appropriated; the parish officers attending and accepting the keys of their respective houses from the mayor, and acknowledging themselves and their several poor to be tenants at will of the Corporation.

The allotment to particular parishes came in time to be disregarded.

All removed to Grove Street.

In 1830 the site of the alms-houses being required for the purposes of the workhouse, the guardians of the poor offered to purchase and convey to the Corporation a piece of land in Grove Street, together

[1] Date of bond by Corporation for payment of L. Sendy's gift, April 30, 1565.

[2] Dr. Speed, Journal, and Liber Niger, fol. 104.

with seven tenements which they would erect on it, in lieu of the old alms-houses; and in September 1831 the town seal was affixed to a deed of exchange, the seven houses having been duly erected. Malortie's houses were then removed, but Butler's—the pest-house, as it was called—which had been marked for destruction in 1773, existed till about 1865. It had been some years previously occupied by a poor burgess, who received a moiety of Sendy's gift, together with an annual rent of £2, 2s. for a portion of the garden which had been built over for workhouse purposes, and fifteen shillings from Malortie's rent above described. An ancient stone bearing the shield of the town and a merchant's mark, with the founder's initials, R. B., and the date 1565, removed from the old buildings, is still to be seen between the first and second of the Grove Street alms-houses. The seven houses consist each of two rooms, and are appropriated to fourteen occupants. They are under the management of the borough charity trustees.

### Section II.—*Care of the Poor.*

Provisions of the Guild.

By the ancient ordinances of the Guild Merchant doles were provided for the sick and poor of the place when and where the Guild should be sitting in the quaint but usual form of so much ale (Ord. 4); forfeits and alms were also awarded to the poor on other occasions (Ord. 7), and members of the Guild were to be assisted in poverty (Ord. 22). These regulations belong probably to the twelfth and thirteenth centuries. Later on we find the 'townys almys' settled on a plan, and lists were kept of the weekly recipients of charity. Thus in the steward's book of 1441 we have 'a remembraunce of the almys (£4, 2s. 1d.) the whych the town yewyth every weke to pore men and women;' then follow the details.

Legislation and town action.

The town books, of course, bear the impress of public opinion as it gradually took shape in reference to the care of the poor. By statute of 1349 (23 Ed. III. c. 7) the giving of alms to sturdy beggars had been strictly forbidden; and by statutes of 1495 (11 Hen. VII. c. 2) and 1503–4 (19 Hen. VII. c. 12) those who could not dig and were not ashamed to beg were sent for that purpose to their native places or to their last settlements. Under this system we come across fines levied on those who lodged 'valiaunt beggers;' and in 1527 the town took to shaving the rogues; thus, 'to iiij berbors for cuttyng of vacabundes here short, iiij$^{d}$.' There must have been heavy work to employ four barbers, but on the other hand the price does not seem excessive. Indigenous beggars had long been permitted by law within certain limits; and about 1529 the town provided sixty-four liveries for its beggars, 'because they should be knowen from straunge beggers."[1] This order probably gives the number of mendicants authorised at that time, when the population of the borough was under 4000. In another order about this period we find the names of thirteen who were admitted to beg every day, and of seven who were allowed the privilege only once a week. Over all these a controller of beggars was appointed, for whose adornment a scutcheon of silver gilt was provided, the other beggars wearing theirs of tin.[2] A few years later we find the 'master of beggars' receiving his fee of 6s. 8d. by the year.[3] The Act of 1531 (22 Hen. VIII. c. 12), under which justices might assign to poor people districts in which to beg, was duly proclaimed in the town; for those who transgressed these limits the stocks were in readiness above Bar.

But the town tried to improve the case of its poor by direct regulations, some of which are sufficiently curious. In 1550 it was enacted that no one 'of the degree of a baylly of the town' should purchase any wood or coal between November 1 and March 25, except what had been brought by water, in order that the poor people might have the fuel which came into the town by carts and get it the cheaper. Brewers and bakers were subjected to a similar restriction in their procuring fuel for the same reason.[4] About this time collectors for the poor were appointed under statute of 1535–36 (27 Hen. VIII. c. 25, ss. 4, 13) to solicit weekly contributions from all householders, the obligation to give something being imperative, the amount being left to discretion. This was further extended by statute of 1562–63 (5 Eliz. c. 3); while a later Act, that of 1572 (14 Eliz. c. 5, s. 16), gave the justices a power of assessment on the inhabitants for the relief of the poor, and dealt with the 'vagrom men' in a summary fashion; the long list of vagabonds including minstrels not belonging to any baron of the realm, and scholars of the Universities of Oxford and Cambridge, who went about begging without authority under seal of those Universities. This last gives a glimpse of the state of our mediæval seats of learning when youths of all classes flocked to them, for whose support various allowances were tolerated and provided by public opinion. Thus in 1579 'John Knightlie, scholard of the universitie of Cambridge, came into this towne out of France, and was licensed by Robert Knaplock, maior, to departe hence to the Universitie of Cambridge, and by the waye to get service, . . . and also to aske the charitie of good people as well in churches as elsewher towards his reliefe and comfort.'[5]

Care of the poor.

Collectors.

License to beg.

[1] MS. temp. T. Overey, sub annis.
[2] Boke of Remembrances, fol. 34.
[3] Steward's Books, 1540.
[4] Court Leet Book, 1550. A century later the town devoted the profits from brewers' licenses to the support of the poor (Journal, September 1659).
[5] Liber Notationum, August 9, 1575.

Apprenticing.

Twenty years later the dawn of the present poor-law system broke with the 43 Eliz. cap. 2, 1601; and we find the town apprenticing lads to the age of twenty-four years, as they were empowered under the statute: they assigned children to be brought up in respectable families at a fixed rate: they parcelled out the aged poor among those who could and would take them: they kept lists of needy people, to whom they allowed threepence or fourpence a week, or sixpence or eightpence monthly. They permitted tradesmen to set up in the town on the understanding that they should take one or more of the town's children. Thus 'Thomas Furlye, shoemaker, is ordered to seek out some boye or maide with whome the towne is charged, and soe he shalbe allowed to sett upp his trade.' Furlye had then to compound with the corporation of shoemakers, who were desired to make the terms easy for him.[1] But the town was often in 'the position of having so many children that it didn't know what to do.' On one of these occasions, the clothiers came forward, and offered to gather in the youngsters who were begging for want of work, and to employ them instead of strangers. This was welcomed as a 'great ease and benefit to the town;' it was therefore ordered that all the able-bodied should be compelled to work for the clothiers or be punished.[2]

Charity Funds.

The charity funds collected in the different churches at this time (1608) were administered under the direction of the Corporation, the mayor giving his receipt to the churchwardens. The amount gathered in each parish weekly at the church doors was husbanded in the chest belonging to each in the Audit-house, and applicable under the supervision of the Corporation to the poor within its own limits in the first instance. On one occasion, October 1648, the mayor not being satisfied with the amount gathered from Holy Rood, a wealthy parish, the collectors were directed to stand at the church door 'as well on Thursdays and att other church solemnityes as on ye Sabboathes to collect ye almes of ye congregation.' Several instances occur of churchwardens being in contempt, and incurring fine for not rendering their accounts to the town with punctuality: thus one of the wardens of All Saints' in 1610. The same year the wardens of All Saints', St. Michael's, and St. John's were warned to make collections for their parish 'plumps'—pumps—notice being given thereof by the clergy in the churches. In July 1625, every Wednesday being now kept as a fast day, it was ordered that two men should in every parish during divine service or sermon collect alms for the poor, to be distributed as the House should direct. In 1644 one of the wardens of St. Mary's had been in prison for

[1] Journal, November–December 1608.
[2] Ibid., January 1614.

refusing to render his account in proper form. Orders were made also on the parishes by the mayor and justices for relief to poor persons, travellers, and others. Under 1716 we find the vestry of St. Lawrence appointing arbitrators for adjusting with other parishes the quota or charge of the poor made on the parish by order of the justices.

The foundation of the workhouse was suggested or accelerated by a bequest of John Major, who by his will, bearing date February 20, 1629–30, directed his executors to bestow £200 for 'building a house of twelve rooms' for the habitation of poor people, or otherwise for setting them to work and maintaining them in labour.[1] From an agreement between the Corporation and Richard Major, the executor of the above John Major, made in 1630, it appears to have been determined that the Corporation should provide the house, and that Major's gift should be devoted to the purchase of land for its endowment. This gift, however, was not enjoyed (see below) for some years. The Workhouse.

In 1632, the town having provided the premises, John Harris was made governor of the workhouse, and covenanted[2] to keep within the house twenty children, who, with himself, formed the body corporate, stipulating that he should have 'noe broken or diseased beastly boye, w^ch^ shall not first bee cured or reformed, putt into the body of the house, nor any under the age of nine yeares, unles with his consent,' he to find the inmates in meat, drink, apparel, and medicine, and to have the benefit of their labour until, with the consent of the overseers, they should severally be apprenticed. At their entrance the town found tools for their work, bedding and clothing, and on their leaving for apprenticeship, provided them with one good suit for workdays and another for Sundays.

The governor's duties were further to teach some forty boys and girls to 'make bonelace, knitt, or to carde or spinne eyther in the greate tourne or the small, as hee in his discretion shall thincke fitt;' he was also to catechise them twice a week, 'soe yt exceede not one houre at one tyme.' In the case of work from the clothiers growing scant, the town was to provide wool, hemp, flax, &c. The hours for those who came to the house for work were from seven till eleven, when they went home to dinner and returned at twelve, leaving work at six in the winter and seven in the summer. The governor was further to keep in a house of correction on the premises such idle vagrant persons, not exceeding twenty in number, as the justices should commit to be punished and kept at work; and the town-crier was to officiate upon their persons as often as need required. House of Correction.

1 Deed reciting will, June 4, 1673.
2 Journal 1632, f. 239, b.

At the end of 1633 Harris received his dismissal, and Nicholas Newbye, clothier, was elected at a salary of £30 per annum, when the establishment was reduced to ten boys in the house. In the latter half of the century the fabric was reported as becoming ruinous,[1] when it experienced a revival by its transformation into St. John's Hospital in 1673. This hospital was due to the recovery by the town, under an order of Chancery, dated 3d May 1665, of the before-mentioned legacy of John Major, together with the accumulation of interest, making in all £728, from Major John Dunch[2] of Baddesley, the heir and representative of John Major. By indenture between the Corporation, Major Dunch, and John Steptoe, with six poor boys, dated June 4, 1673, it was witnessed that the Corporation had erected, founded, and established a messuage now in their possession in French Street, within the parish of St. John, 'for an hospital for poor and impotent people;' and according to the statutes in such case provided, had incorporated the said John Steptoe and six poor boys by the name of the 'warden and poor children of the Hospital of St. John Baptist,' founded by the mayor, bailiffs, and burgesses, and by John Major, Esq.; the common seal of the hospital to bear the crest and arms of the town, together with those of John Major. The Corporation were from time to time to appoint the warden and fill up other vacancies, but Major Dunch and his heirs were secured the privilege of placing one poor boy to be taught and apprenticed by the Corporation as the other boys, but on whom an extra £4 per annum should be expended from the income of the hospital. The visitation of the house was vested in a body of the Corporation, and in Major Dunch and his heirs as representing the co-founder; and its government was placed under such orders as should be made by the founders or visitors. The hospital was further to be used as a workhouse for the employment of other poor people besides the six children, as the visitors should direct.

St. John's Hospital.

The Corporation then by another indenture, dated August 20, 1673, in consideration of the above sum paid them by Major Dunch, granted and confirmed an annuity of £40 per annum, issuing out of certain specified lands, to be paid yearly to the warden and poor children for the above purposes.

St. John's Hospital stood on the site of the recent theatre in French Street. The buildings had a frontage of 24 feet with a depth of 63 feet, and, as described in the deed, were fully of the capacity originally named by John Major.

---

1 Court Leet Book, 1668.

2 Deed of June 4, 1673; also Process detailed in 13 Geo. III., cap. 50 (1773).

In November 1771 the scheme for uniting the parishes of the borough into one poor-law district was entertained; and as it was considered that the Hospital of St. John, with its endowment of £40 per annum, would prove an eligible receptacle for the poor,[1] the consent of Major Dunch's representative was sought, and a petition to Parliament drawn up and sealed in January 1773, for the purpose of uniting the parishes and converting the hospital as proposed. The Act which resulted (13 Geo. III. cap. 50, 1773) took effect from 24th June the same year, uniting the parishes of the town and county of the town, and forming a corporation of guardians, to consist of the mayor, bailiffs, recorder, three senior aldermen, the resident justices of the peace, and other eighteen of the most discreet inhabitants, four from each of the parishes of Holy Rood, St. Michael, and All Saints, and two from each of the parishes of St. Lawrence, St. John, and St. Mary.

Union of parishes for poor-law purposes.

The hospital, which is described as a spacious building, capable of receiving the general poor of the town—we have seen its dimensions—together with the rent-charge of £40 per annum payable to it, was vested in the guardians for the purpose of a workhouse, without prejudice to the rights and interests of the 'six poor boys' for the time being, who were to be taught, visited, and governed as before. By a further clause in the Act the guardians were empowered to purchase any other house in lieu of the hospital, to which the power and authorities given by the Act in respect of the said hospital, the poor boys, and the annuity should extend; and in case of such new purchase, they were enabled to sell St. John's Hospital, and apply the money arising from the sale towards the above purchase, and for other purposes of the Act. It was thought better to take advantage of these powers and erect new premises, when St. John's Hospital was sold to William Daman in 1775, realising the sum of £425. It was advertised for sale again in June 1789, and eventually purchased for the theatre which was built on its site.

The new poorhouse was erected on ground on the north side of St. Mary's Churchyard, and the guardians obtained leave to remove Butler's almshouse, provided they built another 'pest-house' of specified dimensions[2] and fulfilled other conditions; but, for whatever reason, the old house remained standing as we have seen, and the workhouse of 1774 was erected on the ground close by. The endowment of £40

Workhouse of 1774.

[1] Before 1763 for some years Bullhall had been used as a poorhouse, and in that year the lease of it for the same purpose was renewed for seven years (Churchwardens' Accounts, St. Lawrence).

[2] Journal, Sept. 1773.

from the hospital followed the new building, and continued to be applied to the maintenance of the poor, but without respect to the original charity. This union house was more than once enlarged, and latterly became capable of accommodating 240 adults, 100 boys, and 110 girls.

New Work-house, 1866.

But in 1866 a new workhouse on a larger scale was erected, on the site of the former, at a cost of about £40,000. It has room for 500 paupers, exclusively of the large schools on the opposite side of the street. The guardians are fifty-four in number, consisting of the members of the Corporation as above, thirty-one borough magistrates, and eighteen elected ratepayers, thus apportioned, showing the relative change in the parishes; eight for St. Mary's, four for All Saints', two each for St. Michael's and Holy Rood, and one each for St. Lawrence's and St. John's.

## Section III.—*Benefactions.*

The municipal charities are managed by a body of trustees,[1] who act under a scheme bearing date April 6, 1880.

L. Sendy.

Lawrence Sendy gave £20 (see above) to Butler's almshouses; £2 per annum are still paid to the four occupants.

Alms-houses.

*Almshouses.*—The sum of £2, 6s. is distributed annually among the ten occupants of Malortie's almshouses (see above), resulting from three quit-rents of 15s. 4d. each, payable from a house in York Buildings and two in East Street, the leases of which are granted by the charity trustees.

W. Sendy.

William Sendy (October 1533) gave the Corporation £100 for procuring a special quarterly sermon at St. Lawrence's and distributing a shilling apiece to fifty poor persons who should attend and be called 'the fifty poor people of the town of Southampton.' In lieu of this the sum of £10 per annum is given to the Grammar School.

Sir T. White.

*Sir Thomas White's Benefaction*, 1566.—Southampton is one of the twenty-four towns which receives in rotation £104 per annum derived from £2000 given by Sir Thomas White to the Corporation of Bristol, on condition of their purchasing an estate for the support of his charity, to be bestowed in loans of £25 each on poor tradesmen. The benefaction was last received by Southampton in 1878. It is now applied to the Grammar School.

Wallop.

William Wallop, Esq., gave by will (September 17, 1616) £100 as a fund from which loans of £20 for five years should be made to poor young men without interest (see under 'Steptoe').

[1] I have to thank J. E. Le Feuvre, Esq., for much information respecting the Southampton charities from official documents. The following account is otherwise based on the reports of the Charity Commissioners, in which all that is valuable in Dr. Speed's short notice was included.

Lynch's gift (now £210 stock), the accounts of which begin in 1641, was for loans of £10 for ten years. It was probably derived from William Lynch, alderman, whose coat of arms, removed from his house in Simnel Street, and bearing the date 1579, is now to be seen in the hall of the Hartley Institute, or from his son William Lynch of St. Michael's parish (see under 'Steptoe'). Lynch.

John Steptoe, alderman, by will dated February 20, 1667, bequeathed the inheritance of his lands in the parishes of Fawley and Milford to the Corporation in trust, that one-third part of the rents therefrom every year should be bestowed upon the poor, and that the other two parts be lent to 'young beginners' in the town in sums of £10 to each for ten years without interest He also gave £100 to the Corporation, from the yearly interest of which to pay forty shillings to the rector of All Saints' for preaching four sermons before the Corporation on the three Sundays before the 3d of March, and the fourth on that day, after which to give a shilling apiece to sixty poor people. Steptoe.

The original lands at Fawley and Milford were exchanged for land near Romsey in 1840; and this property, consisting of about 21 acres at Mile End, Romsey, and a small farm of 38 acres at Highwood, near Romsey, were sold September 30, 1880, realising about £3621. The sum of £1207, one-third part of the above proceeds, has been devoted to the general charities fund; and the remainder, together with Wallop's and Lynch's gifts, united with Steptoe's by a scheme under the direction of the Court of Chancery, 1862, has been transferred to the Grammar School; the sum of £1000 having been already retained for lending in sums of £50 and under to young beginners in trade.

John Cornish, alderman, who died in 1611, gave £100 for providing seven poor persons, men and women, with a gown apiece each year. The charity consists of £105, 10s. 10d. stock, the interest of which is expended each Christmas in the way directed. Cornish.

George Gollop or Gallop, by will dated April 22, 1650, gave £200 for providing each year a cloth gown of some sad colour to four men and four women. The charity consists of £217, 19s. 8d. stock, the interest of which is spent in the way directed at Christmas. Gollop.

Catherine Reynolds gave by will to the Corporation the sum of £50, received by them January 13, 1615, they having in the previous December covenanted with the Corporation of Sarum to pay one shilling apiece to eighty poor people of Southampton each year on the Feast of the Purification. In place of this, £4 a year are now paid to the Grammar School. Catherine Reynolds.

In October 1635 the Corporation received £20, the gift of Bridget Parkinson, the interest to be distributed quarterly among the poor. Parkinson.

The charity consists of £21, 6s. stock, the interest of which, thirteen shillings, is now paid to the Grammar School.

Rosse. Alexander Rosse, clerk, by his will, proved in 1653, gave £50 to the use of the master of the Grammar School, and £50 to the poor of All Saints, from the interest of which latter sum ten shillings was to be paid to the minister for preaching in All Saints' Church each December 24, on St. Matthew v. 3. The whole of this charity (£3, 5s. 4d.) is now devoted to the Grammar School.

Delamotte. Mrs. Delamotte gave to fifteen poor widows the yearly sum of £1, 10s. This is now paid to the Grammar School. She also gave the yearly sum of £1, 10s. to the vicar of Holy Rood, which goes in the way directed.

Bradsell. Mr. Bradsell gave to the vicar of Holy Rood £1, 4s. yearly. The gift is still received.

Jacomin. Mr. Jacomin's gift consisted of the yearly interest of £50 to a hundred poor people. This gift (£1, 12s. 8d.) is now diverted to the Grammar School.

Mill. Nathaniel Mill, by his will, proved December 10, 1638, gave yearly for ever:—

| | | | |
|---|---|---|---|
| To the poor of Holy Rood parish, 20s. to twenty poor people on January 1st, and 20s. on July 1st, . . . . . . | £2 | 0 | 0 |
| To St. Michael's, 20s. on February 21st, and 20s. on August 1st, . . . . . . . . . . . . | 2 | 0 | 0 |
| To St. John's, 15s. on March 1st, and 15s. on September 1st, . | 1 | 10 | 0 |
| To St. Lawrence, 10s. on April 1st, and 10s. on October 1st, . | 1 | 0 | 0 |
| To All Saints', 20s. on May 1st, and 20s. on November 1st, . | 2 | 0 | 0 |
| To St. Mary's (within the liberties), 15s. on June 1st, and 15s. on December 1st, . . . . . . . . . . | 1 | 10 | 0 |
| To yearly placing four apprentices to some trade at discretion of mayor and assistants, £8 (with each 40s.); and to provide each with a bible, prayer-book, and pen and inkhorn, which should cost 10s., . . . . . . . . | 10 | 0 | 0 |
| To the ministers of the town of Southampton for reading evening prayers, to be divided equally between them; and in case there should be no evening prayers, then the bequest to go to repairs of Holy Rood Church, . . . . . . | 4 | 0 | 0 |
| To the lecture, and in case there should be no lecture on week-days, then to the minister of Holy Rood, . . . . | 2 | 0 | 0 |
| To the repairs of Holy Rood Church, . . . . . . . | 2 | 0 | 0 |
| To the master of the Free School, . . . . . . . . | 2 | 0 | 0 |
| To four people of Southampton, four days before Christmas, four gowns or coats of cloth, costing 16s. each, at the discretion of the mayor and assistants, . . . . . . . | 3 | 4 | 0 |
| To the minister of Jesus Chapel, near Itchen Ferry, . . . . | 2 | 0 | 0 |
| To the repair of Jesus Chapel, . . . . . . . . . . | 1 | 0 | 0 |
| To the poor of the parish of St. Mary, dwelling over the water at Itchen Ferry, Ridgeway, Weston, &c., out of the liberties of Southampton, at the discretion of the minister of Jesus Chapel and the collectors for the time being, . . . . | 2 | 0 | 0 |
| To a poor person of St. Mary's in Itchen Ferry, Ridgeway, Weston, | | | |

| | |
|---|---|
| &c., a gown or coat to be given four days before Christmas at the discretion of the minister of Jesus Chapel and the collectors, . . . . . . . . . . | £0 16 0 |
| To the poor of the parish of St. Lawrence, Winchester, to be given on New Year's Eve to twenty poor people, . . | 1 0 0 |
| And he directed that all the said sums should be yearly paid for ever out of his farm or manor of Woolston to the mayor and three of the most ancient aldermen of Southampton half-yearly, to be disposed of by them as above. And he gave each of them a pair of gloves yearly for their pains, worth 5s. a pair, . . . . . . . . | 1 0 0 |
| By a codicil to his will, bearing date April 20, 1636, he gave to the poor people of the French Church yearly for ever out of his said lands, . . . . . . . . . | 1 0 0 |
| | £42 0 0 |

A deduction of £3, 17s. 6d. for land-tax is made, and the sum of £38, 2s. 6d., the residue, is expended now as follows:—

| | |
|---|---|
| To the Grammar School, . . . . . . . . | £10 18 0 |
| To the poor of the French Church, paid in December, . . | 0 18 2 |
| To four people of Southampton four days before Christmas, four gowns or coats of cloth, and one gown or coat to some person in St. Mary's extra, to be given by the minister of Jesus Chapel, . . . . . . . . . | 3 11 8 |
| To St. Lawrence, Winchester, paid in December, . . . | 0 18 2 |
| To minister of Jesus Chapel for poor of St. Mary's extra, paid in December, . . . . . . . . . . . . | 1 16 4 |
| To minister of Jesus Chapel, paid in December, . . . . | 1 16 4 |
| To repairs of Jesus Chapel, paid in December, . . . . | 0 18 2 |
| To the ministers, paid in December, for reading evening prayers, | 3 12 8 |
| To the lecture, . . . . . . . . . . . . | 1 16 4 |
| To churchwardens of Holy Rood, for repairs, paid in December, . | 1 16 4 |
| Transferred to Taunton's School, December 1881, . . . | 10 0 4 |

Peter Seale, alderman, gave £100 for the apprenticing of poor children. This gift was brought into the Audit-house on October 20, 1654, by Peter Seale, junior, after his father's death. The interest from the stock of this charity, £3, 6s. 2d., is now transferred to the Taunton School. **Gift of Peter Seale, sen.**

Peter Seale, junior, gave the yearly sum of £5 for placing two poor children apprentices for seven or eight years, one to be of St. Lawrence's parish if possible. This yearly sum of £5 is now paid to the Taunton School. **Peter Seale, jun.**

Mrs. Avis Knowles gave by will £50 to the Corporation (received May 30, 1634) for apprenticing two town-born children yearly. The annual interest on £52, 15s. 5d. stock belonging to this gift, namely, £1, 11s. 8d., is now transferred to the Taunton School. **Knowles's gift.**

Richard Taunton, by his will, dated February 15, 1752, gave to the mayor, bailiffs, and burgesses of Southampton £1400 on trust, to **Taunton.**

pay from the interest thereof the yearly sum of £21 to the minister of Holy Rood, on certain conditions (see under that church), and on further trust to apply the residue of the interest in the relief of decayed aldermen of the town or their widows; and failing such cases, to allow the fund to accumulate till such cases should arise. By a codicil to his will he left another £100, from the interest of which to pay the town-clerk for keeping the accounts. The fund having been increased by accumulation, the annual income of the charity is now £140, appropriated as follows:—To the Taunton School, £21; to decayed aldermen and widows, £115, 16s. 8d.; to the Taunton School, £3, 3s. 4d., the interest of the investment of the above £100.

For Taunton's School see next chapter.

Searle's gift.

Richard Searle by his will in 1738 gave to Richard Taunton, Esq., or the Corporation of Southampton, £30 for charitable purposes. By accumulations this sum amounted in 1786 to £66, which was then taken by the Corporation at 4 per cent. The charity now consists of £71, 11s. 7d. stock, the interest of which (£2, 3s.) is devoted to the charity fund.

Knight's gift.

Mr. Alderman Knight having partly rebuilt the cowherd's house on the Common, and made his improvements a free gift to the Corporation, to whom the house belonged, it was ordered by the Common Council (July 1762) that a clear rent of £6 per annum should be paid to the Corporation by every cowherd for his house and office, twenty shillings of this rent being applicable to the uses of the Corporation, and the remaining £5 for distribution among the poor of the six town parishes. In 1786 the Corporation not having obtained the cowherd's rent for some years, set aside from their chest the sum of £115, the amount of twenty-three arrears, from 1762 to 1785, in satisfaction of the charity. This sum they took at 4 per cent., paying the interest as directed in the entry of 1762, together with the annual rent of £5 in respect of the cowherd's house. The charity now consists of £125, 6s. 9d. stock, the annual interest of which, together with the rent of £5—in all £8, 15s. 2d.—is carried to the charity fund. The charity fund is available for everything of a charitable nature arising within the town and county of the town, without regard to the parish in which the recipient may live.

Freeman.

William Freeman, by will dated April 6, 1780, gave to the Corporation £100 in trust, to pay five shillings annually to the town-clerk for keeping the accounts of the trust, and to distribute the remainder of the interest among poor people of the town, not receiving alms, who might happen to be visited in their persons and families with sickness, or should suffer from fire or other calamity, in portions of not less than ten shillings in each case. The legacy was laid out in the purchase of £172, 0s. 10d. 3 per cent. consols, producing £5, 3s. 2d. per annum.

The Corporation having taken this stock to other uses, though always paying the interest as directed, and having similarly taken the principals of Fifield's and Sadleir's gifts (see below), they, by indenture of January 11, 1825, granted to certain trustees a mortgage for two thousand years on the Audit-house, with the open poultry and butter market under it, together with the tolls of those markets, and the shops and sheds on the west side of the Audit-house, by way of securing the principals and interests of these several gifts. In this way are secured the £100 from Freeman's gift, together with £5, 3s. 2d., the dividend of the above stock (£172, 0s. 10d.), previously to its sale by the Corporation; the sum of £1300 from the Fifield gift (see below), with its interest of £44, 4s.; and the sum of £350 from Sadleir's gift, with the yearly interest of £17, 10s.—the total principal £1750. The whole of Freeman's gift, £5, 3s. 2d., is carried to the charity fund.

Silena Fifield, by her will, dated December 8, 1769, gave to the Corporation £1100 in trust, for maintaining from the interest thereof the tombs of her late brother and sister in the chapelyard of St. Mary, near Southampton, and the rails round the same, under the supervision of the mayor and the rector of St. Mary's, who were to receive respectively £1 and 5s. for their trouble on November 1; and on further trust to lay out the rest of the interest on the same day in clothing for poor people not receiving regular parish relief. The testatrix further gave £200 in trust for a distribution of coals annually among the pensioners of God's House; and in February 1773 her executors transferred to the Corporation the sum of £1473, 6s. 8d. 3 per cent. consols in satisfaction of the two legacies. This stock was in April the same year sold out as above (under Freeman's), the principal and interest being subsequently secured by the mortgage of January 11, 1825. The income of Fifield's charity, £44, 4s., is expended in the following manner: To the poor of Holy Rood, St. Michael's, and All Saints parishes, £9, 0s. 6d. each; to the parishes of St. John, St. Lawrence, and St. Mary, £3, 0s. 2d.; to the poor of God's House, £6, 16s.; to the mayor, £1, 1s.; to the rector of St. Mary's, 5s. Fifield.

Richard Vernon Sadleir, who died March 2, 1810, gave to the Corporation by will £350 in trust, to bestow on three poor men and four poor widows or ancient maidens of good character the sum of 20s. each on or shortly before Easter Eve, to enable them to celebrate the Easter festival with pious joy, and to bestow 13s. 4d. each upon four other men and three other women of the same description but inferior grade for the same purpose at the same time. And he further directed that an annual sermon should be preached in the several churches in rotation on 'cruelty to animals,' and that the minister so preaching Sadleir.

should be requested to accept 20s. He further desired that £1 should be given to the town-clerk for keeping the books of the charity, and that the annual surplus of £1, 3s. 4d. should accumulate against a national reduction of interest. The mode of securing this gift and its interest at 5 per cent. (£17, 10s.) has been stated above. The charity is expended as directed, the £1 for keeping the accounts going to the charity fund, out of which a fixed stipend is paid by the trustees to their clerk in respect of the charities.

Pemerton. George Pemerton, as recited in a deed, March 24, 1632, gave to the Corporation £150 under covenant to pay him £12 a year during his life, and after his death to distribute to the poor of Southampton £9 annually as the gift of George Pemerton. One moiety of this gift (£4, 10s.) is distributed at Candlemas, the other (£4, 10s.) at Christmas.

Mercer. Paul Mercer gave to the Corporation by will the sum of £100 (received Nov. 1661), from the interest of which to pay £3 half-yearly for ever to the poor of the French and English churches. Of this bequest, amounting to £6 per annum, the sum of £2 half-yearly is paid to the poor of the English churches, and £1 to the treasurer of the French Church at Lady Day and Michaelmas.

Spinks. Sarah Spinks gave the dividends of £270, 3s. 2d. stock, viz., £8, 2s. 2d., for clothing to the poor of St. Michael's, not being paupers, to be distributed on St. Thomas's Day each year.

Gibbons. Sloane Gibbons of Southampton, who died February 18, 1826, gave a benefaction to the pensioners of God's House. It consists of £693, 13s. 4d. stock, from the dividend of which (£20, 16s.) one shilling per week is paid to the pensioners, and £3 carried to the charity fund.

Bird. Elizabeth Bird by her will, proved in 1820, gave £1200 three per cent. consols to be under the guardianship of the Corporation and the rector of All Saints', to apply the interest, £36 per annum, to the use of her servant during her life, and after her death to the following purposes, viz., to six poor women of Southampton above the age of sixty years, of the Church of England and of good repute, to be called 'the good churchwomen,' and to be provided with and to wear on Sundays and other dress-days silver medals with a device and motto specified by her will, £5 each; the rector of All Saints' to appoint to every fifth vacancy, and to receive £3, 3s. annually to provide for the women a good dinner, the particulars of which are specified, every November 10, at his own house or elsewhere; five shillings to be given to the cook, two shillings and sixpence to the waiter, and £1, 1s. to the rector himself, for his trouble in saying 'grace,' and for his general advice and protection: the remaining interest to be expended in coals for the women. By a further clause she gave another £200 in consideration of income-tax, also to be laid out in coals. The sum of £140 was sold out to discharge legacy duty, and from the interest of the remaining stock the annuitants now receive £6, 6s. each.

**D'Aussey.** Charles D'Aussey, who died October 1, 1781, gave by his will the residue of his property to François Saluces, Anthony Isaacson, and Thomas Guillaume, in trust, to apply part of it to the county hospital, Winchester, part to the Humane Society for recovering persons apparently drowned, and part to the relief of the poor of Southampton, leaving to his executors the proportion and manner of distribution. The trust money consists of £3600 three per cent. consols, from the dividends of which, amounting to £108 per annum, Mr. D'Aussey's tomb at Holy Rood is kept in repair, the residue being expended in annuities of £10 each to poor persons of Southampton, not under fifty years of age, who have lived with credit and fallen into decay.

**Hammond.** The gift of Charles Hilgrove Hammond (see 'Recorders') consists of £700 stock, the dividend from which, £21, is appropriated to annuitants, as in the last charity. D'Aussey's and Hammond's gifts now provide thirteen people with annuities of £10 each.

**Mr. Thorner.** Mr. Robert Thorner, a member of an Independent congregation in London, meeting in Girdler's Hall, who had made a considerable fortune as a merchant, on becoming infirm retired from London to Baddesley, near Southampton, bringing with him letters of commendation from the pastor and deacons of the London congregation, addressed to the Independent congregation in Southampton, of which Mr. Robinson was pastor, and which at that time, or immediately after, met on the present site of Above Bar Chapel. The letters of commendation were dated July 17, 1688, and Mr. Thorner was appointed an elder at the organisation and settlement of the church in August the same year. On the second anniversary of the above letters of commendation, namely, on July 17, 1690, Mr. Thorner died.[1] By his will, dated May 31, 1690, after giving to the officers of the congregation £200 towards maintaining a minister among them, and after giving them in trust his remaining interest in the lease of the house Above Bar, built and then used as a meeting-place for the congregation, provided it should continue to be so used, and a legacy of £500 to Harvard College, New England, he devised all his real estate, consisting of a parcel of land with shops and stalls erected on it in Leadenhall Market, in the city of London, then let on lease for a term of years till 1769 at the annual rent of £80, but of the estimated value of £400 at the expiration of the lease, to Bennet Swayne of London,

[1] Brief Records of the Chapel, by Rev. T. Adkins, pp. 47, 102, 129–132.

Isaac Watts of Southampton, Thomas Hollis of London, and John Brackstone of Southampton, and their successors, upon trust, that £10 per annum should be paid to the uses of the trustees themselves for their trouble, after payment of which, and other legacies and his funeral expenses, he directed that £20 per annum of the proceeds during the lease should be employed towards maintaining a free school in the parish of Litton, Dorset; and that further proceeds from the same should be applied to apprenticing to mechanical labouring trades poor children and youths of Litton, Dorchester, Southampton, and Salisbury, for every child a £5 premium, and £5 to enable him to set up at the end of his apprenticeship; and further, a certain portion of the rent was to accumulate. After the expiration of the lease he appointed £100 per annum to be employed as follows:—One-fourth part to the Free School at Litton, and the other three-fourth parts to the placing and setting up of children as above. The overplus rents were again to accumulate, and the legacy to Harvard College to be paid first; after which the remainder was to be employed in building alms-houses within the town and county of Southampton, for the maintenance of poor widows, each widow being allowed two shillings per week and her house-room, such alms-houses being provided when a convenient sum of money should be raised by the management of the property as before said, and being from time to time increased in number for ever, as monies should arise in the same way out of the lands.

Until the expiration of the original lease at Lady Day 1769 the work of the charity was limited; after that the trustees improved the estate, and after making the payments directed in the will and paying the legacy to Harvard College, they were enabled by accumulations to purchase in 1787, for £450, a site in the parish of All Saints', Above Bar, for the purpose of the almshouses as directed, and the year following to erect them.

The gross annual rent of the trust premises amounted in 1774 to rather less than £400, in 1784 to about £500, in 1794 to about £520, for many years previous to 1819 to rather above £530 per annum, in 1819 to £829, 15s.; at the present time to over £1200 a year.

The alms-houses have been greatly increased since the original building, and are very commodiously arranged on three sides of a large quadrangle of turf planted with ornamental trees and shrubs. They are at present designed for forty-three poor widows, who each receive 5s. per week, and are appointed by the trustees from the inhabitants of the town and neighbourhood. The trustees also expend £100 a year in the payment of apprentice fees and gifts for boys of the above four places, £25 being spent in Southampton. There are four trustees, who each personally appoints his successor during his life, or failing this, the surviving trustees appoint.

The charity will be extended from time to time with the growth of the funds.

## Section IV.—*Medical Charities.*

Passing now to the medical charities: in March 1809 a Dispensary for the poor was started under the supervision of Dr. Middleton, the Corporation subscribing £5, 5s. annually. Medical Charities.

The present Dispensary, formerly held at 146 High Street, was established in 1823, pursuant on a meeting held the previous November under J. R. Keele, Esq., the mayor. The old Humane Society was united with the Dispensary in 1826. The Dispensary is now located in a handsome new building next to the Taunton Schools.

On January 1, 1838, the Royal South Hants Infirmary was established after the previous experiment on a small scale of a casualty ward. The following dates will mark the growth of this valued institution. In 1844 the central building was completed at a cost of £5080, 14s. 6d. In 1851 the east wing was added at an outlay of £1037, 1s. 6d.; and the Bullar wing subsequently at a cost of £1467, 5s. 1d., both from designs of Mr. Critchlow. In 1857 the chapel and offices under were erected by Dr. Oke at a cost of £1330, from funds intrusted to him for charitable purposes by Miss Elizabeth Dowling. The Eyre Crabbe wing was added in 1867 at a cost of £3695, 17s. 11d. The total outlay on the buildings, garden, and land of the Infirmary to the end of 1878 amounted to £17,394, 2s. This hospital has an income from funded and other property of about £915 per annum, and derives a large but fluctuating revenue from subscriptions, donations, legacies, &c. Its funds, however, are scarcely equal to the increasing demands made on this charity.

The Nurses Institute provides a staff of nurses who attend in private houses and also upon the sick poor.

St. Mary's Cottage Hospital, North Front, was founded by Mrs. Black in 1873, for the relief of those suffering from sore and ulcerated legs.

The Homœopathic Dispensary was established in 1873.

The Provident Maternity Society was founded in 1837.

A County Female Penitentiary was settled in the building adjoining Trinity Church in 1828, in place of an older house of refuge which had been formed in 1823. The Penitentiary has now been closed for many years, and the property has been acquired by the vicar of Holy Trinity for church purposes.

It seems needless to particularise the various smaller agencies of public charity still at work.

A Charity Organisation Society was set on foot in 1875.

# CHAPTER VII.

## *EDUCATIONAL.*

### SECTION I.—*The Grammar School.*

THIS foundation was due in the first instance to the bequest of William Capon, D.D.,[1] precentor of St. Mary's, who by his will, dated July 31, 1550, and proved in the Court of Canterbury, October 11, 1550, by his executors, John Capon,[2] Bishop of Salisbury, Christopher Robinson, and William Breton, gave to the town of Southampton £100 towards the erection and maintenance of a Grammar School there; directing that the mayor, recorder, and four of the ancients should have oversight of his bequest, which, in the manner specified, was to produce £10 per annum for the finding of a schoolmaster. And the mayor, bailiffs, and burgesses were to enter into a bond in £100 to the mayor and Corporation of Salisbury rightly to employ for the purposes of the bequest the said £10, which otherwise was to be used by the mayor and Corporation of Salisbury in charitable deeds for the health of the donor's soul.[3]

1553. The school was accordingly founded under letters patent,[4] bearing date 4th June (7 Ed. VI.) 1553, which set forth that, 'at the humble petition of the mayor, bailiffs, and burgesses of the town and county of Southampton,' the king had granted that there should be 'one grammar school in the said town and county of Southampton, which should be called the Free Grammar School of the mayor, bailiffs, and burgesses of the said town and county of Southampton, to endure for ever for the education and institution and instruction of boys and youths in grammar.' The foundation was to consist of one master and an under-master or usher; and the mayor and bailiffs of the town were made a body corporate, under the name of 'The governors of the possessions, revenues, and goods of the Free Grammar School of the mayor, bailiffs, and burgesses of the town and county of

---

[1] Also rector of North Stoneham in 1536.

[2] John Capon, Abbot of Hyde from 1530 to 1538; consecrated Bishop of Bangor in 1534; surrendered his abbey to the king in 1538, and in July 1539 was translated to the see of Salisbury. He died in 1557.

[3] Report of Charity Commissioners, 1840.

[4] Dr. Speed gives the patent at greater length.

Southampton,' capable of receiving and holding lands, &c., not exceeding the yearly value of £40, for the support of the master and under-master. And the mayor, bailiffs, and burgesses were empowered to make, with the advice of the bishop of the diocese, fit and wholesome statutes for the government of the school, and to arrange all other matters concerning it.

"What has been done in consequence of this patent will appear by "the following extracts from the journals. The same year that the "school was established by charter as above[1] [Thomas Pace, of the "town of Southampton, Esquire], Thomas Mille [of the same town, "gentleman], and William Breton [gentleman, one of the] executors "of William[2] Capon, D.D., paid to the Corporation £100, being the "legacy for which they were to pay £10 a year to the schoolmaster, "and by way of security[3] for the payment they conveyed to the said "executors [Jan. 20, 1554, 1 Mary] West Hall and its appurtenances "[together with three other specified tenements], and the parties "above named"—for the maintenance of the school, and that the boys to be taught therein might daily for ever pray for the soul of the said William Capon—reconveyed "these tenements to the mayor and "bailiffs as governors of the school and its possessions." The date of this document is September 26, 1554. "It is plain both from the "price paid and from the practice which immediately ensued, that "these houses were only intended to be made security for the payment "of £10 per annum."

The first master was Robert Knaplocke, who was in office in 1554-55, receiving £3, 6s. 8d. for his board, and his 'wages' of £10. Masters.

"In 1561 [25th Sept., 3 Eliz.] Thomas Diganson was chosen "schoolmaster" at the above salary, with an allowance of sixpence per head from town boys quarterly, and sixteenpence from country boys, 'according to the order of Winchester.'

"In 1569 [1st Oct., 11 Eliz.] John Horlock was chosen," salary £20 per annum, and £6, 13s. 4d. for reading a divinity lecture once a week.

Adrian Saravia, afterwards successively prebendary of Gloucester, Canterbury, and Westminster, must have come into England earlier than the received date;[4] he was master of the Grammar School in

[1] "Liber Niger, f. 111."

[2] The name appears as *John* Capon in the document in Liber Niger, as also in the original deed executed by Pace and Mille, still in the possession of the Corporation. It is an error for *William*, as the name occurs correctly in subsequent clauses.

[3] This is an *interpretation* of the deed; there can be no doubt however of its soundness; the Charity Commissioners of 1840 took the same view.

[4] He was in Southampton in 1570, perhaps before; see under 'French Church.'

1576. Under February (18 Eliz.) that year the notice occurs: 'Paid to Mr. Adrian (sic) for his charges and paiens in his tragedie,[1] by consent xx^s.' In the next year, 'Paid for iiij yardes of broade cloth for a gowne for Mr. Adrian Saravia the schoolm^r. at ix^s. the yarde " xxxvj^s.'[2]

"In 1583 William Davisson [M.A., Queen's College, Oxford] was "chosen schoolmaster [Dec. 2], to be put out at a year's warning if "the mayor and his brethren think fit; to have £20 a year salary, "and no further allowance for an usher."

"In 1595 [Sept. 11] the mayor and his brethren appointed an "usher [John Drake, B.A.], and assigned him £10 a year out of the "master's salary."

"In 1598 the schoolmaster was called before the mayor, &c., "March 16, and warned to provide otherwise for himself by mid-"summer next, they being minded to furnish the place with a sufficient "man." John Drake afterwards became rector of All Saints', and together with Simon Pett (Holy Rood) received a mark of the town's favour in December 1610.

The next master was Mr. Bathe, who left on being beneficed elsewhere.

"In 1601 [18th April] Nicholas Munn [clerk, late of London] was "chosen, to have £20 a year; not to quit under a year's notice, "but to be turned out at half a year's warning."

"In 1610–11 [March 22] Mr. Twiste was chosen," wages as above. In September 1612 a new Bible of the price of ten shillings was ordered to be bought and chained in the Free School.

"In 1616 [April 22] Alexander Rosse, a Scottish man, was "chosen, being recommended by the Earl of Hertford. N.B. in "1654, this gentleman gave £50 to the school, for which the Corpora-"tion agreed to pay £5 a year to the master out of the rent of the petty "customs." This learned writer became rector of All Saints', one of the royal chaplains, and was presented by Charles I. to the vicarage of Carisbrook. He died in 1653.

Mr. Thomas Parker, schoolmaster in Sir Thomas West's house, received the appointment on the resignation of Rosse, September 1, 1620, against the candidature of the usher of the school. The latter

[1] Sir James Whitelocke in his Liber Famelicus, p. 12, about the same period speaks of Mr. Mulcaster, the master of Merchant Taylors' School, presenting yearly 'sum playes to the court, in whiche his scholers wear only actors, and I one among them, and by that means taughte them good behaviour and audacitye.' Plays were acted in the Southampton School till a comparatively late period.

[2] Temp. T. Overey, sub annis.

having procured letters from the Earl of Southampton in favour of his election, which, luckily for Parker, arrived too late, the town, to do the best under the circumstances, presented him with a consolatory £5, which Mr. Rosse, who brought the letters, accepted in his behalf.

"A.D. 1624 [May 7] Mr. Thomas Wareham [M.A. Oxon.] was "chosen" on the resignation of Parker, agreeing to give private notice to the mayor of any intention to resign, and not to publish it abroad, that a successor might 'with conveniencye' be provided. "The same "year Edward Reynolds, Esq., left £20 for the benefit of the school-"master. The Corporation took the money to pay the master 25s. a "year." Wareham left at Michaelmas 1654. His salary had been £10, Capon's gift, £10 Corporation foundation, and £1, 5s., Reynolds' gift—£21, 5s. per annum.

Mr. William Bernard was chosen October 16, 1664, on the same salary. He was rector of Ash, Hants, and vicar of Holy Rood in or before 1653. and so continued till his death, in 1666, at Eling, whither he had retired in consequence of the plague in 1665, himself being in broken health. His widow became the first wife of Dr. John Speed, author of 'Batt upon Batt.' In 1653 he had been chosen registrar of the parish of Holy Rood for marriages, births, and burials under the Act of Parliament of August 24, 1653, and was sworn to his office by William Horne, mayor. He resigned the school in November 1660.

"A.D. [1660, Nov. 16] Mr. [Thomas] Butler [vicar of St. Michael's] "was chosen.

"A.D. 1674–75 [Feb. 13] ordered that Mr. Butler for his neglect of the "Free School shall have no more salary unless he amend. The same year "[Oct. 23], Mr. Butler not giving any satisfaction, the school was taken "into the town's hands; and the next year [March 23, 1674–75] Mr. "Butler resigned." Dr. Clutterbuck (St. Mary's) had interceded for him in January, but without effect beyond that of securing him on his resignation a quarter's salary in advance for his 'good report in the town,' June 1675.

"About this time [Feb. 11, 1674–75] a set of statutes for the school "was sent under the episcopal seal of the Bishop of Winchester."

Mr. Thomas Gubbs, elected September 28, 1666; the appointment was evidently temporary. See last notice.

Mr. Joseph Clarke, B.A., on the resignation of Butler, July 1, 1675.

"In 1676 Mr. John Pinhorne [B.A. Balliol Coll.] was chosen" [Aug. 30] in place of the last deceased, against the candidature of Mr. Floyd or perhaps Lloyd, vicar of Holy Rood. To this gentleman his pupil, Dr. Watts, expressed great obligations. Pinhorne was rector of All Saints', then vicar of Eling, where he died in 1714.

"In 1677 Dr. Edward Reynolds, Bishop of Norwich," a native of the parish of Holy Rood, born in 1599, and brought up at the Grammar school, from which he passed to Merton College, Oxford, "gave "£50 [£100][1] to the school, for which the Corporation agreed to pay "the master £5 a year."

"In 1690–91 [March 6] Mr. Richard Pocock [B.C.L.] was chosen," in succession to Pinhorne. "This gentleman put the school on its present [1760] footing. It had been kept before at a place called the Old "Free school, over against God's House, where silk throwsters now work; "but in February 1694–95 Mr. Pocock entered into an agreement "with the Corporation to have West Hall for a schoolhouse," with permission to alter or rebuild, "and with the old materials to build at "his own cost a house fit for thirty or forty boarders, and to have a "lease for forty years." The total number of scholars was not to exceed one hundred. Eventually a lease (February 26, 1696) of the premises was granted him for ninety-nine years, he having with the assistance of a loan[2] from the Corporation and private subscriptions rebuilt or adapted a portion of the old West Hall, producing a large and regular three-storied house of nineteen rooms, with six windows in each row, and a pedimented doorway in the middle bearing the benediction over the portal, 'Pax huic domui.' A schoolroom of 40 by 35 feet was built out behind.

School removed to West Hall.

Old school premises.

On Pocock vacating the old premises in Winkle Street, which are described[3] as a large tenement or room with three lesser rooms over a cellar in the street or lane leading from the custom-house to God's House gate, they were leased out by the Corporation for seven years at £7 per annum and two good fat capons. However, in April 1700 a certain Mrs. Elizabeth Sambrooke came to the Audit-house demanding possession of 'the loft formerly the schoolhouse near unto God's House gate,' as belonging to her as heir-at-law to John Caplen deceased, it having been discontinued as a schoolroom by the space of four years and upwards. The lady made good her claim, and in September the key was delivered up to her.

Mr. Pocock retained the school till his death; he was in charge of All Saints' in 1699–70, and in 1706 is still described as minister of that church. His burial occurs in the Holy Rood register on November 8,

1 On September 28, 1677, it was ordered that the £100 to be received under the Bishop of Norwich's will, together with £100 to be received by bequest of Alderman John Steptoe, should be paid over (as soon as received) to John Kennell in discharge of his bond of £200 due from the town. On October 1 the writings sealed by the town, and also by Mr. Pinhorne, were ordered to be sent up to Mr. Denton in order to receiving the £100 given by Bishop Reynolds to the Free School; the £100 when received was to be paid to Mr. Kennell as formerly ordered (Journal).

2 Of £300, for which he was to pay £15.

3 Lease.

1710. He was the father of Dr. Richard Pocock, Bishop of Meath, the oriental traveller, who was born at Southampton in 1704. Besides removing the school, he was founder of its library of about 240 volumes, among which is a Chaucer of 1542, bearing the autograph of Bishop Hugh Latimer, a MS. of the Vulgate, and some good classics.

"In 1710 [Nov. 13] Rev. William Kingsman [M.A.] was elected "on Mr. Pocock's death on the terms of his lease;" he was[1] vicar of St. Michael's from 1703 till his death in 1736; he was buried at St. John's on May 22.

"In 1736 [June 17] Rev. William Scott [of Petersfield] was "chosen on the death of Kingsman." In August 1738 it was agreed by the Common Council that the school fee for boys born in the town should be twenty shillings a year, with an extra payment of five shillings to the master, two shillings and sixpence to the usher, and one shilling to the prepositors. Mr. Scott was rector of All Saints'.

"In 1767 [May 20] Rev. Isaac Hodgson was chosen on the death "of Mr. Scott. The Corporation put the house in repair and granted "him a lease with a repairing covenant, remitting the £15 a year "mentioned in the contract with Mr. Pocock, agreeing to pay him a "salary of £30 a year."

The Rev. Richard Mant, M.A., master of New College School, was appointed, in the place of Hodgson deceased, on December 21, 1770; his lease of ninety-nine years bearing date that day. In May 1773 the Corporation gave their sanction to raising the terms to ten shillings quarterly for town boys, with twelve shillings entrance fee, as prescribed by the old statutes, recommending the change to the Bishop. In 1777 and 1778 various enlargements were carried out. Mant's reputation kept his school full; and according to a local chronicler it had become 'one of the most genteel seminaries of learning in the country.' Mr. Mant was rector of Fonthill Bishops, Wilts, and of Ashley, Hants; he was presented to All Saints' in 1793, and proceeded D.D. the same year, resigning the school in 1795. He was father of the well-known Bishop of Down and Connor, who was born in 1776.

Rev. George Whittaker, M.A., master of a school at Alresford, was appointed May 8, 1795. He carried out some improvements in the building, and was a successful master, but, unlike his predecessor, of considerable severity. He was the author or editor of several good school-books. He resigned in 1813.

Rev. Charles Tapp Griffith, M.A., Fellow of Wadham College,

[1] William Kingsman was instituted to Sherfield English on presentation of Edward Keele, patron for that turn, on October 7, 1708, and instituted to West Titherley, February 4, 1708-9.

Oxford, was elected April 23, his lease being dated August 3, 1813. Having obtained the sanction of the Corporation to remove the school to a better site, and failed to secure the position he desired Above Bar, Mr. Griffith contented himself with under-letting West Hall, the present site, and removing the school to Bugle Hall (January–June 1818), where it continued till his resignation at the end of the following year. He was vicar of St. Michael's from 1817 to 1825; master of Warminster Grammar School from 1820 to 1840; rector of Elm, near Frome, from 1825 till his death in 1866, having been made rural dean in 1844, and resigning from infirmities in 1864.

Rev. Thomas Lawes Shapcott, B.A., of St. Alban's Hall, Oxford, was elected October 21, 1819. It had been determined (October 2) before the election of the new master to pull down the old house, which was a remnant of West Hall, and still contained some interesting features. Accordingly a new schoolhouse was erected from plans by Mr. John Taylor, approved August 19, 1820, and carried out by November 1821, the Corporation having expended £1200 on the premises. On the north wall of the present residence an old stone has been inserted under the eaves, bearing the date 1553, a relic and memento of the old foundation, while in a corresponding position on the south side occurs the date 1820, that of the rebuilding. Mr. Shapcott, who was educated under Dr. Whittaker, and afterwards at Marlborough, became vicar of St. Michael's in 1825, holding this preferment with the chaplaincy of the gaol till his death in August 22, 1854. He had been a promoter of improvements in the town.

On the death of Mr. Shapcott no appointment was made to the school for some years; and it will be convenient now to give some account of the statutes under which the school had been worked up to this time.

Old statutes.

They bear date February 11, 1674–75, and were given under the common seal of the Corporation and the episcopal seal of Bishop Morley. Their provisions were to the following effect:—

1. The schoolmaster and usher to be elected by the mayor, bailiffs, and common council, and licensed by the Bishop of Winchester.

2. The master and usher [if any such] to be resident.

3. To read to their boys the following books, as they should deem fit: *Latin*—Lylly's Grammar, Sententiæ Pueriles, Corderius's Dialogues, Walker's Particles and Idiotisms, Æsop's Fables, Ovid's Epistles, Erasmus's Dialogues, Terence, Justin, Florus, Quintus Curtius, Sallust, Pliny's Epistles, Cicero's Orations, Livy, Ovid's Metamorphoses, Virgil, Horace, Martial's Epigrams, Juvenal. *Greek*—Camden's Grammar, Poselii Colloquia, Vigerii Idiotismi, Lucian's Select Dialogues, Isocrates, Demosthenes, Herodian, Musæus, Theocritus, Hesiod, Homer, Pindar, Greek Epigrams.

4. The scholars in the first two forms always to speak Latin, unless permitted to use English.

5. School hours, from 6 A.M. in the summer and 7 A.M. in the winter till 11 A.M., then from 1 to 5 in the afternoon.

6. The boys might play on Thursday afternoons from three o'clock, provided there were no holy day in the week, and on Saturdays from eleven o'clock. Recreation might also be allowed on Tuesday afternoons should a person of quality or learning desire it, provided exercises were set for the next day.

7. The holidays were—from one whole week before Christmas to the Monday after Twelfth Day, from Thursday before Easter to Monday after Easter week, from Thursday before Whitsunday to the Monday seven-night after Whitsun week. Holiday tasks were to be invariably given.

8. Morning and evening prayers were to be used, and to consist of the Confession, and, if the master were a priest, of the Absolution, the Lord's Prayer, some collects, and a special collect relating to the school; one of the upper scholars to read and construe a few verses of Greek Testament, and one of the lower scholars to read the same in English morning and evening.

9. The Catechism was to be taught at ten o'clock every Saturday, and the scholars were to be prepared to answer correctly the vicar or curate of Holy Rood, or of some other parish, whenever the mayor and schoolmaster should appoint an examination.

10. The boys were to meet the master or usher every Sunday or holy day morning, and from thence follow him decently and orderly, two by two, to Holy Rood church; and those who were considered able were required to take notes of the sermon, and give account of it every Monday morning.

11. Two of the best scholars were to be appointed prepositors, one for keeping order in school and taking note of late comers and truants, the other for watching the boys in church. The master and usher were required to correct all boys for misconduct and bad language, but were specially to punish those who were given to lying.

12. The Corporation might appoint free scholars from poor townspeople's children; others were to pay on admission five shillings to the master, two shillings and sixpence to the usher, and sixpence to each prepositor; and instead of gratuities at breaking up, each scholar was to pay to the master, if he were under him, five shillings quarterly, or if he were under the usher, two shillings and sixpence to the usher, and two shillings and sixpence to the master.

13. Registers of entrance were to be kept.

14. None were to be admitted before they could read.

15. The proper endowment was to be paid to the master quarterly, and registers were to be made of the several gifts and bequests to the school, the mayor and the schoolmaster each having a copy: a copy of the statutes was, moreover, to 'remain perpetually' in the school.

16. The schoolmaster being sick and disabled for the time, was to provide a proper substitute, but still to have his salary.

17. So also in case of the school being dismissed on account of contagious sickness in the town.

18. The master or usher might be removed by the Corporation on grave cause.

19. The master might, with leave of the mayor, expel incorrigible scholars.

20. Every year the mayor and bailiffs, and others of the Corporation whom the mayor might invite, were, with the rector of St. Mary's and the other town incumbents, to meet at the school on the Thursday morning before the Whitsun holidays, and there 'inquire into the observance of these statutes . . . and be entertained by the schollars whom the master shall appoint with oracons and declarations in Greeke and Latine or what other exercise he shall enjoyne.'

21. The statutes were to be read publicly in the school every quarter.

22. The mayor, bailiffs, and burgesses might, with the advice and consent of the Bishop, alter or add to these statutes as time and occasion should require.

It had been the custom for many years to grant a lease of the schoolhouse and premises to each newly elected master for the term of ninety-nine years, at a peppercorn rent, upon his covenanting to pay the rates and taxes, to keep the premises in repair, and to observe the above statutes, a copy of which was scheduled to the lease. This was last observed in the appointment of 1819, though the lease was not granted till March 5, 1824.

School reopened, 1860.

The school was reopened in August 1860 under the mastership of Mr. Charles Wright Hankin, B.A., late scholar of Oriel College, Oxford, the premises, with the exception of the master's house, having been rebuilt by the trustees. The school buildings, now considerably enlarged, form with the master's house a parallelogram stretching from Bugle Street on the west to French Street on the east. Convenient dormitories communicating with the master's house are arranged over the principal schoolroom. The further schoolroom has a high-pitched roof, and its east window, the gift of the late Rev. J. W. Cary, D.D., serves as an adornment to French Street. On the north side of this parallelogram is the master's garden,[1] and on the south the boys' play-ground backed by handsome cloisters opposite the school buildings and returned on the east, so that three sides of a quadrangle are formed, the fourth or open side in Bugle Street having a low ornamental wall in which a stone is set recording the date of its erection, 1877, and the name of its donor, J. E. Le Feuvre, Esq., then sheriff. Over the entrance porch of the schoolrooms is the inscription 'Schola Ed. VI^TI^ Regis refecta et amplificata A.D. MDCCCLX. Iterum MDCCCLXXII,' marking the period of renovation; the latter date being that of the rebuilding and opening of the school as it now stands.

The opening ceremony took place in the presence of the mayor and Corporation, the Bishop of Winchester, the Honourable Cowper Temple, M.P., now Lord Mount Temple, the Rev. J. W. Cary, D.D., rural dean and chairman of the trustees, and a large attendance of the clergy and gentry of the town and neighbourhood. Mr. Hankin resigned at the close of 1874; his place having been for some months previously filled by the Rev. Desmond Henry Wynn Sampson, M.A., Magdalen College, Oxford, the second master.

In December 1874 Mr. Thomas Garrett, B.A., of Gonville and Caius College, Cambridge, was elected head-master.

New scheme.

In the following year a new scheme of seventy-five clauses, dated October 26, 1875, was given for the management of the school under

[1] French prisoners are said to have been buried here.

the Endowed Schools Commission by the Charity Commissioners, of which it may be sufficient to give the following abstract:—

Provision is made for the appointment of a body of sixteen governors: of these, the mayor for the time being is an *ex officio* member, six are to be nominated by the town council, two by the School Board of the Southampton district, and seven are to be co-optative. With the exception of the first named, the appointments are for six years, but every third year three members from those chosen by the Council, one of those nominated by the School Board, and three co-optative members retire, as determined by ballot. No religious qualifications are required for the office of governor. From the date of the scheme the 'corporation of the governors of the possessions, revenues, and goods of the Free Grammar School of the mayor, bailiffs, and burgesses of the town and county of Southampton' was dissolved, and their powers transferred to the governors under the present scheme. The visitorial powers were also transferred from the Bishop to the Crown, that is, to the Charity Commissioners, and the jurisdiction of the ordinary as to licensing masters was abolished.

The head-master, who must be a graduate of some University within the British empire, is not required to be in holy orders, nor may he, if in holy orders, hold any cure of souls, or if otherwise, accept any office which in the opinion of the Governors would interfere with his duties to the school. He is to reside in the house assigned him in his official capacity and not as a tenant. Under clause 38 the governors are to prescribe the subjects of instruction, to fix the terms and vacations, the payment of scholars, the number and payment of boarders, the number of assistant masters, and other matters of regulation; but by the next clause they are directed to consult the head-master before settling anything under clause 38. Details of school-working, as to the choice of books, the method of instruction, the arrangement of classes, and generally the whole internal organisation and discipline of the school are left to the head-master, who has the power of appointing and, subject to the approval of the governors, that of dismissing all assistant masters, and determining the proportion in which each shall be paid by the governors. He may also make proposals to the governors as to the improvement of the school. He receives a fixed salary of £150, paid by the Corporation to the governors in consideration of certain ancient charities, besides a capitation grant of not less than £2 or more than £5 per annum on each boy in the school. The governors make regulations as to the reception of boarders, whose payment is fixed at £45 per annum, in addition to the tuition fees. These latter, payable in advance, are £7, 10s. per annum, or £2, 10s. per quarter.

The age of admission into the school is fixed at eight years, there being a preliminary examination in reading, writing from dictation, the first four rules in arithmetic, and the outlines of the geography of England. There is an entrance fee of five shillings. The school is open to the sons of parents of any religious tenets, and there is a conscience clause. No boy is allowed to remain in the school after the end of the term in which he shall have attained the age of seventeen years.

The course of instruction comprises the Holy Scriptures, Latin, French, and German languages, reading, writing, arithmetic, geography, history, English grammar, composition, and literature, mathematics, natural science, drawing, and vocal music. Greek may be taught as an extra at an additional fee of £3 a year for each boy.

By the new scheme the governors are instructed 'to make the teaching and other benefits provided by the Hartley Institution available for the purposes of the school.'

There is an annual examination of the school by examiners appointed by the governors.

Exhibitions. By way of exhibitions the governors are directed to grant exemptions, total or partial, from the payment of tuition fees, for such periods and on such conditions as they may think fit. All such exemptions are given as the reward of merit only, and are liable to forfeiture on account of misconduct or failure to maintain a reasonable standard of efficiency.

The governors are also directed to apply not less than the sum of £35 yearly in providing other exhibitions, each entitling the holder to receive a payment equal to the amount of his tuition fee, with or without further emoluments. These exhibitions are competed for by boys, who have been educated for at least one year at any elementary school in the school district of Southampton.

Mr. Garrett resigned in March 1880, and was succeeded by Mr. James Fewings, B.A., B.Sc., of London University, the present headmaster.

West Hall. Something may now be added about the site of the school. West Hall originally belonged to Gervaise le Riche, the founder of God's House, who gave a charge of two marks per annum on West Hall to his newly founded house; some time later the priory of St. Denys had a charge on it. The earliest document relating to West Hall among the town papers is a covenant for its partition made between the five co-heirs of Thomas le Halveknyght and Cristina his wife, John, Thomas, William Basingrom, and Petronilla (Halveknyght) his wife, Roger, and Walter. A sixth portion is described as belonging to Matilda, the daughter of the Basingroms, by legacy from Sir William le Flemyng; so that in the time of Thomas and Cristina, West Hall and its premises were at least divided into two portions and held by different owners. The boundaries of the property were French Street on the east, Bull (Bugle) Street on the west, certain tenements on the north, and on the south a lane connecting the two streets, part of which is still existing between the Grammar School premises and the ancient building to the south of it in Bugle Street to be mentioned presently. This lane was anciently called 'Narrow Lane,' 'Little Lane,' 'Halveknyght Lane,' &c. The provisions of the covenant between the parties were somewhat curious, and are as follows. The date is 1303:—

John had the painted chamber with the cellars below, another chamber called *La Garderobe*—probably a wardrobe or store-room—the great gate opposite St. John's Church, a bit of green sward, and the courtyard and fountain within the gate.

Thomas had a bakehouse with cellar below, a chamber called *La Criole* over the gate opposite St. John's, and a stable within the gate, behind the aforesaid cellar and bakehouse.

Roger, the third son, had a bakehouse and cellar beside the little lane with an oven, and a little stable behind them; he had also a cellar underneath *La Garderobe*.

Walter had half of the hall, with a solar or upper room, and a shop which ran towards Bull Street, together with a kitchen and oven adjoining that part of the hall; he had also a solar towards Bull Street beside the narrow lane, and over a small cellar running westward, to be spoken of presently.

William Basingrom[1] and Petronilla his wife had the other half of the hall beside the long chamber on the north, with solar and shop; they had also the small cellar running westward under Walter's solar.

These five parties rendered each of them to the Hospital of St. Julian, or God's House, four shillings per annum, in all twenty shillings, and to the Prior and Convent of St. Denys sevenpence farthing each, the fifth not paying the odd farthing, total three shillings. The town paid these sums when the property came into their hands.

The portion which belonged to Matilda Basingrom (as above) was the long chamber with cellars below, a certain void place between it and the tenement of John de Schirlye on the north, with another void space (boundaries given). For this property she rendered to the Hospital 6s. 8d., and to the Prior and Convent twelvepence per annum. All the parties were to have the use of their brother John's gate and fountain.

---

[1] The will of William Basingrom was proved before the Dean of Southampton in Holy Rood Church, August 28, 1316 (Addit. 15,314, f. 50).

The covenant bore the seals of all the parties, and, as was usual, for greater security the seal of the prepositure of the town: the witnesses being Adam le Hordyr, the alderman, William Fughel, the bailiff, Robert le Hordyr, the custumer, John de Schirlye, Thomas Stut, Richard de Bareflet, Henry de Lym, and many others.[1]

Soon after this John le Halveknyght bought his brother Walter's share, and then sold it,[2] together with his own, to John de Schirlye and Felicia his wife for fifty marks, saving the rights of ingress and egress to Roger and Petronilla, and reserving the rents to God's House and St. Denys. The only date is that of the local magistracy. Adam le Hordyr was alderman, William Fughel and Robert le Hordyr were bailiffs.

The second son, Thomas le Demichevalier (half-knight), as he calls himself, also sold his share for twelve marks to the above John de Schirlye and Felicia his wife. Two deeds record the arrangement, one witnessed by Thomas Stone and Nigel de la Wylderne, then bailiffs, and by Robert le Mercer, Peter de Lyons, John de Holebery, John de Bourgoyne, Robert le Barber, John de Puteo, Adam le Hordier, and others; and the second deed by Robert le Mercer, alderman, John de Puteo, Henry de Lym, bailiffs, and others.

Roger, the third son, also sold his share for forty marks, with the same reservation, to the same John and Felicia de Schirlye.

Matilda Basingrom in 1317 granted, for a fine of sixteen marks and an annual rent of 3s. 10d., her two plots (what she did with the Long Chamber does not appear) to Walter de Brackelye, burgess of Southampton, with the usual reservations to the lords of the fee. Walter's widow, Joanna, parted with any rights she might have through her husband to Hugo Sampson in September 1331. We need not follow other changes. The following, however, are important, as throwing light on the nature of that remarkably fine mediæval stone house immediately to the south of the Grammar School cloister wall—the wall of Halveknyght Lane. In a deed of Roger Mascall to Thomas Chapeleyn (October 1365) this building is called the 'Weyhous,' and it was held by John le Clerk. Two years later, namely, in October 1367, this John le Clerk, with Johanna his wife, granted

[1] This document is printed in Madox's Formulare, p. 89, but three of the originals still exist among the West Hall deeds in the Audit-house. One is endorsed 'Participatio facta inter les Halwekynȝtes de la West halle.' The seals are attached to four labels; that of Southampton is on one, two other labels bear two seals each, and a fragment is on the fourth.

[2] Subsequently to this he quit-claimed to Richard Bagge (see below) a tenement in Simnel Street formerly belonging to Richard the Arblaster, which the latter had received by gift of Thomas le Halveknight. The house of the late Richerius le Halveknight is described as on its west side. The deed is dated in March (10 Ed. II.) 1317.

West Hall to Richard Arnewode, rector of the church of St. Cross (Holy Rood); and in a deed of 1388 (11 R. II.) from Robert Bechefounte to Alan Sleddale, Richard Banke, John Penbrok, parson of St. John's, and Robert Falbergh, mention is made of this same messuage of John Clerk, senior, as lately called the 'Woolhouse.' All the above documents, in addition to private seals, bear that of the prepositure of Southampton for greater security. Within the above period three different town seals were in use.

In the fifteenth century West Hall was in the possession of the Corporation. The rent received by them was £13, 13s. 4d. per annum, out of which they paid the quit-rent to God's House of twenty shillings each year.[1]

A portion of West Hall may have been used as a public building in the same century, judging from the fact that the cucking-stool appears to have been kept there. Thus we read[2] under 1475:—

> 'Paid to ij men for theire laboure by John Roper for to carry the scoldyng stoole fro the West Halle to the pillery.'

Under the same date we find the—

> 'Costes doon in makyng of the scooldyng stoole. Furste paid for j pece tymbre boughte of Robert Orchiere for the same stole, x$^{d.}$
>
> 'For carriage of the same fro Hille to the Weste halle, iij$^{d.}$
>
> 'Item, for sawing of the same piece in iij peces, viij$^{d.}$
>
> 'Item, for iij boltes and ij pinnes of iron for the same stoole, vj$^{d.}$
>
> 'Item, for the wheeles to convey the said stole by commaundment of the meyre, iij$^{s.}$ iiij$^{d.}$ Item, paid to Robert Orcherd for the makyng of the said stoole and wheelis for iij days labours to hym and his man, x$^{d.}$ the day. Summa, ij$^{s.}$ vj$^{d.}$'

The total expense appears to have been 8s. 1d.

Under 1563, a plague year, parts of West Hall were rented out, as if under some pressure:—'For ostelage in three sellars in the West Hall for ten weeks at 10$^{s.}$ a week, £5. Ostelage of one sellar in West Hall for fourteen weeks at 2$^{s.}$ 6$^{d.}$ per week, 35$^{s.}$, and for another twenty weeks at 2$^{s.}$ per week, 40$^{s.}$'

From 1695 the history of West Hall becomes identical with that of the Grammar School.

## SECTION II.—*Taunton's School.*

Alderman Taunton (see p. 303) by his will (February 15, 1752) gave to his executors, Peter Dobree and Thomas Harrison, and their heirs, &c., all the residue of his real and personal estates in trust, to apply

[1] Steward's Books, 1457, 1469, 1493. [2] Steward's Book.

the same, after the death of his wife, to such good and charitable uses in the town of Southampton, by the employment and maintenance of poor people there, and bringing up their children in work and industry, fitting them for the sea or otherwise, as should seem to them most useful. He also directed that special favour should be shown to the poor of St. John's parish, the place of his nativity.

Accordingly, in June 1760, a scheme was confirmed by the Court of Chancery, varied in 1771, by which it was provided that six poor persons of either sex, not under fifty years of age, should be received into the charity under the name of 'pensioners,' and each receive £10 as a help, persons being preferred who had some trade or employment; that no more than ten boys should be taken into the charity for education to fit them for the sea, power being given to apprentice to naval trades those who could not be bound for the sea; any surplus, not exceeding £40 per annum, might be applied in giving portions to meritorious servant-maids of the town marrying to satisfaction. By custom a sermon at Holy Rood and a dinner afterwards were annually provided. In 1851 a new scheme for the school, established in 1760, was adopted; but in 1875 (October 26) a further scheme placed the 'Taunton Trade School' under the same management as the Grammar School (see 'Grammar School'), and additional buildings were erected. The scheme provides that the school shall consist of a senior and a junior department under one head-master; it shall supply a liberal and practical education, supplemented by the systematic teaching of such art and science subjects as are applicable to the trades of the district; it shall be in connection with the Science and Art Department of the Committee of Council on Education; the junior department shall be conducted so as to be preparatory to the senior department, and also, so far as practicable, to the Southampton Grammar School. The head-master, who is appointed by the governors, must have the degree of Bachelor of Science in the University of London, or a certificate of the Science and Art Department qualifying him for earning payments on results. The course of instruction is as follows:—(1) Religious; as regulated by the governors and head-master. (2) Secular; in the junior department, reading, writing, arithmetic, geography, English and Latin grammar, English history, drawing, vocal music, drill, and other physical exercises; in the senior department, in addition, book-keeping, mensuration, commercial arithmetic, mathematics, mechanics, chemistry, elementary navigation, and, when specially required, engineering and other sciences relating to a seafaring life, and such other subjects as may seem applicable to the trades of the district. No boy is admitted to the school under the age of seven years, an entrance examination having to be passed in every case; and no boy is retained

New scheme.

in either department after the end of the term in which he shall have attained the age of twelve or fifteen years.

A provision is made for exhibitions, which are granted solely as the reward of merit, by exemptions from tuition fees, boys so exempted being called foundation scholars; special opportunity for competition being given to boys at public elementary schools in the school district of Southampton. Exhibitions.

Under the new scheme for the school, the whole of the Taunton charity property, except the fund for decayed aldermen and the £21 for reading prayers already diverted that way, was applied to the governors of the school, subject to their paying £40 to Taunton's trustees for four annuitants. No sermons, dinners, or marriage portions are now provided, but the school is doing excellent work in harmony with the donor's will.

## Section III.

### *Other Schools and Educational Agencies.*

In 1713 a charity school for the education of thirty boys had been already set on foot, and an annual subscription list of £80 secured; but after some years it fell through.

The next effort was that secured in 1760 under the will of Richard Taunton, Esq. (on whose foundation see above).

In March 1786 Sunday-schools were established in the town, the Corporation subscribing £5, 5s. yearly. Out of these arose an industrial school for twenty-five girls taken from the Sunday-schools, who were trained for service and other occupations. Sunday-schools.

A National School for the town was opened in St. Michael's Square, on the site of the present school of that parish, in 1811, two houses having been converted for that purpose and leased from the Corporation, who subscribed £5, 5s. annually to the school. In July 1819 the committee of management published an account of their work, spoke of increasing success, and of having under education 150 boys and 160 girls, the latter being also taught needlework. National Schools.

British Schools had been established in the Ditches the year before (1810). These were enlarged in 1817 and subsequently, but have now been transferred to the Southampton School Board. Upon renewal of the old lease in 1834 the Corporation returned half of the fine (£21) to the trustees of the school, whose funds were not flourishing, as an encouragement to education, and presented the remaining £21 to the National School in St. Michael's Square. British Schools.

In the following year (1835) the Bedford Place Schools in the parish of All Saints' were built by subscription, the Corporation giving Parochial Schools.

a donation of £21. These schools have for many years served for the district parish of St. Paul's. They cost £556.

In 1839 the first schools in Holy Trinity district were provided, at a cost of £400.

In the following year (1840) the first National School (Grove Street) in St. Mary's was established, at an outlay of £927.

Such seems to have been all the provision of a public nature for the education of the working classes at that period, the population of the borough being 27,744 in 1841. In addition to the above, there were three infant schools in different parts of the town, and a fourth at Hill; but these were probably of private venture.

Order of foundation.

It will now be convenient to group the schools under the various districts, taking them in the order of educational effort from the beginning.

St. Michael's. The old school was enlarged in 1853 at a cost of £691.

Holy Trinity. Large schools with a residence, in place of the old arrangement, were built in 1853 at a cost of £2376. They were subsequently enlarged by the addition of a second boys' school in 1867.

St. Mary's. The Grove Street Infants' School was built in 1845 at an outlay of £640. In 1852 the Deanery Infant School, at a cost of £1300, under Archdeacon Wigram. In 1856 the boys' and girls' schools were enlarged at a cost of £754; and in 1858 the Crabniton Schools erected at a cost of £1458, subsequently to which the workshops were added. The Grove Street Infants' School was converted into houses in 1852. The accommodation in the above schools is for over 1000 children.

St. Luke's, Newtown. Schools were erected here in 1847 at a cost of £1200, and were enlarged at a cost of £1000 in 1859.

Christchurch, Portswood. A school and residence were erected in 1848, and enlarged in 1858.

St. James's, Bernard Street. The schools of this parish were held in rented premises in Orchard Lane for many years, till the present Board schools were built near the church.

St. Peter's School was built in 1856.

Christ Church, Northam. These schools were built, with residence, in 1858 at a cost of £1500; further accommodation was subsequently added.

Holy Rood School was erected in 1861 at the cost of £852.

The following are unconnected with parochial organisation:—

Board Schools.

Under the Southampton School Board, which was formed in 1871, and consists of eleven members, are:—The York Buildings (late All Saints' National) Schools, built in 1849 at a cost of £1354, and subsequently improved; the Houndwell Board School, formerly the Industrial and Ragged School, erected in St. George's Place in 1854 at the cost of £1266, partly to commemorate the Rev. J. Crabbe, taken over by the Board in 1879; the Bevois Town Board Schools; the Eastern District; the Southern District; the Royal British, formerly the British Schools in the Ditches, transferred to the Board; the Northam, and St. Denys' Schools.

Charlotte Place Free School, built in 1856.

Wesleyan Day-School in East Street.

Roman Catholic Schools in St. Michael's Square.

The Peninsular and Oriental Company erected large schools in Paget Street in 1862; they have been enlarged, and now form the District Board School.

The Palk Memorial Home was built in 1876 on a site adjoining the Ragged Schools, in memory of the late Mr. Edward Palk, for many years treasurer of the above schools, churchwarden of Holy Rood, and a promoter of good works in the town. He died in 1872.

The Female Orphan Asylum, established in 1837, under the patronage of the Bishop of the diocese, after having had its first home in Albion Place, was moved into its newly built premises at Bellevue in 1852. The design of the charity is to clothe, board, and train the orphan girls of respectable but destitute poor, and fit them in every way for service. It receives forty inmates. Orphan Asylum.

There is a Servants' Training School in Hanover Buildings.

There are Sunday-schools belonging to all the churches and principal places of worship, but the following buildings specially devoted to the purpose may be mentioned:— Sunday-schools.

The Kell Memorial School, adjoining the Unitarian Church, Bellevue, erected in memory of the late Rev. E. Kell (see under 'Churches').

The Watts Memorial Hall and Sunday-School Buildings, attached to the Above Bar Congregational Church, are said to be the finest suite of Sunday-school buildings in the South of England. They comprise a hall capable of seating 800 persons; an infant class-room to seat 100 children; an elementary class-room for 60 boys too young to be placed in the regular classes; a lecture-room to seat 120, used for Sunday-school classes; eleven class-rooms, each capable of holding from 10 to 30 scholars, and a library to contain 2000 volumes. The cost of the buildings was upwards of £6000. The memorial stone was laid on May 6, 1875, by Samuel Morley, Esq., M.P.; it bears the statement that the first name on the baptismal register of the community is that of Isaac Watts, D.D., 1674–1748, whose father, Isaac Watts, was a deacon of the church for forty-eight years, and transferred to the trustees the freehold of that land.

# CHAPTER VIII.

## ECCLESIASTICAL.

### Section I.—*The Parish Churches.*

### St. Mary's.

In the Domesday record there is no mention of any church[1] or chapel within the borough of Hantune or Southampton. It does not follow that there was none. The Church of St. John certainly existed; and there is some reference to the ecclesiastical position of the town under the account of the manor of South Stoneham. That manor belonged to the Bishop, and was appropriated for the clothing of the monks of St. Swithun's, Winchester, probably by Bishop Ælfwine about 1043; but the manorial church was held by Richerius, the clerk, with two other churches near Southampton, dependent on it as the mother-church. Adjoining this church was a hide of land, and Richerius, who was possessed of holdings elsewhere under the Bishop, owned in right of his benefice all the tithes of the town of Southampton and also of Kingsland. His holdings under the King and under the Bishop were each assessed at twenty shillings.[2] Probably this manorial church was no other than St. Mary's, Southampton.[3] In favour of this opinion is the fact that the precentors or rectors of St. Mary's have possessed the rectory of South Stoneham, and presented to its vicarage, as early as we have any records on the matter.[4] St. Mary's, Southampton, has

St. Mary's probably referred to in Domesday.

---

[1] Dr. Speed takes St. Mary's to have been probably a collegiate church, which came into the hands of the crown at the dissolution of religious houses. Of this latter there is no evidence whatever. He ridicules the idea of its having been the mother-church of the town, in which he is also certainly wrong. It has not been thought necessary to reproduce his account.

[2] Ipse Episcopus tenet Stanham. De vestitu monachorum est. Tempore Regis Edwardi se defendebat pro v hidis, modo pro iii hidis. Terra est ix carucatæ. In dominio est una carucata, et xi villani et ix bordarii cum viii carucatis. Ibi unus servus, et xxiii acræ prati et duæ piscariæ de xxxix denariis. Silva de xx porcis. Tempore Regis Edwardi valebat vii libras, et post iv libras, modo viii libras.

Hujus manerii ecclesiam tenet Richerius, clericus, cum duabus aliis ecclesiis juxta Hantone quæ ad hanc ecclesiam matrem pertinent: et ibi adjacet i hida terræ; et omnes decimas ejusdem villæ, et etiam de terrâ Regis. Valet xx solidos quod de Episcopo tenet, quod de Rege xx solidos.

[3] See also Moody's Domesday of Hampshire, p. 47.

[4] In Reg. Pontiss. (1282), f. 214, 'the church of Suthampton,' as also 'the chapel of the Blessed Mary of Suthampton,' are among those in the Bishop's

also its valuable glebe about the church; it possessed all the tithes of the town, together with those of the whole district probably here described. It should be observed that the tithings of Eastleigh and Allington, which are now comprised within the parish of South Stoneham, are not included in that manor in the Domesday record, but are described separately—Allington, moreover, having a church. The Bishop's manor assigned for the clothing of the Winchester monks was therefore probably Bittern, which had always belonged to the Bishops till it passed to the Ecclesiastical Commissioners in 1869. The King's land, of which Richerius had the tithes, is probably to be identified with Portswood, which we know to have been royal property, and which was afterwards granted to the monks of St. Denys.

It would be impossible to point out the site of the 'two other churches near Hantone' which belonged to this manorial church. The present Church of St. Mary, South Stoneham,[1] was not then in existence, and a church on its site would hardly have been called near Southampton.

Relation of St. Mary's to the other churches.

Passing from the eleventh to the twelfth century, we find Henry II. granting his 'chapels' of St. Michael's, St. Cross (Holy Rood), St. Lawrence's, and All Saints', within the borough, to the monks of St. Denys'; but these chapels must have had relation to a mother-church, which was, no doubt, this important manorial church beyond the walls.

In the time of Bishop Godfrey de Lucy (1189–1204), the clergy of Hampton are referred to in a controversy with the monks of St. Denys about a certain weir, which the former, who were probably therefore a community, had constructed opposite to Munkelonde, injuriously, as the canons averred, to them and their weir, which the king had given them with the possession of Kingsland. The superior of these clergy, Stephen of Reims, was staying at the school in Paris at the time of the alleged trespass, and inquiry into the several rights concerned having been deferred by order of the Bishop till the return of Stephen, the

patronage. Early in the next century the warden (custos) of St. Mary's presents to 'the church of Suth Stonham' (Reg. Woodlock, 1305–16). In 1379 the presentation runs 'to the vicarage of the church or chapel of St. Mary, Suth Stoneham' (Wykeham, i. f. 104 b).

[1] The present Church of St. Mary, South Stoneham, dates from about the end of the twelfth century, the chancel retaining some good original work. On the north side of the nave is the Dummer Chapel, built out in 1728, and on the south a transept and vestry, built by the present vicar, the Rev. William Dann Harrison, in 1854. South Stoneham Church is probably to be identified in Bishop Pontissara's list with one of the chapels of 'Aldinton' (see p. 332), dependent on the 'church of Southampton;' there is no separate mention of it, nor does it occur in the taxation of 1291, nor in the official lists of the rural deanery till late, being probably always included under St. Mary's, Southampton.

latter recognised the right of the canons of St. Denys, spoke of 'my clergy of Hampton,' and ordered the removal of the weir.[1] It seems highly probable that Stephen was the priest of the mother-church, under whom these clergy were living in some sort of community.

1225. A few years after this, Philip de Lucy, 'rector of the church of Southampton,' was in controversy with the prior and convent of St. Denys on the position of the churches in the town. It appears that the Prior and convent, through their chaplains,[2] were in the habit of receiving to divine offices certain parishioners of Philip, and had deprived him of his just dues and tithes. We meet with the matter as brought by Philip de Lucy before Pope Honorius, who, in the eighth year of his pontificate, directed a commission to William de Wenda, the Dean, and Robert, the Chancellor, of Sarum, and to William de Merton, Archdeacon of Berkshire, in the diocese of Sarum, empowering them to examine witnesses and determine between the parties. The inquiry, instituted accordingly in the chapter-house of Salisbury, April 1225, lasted two or more days. Philip de Lucy set forth that the town of Southampton was within the limits of his parish, and that those having domicile or carrying on business within the same ought of common right to be considered his parishioners; notwithstanding which the Prior and convent and their chaplains in the chapels of Holy Trinity, St. Cross (Holy Rood), St. Michael, St. Lawrence, and All Saints had taken oblations and tithes from his parishioners in the town, excepting tithes of corn and of gardens, to the grave injury of the said Philip and his church, on which account he demanded, in the name of his church, that the said Prior, convent, and chaplains should desist from these injuries, and make satisfaction for the past.[3] Three of the chaplains, Masters Roger, John, and Robert, had appointed Brother Rueland, Prior of St. Denys, as their proctor, and the Wednesday after the Feast of Trinity (May 28) having been appointed for a final hearing, on that day agreement was made between the litigants—Philip de Lucy, custos of the church of St. Mary of Southampton, and the clerks[4] serving there, on the one part, and the prior, and convent, and chaplains of the town on the other part—to the following effect, viz., that a common procession of

[1] Addit. 15,314, f. 43.

[2] These were the officiating clergy in the churches of the town. Their appointments were probably not permanent, but rather from year to year, though they were not lightly to be removed (see Constit. Abp. Edmund, A.D. 1236, cap. 25). They became 'perpetual vicars' somewhat later.

[3] Addit. 15,314, fol. 77 b. The document is apparently misplaced, but evidently some of the account has not been transcribed at all.

[4] By a constitution of Archbishop Langton (A.D. 1222) it was ordered that in every parish church there should be two or three priests, according to the size of the parish and the wealth of the church (Lynd., p. 184), who might be appointed by

the town of Southampton, with all the chaplains, should repair to the Church of St. Mary on Ascension Day with crosses and banners, and without these ornaments on the Feast of the Assumption (August 15), and on St. Leodagar's Day (October 2), and there in the rural chapter, the chaplains ministering in the several chapels of St. Michael, St. Cross, St. Lawrence, All Saints, Holy Trinity, and St. Andrews,[1] should each of them swear faithfully to preserve the honour of the Church of St. Mary, and to keep it free, as far as in them lay, from loss of tithes, accustomed legacies, obventions, and wonted offerings for sepulture, all which belonged to the mother-church; saving the right of the chaplains, nevertheless, to the usual dues in their chapels. The Prior and convent, moreover, bound themselves to pay to the Church of St. Mary each year on the Feast of the Assumption, two wax tapers of two pounds weight each, in recognition of the privilege conceded of admitting servants dwelling within the boundaries of their house to the sacraments of the Church and the rights of sepulture.

By a further composition, undated, before the Chancellor of Sarum and the Archdeacon of Berkshire, in which the former concord was recited, Philip de Lucy and his clerks agreed with the Prior and convent and chaplains of the town that the clergy of the 'parochial chapels should receive the tithes from the traffic and fishing of their parishioners, and of pigs within the town walls, as well as from two windmills situated between the town of Southampton and the House of the Lepers, but that all other tithes should be paid to the Church of St. Mary; that the Prior and convent should have the tithe of one watermill near their court (curiam) on the north side, and the tithe of gardens existing within their boundaries at the time of making this agreement; and that in the case of persons dying on shipboard, or in houses within the town unfit for the performance of any service for the departed, the bodies might be carried into the parochial chapels, but that no mass should be celebrated there in presence of the dead, or any service for the departed performed which could not lawfully take place in the house of any parishioner.' In other respects the composition previously made held good.[2]

the principal minister (Otho, p. 28, *propriis personis*), and were, in fact, not unlike stipendiary curates of the present day. The clerks and chaplains of St. Mary's, however, could not have been simply stipendiaries. They joined with the rector, warden, or chanter, in conveying and receiving lands, and acting as a community.

[1] From an exchange (1278) between the precentor, chaplains, and clerks of St. Mary's and the convent of St. Denys we find that St. Andrew's Chapel was in the immediate vicinity of St. Mary's (Addit. 15,314, f. 76). The order for the suppression of the stewes in East Street (15th September 1413) mentions also that they were a nuisance to persons going to the churches of the Blessed Mary, the Holy Trinity, and St. Andrew (Dr. Speed, from Lib. Niger, f. 1).

[2] Addit. 15,314, fol. 77.

Growth of the Town Parishes.

In the above narration the parishes within the walls are seen to be in an incipient stage: there appear to be certain limits or understood districts assigned to the several chapels, in common, however, with those of St. Andrew and the Holy Trinity, whose districts never grew into parishes. The churches are called 'parochial chapels,' that is, chapels of ease; such chapels being created 'parochial' by the bishop, and though still dependent on the mother-church, enjoyed certain privileges, which they were said to hold *ab antiquo*, if they could prove the enjoyment of them for more than forty years. Tithes and parochial rights belonged to a chapel by custom, which could do much in transferring rights from one church to another.[1] The chaplains of the town made no question as to their relation to St. Mary's; the controversies were about the adjustment of rights and dues which had been acquired or conceded, and others which they were endeavouring to obtain, and about the amount of canonical observance to be paid to the chief or mother-church. No mention has been made of the Church of St. John, which belonged (see under that church) to the monastery of Lire, and never had any connection with St. Denys: if the custos or rector of St. Mary's and the clerks there had any quarrel with the parish priest of St. John's, it is simply not reported in the St. Denys chartulary: a century later we find him equally with the other town clergy in controversy with the rector or chanter.

Rural Chapter.

It will be observed that fidelity was to be sworn in the rural chapter at St. Mary's, Philip de Lucy happening to be rural dean, as his successors frequently, though by no means always, were. The Deanery of Southampton in the earliest record (1282) comprised—the old names will be at once identified—the churches of Stanham Abbatis (North Stoneham), Hane (Hounde), Fallely, Elinges with the chapel of Oure, Sirly, Coleworth, Baddesly, St. Michael, Southampton, St. John, St. Cross, St. Lawrence, All Saints, Leteley, Mulebroc [Du]pedene, Bottele, the church of Southampton with all the chapels of Aldinton; the chapel of Esteley, and the chapel of the Blessed Mary of Southampton.[2]

In 1411 it consisted of the following:—The Church of St. Mary, with its chapel, St. Cross, Falelegh with its chapel, Dupedene, Ellyngg and its vicarage, Nusshelyngges, Mulebroc, Baddesle, Stonham Abbatis, Houne with its chapel, St. Michael's, All Saints', Bottelegh, Shirle, St. John's, St. Lawrence's, and Chileworth.[3]

Again, in 1526:—Beaulieu Abbey, vicarage of St. Cross, vicarage of St. Michael, rectory of St. John, rectory of St. Lawrence, rectory of

[1] Lyndwood, p. 238, *capellis par.*, p. 277, *ab antiquo.*
[2] Reg. Pontiss, fol. 157.
[3] Reg. Beaufort.

All Saints', Millbrook, Eling, Dibden, Nursling, the chantry in Southampton Castle, North Stoneham, Botley, Hound, the precentory or Church of St. Mary near Southampton, Fawley, the vicarage of South Stoneham, the chantry of St. Mary.[1] It will be seen above that there were two establishments under the dedication of St. Mary, but clearly under the same authority, 'the church of Southampton' or the 'precentory,' and the 'chapel' or 'chantry of the Blessed Mary.'

The office of rural dean was one of considerable importance. He granted probate of wills, and his seal was often required, like that of the mayoralty, to strengthen documents. Thus in 1247 the seal of Nicholas, the Dean of Southampton, was placed to a grant of Cecilia la Wete, in which she puts herself under the excommunication of the Dean throughout his Deanery, if she at any time trouble the parties to whom she and her husband have just sold certain lands.[2]

**Chanter.** The name of *chanter*, applied to the custos or rector, first occurs in an agreement made on St. Agnes's Day, January 21, 1251, between Prior Rueland and Roger the chanter, about a certain roadway through land belonging to the chanter and clerks, called Munkeslonde, which the convent claimed as belonging to their grange of Northam (written also Norham); and also about the aqueduct of the said clerks, which the latter affirmed to lie in the king's highway, but which the convent asserted to be in their land of Kingsland.[3]

A few years later (December 17, 1258) we read of the warden, chaplains, and clerks of St. Mary's; as, for instance, in a composition about tithes from the mills of Aldyngton and the fishery belonging to the same, settled before Master Geoffrey de Feryng, precentor of Chichester, official of Ethelmar, elect of Winchester, between Prior Nicholas and the convent, and Roger the warden, chaplains, and clerks of St. Mary's.[4]

**Ordinations.** Bishop Woodlock in the first year of his episcopate (1305) held an ordination at Southampton on July 14; it is not further stated where; and on Saturday, June 8, 1308, held one in the chapel of St. Mary's, Southampton.

**Revenues.** In the taxation of Pope Nicholas (1291) the revenue[5] of the Church

---

[1] Reg. Fox., quinta, towards end.

[2] See Madox, Form., pp. 85, 426. Other documents of a similar kind exist among the Corporation papers. The will of John Horn, burgess, dated in 1279, in which he leaves certain tenements to the Prior and Convent of St. Denys, after the death of Rosie his wife was proved in the same year before G. the Dean of Southampton. Addit. 15,314, fol. 58.

[3] Addit. 15,314, f. 76 b.

[4] Addit. 15,314, f. 75 b.

[5] It seems to have stood at about the same amount, or something less, in 1340, two years after the 'invasion' of Southampton (Inquis. Nonarum, p. 125).

of St. Mary with its chapel was returned at £53, 6s. 8d., paying its tenth of £5, 6s. 8d.

Further disputes.

In the time of Bishop Stratford trouble again broke out between the chaplains or rectors in the town and the precentor or warden of St. Mary's;[1] and on May 8, 1331, a mandate issued from the Bishop to Wybert, his official, reciting that the churches or chapels of the town had from ancient time been subject to the Church of St. Mary, and enjoining canonical obedience to the precentor or warden of St. Mary's on the rectors of the churches or chapels of All Saints, St. Cross, St. Michael, St. Lawrence, Holy Trinity, and St. John, and that they should in no way diminish the rights and liberties of that church, on pain of being in contempt. This mandate was but partially successful; and on June 13th a citation was issued against the 'rectors,' Richard of St. Cross, John of St. Michael's, and Henry of St. John's, for disobedience and contempt. Upon this the rectors of St. John's and St. Michael's appealed to the Court of Canterbury, obtaining an inhibition to the Bishop pending their appeals. These, however, were dismissed, April 23, 1332, and the authority of the precentor was confirmed.[2]

Soon after the dismissal of his appeal the rector of St. Michael's exchanged into the diocese of Chichester, and on the institution of his successor, Robert de Bourne, June 29, 1332, the following oath of canonical obedience was taken. Placing his right hand on his breast and looking on the Holy Gospels, he swore[3] 'that he would in no sense diminish ought from the rights, liberties, or customs of the parochial church of the Blessed Mary of Southampton, but that he would be obedient and faithful to the rector or precentor for the time being, as far as he was bound by right, custom, or other special fact.'[4]

Visitation.

On Sunday, November 20, 1334, Bishop Orlton celebrated at St. Mary's, and apparently preached one of his political sermons, his text being 'a king shall reign and prosper, and shall execute judgment and justice on the earth;' and on the following Thursday he held here a visitation of the clergy and people of the Deanery, when he finished his subject, taking for his theme the latter part of the same text.[5]

Disputes revived.

The old controversy between the precentor and the clergy of the

[1] Reg. Stratford, ff. 55, 57, 65.

[2] As also (November 13, 1332) his right to greater and lesser tithes, both within and without the town, against Hugo Sampson and others (Ibid., 75 b, &c.)

[3] This was in pursuance of Archbishop Winchelsey's Constitutions (1305), canon 5, which prescribe such an oath to be taken by stipendiary chaplains before admission to officiate in churches or parochial chapels, if so required. They were not directed necessarily to swear on the Gospels, but on any sacred thing, and touching was not ordered, so that the oath was not called corporal (Lyndwood, p. 110, *inspectis*). See also below for Dr. Alyn's statement.

[4] Reg. Stratford, ff. 129, 129 b.

[5] Reg. Orlton, i. f. 11.

town parishes was revived in the time of William of Wykeham, who, at the instance of Richard de Coleshull, the precentor, issued his commission (September 23, 1370) to John de Wormenhall, official, and John de Ware, sequestrator in the Archdeaconry, to inquire into and give judgment on the matter against the rectors for refusing the oath of canonical obedience to the precentor and withholding his dues.[1] The issue does not appear.

Dr. Alyn and Prior May.

A few particulars as to the relationship of the churches to the precentor may be gathered from a letter of Dr. Alyn, chanter, to Prior May, of St. Denys, written about 1528. It is as follows:—

'The copy of a letter of recognition and knowledge of Dr. Alyn, then being chanter, magister prerogativus, and visitor of all England under my Lord Cardinal and Legate, of wrong suits made against Walter May, then being Prior, for the oblations of our Lady of Grace.

'Brother Prior, I heartily recommend me unto you, so thanking you for my good cheer that ye made me at my Lord Legate's visitation. Sir, according to your letter, I have received 30s. to be delivered unto Dr. Stubbs in part of payment for your procurations of the said visitation; that acquittance whereof the Vicar of Stoneham shall bring unto you. To that ye wrote in the said letter concerning the citation out of my Lord of Canterbury's Audience, whereby ye were cited to appear before Dr. Cockes upon my pretense to have such oblations as were daily made within the Trinity and St. Andrew's chapels, set and being within my parish of St. Mary's without Southampton, Father Prior, Dr. Stokesley informed me of the premises, unto whom, in the beginning, I gave not a little credence, and the rather that he was my predecessor there. But in good faith after I had found in the Black Book of the Chantership two things most notable here ensuing, I left the suit, and had no more courage (refragante conscientiâ) to follow the same. One was a composition real, whereby it well appeared that the said two chapels stood within my parish in like manner as the other four[2] that stand within the walls; of the which all six I should not have oblations, nor yet prime tithes, but all other manner tithes except tithe fish and pigs. The other was a special composition concerning the said two chapels, in the which it is substantially provided for pilgrims that sometime, and then commonly, lay there, that the Prior of St. Denys' chaplains should not go to mass while the parishioners of St. Mary's were at mattins, and thereupon the said chaplains should make manual obedience unto the chanter for the time being without any corporal oath. Now, sir, the premises circumspectly considered, your wisdom shall perceive, first, what made me so fervent in the right of my church, and afterward why I was so cold.'[3]

The arrangement about tithes referred to by Dr. Alyn, and of which no other evidence exists, must have made a fundamental change in the relation of the other churches to St. Mary's.

Ecclesiastical position of Southampton.

The general result from the foregoing notices appears to be that the whole district of Southampton was originally one parish, the centre of which was St. Mary's; that in the Middle Ages the town 'parishes,'

[1] Reg. Wykeham, ii. f. 38* b.

[2] It is not clear why he speaks of only *four*.

[3] Addit. 15,314, f. 78 b.

with their 'rectors' or chaplains or vicars, were in an incomplete condition: they were then acquiring rights, and have become parishes by ancient prescription, like numberless parishes in our land.

The foundation at St. Mary's.

With regard to St. Mary's as a religious establishment, we have seen the 'warden and clerks,' 'the precentor or chanter or warden, chaplains, and clerks,' of St. Mary's acting as a corporate body, and in 1460 the precentor and fellows [1] join in granting a pension to the late precentor for themselves and successors. When and how did the precentory come to an end? We have as little information as of its origin. It was evidently not in existence in Leland's time (see below), and a letter written to the customer of Southampton [2] in September 1529 speaks of the 'chantry' as having been dissolved many years before Dr. Alyn's time, that is, before 1527. No further notice in point has been observed: the registers of the diocese are silent, those of St. Mary's are burnt. It is certain, however, that a considerable establishment existed at St. Mary's as late as 1543 (see under 'Chantries'). The origin of the 'chantry' seems to have been forgotten at this time. When reporting on the Chantry-house in 1547, the Commissioners of Edward VI. stated that they could not discover by whose devotion the 'chantry' had been founded, nor what lands and tenements belonged to it; all that they were able to report was that the house, then belonging to Dr. Capon, had always been called the 'Chantry-house,' which, together with lands 'commonly called the Chantry lands,' was let for £13, 6s. 8d. They make a memorandum that neither Dr. Capon, or his farmer, Crocker, appeared, so that their survey was less accurately made.[3]

The 'chantry' just spoken of was probably a different foundation from the old precentory (see p. 333), though both may have been always filled by the parish priest, who was thus variously called warden, precentor, or chanter, as in other respects he was styled rector. In the Valor Ecclesiasticus of 1536 the precentory of St. Mary, Dr. Capon, precentor, was valued in oblations, tithes, and other casualties at £44, 13s. 4d., from which procurations and other deductions allowed for to the amount of £7, 8s. 1d., a clear value of £37, 5s. 3d. remained, paying its tenth of £3, 14s. 6½d.

Traditionary account and fabric.

Leland (1546) has the following account of St. Mary's, which, dealing with its fabric no less than with its position as the mother-church,

[1] Omnibus, &c., W. Darsset, precentor et socii ecclesiæ B. Mariæ de Sutht. salutem. Noveritis nos unanimi assensu et voluntate dedisse, concessisse, &c., de nobis et successoribus nostris (Reg. Waynflete, i. 105 b.)

[2] Cal. State Papers, September 10, 1529.

[3] Chantry Certificates, Roll 52, No. 54.

may serve as the point of departure for a few paragraphs on the several structures which have occupied the present site:—

'There is a chapel of St. Nicholas, a poor and small thing, yet standing at the east end of St. Marychurch in the great cemetery, where, constant fame is, the old parish church of Old Hampton stood. One told me there that the littleness of this church was the cause of the erection of the great church of Our Lady there now standing by this occasion: One Matilda, queen of England, asked what it meant that a great number of people walked about the church of St. Nicholas? and one answered, It is for lack of room in the church. Then she *ex voto* promised to make there a new; and this was the original St. Marychurch. This Queen Matilda, or some other good persons following, had thought to have made this a collegiate church, but this purpose succeeded not fully. Yet nevertheless St. Marychurch at this day, in token of the ancientness of Old Hampton, is mother-church to all the churches in New Hampton. And in testimony of this the common sepulture of New Hampton is in the cemetery of St. Marychurch. And there be many fair tombs of marble of merchants of New Hampton buried in the Church of St. Mary, as in their mother and principal church.'[1]

According to this account, there was a more ancient parish church somewhat to the east of the then existing 'great church of Our Lady,' the site of which was covered by the chapel of St. Nicholas, 'a poor and small thing,' or that chapel was itself identical with what had been the old parish church. The existing and more important building was due to the piety of 'Molde, the good queen'—Matilda, the wife of Henry I.—for doubtless it was she whom the story pointed out, her countless works of devotion and charity having never been lost from the popular mind. She died May 1, 1118; so that, if there is anything in the tradition, the first rebuilding of St. Mary's on a larger scale of which we have any indication must have taken place in the early part of the twelfth century, and according to the same account the church existing in the first half of the sixteenth century was substantially the fabric of Queen Matilda.

Destruction of the Old Church.

Leland, who presented his report (above detailed) to Henry VIII. in 1546, must have seen nearly the last of 'the great church of Our Lady;' a few years later it was a ruin. From the Court Leet Book of 1550 we get the following dismal notice, suggesting that some dark, unhappy fate had befallen the great church, since its precincts were to be used as a quarry for the public roads:—Ordered that 'so much of the rubbish of St. Mary's Church' should be carted away as would 'serve to make the highway from Bargate and all East Street down to the turning to the chantry.'[2] We have to account for this desolation. The passion-

[1] Itinerary, iii. 105.

[2] In the above year (1550) the 'fermer of the chantry' was presented for not making a bridge between his marsh and Trinity Chapel, and for having removed another bridge leading into his marsh, which he was commanded 'to make again' (Court Leet Book).

less entries of the town records do not help us; the episcopal register is equally silent as to the fabric. However, Speed (1596), the historian, has the following account:—'In the east without the walls a goodly church sometime stood, called Saint Mary's, which was pulled down for that it gave the French direction of course, who with fire had greatly endangered the town; instead thereof is now newly erected a *small* and *unfinished* chapel.'[1] That is to say, the people of Southampton had pulled down their great church to remove from French cruisers in future the direction of a well-known and lofty spire; and this destruction it is not unlikely was perpetrated in 1549 or 1550. In the former of these years the French,[2] after annoying the English coast, had invaded Guernsey and Jersey, though the islanders had given a good account of their foes. It may have been under some local panic, or indeed under a hasty descent of the enemy about this period, that the church was pulled down. Such then was the end of the 'great church of Our Lady,' and it was many years before much was done by way of reparation.

Leases of Rectory.

It had been long the custom for the rectors or precentors to lease out the tithes. On Dr. Capon coming to the benefice in 1529, we find him in controversy with the lessee and with the 'vicar' who was holding the chantorship, begging Cromwell, whose work he had been doing about Ipswich in conjunction with Brabason, that the priest might be sued for the money 'due to us.'[3]

Chancel remaining for divine service.

In 1579, Walter Lambert[4] being the lessee of the rectory and exercising its patronage,[5] a contribution was made towards 'the building of the Church of St. Mary's,' which no doubt gives the history of the 'small and unfinished chapel' spoken of above. Towards this building or rebuilding the mayor paid over to Walter Lambert £44, 8s., and but £24, 9s. 4d. appears to have been collected otherwise,[6]

[1] Theatre of Great Britain (ed. 1650, p. 13), and see below under 'Rectors.'

[2] In 1537 the French had cut out a Flemish ship from Southampton (Froude, iii. 65). In 1545 the French fleet stood before the mouth of Portsmouth harbour, and landed troops on the Isle of Wight at St. Helen's Point. A few days after they invaded the coast of Sussex, landing at Newhaven (Speed, Stow). In this year they also burnt Lymington.

[3] Cal. State Papers, May 7, 15, September 10, 1529.

[4] Third son of Richard Lambert, of an ancient French family which came into England with the Conqueror. The above Walter married (1) Rose, daughter of Sir Oliver Wallop, ancestor of the Earl of Portsmouth, by whom he had Sir Oliver, his heir; (2) Elizabeth, daughter of Sir George Paulet, brother of William, Marquis of Winchester. Of this Elizabeth, when widow, see shortly below in text.

[5] As farmer of the precentory, he granted the presentation to South Stoneham for one turn to James Jefferies, gent., who nominated his relative William Jefferies, May 8, 1582 (Reg. Watson).

[6] Boke of Remembrances, f. 135.

though, of course, there may have been gatherings of which the town books take no account. It is not, however, likely that any extensive work was carried out. This chapel or restored chancel was referred to in the consecration petition of Jesus Chapel (1620), which states that the Church of St. Mary was in ruins, the chancel alone, no doubt this new or rebuilt work, remaining for divine service.[1]

On the death of Walter Lambert his widow Elizabeth [2] received her jointure from the tithes, Sir Oliver,[3] his son, holding the lease. In 1611 (July 19) Sir Oliver sent to the Corporation to inquire if they had in their hands any leases or conveyances granted by the 'chanter, chaplains, and clerks of the church or college of St. Mary's, near Southampton, sealed with their common seal with the picture of our Lady;' a search was ordered for the following Wednesday, but no issue is recorded. Leases of rectory.

After the death of Sir Oliver in 1618, as Baron Cavan, the lease was held at one period, certainly in 1630, by Sir Gerard Fleetwood, probably under Charles Lord Lambert. Five years later we have the following account of St. Mary's from the writer before quoted (p. 65): 'Without the walls [of the town] eastward is a chapel which formerly was their chief church, which, although it hath lost her precedent dignity, yet still it retains a pretty annual revenue, which is no less than £600 per annum,[4] the which a lord (the Lord Lambert) got by lease and enjoyed for some time, and now a knight (Sir Garrett Fleetwood) holds the same for years. A fair house is built thereunto with the ruins of that fair church, wherein the inhabitants (as report goes) cannot rest quiet a-nights; the razing down of churches to rear up mansions with that stuff (say they) is not right; hereupon I heard many pretty odd tales, which I have neither time nor list to insert.'

In the time of the Long Parliament further changes took place. From an order of the Committee for Plundered Ministers, bearing date September 11, 1646, we gather that the tithes and profits of the impropriate rectory or chantry had been sequestrated from the Lord Lambert as a delinquent, and had, by order of July 27 that year, St. Mary's under Long Parliament.

[1] Juxta Southamptoniensem villam ecclesia B. Mariæ collapsa cernitur, solis cancellis ad sacros ritus superstitibus.

[2] '1606, 25th Dec.—Receaved by me Eliz. Lambert, woodow, at the hands of Thomas Stockwell, servante to S^r Olyver Lambert, the some of £20, for my quarter annuitie, due to me out of the parsonage of S. Maries, near Southampton, on the feast of Christmas.'

[3] Knighted at Cadiz by the Earl of Essex; sworn of the Privy Council and created Baron Cavan, February 1617; died July 9, 1618. He married Hester, daughter of Sir William Fleetwood, Knight, of Carrington, co. Beds, and was succeeded by his eldest son, Charles, who was advanced to the dignity of Viscount Kilcoursie and Earl of Cavan, April, 15, 1647. He died in 1660.

[4] Probably an exaggeration (see below).

been committed to the mayor and aldermen on their petition,[1] for distribution among the ministers of the town, whose maintenance was very inadequate. In consequence of this, by desire of the mayor and aldermen, the sum of £40 per annum was appropriated 'to the chapel belonging to the Church of St. Mary, commonly called Jesus Chapel,' the maintenance for which was but £12 per annum, and the remaining profits of the chantry at that time, £250 per annum, were ordered to be distributed in equal portions between the ministers of Holy Rood, St. Michael's, St. John's, St. Lawrence's, All Saints', and St. Mary's. In the case of the chantry rents, amounting hereafter to a larger sum than would give £50 per annum to each church and £40 to the chapel, it was further ordered that the surplus should be devoted to the support of the Thursday lecture at Holy Rood. The Corporation were authorised to let and dispose of the tithes, glebe land, and other profits of the rectory, from time to time to the best advantage, to appoint collectors, and to apply the emoluments as above directed.[2]

In the following year (1647) we find the town entering into an arrangement about the chantry and the chantry-house with Mr. Rought, parson of St. Mary's, and a Mr. Godfrey.[3]

At this time, also, it appears that the Lord Lambert had brought, or was threatening to bring, an action against the town in reference to the chantry; and on May 5, 1648, it was agreed between the Corporation and Mr. Rought 'that the charges of all suits whatsoever in relation to the chantry or parsonage of St. Mary's, now brought in question by the Lord Lambert, should be paid and borne out of the benefice.' It was further agreed, at the same time, that the chantry revenues should be divided into three parts, two of which should remain with the Corporation for the use of the other parishes and of Jesus Chapel, which was to receive its £40, and the remaining third was to belong to Mr. Rought. The above agreement was to continue in force for five years, bearing date from the preceding Michaelmas Day (1647).[4]

On the 24th October 1648, Mr. Rought granted a lease of the chantry tithes to the town for the term of four years, dating from the Feast of St. Michael last past (1648). And on the same day a lease was regranted from the town to Mr. Godfrey of the tithes of the chantry without the town for the same period, while a lease of the tithes within the town was regranted to Mr. Baber and the widow

[1] See also Journal, 17th July 1646.

[2] Order of Committee for Plundered Ministers, September 11, 1646 (Corporation Papers). See further under 'Holy Rood.'

[3] Journal under November 1, December 15.

[4] Agreement between the Corporation and Mr. Rought about the Chantry, May 5, 1648 (Corporation Papers).

Feverell for a like term. The annual rent of these latter tithes was £118, 1s. 6d.[1]

In the same year (1648) the town, acting under the direction of the Committee for Plundered Ministers, ordered the payment on October 30 of certain ministers out of the chantry funds, namely, to Mr. Lamplugh[2] of Holy Rood, Mr. Toms of St. Michael's, and Mr. Robinson of St. Lawrence's, £33, 6s. 8d. each, or £100 in all; the mayor was also directed to receive out of the 'chantry money' £20 towards the payment of certain ministers who had officiated at All Saints' up to the preceding Michaelmas. In an entry of January 2, 1648–49, reference is made to former orders of the Corporation 'for the disposition of the chantry money,' in accordance with which the payment of £10 apiece had been made to the following clergy or ministers for a quarter of the year ending at Christmas past, viz., to Mr. Toms for St. Michael's, Mr. Lamplugh for Holy Rood, Mr. Robinson for St. Lawrence's, Mr. Clifford for All Saints', Mr. Turner for Jesus Chapel. Under Committee for Plundered Ministers.

While the town held the lease, the 'chapel or church of St. Mary's' was found to be 'much in decay.' They therefore committed it to the care of their under-tenant, Mr. Baber, and engaged to allow him for the repairs. The following entry gives a deplorable account of its state:— Further decay of fabric.

> 'St. Maries Chappell. It is this day ordered that the chappell or church of St. Maries, w^ch^ is much in decay, shalbe repayred forthw^th^, and Mr. Baber is desired to get it done, and it is now promised that soe much as he shall dysburse shalbe repayed or abated unto him out of his rent for St. Maries at the next quarter, provided always that he does not disburse above fourty shillings.'[3]

The town's lease having expired,[4] the chantry revenues were in Mr. Rought's hands in January 1652–53, but charged with the payment of £100 a year, by the authority of the before-mentioned committee and with his own consent, 'for the godly ministers of the town,' an engagement which he declined to fulfil till bound to it afresh by Order of Council, dated October 26, 1653 (see under 'Holy Rood'). After the Restoration, in October 1661, releases passed between Mr. Rought and the Corporation concerning the chantry, and in April 1663 an action of ejectment from the rectory of St. Mary's was depending between Thomas Hinton, plaintiff, the lessee of Dr. Clutterbuck, Rought's successor in September 1662, and William Wakefield, St. Mary's after Restoration.

1 Journal, 27th October 1648.

2 Thomas Lamplugh lent himself with equal zeal to the League and Covenant, to Charles II., James II., and afterwards to William III. He was of a good Yorkshire family. See under 'Holy Rood;' see also 'Notes and Queries,' 2d series, vol. iii., pp. 190, 258.

3 Journal, 30th December 1650.

4 It had been granted for four years from Michaelmas 1648.

defendant. The case was ordered to be heard in London, the burgesses on the jury having leave to serve there.[1] It appears that the new rector was ultimately successful in his suit.

Church rebuilt by Dr. Brideoake.

In spite of the vigour of Dr. Clutterbuck, the fabric remained in a wretched condition till the time of Archdeacon Brideoake, who in 1711 succeeded in rebuilding the church, the Corporation granting £40, and several other notable subscriptions being raised. The renewed church consisted of a nave fitted to the old chapel or chancel mentioned above, at the cost of about £920; and in 1723 he rebuilt the chancel for about £400. A brass tablet,[2] the memorial of the Archdeacon's work, is preserved in the vestry of the present church. According to it, the received tradition was that the French themselves had destroyed the church, and probably this was supposed to have taken place in the time of Edward III., in whose reign, as we know, part of the town had been burnt by foreigners — a circumstance never forgotten. Leland, however, whose works were not easily accessible in the time of Brideoake, knew nothing of this tradition in regard to St. Mary's, and, on the contrary, has described 'the great church of Our Lady' as existing when he wrote.

The Archdeacon's fabric seems to have been strong and honestly built; that it went beyond this, the date of its erection forbids us to suppose. It met with a panegyrist in Dr. Hoadley, Brideoake's successor, who in his will (see below) in 1763 speaks of it as built 'in a substantial, yet in a very expensive manner, and on a much larger scale than the use of that parish alone required.' As to the population at this time, a copy from the rate-book for St. Mary's parish of the year 1779 gives the total number of rateable houses at fifty-seven.[3] The number of inhabitants was very small, the town of Southampton being substantially within the walls.[4]

---

[1] Journal, April 3, 1663.

[2] 'Ecclesiam Beatæ Mariæ, cujus fundamenta hostili Gallorum manu olim eversa inanis proavorum reposuit labor, serva nepotum pietas feliciter restituit. A. X$^{i.}$ 1711. Idem rector cancellos hosce quadringentis circiter libris operi impensis in Dei honorem de novo struxit. A. X$^{t.}$, 1723.'

[3] The number of houses was as follows:—

| | | | | | |
|---|---|---|---|---|---|
| Bevis Mount | 1 | Love Lane | 7 | Orchard Lane | 4 |
| Northam Farm | 1 | Opposite Churchyard | 2 | Golden Grove | 2 |
| Northam | 3 | Causeway | 2 | Irwin's Garden Three-Field Lane | 1 |
| Chapel | 2 | Bag Row | 23 | | |
| Cross House | 2 | Kingsland | 7 | | |
| | | | | Total, | 57 |

The name of the occupiers are of course given.

[4] There was, it is to be remembered, a somewhat extensive suburb on the north, Above Bar, in the parish of All Saints'.

Archdeacon Brideoake's church remained as he left it till the year 1833. Under the pressure of a growing population it was completely transformed in the incumbency of Francis North, Earl of Guildford. The walls of the nave were pulled down, and the roof supported by nondescript columns of brickwork, wood, and stucco; huge aisles were thrown out, in which the seats, rising gradually towards the back, faced into the nave north and south, and over all heavy but capacious galleries were added. A plain wall with two ranges of windows of the meanest carpenter's Gothic enclosed and added materially to all this ugliness, affording some elevations hardly to be matched in the county. It was, however, considered a masterpiece of arrangement in its day. The Corporation granted £50 towards it, and the Bishop (Sumner) opened it in state on Friday, July 12, 1833. Church transformed in 1833.

During the incumbency of Archdeacon Wigram, afterwards Bishop of Rochester, an east window of stained glass was presented to the church in memory of Admiral Ayscough, and a vestry was added on the south side of the chancel.

Upon the appointment of the present rector, on the death of the Rev. Mark Cooper, on February 28, 1871, such further improvements as seemed possible to the existing fabric were effected at once, and a handsome reredos by Earp was placed beneath the Ayscough window. Meanwhile the badly constructed fabric of 1833 was beginning to show signs of dilapidation; and by desire of the Bishop the advice was sought of the eminent architect, the late Mr. G. E. Street, who condemned the building, as not only incapable of improvement, but almost ruinous in condition.

The sudden death of Bishop Wilberforce on July 19, 1873, gave a shock to the diocese and to the whole Church, but the event, which might have seemed so likely to retard the rebuilding of St. Mary's, only strengthened the determination of the rector to carry out what had been often an expressed desire of the late Bishop. The rebuilding of St. Mary's.

There was no intention at first of making the church a public memorial to Bishop Wilberforce, but, in point of fact, most of the offerings made for the proposed new church were distinctly associated by their donors with his name, and it seemed desirable ultimately to yield to the wishes of very many, and make the new church a distinct memorial to the Bishop. With this view his Royal Highness the Prince of Wales consented to lay the first stone, and appointed Monday, 12th August 1878, for the ceremony. On that day the Prince and Princess, with their two sons, Prince Albert Victor and Prince George, were received at the pierhead by the mayor (A. H. M'Calmont, Esq.) and Corporation, the members for the borough (Sir F. Perkins and Alfred Giles, Esq.), and others. An address suitable to the occasion was read by the town-clerk (R. S. Pearce, Esq.), to which his Royal Highness made the following reply:—

'The Princess of Wales unites with me in thanking you for your address and hearty welcome to Southampton. It is a source of satisfaction to us to find that the pleasing duty which I am about to undertake to-day in memory of my lamented and valued friend, the late Bishop Wilberforce, has been the means of enabling us to visit your important and thriving town. Our warm acknowledgments are due to you for the kind and flattering terms in which you have alluded to us; and let me assure you that the Princess of Wales and I are united in an earnest desire to promote any object tending to advance the happiness and prosperity of the community.'

Foundation-stone laid.

On arriving at the church, the royal party was received by the Bishop of Winchester, the archdeacon, the rector, and the churchwardens, and having been conducted to the dais prepared in what would afterwards be the north chancel aisle, the special service for the occasion was performed by the Bishop and the rector, the Prince at the appointed place laying the memorial stone, and saying, 'In the name of the Father, and of the Son, and of the Holy Ghost, I place this dedication stone in memory of Samuel Wilberforce, Bishop of Winchester.' This stone, in one of the pillars of the north chancel aisle, bears an inscription on a brass plate recording the fact.

After the ceremony their Royal Highnesses honoured the rector with their presence at the 'Deanery,' and embarked again for Osborne precisely at six o'clock.

The portion of the new church which it was proposed to erect at this time was the chancel, with its aisles and vestries, the transepts, and one bay of the nave, with its aisles, the new portion being joined to the main body of the old building till the whole design could be completed. At the time of laying the memorial stone, the surrounding walls were already some 20 feet high, and by Thursday, the 21st of June 1879, the church was ready for consecration. The ceremony, which was attended in state by the mayor (J. B. Thomas, Esq.) and Corporation, was performed by the Bishop of the diocese, who was accompanied by the Archbishop of Canterbury (Dr. Tait), the preacher on the occasion. His Grace took for his text Rev. iv. 1, and made much reference to the late lamented prelate with whose memory the church was to be connected. The sermon in the evening was preached from St. John xviii. 37 by the Archbishop of York, who had also undertaken the duty of preaching in consequence of the memorial character of the work.

The church is of noble design and proportions as far as now carried out,[1] and fully maintains the reputation of its late lamented architect, Mr. Street.

[1] The whole design is now (June 1883) to be carried out and completed by the middle of next year.

No foundations of any importance or suggestiveness were discovered in the above works. This may partly be accounted for by the fact before related, that at one period the ruins of the church and chantry buildings were used as a quarry.

Among ancient bequests to St. Mary's occur those of Agnes le Horder,[1] by will, January 1348–49; William of Wykeham,[2] who gave £20 to John Keton, the precentor, and a pair of vestments and chalice to the church, by will, July 24, 1403; John Renawd,[3] October 27, 1422. Bequests and Charities.

The bequests and charities of more recent times are as follows:—Mill's and Fifield's gifts, see under 'Town Charities;' for Smith's gift and Hill's bequest see under 'Holy Rood.'

Dr. Hoadley, rector of St. Mary's, by his will subsequent to 1763,—

Reciting that he had observed that the parish church was built, though in a substantial, yet in a very expensive manner, and on a much larger scale than the needs of the parish required, and that the inhabitants were chiefly poor persons, so that in process of time the repair of the church was likely to become a heavy burden to them, gave to the succeeding rector and his successors for ever, £100 on trust, that it should be laid out in the public funds at the discretion of the said rector, and never on any account be broken in upon, but that the dividends only should be reserved and applied for the uses of the trust, and that such dividends should also be laid out in the funds for the increase of the principal, and that no part of it should be expended until it should amount to the full sum of £50, the said church being, at the time of his making his will, in good repair. And he recommended that his money should not be laid out in trifling repairs, but reserved for such as were more material, such as roofing, timber, main walls, iron work, &c., at the discretion of the rector for the time being. And he hoped that with a little care his legacy might be a great ease to the parish, and in time perhaps sufficient to answer the whole expense of the repairs of the church. Hoadley's gift.

Mrs. Mary Baker, widow, late of Southampton, who died February 16, 1872, by her will, proved March 12 the same year, bequeathed the sum of £2000 consols to the Southampton poor of the parish of St. Mary, and a like sum of £2000 consols to the poor of the parish of Millbrook; the distribution of the interest in the respective parishes is made every Christmas to poor but industrious persons above the age of sixty years. The first intention of the donor had been to found almshouses. Baker's gift.

The ancient books of the church have unhappily been destroyed in the disastrous fires which have twice wrecked the chantry or rectory- Registers.

---

1 Addit. MS., 15,314, fol. 85 b.

2 Lego Ecclesiæ Beatæ Mariæ Southampton unum par vestimentorum cum calice (Will of William of Wykeham, in Lowth's Life, pp. 392, 394). He also left twenty marks towards the repairs of the Priory Church of St. Denys.

3 See under 'Holy Rood.'

house. The entries in the register book prior to 1706 are made from notes taken by the clerks and churchwardens.

The Deanery.

The rectory-house of St. Mary's, now called the Deanery, stands in its ample grounds on the site of the two former houses, both destroyed by fire, one in 1706, its successor in 1801. It occupies part of the site of the old chantry buildings. No plan of the chantry is known to exist beyond that in Speed's (1596) map, which shows the principal entrance by an ample gatehouse in Marsh Lane, admitting between double walls to another building through which was the entrance into a walled quadrangle, opposite being the main buildings of the house, forming three sides of a square, beyond and admitting into which was another entrance where are now the Deanery gates; at the side was a small building like a lodge, a fragment of which remains. The name 'Deanery' applied to the rectory-house of St. Mary's is of no antiquity; and for want of a better reason the popular one may serve, which attributes it to the fact of a Dean (Ogle) having lived there. The term being modern, can have no connection with the rural deanery of the Middle Ages, though the rural dean may not unfrequently have resided at the chantry (see above on 'Rural Deans').

The revenues of St. Mary's are derived from the rectory of South Stoneham,[1] commuted in 1845 at £1430, and from the valuable rectorial property of St. Mary's in the town and neighbourhood.

Endowments from Rectory.

For several years now—since the retirement of the Earl of Guildford in 1850—under the arrangement of the successive Bishops of the diocese, and with the concurrence of the rectors, the revenues of St. Mary's have been much employed in the endowment of new districts in St. Mary's and within the rectory of South Stoneham.

The following are the dates of the nine churches within its limits:—

Jesus Chapel, St. Mary Extra, 1620, now (1881) endowed from the rectory on its patronage being made over to the rectors.

Holy Trinity, Southampton, 1829.

St. Luke, 1853.

Christ Church, Northam, 1856.

St. James, Bernard Street, 1858.

St. Mark, Woolston, 1863.

Holy Trinity, Weston, not endowed from the rectory; built at the cost of Rev. W. P. Hulton, 1865.

St. Mary, Sholing, 1866.

St. Matthew, St. Mary's Road, 1870.

The churches and districts within South Stoneham are:—

St. James, West End, 1838.

[1] The vicarage of South Stoneham was commuted at £500 a year.

Christ Church, Portswood, 1847.

Holy Saviour, Bittern, 1853.

St. Denys, Portswood, 1868.

The Resurrection, Eastleigh, 1868.

A notice of such of these churches as are within the limits of the town and county of the town will follow.

The rectory of St. Mary's is in the patronage of the Bishops of Winchester.

*Rectors or Precentors of St. Mary's.*

Richerius, in 1086 (Domesday).

Stephen of Reims, c. 1200 (Addit. 15,314, f. 43).

Philip de Lucy, precentor in 1225 (ibid., ff. 76, 77, &c.)

Nicholas,[1] Dean of Southampton in 1247 (see Madox, Form., p. 85).

Roger, precentor in 1251 (Addit. 15,314, f. 76 b); 1258 (f. 75 b).

Robert, in 1278 (f. 76).

G.,[1] Dean of Southampton in 1279 (f. 58).

Simon de Farham, admitted to church or chantry of St. Mary's with chapel adjacent on collation of Bishop, September 25, 1304.[2]

Galfrid de Hotham, S.T.P., collated December 1, 1312.

Thomas de Becford, priest, collated December 23, 1330.

Thomas de Crosse, priest, custody of the precentory committed to him in commendam, to hold during the vacancy and the Bishop's pleasure, February 18, 1346–47.

John Payn, priest, receives the church or precentory of the Blessed Mary in commendam, September 23, 1348, letters for his induction being issued to Master John de Ware, sequestrator, and Dean of Southampton; on January 10, 1348–49 he was collated to the rectory or precentory, letters for induction being issued as before;[3] steward of St. Cross Hospital, Winchester, in 1337; collated to South Waltham, June 20, 1346, which he resigned for this precentorship in 1349; collated to Church of Blessed Mary of the Valleys, Winchester, May 26, 1361, which he immediately exchanged for rectory of Radipole, county Dorset[4] (see next entry).

John de Bleby, rector of the church of Meonstoke, on exchange with Payn, concerning which there was a contention, made precentor April 17, 1358.

Walter de Sevenhampton, priest, on resignation of John de Bleby, collated April 30, 1358;[5] steward of St. Cross Hospital in 1352–53.[4]

Robert de Wychford, clerk, collated June 17, 1359, on death of John Payn (sic), late rector or precentor.

John de Staunton, rector of the church of Houghton, on exchange with last, collated July 2, 1359.

Thomas de Ocle . . .

Richard Coleshull, collated January 24, 1368–69, exchanging with last the rectory of the church of Winterbourne, Wigorn; his will was proved

[1] Placed doubtfully among the rectors.

[2] This and the following entries, as far as regards St. Mary's, are from the registers of the various Bishops.

[3] Reg. Edyngton, prima, ff. 36 b, 42 b.

[4] History of Parish of Wyke, by Mr. F. J. Baigent (1865), p. 31.

[5] Reg. Edyngton, prima, f. 95.

September 18, 1389; he desired to be buried in the chancel before the white image of the Blessed Virgin.

John Keton, collated November 9, 1389.

Peter de Allcobasse . . . afterwards (1422) canon of Windsor.

John Ikelyngton, collated December 15, 1411, exchanging with last the rectory of the church of St. Columba Major, Exon; seems to have been a prebendary of York; installed November 18, 1396; Archdeacon of Wells, 1398.

William Prentyse, S.T.P., precentor in May 1445 (deed of William Prentyse, precentor, &c., to Walter Fetplace, mayor, and William Blake, vicar of St. Cross, May 8, 23 Hen. VI.)

William Whiteling . . . prebendary of Southwell in 1443; his will was dated June 19, 1453, proved June (July?) 12th same year; he left a breviary to St. Mary's, also a missal and five marks.

John Holand, Sac. Paginæ Prof., collated June 20, 1453, on death of Whiteling; seems to have been prebendary of Lincoln in 1451; a pension of twenty marks a year from the fruits of the precentory was assigned him, after his resignation through infirmity, by the 'precentor and fellows,' November 24, 1460, in recognition of his services and costs on repairs to the precentory.

William Darsset, LL.D., collated November 12, 1460, by papal letters of dispensation to hold three incompatible benefices, on resignation of Holand by his proctor Thomas Gyan; letters to induct William or his proctor Thomas Darsset (see 'Vicars of St. Michael's') directed to John Cliffe, perpetual vicar of St. Cross; seems to have been prebendary of Hereford in 1462.

John Waynflete, LL.B., collated February 14, 1470–71, on death of last; may have been prebendary of Kentish-town June 1454, which he exchanged for sinecure rectory of Fulham, November 1465, resigning it in May 1475.

Stephen Tyler . . .

David Hopton, collated November 5, 1489, on death of Tyler; perhaps canon of Windsor, August 1471.

John Coryngdon, collated January 22, 1491–92, on death of Hopton.

Richard Gardyner . . .

John Stokesley, S.T.P., collated January 4, 1518–19, on death of last; Principal of Magdalene Hall, Oxford, 1502; Archdeacon of Surrey; chaplain to Bishop Fox; Archdeacon of Dorset, 1521–22; Bishop of London, 1530; resigns St. Mary's, January 29, 1518–19: so the Register of Bishop Fox; but from Precentor Alyn's letter to Prior May a longer tenure might be inferred (see above).

John Dowman, LL.D., collated September 9, 1522, on resignation of Stokesley; prebendary of London, resigning in 1514 Portpoole for Twyford; Archdeacon of Suffolk, resigning 1526, his will being proved the same year; prebendary of Lichfield, March 1509 to August 1525.

John Incent, LL.D., collated November 11, 1526, on death of Dowman; previously rector of All Saints'; Bishop's commissary and president of Consistory Court about 1513; Master of St. Cross, Winchester, 1524–45; on July 20, 1530, Dr. Capon, then rector of St. Mary's, writes to Wolsey, 'This day I repaired to Hampton'—he had been at Ipswich, and speaks of the King's intention to dissolve the College there—'to commune with Dr. Incent of the benefice he gave me' [probably North Stoneham], 'near Hampton,' (Cal. State Papers); Dean of St. Paul's, June 1540; died before September 4, 1545.

John Alen or Alyn, LL.D., collated March 13, 1526–27, on death (so the Register, but almost certainly by error) of Incent; chaplain to Cardinal Wolsey; judge of his courts, not without protest of Archbishop Warham; assisted Cardinal in visiting first, and afterwards dissolving, forty small monasteries in order to found Cardinal College (Christ Church) at Oxford; in 1525 incorporated LL.D. at Oxford, having been previously LL.D. of foreign university, though an Oxford man; for his letter to Prior May, see above; consecrated Archbishop of Dublin, March 1528–29; murdered, July 1534.

William Capon, S.T.P., collated probably March 1528–29, on cession of Alyn; prebendary of Wells, 1537; prebendary of Bangor, 1543; rector of North Stoneham (see above and 'Valor Ecclesiasticus'); he was brother to John Capon, alias Salcote, Bishop successively of Bangor and Salisbury (of whom elsewhere), and founder of the Grammar School at Southampton (see under 'Grammar School').

William Burton, clerk, collated October 12, 1550, on death of Capon, on presentation of John Mill and George Mill, Esqs., who must have obtained the patronage from the crown, Bishop Gardiner being at this time a prisoner in the Tower, and hindered from the office of his See; his deprival followed in February 1551.

Robert Raynolde, LL.D., precentor in February 1558–59, when he presented John Payne to the perpetual vicarage of the church of South Stoneham with the chapel of St. Mary, near Southampton; so that apparently the ruined chancel of 'the great church of Our Lady' (see above) was held with South Stoneham, the precentor possibly himself being non-resident.

John Hillyard, S.T.B., resigned October 14, 1631.

Walter Rought, M.A., collated October 26, 1631, on resignation of last; on April 4, 1631, had been licensed to curacy of South Stoneham, and made sequestrator on death of Thomas Ely, late vicar, in succession to whom Rought was appointed, May 7, 1631, on presentation of John Hillyard, rector or precentor; Rought continued rector of St. Mary's till after the Restoration (see above). Walker says (Sufferings, &c., p. 98): 'In and about Southampton was one Rout, who, on the Restoration, appeared to be a Papist;' query whether he refers to this rector?

Thomas Clutterbuck, S.T.P., collated September 2, 1662, and vicar of South Stoneham; Chancellor of York, 1660; rector of Leckford, February 11, 1661–62; Archdeacon of Winchester, July 1684.

George Fulham, S.T.P., collated November 5, 1700; Archdeacon of Winchester, November 1700; died 1702; prebendary of Winchester, February 1692–93, till death.

Ralph Brideoake, M.A., collated November 25, 1702; Archdeacon of Winchester, November 1702; died March 1742–43; grandson of Ralph Brideoake, Bishop of Chichester.

John Hoadley, LL.B., collated June 9, 1743, on death of last, by presentation of Martin Folkes, Esq., and Samuel Lisle, D.D., executors of the late Lord Archbishop of Canterbury (Wake), patrons for this turn by virtue of the Archbishop's option. On July 27, 1756, the Bishop confirmed a lease of the rectory to Andrew Fielder of Southampton, Inn Holder, for forty years. Hoadley, son of Benjamin Hoadley, Bishop of Winchester, was chancellor of the diocese, November 1735; ordained deacon and priest by his father in December the same year, being then twenty-four years old; chaplain to Prince of Wales same year and month; chaplain to Princess Dowager of Wales, May 1751; collated to rectory of Alresford, November 1737; to Overton (sinecure), December 1746. On receiving St. Mary's, Hoadley resigned the sinecure of Wroughton, Wilts, in favour of a relative of Archbishop Wake; appointed Master of St. Cross, May 1760. All these preferments he held together.

Newton Ogle, D.D., collated March 26, 1776, on death of last; Archdeacon of Surrey, 1766; resigned 1769; prebendary of Durham, 1768; Dean of Winchester, 1769; resigned St. Mary's, June 28, 1797; died 1804.

Francis North, M.A., afterwards (October 1827) Earl of Guildford, son of the

Bishop; rector of Alresford; collated to St. Mary's, July 21, 1797, on resignation of last; Master of St. Cross, 1808; these preferments he held together; resigned St. Mary's, December 4, 1850.

Joseph Cotton Wigram, M.A., collated January 18, 1851, on resignation of last; inducted January 21, 1851; Archdeacon of Winchester, 1847; Bishop of Rochester, 1860.

Mark Cooper, M.A., instituted July 7, 1860, on presentation of Queen by virtue of ancient prerogative, on promotion of last; general mandate to induct same time; had been vicar of Bramshaw, 1840–60; died February 28, 1871.

Albert Basil Orme Wilberforce, M.A., collated on death of last; inducted April 3, 1871; honorary canon of Winchester, 1876.

PARISHES FROM ST. MARY'S WITHIN THE TOWN AND COUNTY OF THE TOWN.

*Holy Trinity, North Front, Kingsland.*—The church of this ecclesiastical parish, which was formed out of St. Mary's in 1848, was originally intended to be the chapel of the female penitentiary adjoining, though open also to the public. It was erected in the pseudo-Norman style of brick and stucco in 1828–29, at a cost of about £1250. In view of the assignment of a district it was much enlarged, and consecrated by the Bishop of Winchester, April 15, 1847; it has been very much improved of late years during the incumbency of the present vicar. It now contains about 1260 sittings. The register commences in April 1842. The population of the parish in 1871 was 5235; in 1881 it was 5421. The living is a new vicarage in the patronage of the Bishop. There is a good vicarage-house.

*Incumbents.*

Henry Bisse, August 15, 1829.

George Darby St. Quintin, July 11, 1834, on resignation of last, on nomination of trustees.

Charles Simon Faithfull Fanshawe, April 11, 1837, on resignation of last, on nomination of trustees.

Alexander Watt, M.A., October 13, 1846, on cession of last.

Stephen Butler, December 22, 1847, on nomination of trustees.

Joseph Baldwin Meredith, April 30, 1856, on date of last.

Alexander Bradley Burton, November 27, 1857, on resignation of last, on nomination of trustees.

Cresswell Strange, collated August 2, 1872; inducted August 30, on cession of last to West Meon.

*St. Luke's.*—This ecclesiastical parish was formed by Order of Council, August 8, 1853, the district having been arranged in 1851. The church, erected in 1852–53, was enlarged in 1860; a chancel was added in 1873, and consecrated on December 23d, many improvements having been carried out about the same time. It contains about 1400 sittings. The register commences in December 1854. The benefice is a new vicarage in the gift of the Bishop. A small house belonging to the incumbents adjoining the church was sold in 1876 for the good of the benefice, the proceeds being held by Queen Anne's Bounty toward providing a suitable vicarage-house.

*Incumbents.*

Frederick Russell, M.A., licensed to proprietary chapel (Newtown), of which he was proprietor, on his petition, July 31, 1850; afterwards licensed as perpetual curate of St. Luke's new parish by appointment of Bishop.
William Jebb Few, M.A., 1872, on death of last.
Frederick Hermann Bowden-Smith, inducted July 7, 1875, on cession of last to St. Nicholas, Guildford.
William Willcox Perrin, collated and inducted November 2, 1881, on resignation of last.

*Christ Church, Northam.*—The church of this parish was erected in 1854, a badly built and poor fabric, which is now being superseded by a handsome building from the designs of Mr. Woodyer. Its district was arranged in 1851, and formed by Order of Council in 1853. The population in 1871 was 3631; it now amounts to 5000. The living is a new vicarage in the patronage of the Bishop. There is a good vicarage-house close to the new church.

*Incumbents.*

John Willis Grane, 1851.
Cornelius William Wilson, November 19, 1858, on cession of last.
George Staunton Barrow, April 16, 1863, on cession of last to Colbourne.
Samuel Kelson Stothert, 1872, on cession of last to Knights Enham.
Henry Eden Trotter, inducted October 31, 1873, on cession of last; resigned 1883.
Henry Mitchinson Coverley Price, inducted August 24, 1883.

*St. James's, Bernard Street.*—The church of this parish was built in 1857–58, on a site given by Queen's College, Oxford, who also gave land for a parsonge adjoining the church on the east side. It was consecrated on October 4, 1858, by Bishop Sumner, and has accommodation for about 830 persons. It has been much improved during the present incumbency. The district was arranged in 1851, and formed by Order of Council, August 8, 1853. The parish includes all that part of the original parish of St. Mary within Canal Walk, Union Street, Orchard Lane, East Street, and Marsh Lane leading to the Floating Bridge and the Docks. The population in 1871 was 7029; in 1881 it was 7314. The register commences in 1858. The living is a new vicarage in the gift of the Bishop.

*Incumbents.*

John Scotland, 1851.
William Hopkins White, June 11, 1856, on resignation of last.
William Sealy, May 31, 1862, on resignation of last.
George Allen Procter, March 28, 1863, on resignation of last.
Carston Dirs Kebbel, inducted August 5, 1871, on resignation of last, and by exchange with him from Hatherden and Smannell.

*St. Matthew's, St. Mary's Road.*—This parish was formed in 1866. The church, in the Norman style, was built in 1869–70, and subsequently enlarged by the addition of an aisle in 1874, the original site having been given by the late Mr. G. S. Brinton (see under 'Mayors'). It will accommodate about 800 persons.

*Incumbents.*

John Bullen, M.A., 1866.

Richard Hughes, M.A., inducted August 10, 1881, on resignation of last, and exchange with him from Southam.

The parishes formed from South Stoneham within the town and county of the town are as follows:—

*Christ Church, Portswood.*—The church of this district, formed in 1848, was built in 1847, consisting of nave, chancel, and south aisle, part of the endowment being found by the vicar of South Stoneham, Rev. W. D. Harrison, who at first held the patronage. In 1856 the church was considerably enlarged by the addition of a north aisle out of all proportion with the original building, the existence of which governed the recent alterations, of which below. Further works were carried out in 1868, and in 1878 a considerable addition was made to the church by building a second aisle on the north similar to that on the south side, and by the construction of a much larger and wider chancel. The church now presents the unusual appearance of a double nave—the old nave and the aisle originally added as above having been brought into harmony—flanked by an aisle on either side; the wide chancel with its aisles being fitted on to the two naves, so that the easternmost pillar of the mid-nave arcade stands exactly in the middle at the entrance of the chancel. The plan is a bold one, and was due to the suggestion of the Rev. H. Bothamley, accepted and approved by the late Mr. Street. The works were carried out chiefly at the cost of the Rev. F. S. Wigram, incumbent. The living is a perpetual curacy in the gift of the Bishop. There is a large and handsome parsonage-house, originally built in 1853, but subsequently much increased and improved by the late incumbent.

*Incumbents.*

| | |
|---|---|
| Philip Raulin Robin, M.A., . . . . . . | 1847 |
| Gerald Stephen Fitzgerald, . . . . . . | 1852 |
| Frederic Edward Wigram, M.A., . . . . . | 1864 |
| Edgar Silver, M.A., . . . . . . . . | 1880 |

*St. Denys.*—This parish was formed in 1867. Its church, erected in 1868, is a handsome building in red brick and stone, consisting of nave, north aisle, and chancel, from the designs of Mr. Scott. The living is a perpetual curacy in the gift of the Bishop.

*Incumbents.*

| | |
|---|---|
| Tobias de Rome Bolton, . . . . . . . . | 1868 |
| Thomas Plunket Mooney, . . . . . . | 1874 |

## Holy Rood or St. Cross.

The Church of Holy Rood or St. Cross stood originally in the middle of the High Street, in front of its present situation. Having fallen into a ruinous condition in the early part of the fourteenth century, and been for some time past no small inconvenience to the townsfolk, a wealthy burgess, Thomas de Bynedon, made fine with the crown (1318) for permission to grant to the Prior and convent of St. Denys, the patrons of the benefice, a certain void plot of land, measuring 140 feet in length by 120 feet in breadth, for the purpose of a new church and cemetery.[1] The transference of site being arranged, the church was removed (1320) to its present position; a stone wall was thrown round its area or cemetery, and the old site in subsequent time became occupied by the Audit-house.

Ancient site.

Church removed.

Shortly after the church was opened, a cause was moved between Thomas de Beckford, precentor or rector of St. Mary's, and Richard de Kyngeston, 'rector' or chaplain of St. Cross, on the right of interment both within and without the church, when, by decision of Bishop John de Stratford (December 4, 1333), such right was entirely denied to the rector of St. Cross, who obtained, however, permission for the interment of himself and his successors within the church, as also for Roger Norman, Thomas de Bynedon, Henry de Lym, and Hugo Sampson, on the ground of their having assisted largely in the building of the church. Still the dues were to go to St. Mary's; all other sepulture was forbidden.[2]

Rights of interment.

In 1291 we find, from the taxation of Pope Nicholas, the revenues of this church were worth £4, 6s. 8d. per annum, its tenth being six shillings and eightpence.

Revenues.

Soon after the rebuilding of the church, the convent made an arrangement for the increase of the benefice; and in the time of Bishop Beaufort, May 16, 1408, this church having been, as was also the Church of St. Michael, appropriated to the Priory (1405), a further agreement with the same view was made between the Prior and convent and the perpetual new vicar.[3] All ecclesiastical rites for the parishioners were to be performed by the vicar and his chaplains; the house and garden provided in time past for (pro) the rector being assigned for his use and that of his successors; the vicar was, moreover, to receive £8 per annum from the convent, and arrangements were

Vicarage.

1 Pat. 14 Ed. II. (December 30, 1320) p. 1, m. 1. This was afterwards exemplified at the instance of the convent, June 20, 1409.

2 Reg. Stratford, f. 87 b, 88.

3 Perpetuus vicarius modernus. It is something like the titles of new-rector, new-vicar, for the titular rectors and vicars under Bishop Wilberforce's Act.

made between the parties as to legacies and obits. The vicar and his successors at their admission were to swear fidelity to the Prior and canons; the latter were to receive oblations in money, wax, and other items, but were also to bear the burdens of the church.[1] In 1474 (April 4) a further arrangement was made before Bishop Waynflete, in consideration of the poverty of the vicarage, by which the new vicar and his successors were to have the cure of souls, enjoy the house and garden provided by (per) the rector, and receive £10 per annum from the fruits of the church; while all other oblations, obventions, tenths, altar dues (altaragia), mortuaries, &c., belonged to the Prior and convent, who were bound to support all the ordinary and extraordinary duties.[2]

Valor Ecclesiasticus.

The ecclesiastical valuation of 1535–36 (27 Hen. VIII.) shows this vicarage, John Fawne, vicar, as being worth, in the rent of glebe lands, tithes, oblations, and other casual gifts, £15, 10s. 0½d., from which procurations and other payments amounting to £3, 8s. 3½d. had to be deducted, leaving £12, 1s. 9d. as the annual value, which paid its tenth, £1, 4s. 2¼d., to the king.

Pension.

A pension in this church belonging to the Priory of St. Denys was purchased of the crown, among other possessions, by Richard Freston, December 9, 1546; and in 1548 (June 24) William Ward and Richard Venables purchased certain rents late belonging to the parish church.[3]

"This church has received several augmentations. First, from Dr. "Morley, Bishop of Winchester, as follows:—

Augmentations.

"This indenture tripartite, made 29th January, 34 Chas. II. (1683), between "the Rt. Rev. Father in God, George, Lord Bishop of Winchester, on the "first part; Francis Morley, of Farnham, in the county of Surrey, Esq., and "Charles Morley, eldest son of the said Francis Morley, on the second part: "the worshipful Richard Meggott, D.D., Dean of Winchester, John Nicholas, "D.D., Warden of Winchester College, and William Hawkins, D.D., Pre-"bendary of Winchester, on the third part: witnesseth that the said George "Lord Bishop of Winchester, Francis Morley, and Charles Morley, do hereby "mutually agree that the said Francis Morley and Charles Morley, and their heirs, "&c., shall stand seized, &c., of certain annual fee-farm rents of £56, 2s. 0½d., and "other premises therein mentioned, and the reversion and remainders thereof, "under the trusts hereinafter mentioned, that is to say, that they shall pay, &c., "to St. Maurice Church at Winchester. And upon this further trust, that they, "the said R. Meggott, J. Nicholas, W. Hawkins, F. Morley, and C. Morley, and "survivors, heirs, &c., shall also yearly for ever pay the clear sum of £20 yearly "out of the said fee-farm rent to the vicar, for the time being, of the parish church "of Holy Rood, keeping his or their residence in the parish, until the said Lord "Bishop shall procure a greater augmentation to the said vicar, and so long as the "inhabitants of the said parish of Holy Rood, or of any other parishes in the town "of Southampton, shall jointly or severally, by subscription, &c., yearly raise a "like sum of £20, over and above all customary dues, &c., for the vicar for the

[1] Addit., 15,314, f. 44 b. [2] Reg. Waynflete, ii. f. 130 b.
[3] Particulars of Grants, &c.

"time being of the said parish church. And in case of the said Lord Bishop pro-"viding a better augmentation, or failing the inhabitants to make their payment of "£20 yearly as is aforesaid for one whole year, in either of these cases the said "£20 from the fee-farm rent shall be no longer paid to the vicar of Holy Rood; and "then, in either of these cases, these presents are on this further trust, that they, "the said Richard Meggott, &c., shall pay the £20 to the vicar successively for the "time being of the parish church of Farnham, Surrey, in augmentation of his "maintenance."[1]

Taunton's foundation.

"In 1752 Mr. Richard Taunton, merchant, alderman of this town, "left by his will [see under 'Charities'] £21 a year to the minister of "Holy Rood parish, to read prayers thrice every day in the year at "that church; and if he misses twelve times in any year, the benefac-"tion is to go to the minister of St. Lawrence parish on the same "terms; and if he misses twelve times in a year, it is to return to Holy "Rood, and so on for ever from one to the other.

Further augmentations.

"This parish has likewise had Queen Anne's bounty, with which "has been purchased an estate of £20 a year.

"And Queen's College, Oxford, who have been the patrons [but "see below] of this church since the year 1609, have of late years "annexed the stewardship of God's House to it, which brings in £21 "a year, besides a very good house for the steward in the hospital, and "some perquisites from the stewardship.

Vicarage-house.

"There is another article which used to be looked on as part of the "vicar's income, which has lately been the subject of much dispute: "it may therefore be of use to set it in its true light.

"The site of the original vicarage-house[2] was part of the ground "on which the great house[3] on the north side of the church now "stands, and was alienated in the year 1551,[4] for four terms of ninety-"nine years each," dating from June 12, 1551, "to a person[5] who "built that great house upon the ground, and covenanted to maintain "the vicar in the possession"—during those terms—"of another "house"[6]—then newly built—"which he, the alienee,[7] held by lease

[1] "From a copy in the hands of Mr. Daman, agent for the trustees." The document is here somewhat abbreviated.

[2] On August 3, 1441, the town audit was held in Holy Rood Vicarage, when the usual festive expenses occurred (Steward's Book).

[3] Holy Rood House, subsequently the residence of Dr. Speed's father, and afterwards his own; now Mr. Lankester's iron-foundry, and of course much altered. This fine house still retains within it portions of the old stone-built vicarage-house.

[4] John Griffith, vicar, and John Capelin, patron.

[5] Robert Evans, merchant.

[6] Immediately to the south of the church, in which house the vicar was then living. It is stated in the indenture that the vicar was too poor to repair the original house, which had fallen into bad condition during the incumbencies of Dr. Fawne and John Hichen.

[7] He also covenanted to relieve the vicar, during his terms, of a pension of forty shillings to the king on the vicarage, or to get the pension released for ever.

"from Queen's College. When that College became patrons of this "church they did not renew the lease of the above house, but let it "run out, and at the expiration of it granted a new one to the vicar. "About the year 1642[1] the vicar,[2] to save his house from the Parliament sequestrators, assigned the lease of it to a layman;[3] and the "vicar being sequestered from the church, the layman kept the lease, "and afterwards renewed it in his own name, by which means the "house was quite lost to the vicar. About January 1, 1643–44,[4] the "then owner[5] of the great house shot himself, and the house escheated "to the Corporation by their charter,[6] so that they now became "parties to the covenants of the deed of alienation, and the next "vicar applied to them to recover the lost house for him. They compounded the matter by agreeing to pay him a certain yearly sum by "way of rent for a house, or, as it is expressed in their Journal, 'in lieu "of a vicarage-house, to be paid till a vicarage-house is found him.' "This went on about threescore years, and then the College and the "Corporation joined to buy another house[7] for the vicar, and from "that time the payment of the above compensatory rent should have "ceased; but as in the course of so many years the reason of its being "paid was forgot, they continued to pay it for fifty years after this.[8] "But then a new vicar made fresh application to them to recover the "lost house for him. This put them upon looking back into their "journals, where they found the true reason of the payment; and as the "reason had long ceased, they resolved to pay it no more.

[1] Dr. Speed has 1640, but the statement of Dr. Perkins, a former vicar, whom he otherwise follows, has 1642, probably the true date.

[2] Henry Edmundson.

[3] Mr Cornelius.

[4] Dr. Speed has 1642.

[5] John Parkinson, Esq.

[6] See Journal, February 13, 1643–44.

[7] 'October 12, 1705.—Holy Rood.—This day at Mr. Bernard Brougham's request, Queen's College have given him £100 towards the purchase of a house, &c. The Corporation of this town and county do freely give him £100 more, being the full purchase of the same house.'

'August 8, 1706.—Holy Rood Parsonage.—This day a release and confirmation of the inheritance of a house in Holy Rood, in trust for the vicar of Holy Rood, with an assignment of the premises for the residue of the term of years for which it is held, was this day brought into the House and put into Holy Rood box' (Journal). The deed, among the Corporation papers, is dated January 25, 1705–6. The house had a double gable and a vault underneath. Englefield further described it in his 'Walk,' and attributed it to the time of Henry VIII., if not earlier. It has long since been pulled down, and its site is now occupied by No. 106 High Street.

[8] In May 1755 we find paid to the vicar 'a benefaction of the Corporation in lieu of a vicarage-house till provided, £6. Mr. Bradsell's gift, £1, 4s. Mr. Delamott's, £1, 10s.—£8, 14s.' This was the annual sum which used to be paid in half-yearly payments.

"All the above articles, together with the dues, amount to about £160 per annum."

Patronage.

The patronage of this church remained with the College till 1871, when an exchange was effected (June 29) between the College and the Bishop of Winchester (Wilberforce), the former resigning to the Bishop the patronage of Holy Rood, together with the benefices of Knights Enham, Newport, Milford, and Hordle, and receiving in exchange the rectory of Crawley, with the chapelry of Hunton annexed.

The population of the parish is 1507.

Historical Notices.

It has been usual to hold episcopal and archidiaconal visitations in this church. The celebrated Dr. Nicholas Harpesfelde, as official of the Archdeacon, held a visitation for the Southampton Deanery on April 5, 1543.[1]

Visitations.

King Philip.

On July 20, 1554, Philip, Prince of Spain, who had arrived in our waters the previous day escorted by the combined fleets of England and Spain, heard mass in this church, and remained at Southampton till the 23d, when he rode to Winchester with a splendid retinue, and was married to Queen Mary in the cathedral on St. James's Day, July 25.

The Churches of the town under Edward VI.

The churches here are little likely to have escaped the plunder of the late reign, especially that enjoined towards its close. It was notorious that in many instances, under whatever colour, the houses of the avaricious reforming nobles and gentry had become furnished with altar-pieces, chalices, and sacred ornaments looted from the churches; in consequence of which, in the last year of Edward VI., commissions were issued through the length and breadth of the land with a view to cutting off this lust of private embezzlement and securing finally the remainder of the booty. On 21st April 1553 (7 Ed. VI.) a missive[2] similar to that directed to every county in England had been issued from the King and Council to Sir Francis Fleming, knight, mayor of Southampton, Thomas Pacye, Thomas Mille, Robert Reyneger, and Thomas Goddard, empowering them to take view of and receive all church goods, plate, jewels, ornaments, and the like, within the town to the king's use, leaving but one chalice in each church, or in the case of large churches two; and, further, to sell all the vestments and rich furniture, and apparently to rob the sacred edifices of almost every vestige of their solemn use and dedication.

Commission, 1553.

Under Mary and Elizabeth.

There is little or no local trace of the reaction under the reign of Mary, but a commission in reference to that period, bearing

[1] Addit., 12,483.

[2] Orig. doc., Corp. Archives. See also Collier, ii. 335, 336.

Commission, 1559. date 21st September (1 Eliz.) 1559, was directed to the mayor and others from Thomas Beacon, B.D., Robert Weston, LL.D., and Robert Nowell, Esq., visitors of the dioceses of Rochester, Canterbury, Chichester, and Winchester, authorising them to act in their behalf within the town and deaneries of Southampton, and to make inquiry as to all religious abuses. In the case of clergy having preached any peculiarities of Romish doctrine, they were to exact a public recantation, to be made before the congregation according to a form scheduled to the instrument of commission.[1] Here again we do not know what action was taken.

Thursday Lecture. A lecture was formerly held in Holy Rood Church. It was filled in 1607 by the town lecturer, Mr. Hitchcock, whose appointment was continued, subject to the Bishop's approval, December 20, 1611. But in 1615 it was agreed that the four incumbents of the town—St. Lawrence and St. John being then united—should keep the lecture at Holy Rood on Thursdays, they having made some representation on the matter; and contributions were ordered from each parish in aid of the lecture.[2]

Lecturers. From a paper of instructions issued by the Archdeacon of Winchester to the ministers and churchwardens of the several parishes we gather particulars in reference to lecturers, and generally as to the discipline of the time. The instructions, which are undated, were probably put forth soon after the royal declaration of Charles I. prefixed to the articles to which they refer. The following is the substance of them:—

(1.) His Majesty's declaration published in 1628 [January 1629] is to be strictly observed. (2.) Special care is to be had concerning lecturers in every parish for whom these directions are to be followed:—(*a.*) That the afternoon sermons in parish churches be turned into catechisings by question and answer where there is no great cause to break that ancient and profitable order. (*b.*) That every lecturer read divine service according to the Liturgy of the Church in his surplice and hood before the lecture. (*c.*) That wherever a lecture is set up in a market-town, the same be read by a company of grave and orthodox divines near adjoining, in the same diocese, and in their preaching gowns, and not in cloaks, as many use to do. (*d.*) That if a corporation maintain a single lecturer, he be not suffered to preach till he profess his willingness to take upon him a living with cure of souls within the corporation, and that he do actually take such benefice or cure so soon as it shall be fairly procured for him. (3.) The ministers and churchwardens of every parish are to certify to the Archdeacon or his official the names, quality, and degree of every lecturer in their parishes. (4.) They are further to certify the names of such persons as, not being qualified by law, do keep chaplains in their houses. (5.) And also to signify the names

[1] Original document among Corporation Papers, endorsed 'A letter to order and determine ecclesiastical matters.'

[2] Journal under years.

of all such as absent themselves from, or are negligent in coming to, divine service, as well prayers as catechisings and sermons; and (6.) That they carefully preserve a copy of these instructions for reference.[1]

The following documents concern the Thursday lecture at this church. The first is a petition in the Puritan interest against the action of the mayor and of Mr. Bernard, then vicar of Holy Rood; the second is the answer of the Council of State providing a committee for supplying the several vacant churches and the Thursday lecture at Holy Rood with 'godly and able ministers,' and for taking care that Mr. Rought, the incumbent of St. Mary's, fulfilled his engagement of supplying £100 per annum out of the chantry money towards 'the maintenance of the godly ministers of Southampton;' the Council also requires the mayor and aldermen to permit the committee's nominee free access to the pulpit of Holy Rood. Lecture under Long Parliament.

*To the Right Honor^ble^ the Counsell of State.*[2]

The Petition of many well affected in the Towne and County of Southampton humbly sheweth,— 1653, October 26.

That the Thursday lecture in Rhoodes church being under sequestration in the s^d^ towne, was by order from the comm^tee^ of plunder'd ministers, dated January 1647–48, committed to the care of Col^l^ Rich. Norton, Rich. Major, John Hildesley, Esq., and others, to the end it might be supplied with godly and well affected ministers, who by their order, dated 24th January 1647[–48], appoynted M^r^ Nath. Robinson and others to preach the s^d^ lecture. But since the dissolution of the s^d^ committee of plunder'd ministers, the mayor and aldermen, togeather with M^r^ Bernard, a minister elected ther by themselves, denied M^r^ Robinson to preach the s^d^ lecture ther, but he eyther preached it himself, or some other by his procurement, who have beene for the most part most notorious enimies to the Common Wealth, or scandalous ignorant men.

Your petitioners farther humbly sheweth that ther was by order of the s^d^ com^ttee^ of plunder'd ministers, dated 14th January 1652,[3] an augmentation of 100^lb^ per ann., issuing out of the chantrie of Maries, with the cõnsent of M^r^ Rought, the incumbent, allow'd and settled towards the maintenance of the godly ministers in Southampton afores^d^, w^ch^ since the dissolution of the s^d^ com^ttee^ of plunder'd ministers the said M^r^ Rought neglecteth to pay. And your petitioners knowing noe wheare to complaine for redress but this hon^ble^ Counsel,

Humbly therefore prayeth that you will be pleas'd by your order to recommend the care of the s^d^ lecture to M^r^ Nath. Robinson, M^r^ Behaute, M^r^ Terry, M^r^ Crandon, and M^r^ Cox; and that neither the mayor nor M^r^ Bernard doe oppose them in preaching thereof, and that M^r^ Rought be order'd to continue the payment of the s^d^ augmentation, according to the s^d^ order of the com^ttee^ of plunder'd ministers.

---

1 Paper among the documents of the parish of All Saints, Southampton.

2 These documents are given by Dr. Speed. The reply of the Council is still among the State Papers, but I do not find the petition.

3 The original order from the committee may have been made some years before this. Certainly the ministers were paid in 1648. The above date may have been simply that of Mr. Rought's consent to the arrangement.

*Wednesday*, 26*th October* 1653.

Att the Counsell of State at Whitehall.

Upon the readinge of a petition presented to this Counsel from many of the well affected in the towne and county of Southampton, settinge forth that by virtue of several orders from the late com$^{ttee}$ of Parliam$^{t}$ for plunder'd ministers, appoynting Col$^{l}$ Rich$^{d}$ Norton and others to take care y$^{t}$ the several voyd churches and the thursdays lecture in Rhood's parish in the towne afores$^{d}$ might be supplied with godly preachers, the s$^{d}$ Col$^{l}$ Norton, with the rest, did appoynt M$^{r}$ Robinson, with others, to preach the s$^{d}$ lecture, who continued their s$^{d}$ exercise ther, till they were disturbed therein by one M$^{r}$ Bernard, a minister ther, elected by the mayor and some of the aldermen, and that the augmentation of 100$^{lb}$ per annum, made and allow'd by order of the s$^{d}$ com$^{ttee}$ for plunder'd ministers out of the chantry or rectory of Maries, with the consent of M$^{r}$ Rought, the incumbent, towards the maintenance of the godly ministers in Southampton is allsoe since the dissolution of the s$^{d}$ com$^{ttee}$ deteyn'd and witheld, and therefore craves the Counsel's order touchyng the premisses. Upon consideration whereof, and the state of the bussines as it is therebie represented to the Counsel,

*It is ordered* that Col$^{l}$ Rich$^{d}$ Norton, Rich. Cromwell, Rich. Major, Jn$^{o}$ Hildesley, Pet$^{r}$ Murford, Esq$^{rs}$, Ro. Wroth, Pet$^{r}$ Legay, Jn$^{o}$ Barton, Da. Hersent, gents, or any 3 of them, be appoynted a com$^{ttee}$ to take care for the supplying the sev$^{l}$ voyde churches, and the Thursday's lecture at Rhoode's church in the towne of Southampton with godly and able ministers, and allsoe to take care that the augmentat$^{n}$ of 100$^{lb}$ per annum, made and allow'd out of the chantry or rectory of Maries as afores$^{d}$ may be dewly rece'd out of the profitts of the s$^{d}$ place, and applied toward the maintenance of the s$^{d}$ godly ministers of Southampton. *And* to the end the s$^{d}$ com$^{ttee}$ may be enabled to doe anything that is committed to them in as ample manner as the com$^{ttee}$ formerly appoynted by the com$^{ttee}$ for plunder'd ministers was, *The Counsel* doth hereby give to the com$^{ttee}$ now nam'd by them the same powers w$^{ch}$ were given by the s$^{d}$ com$^{ttee}$ for plunder'd ministers to the persons appoynted by them to this service. *And* the mayor and aldermen of the s$^{d}$ towne of Southampton are herebye requir'd to give order and take care that the preaching place in the church of Rhoodes wherein the s$^{d}$ lecture hath usually beene preacht, may be free to such persons to exercise in as shal be appoynted by the com$^{ttee}$ herein nam'd, or any 3 of them, to preach the s$^{d}$ thursdayes lecture.

JO. THURLOW, *Sec$^{r}$.*

Under Charles II.

After the Restoration, Holy Rood still remained the favourite church. Hither the mayor came in state to listen to coronation sermons, as at the accession of Charles II., and to discourses on various public occasions. It appears, however, by a decree of Sir Mountford Bramston, Chancellor of the diocese, given in September 1670, that some unpleasantness had arisen between Dr. Pittis, then vicar, and the mayor, John Winder, Esq., from which again we shall gather a picture of the times worth preserving. The Chancellor's order was as follows:—

'1. That the mayor for the time being shall be constantly prayed for in the parish church where he shall usually resort in his formalities on Sunday mornings, by the title of the Right Worshipful, as formerly it hath been accustomed to be done, whether he be present or absent. 2. That the morning prayers and sermon on Sundays shall be constantly used, performed, and observed in the parish church where the mayor for the time being shall resort in his formalities. 3. That the election and session sermons be, according to the ancient custom, preached in the parish church of Holy Rood by such an orthodox, lawful, and licensed minister as the mayor for the time being shall make choice of. 4. That the minister of the parish church where the mayor for the time being shall resort and come unto in his formalities shall stay a continent time after the end of the tolling of the bell before he begin prayers, whilst the mayor is coming to the church with his brethren.'[1]

Election and Sessions Sermons.

In 1754 Mr. Perkins, then vicar, refused to allow the mayor's nominee, Mr. Scott, to preach the election sermon in his church, upon which the sermon was delivered at All Saints', and the matter subsequently referred to the Chancellor. After this the sermon became occasionally movable.[2]

Daily service.

It was the practice for the clergy of the town to keep up a daily service at Holy Rood. Thus in September 1661 they were begged to 'revive and continue the *ancient* and laudable custom of reading divine service within the Church of Holy Rood in their several turns, at six o'clock every evening from Michaelmas to Lady Day, and at six every morning from Lady Day to Michaelmas'[3]—Sundays and festivals only excepted, when each had his special work. Alderman Taunton's bequest in the next century (as above) provided for a double daily service; and in 1781 Holy Rood is described as the fashionable church of the town, with service twice a day.[4] Taunton's bequest continued to be received till of late years, when it was declined by the vicar, and the charity became diverted to the Taunton School (see p. 304).

Houselling cloth.

The old custom of the houselling cloth spread over the communion rails at celebrations of the Holy Communion was retained in this church till the death of Dr. Wilson.

Fabric. Proclamation-house.

From an early period the western porch or cloister of Holy Rood Church was used by the town for proclamations, in consequence of which the Corporation always repaired that part of the church, called the 'Proclamation-house,' and paid some acknowledgment for its use. In November 1608 the Corporation rebuilt this porch or cloister, and in September the following year agreed to an annual rent of ten shillings, and 'to repair that part only next to Mr. Pitt's house.'[5] Payments for the rent and repairs of this portico constantly occur, and in September

[1] Original order of the Chancellor and Corporation Journal.

[2] Journal. [3] Ibid. [4] Ford's Guide for 1781.

[5] Journal. This was the house, long since pulled down, immediately to the south of the church, in which formerly the old vicars had lived after the alienation of the ancient vicarage-house and premises on the north side. Its occupancy by Mr. Pitt gave his name to the lane (Pitt's Lane), which ended simply at the town walls, and was widened into Bridge Street at the commencement of this century.

1755 the parish obtained permission to extend farther into the street—two and a half feet—the 'paved court or walk before the church, enclosed with palisades, and called the Proclamation-house;' and in consideration of the town's use of the same for hustings and proclamation purposes, the Corporation paid to the parish ten guineas. The 'palisades' were eight pillars of Portland stone—the whole being meant for a handsome work.

Town assembly and curfew bells.

At this church were rung the assembly bell for the town in the early morning and the curfew at night. In 1456 and 1461 the clerk of Holy Rood was paid for ringing 'kerfu and semly belle;' so in many subsequent years for the 'day bell and the curfew.'[1] From the Court Leet Book of 1569 we find that the clerk was ordered, on pain of eightpence, to ring the bell at four o'clock every morning and at eight o'clock every night.

Peal of bells.

This church also, in the opening of the sixteenth century and later on, possessed the chief peal of bells in the town. In November 1715 an effort was made to recast the five old bells into six new ones, the mayor being authorised to contribute £20; and in the following year the All Saints parishioners obtained a promise of £10 from the Corporation for making their two bells into five. The parishioners of Holy Rood, in difficulty about funds, recalled the capital of Archbishop Lamplugh's[2] benefaction of £20 to the poor, undertaking to pay twenty shillings a year for the same, and obtained £40 from Thomas Missing, Esq., M.P. In 1742 their six bells were sent to London and turned into eight, towards the cost of which the Corporation gave £50 out of a gift to the town of £500 from Peter Delmé, Esq. Enough has been said of the bells.

Lamplugh's gift.

Interior church.

As to the interior arrangements of the church, we have no records but what are late. The wardens' accounts give the several changes of the last century. In 1711 leave was given to certain parishioners for building a gallery on the north side of the church fronting the pulpit at their own expense, for themselves, their heirs, and assigns. In 1727 the pulpit was moved eastward, leave being given for building family pews on the place where it stood. In the same year the chancel screen was thrown back one bay. Two years later the north aisle was ordered to be seated like the south aisle.

Pew system.

The pew system was rigidly worked. Under February 1741–42 it was ordered that the churchwardens take off the lock of Mr. de Vaux's seat and carry it to him, and tell him that if he sends his cook-maid or any other servant to sit in that seat for the future, the parish are determined to dispose of it to some other family.

1 Steward's Books.

2 See below under 'Vicars.'

In 1759 it was proposed to construct a gallery on part of the north side; and in December 1780 a vestry was held for the purpose of erecting one over the whole of that aisle, the seats being saleable to the parishioners. A faculty for the erection was issued the following year (March 1781), and the vestry gave permission to Mr. Halton, the vicar, to build the gallery as he had proposed, on the understanding that a lease of it should be granted to himself and his *heirs* for the full and free disposal of the seats therein for the term of ninety-nine years. The vicar, finding this condition illegal, offered to the vestry in June 1781 to erect the gallery, with the proviso that the right of disposal of the pews should be vested in himself and his *successors*, vicars of the parish, for the above term of years. This was arranged, and the old tablet recording the transaction was subsequently removed to the north gallery of the rebuilt church. North gallery.

In 1792 a small gallery was erected on the south side of the church.

This church had, of later years, the benefit of an organ before others in the town, toward the erection of which, in 1729, the Corporation devoted £105 out of a gift of seven hundred guineas presented for the public good by William Heathcote, Esq., M.P. For the same purpose, and at the same time, Michael Gray, Esq., gave £300, and the vestry directed the vicar and wardens to decide on the builder and on the position of the instrument in the church as they should be advised by a master well skilled in music.[1] From this time the Corporation used to subscribe towards the organist and singing-boys. Organ.

The fabric having fallen into great decay, a faculty, dated October 17, 1848, was obtained from the Episcopal Court for pulling down and rebuilding the church. The old tower was fortunately preserved, but the nave, aisles, and chancel were rebuilt (1849–50) strictly on the old plan and partly on the original walls. The cost of the renovation was about £4500. The church has a good western elevation, but the effect of its central canopied doorway is somewhat marred by two large tablets commemorating by name twenty-two brave men, whose lives were sacrificed in attempting to check the ravages of a disastrous fire on the night of November 7, 1837, on the site of the premises of Messrs. Lawrence at the lower end of the High Street, which also were totally destroyed by fire on July 13, 1878, but without loss of life. Church rebuilt.

The tower, which was in imminent danger of reconstruction in 1791, is of good proportions, at the south-west angle. It is crowned by a spire, and contains the eight bells which rang their first peal after the renovation, August 28, 1849. It bears also an illuminated clock with two dials, each 5 feet 4 inches in diameter, by Mr. J. Blount Thomas, Town and clock.

[1] Town Journal; Churchwardens' Accounts.

of the High Street, erected in 1875. Previously to this date the quarter chimes had been struck by a couple of little automatons of some antiquity—they are mentioned in 1760—within a square niche made for them on the face of the tower. These have unfortunately been removed, their work being now performed upon half-ton bells by a driving power of over half a ton, while the hours are struck on a bell weighing nearly a ton, the weight of the hammer being forty-two pounds.

Interior. The interior of the church has now (May 1883) been greatly improved by the removal, under a faculty, of the lateral galleries constructed at the rebuilding of the church. The font is modern. The lectern, a handsome work of the fourteenth century, represents an eagle standing on a globe, supported by a battlemented tower; beneath the claws of the eagle a dragon raises its head to dart at her breast. The tower or pedestal stands on a triangular base, carried by three lions. Passing into the chancel, some ancient stalls are to be noticed with the motto of Bishop Fox, 'Est Deo Gratia,' in bold relief. An esquire's helmet, about which no tradition exists, hangs on the north wall.

Bequests. John Renawd, burgess of Southampton, by will dated October 27, 1422, desired to be buried in the cemetery of St. Mary's, and left to the fabric of that church twenty shillings. He gave to each poor man coming to his funeral a penny in bread or money, and the same to those who kept his anniversary. Among his legacies he left to Thomas Tellar, vicar of St. Cross or Holy Rood, five marks; to the Prior of St. Denys, for forgotten tithes and oblations, one hundred shillings; to Master Bartholomew, vicar of St. Michael's, forty shillings; to Master William, rector of St. John's, forty shillings; to William Green, clerk of St. Cross, twelvepence; for a chaplain to celebrate for his soul and for the faithful departed, ten marks; for vestments for St. Cross, £10; to the church of the Friars Minor of Southampton, 13s. 4d.[1] A few minor ancient bequests are to be found in Liber Niger.

Property. The church property has been already spoken of, and will come under notice below among the parish charities. At the beginning of the sixteenth century the parish appears to have had some interest in the Dolphin. Thus in June 1506, a tenant came before John Godfrey, mayor, and before the churchwardens and parishioners of Holy Rood, and 'bound himself sufficiently to repair all such building as is now in the house that he dwelleth in, called the Dolphin, upon pain of forfeiting his indentures of the same house.'

The present Dolphin Hotel is partly in Holy Rood parish and partly in St. Lawrence's, a former owner having thrown two houses

1 Among his properties he owned Bull Hall (Madox, Form., 430–432). It may be noted that the date given in Madox (1322) is a misprint.

into one by joining to his hotel, which was in Holy Rood parish, a wine merchant's shop contiguous in St. Lawrence's parish.

The parish registers commence in 1653—that for marriages on November 20, for baptisms on December 27, and for burials on November 28. A note at the beginning of the earliest register sets forth that the Rev. William Bernard, vicar of Holy Rood, was at a meeting of the parishioners on [blank] 1653 chosen, according to the Act of Parliament, to be registrar of the parish touching marriages, births, and burials, and to keep the register-book for the said parish. He was sworn thereto by William Horne, mayor. Registers.

The registers, valuable of course for family history, contain otherwise little worth noting. A remarkable frost is recorded among the baptisms in February 1683-84, which commenced before Christmas, and by the third and fourth days of February the 'river of Southton was frossen all over and covered with ice from Calshott Castle to Redbridge, and Thomas Marteine, master of a vessell, went upon y^e^ ice from Berry neare Marchwood to Millbrook Point. And y^e^ river at Ichen Ferry was soe frossen over that severall persons went from Beauvois hill to Bittern farme forwards and backwards.'

No churchwardens' accounts are preserved earlier than 1699-1700; from that date they are continuous. They have been used in the foregoing narrative, but two or three further extracts may be added. Church-wardens' accounts.

A charge for decking the church with boughs at the proper seasons constantly occurs, as is usual in such documents.

George Herbert refers to this old custom in his directions to the country parson. Among other things, he is enjoined to see 'that the church be swept and kept clean, without dust or cobwebs, and at great festivals strewed and stuck with boughs and perfumed with incense.'

At the end of the first volume occurs a note concerning the charity in bread of Thomas Lewis, Esq.,[1] February 13, 1714-15, about which and its duration we have no further account. Ten shillings' worth was distributed each Sunday at one of the churches according to an agreed rota. Lewis's gift.

Katherine Wulfris, by her will, bearing date December 30, 1665, gave the yearly rent of an orchard in Southampton worth forty shillings per annum, with all improvements which should be thereafter made upon it, to be yearly paid into the hands of the churchwardens of Holy Rood, the parish in which she was born, for the clothing and placing out one poor maid of the same or any other parish within the town to some apprenticeship or service, at the appointment of her daughter and executrix, Katherine Wulfris, during her life, and after- Charities. Wulfris's gift.

[1] See under M.P.'s for the borough.

wards at the appointment of Jane Stanley, also daughter of the testatrix, and successively to each of their heirs, and for want of such, at the appointment of the churchwardens and overseers of Holy Rood parish for ever.

The property, afterwards called Giddy Bridge, continued to be of small annual value. In 1770 Mr. St. André, whose lease expired that year, offered to pay £5 per annum, provided the parish for the future applied the rent in accordance with the will of Mrs. Katherine Wulfris, and from this time the rent of £5 was always applied in apprenticing a girl. In 1790 the parish received £25 rent for Giddy Bridge from Sir Richard King; and on June 25, 1792, the churchwardens, with a view to improve the rent, put to auction a lease for ninety-nine years, when J. Simpkins became the purchaser at a rent of £51. The matter having been subsequently referred to Chancery, a lease to Simpkins at the above rent was granted on July 29, 1794, dating from the preceding Midsummer Day, the lessee covenanting to keep in repair all buildings which might be erected on the premises during his tenancy, and deliver up the same to the churchwardens at the end of his term. The demised property is described as a piece of garden ground or orchard situate in the parish of All Saints, adjoining to and making part of the pleasure-grounds of Sir Richard King, Bart., containing in length from east to west on the north 165 yards or thereabouts, and on the south 145 yards, and in depth from north to south on the east 43 yards and 1 foot, and on the west 15 yards, bounded by the garden occupied by the said Sir Richard King, Bart., on the north and east, by the turnpike road leading from Southampton to Winchester on the west, and by a common field called East Maudlin field on the south.

In August 1803 a new scheme was approved by the Court of Chancery, in pursuance of a resolution of the vestry of Holy Rood, empowering the trustees to employ the above rent in placing out annually five—the vestry had suggested six—poor children of the said parish, boys or girls, to some apprenticeship or service, at the discretion of the minister, churchwarden, and overseers of the poor. The premium with each child was not to exceed £10.

The actual practice at the present time is to put out six children every year, boys or girls, of the parish of Holy Rood in the first instance, but failing that, then of any other parish in the town. The premium of £8 is paid with each, and every fifth year a seventh child is put out. Applications are made to the churchwardens by persons desiring the benefit of the charity for their children.

Brunswick Place.

The Wulfris charity land is now built over with good houses called Brunswick Place, so that at the expiration of the above-described lease a few years hence, this charity will become one of the wealthiest in the town.

Bishop's gift.

John Bishop, a baker, residing on the west side of the High Street, in the parish of Holy Rood, by his will dated November 18, 1796, and proved in the Prerogative Court of Canterbury in 1800, left £10,000 stock three per cents., out of which, after making provision for his two sisters to the extent of two-thirds of his property, he gave the interest of the remaining third to five annuitants, which, with the principal, should ultimately revert to any issue of his above sisters. Failing this, he directed that the said principal should be invested in the names of his executrix and two trustees, their executors and administrators for ever, together with the four guardians of the poor of the parish of Holy Rood, for the time being, and the two churchwardens, to be appropriated by them from time to time to five poor decayed tradesmen of the parish of Holy Rood only, their widows or maiden daughters, in yearly payments of £20 each, to be chosen by the above nine persons, or a majority of them. Bakers and their widows or maiden daughters to have the preference before other trades, as was also any journeyman baker of good repute who had served seven years as an apprentice.

The charity consists now of £3116, 3s. 9d. stock three per cent. consols, producing a dividend of £93, 10s. 2d. per annum, which is divided among five persons each year, who, when they are once elected, are considered life-annuitants. Each thus receives £18, 14s. per annum, payment being made in half-yearly instalments, due on February 2 and August 2. The charity is worked on the following scheme:—

Class I.—Bakers and their widows or maiden daughters, or journeymen bakers having served apprenticeship in the parish of Holy Rood for seven years, resident in the parish, and having acquired and retained a settlement there.

Class II.—The same description of persons as Class I., *not* resident in the parish, but who shall have been parishioners, and acquired and retained a settlement there.

Class III.—Decayed tradesmen, *not* being bakers, or their widows or maiden daughters, resident in the parish of Holy Rood.

Class IV.—The same description of persons as Class III., *not* resident in the parish, but who shall have acquired and retained a settlement there.

Smith's gift.

Henry Smith, of Silver Street, in London, Esq., by his will, dated 24th April 1627 (3 Charles I.), and proved 23d January 1627–28, left extensive charities, and gave powers to his executors to develop some portions of his estate for the benefit of poor towns. The Southampton parishes came in for the charity after Mr. Smith's death. The allotment to Southampton, among other places, is from the estate of Telescombe[1] in the county of Sussex, amounting to 217 acres, the share falling to this town of the annual rents amounting to about £29, 15s. The object of the gift is a distribution of clothing, bread, flesh, or fish, the proportions being assigned to the different parishes according to their supposed needs.

Trim's gift.

Mary Trim by her will left ten shillings annually to the vicar and churchwardens of Holy Rood for keeping in repair the tomb of her father, Cornelius Trim (died March 14, 1823), in St. Mary's churchyard.

Hill's bequest.

Ann Lance Hill, widow of the Rev. Hugh Hill, D.D., by her will, proved October 21, 1848, left £500 consols for keeping in repair the tomb in St. Mary's churchyard (in which she herself was subsequently buried), containing the remains of her mother and sister, Mrs. Ann Newall and Bridget Lance Hill; also for the repair of a tablet in Holy Rood Church to the memory of Dr. Hill. After these purposes the remainder is to be distributed to the poor of Holy Rood and St. Mary's parishes.

Cushen's gift.

Edward Cushen by his will, dated May 18, 1833, and proved with two codicils April 10, 1837, left under the first codicil, dated January 1, 1835, for each of the parishes of Holy Rood and St. Michael the sum of £200 sterling, to be invested by his executors for the benefit of those parishes, the interest being paid to the churchwardens, to be laid out and distributed in gallon loaves of bread each 8th of December to poor persons, the elderly being served first. The distribution is made each December in old-fashioned gallon loaves, 8 lbs. 9 oz.

For Mill's, Gibbons's, Bradsell's, and Delamotte's gifts, see under 'Municipal Charities.'

## *Vicars of Holy Rood.*

Robert de Puteo, October 28, 1283.
William, in 1306.
Thomas de Portesmuth, chaplain, July 23, 1311.
Richard de Kyngeston, December 20, 1316; mandate of induction to Dean of Southampton same day.
Adam de Sunnynges, March 12, 1348–49; by presentation of King, Priory of St. Denys being vacant when benefice became void (see under 'St. Denys'); was rector of St. Lawrence.
Henry de Chippenham, April 22, 1349; rector of St. John's (q.v.)
John de Upton, September 20, 1349.
Richard Ernewode, September 1, 1361.
Philip Stone, September 28, 1376.
John Bussh, October 5, 1377.

[1] Mentioned in Journal, May 26, 1679; April 2, June 18, August 27, 1680, &c.

William Salesbury, September 19, 1390.

William Wynwyk, March 11, 1391–92, on resignation of last, exchanging with him the wardenry of the free chapel of St. Radegund, in St. Paul's, London; resigned September 2, 1407.

Thomas Teller, December 27, 1407, on resignation of last.

Peter Osmond, vicar in 1430 (deed of William Balvayr, in mayoralty of Thomas Belle, John Emory, bailiff, December, 9 Hen. VI.)

William Blake, vicar in 1445 (deed of Dr. Prentyse, see under 'St. Mary's').

John William *alias* Mershfield, chaplain, August 5, 1452; on resignation of Blake.

Thomas Gardener . . .

John Clyffe or Cleve, chaplain, August 3, 1457, on resignation of Gardener.

John Lonyer, March 20, 1487–88, on death of Clyffe.

William Skynner, M.A.; the name of William Morrowmas, perhaps a nickname, occurs in Journal of 1490.

Christopher Ward, LL.B., May 14, 1507, on resignation of Skynner.

John Wilcok, D.D., June 10, 1508, on death of last; successor not named; admitted to Guild of town, 1510.

John Fawne, D.D., December 10, 1522, on collation of Bishop, to whom turn had been granted (June 11, 1522) by convent, on resignation of last; he resigns in January following, and receives the church 'in commendam' for half a year, January 26, 1522–23; admitted July 16, 1523, on presentation of Gilbert Burton, bachelor of decrees, to whom and to Gilbert Piers, LL.D., convent had granted it (January 3, 1522–23) for one turn.

John Ichyn or Hichen, December 22, 1536, on death of Fawne, by presentation of Stephen Quiedeux through grant of convent.

John Griffith, M.A., May 25, 1548, on death of Ichyn, by presentation of John Capelyn, who had acquired patronage on dissolution of Priory.

Richard Wodlocke, September 10, 1554.

Robert Leybourne, May 17, 1560.

Henry Hopkins, M.A., September 8, 1574, on death of Leybourne, by presentation of John Capelyn, gentleman (see also Cal. State Papers, Elizabeth, undated).

Simon Pett, March 8, 1586–87, by cession of last, and presentation of Anthony Lisle, Esq.

James Rowlandson, M.A., November 9, 1611, on death of Pett, by presentation of Queen's College, Oxford; also rector of St. Lawrence; afterwards rector of East Tisted; Master of St. Mary Magdalene Hospital, Winchester; chaplain to Charles I.; D.D. 1636; canon of Windsor, November 1638; died May 9, 1639; he preached at consecration of Jesus Chapel by Bishop Andrewes, September 17, 1620 (see further in 'Wood,' &c.)

Christopher Brownrigge, M.A., October 30, 1615, on cession of last, by presentation of Queen's College.

Alexander Rosse, M.A., July 7, 1628, on death of last, by presentation of King Charles I. (see under 'Grammar School').

William Hicks . . .

Henry Edmundson, M.A., August 26, 1637, on death of Hicks, by presentation of Queen's College; sequestrated by Long Parliament, probably in 1642; afterwards (1655) appointed by provost and fellows to Northlech School, then well endowed, where he continued till death, July 15, 1659 (see 'Wood,' &c.)

Mr. Mason, in this vicarage in 1647, receiving the allowance in lieu of a vicarage-house.

Thomas Lamplugh receives a share of St. Mary's chantry-money as minister of this church in 1648; fellow of Queen's College, afterwards D.D.; Archdeacon of London, May 1664–76; Principal of St. Alban's Hall, August 1664; resigned 1673; prebendary of Worcester, June 1669–76; vicar of St. Martin-in-the-Fields, 1670–76; Dean of Rochester, March 1673-76; Bishop of Exeter, November 1676; Archbishop of York, November 1688; died May 5, 1691.

William Bernard, in the vicarage in 1653 (see under 'Grammar School').

Thomas Pittis, instituted June 19, inducted June 20, 1666, on death of Bernard, by presentation of Queen's College; also rector of St. Lawrence and St. John.

John Lloyd, instituted May 20, inducted May 22, 1675, on resignation of last; also rector of St. Lawrence and St. John.

Roger Farbrother, August 31, 1682, on death of last; rector of St. Lawrence and St. John; died December 1, 1698.

Anthony Poole, April 12, 1699, on death of last; died August 5, 1702; vicar of South Stoneham in succession to Roger Turner, October 29, 1668, on presentation of Dr. Clutterbuck, from which he removed to Holy Rood; also rector of St. Lawrence and St. John; also perpetual curate of Jesus Chapel, where he was buried the day after his death, August 6.

Bernard Brougham, instituted October 15, 1702, on death of last; rector of Millbrook, as well as of St. Lawrence and St. John; he died September 25, 1750.

Daniel Perkins, M.A. (afterwards D.D.), instituted March 9, inducted March 12, 1750–51, on death of last; also rector of Church Oakley in gift of Queen's College.

Miles Halton, M.A., instituted January 19, 1773, on death of last; also instituted to Church Oakley, January 1, 1773.

Hugh Hill, D.D., instituted July 25, 1792, inducted July 27, on death of last; instituted to Church Oakley, July 21, 1792.

William Wilson, D.D., instituted July 28, inducted July 29, 1824, on death of last; canon of Winchester, February 3, 1832; died August 22, 1873.

John Aston Whitlock, M.A., instituted 1873; inducted January 17, 1874, on death of last, on presentation of the Queen by reason of the See of Winchester being vacant at the time of the voidance of the benefice, the patronage of which had now by exchange (see above) passed to the See of Winchester.

## St. Lawrence and St. John.

St. John's. The Church of St. John seems to have been granted by William Fitz-Osbern, kinsman and marshal of William the Conqueror, and Earl of Hereford, to the Abbey of St Mary of Lire, which he had founded in the diocese of Evreux: he also gave a rent-charge of £9, 5s., together with a burgage in Hampton, to the same monastery. This must have occurred soon after the Conquest, when he had probably himself received the grants from the king. He died in 1071. These several gifts, together with the Priory of Carisbrook, were confirmed to the abbey by charter of Henry II.[1]

Patronage. The Abbot and convent of Lire continued to present to the rectory of St. John's till an interruption occurred in the French wars of Edward III.; however, after this the convent presented again (see below) through the Prior of Carisbrook, as their proctor, for at least one turn.

[1] Mon. Angl., ii. 906, 985, 987.

The rectory of St. Lawrence continued in the patronage of the Prior and convent of St. Denys from the date of its grant to them by Henry II. to the suppression of that house in 1536: it is now in the gift of the crown. St. Lawrence's.

Neither St. John's nor St. Lawrence's occurs in the taxation in 1291. In the 'Valor Ecclesiasticus' of 1536 the rectory of St. John appears as worth in oblations, tithes, and casual offerings, £5, 6s. 8d., its tenth to the king being 6s. 8d. St. Lawrence was worth £8, 4s. 9d., which, after deducting procurations and a certain pension, yielded £7, 9s. 9d., its tenth being 13s. 9¾d. In 1723 the rectory of St. John stood in the king's books at £6, 13s. 4d., but only gave the clear annual value of £2: the rectory of St. Lawrence stood at £7, 10s., with the clear yearly value of £11. Dr. Speed, in the only sentence in which he mentions these churches, thus gives the value of the united benefices: "Dues £13, Queen's bounty £20. Total £33 "per annum." Revenues.

The two benefices were held together in 1614, and have so continued since that date. A further union was attempted half a century later, owing to the poverty of the town benefices. In April 1663 the town council addressed the Bishop on the subject of uniting the churches of St. Lawrence and St. John with Holy Rood, and that of All Saints with St. Michael's, in order to secure the maintenance of two able ministers within the Corporation: the parishioners of each old parish were still to support their parish church. The recommendation was not carried out, though practically (see lists of incumbents of the various churches) the benefices were frequently held together. Benefices held together.

But the Church of St. John having fallen into a ruinous condition, and its poverty considered, it was proposed at the beginning of the following century to take advantage of the provisions of 17 Car. II., cap. 3, 1665, 'for uniting churches in cities and towns corporate,' and obtain an ecclesiastical union of the parishes of St. Lawrence and St. John, their joint value not exceeding £12 per annum. On February 25, 1705-6, the town seal was placed to a petition for this purpose, and the vestry having taken separate action with the same view, the parishes were united under a faculty from Trelawney, Bishop of Winchester, dated September 3, 1708, the instrument being brought into the Audit-house on October 22 the same year. After this the Church of St. John was pulled down as ordered by the faculty, the parishioners of St. John being henceforth bound to repair and support the Church of St. Lawrence; the area of the church then became appropriated as a burial-ground for the united parishes, the church-walls being lowered to the height of eight feet all round, and coped with stone by order of vestry, September 18, 1721. Union of St. Lawrence's and St. John's.

The two churches were held with Holy Rood from the time of the Restoration to the death of Mr. Brougham, who was also rector of Millbrook, in 1750: they were held with St. Michael's from 1793 to 1817.

Site of St. John's.

St. John's Church stood in French Street; its site, the now disused burial-ground, having been lately put in order. Its ancient history seems past recovery. In 1538–39 it was the scene of a consecration of a bishop, Abbot John Bradley being here consecrated Suffragan of Shaftesbury on March 23, by John Salcote alias Capon, Bishop of Bangor, assisted by John, Bishop of Hippo, and by Thomas, Suffragan of Marlborough.[1]

No plan or drawing of the church has been discovered: its site is an irregular cross, measuring from east to west 90 feet 10 inches, made up thus:—Length of chancel, 26 feet; depth of transept, 17 feet 4 inches; length of nave, 47 feet 6 inches. From north to south the width at the transepts was 70 feet, the width of the chancel being 29 feet 5 inches, that of the nave and aisle 44 feet 6 inches.

Rectory-house.

In the angle formed by the transept and aisle wall on the south are buildings in St. John's Court belonging to the church, and said to have been the ancient parsonage. Here is a mission-room, in which service has been for some years conducted.

Within the site of the church is a Tudor monument, quite defaced; also memorials to Richard Taunton, the benefactor of the town, who was buried here, April 7, 1752; to Dr. Mant, rector of All Saints'; William Smith, collector of customs, and twice mayor; and many others.

The population of St. John's parish is 613, that of St. Lawrence 313.

Notices of St. Lawrence.

The following notices are gathered from the churchwardens' accounts, which include visitation fees,[2] Pentecost-money accounts, other expenses and receipts,[3] and notices of meetings. An inventory of church property was handed down from year to year. The lists are of no special interest. The sacred vessels in the earlier entries appear to have been but a chalice[4] and cover, that is, a paten; later on a flagon and a second chalice and paten were provided. The vestments were simply the surplice. The bells were three in number. In 1606

[1] Strype's Cranmer, p. 71; Stubbs' Episcopal Succession.

[2] *E.g.*, Payd at y[e] vysitacion xvij days after Easter 1569, for o[r] byll making and delyveryng up y[e] same, vj[d.] Item, Peter Jambryng (he was one of the churchwardens) laid out at Wynchester to discharge oure excomywnycacion, xx[d.]

[3] Under 1568 and subsequently there is an account of 'money gathered by the wives at Hocktide.'

[4] See the Commission of 1559 under the account of 'Holy Rood.'

'a running glass' was bought for the pulpit, 'with a stander to set him in.' This was the hour-glass, which regularly appears in the inventories, and in 1634 a half-hour glass was added, as if to hint of moderation. After 1660 they are heard of no more. Besides these articles the inventories generally included a list of the church deeds and papers.[1]

Books for the church.

Under 1567, the earliest year of these entries, we find a note of the changes which had been passing over the church, in a purchase of a 'paraphrase of Erasmus,' bought of a Mr. Webb for 13s. 4d. After which occurs the entry, 'Layd out for iiij songe bookes for y$^{e}$ queer [choir], v$^{s.}$' Under February 1569–70, 'Layd out for a booke of prayer and homyles, to be yowsed at sartayne tymes, iiij$^{d.}$' Under 1572, 'Payd for a newe Byble in London for our churche, xxvj$^{s.}$ viij$^{d.}$; for carriadge of y$^{t}$ from Powlis to Fanchurch, and thence to Holborne, and from Holborne to Hampton, to the carier, vj$^{d.}$' This was probably the 'Bishops' Bible,' which had just appeared. 'P$^{d}$ to the sumoner the 28 of Novembre 1572, for ij small bookes of praier for the churche, xij$^{d.}$' In 1636 a new service-book and its carriage from London cost 8s. 3d. Various other entries occur for service-books and others at different times. In 1592 a book of prayers for her Majesty's life was purchased at the cost of fourpence. Notices of royal visits occur from time to time under payments for ringing the bells. For instance, under 1570, for the Queen's visit on the previous year, when also payment was made to the men who sang for the Queen. Under 1660, 'Paid for ringing upon the occasion of the King's being voted upp in Parl$^{t}$., 3$^{s.}$ 6$^{d.}$ Paid for ringing when the king was proclaimed, 5$^{s.}$; do., on the thanksgiving-day, 4$^{s.}$' Under 1669, 'Paid for ringing at the King's reception, 3$^{s.}$' Again, 1687, 'When his Majesty (James II.) was here, 1$^{s.}$ 6$^{d.}$'

St. Lawrence's Cross removed.

In 1570 the cross in front of the church was pulled down,[2] while within the church the choir screen was removed. The walls were decorated with choice passages of Scripture, and the ten commandments were set up at the east end. The altar-table was covered with a carpet as ordered; one was bought of Richard Etuer[3] in August 1573.

---

[1] Among the documents handed on to the new churchwardens in 1599 occurs the following, now lost:—'Item more, one antiente deede indented, whereby Mr. Grigorie his howse is bounde for the mayntenance of the gutter on the north side of the churche, and to cleere and discharge the churche of all duties thereto belonginge, granted in King Edward the third's tyme, in the xxxij yeare.' The same occurs under subsequent years. Under 1577 occurs a reference to the older church book, now lost.

[2] See under 'Markets.'

[3] Recently churchwarden. He was of a local French family, and probably the donor of the town seal in 1587. In the register of God's House the name frequently appears as Richard Estur. He was a burgess of Hampton, and closely connected with the French Congregation.

The old organ.

Several charges occur for mending the organ in 1575 and subsequent years, and we discover the end of the old instrument under 1613. Certain ratepayers have signed the book, against whose names is written, in a contemporaneous hand, 'A pack of knaves,' and underneath the signatures occurs the note, 'Delivered to the two new elected churchwardens in organ pipes of metal, 35 lb.' Doubtless some controversy about the old organ had led to the above expression of opinion. In 1618, 65 lb. weight of organ pipes was sold, at the rate of ninepence per pound.

The following entry under 1595–96 speaks for itself:—'Received of M^r. Malerie, skoulmaster, to paie for spoilles made by hym and his skollerdes in y^e churche y^e 7^th Feb. 1595, vj^d.'

Lecture.

In 1596 a lecture appears to have been established in the church.

Mr. Robinson.

For the intrusion of Mr. Nathaniel Robinson into this living, see under 'All Saints.'

Brief.

We find the parish contributing in 1678 to the erection of St. Paul's Cathedral. We are not told the amount,[1] but the cost of carrying it to London was one shilling.

Request of French Congregation.

In 1723 the French Congregation from God's House, who had before this joined the Anglican communion, applied to the vestry for the use of St. Lawrence's Church.[2] The request, however, was negatived by a majority of eighteen to three. This entry also occurs, 'Item, paid when the parish met for the French gentlemen, 10^s.'

Spire taken down.

In 1775 the spire, which had been threatened for some six-and-twenty years, was taken down as far as the tower under a faculty, after which two of the three bells were sold, and a clock procured for the tower.

Agreement as to services.

Under the above year we find an agreement between the rector and parishioners 'that divine service and a sermon shall be performed and preached every Sunday morning throughout the year,' in consideration of a subscription being raised for that purpose, the account of which was left with the churchwardens. This was repeated in subsequent years.

In 1814 it was agreed to pay the rector fifty guineas a year, including the clerk's salary, for performing the additional duty at the church, namely, the whole of the divine service three Sundays in each month at the least, and an evening lecture, to commence from the first Sunday in November to the last in February Probably, therefore, owing to the circumstance of this church having been frequently

[1] A collection made in the church, September 1684, for the building of Portsmouth church produced 6s. 2d.

[2] See the circumstances under 'French Church.'

held with others, the regular services had for a lengthened period been reduced to a minimum. The scanty population of the town may, however, be remembered, and the ample size of the other churches.

The Old Church.

The inventory of 1777, in bold defiance of the canon, presents us with a novelty in fonts—'a neat moveable wood font.' After this we read of the front of the church being 'ornamented' in 1780 'with a plaster called stucco.' A northern gallery was added to the interior by a faculty in 1796. We may now finish the description of the old church. Its west front exhibited a low included tower at the south-west corner, forming the end of the south and only aisle, and making one-third of the church's width. The upper stage of the tower was pierced by a single lancet window, immediately below which was the clock; it was surmounted by a battlement-table with an open wooden cupola to carry the bell. A door opened into the basement of the tower. The west window of the nave, beneath which was the chief entrance, had exchanged its ancient tracery for three plain vertical wooden mullions. The west wall had been carried up nearly to the level of the tower in order to give the building height with a view to its surroundings; it was finished above by a course of battlements. A colonnade on five pillars, probably added in 1727, when two shops were removed (see below) from the front, ran the whole width of the church. A painted east window was the gift in part of Dr. Speed in 1776; but the church contained nothing of beauty or antiquity. Under constant patching it had become an incongruous and inconvenient mass, past further repair, and being pronounced dangerous into the bargain, it was, after the necessary preliminaries, pulled down in 1839.

The New Church.

The new church of white brick, erected at a cost of about £3000, and consecrated on 31st March 1842, was built too soon for strict architectural propriety. It has now, however, a pleasing interior, improvements having been carried out of late years. The windows in the apse were the gift of the Rev. Edward Horne, rector, who contributed otherwise largely to the rebuilding. The font was also a gift. A good broad spire was added to the tower in 1861.

Registers.

The records of St. John's parish are mostly lost; what remain are in the custody of the rector and churchwardens of St. Lawrence.

St. Lawrence.

The earliest entry in the St. Lawrence books is dated July 5, 1751, the registrations for a lengthened period before this time having been made in the books of Holy Rood, with which church the united parishes were held from 1666 to 1750. The Church of St. Lawrence, however, possesses a series of churchwardens' minutes and account-books which are of some value. The earliest of these volumes, already mentioned, ranges in an unbroken series from 1567 to 1742. There are also several ancient deeds relating to the church houses in the High

Church property. Houses.

Street, latterly two in number—one on the west side, No. 145, which still belongs to the parish; the other on the east, No. 25, some time in the occupation of Messrs. Atherley & Fall, bankers, and now of Mr. Patstone. The following is a notice of the deeds.[1]

Site.

1. Thomas Bagge quit-claims to his father, Richard Bagge,[2] all his right to the plot of land (described) on the west side of English Street. Date, 6th June, 48 Ed. III. (1374).

2. Quit-claim of Richard Bagge to his father, Richard. His own seal and that of the prepositure of Southampton for greater security. Date, Saturday before St. Luke, 2 Rich. II. (1378).

3. Robert Parker, parson of St. Lawrence, and another, grant to Richard Mey and Agnes his wife the above plot of ground, lately received by gift of Richard Bagge, junior. The seals of Parker, &c., and for greater security that of the mayoralty. Date, Tuesday before St. Katharine V., 4 Rich. II. (1380).

House is built.

4. Agnes Mey, widow of Richard Mey, grants to John Grey and to Agnes his wife, daughter of the said Agnes, the reversion of a tenement on the west side of the street, &c. The property extended from English Street on the east to the Castle ditch on the west. Her own seal and that of the mayoralty, John Polymond, mayor, Date, July 30, 16 Rich. II. (1392).

5. Elena, spinster, daughter and heir of Agnes, wife of John Grey, quit-claims all rights in the above tenement to her father. Her own seal, and for greater security that of the mayoralty. Date, 27th April, 2 Hen. IV. (1401).

6. Will of John Grey, burgess, dated 26th April 1403. He desires to be buried in the church of the Friars Minor of Southampton, near the tomb of his wife; and leaves to the fabric of that church 12d.; to the rector of St. Lawrence 20d. sterling, and the same amount to John the parish clerk. He leaves to the Fraternity of St. John 12d., and the same to the Fraternity of St. Thomas, both in the Church of St. Cross (Holy Rood); and seven pounds of wax are to be bought and burnt round his body on the day of his sepulture. He bequeaths to John Mascall, burgess, and to Thomas Tredington, clerk, the above-described tenement, in which he was living. Will proved before the Dean of Southampton, 9th May 1403.

Fraternities.

7. John Mascall quit-claims to Thomas Tredington his right in the above property. His seal and that of the mayoralty, Thomas Midlyngton, mayor. Date, 19th June, 4 Hen. IV. (1403).

8. John Bagge of Whippingham, Isle of Wight, quit-claims to Richard Bradewey, burgess of Southampton, all right to the tenement, &c., which John Grey left to Mascall and Tredington. His seal and that of the mayoralty. Newport, 5th March, 6 Hen. IV. (1405).

9. Richard Bradewey, burgess, grants the tenement, &c., to William Niewe of Fareham. His own seal and that of the mayoralty. Date, 27th October, 3 Hen. V. (1415).

10. Release from R. Bradewey and Alice his wife to the same party at the same date.

11. An inspeximus of John Benet, mayor, with an exemplification under the seal of the mayoralty of a charter of feoffment, under which five tenements and three messuages with shops are sold by William Weygant, executor of the will, dated 6th December 1415, of Richard Bradewey, to John Mascall and Walter

[1] These are what remain of twenty-three poll deeds which used to be preserved in an ancient sealed box, and handed on with other church properties by the outgoing to the incoming churchwardens.

[2] Bagge Row was probably named from this family.

Fetplace. His own seal and that of the mayoralty. Date, Saturday before St. James the Apostle, 6 Hen. V. (1418). Date of exemplification, 4th July, 7 Hen. V. (1419).

(Same skin.) Walter Fetplace quit-claims to John Mascall all his rights to four of the above tenements, two together on the west, and two together on the east side of English Street. His seal and that of the mayoralty. Date, 4th July, 7 Hen. V. (1419).

(Same skin.) Release of the same four tenements from Richard Bradewey, son and heir of Richard Bradewey, jun., son of Richard Bradewey, sen., to Margery, wife to John Mascall, late burgess of Southampton. His seal being little known, he has caused that of the mayoralty to be affixed. Date, 13th March, 7 Hen. VI. (1429).

12. Thomas Michell, late rector of All Saints', quit-claims to William Nitinynhalve[1] and Cristina his wife, formerly wife of William Colles, and executrix of his will, all his right to the tenement on the west side of the street, &c., which he had by gift and feoffment of the said Cristina when in her widowhood. His seal. Date, Wilden, Bedfordshire, 1st May, 8 Ed. IV. (1468).

13. Cristina Colles, widow, grants to Massia Salmon (the name Robert Bushup is written over that of Salmon, but there is no erasure), and three others, her tenement on the west side of the street, &c. Date, 11th March, 1 Rich. III. (1484).

14. Richard Ludlowe, son and heir of Richard Ludlowe, lately of the town of Southampton, Esq., quit-claims to Massia Salman and the others, now in peaceful possession, and to their heirs, all right and interest in the above tenement. His own seal, &c., before John Walker, mayor, &c. Date, 14th March, 1 Rich. III. (1484).

We must now turn to the minute-book.

Parish house on west side of High Street, No. 145.

The first notice of the parish house on the west side of the street occurs under 1567, when it was inhabited by David Morell; the rent appears as £1, 6s. 8d. In 1576 the lease was renewed to him, at a fine of £20 and an annual rent of £2, for sixty years. The rent, fines, and occupation of the premises are easily to be traced in the church books to the present time. The premises are now held by Mr. Emanuel under a lease of twenty-one years bearing date March 25, 1870.

Former Parish house on east side of High Street, No. 25.

The parish became possessed of the house on the east side under the will (see under 'Chantries') of Richard Mylles, who, upon certain contingencies and conditions, bequeathed his dwelling-house to the Church of St. Lawrence. In 1564 it stood at the rent of £1, 6s. 8d.; an allowance of ten shillings per annum out of this amount being due to the poor in bread. This was, no doubt, by way of carrying out the will of the testator. Early in the next century the bread money dropped through. The history of this property can also be perfectly traced to the present time. It may be sufficient to mention that in 1826 the lease was renewed by Messrs. Atherley & Fall, in succession to Mr. Hilgrove and Mr. Richard Vernon Moody, and that they continued doing so every seven years until 1862, when the parish authorised the sale to the same gentlemen of the reversion in fee expectant on the determination of their lease, which was dated Decem-

[1] For the family of Halveknyght see under 'West Hall,' p. 320.

ber 14, 1854, for the sum of £350, or upon deduction of £43 already paid by the lessees for the redemption of the land-tax, for the reduced sum of £307. This projected sale of the fee-simple was approved by the Charity Commissioners in April 1862 and concluded, the purchase-money being invested in three per cent. consols in the name of the official trustees of charitable funds, the dividends of the purchase-money (about £9, 14s. 4d.) being thenceforward regularly paid to the churchwardens for the time being through the bank of Messrs. Maddison, Atherley, Hankinson, & Darwin, the parties authorised to receive the same in their behalf.

Parker's annuity.

Formerly the church of this parish enjoyed an annuity of thirteen shillings and fourpence by deed of Mr. John Parker, dated May 30, 1603, issuing out of his house on the west side of the High Street in the parish of St. Lawrence, in lieu of church rates.[1] This deed he executed in fulfilment of an agreement in the vestry April 19, 1600. The annuity was regularly received by the churchwardens from the various occupants of Parker's house till 1816, after which the parish collected church rates from it which really amounted to more than the thirteen shillings and fourpence per annum, and the rent was virtually abandoned.

Two shops now pulled down.

Another source of former parish income was the rent of a couple of shops built against the west wall of the church, one on each side of the porch. In 1572 these shops were rented at one shilling each per annum, and about the year 1605 had risen to the value of ten shillings and nine shillings respectively. They remained at this figure till 1727, when the vestry happily ordered them to be pulled down and not rebuilt, the churchwardens being directed to fit up the front of the church in a decent manner according to their discretion.

Lease of the Vestry.

Another strange source of income at one period was the lease of the vestry. In 1586 Henry Massey, the occupant of one of the above shops, obtained a lease of the vestry for a fine of £2, 10s. at an annual rent of twelve pence. The last payment for the vestry occurs, I think, in 1626.

Parsonage.

The old parsonage of St. Lawrence adjoined the church on the south side. It is mentioned under 1592, when some small stone-work repairs were carried out. In 1646 it was rented out to one James Mudge at £2 per annum. He appears to have entered upon it in the latter part of 1645, and continued to enjoy it for upwards of twenty years, paying rent for it to the parish in 1647, and apparently in the

[1] The original deed is still among the St. Lawrence documents. There is also an old deed not hitherto mentioned— an indenture of agreement on the joint use of a well, bearing date 3d May, 35 Hen. VI. (1457). It must have concerned parish houses.

first part of 1648; after this he probably paid Mr. Nathaniel Robinson, who had at this time been intruded into St. Lawrence's, and was afterwards put into All Saints. On April 30, 1660, Mudge was directed to pay the rent to the churchwardens. This he continued to do; but in 1667 we find Mr. Pittis, the rector, who was also vicar of Holy Rood, receiving Mudge's rent; and it is to be presumed that after this the house was occupied by the rectors, as no further rent was received for it on the parish account. In 1742 the south wall of the church was found to be perilously overhanging the parsonage garden, when the churchwardens were authorised to remove the stone buttress from the south-east corner of the church, and build it farther westward against the south wall; in the event of a buttress being still needed at the south-east angle, they were to replace the stone with brick. The old rectory or priest's house was latterly inhabited by the parish clerk, and was, with the consent of the Bishop, the patron, and the rector, pulled down in 1839, when its site and garden were applied to the enlargement of the church.

New Rectory-house.

The new rectory-house, acquired under the late rector, is situated within St. Peter's parish, near to the Commercial Road, and facing the West Marlands.

Little Somborne.

The rector possesses, in right of his rectory, a farm at Little Somborne.

Windsor's gift.

The rector of these parishes receives the dividends of £100 three per cent. consols, standing in the name of the Corporation of Romsey, which stock is believed to have been given by Brigadier Windsor for the administration of a monthly sacrament in St. Lawrence's Church. (See also under 'All Saints.')

For Mill's and Sendy's gifts see under 'Town Charities;' for Smith's charity under 'Holy Rood.'

Priaulx's gift (lost).

Robert Priaulx, of the city of London, merchant, by his will bearing date August 23, 1681, gave to the poor of St. Lawrence's parish, his native place, £20, as acknowledged by the churchwardens in vestry, November 20, 1683, when it was determined that the interest should be distributed to the poor at celebrations of Holy Communion at Christmas, Easter, and Whitsuntide. This charity became lost in 1723 by the holder of the capital becoming insolvent, when the churchwardens with the other creditors accepted five shillings in the pound.

### *Rectors of St. Lawrence's.*

Roger le Rous, instituted June 6, 1295.

Jeoffrey Nel, acolyte, instituted at Bitterne, December 23, 1305.

Adam de Sonnynges, priest, December 29, 1330; swears fidelity to chanter of St. Mary's; afterwards vicar of St. Cross or Holy Rood.

Ralph de Stapenhull, April 4, 1349, on cession of last.
Nicholas Poleyn, February 27, 1352–53, on resignation of last.
William Noble, November 6, 1353, on resignation of last, exchanging with him the rectory of the church of Bixe Gybewyne, diocese of Lincoln.
Stephen de Bottlesham, March 27, 1365.
Roger Barry, October 9, 1369, on resignation of last.
John Stawell, August 11, 1370, on death of last.
Robert Perker [1] (sic.) . . .
Richard Merston *alias* Palmer, May 26, 1383, on resignation of last, exchanging with him the perpetual vicarage of Kentebury, Sarum diocese.
Walter Harden, August 7, 1385, exchanging with Palmer the church of Chilton Candover.
Adam Stakepolle, May 8, 1395, exchanging with last the church of Fynchamstede, Sarum diocese.
William Olyver, November 8, 1413.
Robert Walwyn . . .
Thomas Grysthwayt or Gristwood, chaplain, July 11, 1464, on resignation of last.
William Nicholson, August 19, 1483, on death of last.
Edward Chamber, . . . resigned June 28, 1527.
William Smyth, chaplain, June 30, 1527.
Thomas Whitehead, April 26, 1543, on resignation of last, by presentation of King, the Priory of St. Denys having been dissolved.
Thomas Brane . . .
William Morrell, April 14, 1557, on resignation of last, by presentation of Philip and Mary.
Henry Willet, September 8, 1565, on death of last, by presentation of Queen Elizabeth.
Thomas Husse, November 12, 1567, by presentation of Elizabeth.
Humphrey Piggott, February 8, 1581–82, on death of last.
Henry Hopkins,[2] rector in 1592.
Thomas Smith,[2] in 1602.
James Rowlandson,[2] in 1614; also vicar of Holy Rood (see under that Church).

## *Rectors of St. John's.*

Robert de Broughton, March 11, 1309–10.
Henry called Chippenham of Winchester (Henry de Chippenham, see under 'St. Mary's'), December 7, 1327, by presentation of Brother John Poucyn as proctor for Abbot and convent of Lire, diocese of Evreux; vicar of Holy Rood (q. v.)
Maurice Brut de Sydenham, November 13, 1361, on presentation of Abbot and convent of Lire.
Robert de Milverton or Wager, March 11, 1372–73, on resignation of Brut, exchanging with him the vicarage of the church of Ellingham, by presentation of Edward III., the temporalities of the abbey being in the King's hands on account of the war.

---

[1] The name of Robert Parker, rector of St. Lawrence, occurs in the deed (above) dated November 1380, also in deed of John atte Bere dated 18th September 1395, though he was not rector at that date. The Episcopal Register mentions his exchange.

[2] Churchwardens' Accounts. All the preceding entries are from Episcopal Registers, which are here defective.

John Penbroke, October 14, 1376, by presentation of King for same reason.

William Hunderlythe, chaplain of the town, December 19, 1391, on presentation of Richard II. for same reason.

Richard Croucheston, January 28, 1399–1400, by presentation of Prior of Carisbrook, as proctor for Abbey of the Blessed Mary of Lire.

William Sweyn . . .

John Granger, April 15, 1405, on resignation of Sweyn, exchanging with him the church of Hiwissh, Sarum diocese, by presentation of John Lord Lovell and Holand.

John Holand, October 26, 1405, on resignation of last, by presentation of King.

William Gernyngton, April 11, 1407; exchanging with Holand the church of Dauntsey, Sarum diocese, by presentation of King.

Thomas Geffrey, January 20, 1407–8, by presentation of King.

William Goldsmyth, December 9, 1412, exchanging with last rectory of parish church of Eston Gray, Sarum diocese.

William Russhall . . .

John Godeston or Godestowe, chaplain, September 3, 1455, on resignation of last; by presentation of King.

Richard Hodges or Hegge, chaplain, May 27, 1479, on death of last, by presentation of King; admonished by Chancellor David Husbond (May 28) to appear personally in parish church of Waltham that day year to undergo examination by the Bishop or his commissary.

William Byrt or Burde, chaplain, March 20, 1490–91, on death of last, by presentation of King.

Alexander Holden, September 6, 1529, on death of last, by presentation of King; retired into a convent.

John Vaughan ap Griffith ap Rhes, chaplain, June 7, 1532, on retirement of last, by presentation of Thomas Hatcliffe and Nicholas Leghe, controller of customs at Southampton, through grant of King.

John Newton, October 30, 1532, on resignation of last.

Adryan Mason, in 1550; name occurs in Court Leet Book.

*Rectors of St. Lawrence and St. John.*

Stephen Venyng, B.A., April 26, 1614; not stated how vacancy occurred, or by whom presented.

William Pyne, March 27, 1615, on presentation of James I.

Walter Norman, M.A., November 3, 1631, on cession of last, by presentation of Charles I.; he had been (September 28, 1630) licensed as curate in the parish church of St. Mary, near Southampton.

Nathaniel Robinson,[1] presbyterian, intruded about 1648.

Thomas Pittis, S.T.B., instituted June 10, 1666; vicar of Holy Rood.

John Lloyd, instituted May 20, 1675; vicar of Holy Rood.

Roger Farbrother, instituted August 31, 1682; vicar of Holy Rood (q. v.)

Anthony Poole, instituted April 12, 1699; vicar of Holy Rood (q. v.)

Bernard Brougham, instituted October 15, 1702; vicar of Holy Rood (q. v.)

James Scott,[2] instituted June 4, inducted June 5, 1751, on death of Brougham; licensed to Jesus Chapel, September 6, 1768, on nomination of James Mylles, Esq., upon death of William Bartholomew; died in Welbeck Street, April 6, 1794, at house of Earl of Oxford, who had married his daughter, March 3, same year.

---

[1] The preceding entries are from the Episcopal Registers; this and the following, till James Scott, are from the Town and Parish Books.

[2] This and the following are from the Diocesan Registries.

Thomas Mears, instituted September 9, inducted September 17, 1794, on death of last (see also under 'St. Michael's' and 'All Saints').
Edward Horne, instituted July 15, 1835, on death of last.
Eldred Woodland, instituted January 18, 1847, on resignation of last; rector of Stone, diocese of Lichfield, 1854–77; vicar of Milton, diocese of Winton, 1877.
Gibson Lucas, instituted June 30, 1854, inducted July 11, on cession of last.
Henry Horace Pereira, inducted July 1, 1876, on death of last.

## St. Michael's.

The church of this parish is architecturally by far the most interesting in the town. Its patronage, with that of the other churches except St. John's, was made over by Henry II. to the Prior and convent of St. Denys; it is now in the gift of the crown.

Revenues. In the taxation of Pope Nicholas (1291) it was valued at £4, 6s. 8d., its tenth being 8s. 8d.; a pension settled here was worth £3, and paid its tenth of 6s. This church was appropriated to the Priory in 1405 (see under 'St. Denys'), when, as required by law, a proper arrangement was made for the vicar. In the 'Valor Ecclesiasticus' the vicarage appears worth £13, 6s., or, after deductions, £12, 11s. 8½d., which paid a tenth of £1, 5s. 2¼d. In 1723 it stood on the King's books at £12, 11s. 10¼d., and was stated to be of the clear annual value of £20. In the seventeenth and eighteenth centuries the dues collected from the parishioners amounted to about £25—the sum stated also to have been the amount in his time by Dr. Speed in the only mention he makes of this church, except what will be found quoted below. The population of the parish is 1943.

Notices. This church suffered in the locally disastrous French invasion of October 1338, when a portion of the south-west quarter of the town was burnt. The flames seized upon certain wooden buildings attached to the church, and the sacred edifice itself became a scene of terror, violence, and bloodshed. The church having thus become polluted by the effusion of blood and by homicide, was reconciled by the Bishop of Sarum, under a faculty from Bishop Orlton, dated June 11, 1339.[1] In 1351 the church becoming again defiled with blood, though under what circumstances does not appear, a faculty dated November 27 was granted by Bishop Edington to the rector, Peter de Malmeshull, empowering him to get any Bishop of the province, or the Archbishop of Nazareth, then Suffragan of Canterbury, to perform the office of reconciliation.[2]

Polluted by bloodshed.

Among the earliest notices of this church in the town books are

[1] Reg. Orlton, i. f. 70.

[2] Reg. Edington, ii. f. 24. The same Bishop granted a license, dated October 21, 1352, to John Aunger, burgess of Hampton, for the celebration of

Clock and chimes.

those connected with its clock and chimes. The town took its time from St. Michael's, though roused from its sleep by the bells of Holy Rood. In consequence the parish clerk was paid (1456, 1461, &c.) as a town official for attending to the clock and chimes. In 1575 the court leet presented that 'the chyme doth not gooe, which is a very comfortable hearing to all the inhabitants.' Whether on this account or not, the custody of the chimes was given to one of the town gunners in 1594, who was to keep clean the callivers in the Audit-house at £1, 6s. 8d. per annum, and for a like salary to attend to the clock and chimes of St. Michael's, 'and he hath promised to alter the chymes into so good a note and tune as shalbe liked of by the towne, and into good harmonie.'[1] In later times the office devolved upon the sexton, whose duties in the seventeenth century were providing boughs for and dressing the church, washing the linen, scouring the eagle, cleansing the church plate, and, among other duties, most disastrously, writing the church books and registers.[2]

Notices. Case of Hancock.

At the close of 1547 or commencement of 1548, Thomas Hancock,[3] who, in consequence of an inflammatory sermon preached by him at St. Thomas's Church, Salisbury, had been bound over for his good behaviour, himself in £90, with ten sureties at £1 apiece, came to Southampton with a letter obtained from the Duke of Somerset to the Lord Chief Justice, Sir Richard Lyster, requesting the discharge of the bonds. While Hancock was with Sir Richard, the bells of St. Michael's[4] rang out for the sermon, for it seems that he had been asked to preach on the occasion of his visit. However his sermon was not to be permitted. To follow Hancock's narrative:—

'My Lord said unto me that Hampton was a haven town, and that if I should teach such doctrine as I taught at Sarum, the town would be divided, and so should it be a way for the enemy to enter in, and therefore he commanded me that I should not preach there. I answered that I would not take that for a forbidding, but that for so much as the people resorted to the church at the ringing of the bell to hear the word of God, they should not return home again void of God's word. My Lord said again unto me that I should not preach, and that there was one in the Tower (meaning Bishop Gardiner) that he would believe

---

divine offices in an oratory attached to his house in the parish of St. Michael's (Ibid., f. 26). A similar license was granted by Bishop Waynflete to Johanna, the relict of Nicholas Holmehegge, December 26, 1461 (Reg. Waynflete, i. 69* b).

[1] Boke of Remembrances, fol. 177.

[2] Churchwardens' Accounts.

[3] He took B.A. degree, Oxford, in 1532, and proceeded M.A.; was curate of Amport near Andover, and suspended in 1546, under Bishop Gardiner, for breaches of the Six Articles, but was licensed to preach by Cranmer in the first year of Edward VI. (Autobiography, p. 75, &c.)

[4] The church was apparently St. Michael's, though it is not expressly stated.

before four hundred such as I was. I answered him that he spake those words betwixt him and me, but if I had record of them, he would not speak them. So my Lord sent for the Mayor and his brethren. Mr. Mayor asked me whether I would be content that another should supply the room for me. I answered, Yea; and that I was as willing to hear the word as to preach myself. So did Mr. Mayor send to one Mr. Griffith,[1] who did preach; and my Lord being present, he challenged him that he, being Chief Justice of the law, did suffer the images in the church, the idol hanging in a string over the altar, candlesticks and tapers on them upon the altar, and the people honouring the idol, contrary to the law; with much other good doctrine. I praised God for it. And thus were my friends of Sarum that were bound for me discharged their bonds.'[2]

Sixteenth century changes.

From the Court Leet Book of the Corporation for 1576 we gather that the rector of All Saints' and the vicars of St. Lawrence's and St. Michael's, at least, were slow to adopt recent changes.

Sir Thomas presented.

'Item, we present that Mr. Stere, Mr. Husse, and Sir Thomas of St. Michael's do use to administer the communion with wafer or singing bread, which is contrary to the statute and Book of Common Prayer, for it appeareth by the said book that for the avoiding and taking away of superstition the communion ought to be administered with the finest "whyte bread" that may be gotten, and such as is usually accustomed to be eaten at men's table.'

In the margin is written 'To be considered;' no result of the presentment appears.[3]

From a notice in December 1611 we learn that during the voidance of the vicarages of Holy Rood and St. Michael's the vacancy had been partly filled by Mr. Hitchcock, the town lecturer, whose fervent preaching was said to have had great effect.

During the Puritan period St. Michael's continued to be held by the vicar, John Toms, M.A., who was instituted October 4, 1628, and was buried as minister of this parish on July 2, 1652.[4] On his death it is probable that Giles Say, a Presbyterian, was intruded; but if so, he was then only twenty years of age.[5] There are, however, several

[1] Probably John Griffith, vicar of Holy Rood.

[2] Hancock's Autobiography, Camden Soc., p. 76. Hancock was bound over by the Mayor of Salisbury, and subsequently tried as above under the statute of 1 Ed. VI. cap. 1. 'An Act against such as shall unreverently speak against the Sacrament of the Body and Blood of Christ, commonly called the Sacrament of the Altar, and for receiving thereof in both kinds.' A proclamation, founded on the above, dated December 1547, threatened any one who should 'revile, contemn, or despise the said sacrament by calling it an idol,' as Hancock had done at Salisbury, and as Griffith, we see, did here. We do not know Sir Richard Lyster's comments on this sermon.

[3] When Mr. Husse himself was married, October 12, 1572, the charge for the elements at the celebration that day is entered for 'breade and wyne, $ij^{d.}$,' though this would not decide as to the kind used.

[4] The Mr. Martin said by Walker to have been sequestered by the Long Parliament must have belonged, apparently, to some other St. Michael's (see Reg. Bishop Neile, and Reg. St. Michael's).

[5] Walker (Sufferings, part i. p. 98) says he was a weaver by trade.

instances of intruded ministers at this period having been even younger. He was born in Southampton in 1632. His mother was of Huguenot extraction, and it is not improbable that his father was the same, since the name of Say occurs on the register of the French Congregation at God's House. In 1660 Mr. Say received Presbyterian ordination at Bishopstoke at the hands of Mr. H. Cox, minister there, and of others. Not being a member of the Church of England, much less in episcopal orders, and being unwilling to receive ordination, he was ejected from St. Michael's in 1662, after which he preached in several places as opportunity occurred. It appears that he was offered the living of Wellow by the lay patron if he would conform and procure ordination. Upon King Charles II.'s declaration of indulgence in 1672, he opened his house in Southampton for worship, and received a license for that purpose, dated May 2 that year, in which he is described as of the Congregational persuasion. On the revocation of this indulgence he is said to have been imprisoned. When he left the town does not appear, but a daughter was born to him in December 1684, in a house 'in Lord's Lane, next to the Blue Anchor, on the east side,' in the parish of St. Michael. After the liberty granted by James II. he was chosen pastor of a congregation at Guestwick, Norfolk, where he continued till his death on April 7, 1692.[1]

The recent history of St. Michael's will come more conveniently under the description of the fabric; we turn now to the registers and churchwardens' accounts.

The earliest register commences with April 8, 1552, and ends with January 9, 1652–53. Each year is headed with the names of the mayor and sheriff, and very frequently with the Sunday letter. Register, vol. i.

In the first year the burial of Sir Richard Lyster, knight, is recorded on March 17, 1552–53 (see above).

In 1560, 'The same yaere Poulles (St. Paul's Cathedral) styple was burne with thonder the iiij day of June.' This is entered twice—so, and in another place against 1561. The latter seems the correct date.

Against the year 1560 a royal visit is recorded: 'The quenes majesties grace cam from the castle of Netley to Southampton the xiij day of August, and from thence she went to Wynchester the xvj day.'

Under 1604 an extraordinary number of burials is recorded. In July no less than 107, and in August 60 occurred; very many of these died of the plague.

Volume II. commences with March 25, 1664, but beyond what have been incorporated elsewhere there are few incidental notes.

[1] See Rev. T. Adkins's Brief Records, pp. 106–110; Palmer's Calamy's Nonconformist Memorial, vol. ii. pp. 279, 280.

Volume III. commences with January 17, 1762.

Bugle Hall.

Under 1791 Mr. Mears, the rector, notes the destruction by fire of Bugle or Bull Hall, which occurred in the early morning of November 16, owing it was supposed to some carelessly made-up fire, the house being at the time uninhabited and undergoing repairs. A fierce wind was blowing, and notwithstanding every exertion, favoured by the state of the tide, the spacious and venerable building was reduced to a heap of ruins in about six hours, the adjacent houses suffering little damage. Formerly the residence of the Earls of Southampton, Bugle Hall was at this time the property of William Gunthorp, Esq. Its front extended along the pavement of Bugle Street, and on the other side was bounded by Westgate; it enclosed a spacious quadrangle with ancient hall adorned with wainscoting and stained glass.[1]

The owner built another house of smaller dimensions on part of the site, which bore the old name, but had no resemblance to its predecessor.

Swearing into office.

Under 1795 is mentioned the swearing into office of James D'Auvergne, Esq., as mayor, according to annual custom, on St. Michael's Day; Nathaniel Heywood, Esq., being sheriff, and Frederick Breton and Noah de Cras, Esqs., bailiffs; and it is noted of the latter gentleman that he resided at Eling, having lately quitted his house in the town, and 'is perhaps the first instance of a person living without the liberties of the town serving an office in the Corporation.'

Baptisms, &c.

In the same year sixty-one persons were baptized and sixty-two were buried. Of these numbers, twenty-nine males were baptized and twenty-nine were buried; of females, thirty-two were baptized, thirty-three were buried.

In 1797 there were eighty-four candidates for confirmation: in 1802 there were fifty-three: in the same year forty-five were baptized and twenty-six buried. In 1807 the candidates for confirmation were sixty-four in number: in that year fifty-nine were baptized and fifty-three buried. In 1812 sixty were confirmed.

Volume IV. (1755 to 1787), Volume V. (1787 to 1804), Volume VI. (1805 to 1816), contain no special notices. All the later church-books have been, as usual, very regularly kept, though they lack, of course, any mention of extraneous incidents.

Church-wardens' accounts. Church houses.

The churchwardens' accounts commence with the year 1686. They preserve the rentals of the church houses which formerly belonged to the parish. These appear to have been six in number, in addition to

[1] Mr. Dottin, one of the M.P.'s for Southampton, afterwards lived at Bugle Hall. At an earlier date again (April 17, 1725), the Register of St. Michael's records, 'Mr. Benjamin Tichborn, son of Michael John, was born att y[e] house of Bugle Hall in this parish.'

which were a couple of stables, for which the parish received rent. Of these houses, four remain in existence. Concerning one of the houses removed, originally a chantry chapel attached to the church, see below under 'Fabric.' Another was the Robin Hood in French Street.

The remaining houses, situated respectively in Bugle Street (No. 55), in St. Michael's Square (next to old vicarage), in Pepper Alley (White's Court), and in Simnel Street (The Sailor's Return), are held upon twenty-one year leases, which will shortly (September 1882) expire. The oldest document relating to them is a lease dated 1575.

The churchwardens' accounts contain the usual official payments, together with a few notices of political events, briefs, agreements for the erection of pews, &c., which need not be recorded here.

The church was originally cruciform in plan. To its earliest period that portion of the tower which is seen within the building may be attributed, also a portion of the east, west,[1] and old south transept walls. In the east wall is a triple-arched piscina with double bason, which may perhaps belong to the time of Henry II. The fabric.

It would seem that in the Early English period a large addition was made to the church on the north side; and late in the fifteenth century Perpendicular tracery was supplied to the Early English windows on this side. The old cruciform church was then enclosed within a large parallelogram by the addition of chancel, aisles, and a south aisle to the nave. At the same time every other column of the Norman arcades in the nave was taken away, and arches of considerable span turned over the remaining pillars. The ancient tower, supported on its four round arches of rugged masonry totally devoid of ornament, was left standing in the midst like a triumphal arch before the chancel entrance, an arrangement extremely singular. Such was the condition of the structure in the latter part of the fifteenth century.

Subsequently to this a chantry chapel was built out on the south side of the south chancel aisle. This in time became desecrated, turned into a dwelling-house, and let on lease as one of the parish houses. It is probably mentioned in 1689, and a notice of it occurs under 1737. The occupier in 1764 was charged by the vestry with having made several alterations in the structure for the purpose of blinding a jury hereafter to the fact that the house was really part of the church. Subsequently the parish sold the house, though such was its history. Within living memory this desecrated chantry was a barber's shop; it has now for some years been pulled down, and the archway into the church roughly filled with the old stones.

[1] At the beginning of the century Sir Henry Englefield noticed remains of the original masonry in the west wall.

Corporation Chapel.

The north chancel aisle was called the 'Corporation Chapel,' and here the mayors used to be sworn. "It was customary for a sermon "to be preached on the occasion by the minister of the parish, who had "a guinea for his pains; but [Oct. 1] 1677 an order is entered in the "Journal that because Mr. Butler had abused the Corporation in the "swearing sermon, there should be no sermon at swearing of the "mayor, and that the mayor may be sworn at which church he pleases; "which order was repeated [Sept. 29] 1691. Notwithstanding which, "the custom has revived; but a few years since was discontinued again "on a like occasion,[1] and on account of some other squabbles with the "minister of that parish is discontinued still. But the mayor is still "sworn at this church."[2] In 1828 (of this date, see below) the Corporation voted £35 for a painted glass window for their chapel with the Southampton arms in it, and subsequently gave £15 more.

The south chancel aisle—now the vestries—to which the chantry chapel above spoken of was applied, was at one time called Fashin's chancel, possibly from money laid out on it by George Fashin, or from a distribution of bread owing to a legacy by him, mentioned in a note of 1687, to continue for nineteen years.

Pews.

The minute-books record the gradual but destructive changes in the interior caused by the erection of private pews (*e.g.*, 1705 and onwards) wherever fancy led wealthy parishioners to build them, with consent of the vestry and ecclesiastical authorities, by the blocking-up and opening of doors, by the erection of a gallery for the 'charity boys' in 1714, by the movement of the church furniture into different positions. For instance, in 1737 Mr. George Hammond obtained leave to remove at his own expense the 'reading-desk' into the body of the church under the pulpit, and to add a clerk's desk—in fact, to fit up a 'three-decker'—retaining the old reading-pew for his private property; an arrangement which Archdeacon Brideoake thought commodious and decent. This gave rise to other alterations. In the same year the churchwardens were authorised to have the three aisles of the church 'to be parted of eight-feet deal in a workmanlike manner.'

A visitor in 1719, whose notebook survives,[3] describes St. Michael's as the largest and most beautiful church in the town, with its three

[1] In September 1751 the privilege of choice as to the preaching at the swearing-in of the mayor was requested from Chancellor Hoadley. See precedent, under 'Holy Rood.'

[2] With the Municipal Corporations Act, 1835, the swearing-in of the mayor as above was discontinued. The foregoing is the only notice Dr. Speed has of this church, excepting the remark as to dues already quoted.

[3] Addit., 14,296.

broad aisles, a fine brass eagle standing in the midst, a rather handsome altar-piece, the gift of James Parker in 1672, its ancient font, which then had the four supporting pillars, and its six bells. The monument to Sir Richard Lyster is mentioned, but without the name; it was then, as till recently, in the north chancel aisle. Close by a black marble stone was inscribed to George Freke, gentleman, 1664, with a metrical epitaph which the writer suspects to have been the work of Dr. Speed —that is, the author of "Batt upon Batt." A rough drawing of the church is given, which shows a rather stunted spire, subsequently taken down for the present lofty one.

Monument of Lyster.

Alterations, 1828.

Structurally the fabric remained much as the fifteenth-century architect had left it. Still, under constant and ruthless alterations of the interior, the church had become sufficiently inconvenient by 1828, when, under the incumbency of the Rev. T. L. Shapcott, it was determined to rearrange it. It was thought necessary to add spacious galleries round the church, and to accommodate these a greater altitude was essential, the walls were therefore raised some three feet, and unfortunately the nave arcades removed, and the present flimsy arches and pillars of cast-iron, brick, and stucco substituted. The north aisle, which, until this period, had not extended as far westward as the end of the nave, was now lengthened, and the whole west front renovated in the Gothic of the period. These extensive alterations, under Mr. Goodwin as architect, were completed in April 1828, and the church was re-opened on the 16th of that month by the Bishop of Winchester, who had been previously sworn in as a magistrate and burgess at the Audit-house. He preached on John iv. 23. Not long after it was discovered that the proportions of the fifteenth-century architect had been too hastily abandoned, and the walls began to spread under the thrust of the flattened roof.

1872.

The changes detailed above were not destined to last half a century. When the present vicar came to the parish in 1870, serious repairs had become imperative, and it was again determined to restore the church. In 1872 roof and fabric were made firm, all the pewing and the galleries were taken away, the walls were cleaned down, and divested of every particle of whitewash and plaster. The church was reseated with convenient open benches, the font removed from the tower and placed appropriately at the west end of the church; the chancel was renovated, and the choir seats placed under the arches of the tower. The mayor's or north chancel was fitted for worship as a morning chapel, the tomb of Sir Richard Lyster, which at some period had been removed from its unknown original site to an inconvenient position between the north and central chancels, was carried to the west end of the north aisle, where at all events the recumbent figure lies in the usual direction, which it did not before.[1] The walls throughout the church are still in their rugged state, so that every change in the history of the fabric may be detected. Mediæval architects never intended that their surfaces should be left in this condition, but in the present instance we cannot regret it. In the renovations of 1872 the tower, spire, and bells were not touched. These were taken in hand as a public work towards the close of 1877, and by the end of May in the next year the whole had been finished. The appearance of the spire, originally built about 1745,[2] was considerably improved by the addition of nine feet to its height, as was the tower, which now (1881) contains a good peal of eight bells, by the insertion of a window in its upper storey in each of the four walls. Mr. Colson of Winchester was the architect, and Messrs. Stevens & Son of Southampton the builders. On the completion of the works, which included the addition of two bells to the old peal of six, the Corporation attended the church in state.

Font. The font is the original Norman one of about 1150, and is of the same general character as those in Winchester Cathedral and in East Meon Church. The bason is cut in a block of black marble about three feet four inches square, supported by a central shaft—originally there were also corner shafts—the whole standing upon a base of black marble.

Lectern. The brass lectern—an eagle standing upon a globe borne by an enriched shaft set on a base circular in plan and carried on three lions—is an inferior work to that at Holy Rood; it dates from about 1450.

[1] The monument is of some interest, but is in an imperfect condition, though not more so than in 1719. It was erected by his widow Elizabeth some few years after Sir Richard's death, as we gather from what is left of the inscription on the frieze:—'Et dicto Elizabeth hoc in viduetate suâ cuzavit 18 die Marcie 1567.' At the back of the monument, below the canopy and over the recumbent figure, a shield of arms is seen, with the date 1567 over it and the initials R. L. beneath. Remaining in the north chancel aisle are the fragments of an ancient figure of a bishop giving the benediction; the head is gone; also an ancient stone-coffin lid with floriated cross. In the reveal of the north window of this chapel is a square sunk panel, within which is a shield bearing a merchant's mark, the emblem no doubt of the donor of the window. On the wall of the south aisle of the nave is a memorial to Bennet Langton, for whom Dr. Johnson had such admiration. The stone bears the sentence which Johnson once uttered in reference to his friend, 'Sit anima mea cum Langtono.' He died on a visit to the town. There are many other memorials of interest.

[2] Unfortunately the Minute-Book of this period is lost. It may interest some to know that the weather-cock appears to have come from the old spire. It was taken off by Mr. Garrett, stonemason, on November 5, 1822, and was found to measure 3 feet 3 inches from beak to tail, and to weigh 18½ lbs. On the upper part of the tail was the date 1733, on the lower part 1782, and on the head 1792 When lately taken down something fresh was added.

The present vestry in the south chancel aisle is enclosed by remains of Perpendicular screen-work removed to their present position. It contains a handsome press, brought from the mayor's chapel, with the inscription 'John, the sonne of John Clungeon of this towne, alderman, erected this presse and gave certain books, who died anno 1646.'

There is a desk with four books chained to it, viz., Fox's 'Book of Martyrs,' 2 vols. folio, titlepages gone; these books, bound in 1712 at the cost of £1, are called the two church-books of martyrs. Also two vols. small folio, 'Annotations upon all the Books of the Old and New Testament, second edition, London, printed by John Legatt, 1651.'

There is a large coffer of about the same period. Also a chest concerning which probably an order exists, dated June 1741, that the churchwardens should bring into the church 'a chest with three locks as the law ecclesiastical directs, and demand all the writings belonging to the said parish of all persons in whose hands soever they are lodged, that they may be secured in the said chest for the use of the said parish.'

The numerous oak stalls which remained in the chancel in the time of Sir Henry Englefield, others being in different parts of the church, seem all to have disappeared in 1828.[1]

A portion of what is now St. Michael's Square, at the west end of the church, where had been the fish-market, was enclosed and planted with trees about 1711; we also read of the old well, which still exists beyond the west end of the church.

The Vicar's residence.

We first meet with the vicar of St. Michael's residing at St. Michael's prison, but not at the borough's expense. Under 1469 we find, 'Receyvyd of the vycary of Seynt Michell for rent of the house above the prison, vi$^s$. viij$^d$.' Again the same in 1488. After this the Prior and convent as patrons, with consent of the Bishop, granted in 1497 to William Dorset, clerk, perpetual vicar of St. Michael's, and his successors, a certain tenement of theirs situated on the west side of Fish Street, between a tenement of a certain Thomas Crekewoode on the south, and a void place belonging to John Fetteplace on the north, and running back from the street on the east to a certain long house of the late John Williams on the west. This description bears on the position of Fish Street. The said vicar and his successors for ever were to enjoy the above property at an annual rent of ten shillings during the lifetime of William Dorset, after that the rent was to be thirteen shillings and fourpence The vicars were to repair, and the convent to re-enter if the rent remained in arrears above a month. After this

[1] See 'Visit to Southampton in 1828' (Gent. Mag., Sept. 1830).
[2] MS. Addit., 15,314, f. 68 b.

St. Michael's prison.

we hear no more of the vicar of St. Michael's prison. The house over it, however, still continued to be let to various tenants at the old rent. This prison stood on the site of, and was in part identical with, the ancient stone and brick edifice with curved gables in St. Michael's Square at the corner of West Street, opposite the north chancel door of the church. There are many entries concerning this building.[1] It was an unwholesome place, and constantly out of repair. Before 1609 it had actually fallen to pieces, but its re-erection having been presented year after year by the court leet jury as highly convenient for the town, it was agreed in the above year to rebuild and construct a tenement over it as before.[2] In 1670 the prison was again in decay, and the roof of the tenement ready to fall in. Five years after the house over the prison was ordered to be pulled down as ruinous, and the lock-up, it is to be presumed, was strengthened. Repairs were again ordered in 1704.

Old Vicarage.

It does not appear at what time the parsonage in St. Michael's Square was acquired; it is the house next but one to the parish school, and on the east side of it. The churchwardens' accounts for 1686 contain an entry which probably has reference to the house which occupied this site, 'To surveying the parsonage-house by workmen with a lawyer, 7s. 6d.' Subsequently, during the incumbency of Mr. Kingsman, this house was pulled down by his direction; and in 1735 the vestry sanctioned the employment of a proctor to back the churchwardens' presentment of this offence. The year following Mr. Kingsman died, and in June 1737 it became a question with the parish whether his widow was not liable for the rebuilding of the house. By the next month nothing had been done apparently, as an entry in the minute-book permitted Captain Lowder to have for £4, 10s. 'a quantity of stones that came down out of the old spire, and also the stones that are in the parson's ground.' It is probable that the house was re-erected soon after this. It was again rebuilt in 1853, during the incumbency of Mr. Shapcott.

New Vicarage. Moxins.

Modern requirements have outgrown most of the ancient parsonages, and the vicarage of St. Michael's has not been tenanted by a vicar for many years. It still, under the name of the old glebe-house, belongs to the vicars, but in 1879 a spacious vicarage, No. 9 Portland Terrace, was obtained for the benefice on the old estate called Moxins, from which a charge of £5 per annum is payable to All Saints parish (see under 'All Saints'). The vicar of St. Michael's now pays this charge.

[1] Repairs for this building occur under 1441 (Steward's Book) and 1485, &c.

[2] A garden next to St. Michael's prison was rented by John Speed in 1641–42, at five shillings a year (Steward's Book).

See under 'Town Charities' for Spinks's, Mill's, Fifield's, and Sadleir's gifts; under 'Holy Rood' for Smith's and Cushen's. Charities.

*Vicars of St. Michael's.*

Nicholas, c. 1237 (Madox, Form., p. 378).
William de Arundel, in 1248 (ibid., p. 378).
William Sweyn, instituted October 21, 1305, on presentation of convent.
Robert de Hanydon, August 17, 1309.
John de Penbroke, September 23, 1316, on death of last; on February 26, 1316–17, obtained license to attend obsequies of the Lady Mary, daughter of the late King Edward I., who had as a child taken the veil at Amesbury, and for whose wine and oil the port of Southampton had been charged; leave of absence for year from date; on September 15, 1318, license for another year.
John de Lekford, October 9, 1324, on resignation of last, exchanging with him chapel of Wodynton, Isle of Wight (see under 'St. Mary's').
Robert de Bourne, June 29, 1332, on resignation of last, exchanging with him the rectory of Erneley (see under 'St. Mary's').
John de Tadcaster, October 25, 1339, on resignation of Bourne.
Peter de Malmeshull was vicar in 1351 (see above).
Robert Gerneys, May 3, 1376, on death of Malmeshull; obtains license to pursue his studies for a year at Oxford, June 15, 1377.
Gilbert Waryn, February 25, 1379–80, on resignation of last, exchanging with him church of Wychampton, Sarum.
Walter Staward, April 24, 1383, on resignation of last, exchanging with him church of Morchirchille, Sarum.
Richard Howey, November 11, 1387, on resignation of last, exchanging with him church of Spryngfelde, London.
Lambert Threkyngham, . . . Chancellor of Chichester.
Robert Keten, November 9, 1393, on death of last; obtains leave of absence (November 16, 1393) for three years for purposes of study in any approved centre in England (ubicunque in Angliâ illud [sc. studium] viget generale).
Joceus Bayly, May 22, 1404, on resignation of Walter Aude, 'last rector of the same.'
Walter Aude, June 1, 1404, on resignation of Joceus Bayly, 'last rector of the same.' It does not appear with which instituted vicar possession remained.
John Roberte . . .
Thomas Darsset, August 11, 1456, on resignation of Roberte.
William Darset, June 10, 1485, on death of last.
John Orpyt, probably from All Saints, in 1502; admitted into the Town Guild—*i.e.*, Corporation—by common assent, 'because he hath always been a helper of the town,' 1510 (Burgess Book).
Thomas Tomson, vicar in 1525 (Valor Ecclesiasticus).
William Aude, in 1550 (Liber Niger).
Lawrence Sutton . . .
Thomas Banester, February 19, 1557, on death of Sutton, by presentation of King (see above for presentment of Sir Thomas in 1576).
Simon Pett, 1588—no day or month—on resignation of last incumbent; similar entry occurs under November 15, 1591.
John Slatter, M.A., October 24, 1611, on death of last incumbent.
George Vernon, B.A., April 4, 1614; resigned September 16, 1628.

John Toms, M.A., October 4, 1628; buried at St. Michael's, July 2, 1652, 'minister of this parish' (Church Register).

It has been commonly said, on the authority of Walker (Sufferings, &c.), that a Mr. Martin was sequestrated from St. Michael's during the Puritan usurpation. This could hardly have been the case (see just above). Walker has probably mistaken the locality.

Giles Say, Presbyterian, intruded; ejected 1662 (see above).

Thomas Butler, instituted July 11, 1666, inducted September 1, on death of last incumbent—who this was does not appear—by presentation of King (see under 'Grammar School'); had been collated vicar of Millbrook and inducted September 3, 1662.

William Kingsman, vicar in 1703; buried at St. John's, May 22, 1736 (see under 'Grammar School').

William Budworth, vicar in 1737; sermon by him on Rebellion of 1745.

Robert Rooke, instituted and inducted July 23, 1752, on death or cession (sic.) of last; also rector of All Saints.

Thomas Mears, instituted and inducted November 13, 1793, on death of last (see under 'All Saints').

Charles Tapp Griffith, M.A., instituted May 10, inducted May 14, 1817, on cession of Mears to All Saints (see under 'Grammar School').

Thomas Lawes Shapcott, B.A., instituted December 3, inducted December 5, 1825, on cession of Griffith; died August 22, 1854 (see under 'Grammar School').

Edward Edmunds, instituted January 5, inducted January 8, 1855; died August 1864.

Stephen Mountcashell Innes, M.A., inducted October 24, 1864.

Francis Maundy Gregory, M.A., inducted September 1, 1870, on death of last.

## All Saints.

Patronage. The patronage of this benefice, formerly belonging to the convent of St. Denys, is now vested in the Bishops of the diocese.

Value. No mention of this church appears in the taxation of 1291, but a settled pension there of £1, 6s. 8d. yielded its tenth of 2s. 8d. In the 'Valor Ecclesiasticus' of 1536 the benefice was worth £9, 10s., which, after deducting procurations and a certain pension amounting together to £1, 8s. 3½d., gave a net value of £8, 1s. 8½d., paying its tenth of 16s. 2¼d.

In 1723 it stood in the King's books at £8, 1s. 10½d., and was of the clear yearly value of £18. Dr. Speed, in his only sentence about All Saints, gives the revenue thus: "Dues, £32; Queen's bounty, "£9; Mr. Windsor's legacy, £4; total, £45 per annum."

Notices. Notices of this church are scanty. Under April 1461 we find a payment[1] for watchmen at the church of All Hallows 'to kepe a manne þt hadde take sentwery;' but no details are given.

On March 17, 1463–64, an ordination was held here by William, Bishop of Sidon, suffragan of Winchester, and rector of this parish, when one acolyte and seven deacons were admitted.[2]

[1] Steward's Book.

[2] Regist. Waynflete.

Nothing of the history of the parish during the controversies of the following century has survived: in those of the next the ejectment of Mr. Robinson in 1662 claims some notice. Nathaniel Robinson appears to have been in Southampton in 1643, where on a fast-day, according to Walker, he delivered himself in an unbecoming manner.[1] We meet with him in the town books under January 18, 1646–47, where the following entry occurs:[2]—

'That Mr. Robinson bee sent for to the Audit-house, and bee advised to preach noe more excepte hee procure himselfe to bee legally ordained according to the ecclesiastical lawe of the realme. But answere was returned that hee was gone out of towne.'

Two days after this (January 20) the Town Council met again—

'To consider what course is fitt to be taken with Mr. Robinson, who is not an ordained minister, and yett preacheth publiquely. And ordered that this business bee respite untill Major Murford doe come to towne, and soe knowe of him whether hee will assist them in this service as the Parliament by theire declaration doe require, provided hee come to towne within this weake. Item, the constables of this towne were ordered to bee sent for and charged to forewarne some suspected inhabitants of this towne, that from henceforth they doe not meete at any conventicles or unlawfull assemblies to heare the worde of God preached or expounded by any person whatsoever that is not lawfully ordayned for the ministry.'

Mr. Robinson then was not in holy orders, and it is very certain that he never afterwards received episcopal ordination. In October 1648, however, we find that he been intruded into St. Lawrence's, and received from the town a share of the 'chantry' money—namely, £33, 6s. 8d.—in common with Mr. Lamplugh of Holy Rood and Mr. Toms of St. Michael's, who each were paid the same amount. At this period All Saints was being served by different ministers, who received payment from the same source up to Michaelmas 1648. In the following January (1649) Mr. Robinson was still at St. Lawrence's, the other ministers remaining as before at Holy Rood and St. Michael's, but a Mr. Clifford had been put into All Saints. It is to be presumed, since no evidence is forthcoming on the matter, that on the avoidance of All Saints Mr. Robinson was moved there. He has left no mark in the parish books beyond a note, at the end of Register I., bearing date 30th November 1653, concerning a disastrous fire which had occurred at the house of the roper Above Bar. After his ejectment from All Saints in 1662 Mr. Robinson's history became bound up with that of the congregation Above Bar (see under 'Above Bar Church').

The church originally possessed a peal of five bells, but from a curious notice of September 1682 we learn that three of these were stolen on Tuesday, August 29, between twelve and one at night. Fabric. Bells.

[1] Sufferings, pt. i. p. 18. [2] Journal.

Persons having any knowledge of the whereabouts of the bells, or of those who committed the theft, were desired to give notice to Dr. Speed, the mayor, or to Mr. Christopher Smith, alderman.[1] The parishioners went on with their two bells till 1716, when an effort (see under 'Holy Rood') was made to provide the original number.

Description of old church.

The old church consisted of a chancel and nave with north aisle, at the west end of which was an included tower of good form in three stages; in the lower of these was a three-light window, in the middle a clock, and in the upper a double lancet. The newel staircase of the tower was at the south-west angle, and above it was a simple bell cupola. There was a modern western porch, above which was a large Pointed window deprived of its original tracery.

Rebuilding.

The ruinous state of this church and the scantiness of accommodation having for some time engaged attention, plans were provided in May 1790 for rebuilding on an enlarged scale; and on May 13, 1791, a local Act 'for the taking down and rebuilding the parish church of All Saints, and for purchasing land for the purpose of a churchyard for the use of the parish,' received the royal assent. The Act appointed trustees for carrying the work into effect; and two other Acts amending the former were subsequently passed in 1793 (33 Geo. III. cap. 101) and in 1797 (38 Geo. III. cap. 1). The first of these Acts empowered the trustees to let, sell, or otherwise dispose of, for the objects of the Act, any part of certain lands and tenements then belonging to the parish.

Old parish property.

These consisted of two messuages or tenements with gardens, situated one on each side of Above Bar Street,[2] and of two other tenements, together with a shop which adjoined the church, on the north side of East Street. The above estates were now vested in the trustees for the purposes of the intended purchase and rebuilding, and in consequence the houses in Above Bar Street were sold, and those in East Street, with the shop, were taken down, and their site became partly occupied by the new church.

At one period there were two shops along the south side of the church.[3] In April 1615 the vestry chamber of the church, which had a room over it, was leased out with the adjacent property.

---

1 London Gazette, September 4–7, 1682, in Skelton's Guide, 1805.

2 That on the east side, by deed of gift, dated 20th February 1497 (12 Hen. VII.), from Richard Hilton, who also conveyed to the parish the two tenements on the north side of East Street, the site of which he had obtained from Peter Gruet in 1478; the shop had been built on church ground, a lease of which exists, bearing date in 1460 (38 Hen. VI.) The property on the west side of Above Bar Street is described in a lease of September 6, 1585.

3 The parish still possesses a large number of deeds and leases relating to the old property, as also an accurate account of the tenants, their fines and rents, for a considerable period.

The new church was commenced in the spring of 1792, and on August 3d the first stone was laid at the south-west corner by the Grand Master Provincial and brethren of the Freemasons, the mayor (Sir Yelverton Peyton, Bart.) and Corporation assisting. All the local clergy were present with the exception of the rector, who from infirmities did not attend. Preparatory to the ceremony divine service was performed and a sermon suitable to the occasion preached by the Rev. James Scott, rector of St. Lawrence and St. John. During the service the poet-laureate, H. J. Pye, Esq., occupied himself in the church porch [1] by writing an ode on the occasion, of which it will probably be sufficient to quote the first six lines:— The present church.

'Tho' Ambition (oft deck'd in false Glory's gilt robe)
Stirs the nations to war and unpeoples the globe,
Awhile let the trumpet of Insolence cease,
And be sacred this day to the triumph of Peace.
On the stone this day laid may a fair pile be rear'd,
By Religion protected, by Virtue endear'd.'

The church was consecrated on November 12, 1795, by William, Bishop of Exeter, in place of Bishop North, who was as usual abroad. The sermon at the consecration was preached by the rector, Dr. Mant, who took for his theme the value of liturgical forms of worship; it was attacked by Mr. Kingsbury of Above Bar Chapel, who in answer produced a pamphlet on the manner of worship of the Protestant Dissenters. Description.

This church, from the designs of Mr. John Reveley, a pupil of Sir William Chambers, and carried out by Mr. John Hookey, builder, of Southampton, has a west frontage in the High Street of 66 feet 6 inches. The building is in two stages throughout. Its front is adorned with a pediment supported by four three-quarter columns of the Ionic order, four feet in diameter and thirty-six feet high. In the basement are three entrances into the vestibule of the church, which is lighted by fan-lights over the doors. The upper stage of this front is furnished with five empty niches, the absence of windows on this side being intended for shutting off the noise of the street. The south side is pierced with sixteen windows in two ranges, the lower of which admit light under the gallery, and are six feet square; the windows in the upper range are thirteen feet high by six broad. On the north side houses abut on the church. The whole body is of brick stuccoed, with the exception of the footing on the south side and the plinths of the great columns. Rather a handsome cupola at the east end, also of stone, is supported by the arch which covers the altar. It consists of six Corinthian columns fifteen feet high, standing on a square basement in three groups of two each supporting a circular entablature,

[1] Salisbury and Winchester Journal.

above which three large clock dials are contrived, the whole being surmounted by a dome, from which again rises a small Attic order, finished by a gilt pine-apple and vane. The effect of this structure is greatly lost by its position at the east end. The dimensions of the interior of the church are: width, 61 feet; length, including vestibule, but excluding the altar recess, 95 feet; height to the spring of the segmented ceiling, 39 feet; the rise of the arch, 8 feet,—thus giving a total height of 47 feet. This roof is the chief feature in the building; it is framed together without any support from columns over a span of 61 feet, and is adorned with sunken panels after classical models. There is a wide gallery round three sides of the church, a fine organ being placed at the west end. The recess for the altar, raised three steps, is lighted simply by a window on each side, an arrangement intended to accommodate a picture, for which an arched space was prepared on the east wall. This church was more admired some years ago than it is at present. The architect, however, had to solve a problem in which he certainly succeeded: how to provide for the greatest number at the least cost? The result was the above-described parallelogram, accommodating 1400 people, at an original outlay not exceeding £6000. Since the church was opened about £4000 have been spent upon it; much has been done in late years, and the accommodation has been increased.

Interior.

Catacombs.

Catacombs were constructed underneath the church. They are now disused, but are already largely tenanted. Here, among many others locally well known, are the remains of Admiral Philip Carteret, the circumnavigator, buried July 28, 1796, aged sixty-three; of Bercher Baril, a well-known member of the Corporation, in the same year; of Colonel Philip Fall (Governor Fall) of Jersey, in 1797; of General D'Auvergne, who in 1795 was mayor, and to whom a tablet is erected, in 1800; of Sir Yelverton Peyton, Bart., who lived where are now the Philharmonic Rooms, and was thrice mayor, in 1815; of Bryan Edwards, author of the "History of the West Indies," 1819, 5 vols. 8vo; and of Lord Lisle, in 1834.

Churchyard.

The churchyard, now closed, is situated at the Back of the Walls, a little south of East Street.

Rectory.

The ancient rectory-house in East Street (now No. 3, occupied by Mr. Carter) seems to have been acquired by Thomas Michell, rector,[1] who rebuilt it in stone, probably about 1470. The property was sold in 1858, and with the proceeds, together with a sum specially raised, the present rectory-house, 16 Anglesea Place, was provided.

The house No. 179 High Street belongs to the rectory of All Saints, but the garden is Corporation property.

[1] So stated in grant of Peter Gruet to Richard Hilton, 1478 (see above).

The population of All Saints in 1881, apart from the ecclesiastical parishes of St. Peter and St. Paul, was 6903. Population.

Mrs. Alice Palmer, by her will, bearing date September 5, 1709, gave to John Gully and his heirs an orchard called Moxins, in the parish of All Saints, on trust, to pay yearly to the churchwardens of All Saints and their successors £5, to be distributed by them for the use of the poor of the parish, with power to the churchwardens from time to time, in case of non-payment of the annuity, to enter upon the said orchard and receive the profits of it for the purpose above stated. The site of this orchard is now occupied by St. Michael's vicarage in Portland Terrace, which is charged with the above annuity. The distribution is made in bread. Palmer's Gift.

The Honourable Andrews Windsor[1] of Southampton, by indenture[2] bearing date 1st May (22 Geo. II.) 1749, conveyed to the Corporation three acres of arable land, commonly called Littlefield, and one of meadow, lying at a place called Prior East Mead, all in the parish of Breamore, in trust, for the benefit of the rector of All Saints Church, for maintenance of an additional monthly sacrament at the Church of All Saints, namely, on the third Sunday in every month, and for prayers on three mornings in the week preceding each such celebration. Failing strict compliance on the part of the rector, the mayor and Corporation were desired to pay the whole of the trust rents to the vicar of Reigate, and the overseers of the poor of that part of the parish of Reigate called Uplands and Foreigners, to be distributed by them to poor housekeepers, being communicants. The grantor directed this disposition, on failure of the conditions at All Saints, in consequence of Flanchford, the residence of his late father, Thomas, Earl of Plymouth, being situated in that part of Reigate. There has apparently been a miscarriage of this gift. In Dr. Speed's time the rector of All Saints received the benefaction, but nothing is known of it at the present day; nor does the parish of Reigate receive it in any shape or form; nor does the Corporation of Southampton now possess any land in the parish of Breamore, or has possessed any within living memory: and by another most singular circumstance the site of the old family mansion of the Windsors in the parish of Reigate is unknown. Windsor's Gift.

For Mill's, Sadleir's, Fifield's, and Bird's gifts, see under 'Town Charities;' for Henry Smith's, see under 'Holy Rood.'

The earliest register-book was procured for the 'recording of marriages, births, and burials according to an Act of Parliament dated Register Books.

---

[1] Andrews Windsor, fourth son of Thomas, Earl of Plymouth, born about 1679; brigadier-general, February 11, 1711.

[2] Conveyance and title-deeds in possession of Corporation.

August 24, A.D. 1653.' The first marriage (January 24, 1653–54) was performed by Mr. Peter Seale, senior (see under 'Mayors'), marriage being at this time simply a civil contract. The births in the register begin May 1650: the registration is that of *birth*, though *baptism* sometimes is mentioned. An interesting instance is that of Samuel, son of Mr. Henry Coxe, minister, who was born June 19, 1661, and baptized on the 23d of that month. Henry Coxe was, no doubt, the Presbyterian minister at Bishopstoke, and the officiant at his child's baptism was possibly his friend, Nathaniel Robinson, who was at this time at All Saints (see above). The formal registration of baptism does not commence till 1663. The register of burials commences September 30, 1653.

*Rectors of All Saints.*

William de St. Denys, instituted October 9, 1305, on presentation of convent.

Thomas le Barbur, December 23, 1305. This rector must have been previously appointed in some form, since we find the matter of the presentation in dispute with his predecessor; a citation in this cause issuing out May 10, and a commission appointed July 11, 1305.

Roger Balvair, August 27, 1307, on resignation of last, by collation of the Bishop, lawful patron for this turn.

William de Swyna, November 27, 1334, by presentation of convent.

John Dunstan, June 28, 1337, on exchange with last of perpetual chaplaincy in College of St. Edmund, Sarum, by presentation of convent.

Adam Waleys, March 10, 1341–42, exchanging with last perpetual vicarage of the church of Wambergh, Sarum diocese.

Thomas le Blount, January 8, 1347–48, receives license for studying for a year from date, a period subsequently extended to enable him to take a further step in Holy Orders.

John de Upton, July 29, 1349.

Peter de Ravenwyke, September 25, 1349, on resignation of last.

John Tonge, May 8, 1373, exchanging with last from rectory of church of Stodleye, Exon.

Peter Trewens, September 10, 1374.

Roger Oliver, May 24, 1394.

Thomas Michell (see under 'Rectory House').

William Donys or Doyns, June 19, 1457, on resignation of last.

William Westcarre, S.T.P., Bishop of Sidon, February 9, 1463–64, on death of last; Bishop Suffragan of Winchester (1457–86); Prior of Mottisfont; he probably resigned All Saints in view of St. Martin's, Ludgate, to which he was preferred, October 30, 1465.

John Halshall, May 7, 1465, on resignation of last.

David Kemys, Bachelor in Decrees, July 16, 1466, on resignation of last.

Leonard Wherton . . .

William Surteys, April 28, 1480, exchanging with last from the church of Wambergh, Sarum.

Sir Richard[1] . . .

[1] Placed doubtfully among rectors. Under 1488 (temp. T. Overey) mention is made of 'Sir Richard, preste of Alhalowen,' who was fined for violent language against Mr. Mayor. There was a Sir Richard, the Guild priest, at the same time.

Thomas Shortryge . . .

John Newman, LL.B., June 24, 1491, on death of last, by presentation of Archbishop of Canterbury, through grant of convent.

John Orpyt (see under 'St. Michael's').

William Norbury, November 23, 1502, on resignation of last.

Edmund Banners, c. 1505, on resignation of last (Addit. 15,314, f. 101).

William Cotton . . .

Richard Wakefield, November 24, 1509, on death of Cotton.

John Incent, LL.D., . . . resigns October 20, 1521, and receives pension from this church till another benefice shall be provided (see under 'St. Mary's').

Edward Redford or Redfal, April 10, 1522, on resignation of last.

John Croke, May 10, 1551, on death of last, by presentation of King, the Priory being now suppressed.

Thomas Steere, November 20, 1562, on resignation of last.

Mr. Calvert [1] . . .

Henry Hopkins, M.A., May 27, 1589.

John Drake, August 28, 1600, on death of last (see under 'Grammar School').

Nicholas Plummer, M.A., June 2, 1613.

Alexander Rosse, D.D., July 7, 1628; he signs a receipt for Mill's charity as 'rector,' May 4, 1647; in the body of the document he is oddly called 'minister of All Hollands' (Church Register); see under 'Grammar School.'

Mr. Clifford was at All Saints in January 1648–49 (Town Journal).

Nathaniel Robinson intruded (see above and under 'St. Lawrence' and 'Holy Rood').

John Pinhorne, M.A. . . . (see under 'Grammar School').

Richard Pocock, LL.B., appointed probably in 1700 (see under 'Grammar School').

William Purbeck, instituted May 31, 1716.

William Scott, instituted May 29, inducted May 31, 1740 (see under 'Grammar School').

Robert Rooke, B.A., instituted May 1, inducted May 2, 1767, on death of Scott; also vicar of St. Michael's.

Richard Mant, D.D., rector of Fonthill Bishops; certificate of value and distance, October 11; instituted to All Saints, November 13, 1793, on death of last (see under 'Grammar School').

Thomas Mears, instituted April 28, inducted April 30, 1817, on death of last (see under 'Guild Chaplains,' also 'St. Michael's' and 'St. Lawrence').

John Emylius Shadwell, M.A., instituted May 15, inducted May 18, 1835, on death of last.

Henry Almack, B., afterwards D.D., instituted May 18, inducted May 20, 1843, on death of Shadwell; also rector of the sinecure rectory of Aberdaron, diocese of Bangor, 1843; rector of Fawley, Henley-on-Thames, 1846.

Charles Simon Faithfull Fanshawe, M.A., instituted January 23, inducted January 24, 1846, by cession of Almack and by exchange with him from Fawley; went to Upham.

---

[1] Placed doubtfully among the rectors. The Court Leet Book of 1587 contains a presentment of Mr. Calvert 'because he has a house and a skelyng in the backside of his parsonage-house in All Hallow's parish, thatched.' John Calvert, M.A., was at this time rector of Millbrook, to which he was admitted February 3, 1586–87. He may have been also rector of All Saints; or his house may have been called a parsonage because he lived in it.

Henry Carey, M.A., instituted February 16, inducted February 19, 1855, on cession of last to Upham; went to North Waltham.

Arthur Bradley, M.A., instituted March 2, inducted March 17, 1863, on cession of last to North Waltham, by collation of Bishop, the benefice being now in patronage of the see of Winchester; formerly perpetual curate of Hale, Farnham.

### District Parishes separated from the Parish of All Saints.

*St. Paul's.*—This ecclesiastical parish was formed February 3, 1863, a conventional district having been arranged in April 1860. In 1871 its population was 2068, in 1881 it was 2285. St. Paul's was the first projected of the new churches in Southampton, and in March 1824 the Corporation offered a hundred guineas towards its erection. It was, however, carried out as a proprietary chapel. It was built of brick and stucco in the Perpendicular style of the period, from designs of Mr. Benham. A critic in February 1828, viewing the new church in its nearly completed state, pronounced that it might form a picturesque object at the entrance to the town—Mile End the locality was sometimes called—but that its half-warlike, half-religious appearance would prove a monument of the growing corruption in architectural taste. The church was consecrated after the formation of the parish on October 18, 1863. A handsome new chancel was added by Rev. J. W. Cary, D.D., in 1862, the stained glass of the east window being given by his former pupils. The church was reseated in good taste in 1871. The long Perpendicular windows of paltry work were gradually replaced by stone-work of good design filled with stained glass, as opportunity occurred, by the same incumbent. Since his death another window has been added to his memory, and the church is becoming by degrees an example of what may be done with a parallelogram of mean design.

There is a vicarage-house, lately acquired, situated in Carlton Crescent.

The baptismal register dates from 1860; that for marriages from 1863.

The benefice is a new-vicarage in the gift of the Bishop.

#### *Incumbents.*

William Bettridge, B.D., . . . 1828, formerly distinguished in the army; served under Wellington; born 1791; ordained 1824; offered Bishopric of Huron; died August 1882.

William Preston Hulton, M.A., September 23, 1834, on resignation of last, on nomination of trustees; subsequently in 1864 built at his own cost Holy Trinity Church, Weston, which he served till his death.

Robert Dampier, M.A., . . . 1851.

Peter Harnett Jennings, M.A., . . . 1853.

James Walter Cary, D.D., March 12, 1859, on cession of Jennings; patronage vested in Dr. Cary, April 12, 1862; it was subsequently exchanged under Bishop Wilberforce.

George Cecil White, M.A., inducted December 21, 1877, by collation of Bishop, on resignation of Dr. Cary.

*St. Peter's.*—This ecclesiastical parish was formed by Order in Council, February 4, 1861, from which year the parish registers date. The population of the district amounted to 1765 in 1871, and to 1866 in 1881. The Church of St. Peter's, Commercial Road, in the Norman style, was finished in 1845, very much owing to the exertions of Rev. John Langley, the first incumbent. The church is well placed, and presents a good exterior. It has been further improved of recent years. The living is a new-vicarage in the gift of the rector of All Saints.

*Incumbents.*

John Langley, M.A., May 25, 1846; had been curate of All Saints; on the vacancy in that church in 1835, Corporation petitioned that Mr. Langley might be appointed.

Charles Edward Steward, M.A., May 1869, on resignation of Langley; formerly perpetual curate of Churt, Farnham, 1865–69.

## French Church.

It has been a constant tradition in the Congregation that a French Church was established at Southampton by letters patent of King Edward VI.;[1] but no such letters are forthcoming. The earliest notice of the foreign congregation in this place is probably to be derived from a petition[2] to the Corporation bearing date May (?) 1567, proffered by a body of Walloons who had obtained permission from Queen Elizabeth to settle in the town. The petitioners speak in the name of many in the Low Countries of Germany, who are so oppressed in their consciences, especially with the 'intolerable clog of the Spanish Inquisition,' that they are determined to give up goods and fatherland and seek an asylum where they may live 'quietly and Christian-like' either in England, France, or Germany. They further say :—

1567. Walloon petition to Corporation.

That on the arrival of several of their number in England, they were received with such courtesy and liberality that they could have no other wish than to be permitted to remain; that on petition to Queen Elizabeth she had favourably entertained their suit and directed them to Southampton : 'shee appointed us unto this youre towne, where wee should freely and peaceably make our abode and quietly exercise marchandizing.' Lest, however, their coming should appear 'noisome' to their worships the mayor and Corporation, and their 'occupations' new and strange, they think it good to make their request and explain their needs in writing :—

[1] Case respecting Mercier's Legacy, December 11, 1749, which set forth that the Church was settled at God's House by letters patent of Edward VI.

[2] Vespasian F. ix. fol. 259.

1. In the first place, they desire to have a church assigned them, 'within which it may be lawful to have sermons and other service and sacraments to be used apperteyning to the Christian religion and administration, as it was used in the time of the noble prince of famous memorie King Edward the Sixte,[1] and is now at this present.'

2. They ask leave to exercise their trades of whatever kind in the town and neighbourhood, or if that appear unreasonable and contrary to local privilege, at least 'such misteries and occupacions' as had not been practised in the country before; and they beg permission to employ in their houses as many hands, male and female, of their own people as may be necessary, since unskilled labour would be prejudicial to their trade, and so to the town.

3. They request the Corporation's influence with landlords and house-owners to exact no more rent than had been paid for the last two years.

4. In case of not finding a market for all their goods, they ask the privilege of exportation, stating that they are willing to pay reasonable custom, and an augmentation after twenty years at the Queen's pleasure.

5. Should their expectation in the number of artificers ready to join them prove unfounded, and the quantity of sayes and other wares manufactured be insufficient to enable them to maintain a dyer with his family, they ask that they may send their fabrics over the sea undyed.

6. And lastly, should it not be lawful for shoemakers, tailors, and other like artificers 'to occupy their sciences' within the liberties of the town, they request that their countrymen may be permitted to compound and agree reasonably with their worships on such matters.

Having begged the good offices of the Corporation with the Queen's Council and with the Bishop of Winchester, out of the 'humanity' which they bore 'towards the afflicted for the gospel's sake,' they concluded by assuring the Corporation that their settlement within the town would soon be found a public benefit, and that they were able and willing 'to pay such taxes and talents and other impositions' for the maintenance of the town as should be thought good and expedient.

To this the Corporation replied—(1.) That the request for a church should be made to the ordinary. (2.) That they might practise within the town trades hitherto unknown, but that servants from their own country could not be allowed. (3.) That they would find landlords reasonable. That to the 4th and 5th sections they had no answer to return, the matter belonging to higher authority. (6.) That as for shoemakers and tailors, there were too many in the town already.

Judging from the notes by Cecil upon the above petition and reply, we do not gather that the strangers had full success with her Majesty's Council at first. They appealed to Bishop Horne, who recommended their case to Cecil on June 30, 1567, and again on September 19; after which we find the reply of the Council to the following effect:—

Twenty families of strangers might be permitted to settle in the town, with ten men-servants in each household, on condition that each retained and instructed for seven years in their sciences two English apprentices, and that after seven years for every two strangers they kept one Englishman. During seven years they should pay but half strangers' subsidies for wares made in Southampton, to be carried out only from that port. The same for any new commodities made by

[1] The reference is to the description and kind of service, and not to their having enjoyed it at that period, any more than they were so doing at the date of their petition.

them on which no custom was appointed. They were to have the same privilege for strangers as Sandwich had.[1]

Accordingly we find a congregation of Walloon strangers settled in the chapel of God's House before the close of 1567, at which period (December) the register of the French Church commences, and, as we learn from several entries in that volume, the same year was that of their admission into Hampton. We do not know by what several steps they obtained footing within the chapel of God's House, or many questions might have been avoided in times past. Letters patent from Queen Elizabeth have been alleged,[2] under which it was believed that this Congregation was established as one of the seven Walloon churches, and somehow or other gifted to a great extent with the hospital chapel; but no such letters can be found, and we conclude that the congregation, as such, was simply protected by a royal license, while for the place of their meeting they must have obtained the permission of Queen's College, to which body (see under 'God's House') the entire hospital, and so its chapel or chapels, belonged.

Congregation dates from 1567.

The earlier history of the French Congregation is to be derived from their register,[3] the order of which it will be convenient to follow. The volume is divided into sections recording the admissions to the Lord's Supper, the baptisms, marriages, and deaths, and the fasts of the community. The first entry gives 'The names of those who have made profession of their faith and are admitted to the Supper, the 21st December 1567.' Then follows a list of those received to the Supper the 5th April 1568. The settlers appear mostly to have come from Lisle, Valenciennes, and other places in the Low Countries, from Normandy and the Channel Islands; their occupations being various. The Supper appears to have been celebrated four times a year, afterwards for a short period it became more frequent. None were admitted to join the Congregation of whose good intentions the authorities were not satisfied, and the Communion was withheld from their own members when discipline so required. Against many names the word 'messe' is written, which implies that such persons before leaving the Continent had heard mass in order to avoid persecution or to facilitate their escape, and were now required publicly to express their sorrow. New-comers were required to produce witnesses of their having belonged to 'the religion' before leaving France, for fear of spies under colour of brethren; this caution was, moreover, enjoined by the magistracy of the town. Among the communicants there occurs a large number of

History from Register.

Admissions.

[1] Cal. State Papers, 1567 (Addenda, vol. 1566–79).

[2] Case respecting Mercier's Legacy, December 1749.

[3] Original Register Book, in the custody of the Registrar-General, Somerset House.

ministers from abroad, probably, for the most part, passing through the town, but some were settled. One of them, a M. du Plantin, otherwise Antoine Ylot, seems to have kept a school; seven of his young scholars are mentioned as communicating. Various names of interest in subsequent town history occur.[1] It seems that the family of Saravia were settled among these early refugees. In the list of July 1569 we have Christopher de Saravia and his wife. These were the father and mother of the celebrated Adrian de Saravia, who was master of the Grammar School soon after this. The death of Christopher, who is described as a Spaniard, took place on May 27, 1572; that of his wife, Eliza Boulangier, on December 28, 1578. In the list of January 1570 the wife and servant of Monsieur Mestre Adrian Saravia are recorded as among those admitted to the Supper; while in that of April 1572 appear two of his scholars,[2] Nicholas Essard and Nicholas Carye. In June 1571 Saravia was witness at the baptism of a daughter of Louis du Bois. In this entry he is described as 'ministre,' and it is possible that at this period he may have officiated as pastor of the congregation. The former minister, Wallerand Thenelin, was still living, but he ceases to be described as minister of the church after the end of 1570. Saravia again appears as a witness at a baptism in June 1576, but not described as minister.

Saravia.

It appears that a few English were admitted into the Congregation; thus in 1582 there is mention of one Cornice, maistre de navire, Anglois, and afterwards la femme Cornice. Under January 6, 1628–29, after the fall of Rochelle in the previous October, we have refugees from the Isle of Rhé received to communion of the church and to the Supper. At the same time several from other quarters were received. This portion of the volume ends with the year 1665, when Captain James Clungeon, Mr. Nicholas Caplain, and Mr. Richard Blackford were received.

Baptisms.

The baptisms commence with 1567, Wallerand Thenelin being minister. As a witness to a baptism in 1573 occurs the name of Richard Estur, the donor of the present town seal, who is described as a native of Southampton and a burgess. In 1584 three baptisms were performed by Mr. Hopkins, an English minister—perhaps vicar of Holy Rood. On November 1, 1663, was baptized Adam, son of Mr. Adam de Cardonnel of Caen, an elder of the church, and of Madame Marie Pescod, his wife; this Adam de Cardonnel, the father, being customer and collector of Southampton. He died January 20, 1710–11, aged ninety years; Marie Pescod, daughter of Nicholas Pescod, alder-

[1] Such as Malortie, Clungeon, Le Pork, Brock, La Motte, Lempriere, Priaulx, Le Feuvre, Estur, Le Say, and many others.

[2] 'Tous deux escolliers a Mestre Adrian Saravia.'

man, of Southampton, having preceded him on July 27, 1708, at the age of seventy-eight years. Both were buried within the chapel, close to where is now the altar. Under 1665 we have a notice of the plague. The greater number of the town's people had abandoned their houses, and Mr. Bernard,[1] their minister, compelled by sickness, had himself sought change of air in the country, and was still away; in his absence, by desire of the mayor, M. Courand, the French minister, had baptized a little English infant by the name of Nicholas. The entry says that the baptism was performed in the French Church, but a note immediately below says it was at St. John's. Anyhow it occurred on July 23; and after this, in November, Mr. Courand baptized a few more children in Mr. Bernard's continued absence, some at the French Church, others at Holy Rood. A few years after this a fresh stream of refugee immigration seems to have set in.

M. Courand and the plague

In the marriage section of the register, under November 1665, we find M. Courand, by permission of the mayor, blessing the marriages of William Farmer and Elizabeth Baker, and of John Chapman and Sarah Taylor. The deacons of the church, who seem to have kept the register, enter next the marriage, on December 4th, of Jacob Berger and Sarah Baylie, accompanying the entry with the sad remark that these two English people 'received the benediction of their marriage from our pastor at the Church of St. John, the English clergy having abandoned their flocks on account of the plague then desolating the place.' On the other hand, we have the union of Jean Ralins, a deacon of the church, with Anne, the daughter of Joseph De la Motte, an elder, blessed at St. John's Church in September 1669 by Mr. Thomas Pittis, vicar of Holy Rood; and in July 1671, when the same Jean married Judie, daughter of M. le docteur Philippe de Carteret,[2] of Jersey, they received the benediction at Millbrook Church from Mr. Thomas Butler, vicar of St. Michael's and late of the Grammar School.

Marriages.

In the register of deaths we have proof of the fearful amount of mortality in plague years. Under April 1583 occurs the note in the margin, 'La peste a commencée,' between which date and April 1584 no

Deaths.

---

[1] He was at his brother's house, Eling Vicarage, where he died March 31, and was buried April 2, 1666. Dr. Speed ("Batt upon Batt") married his widow, Elizabeth, the daughter of a Mr. Baker, probably in the following year. Mr. Bernard was vicar of Holy Rood, within which parish God's House is situate. Paul Mercier (see below) left him a legacy of £5 as a mark of regard.

[2] Members of the old Jersey family of Carteret were frequently resident in Southampton. Some of their relatives lie buried at God's House. Rear-Admiral Philip Carteret, as we have seen, was buried at All Saints. His son Philip, by Mary Rachel Silvester, became also a distinguished naval officer and C.B., and assuming the surname of his uncle, Sir John Silvester, succeeded him in the baronetcy in 1822. He died without an heir, having never been married, in 1828.

less than seventy-one persons are noticed as having died of the plague, the annual average otherwise being very small. In 1604 the plague entries commence on June 1st, between which day and the end of the year one hundred and fifty persons are marked as its victims.[1] During the visitation of 1665 it is somewhat strange to find only twenty-four persons recorded as having died of the *peste*, the first entry occurring on July 15th; registration may have been imperfectly carried out. Under 1661 an affectionate record is made of the death, on August 22d, and the burial within the chapel, of Paul Mercier, 'one of the great pillars of the church and full of alms-deeds.'

Fasts.

The section devoted to the public fasts held in times of trouble, 'according to the custom of the churches of God,' notices about seventy of such acts of humiliation. The first was on 3d September 1568, when the refugees besought God's blessing on the Prince of Orange in his descent upon the Low Countries to deliver the 'afflicted Churches' there. In 1570 another fast was held upon the defeat of the Prince de Condé, to pray God's help for their suffering brethren. Again, in 1572, after the horrible massacre of St. Bartholomew's Day, when twelve or thirteen thousand of the faithful were killed in one night.[2] In 1576 a fast was held to implore God's blessing on the friendship of Queen Elizabeth with the Prince of Orange, as bearing, of course, on the safety of the Protestants. The portent of the earthquake is recorded in April, and that of the comet in October 1580. The great plague year of 1583 was marked by a solemn fast on September 12, for beseeching God's pity on His poor Churches: (1) those of France, in great affliction by menace of war; (2) those of Flanders, persecuted by the Spaniards, who set up again Papistry and idolatry; and (3) the church within the town, which for the last five or six months has been sorely stricken by the plague; about fifty persons of the church having already died, and about four hundred of the town, and it continues still. In November 1588 thanks were returned for the dispersion of the Spanish Armada; and in the next month a fast was held for beseeching like mercies on the Churches of France and Flanders which had been shown to England.

Interview with Queen Elizabeth.

On September 4, 1591, Queen Elizabeth visited the town with her full court, and stayed till the 7th about mid-day, when the foreigners placed themselves in her way, determined on an interview in the

[1] It appears that the states of Jersey sent some assistance to the burgesses under their affliction, and a reference to their letter of thanks as a memorial of mutual friendship is made in the Jersey records, April 8, 1607 (livre i. p. 34). (Extract furnished by H. M. Godfray, Esq.)

[2] This purports to be the number of those who were massacred in Paris alone.

fulness of their gratitude. 'When she was gone and was without the town, not having been able to get access to her Majesty before, we thanked her for having enjoyed her protection in this town for more than twenty-four years.' She replied very kindly, blessing God that it had been in her power to afford protection to the poor strangers, whose prayers, she knew well, had served much to the preservation of her dominions.

The last fast recorded in regular sequence was on June 19, 1667, under the pastorate of Courand. One more occurs on December 16, 1720, and the next and last on December 8, 1721.

Deputation to Bishop.

The volume closes with a notice of a deputation from the Congregation on July 13, 1584, to the Bishop of Winchester, Dr. Thomas Cooper, who had been translated from Lincoln to Winchester in March that year, consisting of the minister, Matthew Sohier, William Hersen, and Peter Le Say, praying him to continue the kindness in maintaining their church which his predecessors had afforded. This the Bishop promised, together with his full protection. Probably on every occasion of a vacancy in the See the French Congregation took care to approach the new Bishop in a similar way, though the above is the only instance recorded.

Archbishop's Visitation.

In 1635, at a visitation of the Archbishop's commissary and vicar-general, Sir Nathaniel Brent, we gather from the examination of Daniel Sauvage, minister of the French Church, John Clungeon and Peter Seale, aldermen, being present, that more English than French families attended the chapel. This was ordered to be reformed: aliens were to be permitted the liberty granted them, but the English were to frequent their parish churches, which was promised. The commissary adds, that on the day of his visitation (June 25) the mayor offered him a burgess's place, which he declined, because the mayor had not first called upon him. In reference to the town he says, 'I found no Puritans in this place on whom anything could be fastened, yet there are many that do straggle to other parish churches from their own.'[1]

The account of Dr. Speed, who had no access to the earlier history of the French Congregation, is as follows:—

"In the year 1668 there was a scheme for settling some French "Protestants in this town to carry on a silk-weaving manufacture, but "it did not succeed. However, about that time, or a few years after, "enough of them had settled here to form a congregation, and they "had, and still have, by the leave of Queen's College and the license "of the Bishop of Winchester, the use of the chapel at God's House, "which is therefore usually called the French Chapel or French Church.

[1] Cal. State Papers, 1635, June 25.

"They were all of them Dissenters, and in the year 1683 a complaint "was made to the Bishop by the magistrates of the town, that other "Dissenters made this chapel, being a licensed one, a kind of asylum "to protect them from the laws then in being against Nonconformity, "and the people of better sort of the islands of Guernsey and Jersey "complained that their countrymen, who frequented this chapel when "they came to Southampton, frequently returned greatly prejudiced "against the Liturgy (which was then, and I think is still, [not] alto- "gether used in those islands), praying, therefore, that the minister "of this chapel may be ordered to use the Liturgy of the Church of "England in French, as at the Savoy in London."[1]

On the revocation of the Edict of Nantes, October 22, 1685, a considerable addition was made to the foreign community in Southampton. From an undated letter,[2] to be assigned to 1694, addressed by the administrators of the foreign refugee fund to the mayor (Dr. Speed) and the Common Council of the town of Southampton, we gather that the Council had applied for assistance through Sir Benjamin Newland, one of the members for the borough, to enable the settlers at Southampton to establish a silk manufacture after the fashion of Tours and Lyons. The Council were informed in reply—

Establishment of silk manufacture.

That the setting up of trade was a secondary consideration with the administrators, immediate relief to the sufferers being the first, and so great was the demand on the fund that fears were entertained of its not holding out. They had, nevertheless, consulted Mr. Paul Grimpé, who had viewed the town with special reference to starting this industry, and from him they had understood that many of the town authorities, especially Mr. Cardonnel, had proposed that a fund should be gathered in the place itself, provided a considerable number of artists should be found willing to settle there. The administrators were willing to encourage such a settlement, believing that it would be a public benefit and of great service to the Corporation, as the settling of this and other manufactures had certainly been to Canterbury, London, Colchester, Maidstone, Norwich, and other places. They suggest the employment of thirty looms as a beginning, which would give occupation to over a hundred persons; anticipating a speedy increase in the works, since 'this Grimpé,' who, though not a refugee himself, was willing to head the undertaking at Southampton, had succeeded well in London for some years past, where provisions and labour were dearer than in Southampton. Materials of silk and grogrin[3] yarn might be supplied at first on credit from London. In conclusion, provided the town authorities receive a sufficient number of families to carry on the silk trade, the administrators promise their best towards providing 'utensils for them at their first settling;' they add what another Corporation has found to be an inducement 'to some of these poor people

[1] "In consideration of the use which the islanders make of this chapel when "they come to Southampton, the following dues have been appointed to the "minister:—The French minister's dues in the port of Southampton from the "inhabitants of Jersey, Guernsey, Alderney," &c. [The tariff is not here produced.]

[2] Original letter.

[3] Coarse grain.

in order to the settling a linen manufacture'—the magistrates have offered to give them £100, to pay the interest of £1000 for three years, to ease them as to house rent, and free them from all parochial charges.

With this broad hint to the Corporation the writers remain their very loving friends, J. Warde, H. London.

The sequel does not appear, but the trade was settled in the town and carried on in Winkle Street. We may now return to the community in their ecclesiastical relations. Three years previously to the date of the above correspondence, a petition,[1] bearing date June 18 (3 Will. and Mary), 1691, had been presented by the ministers, elders, and members of the French Congregation to the Court at Whitehall, praying for a confirmation of their ancient rights and privileges 'as they were confirmed to the Church of Canterbury and are now enjoyed in London;' but the result of this petition does not appear.

Petition to Whitehall.

The present minute-book of the French Church commences with the year 1702, Antoine Cougot, doctor of medicine, being minister, Messrs. de Cardonnel, De Gruchy, De Veule, and Guillaume, the elders, and Messrs. Le Blanc, Courand, and Lavand, deacons. It will be interesting to abridge consecutively a few of the consistory and general meetings. The first entry is dated March 24, 1701–2: it is of a consistory. After the invocation of the sacred name, it was resolved that the Supper should be celebrated on Easter Sunday, and that the preparation sermon should be preached on the preceding Friday—Good Friday as such not being observed—and on the same day M. Le Blanc would distribute 'les marraux,' or the passes of admission to the sacred rite. The Congregation were to be apprised of this resolution on the Sunday next after its adoption. The meeting then adjusted a matter of difference between Adam de Veule, an elder, and Paul Courand, a deacon, censuring both parties; after which exercise of discipline, M. Cougot was requested to enter in the new minute-book, which would last many years—the volume is still in use—an account of the privileges of the Church; an instruction never carried out, or the entry has been removed. At the next consistory, that of May 5, a certain M. La Combe appeared and confessed that, under the violence of persecution, he had heard mass in France, and desired to give proof of his repentance; upon which, after an earnest exhortation, he was ordered to appear publicly after the second, or evening, preaching on the next Sunday, to be received to the peace of the Church. At the following consistory on August 3, two natives of Havre, who had been captured by one of the Queen's ships, were present to express sorrow for having yielded to the persuasion of terror and heard mass. They were

History from minute-book.

[1] French Church Papers.

examined on the 'points of our holy religion,' and having promised to return no more to France, at least till liberty of conscience should be proclaimed, their reception to the peace of the Church was arranged for the following Sunday (August 9), after the second preaching. On Sunday, August 23, Courand retired from the office of a deacon with the thanks of the community, and Francis Cabot was chosen. The minute-book records the retirements from time to time of the elders and deacons, generally after a service of some years; but these changes need not further be mentioned. At the next meeting on Sunday, September 6, 1762, two more public confessions were made of having been at mass. On November 8, two natives of Amsterdam confessed to having been at mass, and Philippe Algon of Ostend, a prisoner, having been adequately instructed, abjured the Roman Catholic faith, and was received. On December 1, 1702, it was arranged in consistory that the Supper should be celebrated on Sunday, December 27, the sermon of preparation preached on Christmas Day, and 'les marraux' distributed by M. Lavand from two o'clock till four. On January 24, 1702–3, a certain prisoner taken by one of our ships desired to express publicly his grief that during youth he had sometimes 'assisted' at the catechism in Papistical churches in order to avoid persecution. He appeared 'in our temple,' and was received to the peace of the Church. On the same day three persons abjured the Roman faith after evening preaching. On January 31 another abjured, and on February 21 another. On March 2 the Supper was ordered to be celebrated on Easter Day, the preparation sermon to be preached on the Friday previous, and 'les marraux' to be distributed as usual. On March 7, a native of Brest, Christopher de Moulin, renounced the Roman faith with the usual forms. These were the meetings for that year.

General discipline of Congregation. The elders.

The consistory was composed, as we have seen, of 'les anciens,' that is, the elders, and the deacons; but in February 1705–6, for whatever reason, the body was reconstituted, to consist of eight elders without any deacons. The eight then chosen were M. Cardonnel, De Gruchy, Jean Sorré, M. Bervallées, John Thomas, Pierre Boyer, Richard le Blanc, and Daniel Pinsun. On notice being given, according to form, to the whole community, exception was taken to the name of John Thomas, because, contrary to the discipline of the Church, he had held public plays in his house; the name of Jean Barbot was therefore substituted. Among the elders were always two natives of Jersey or Guernsey, to represent those islands, so important to the community, both for kinship and for financial reasons. This rule was reaffirmed in January 1708–9, when also four elders desiring to retire, and leave being only given for half that number, lots were permitted to be cast to determine which two should have their liberty. We gather from the same entry that Mr. Cardonnel, then in extreme old age, had made up his mind to continue for life. In 1712, as will be seen, the community conformed to the Anglican Church, but their property and charities continued to be managed by the elders or trustees. These are stated [1] to have been four in number in 1749, and we gather that such was the ordinary complement. Latterly there were but two. The formality of the election of an elder consisted in his being nominated after serious deliberation in the consistory; his name was then published in the church on three consecutive Sundays, after which, there being no objection, he was received by the minister and the rest of the body, into which he was then introduced.

Besides the minister, elders, and deacons there was a reader, whose duty it was to be at church at every exercise, to read there the Word of God, to chant the psalms, to read the prayers in case of the absence of the minister, and to accompany him to funerals. **Reader.**

Notices of the fabric are scanty. The repairs were carried out by the congregation; and from an entry of June 1707 we learn that there were separate seats assigned to men and women, strangers 'from the neighbouring isles,' in recognition of the help to the ministry so long afforded by those islands: other seats were let. **Pews.**

Between March 1702–3 and March 1711–12 several persons did public penance for having been at mass under fear of persecution, and a few renounced Romanism, most, if not all, of those received in each case having been taken prisoners of war by English ships. Among those who abjured was the Sieur Jean Claude Pugin, an ecclesiastic, a native of La Roche, Savoy, who having been taken in July 1704, was received into the French Congregation, with the usual forms, in September 1705.

**Question of conformity to Anglican Church.**

From whatever causes, the question of conforming to the Anglican Church had for some years been occasionally before the congregation. Their respected minister, M. Cougot, must have been in Anglican orders, having been instituted by Bishop Mew so long before as June 20, 1702, to the rectory of Millbrook,[2] and the natural leanings of M. Cougot had made themselves felt. Nor had he been altogether silent on the matter; and in the consistory of September 1703 he was desired to explain some doubtful utterances. Many persons in his flock had understood him to be intending to introduce the English Liturgy in place of the discipline of the Churches of France. On this, however, M. Cougot satisfied his flock, replying that he had 'always proposed to keep good faith with the article inserted on that subject at his reception

[1] Paul Mercier's Case.

[2] Book of Institutions, Record Office.

without changing anything of himself as long as they chose to retain the French Liturgy.' The question had, therefore, been mooted in some form in 1690, the date of M. Cougot's appointment.

The entries are defective at this period, and we have no means of completely following the steps which led to the conformity of the French Congregation. It appears [1] that early in 1712 the authorities of Queen's College had given notice through their agent, the vicar of Holy Rood, to the French elders that the use of the chapel would not be permitted beyond the 25th of March unless they conformed to the Anglican rite, adding somewhat ungraciously that they considered their chapel had been put to a bad use in serving for their assemblies.

A special meeting of the minister, elders, and heads of families supporting the ministry was accordingly convened on or before 5th of March [2] to consider the whole question. M. Cougot, after opening the discussion, stated that as proposals might have to be made affecting his own private interest, he would withdraw for a time, begging them first to appoint a chairman to conduct the business in his absence.[3] The choice fell on M. Pinsun, upon which M. Cougot retired, exhorting them to peace and unity. The chairman went at once to the point, and proposed the admission into their church of the Anglican Liturgy, under which phrase was really meant conformity to the English Church. This was affirmed by a plurality of votes, though at the same time opportunity was given to the Walloon Church in London and to their friends in the Channel Islands to stay proceedings if they could help them out of their difficulty. Letters detailing what had passed were ordered to be written to London, to Jersey, and Guernsey, referring specially to the Act of that present session of Parliament 'For better affirming the Church of England,' [4] and pointing out that it would be necessary to obtain a precise and particular exemption from its operation for their church; for themselves, however, they were prepared to introduce the English Liturgy on the 25th of the month, and in default of reply before that date, would consider their line of action approved. It was further resolved that immediately after 25th March a petition should be presented by the consistory to the Bishop of the diocese in the name of the heads of families, begging to be received into the Anglican Church after the manner of the French conformist churches in London. Messieurs Pinsun, Rufane, De Vallée, and De Cosne were nominated from among the heads of families to sign conjointly with

Resolution for reception into Anglican Church on basis of Savoy.

1 Letter from Walloon Church, dated March 11, 1711–12.
2 Letter from Guernsey, dated March 10.
3 Minute, dated March 13.
4 The royal assent was given February 9, 1712.

the consistory the letters to London and the Channel Islands, and the requisition to the Bishop.

This action of the congregation was protested against by some whose written disclaimer was allowed to be entered on the minutes. The objectors were Daniel Guyon, Isaac Susson, Thomas Gariot the reader of the church, Pierre Louis Beranger, and Jean Sorré, whose consciences would not allow them to relinquish the rights of the old French Congregation; they were opposed to what had passed, and were intending to provide themselves with a minister and a church to enable them to continue as before. The supporters of the resolution comprised names of greater weight: these were Antoine Cougot the minister, Richard le Blanc, P. Pasquereau, Jean Barbot, Isaac du Vit, Mathieu Herrivet, Dan. Pinsun, Duchesne Rufane, Pierre de Cosne, De Falaeseau de Vallée, De Castelnau.[1] Protests.

The answer of the Walloon Church in Threadneedle Street,[2] apparently by the hand of Mr. Primerose, the superior minister, and dated March 11, is a lengthy document strongly disapproving of the action of the Southampton body.

They cannot, they say, give them credit for sincerity in their desire for change; they were frightened by the act of the preceding December, which, after all, need not affect them, nor does it touch M. Cougot.[3] Their conduct will add affliction to the brethren, and scandalise many good souls by their attachment to the things of this world; they are disregarding the command of St. Peter to 'love the brotherhood,' and are cutting themselves off from the communion of the Churches in which God has placed them, to say nothing of their own antecedents for the last hundred and forty years. As to Messieurs of the islands, they will probably remember that they received the Reformation from the Churches of France, and will neither approve the present step of the Congregation or continue their support. True, they have received a letter from Queen's College; but it bears evidence of having been drawn from that body with a purpose, and would certainly be revoked if the College were properly approached. And at the worst, can they not find another place of meeting? But the College would never refuse in face of the view taken in the Articles of Religion and the preface to the Prayer Book regarding foreign bodies of Christians. Even the Act of Uniformity is by no means against their position. Certainly the Oxford authorities will never think their chapel dishonoured if they are reminded of the sentiments of Bishop Horne, no favourer of dissentients, who yet welcomed the foreign congregation to his diocese, or of the illustrious Bishop Andrewes, who otherwise spoke boldly of the claims of foreign Protestants; nor will the College disregard the present temper of the Church of England towards the Reformed Churches of France and

[1] The above important minute is entered on a sheet of paper, now fastened in the book, dated March 13, 1711–12; otherwise there is no entry from September 4, 1711, to March 2, 1713–14.

[2] The French Church in Threadneedle Street, the oldest in London, was in a measure the 'cathedral church' of the Huguenots (Smiles, p. 264). It was the chapel of St. Anthony's Hospital, assigned to the French by Edward VI.

[3] 'Car il ne touche mess$^{rs.}$ du clergé, et il ne defend point de faire a l'avenir ce qu'ils pouvent faire presentement.'

elsewhere, or fail to notice the deference paid to the Church of England by those congregations. When lately at Geneva, the Bishop of Salisbury [Burnett] had been offered the use of a church if he desired it, and the newspapers report from Utrecht that the English service has just been adopted in one of their public temples. The letter concludes by fearing that conformity to the Anglican Church is a foregone conclusion which no argument will touch.

Consent of the Islands.

Judging from a letter of Mr. Martin from Guernsey, dated March 10, as also from continued support, their friends at the Channel Islands viewed the matter in a different light. M. Gomare, the rector, had summoned the chiefs of families to meet in the church, hear the letter, and give their advice, when the votes were found to be in favour of the Southampton resolution. For himself, the writer says, he is full of joy, and has hope that many English Nonconformist congregations may follow their example, and join themselves to the Anglican communion, 'which is most conformed of all to the Primitive Church.'

Petition to Bishops of Winchester and London.

We next find the community in correspondence with M. de Blagny, who had been intrusted with the petition to the Bishops of Winchester and London, praying that the Congregation might be received on the same terms as the Savoy Church in the metropolis. Evidently no time had been lost in forwarding instructions. M. de Blagny, as in duty bound, waited first on the Bishop of Winchester, who gave his hearty approval, and at the suggestion of the former wrote a few words of consent at the foot of the petition. With this sanction of the diocesan he went to the Bishop of London, who also at his request signified his approval on the petition itself, expressing at the same time more fully his consent to the congregation at Southampton being placed on the same footing in every respect as that of the Savoy. 'Having the approbation of these two prelates,' writes M. de Blagny on 27th March, 'I do not think, Messieurs, that anything hinders you from proceeding next Sunday to the change which you design to make.'

Congregation conforms, March 1712.

The French Congregation was now put formally in communion with the Anglican Church.[1] The minute-book here is provokingly imperfect, and no loose papers have survived. From March 1713–14 no entry occurs, with the exception of one, dated October 1, 1717, recording the retirement of the elders, Pinsun and Castelnau, and the appointment of Rufane and De Cosne, till November 19, 1719, when we find the consistory assembled to make arrangement on M. Cougot's declining health by appointing a coadjutor.

Their choice fell on M. Pierre Deneveu de St. Denis, doctor of theology, who, with M. Cougot's full consent, was accepted as colleague

[1] The first baptism according to the Anglican rite was administered 21st April 1712.

of equal authority with him. He was to perform the duties of the church, receiving as his stipend all the contributions from the heads of families, while M. Cougot retained such offerings as Messieurs of the Islands[1] might see fit to give. Cougot signs the minute with very shaky initials, against which another hand has written 'Marque de M. Cougot, ministre.'

M. de St. Denis having accepted the appointment, arrived in December, and was formally received by the Congregation in January 1719–20 on the above terms, excepting that when God 'disposed' of M. Cougot, he would further receive the offerings from the Islands, having the right of succession. His duties were to give one sermon every Sunday, to use on Sundays, morning and evening, prayer according to the English office, to follow the doctrine and discipline of the Anglican Church, and to administer the sacraments as prescribed by her formularies. To this Cougot's mark and St. Denis's signature were affixed.

In May 1720 the islands of Jersey and Guernsey agreed, by the written consent of about fifty merchants, to pay one penny per tod of wool towards the support of the ministry of the church. Their letter contains the warmest expressions of sympathy. They regret to hear of the illness of Cougot and of the need of a successor. Their ancestors, moved by a veritable zeal towards God and charity towards their neighbours, had in time past helped to maintain that church, and they, their successors, could never consent to do less, or see without grief a church which was so useful to their travellers destitute of proper support.

M. Cougot was now fast declining. Suffering from paralysis and expecting his end, he had returned to the consistory such books and papers belonging to the church as had remained in his hands; and in August concluded a fresh arrangement with his successor to resign at once the offerings of Jersey, the wealthiest of the islands, retaining the residue for himself. His change happened to him on May 14, 1721, and he was buried on the Friday following in Millbrook Church. Though rector of Millbrook, he appears to have died in comparative poverty, and aid was extended to Madame Creanton, his daughter. He seems to have been deeply respected by his people, and there remains this record of him in the French register, 'He served this church to their edification for thirty years.' A notable member of the community had just preceded M. Cougot. This was M. Philibert d'Hervart, Baron d'Huningen, formerly ambassador from William III. at Geneva, who departed this life on 30th April 1721, at the age of seventy-six, and was buried within Holy Rood Church, followed to

Death of M. Cougot.

[1] Jersey, Guernsey, Aurigny (Alderney), and Sark.

the grave by all the French and English clergy. He was a man of large charity, a benefactor to the French Hospital in London, and to the ministers and poor of the French Church at Southampton.

Dissensions.

After the death of Cougot the affairs of the congregation fell into confusion. M. de St. Denis proved very unpopular, and charges of a varied nature were brought against him, which it will be unnecessary to follow. The English clergy at first seem to have supported him, and the Archdeacon, acting on an *ex parte* statement of the minister, and ignorant, it was said, of the custom which the French Congregation had been permitted to retain, advised the appointment of churchwardens after the English fashion, since it was stated falsely, as was afterwards replied, that the elders had relinquished their duty, while the concerns of the church needed management. In consequence of the above advice, M. de St. Denis had appointed churchwardens, two for Jersey and two for Guernsey, having secured a packed congregation of Jersey sailors. This was in April 1723. Complaint was made to the Archdeacon by the congregation, who represented the terms under which they had been permitted to conform by the Bishops of Winchester and London. By these they were allowed to retain their consistory, the choice of their minister, and the distribution of their charities as before. They further applied to the consistory of the Savoy, who advised an immediate appeal to the Bishop. Accordingly, in May, M. Brissac waited upon the Bishop on their behalf, requesting that if the Bishop should not see fit to inhibit M. de St. Denis, against whom they exhibited other complaints, he would not refuse them another church for worship, under a minister whom they would respect. The Bishop was inclined to grant them the use of St. Lawrence's Church, but on the matter being referred to the parishioners by desire of the Archdeacon, they expressed so strong an objection that it was no further urged. A commission was now issued to Archdeacon Brideoake, rector of St. Mary's, directing him to inquire into and report on all the circumstances of the case; the ultimate result of which was that M. de St. Denis was inhibited, and the congregation elected M. David Duval on June 17, 1723.

Application for St. Lawrence's Church.

French Nonconformist Congregation.

In the above decision M. de St. Denis was far from acquiescing, and upon the Bishop's death in August he refused to deliver up the register-book[1], and claimed payment as minister from d'Hervart's

[1] The last entry signed by M. De St. Denis is in December 1725, at which time he must have been officiating for a French Nonconformist congregation. After the above-dated entry M. Duval in the marriage register makes a couple of back entries. The book was in possession of the Conformist body probably soon after the first-mentioned date, at which period it is not unlikely the Nonconformist body ceased to exist.

legacy, while at the same time he had allied himself with the French Nonconformist congregation. The affair was then carried before Dr. Willis, the new Bishop, but not to the advantage of M. de St. Denis, who in the following year appealed unsuccessfully to the law for reinstatement in his former position.[1]

M. Duval had undertaken the charge of the congregation on much the same terms as his predecessor, and was to follow the discipline of the Church of England according to the usage of the Savoy. At the instance of M. Duval the mooted question raised by the Nonconformist French body as to the legacies of Mill and Mercier, bequeathed before 1712, was settled on February 11, 1723–24 by an agreement to divide them equally between the two churches as long as they existed. We have no further notice of the Nonconformist body.[2]

In the spring of 1736 M. Duval left the neighbourhood, having recommended to the consistory as his successor M. de Barnouin, who was accordingly elected and entered on his duties in June. From this time the entries in the minute-book became less frequent, chiefly recording the retirement from time to time of the elders or trustees. Among these from 1751 to 1761 the names occur of Jacques Dulamon, Brissault, Turquand, W. Seward; April 1761, Vignoles, Palairet, Saulnier, on the retirement of the three first of the above; Bercher Baril in 1763, in place of Pierre Saulnier deceased; 1786, Philip Seward and Philip Le Feuvre; 1790, Thomas Pipon, on the death of W. Seward; 1802, Thomas Durell, on the death of Pipon; 1814, Samuel Le Feuvre; 1829, George Atherley; 1833, Nicholas Bienvenu, on the death of P. Le Feuvre. There are also in the same period a few bequests, which will be mentioned below. In February 1753 Madame Susanna Louise Grossard made the elders her executors and guardians of her grandson, Henry Grossard, under promise of a legacy of £50 to the French poor in case of the boy dying before the age of twenty-one. The legacy did not fall in.

**Elders or trustees.**

On the death of M. de Barnouin, March 20, 1797, Edward Dupré, D.D., afterwards Dean of Jersey, was elected. He was constantly non-resident, and served the church through his brother, the Rev. Michael Dupré, as his substitute. The elders, however, in January 1802, reminded him of the 'rule that the rectors should reside on the spot,' and added further that they had elected his successor, but were ready to withhold action should Dr. Dupré come into residence at once. This the 'rector' apparently declined, and on 9th July the Rev. George Le Feuvre, B.A., succeeded as incum-

[1] Letters and Papers belonging to the French Congregation.

[2] See note on opposite page.

bent. He also became non-resident, and on November 11, 1824, the Rev. Frederick Vincent was chosen. During the latter portion of Mr. Vincent's incumbency, in addition to the usual French services, there was a Wednesday evening lecture in English; the chapel was also used for a congregation from St. Mary's parish till a district church could be built. This was prior to the erection of St. James's Church. After the death of Mr. Vincent in May 1853, no appointment having been made, a memorial signed by fifty-eight persons was in July presented to the remaining elders or trustees, Messers. Atherley and Bienvenu, and to Dr. Wilson, as vicar of Holy Rood, praying that steps might be taken for appointing a minister for the French Congregation. The memorial was forwarded to the French Protestant Ecclesiastical Committee with a request for their continued support, which they declined, and the service remained in abeyance.

Change of trust.

The elders now sought the advice of the Charity Commissioners, requesting to be discharged of their trust, and having received their certificate after a thorough investigation into the affairs of the church and its charities, a meeting was convened, as authorised, of the above memorialists and others interested in carrying on the services, to be held on April 22, 1856. At this meeting a new body of trustees was elected, subject to the approval of the Court of Chancery, viz., Rev. William Wilson, D.D., vicar of Holy Rood and steward of the Hospital of God's House; Rev. Henry Carey, rector of All Saints; Robert Rouby Oke, Esq., and Mr. Edward Palk; and a new scheme was adopted, subject to the same approval. Accordingly, by order of Chancery, dated 7th July 1856, it was provided—

(1.) That vacancies in the trust should be filled up at a meeting, called for the purpose, of the remaining trustees and persons frequenting the church; (2.) that the minister should be a priest in orders of the Church of England, and be appointed by the trustees; (3.) that 'as long as the congregation' were 'permitted to enjoy the chapel heretofore used by them,' the income of the church and its charities should be applied as follows :—£75 to the minister per annum —this was afterwards increased to £85 by order of the Charity Commissioners, dated October 29, 1878, in partial variation of the previous scheme; £12 to the clerk; £4 to the sexton; and the remainder, at the discretion of the trustees, to the relief of poor French Protestants and natives of Jersey and Guernsey frequenting the church; and also, if there were any surplus, to the relief of poor foreigners and natives of the Channel Islands, being in Southampton and in distress, preference being always given to natives of France and of the Channel Islands.

The affairs of the Congregation being thus placed on a new footing, the trustees on October 14, 1856, appointed the Rev. Hubert Napoleon Dupont as minister, and the chapel was opened for divine service on the following Sunday, October 19. In 1863 certain alterations were made in the interior of the chapel by Queen's College, with a view to the better accommodation of the brethren and sisters of the hospital; the old pewing was removed, which it seems had been placed in the chapel by Dr. Wilson in lieu of the decayed benches of ancient time, and the French Congregation found themselves without any seats, provision having only been made for the hospital. The Congregation remonstrated, with the usual reference to their (supposed) letters patent of Edward VI. and Elizabeth; upon which the College replied, in February 1864, that while they had no objection to the use of the chapel as before by the French Congregation, they declined to replace the pews. Subsequently they returned the value of what had been removed. The trustees then renewed the benches, and the College their loan of the chapel by a formal permission under their corporate seal, dated June 15, 1864, 'at such times as the said chapel may not be required for the use of the brothers and sisters of the Hospital of God's House.'

After the death of M. Dupont on July 30, 1875, the trustees were requested, by memorial of about forty persons in October that year, to supply the vacancy; and in November they met to consider whether, as had been proposed to them, the chaplaincy to seamen in the port could be joined to the pastorate of the French Congregation. No difficulty under the terms of the trust having been found, the appointment to the French Church was offered (December 31, 1877) to the Rev. Alphonse Auguste Dupont—no relation whatever to the last incumbent—who accepted the post on 28th March, and the church was re-opened on 7th April 1878.

The present trustees are Robert Rouby Oke, Esq.; Robert Chatfield Hankinson, Esq., June 1868, on the death of Mr. Carey; Rev. Frederick Edward Wigram, April 1873, on the death of Mr. Palk; Rev. J. Aston Whitlock, vicar of Holy Rood, February 1875, on the death of Dr. Wilson.

The following bequests have been made to the French Church:—

Nathaniel Mill (see under 'Town Charities').

Paul Mercier, by will dated 6th June 1661, left a share in the interest of £100 deposited with the Corporation for the benefit of the French and English poor at Southampton.

Philibert d'Hervart, Baron d'Huningen, by will in 1721, left (capital of £483, 6s. 8d.) £12 per annum to the minister of the French Conformist Church, and £2, 10s. per annum to the poor.

M. de Belleau, by will dated December 6, 1738, left £150 sterling to the church; a legacy never realised, owing to the insolvency of the person with whom it was placed.

David Roque, by will dated April 15, 1742, left the interest of £150 for the minister.

François Fradin, by will dated July 14, 1746, left the interest of £50 for the minister.

Madame Anne Castanier, by will dated April 12, 1749, left the interest of £100 for the minister.
Isaac Gignoux, by will in 1754, left the interest of £150 for the French poor.
Jacques Dulamon, by will dated August 13, 1761, left the interest of £150 stock to the French Church in Southampton and French Hospital in London.

*Ministers.*

1567. Wallerand Thenelin.
1571. Adrian de Saravia (?).
1576. —— Morel,[1] removed to Rye, 1583.
1584. Mathieu Sohier[2] (?).
1586. Philippe De la Motte, died May 6, 1617.
1619. Elie Durande,[3] died May 13, 1633.
1633. Daniel Sauvage,[4] died June 21, 1655.
1655. Gabriel Du Perrier.
Jean De la Place,[4] died March 6, 1663–64.
1665. Jean Courand, still minister in April 1688.
1687. Isaac D'Huissaux, perhaps at first coadjutor.
1690. Antoine Cougot, M.D.,[5] died May 14, 1721.
1719. Pierre Deneveu de St. Denis, Theol. Doct.; removed June 1723.
1723. David Duval, resigned May 1736.
1736. Isaac Jean de Barnouin, died March 30, 1797.
1797. Edward Dupré, D.D., displaced for non-residence July 1802.
1802. George Le Feuvre, B.A., displaced November 1824.
1824. Frederick Vincent, died May 1853.
1856. Hubert Napoleon Dupont, died July 30, 1875.
1878. Alphonse Auguste Dupont.

## SECTION II.—*Chantries.*

"It was a common thing for people to leave at their death some " stipend for a priest to sing for their souls. In this town they gener- " ally made the Corporation trustees, and some estate of house or land " was settled to provide for the payment, and this was called a " chantry.

"There were several of these appointed at different churches in this " town, some of which were only for a term of years, but others were " perpetual. Among these latter were the following:—

"'Pd. to Sr. Thos. that syngyth for Holmage at St. Mary's, £6, 13s. 4d.'

"'Pd. to Sr. Robt. that syngs for Thos. Peyne at Holy Rhood,[6] £6, 13s. 4d.'"

---

1 According to Burn, 'Refugees,' 1846.

2 Burn has him in this position; the only authority for the name is the note given above in the text, p. 409. He was possibly only an elder.

3 Buried at St. Mary's.

4 Buried within God's House Chapel.

5 Buried in Millbrook Church.

6 "The nomination of the chantries of St. Mary's and Holy Rood was granted " by the mayor and his brethren to Thomas Wriothesley, Esq., 29 Henry VIII." [January 6, 1538].

Holmage or Holme-hegg.

The former of these foundations was settled under the will of Johanna,[1] widow of Nicholas Holmage or Holmehegg, bearing date May 6, 1462 (2 Ed. IV.), by which she left to the Corporation eleven messuages, with cellars, solars, and gardens, for the establishment of a chantry at St. Mary's, to consist of one priest, who should celebrate each year on her anniversary, that is, on the day of her death, for the soul of herself, her husband, her parents and ancestors. She thus provided for her chanter a stipend of ten marks, or £6, 13s 4d., and desired that Andrew Arthur, her chaplain, should have the appointment for life. On the day of the obit the sum of £1, 6s 8d. was to be distributed as follows:—To the mayor, 3s. 4d.; to the seneschal, 2s.; and the remainder among the priests, clerks, and poor of St. Mary's. She further directed that two other messuages, besides the above, should be sold, and the proceeds devoted to the poor.

It appears that the total amount of the chantry was £9, 0s. 8d.; the remainder, £1, 0s. 8d., not accounted for above, going to the repairs of the tenements connected with it.[2]

Sir Andrew held the chantry apparently till 1490, when Sir Thomas was appointed, and paid the fine of half a mark for the town seal to his chantry. Sir William, who was also mayor's or guild priest, was singing for Holmage in 1509, and continued to do so for some years.[3] Perhaps he was the William Bifelde who was the Holmage chanter in 1536, the particulars of whose stipend are given in the 'Valor.' John Baker appears to have succeeded: he was certainly holding the chantry in 1543, and in 1553 received a pension of £6 as its incumbent.

The following is a specimen of this obit:—

The mynd of Nycolas Holmage and Jone, hys wyfe,[4] holden in the chyrche of Sent Mary's, the 18th day of June.

| Paid | | | | | | | |
|---|---|---|---|---|---|---|---|
| To the chanter for his wax | £0 | 0 | 8 | To iiij c of whyt bonys . | £0 | 4 | 0 |
| To ij prests there . . | 0 | 1 | 4 | To ij c of spysyd bonys . | 0 | 2 | 0 |
| To ij clarks there . . | 0 | 0 | 8 | To spyse and butter . | 0 | 0 | 10 |
| To v ceurats of the towne | 0 | 2 | 6 | To j dos. and halfe of gud | | | |
| To v clarks . . . | 0 | 1 | 8 | ale . . . . . | 0 | 2 | 3 |
| To iiij chylds. . . | 0 | 0 | 4 | To j dos. of peny ale . | 0 | 1 | 0 |
| To pore men . . . | 0 | 0 | 9 | To j galon of wyne . | 0 | 0 | 8 |
| To the frerys . . . | 0 | 2 | 6 | To beyryng of all y$^e$ stufe | | | |
| To Mr. Meyre . . | 0 | 3 | 4 | to St. Mary's . . | 0 | 0 | 4 |
| To the steward . . | 0 | 2 | 0 | To the bedmen . . | 0 | 0 | 2 |

Nycoll, Thomas, and Payne.

The chantry at Holy Rood was founded after 1452 or 1472 for the souls of William Nycoll, and of Anneys and Alice his wives, and of

[1] Liber Niger, fol. 71.
[2] Chantry Certificates, Roll 51, No. 1.
[3] Steward's Books under dates.
[4] Dr. Speed has this extract from Steward's Book, 14 Hen. VII. (1499).

Richard Thomas and Thomas Payne. It seems to have been worth originally, as founded by William Nycoll, £8, 13s. 4d., the stipend of the priest being £6, 13s. 4d.; on the obit £1, 6s. 8d. was spent, the remaining thirteen shillings and fourpence being appropriated to repairs.[1] The anniversary was kept on 25th April. Subsequently the foundation was enlarged by his wife or wives for two stipendiaries, who were to receive £6 and £6, 13s. 4d. respectively. An additional obit seems also to have been kept at a cost of ten shillings; a residue of fifty shillings was then left, the worth of the whole foundation being £15, 13s. 4d.[2] In 1493 Sir Robert was singing for the above. In 1501 Sir Thomas was the chaplain. He held the office in 1515, when a townsman was fined thirteen pence 'for gevinge Sir Thomas a blowe on the nose.' Under 1553 we find pensions of £6 and £5 paid respectively to Thomas Greene and John Teyle, stipendiaries at Holy Rood.

Gunter. William Gunter—apparently after 1493—founded a chantry in the Church of Holy Rood for the souls of his parents and himself. His priest was to have £6, and £1 was reserved for repairs of tenements belonging to the chantry. No provision seems to have been made for the obit, the whole being worth £7.[3]

The following obits were also connected with the town:—

Malmesylle or Maunsell. 'The mynd' of William Malmesylle[4] and of Margaret his wife, founded after 1378—the name appeared afterwards as Maunsell:—

A remembrance of the seconde daye of Septembyr of the spenses that was ymade in the chyrche of Seint Mychelle for Wylliam Malmesyll ys mynd.

| | | | |
|---|---|---|---|
| Item payd the v curates of the towne for dyvers, . . | xv$^{s.}$ vi$^{d.}$ | Item payd to bedman, . . | ij$^{d.}$ |
| Item payd to the meyre, . . | ij$^{s.}$ | Item in moneye ydelyd to pore ffolkes, . . . | ij$^{s.}$ ix$^{d.}$ |
| Item payd to the stywarde, . | ij$^{s}$ | Item payd for iij dossyn bred, . . . . . . . . | iij$^{s.}$ |
| Item payd to the clerk of | | Item payd for ij dossyn ale, . . . . . . . . | iij$^{s.}$ |
| Sent Mychell, . . . . | vj$^{d.}$ | Item iij chesys, . . . . | j$^{s.}$ |
| Holy Rode, . . . . . . | vj$^{d.}$ | Item payd for a gallon wyne, . . . . . . | viij$^{d.}$ |
| Sent Laurens, . . . | iij$^{d.}$ | | |
| All Hallyn, . . . . . . | ij$^{d.}$ | | |
| Sent Johnes, . . . . | ij$^{d.}$ | | |

Mascall. The mind of John Mascall and Margery his wife,[5] kept on 10th November, at the annual cost of £1, 0s. 9d., at the Church of Holy Rood.

Florans or Floryse. The mind of Robert Florans and Ellen his wife,[6] founded after 1436, yearly in the Church of St. Michael's on 22d February.

Smale. The mind of Thomas Smale and Joane his wife,[7] yearly at St. Mary's on 9th April.

[1] Chantry Certificates, Roll 51.
[2] Ibid., Roll 52.
[3] Ibid., Roll 51.
[4] Steward's Book for 1441.
[5] Ibid. for 1457.
[6] Ibid.
[7] Ibid.

The mind of John James, burgess,[1] who by his will, dated September 2, 1471, gave certain legacies to all the churches, and left to Alice his wife a life-interest in certain properties on condition of her holding his anniversary in the Church of Holy Rood; on her death the property was to pass to the Corporation with the same proviso. James.

The mind of Margery Marsh, kept at Holy Rood. Marsh.

The mind of Adam March and Joane his wife,[2] founded after 1425, yearly at the Church of St. Lawrence on the Sunday after St. Lawrence's Day (August 10). March.

The mind of John Sylder,[3] yearly in the Church of All Saints on St. Paul's Eve (January 24), founded after 1427. Under 1543 we find that it was kept on February 16 at St. Mary's— Sylder.

> 'Because the curate of All Hallows would not kepe ytt mynyshynge anythinge of hys olde dewty acustomyd. So to the curatte of Saynct Mares for hys labor and the waste of hys wax, x$^{d.}$ Item to Sir John Baker (who was the Holmage priest) 4$^{d.}$, to Sir Thomas Gryme 4$^{d.}$, to Sir Crystoffer 4$^{d.}$, to Sir Ector 4$^{d.}$' (Sir Hector was also mayor's priest).

These were the St. Mary's clergy,[4] four in number, besides the chanter, here called the 'curate,' as the rector of All Saints is also called.

The mind of John (?) Shropshire,[5] yearly in the Church of All Saints, after 1479, on July 8th. The mayor was to receive two shillings, the steward twenty pence, and the friars two shillings and sixpence. Shropshire.

The mind of Richard Gryme and Margery his wife was kept at All Saints after 1459.[6] Gryme.

Besides the obits for which the town acted as trustees there were others.

In 1273 (1 Ed. I.), under an agreement between Robert, Prior of God's House, and the brethren there, on the one part, and Robert Bonhayt, burgess, on the other, the Prior and brethren undertook to find for ever a chaplain, and to board and lodge him as one of their own chaplains, and give him twenty shillings per annum, for the purpose of celebrating each day one mass at the altar of St. Theobald, in the Church of St. Michael, for the soul of Alice, daughter of Walter Flandrensis (Fleming), and late wife of the said Robert, and for the souls of all the departed. For the above foundation Robert Bonhayt gave to the Prior and brethren certain properties, viz., the house in French Street in which he had lived with his wife, opposite the great houses of the late Richard de Leicester, and a quit-rent of nine shillings from a bakehouse on the east side of English Street towards the sea, and between a messuage which Nicholas Beket was holding of God's House, and another vault in the Bonhayt.

[1] S. B., Liber Niger.
[2] Steward's Book, 1486.
[3] Ibid., 1543.
[4] See above.
[5] Liber Remembranc. H., fol. 107.
[6] Steward's Book, 1512.

tenure of Giles le Fleming. The agreement was signed with Robert's seal, and for greater security with that of the community of the town, also with the seal of God's House, and with that of Prior Nicholas of St. Denys, since in the event of God's House failing to appoint within twenty days after any vacancy, the Prior of St. Denys was empowered to put in a chaplain for a year, and the Prior of God's House was bound to admit him.[1]

Beket.

Soon after this a chantry was founded in St. Mary's for the above Nicholas Beket, who died before 1287,[2] and Agnes his wife, the warden of St. Mary's, from time to time, being bound to find a chaplain for the purpose. Nicholas Dykeman was probably the first. William de Hamme succeeded October 18, 1306; on death of whom, John de Borne, December 21, 1309.[3]

Renawd.

In 1422 John Renawd, burgess, left ten marks for a chaplain to celebrate for his soul and for the souls of the faithful departed in the Church of Holy Rood;[4] and left to every poor man coming to his anniversary one penny, either in bread or silver.

Mylles.

Richard Mylles bequeathed his dwelling-house in St. Lawrence's parish[5] to his widow, Bessamy, for life, and then to his daughter Elizabeth, and to her heirs, and failing them to the parish of St. Lawrence, in order that the churchwardens of the parish church of St. Lawrence for ever should yearly keep his obit with dirge and requiem in the said church, with all the curates and parish clerks in Hampton, and with the curate and parish clerk of St. Mary's. Every curate was to have for his labour eightpence, every clerk sixpence, but the curate of St. Lawrence was to have for his dirge his mass and his wax sixteenpence. The churchwardens were to distribute bread and ale to the poor at the said obit to the value of six shillings and eightpence. Failing their duty in reference to the above conditions, the Provost of God's House, with his brethren, was to enter into possession of the tenement on undertaking the obit.

Chantries time of Ed. VI.

The greater number of the above chantries had disappeared before the Commissioners of Edward VI. reported on such foundations. The following were enumerated by them:—The Holmage chantry at St. Mary's; the Nicholls and Gunter chantries at Holy Rood; the chantry in the castle; the Maunsell and Florans at St. Michael's; as also a small foundation worth four shillings and twopence for two obits by Thomas Crikelwood and Robert Floryse (Florans). Two other unknown obits are mentioned, one at St. Lawrence, the other at All Saints.

1 Addit., 15,314, fol. 68 b.
2 See under 'St. Denys's Priory.'
3 Reg. Woodlock, fol. 47, 106, 175.
4 Madox, Form., p. 431.
5 See under 'Account of Parish Property.' The above is from extract of his will, in which no date is given, and I have failed to ascertain it.

In reference to Holy Rood the Commissioners state that as there are 'in the said parish xvij$^{xx}$ [*i.e.* 340] houselling people, besides great repair of mariners,' they think that more than one minister must be left.[1] Under the Act of 1 Ed. VI., 1547, "these chauntries "came to the Crown, and the income of them was paid to the "Crown.

"'1 Eliz. [1558–59]. Paid to John Harrison for the two chauntries, "'one at S$^{t.}$ Marie's, and the other at Holly Roddes, the which ys dew "'to the Quen's grace at the Feste of S. Michel the Archangel, "'summa, £13, 6s. 8d.'"

About the middle of the sixteenth century[2] the liability of the town for chantries amounted to £17, 12s. 2d., as follows:—From lands belonging to the Holmage chantry at St. Mary's for the stipend, £6, 13s. 4d.; and from the same for maintenance of the obit, ten shillings; amount payable for the Sylder obit at All Saints, ten shillings; from lands and tenements in St. Lawrence for the obit of Adam March, eight shillings; from lands and tenements given by John James and Margery Marsh for two obits in Holy Rood, £1, 3s. 4d.; from the foundation of William Nycoll and his wives at Holy Rood for the stipend, £6, 13s. 4d.; and for maintenance of the obit, ten shillings; from lands and tenements in St. Michael's for the obits of William Marmsell and W. Flower (R. Florans?), ten shillings for each; and further rent from two cottages in St. Michael's belonging to these two obits payable by the wardens, four shillings and twopence. Town's liability for chantries.

In 1650–51 (March 10) the above rents, amounting to £17, 12s. 2d., were sold by the trustees of Parliament,[3] as 'parcel of the possession of the late Crown of England,' to John Bankesford, Esq.; after which the rents were regularly paid to Colonel John Barkstead,[4] the purchaser and holder of the episcopal manor of Bittern in 1649, till the Restoration, when that manor reverted to its episcopal lords, as did these rents to the Crown. They were received by Colonel Barkstead from May 1651 to May 1660. In 1661 and 1662 they were accounted for to the Crown. Sold. Resumed.

"A.D. 1665 [April 14], arrears of these chauntry rents [for two "years] were order'd to be paid to the King's receiver at Andover.

"About this time the Corporation got a release from the Crown "from the future payment of them." Town released from payment.

---

[1] Chantry Certificates, Roll 52, n. 60.

[2] Boke of Remembrances, fol. 91 b. The date of the document here extracted is about 1560.

[3] Journal, vol. 1642–97 at end.

[4] Journal under dates.

## Section III.—*Nonconformist Congregations or Churches.*

Congregational.

*Above Bar Congregational Church, formerly called Above Bar Chapel.*—The congregation established here is the oldest Nonconformist body in the town. It had its origin soon after the passing of the Act of Uniformity in 1662, and was due to the labours of the Rev. Nathaniel Robinson, formerly intruded successively into the benefices of St. Lawrence and All Saints (see under those churches), and ejected from the latter as not being in holy orders, and being unwilling to receive ordination and to conform. It seems that the society met first in private houses as occasion offered, but after the extension of statutory relief to Protestant Dissenters, a congregation was organised and settled, Mr. Robinson being pastor, on August 3, 1688, upon the following basis:—

1. The town of Southampton was to be the seat of the gospel church then established, as being the place of its first foundation.

2. The Lord's Supper was to be administered on the first Lord's day of every month.

3. Although Mr. Nathaniel Robinson was 'not in all points satisfied concerning the office of ruling elders,' yet on his referring the matter to the church, they, 'to satisfy themselves therein, unanimously proceeded to the election of such elders, viz., Mr. Robert Thorner (see under 'Alms-houses') and Mr. John Lee, and desired them to undertake the sacred office, and therein to act in all things as occasion shal require, until either God shall persuade our said pastor, or else some other opportunity shall present for their actual ordaining, according to the rule of the Word.'

4. Several of the members residing at Romsey and thereabouts, it was thought advisable for the better inspection of the poor that two deacons should be chosen for those parts as well as two for Southampton. Accordingly, Isaac Watts, the father of Dr. Watts, and Abraham Johns were elected for Southampton, and Arthur High and Peter Hollis for Romsey. Collections, however, were to be received and accounted for by the deacons at Southampton, who should disburse to the others as occasion required. On August 24 the four above named were solemnly set apart by prayer, and entered upon their office.

At this period of their organisation the congregation worshipped in a meeting-house in front of the site of their present chapel, built or adapted for that purpose, and held on lease by Mr. Thorner, who by his will (May 31, 1690) bequeathed the remainder of the lease to the officers of the church in trust for the church's use, provided the premises continued to be used as a meeting-house. The gift was acknowledged after Mr. Thorner's death by a minute in the church records dated July 17, 1690. He also gave a benefaction of £200 towards maintaining the ministry. The freehold of this building, together with adjoining ground, was purchased by subscription in 1719, and a few years later, the old chapel having become decayed, a new and more commodious building was erected in 1727. This chapel in its turn, after various smaller changes, and being considerably enlarged in 1802—during which period the congregation met in the Long Rooms—was removed in 1819 to make way for the present structure. The spot selected for the new fabric was in the rear of that occupied by the former chapel, so that the worship of the congregation was not interfered with till within six weeks of the completion of the new building. During these weeks the congregation met in the Baptist Chapel in East Street, by arrangement with the Baptist congregation.

The first stone of the new chapel was laid by the pastor on April 1, 1819, and on April 26, 1820, it was devoted to the service of God by appropriate services, the sermon in the morning being preached by Rev. W. Jay of Bath, and in the evening by Rev. George Clayton, who had been coadjutor with the late pastor, Mr. Kingsbury, from March 1802 to January 1804, and had been much instrumental in the enlargement of that period. This chapel has been also subjected to various improvements and additions, especially of late years under the present pastorate.

In the early and troubled days of the congregation monthly fasts were held, at which collections were made for the poor, and from these resources contributions were made to the brethren in other towns, and occasionally to the Protestants of Ireland and France.[1]

The first pastor, Mr. Robinson, died at an advanced age in May 1696; the entry of his burial thus occurs in the register of All Saints Church:—

'Mr. Nathaniel Robison (sic.) interr'd May 27, '96' (sic.) His wife had preceded him a few years: 'Buried 2d June 1691, Elizabeth, wife of Nathaniel Robinson.'

The succession of pastors has been as follows:—

Nathaniel Robinson, before 1688.
William Bolar, 1694; died September 25, 1734.
Henry Francis, co-pastor from August 19, 1726; died November 7, 1752.
John Bertram, 1753; left in 1763.
William Kingsbury, 1764; resigned 1809.
Thomas Adkins, 1810; died December 9, 1868.
Henry Hermann Carlisle, LL.B., co-pastor from July 1859.

[1] Brief Records of the Church of Christ of the Independent Denomination at Southampton, by Rev. T. Adkins.

Congregational.

*Albion Chapel, St. Mary's Street.*—The congregation worshipping here is an offshoot from that of Above Bar Church, formed in 1844; the old infirmary being purchased, converted into a chapel, and opened September 15, 1844. The present chapel is a spacious building, adorned in front with a classical pediment, in which is inserted a most useful clock.

*Pastors.*

Thomas Pullar, 1845, resigned July 1850.
Joseph W. Wyld, March 1851, resigned November 1853.
William Roberts, September 1854 to March 1862.
Septimus March, October 1862 to July 1877.
Samuel Barnes Driver, April 1878 to December 1879.
Stephen George Matthews, B.A., April 1881.

Congregational.

*Kingsfield Chapel, West Marlands.*—This congregation came from Albion Chapel, the church being established in 1853, and meeting first in the Victoria Rooms. The present building was erected in 1861.

*Pastors.*

Joseph Wyld, November 1853 to April 1855.
Peter Turner, January 1856 to July 1861.
John Hill, M.A., November 1861 to April 1864.
Thomas Sissons, January 1865 to August 1867.
R. G. Harper, January 1868 to March 1870.
Samuel B. Stribling, July 1870.

Congregational.

*Belvedere Independent Chapel.*—The congregation meeting here was first formed in 1847, the present pastor moving into Belvedere Chapel in 1854. Pastor, Rev. George Westbury Fuller Gregg.

Baptist.

Notice occurs of a *Baptist congregation* existing in Southampton in the years 1689 and in 1703, under the pastorate of Mr. Richard Ring,[1] their meeting-house being in Blue Anchor Lane. Previously to this, in 1646, a Mr. John Sims, a Baptist minister, resided at Southampton, but no mention occurs of any regular congregation. From the records of the present church it is gathered[2] that a congregation existed before 1750, worshipping in a meeting-house which was sold in 1764, a new one being erected the same year on part of the ground now covered by Albion Chapel, in the parish of St. Mary's. It was only occasionally used, the church being without a pastor from 1764 to 1796. In the latter year Mr. Edward Rowcliffe accepted the pastorate, and the little meeting-house being found too small, a new one of some kind was

[1] Ivimey's History of the Baptists, vol. ii. p. 214, &c.
[2] Account by Rev. H. Carrington Lake.

erected by the end of the same year (1796). In consequence of dissension, Mr. Rowcliffe resigned in January 1800. In the same year it was resolved to move the chapel to a more favourable site, and on September 12 a site in East Street, given by Mr. Saunders, who had acted as temporary pastor, was selected, and by April 17, 1801, the new chapel was finished on ground in the rear of the present chapel, where the school-room now stands. In January 1805 Mr. Richard Owers accepted the pastorate. In 1815 a serious division shook the church, but shortly after it was determined again to rebuild the meeting-house on a site bought from Mr. Roe, and on May 27, 1818, the present chapel was opened. Mr. Owers died May 4, 1820. The pastorate was then offered to Rev. B. H. Draper, who commenced his work October 5, 1820. He died October 12, 1843, after whom the following is the list of pastors:—Rev. T. Morris, began May 1844, resigned April 1851; Rev. S. S. Pugh, June 1853, ended May 1858; Rev. R. Cavan, September 1859, resigned April 1875; Rev. J. H. Patterson, July 1875, resigned March 1880; Rev. Harris Carrington Lake, August 15, 1880.

*Portland Chapel.*—This church is an offshoot from Dr. Draper's hearers in East Street, who formed themselves into a congregation in 1840, and met for worship in the Victoria Rooms, under the pastorate of the Rev. John Pulsford, who eventually removed to Edinburgh. Soon after the settling of the congregation the chapel in Portland Terrace was erected, but in 1843 it had to be sold in order to satisfy the claims of the mortgagee, and was purchased, February 8, 1844, by the founders of the present congregation for about £1350. The chapel was re-opened on February 25, 1844, under the ministry of the Rev. John Ford, who had entered upon the charge of the congregation in the previous year, and on March 31 the church was formed, commencing with twelve members. In 1845 the Rev. Alexander M'Laren was chosen minister, under whose able preaching the congregation became very numerous. In 1858 Mr. M'Laren, on June 14, took leave of his congregation on removing to Union Chapel, Manchester. In April 1859 the Rev. J. A. Spurgeon became pastor, and the chapel was enlarged considerably, after which a division took place, and in 1860 Mr. Spurgeon carried off the greater part of the congregation, who located themselves in the Carlton Hall. The Rev. M. Hudson became pastor of Portland Chapel in 1860, and was succeeded by Rev. Charles Williams, who in 1868 wrote a brief sketch of the history of the congregation, from which this account is drawn. After Mr. Williams, Rev. William Emery became pastor, and was followed by Rev. H. O. Mackay in 1875.

*Carlton Chapel.*—The congregation from Portland Chapel, under Mr. Spurgeon, worshipped in the Carlton Hall till 1865, when they became settled in Carlton Chapel, Belle Vue Road, erected and opened in that year. Pastors, Rev. J. A. Spurgeon, May 1, 1861, resigned May 4, 1863; Rev. J. Collins, July 4, resigned February 2, 1871; Rev. Edwin Osborne, January 6, 1872.

The *Particular Baptists* have a meeting-place in Ascupart Street, and the *Calvinistic Baptists* in St. Andrew's Road.

The *Bible Christians* have a chapel in Melbourne Street, built in 1864, and another in St. Mary's Road, built in 1874.

Presbyterians. *St. Andrew's Presbyterian Church of England.*—This congregation was organised in 1849, and from that time till 1853 met regularly for worship in the Victoria Rooms; in the latter year the present church was built on ground given by the late Mr. Alderman A. Lamb. Ministers—Rev. W. Hunter, April 1851; Rev. John Grant Wright, LL.D., November 1855, died February 11, 1880; Rev. Robert Vint, M.A., B.D., October 15, 1880.

Society of Friends. The meeting-house of the *Society of Friends* was originally in St. Michael's Square; it is now in Castle Square. They have possessed their burial-ground in the Avenue since 1680.

Jews. The *Synagogue* is now in Albion Place, and was formerly in East Street.

Wesleyans. *East Street Chapel.*—The place of worship belonging to the Wesleyan Methodists was formerly in Canal Walk or the Ditches, the society itself having been formed, it is believed, by John Wesley during a short visit to the town in August 1787, when on his way to Guernsey. The present commodious chapel, situated in East Street, was erected of white brick and stone in the Decorated style in 1850, at a cost of about £6750. The ministers are Rev. George Mellor[1] and Rev. T. W. Cook.

*Bevois Town Chapel* was originally a small structure erected in 1858; it has since been enlarged.

*Independent Wesleyan Chapel,* Broad Street, Kingsland. Pastor, Rev. J. Williams.

*Primitive Methodists.*—The Chapel in St. Mary's Street was erected in 1838 by the Association Methodists, and was purchased by its present congregation for £400 in 1841, after which it was enlarged and improved at a cost of £520. Minister, Rev. J. Herridge.

---

1 Mention may be permitted of the very extensive collection of brass rubbings from nearly every county of the United Kingdom made by this gentleman. A few specimens were exhibited at the Hartley Institute during the meeting of the British Association.

*St. John's Free Church, Clifford Street.*—This congregation was formed about 1872. Pastor, Rev. E. J. Boon. Free Church.

*Catholic Apostolic Church.*—This congregation was formed in 1834. It is ministered to by Rev. Richard Symes, appointed in 1860. Irvingite.

Unitarians first met for public worship in the town in the rooms of the Philosophical Society in St. Michael's Square, April 19, 1846, under Rev. Edwin Chapman. In 1851 the old Methodist chapel in Canal Walk was purchased by Rev. E. Kell, and opened for worship on September 25 that year, the sermon being preached by that gentleman, then minister at Newport, Isle of Wight. Subsequently Mr. Kell was invited to take charge of the congregation, and did so from June 19, 1853. By his exertions the present 'Church of the Saviour' was erected from designs of Mr. Philip Brannon, one of the earliest members of the connection, and opened in March 1860. The Rev. Edmund Kell, whose antiquarian researches are well known, died January 17, 1874, on the eve of his seventy-fifth birthday, and was succeeded, October 8, 1874, by Rev. Iden Payne, who resigned at Christmas 1876. Rev. D. Amos took charge April 14, 1878, and left March 19, 1882. The Rev. Henry Shaw Jolly, M.A., commenced his ministry October 8, 1882. Unitarian.

The original Chapel of St. Joseph's Mission, Bugle Street, was built on the present site in the time of the Rev. Father Watkins, who was succeeded in 1834 by the Rev. William Hunt, now Provost of Westminster. The Rev. Father Siddon was appointed in 1843, and the chancel of the present church was erected in 1847 by the elder Pugin. The appointment of the Rev. Robert Mount dates from November 1849; and the church was completed from designs of Mr. J. G. Poole in 1850–51. Roman Catholic.

## SECTION IV.—*Religious Houses.*

### PRIORY OF ST. DENYS.

A solitary fragment of grey ruined wall on the right bank of the Itchen, about three miles above the present dock entrance, is the sole relic of St. Denys's Priory, a house of Black Canons of St. Augustine, founded by King Henry I. about the year 1124, or at all events between the date of the consecration of Archbishop William de Corbeuil in February 1122–23 and the death of William de Giffard, Bishop of Winchester, in January 1128–29, both of those prelates being concerned in the execution of its earliest charter of endowment. Founded c. 1124.

By this charter, directed to William, Bishop of Winchester, William de Pontearch, sheriff, Warin of Hampton, and the burgesses of that place, as well as to all his barons and faithful subjects, French and

English, of Hantescira, King Henry I. granted to God and the Church of St. Denys, and the canons serving God there, a parcel of his land between Portswood and the Itchen, the rent of which was valued at eleven shillings and sixpence per annum. The grant also conveyed to Girard, the canon, no doubt the Prior, and to the brothers of the house, that parcel of the King's land of Portswood which lay near the sea on the east part of Hampton, the rent of which had been forty-one shillings and sixpence.

Portswood.

King Stephen confirmed to the canons the grant of Betheslega (Baddesley) made to them by Robert de Limesey.[1]

William, son of Audoenus, made over to the convent in 1151 his patrimony of Northam, giving seisin by the knife in the presence of Adelard, the Prior, and the whole convent. This grant of the manor of Northam was confirmed by King Henry II.; again by John, the marshal of the King, tested by Richard,[2] the treasurer; again by Henry de Blois, Bishop of Winchester (1129–71); again by Thomas Beket, Archbishop of Canterbury[3] (1162–70); and finally by Edward IV., February 20, 1465.[4]

Northam, 1151.

King Henry II. granted to the Priory his chapels within the borough, St. Michael, St. Cross (Holy Rood), St. Lawrence, and All Saints, with all that belonged to them. For a further gift of land by this king see above, p. 30.

Chapels within the borough.

The possessions of the Priory at this time consisted of three ploughlands of ground in Portswood, three groves of woodland, one hundred acres of pasture, forty of meadow, and forty of marsh.[5] Their property was enlarged in the following reign.

King Richard I. gave to the canons (September 8, 1189) Kingsland[6] and the wood called Portswood, with all that pertained to them, on account of which grant the burgesses subsequently obtained a remission of £5 per annum from their fee-farm, an immunity which they do not appear to have long enjoyed.

Kingsland and Portswood.

We have already seen that a portion of the royal land at Portswood had been granted to the canons by King Henry I. The chartulary of the house[7] notices the customary work which the 'men of Portswood' performed for the King 'before the Church of St. Denys was founded, in the time of King Henry I., who was himself the founder.' From

Tenants of Portswood.

1 The above charters are in Dugdale, Mon. Angl.

2 Richard Fitz-Neal, for whom his father, Bishop Nigel of Salisbury, had purchased the reversion of his own office as treasurer for £400. Richard was the author of the "Dialogus" (Stubbs, i. 384, 468), and afterwards Bishop of London.

3 The above from Addit., 15,314, f. 95.

4 Pat. 4 Edw. IV., p. 4, m. 22.

5 Addit., 15,314, f. 100.

6 Addit., 15,314, f. 100.

7 Ibid., ff. 99 b, 100 b.

St. John Baptist's Day (June 24) to St. Peter ad Vincula (August 1) they cleaned half an acre of ground daily. In the month of August they reaped half an acre, and each one had a sheaf. After the harvest they collected clay for repairing their houses till Michaelmas. In Kingsland and in the ground beyond the Wood after Michaelmas they gathered the apples and made cider; at Martinmas (November 11) they paid their church dues and custom for the rights of pannage; then they trenched the land and made up the fences. On the Vigil of Easter they carried rushes to the house of the reeve or bailiff (præpositus) at Hampton, and did the same before the other festivals. They cut the meadows, carried the hay, and stored the harvest in the barns; they sheared the sheep, measured out the folds, and repaired the King's weir. They did no suit in the county or hundred, but only in the court at Hampton, and were quit of murder fines. The duties subsequently rendered to the Prior were similar to those which had been performed for the King.

In reference to the tenants at Portswood it was arranged, under a final concord,[1] dated May 1397, that the inhabitants of Portswood should attend the court leet at Cutthorn or elsewhere within the liberty of the town once or twice a year; that the Prior and convent should have two-thirds, and the mayor and community one-third of the fines and agreements there made by the inhabitants of Portswood; but that the mayor and community should have two-thirds, and the Prior and convent one-third of felon's goods and forfeitures happening in Portswood. The agreement also directed that Portswood should be rated for the King's supplies with the town of Southampton, and that their proportion should be for every fifteenth, £1, 6s. 8d., to be collected by the alderman of Portswood; and the Prior and convent quitted claim to a certain rent of forty shillings a year due from the town of Southampton, of which 32s. 2d. was for the lepers in the hospital of Southampton, and 8s. 2d. was issuing from the lands of Southwyk, near Portswood.

To resume the charters:—Hadewis, Abbess of Romsey (1130–55), granted a corrody, or allowance of meat and drink, in perpetual alms from the Abbey of Romsey to the canons of St. Denys.[2]

Geoffry de Hose, one of the justices of Henry II., granted them a moiety of the land which he had bought of Walter de Chalke in Edboldington, for the health of King Henry II. and the good of his own soul.[3] He also gave to the canons the church of Little Fageham (Faccombe), and died 1199. Cir. 1190.

[1] Document in Corporation Archives; also Addit., 15,314, f. 83 b.; Merewether and Stephens, 751.

[2] Madox, Form., p. 241.

[3] Madox, Form., p. 248.

Cir. 1200. Gundred de Warenne, widow of Geoffry de Hose, ratified the gift of the church of Little Fageham, which had belonged to her dower.[1]

King John, on 9th January 1201, confirmed to them Kingsland and the wood called Porteswud.[2]

1204. Bishop Godfrey de Lucy, on August 25, 1204, confirmed the gift of William Aliz, consisting of the tenth penny of his yearly rents in Aldington, five shillings annually from the mill of the same place, a tenth of his pannage, and free range in his woods for thirty hogs.[1]

Walter de Chalke (see above) and Beatrice his wife gave to the canons in perpetuity two bezants[3] of annual rent issuing out of property at Eblington.

Humphrey de Bohun, Earl of Hereford, Constable of England, confirmed (c. 1300) the gift made by his father, Humphrey de Bohun, of Chilworth. the church of Cheleworth (Chilworth), with its lands, liberties, and customs, the canons being bound to provide a chaplain. Milo the chaplain was first among the witnesses.

William Musard (c. 1290) gave to the canons three shillings of annual quit-rent in the village of Elleden (Eldon, near Michelmersh), on condition of their burning for ever one wax taper before the altar of the Blessed Virgin in the convent church wherein the body of his wife Isabella was buried. Among the witnesses was Hugo de Chekehull, sheriff of Hants in 1294 and subsequent years.[4]

Walter Basset about 1253 granted two acres in Lokerlegh[5] (near Mottisfont).

Hoglands. John de la Bulehuse and Bartholomew, his son, about the same time granted and confirmed certain land in Hoggeslonde.[6]

Bartholomew de la Bulehuse gave his tenements at Levedon and the Strand, together with his tenants, their lands and tenements. Levedon, Lufefedon, or Lovedoune appears to have been the name of the rising ground about the Polygon.

Polygon and Water-house Lane. The property granted by Bartholomew is described as lying at Lufefedon, in the north suburb, between the present boundary stream, then called Rollebroke, which descended to the sea at Achard's Bridge, and Goswell or Waterhouse Lane, then called Goushanewell Lane, which led to the shore.[7] In a later document Prior Henry (c. 1290) leased to Adam le Hordyr a certain hill in the suburb called Leueuedon upon the Strand.[8] The locality is further pointed out by other deeds; one speaking of a house at la West Strond, under Levedon; another

[1] Dugdale, Mon. Angl. [2] Chart. 2 John, m. 16.

[3] Gold coins, so called from Byzantium, or Constantinople, where they were first struck.

[4] The three preceding documents are in Dugdale.

[5] Addit., 15,314, f. 88 b. [6] Ibid., f. 23 b. [7] Ibid., f. 72 b.

[8] Ibid., f. 72 b.

of the same tenement as in the suburbs on the Strand, south of Levedone; a later document (1410) mentions certain acres as lying upon the Strand between the hill called Lovedoune on the north and Gosenwellane on the south.

The Marlands.

The convent possessed land in the East and West Garstons, in Lubery Mead, and in Pedelond.[1] They held also six acres in Rockesdone, the gift of William de Rockesdone.[2]

The holdings within the town were very numerous; a few of them were as follows:—

Roger de Hampton, probably the son of Gervaise le Riche, the founder of God's House, granted (c. 1228) a rent of fifteen shillings in Southampton to the infirmary of St. Denys. Walkelin was Prior; but there is no other date.[3]

Benedict, the son of Azon, gave certain rents from his tenements in French Street, and from his cultivated ground behind the Lepers' Hospital, also from another field of half an acre to the south of the hospital, which had its length upon the street leading from Houndwell Cross to the Strand. His son John confirmed the two-shillings rents from French Street, added two shillings more for his father's soul, and made some further grants by deed of December 1221.[4]

Michael, son of Alice Fortin, gave (c. 1230) a messuage worth five shillings per annum in the parish of St. Lawrence on the east side of English Street.[5]

Michael, son of Richard le Franceis, gave (c. 1237) three stalls (stagia) near the Friars' Gate, and two shillings quit-rent from the land on which the Friars' dwelling stood. Among the witnesses were Benedict, the son of Azon, then mayor, Walter le Flemyng the bailiff, and Luke the clerk.[6]

Among other benefactions were those of Thomas Daunger and Matilda his wife (c. 1237).[7] Robert le Moynes, burgess, who gave (1249) two messuages in the suburb of Southampton at the north end of Niwetone Street (now Orchard Lane) and other properties.[8] Arnold de la Mote, the Gascon, who bound himself to a yearly quit-rent of half a mark in silver from the house lately in the occupation of the Lady Claremunda, for the good of her soul, June 1263.[9] Nicholas Beket, who gave by will (c. 1287) ten shillings annual quit-rent on some property at West Quay, to the north of which was a lane called Grantteslane, possibly that now called

[1] Addit., 15,314, ff. 13, 35 b.
[2] Ibid., f. 95 b.
[3] Ibid., f. 69.
[4] Ibid., ff. 69, 70 b.
[5] Ibid., f. 48; Madox, Form., p. 278.
[6] Madox, Form., p. 196.
[7] Ibid., p. 378.
[8] Addit., 15,314, f. 31.
[9] Madox, Form., p. 358.

Blue Anchor Lane.[1] Sir Thomas Peverel, who about the same time gave an annual rent of five shillings from a tenement in the parish of St. Lawrence, to maintain an anniversary for the soul of his father, Andrew Peverel, in the convent church.[2] William de Arundel gave a messuage and four shops in 1311.[3]

By grant of 6 Edw. III. (1332) the convent was empowered to receive from the king's butler in the port of Southampton one cask of red wine annually for the celebration of the mass.

In 1342 Roger de Petersfield and others gave to the convent six messuages in the town of Southampton.[3]

Roger Haywoode, in 1371, left a house in Southampton for a chaplain to celebrate for his soul every day.[3]

For William of Wykeham's bequest, see p. 345; and for mediæval controversies[4] about the churches of Southampton, see pp. 330–335.

Revenues. The house never was wealthy. In the taxation of 1291 the property appears as follows:—At St. Denys, £10, 13s. 4d.; Lockerley, £1, 13s. 4d.; rents at Winchester, £1, 10s.; giving a total of £13, 16s. 8d., paying its tenth of £1, 7s. 8d. In the Archdeaconry of Sarum the Priory held land at Bereford worth £4, at Fogheleston and Bymerton, £2, 4s. 8d., and at Chureneston, £1.

In the Deanery of Marlborough the rectory of Chiselbury brought in £2, 13s. 4d.; and there was a holding at Burbach (Burbage) worth ten shillings.

Poverty. In April 1294 the canons, on account of their poverty, obtained license to serve the appropriated churches[5] of Shirley by a secular chaplain.[6]

We have elsewhere mentioned the respites granted to the house by Parliament in consequence of their losses at the burning of the town in 1338: their poverty frequently appears in charters.

On the same plea the house obtained by charter,[7] April, 4, 1405, the appropriation of the churches of St. John in the Soke, Winchester, and St. Cross and St. Michael, Southampton, the advowsons of which churches they had previously held. These appropriations, it was believed, would bring them in some fifty marks per annum after the payment of the vicars; the endowments of these

1 Addit., 15,314, f. 71. 2 Ibid., f. 49. 3 Inquis. ad q. d.

4 A few local names occur in a case of re-entry in 1385 given by Madox, Form., p. 121.

5 The site of these churches, called also chapels, is lost. There was a church in the manor of Shirley at the Domesday Record.

6 Reg. Pontiss., f. 13 b.

7 Pat. 6 Hen. IV., p. 2, m. 18.

latter being secured according to the statute,[1] together with the distribution of certain annual sums among the poor.

In the 'Valor' of 1536 the revenue of the Priory is given as £91, 9s., with a net income of £80, 11s. 6d. The particulars of its possessions were returned on the roll of the King's Commissioners as follows:—[2]

*County of Southampton.*

| | | | | |
|---|---|---|---|---|
| Southampton. | Profits from the manor of St. Denys, with the Grange there | £13 | 6 | 8 |
| ,, | Assessed (or fixed) rents of freeholders | 2 | 16 | 7½ |
| ,, | Rents of customary tenants (or copyholders) | 1 | 7 | 8 |
| ,, | The farm of tenements, cottages, and gardens let at will | 12 | 2 | 4 |
| ,, | The farm of tenements, cottages, and gardens let by indenture (or lease) | 18 | 7 | 9 |
| Northam. | The farm of the manor | 9 | 6 | 8 |
| Southampton. | Pension on the vicarage of St. Cross | 2 | 0 | 0 |
| ,, | Pension on the vicarage of All Saints | 0 | 13 | 4 |
| ,, | Pension on the rectory of St. Lawrence | 0 | 13 | 4 |
| ,, | Pension on the vicarage of St. Michael | 0 | 13 | 4 |
| ,, | Dues for pannage | 0 | 2 | 2 |
| ,, | Perquisites from the manor court | 0 | 1 | 10 |
| Shamelhurst. | Farm of the grange | 3 | 6 | 8 |
| ,, | Farm of various lands there | 1 | 6 | 8 |
| Aldington (Allington). | Rents of free and customary tenants | 2 | 14 | 4 |
| Portswood. | Rent and farm, (and one red rose) | 5 | 10 | 4 |
| Leverley (Lockerley). | Farm of the manor | 2 | 13 | 4 |
| East Dean. | Rents from the customary tenants | 1 | 0 | 0 |
| Broughton. | Assessed rents | 1 | 0 | 0 |
| Houghton. | Farm of tenements there | 0 | 7 | 0 |
| Estudderley (East Tytherley). | Farm of the rectory | 1 | 6 | 8 |
| Chilworth and Shirley. | Farm of the rectories | 8 | 0 | 0 |
| King's Sombourn. | Pension from the rectory | 2 | 13 | 4 |
| ,, | Pension on the rectory of All Saints church | 1 | 0 | 0 |
| Romsey. | Corrody at | 2 | 0 | 0 |
| Ablington. | Assessed rents, &c. | 6 | 8 | 0 |
| Appulshawe. | Assessed rents | 0 | 3 | 0 |
| Burbage (near Marlborough). | Farm of a tenement | 0 | 10 | 0 |
| Chesbury. | A portion of the tithes | 0 | 6 | 8 |
| Berford (Barford, Salisbury). | Farm at the manor | 5 | 0 | 0 |
| Shreton (Shrewton, Devizes). | Farm of a tenement | 1 | 5 | 0 |
| Stapleford (near Salisbury). | Farm of a tenement | 0 | 5 | 0 |
| Bemerton and Quidhampton (near Salisbury). | Farm of the manor | 11 | 0 | 0 |

*County of Wilts.*

| | | | | |
|---|---|---|---|---|
| Wilton. | Pension on Holy Trinity Church | 0 | 2 | 0 |

*County of Dorset.*

| | | | | |
|---|---|---|---|---|
| Sturminster and Lichette (probably Sturminster-Marshall near Wimborne, and Lytchet-Minster near Poole). | Assessed rents | 0 | 18 | 0 |

[1] Stat. 15 Rich. II. c. 6, and 4 Hen. IV. c. 12.

[2] See Caley's Dugdale's Mon.

Priors.

It will be convenient to arrange the remaining notices of this house under the succession of its Priors.

Girard the canon was probably first Prior, c. 1124.

Adelard, Prior in 1151.

Walkelin, mentioned in a deed October 7, 1228.[1]

Rueland, mentioned, first time observed, January 14, 1230;[2] last time, January 21, 1251.

Nicholas, June 29, 1263;[3] October 1278.

Henry, Prior in 1290; obtains license from the Bishop to vacate his Priory on account of infirmity, August 18, 1294.[4]

Richard de Chacombe. The royal assent, Bishop's mandate to Archdeacon for induction, and to the convent (as usual), requiring obedience to the new Prior, are dated August 22, 1294.[5] Under this Prior the selling of corrodies without the episcopal license was ordered to be reformed, March 13, 1306–7. Later in the same year (September 5), Bishop Woodlock wrote about the internal management of the house, and in the following April (1308) held a visitation of the Priory, when certain statutes were given for its regulation. The house was again visited by commission in May 1309.[6]

Peter or Robert de Stoneham. Bishop Stratford writes, January 24, 1327–28, that being about to attend the Parliament at York, he cannot immediately attend to the reformation of the defects found in the monastery at his visitation, but he will do so, the Lord willing; meanwhile, he commands that none be permitted to leave the house without leave of the Prior or Subprior.[7]

Thomas de Newton was elected on the resignation of *Peter* de Stoneham on May 14, 1328; but objections being taken to his election, Brother Thomas submitted to the ruling of the Bishop and resigned. Upon this the Subprior and convent, on June 28, put the selection of a Prior from among the canons into the hands of the Bishop.[8]

William de Warham was accordingly appointed, receiving the episcopal benediction and the obedience of the convent in the chapel at Marwell, July 13, 1328; the royal letters bearing the same date, the mandates for induction and obedience, July 26.[9] Two days later the Bishop wrote to his nominee on certain reformations which he had lately enjoined upon *Robert* de Stoneham, then Prior. These had not been attended to, and he desired there might be no further delay.[10]

Bishop Orlton made a visitation of the Priory on November 22, 1334, preaching in the chapter-house on the text 'Israel shall dwell safely;' two days after which the appropriations of the churches of East Tytherley and of the vicarages of Shirley and Chilworth, and the chapels of Holy Trinity and St. Andrew, Southampton, together with pensions at St. Michael's worth 60s.; at St. Cross, 13s. 4d.; at St. Lawrence, 13s. 4d.; and at All Saints, 26s. 8d., were secured to the Priory.[11] In 1346 some addition was made to the buildings, and Bishop Edington licensed for celebrations (July 13) an oratory lately constructed over the outer gate in honour of St. Katherine.[12]

Richard de Staunford (Stamford) succeeded on the death of Warham, March 9,

---

1 Addit., 15,314, f. 93 b. 2 Ibid., ff. 48, 76 b. 3 Ibid., ff. 93 b, 76.
4 Reg. Pontiss., f. 14. 5 Ibid., f. 14 b.
6 Reg. Woodlock, ff. 56, 64 b, 152 b, 107 b.
7 Reg. Stratford, f. 34 b. 8 Ibid., ff. 108 b, 109 b.
9 Ibid., f. 110. 10 Ibid., f. 40.
11 Reg. Orlton, i., ff. 11, 12 b. 12 Reg. Edington, ii. f. 2 b.

1348–49.[1] A visitation of the Priory, as also of the precentory of St. Mary's, was held by commission of Bishop Wykeham under letters dated September 27, 1381.[2] A few months after this, Prior Richard having become very infirm, John Staunford was chosen coadjutor, and admitted by the Bishop, March 14, 1381–82.[3]

John Staunford (Stamford), on the death of Richard, received royal letters, mandates, &c., on March 22, 1390–91;[4] he died December 1397.

John Ryall, succeeded December 6, 1397,[5] the usual mandates being issued December 20.

Thomas Winchester, on the death of Ryall, elected April 20, 1412; mandates, &c., April 28.[6]

Thomas Arnewode, elected April 5, 1435; died January 4, 1456–57.[7]

William Norman, Subprior, elected January 8, 1456–57; receives confirmation, &c., January 12.[8]

Thomas Robyns or Revys, elected November 4, 1462;[9] temporalities, &c., November 9. The name is written Revys in deed of grant to William Gunter, merchant, of twenty shillings rent from the manor of Bemerton, Wilts, dated April 1, 1476.[10]

John Foster, elected April 9, 1490.[11]

Robert Wode or Wodd, temporalities, &c., August 29, 1499.[12]

Walter May, on the death of Wode,[13] February 10, 1508–9; pardon for entering into said Priory, October 20, 1509.[14]

The injunctions given to the house by Bishop Fox may serve as an example of other visitation articles from the Bishops. In order to the true service of God, it was enjoined that the nocturnal and daily offices, the celebration of masses, the ceremonies and hours according to rule in choir and convent be duly observed; that since ignorance is the mother of error, the rule of public reading and exposition be diligently kept; that no meetings with women be permitted in the church, and none but honest women admitted within the convent; that the brothers go about two by two, and never frequent taverns, nor go to Portswood or Southampton to dine, except by leave, lest by secular conversation their quiet be disturbed, and they be tempted to worldly thoughts and desires; that when at home they exercise themselves in reading, &c.; that doors be shut at proper times and safely kept; that no drinking be allowed in the refectory; that the brethren use the dress of the order and no other; that they make no dissensions in the house; that the accounts of the convent be rendered openly before all at least once a year. These, with several other useful regulations for the ordering of the house, avoiding abuses, and living by the strict rule they had

[1] Reg. Edington, i. f. 43 b.
[2] Reg. Wykeham, ii. f. 190.
[3] Ibid., f. 194.
[4] Ibid., i. f. 211.
[5] Addit., 15,314, f. 80; Reg. Wykeham, i. ff. 280, 281 b.
[6] Reg. Beaufort, f. 38 †.
[7] Reg. Waynflete, i. f. 82.
[8] Addit., 15,314, f. 79 b; Reg. Waynflete, f. 82.
[9] Ibid., f. 123 b.
[10] Deed *penes* Corp.
[11] Reg. Courtenay, f. 11.
[12] Addit., 15,314, ff. 94 b, 101.
[13] Reg. Fox, ii. ff. 108 b, 110.
[14] Brewer's Letters of Hen. VIII.

chosen apart from the snares of the world, made twenty-four articles altogether.[1]

The Dissolution, 1536.

Walter May was Prior at the dissolution, the canons at that time being nine in number. The house and site of the Priory were granted by Henry VIII., after its suppression in 1536, under 27 Hen. VIII. cap. 28, to Francis Dawtrey, Esq., on August 26 (30 Hen. VIII.), 1538, together with the manors of Portswood, Northam, and Lockerley, lands in East Dean, &c. On July 10, 1543, Thomas Hobson petitions to exchange, among other possessions, the farm of St. Dyonyse Oldehouse in the town of Southampton, and certain rents and farms in the parish of All Saints, and in other parts of the town, lately possessions of the Priory.

In 1549 (February 3) the farm of the rectory of Chilworth and Shirley passed to Roger Prideaux of the Inner Temple. In 1557 (June 26) Andrew Lame acquired certain holdings late of the Priory; and in 1563 (July 22), other possessions late of the same passed to Thomas Gardiner and John Devyke.[2]

In 1730 the Priory came,[3] with the estate of Portswood, into the possession of Charles, Earl of Peterborough, in whose literary circle, at his neighbouring seat of Bevois Mount, were included Pope, Swift, and other celebrities. It then passed into the hands of Thomas Wood, Esq., of London, the owner in Dr. Speed's time; it was afterwards purchased by General Giles Stibbert, of the Bengal Presidency, for whom, 1771, Portswood House was built after designs from Mr. Crunden; it was pulled down a few years ago for the erection of villas. St. Denys afterwards underwent several changes of possession till purchased with Portswood House, about 1830, by Mr. George Jones of Manchester, who destroyed most of the remains, which were considerable, in the early part of the century. Shortly before 1859 the Priory was bought by Mr. Alfred Skelton,[4] with a view to its preservation. It is now the property of Mr. W. H. Baigent.

## The Convent of Friars Minor.

From a document printed by Madox,[5] we find that this house of Franciscan or Grey Friars, so called from St. Francis of Assisi, their founder, and the colour of their habit, otherwise styled by themselves in humility Friars Minor, as being the youngest and the humblest of the

[1] Reg. Fox, ii. f. 119, &c.

[2] Particulars of Grants, &c. (Record Office).

[3] Journal Brit. Arch. Assoc., vol. xv. pp. 278–280.

[4] In 1857 this gentleman issued coloured engravings of the encaustic tiles from the convent in his possession in thirty-eight plates; only four copies of the work were printed.

[5] Formulare, pp. 196, 279.

religious orders, was in existence during the mayoralty of Benedict the son of Azon, Walter le Flemyng being prepositus. This document is undated, but another executed in the same mayoralty, when also Walter le Flemyng was bailiff, bears the date of 1237. It is possible that these instruments may not belong to the same year, since in the former Luke was the clerk, and in the latter Samson. But whatever may have been the exact year of the first-named deed, the house was settled at that time, and thus was probably one of the earliest of the order established in England, the Minorites not having been introduced into the country before September 1224. Foundation.

The office of the Minorites was to minister to the poor, the sick, and the afflicted in towns, and they chose their places of abode in the immediate vicinity of poverty and wretchedness. Here they were located close to the hospital for the poor (God's House); the back of their premises adjoined the town wall or ditch on the east, about which and beyond, in the suburb of Newtown (see under 'God's House'), a poor population had sprung up. In front, their entrance, which was either at the High Street end of Sugarhouse Lane or in the street leading to Gloucester Square, was choked, as it continued to be, with sheds, stalls, and shops, some of which belonged to the canons of St. Denys.

The Franciscans assumed the most abject poverty that they might be the more acceptable to the neglected classes to whom in the first instance they ministered. Barefooted and scantily clothed in the coarse dress of their order, they begged their bread from house to house; at the same time they were bound to be of ready wit and completely learned, no less than of general aptitude for the edification of the people. They soon took their place as foremost teachers, and among the divinity readers in the University of Oxford a Southampton brother (Walter) appears as fifty-third on the list.[1] Poverty.

The possession of wealth and costly buildings was alike inconsistent with their rule of poverty. Their earliest houses and chapels were hovels of clay and wood, nor might they surround their humble possessions with anything more pretentious than ditch or fence. The liberality of their friends was constantly tempting the Friars to exceed what was lawful in the style of building. At Southampton we find that the cloisters had been erected in stone through the goodwill of the burgesses, who sorely opposed the strict measure of Brother Albert of Pisa, the minister-provincial of England, when he ordered the destruction of the fabric, and eventually carried his point.[2] This was about 1236. Buildings.

[1] Monumenta Franciscana, p. 534.

[2] Mon. Francisc., p. 55. The same Brother Albert invoked the thunders of Heaven upon the new chapel at Reading, which he dared not himself destroy,

Government.

The Franciscan body was governed by a minister-general, under whom were provincials, with their subordinate wardenries; the house of St. Mary, Southampton, being included within the wardenry of London.

Register of the House.

A short register of this house existed among the Corporation archives in the middle of the last century. It is not now to be found; but fortunately Dr. Speed has preserved a transcript, which, though manifestly not *verbatim*, gives probably the chief features. From this document, printed below, and from other surviving notices, we collect the following facts:—

Isabella de Chekehull,[1] who died in 1253, was considered the chief foundress of the house, having bestowed on the Friars a plot of building ground. Walter le Flemyng, bailiff of the town in 1237, appears among the earliest benefactors. By an exchange with the canons of St. Denys he gave the Friars in 1241 a small parcel of land;[2] his own dwelling being close by.

The Chapel.

The first stone of the chapel was laid on July 8, 1280, the rigidity of the order as to buildings being somewhat relaxed; and on the Feast of St. Francis, July 16, 1287, the Friars entered their new church for the first time, and on the same day were entertained by John, bailiff of the New Forest, and Petronilla his wife. The site for their chapel had been given by Robert le Mercer, whose death took place in 1314. Within this chapel an ordination was held by John Sandale, Bishop of Winchester, in Lent (March 18) 1317, when a large number were admitted as acolytes, sub-deacons, deacons, and priests.[3] Interment was frequently sought within the convent chapel, and gifts and legacies were bestowed upon it by the burgesses among the other churches of the town. Later on a curious instance occurs of the manner in which our churches were sometimes used for lay business. In 1496 Thomas Overey, the gauger of wine and oil, having claimed, by virtue of the king's authority, for every pipe twopence, for every tun fourpence, and for every tun of oil eightpence, it was agreed (October 8) in the church of the Friars, before John Walsh, mayor, John Dawtry, custumer, Thomas Thomas, controller of customs, William Justice, sheriff of the town, that he should take half the duty from the men of the town and other Englishmen, according to the custom of the town, 'and as for other aliens and strangers, they to sue themself for their remedy.'[4]

Curious business.

as it had been erected by the King. Several stories are told illustrative of the suspicion with which the early Friars regarded a taste for building (Ibid., 18, 34, 37, &c.)

[1] Chickenhall, Chignall, in the parish of North Stoneham.

[2] Addit., 15,314, f. 57 b.

[3] Reg. Sandal., ff. 57 b, 58.

[4] Liber Niger, f. 45.

In 1291 the Friars entered their new dormitory, and in the same year the chapter-house was built. Before this period the needs of the fraternity were probably satisfied in the humblest manner.

John le Forester of Romsey and William Putton joined in giving the warden and brothers in 1368 (42 Ed. III.), for ever, one toft, with its belongings, towards the enlargement of their house and premises, a gift confirmed by royal license in 1374.[1]

Soon after this the convent obtained license for adding to their cemetery an area 120 feet long by 100 feet wide, on the west side of their church, and adjoining the High Street, for the consecration of which by Thomas, Bishop 'Achadensis,' probably a suffragan of Winchester, a commission was issued by William of Wykeham in April 1381.[2]

In 1290 Nicholas de Barbeflet granted to the Friars the fountain in his manor of Shirley spoken of above, p. 114. Why they did not make immediate use of this grant does not appear; but in 1304 they began to bring the water down to the convent, and on June 2, 1309, commenced their works at the conduit-head, owing to the liberality of Henry de Bluntesdon, Prior of God's House, who died about September 1316.

In 1382 Richard II. took the house, their church, aqueduct, garden, and premises into his protection by his royal patent.[3]

Benefactors.

Among the chief benefactors to the convent were reckoned:—Isabella de Chekehull, the chief foundress; Nicholas de Barbeflet, with Agatha and Alice, his wives, who gave the spring at Hill or Colwell; Henry de Bluntesdon, who enabled the Friars to appropriate the gift; Robert le Mercer, who gave the site of the chapel; Robert Stenigg, who did them much good, especially after the burning of the town; and Henry Flemyng, who remembered them in his will, bearing date 1357.

Priors, &c.

The license to preach and hear confessions granted by Bishop Stratford in February 1325 has preserved a few names of the brethren:—Jordan of Dounton, the warden or prior; John of Pageham, the reader; Jordan of Kingston; Nicholas of Dounton; and John of Romsey.[4] For Prior Robert Horewood in 1420, see p. 115.

Reformed into Observants.

In July 1499 this house of conventual Friars Minor was reformed into Observant Franciscans by King Henry VII. From letters of April 1534 addressed by the mayor and Henry Huttoft to Cromwell it appears that an order for the arrest of the warden of this house, Friar

[1] Inquis. ad. q. d. 42 Ed. III.; Pat. 48 Ed. III. p. 1, m. 8.

[2] Reg. Wykeham, ii. f. 194.

[3] This patent, given at length by Dr. Speed, is not here produced; its gist is simply as above, without any historical notice. It is Pat. 5 Rich. II., p. 2, m. 11 (June 6).

[4] Reg. Stratford, f. 15.

Gilbert Pecock, had been issued; he was then away preaching, but the town authorities promised he should appear, and begged Cromwell's favour to him. On July 16 Pecock himself wrote to Cromwell giving account of a pretended visitation of the house which had occurred the day before by a Father Black Friar, who took the keys from the porter, assembled the brethren in the chapter-house, and read an instrument by which authority had been given to Dr. Browne, provincial of the Augustine Friars, and Dr. Hylsey, provincial of the Black Friars, to be visitors. It appearing, however, that this Black Friar had no sufficient authority for himself, his further intrusion was resisted. The issue does not appear.[1]

After the dissolution the site passed by purchase, on their petition, January 6, 1545, to John Pollard and William Byrt, and June 23, 1551, to Sir A. Darcy.[2] The property has gone through many changes since. Scarcely a vestige of the Priory now remains.

Philosopher's Stone.

Among the Corporation archives is a metrical treatise on the Philosopher's Stone, which Dr. Speed, in a note attached to it, supposes to have been found in the Friary; a suggestion which possibly gave rise to the assertion of a later writer that this was the only book found in their library at the dissolution.

The following is Dr. Speed's transcript:[3]—

"The register of this house . . is preserved in the Audit-house. . . "I shall transcribe it at large, both as a curiosity and as the most "authentic account, so far as it goes, of this convent:—

"Isabel Chekehull died, who gave to the Friars Minors of this place "one plot of ground, A.D. 1253, and who was the chief foundress of "this convent.

"Here follow the buildings (constructiones) of the same convent.

"A.D. 1280. On the morrow after the translation of St. Thos., the "Martyr, the first stone of the foundation of the chapel of the Friars "Minors of Southampton was laid.

"A.D. 1287. On the Feast of St. Francis the brothers first entered "their new church at Southampton, and John the son of Thos., then "bailiff of the New Forest, and Petronilla his wife, gave a treat to the "brothers and all their friends that were there that day.

"A.D. 1291. On the Nativity of our Lord the brothers entered "their new dormitory.

"A.D. 1291. The Chapter-house was built.

"This day [no day mentioned] they began the watercourse, A.D. "1304.

---

1 Brewer's Letters. 2 Particulars of Grants, &c. (Record Office).

3 His translation is given; want of space forbids the production of the text, which, however, presents no difficulties.

"Here follow some things which concern the good of the convent "of Friars Minors at Southampton.

"Imprimis, A.D. 1309, on the 4th of Nones, that is, the 2d day of "June, the Friars began to work on the conduit-head given to them "by the charity of Henry de Bluntesdone, Prior of God's House and "Archdeacon of Dorsetshire, and formerly almoner to the most famous "Edward, king of England, son of our Lord Henry III., formerly "king of England, and Eleanor his wife, who took the habit of a nun "at Ambresbury,[1] and was buried there, and her heart was with "venerations interr'd at the Friars Minors' convent in London.

"Consecrations follow.

"Anno Domini 1311, several altars were consecrated.

"A.D. 1382, the churchyard was consecrated.

"Then follows as under:—

"Robert Meucir [le Mercer?] died, who bought for the Friars the "ground on which their chapel stands, A.D. 1314. Henry de Bluntes-"done died A.D. 1316. It was he that brought the water from Cole-"welle to the house of the Friars.

"This day the Friars ought particularly to pray for the souls of "Nicolas Barnfleet [de Barbeflet], and those of Agatha and Alice, his "wives, for the spring of Colewelle, as appears in their deed of gift of "the said spring.

"This has no date.

"A.D. 1336. The third day after the Feast of St. Michael the Arch-"angel, at one o'clock, there came about 40 galleys and about 20 pin-"naces, and took the town of Southampton, and burnt it the next "day, the year above said.

"Robert Stenigg died, who was a great benefactor to the Friars a long "time, and especially after the burning of the town of Southampton.

"This has no date.

"Henry Flemyng died, who was a great benefactor to the Friars in "his will, A.D. 1357.

"A.D. 1499. On the 26th day of July, being the Festival of St. Anne, "the mother of the glorious Virgin, this Hampton convent, being "then under conventual Friars Minor, was reformed, and Observant "Friars were introduced to live there by our most serene Lord Henry "VII., king of England.

"Here ends the register."

"The sugar-house [built 1740] stands on the site of the chapel, and "the place called Gloucester Square on that of the main body of the "abbey, and a few other houses on other parts of the ground."

[1] The Queen's profession took place at Ambresbury (Amesbury) in 1284.

## Hospital of St. Mary Magdalene.

Founded c. 1173.

The Hospital of St. Mary Magdalene[1] for lepers, commonly called Le Maudeleyne, was founded by the burgesses at their own cost in the twelfth century, in or before the 20 Hen. II. (1173–74),[2] and was confirmed by Pope Alexander III. in 1179, among other possessions, to the Priory of St. Denys by the name of the chapel of St. Mary Magdalene; but it does not appear that the Priory derived any benefit from the hospital till the reign of Edward III.

In consequence of its foundation by the burgesses, they at first exercised the patronage. Towards the end of the thirteenth century, however, the crown claimed the advowson, and appointed William Balweys, an intrusion which the burgesses resented, as did also the Bishop of Winchester, John de Pontissara, who also, it seems, claimed the presentation, and at the instance of the burgesses appointed (April 1285) Robert de Puteo, rector of St. Cross (or Holy Rood),[3] ousting the nominee of the crown. Upon this the Bishop was charged with purpresture against the King in appropriating the advowson; but on a trial which ensued, the jury affirmed the right of the burgesses (Easter 1291), and found that, owing to the circumstances of the foundation, neither king nor bishop had hitherto interfered with the patronage. After this the Bishop resigned all jurisdiction over the hospital, except that of ordinary, and W. Balweys was left in possession.[4]

It appears that when the burgesses founded Le Maudeleyne they also settled in it a chantry for a priest to celebrate on certain days, and arranged that the Prior and convent of St. Denys should support all other burdens.

Appropriated to St. Denys.

In 1347 (June 1) the hospital, together with all its possessions, was appropriated by Edward III. to the convent of St. Denys in consideration of the poverty of that house, with the usual proviso that they should perform the duties belonging to the hospital.[5] This grant of annexation was confirmed by Richard II. in 1390, the condition being repeated of the convent supporting the hospital and chantry, together with the poor and infirm thereto belonging, according to the terms of its founda-

---

1 Dr. Speed quotes chiefly Bishop Tanner for his notice of the house. He believed, erroneously, that it stood in French Street, and was called 'Little St. Denys,' from the tradition that the Friars latterly occupied it when they came to town to serve the churches. He adds that the old house was standing a few years ago, when one Mr. Matthew Woodford built a new one on the ground, in which their family were then living. A pencil note on the MS. dated 1820 adds 'Now called Hampton Court.' Here was the birthplace of Dr. Watts.

2 See above, p. 30.

3 Reg. Pontiss., f. 77.

4 Rot. Parl. i. 45; Abbrev. Plac. Hillary and Easter, 19 Ed. I.

5 Pat. 22 Ed. III. p. 1, m. 1.

tion from ancient times. It appearing afterwards on inquisition that these terms had not been carried out, the hospital was granted to John Newport, clerk, whose letters patent were, however, revoked at suit of the convent in 1398.[1] It is true that in the next reign the above neglect on the part of the convent was disavowed, but undoubtedly for some years past Prior Stamford had ceased to support the hospital and its chantry as heretofore, and had let the buildings fall much to decay. The use of the hospital, therefore, as a charitable institution was grievously curtailed; nor were matters mended when Henry IV. in his second year (February 10, 1401) confirmed the hospital to the convent on the sole condition of praying for his health while he lived and for his soul after death.[2]

Property.

The property of the house in the fourteenth century consisted of eighteen acres called 'Le Maudelayne,' three acres in Bove-barre Street, four cottages in Foleflode, without the bars of the town, and a few rents in the town and neighbourhood.[3]

Perquisites.

Under the old laws of the Guild the lepers 'de la Maudeleyne' were remembered in the charity of the town, and they enjoyed from ancient time an impost of a penny on every tun of foreign wine landed at the port; a privilege which passed to the convent of St. Denys in right of the hospital annexed to it.

Site.

The following transactions bear on the site of the hospital. About 1250 an exchange was made between Prior Rueland of St. Denys and the hospital of an acre of land belonging to the latter in Bockland[4] for an acre in la East Garston,[5] conveniently situated for the hospital as adjoining their garden. East and West Garston, of which we read in connection with the hospital, are to be identified with the Marlands, called in the last century the Magdalen or Maudlin Fields; the above-mentioned acre in la East Garston was immediately to the right of the Winchester Road, and had the lepers' garden on the south; it was further described as opposite to the house of the Blessed Mary Magdalene of Southampton, so the hospital itself was in la West Garston, or the West Marlands. And it had a garden and enclosure round it. An acre given by Robert Pede of Pedeland in the northern suburb is described[6] as on the north side of the garden of the lepers, and stretching thence along the west side of the king's highway (Winchester Road) towards Lubery Cross (see p. 51). And in another deed Prior Nicholas,

[1] Pat. 21 Ed. III., p. 1, m. 1.
[2] Addit., 15,314, f. 12 b; Pat. 2 Hen. IV., p. 3, m. 6.
[3] Pat. 22 Rich. II., p. 2, m. 37; Madox, Form., p. 399.
[4] 'In campo qui vocatur Bocland.'—Addit., 15,314, f. 20 b.
[5] Garston means, probably, enclosed grass-land.
[6] Addit., 15,314, f. 13, also another document, 19 b.

granting to Richard le Bretun six acres formerly held of the convent by Benedict Ace, describes them [1] as in the west field behind the house and garden of the lepers of St. Mary Magdalene in the suburbs, and as stretching from their buildings to another acre formerly held by Benedict.

The house and enclosures then stood in the West Marlands to the north of Anglesea Place, the Winchester Road passing through its premises; another garden and the church apparently being on the opposite side, or in the East Marlands.

The church is frequently mentioned; its site seems pointed out [2] by a grant of an acre (no date) in the suburb outside the north gate, above the Church of the Magdalene on the east side of the street. The Winchester Road about here seems to have been sometimes called 'Magdalene Street,' [3] and the house of Simon, the chaplain, was on the east side of it, probably adjoining the church.

Some land in a croft called Burestwoldesland or Briȝtwoldesland is said to stretch from the great street called Hundewelle Street to the stone wall of the lepers.[4] This 'great street' was the highway leading from Houndwell Cross to the Strand [5] (western shore) through what is now called Regent Street, and was formerly called Windmill or Canshut Lane; so that the land referred to might have been in the West Marlands, in which the greater portion of the hospital's property may have been situated. The boundary of la West Garston towards the north seems to have been 'Gosenelkellestrete,' [6] Goswell Street, now (part of it) Waterhouse Lane; one of the conduits in this lane being the Gosen Well or Goose Well, which gave its name to adjacent land no less than to the street or lane.

The hospital is spoken of as a house for male lepers, but (see under 'God's House') females were at one time admitted. At the dissolution [7] it was worth £16, 16s.

## The Hospital of St. Julian, or God's House.

Foundation.

This hospital, designed originally for the poor, to whose use it is still dedicated, was founded in the reign of Richard I. by Gervaise le Riche, burgess of Hampton and præpositus of the town, in 1185 (31 Hen. II.), who, according to tradition,[8] conferred the wardenship on his brother Roger, having endowed his new foundation with various estates in houses, rents, and lands both within and without the town.

[1] Addit., 15,314, f. 20 b.
[2] Ibid., f. 18.
[3] Ibid., f. 18 b.
[4] Ibid., f. 22, also f. 28.
[5] Ibid., f. 26 b.
[6] Ibid., f. 22 b, 34 b, &c.
[7] Speed, Catalogue of Religious Houses, 1073.
[8] Rot. Parl., i. 18.

These properties were confirmed to the hospital by his son Roger, who also added to the endowment by a similar grant of lands, rents, and tenements in pure and perpetual alms.

Charters, &c. — West Hall. — Padwell. — Gussage. — Hickley. — Cofham. — Werrore. — Saltmarsh.

(1.) The earliest known charter is a grant and confirmation by Richard I.,[1] dated September in the eighth year of his reign (1196), and renewed, on account of the royal seal having been changed, on 17th December in the tenth year (1198), securing to the Domus Dei or God's House of Southampton and the poor residing in it the properties given by Gervaise.[2] These were a rent of two marks on the house in which he had lived in Hantone—West Hall (see p. 320)—payable after the death of his widow by his nephew or grandson (nepos) Walter and his heirs for ever. Among the houses granted by Gervaise was a stone house acquired from the wife of Hugo Cole, so described no doubt as forming an exception to the greater number of domestic buildings, which were probably of wood. Other houses or rents given by him were also confirmed to the hospital. Mention is made of land in the neighbourhood of the town called 'Siwldeslant,' and of 'Padewlle' (Padwell), which passed with other acres belonging to Gervaise in the suburbs. Besides the above, there were grants at a distance from the town. In Portsmouth, the house and land once belonging to Ralph the miller, and a certain void plot of ground which, after the death of Gervaise, was obtained from the king by Hugo de Bosco, the sheriff, and by him conveyed to the Prior of Portsmouth, between whom and the warden of God's House, Southampton, there was a trial at law, when it would seem the right of the sheriff was disallowed. In Dorsetshire, his estate of Guersich (Gussage), formerly in the possession of William de Huecon, but which had escheated to John, Earl of Mortaine, brother of Richard I., afterwards King John, by whom in 1192 (3 Rich. I.) it had been conveyed to Gervaise in consideration of money lent by him to the Earl.[3] Gervaise had also given a yard-land in the same place which he had obtained from Nicholas de la Pentiz. Nearer Southampton again, he had bestowed on his foundation Heckeleia—that is, Hickley Farm, between West End and Botley; in the Isle of Wight, the land which formerly belonged to Peter de Cofham, and also Werore. Returning again to the town, the deed mentions Saltmaris (see p. 52) as passing to the hospital under the grant of Master Roger, together with the house in which he lived, and certain other gifts.

Confirmation.

(2.) Nicholas de la Pentiz[4] confirmed to the hospital the above yard-land in Gersiz (Gussage), which Turstin held, including in the convey-

[1] The hospital paid £206 for having possession and confirmation by the king (Rot. Cancel. 3 John).

[2] Deed in Append. to Fourth Report of Hist. MSS. Commiss., p. 451.

[3] Ibid., p. 452.

[4] Ibid., p. 453.

ance Turstin himself and all his belongings. No date. First among the witnesses is Master Roger of Hampton.

(3.) William de Chelegrave granted the whole land of Hickley for ever at an annual rent of five shillings for service, the hospital also rendering to William de Baggeworde, son of Azon, son of Roger of Hampton, or to his heirs, annually a pair of gilt spurs or fourpence, and to Ralph his brother, or his heirs, a pound of cumin. First among the witnesses was Hugo de Bosco, sheriff (1195–1200).

(4.) William de Redvers, Earl of Devon (1194–1216) granted[1] rights of pasturage and fuel, excepting for six weeks each year, over the whole land of Werrore which belonged to his fee, and is described as lying within Parkhurst, Northwood, Carisbrook, and the Medina. For this the hospital agreed to pay a rent of two shillings per annum, paying the Earl for the present grant of confirmation through Vincent the Warden (custos) ten marks of silver, together with golden spurs to Baldwin, his son and heir.

Vincent the Warden.

(5.) Roger, the son of Marcus[2] (*c.* 11 John, 1209), confirmed to the hospital for the support of the priests, brethren, and sisters therein dwelling, and in subsidy of the poor thereto resorting, his father's gift of the whole land of Werole, with all its appurtenances, at the annual rent of sixpence in lieu of service, and for a fine of twenty-eight marks through Master Roger.[3] Among the witnesses were Walter Fortin, Simon de St. Lawrence, William his brother, Goce, then præpositus of Hampton, &c.

Royal protection.

(6.) King John, by charter[4] dated from Les Andeleys (21st October, no year), took the hospital into his special protection.

(7.) Henry III. did the same,[5] Westminster, 6th February, 18 Henry III. (1234).

(8.) King Edward III., on September 20, 1332, recited and confirmed previous gifts. Those of Gervaise and of Roger his son; those of Margery de Redvers, consisting of lands at la Hore (Ower?), Apeldore, and a bit of wild ground near Hickley; quit-rents at Southampton worth nine shillings per annum, the gift of Robert Bonhayt, burgess; and of John, the son of Hugo of Southampton, worth four shillings; a plot of land in the suburb, the gift of James Isembard, burgess; rents from Adam, the son of Isabella Kampeline, and from John, the son of Azon of Hampton, worth respectively twelvepence and two shillings per annum; the grant of a messuage and garden in

1 Deed in Appendix to Fourth Report of Hist. MSS. Com., p. 454.

2 Ibid., p. 452.

3 Probably the relative of the founder, under whose care the hospital may have remained.

4 Deed in Appendix to Fourth Report of Hist. MSS. Com., p. 452.

5 Ibid., p. 452.

Newetune (Newtown), and of a parcel of land at Newelond, both by William Patrick of Southampton; a parcel of land in Kyngescroft given by William de Rokesdune; a cellar in St. Michael's parish, and two acres in Nywetune, the gifts of Golditha, daughter of Vitalis; two pounds and a half of pepper in Southampton from Ralph le Futur and Juliana his wife; a plot of land in the town from Robert le Fleming and Cecilia his wife, who also gave a piece of land in Newetone; half a pound of cumin per annum and a quit-rent in Nywentune from John, son and heir of Denys Fortin; the donation of all his land of Hekéleia by Ralph the son of Azon; and the confirmation by William de Chelegrave (see above); also that of Henry Biset; the gift by Margery de Redvers of land and a tenement, with messuages, &c., formerly held by Roger de Garden in Shamelherst (Shamblehurst), and the whole land called Bernardsland; the confirmation of Roger de Saunford for the property of Heckel (Hickley) which belonged to Ralph the son of Azon, and for a croft called Losle (Lowsley) with Losle Moor and Peter's Moor; also for a tenement called Herberdeslond, and for two acres of meadow land in Manebrig (Mansbridge), also for rights in Shamelhurst which Roger de Garden formerly held of the predecessor, of Roger de Saunford, lords of Manebrig; further the confirmation of Bernard's land with the possessions which his predecessors had given to the hospital; the grant by Roger Alis of a yard-land in Alditone (Allington), with moors, &c., and of a croft called Blakedune; also of all that land alongside the property of John de Stanham towards the east and south, and of the land between that of John de Stanham and of Sandhurst; also of all that which William the son of Edulph held, lying eastward of Sandhurst between two ways, and of an acre of cleared land in his wood *ad bellam spinam;* also of a right of way before his court through the cultivated land and through the wood to the before-mentioned acre of cleared land at Malmand, and through the land of Pharewy beside the Smith's hedge to Pharewyse ford; the gift also of Nicholas de la Pentiz (see above) of the yard-land in Gersic. All the above, and other specified gifts, were now confirmed. Newtown.

(9.) The same king, by charter[1] in the seventeenth year of his reign (1343), granted the custody of God's House to the provost and scholars of Queen's Hall, Oxford, then recently founded under royal license (January 18, 1341) by Robert de Eglesfield, chaplain to Queen Philippa, and named after her Queen's Hall; the foundation itself being commonly ascribed to that queen in the charters. The house with all its possessions and rights thus passed to the college, with the provision that the Provost and scholars and their successors should support all

Custody granted to the Provost and Scholars of Queen's Hall.

1 Dugdale, Monasticon.

the burdens required by the original foundation, and out of the surplus of the proceeds, if any, should provide a receptacle and habitation for any scholars of the hall afflicted either with incurable malady or lasting infirmity, and should also, the surplus admitting it, permanently increase the number of scholars at the said hall. The last clause provides that the provost and scholars shall enter on the custody of the hospital immediately on the removal, by death or otherwise, of the then present warden.[1]

Provision for afflicted scholars.

Custody confirmed.

(10.) The same king, by charter November 18, 1347, repeated[2] his former gift of the custody to Queen's Hall or College, the charter reciting that in consequence of a great part of the hospital having been burnt by foreign enemies invading Southampton, in which calamity its records had also been destroyed, the king, in relief of its depressed condition, granted it to the provost, the warden, scholars, and brothers and sisters of the said hospital and their successors for ever, with all its lands, &c., in free, pure, and perpetual alms, quit of toll, pontage, pavage, murage, passage, and of prizes of corn, hay, horses, carts, &c., as also of taxations, tallages, &c., belonging to him or his heirs on the aforesaid lands, tenements, &c.

(11.) The above was confirmed[3] by Richard II., November 15, 1378, who also in 1385 exempted Queen's Hall from the payment of tenths and fifteenths for that time in respect of the God's House property in the county of Southampton.

(12.) The hospital was further confirmed[4] to Queen's Hall in the 1 Henry IV. (October 18), 1399; in the 1 Henry V.[5] (May 30), 1413; and in 8 Henry VI.[6] (November 18), 1429.

Priory of Sherborne granted to God's House.

(13.) Edward IV., by charter[7] of 16th February in the first year of his reign (1462), granted to the warden, chaplains, and brothers of God's House and their successors for ever the Priory of Sherborne in the county of Southampton, which having been founded in the time of Henry I. by Henry de Port, and by him given as a cell to the Abbey of St. Vigor at Cerisy-la-Foret in Normandy, was now in the king's hands.[8] The object of the grant was to secure the increase of divine worship within the Hospital of St. Julian or God's House, and to oblige the warden, chaplains, and brothers of the hospital for ever to pray for the king and his successors, and also 'for the souls of Richard,

[1] The warden seems to have been Robert Eglesfield, the founder of the college (see below).

[2] Cart. 21 Edw. III., n. 5.

[3] Pat. 2 Rich. II., p. 1, m. 19.

[4] Pat. 1 Hen. IV., p. 1, m. 21.

[5] Pat. 1 Hen. V., p. 1, m. 20.

[6] Pat. 8 Hen. VI., p. 1, m. 14.

[7] In Dugdale's Monasticon.

[8] This Priory had been given by Henry VI. to Eton College; by Edward IV. (above) it was given to God's House; by the same king in his thirteenth year to Eton College; after which it was restored to God's House (Tanner).

late Duke of York, our father of famous memory, and of Richard, late Earl of Cambridge, our grandfather, who lies buried within the same hospital.' Thus the Priory of Sherborne, with all its possessions of whatever kind, passed to God's House, in which hospital the benefit of the gift was intended to take effect; but as this foundation itself had long been made over to Queen's Hall or College, the lands together with the muniments of the Priory really became the property of the college. The advowsons of churches belonging to the Priory were those of West *alias* Monk's *alias* Prior's Sherborne, Bramley, Upton Grey, and Chineham. The church of Chineham has long disappeared, but the tradition of its locality remains. The patronage of the other churches continue with Queen's College.

Earl of Cambridge buried here.

Advowsons.

The property of the hospital within the town of Southampton in the thirteenth century consisted of houses, cellars, vaults, sheds and warehouses, and certain plots of ground. The following notices bear on localities. Among the early tenants[1] (1273), John de Shirley pays the two marks (see p. 320) for West Hall; John de Worth owes for the 'Bole-hous' (afterwards Bull or Bugle Hall, in the street of that name). The rector of St. Michael's pays the yearly rental of eleven shillings and tenpence for his rectory; Roger Halfknyt (see under 'West Hall') a rental of four shillings. William Basingrom, the younger, holds half the vault near St. Michael's Church. Henry de Lym pays a mark per annum for the Gympe-house, so called from one John Gympe, a former tenant. The warden of Magdalen—that is, of the lepers' hospital—pays a yearly rent of fourpence; Adam le Horder pays three shillings yearly for three acres in 'Leyham;' Robert Chopyn pays seven shillings and sixpence for an acre and a half in Le Garston (see p. 449). The relicts of John and William Lobery (see p. 147)—a little later we hear of Walter Lobery—pay each one penny yearly. Mention is made of the gaol in Fish Street, probably that known afterwards as St. Michael's prison (see p. 392).

Notices from the early Computus Rolls.

Under 1278 we hear of Simenelestret. William le Horder rents the plot where 'the windmill is built in Fulflod.'

Under 1297 expenses occur for an earthen wall between the court-yard and Nywyntone (Newtown, immediately to the east), and for an earthen wall on the east side of the bridge in Nywyntone near the street—the street in Nywyntone, it is called elsewhere—that is, no doubt, the modern Orchard Lane or Street, formerly called Newtown Lane.

Newtown

In 1299 eighteen boat-loads of stone were bought at a cost of

[1] See Mr. Riley's Examination of the God's House Computus Rolls, Appendix to Sixth Report of Historical MSS. Commission, pp. 551–569.

The chapel.

twenty-eight shillings and sixpence for making a new quay opposite the chapel near the sea; so that at this period there was no town wall immediately south of the hospital, and the chapel-side of the quadrangle was open to the water. Seven boat-loads of stone were also procured for making a quay towards the Master's Close in Nywyntone; the Close may have been the modern 'Bowling Green,' and the quay a rudimentary 'platform.'

The gate of Nywyntone, which occurs at this period, may have been the town gate, subsequently and to this day called God's House Gate, or it may have led directly from the house into the east suburb.

Under 1315 contributions are mentioned towards a new bridge beyond the street on the east side of the courtyard of God's House towards Nywyntone. Evidently this street to the east of the quadrangle was that now known as the Back of the Walls, and the bridge crossed into what was called afterwards variously God's House or Bowling Green.

Back of the Walls and Orchard Lane.

We meet with Brode-lane and Bule-strete in 1325, the family of Balvayr, and 'two leprous sisters of the Maudelyne.'

Under 1340 a tenement is described as 'near the Flood-gate' (see p. 97). Thomas atte Marche holds two-thirds, and Walter de Brakele one-third, of West Hall, which 'when whole belonged to Gervaise le Riche.' Thomas atte Marche again pays five shillings for a certain house at Westhuthe (West Quay) towards the castle, which formerly belonged to Hugo Sampson, situated between the Jew's House and that of John Twyg. About this time rents were in arrears, and were constantly forgiven on account of the late disastrous 'burning of the town' by the French in 1338. In the year from Michaelmas 1341 to Michaelmas 1342, the rental remaining the same, the arrears due to the hospital from the five parishes of Holy Rood, St. John, St. Michael, St. Lawrence, and All Saints within Bar were £155 against £127 two years before.

Burning of the town.

The destruction in the town, however, was by no means as great as has been represented. For instance, exclusively of vaults, cellars, and vacant places, the hospital possessed a hundred and eight houses, and of these only twenty-nine had been burnt, which were thus distributed:—Of seventeen houses in Holy Rood parish only one was destroyed; of eighteen in St. John's, four were burnt; of thirty-seven in St. Michael's, seventeen; of six in St. Lawrence's, four; of nine in All Saints within Bar, three were burnt; of sixteen in All Saints above Bar, none; of five in St. Mary's, none.

Under 1340 we have mention of a 'little lane called Rochel-lane' in French Street, perhaps from a family, 'De Rochelle,' formerly living in the town, and of other localities which have occurred before.

Interior history of the house.

Turning to the interior and domestic history of God's House, at the earliest period its members seem to have consisted of a custos or warden, two priests, two or three brothers, from three to nine sisters, three or more poor men and women, sometimes a clerk, various indoor and outdoor servants, such as a cook, laundress, dairymaid, brewer, ploughman, cowherd, shepherd, and swineherd.

The Warden.

The warden comes first under notice at the death of Robert de Knowell or Knoel, about Christmas 1285, when Queen Eleanor, the king's mother, who held the town in dower for life, took possession of the hospital by her bailiffs, and conferred the wardenship or chaplaincy upon Robert le Stock, or le Aumoner, so called from his office. It appears, however, that the Bishop of Winchester, John de Pontissara, had previously to this made good against the town in the King's Bench a claim to the right of advowson; and relying on this decision, and acting through the sheriff of the county, he now obtained the ejectment of Robert, appointing instead John le Flamang, January 3, 1285–86, and afterwards Roger de Multon, on July 11, 1286, the mandate for induction and for the obedience of the house to him being dated that day.[1] On the question being brought to trial (May 23, 1290) before Gilbert de Thornton and John de Metyngham, the king's justices, the Bishop, on the score of his recent lawsuits with the burgesses, and having still in contest with them a question of right to free toll for his men, objected to a Southampton jury; and finally, though he did not carry his point completely, obtained the removal of the well-known names of Robert le Mercer, Robert le Barber, and John de la Barre. In the issue it was decided that the patronage did not belong to the Bishop, against whom £20 damages were given, and Robert le Stock was reinstated.

The wardens were constantly non-resident, probably because the hospital was generally held with other and more important preferments. Warden Henry de Bluntesdon procured and furnished, partly at the expense of the hospital, a residence at Blunsden, near Highworth, which may have suited him better as Archdeacon of Dorset. Other wardens lived on the estate at Gussage, at Finchamstede, near Wokingham, at Salisbury, Winchester, and Odiham.

The Priests.

From the time of Edward IV. (see p. 454) the establishment consisted of at least three priests; in the earlier period there were two, one acting as steward, the other as chaplain.

The Brothers.

The brothers of the house, three or four in number, no doubt lay, served as under-stewards in various manors. They seem to have received no fixed allowance, living on the produce of the farms; but

[1] Reg. Pontiss., ff. 4, 5.

payments were frequently made to them in the shape of materials for clothing, shoes, hose, &c.

The Sisters.

The sisters, who varied in number, probably had their meals in common in their own hall, and received each of them a farthing per day as an allowance for clothing. Exceptional allowances also occur: thus under 1297, 'the pittance of Sister Joan, who does not eat flesh throughout the year, was 7s. 7¼d.,' that is, a farthing a day. Again, Sister Elena, who 'ate nothing that had suffered death' from the end of February to the 14th April, received in lieu sixteenpence or a farthing a day. They sometimes shared with the brethren in so many ells of russet.

The poor inmates.

The poor inmates or paupers, besides their food, had an allowance of one farthing each for every two days; but on making themselves useful and saving the house expense, their doles were increased. Thus one of them in 1306 took the place of gatekeeper for the year, and lent a hand at reaping in the autumn, for which he received two pairs of shoes at twelvepence. At this period two pairs of shoes bought for Emma, a kinswoman of the master, cost tenpence.

Reception into Fraternity.

Secular persons were received into the Fraternity[1] after an orderly form which is set forth in the register, but cannot be produced here. Directions are also given as to the recitation of the Lord's Prayer and angelic salutation by every brother and sister so many times at the various hours—in all, a hundred and eighty times a day.

The rule of the house, enforced by an oath or declaration, bound the brethren and sisters to be obedient to the Prior or his deputy, to assist in counsel if called upon, to be helpful in the burdens of the house, to keep its secrets and generally study its welfare.

Buildings.

A few slender notices of the buildings appear in the earliest account rolls.[2] From the computus of 1299, we gather that the sisters dwelt in a separate house from the brothers, probably much as in the present arrangement. Under the same year we have mention of a 'new door for the new chapel, towards the west.' The present chapel seems a century older than this date—it may have been 'renewed.' The chapel faced the water (see above), and had a quay opposite. The curtilage belonging to the master, mentioned in the same year as stretching to the premises of the Friars Minor, and divided from them by an earthen wall, was probably identical with the garden formerly attached to the house on the west side of the quadrangle, assigned till comparatively lately for the residence of the steward.[3] On this west side of the quad-

[1] Transcripts from Register of St. Julian, *penes* Rev. Sumner Wilson.

[2] Mr. Riley's Appendix, as above.

[3] Dr. Wilson (Holy Rood), the last steward, occupied this house during the early part of his incumbency, as did Dr. Hill, the preceding steward. There was a good garden.

rangle the master's lodgings may have been arranged, the halls on the west and north. Under 1321 we read of a chamber between the hall and the sea. There is also mention of the study near the master's chamber; and under 1324 are charges for claying the floors of the master's and chaplain's chambers.

The present buildings.

The chapel and gate tower adjoining are on the south side of the quadrangle, and are substantially of the date of the hospital, namely, about 1195, though their ancient character has suffered much under modern restorations: the gateway had been remodelled in the Late Perpendicular period.

The interior measurement of the chapel is about 57 by 19 feet; it is lighted by plain Norman windows, the chancel arch being now the only remarkable feature in the building. A brass belonging probably to one of the former priests is still preserved in the chapel. The other memorials relate almost exclusively to its French occupation.[1] A tablet on the south side commemorates the interment of the conspirators against King Henry V. It was erected by John, Earl Delawarr, who died in 1766, and is as follows:—'Richard, Earl of Cambridge, Lord Scrope of Masham, Sir Tho. Grey of Northumberland, conspired to murder King Henry V. in this town, as he was preparing to sail with his army against Charles VI. of France; for which conspiracy they were executed, and buried near this place, in the year MCCCCXV.'

In the rounded south-west corner of the chapel, outside the gate tower, was a quatrefoil insertion, breast-high, which has now disappeared, serving the purpose of a view of the interior without entering the building. Remains of a considerable building, of the date of the foundation, the nature of which is not determined, exist in the north wall of the quadrangle.

The old domestic buildings of the hospital, which seem to have been coeval with the foundation of the house, were removed in 1861, to the grief of archæologists, and the present somewhat feeble though more commodious buildings erected in two blocks; that on the east side of the quadrangle being assigned to the brothers of the hospital, that on the north to the sisters. Each block, designed for four inmates, has a frontage of about 50 feet, with a depth of 25 feet, and contains four small houses or sets of rooms in flats, two being on

[1] Here were buried Mary, daughter of Nic. Pescod, wife of Adam de Cardonnel, of Caen, customer and collector of the port, who died July 27, 1708; also the above Adam de Cardonnel, who died January 20, 1710, aged ninety years; Colonel Lewis de Belleau, died February 17, 1739; Peter de Vaux, Esq., died December 3, 1742; Rev. Benj. Franc. Housselmayne du Boulay, late minister of French Church in Threadneedle Street, died June 17, 1765, aged forty; Peter Mercyer, gent., died June 20, 1630, aged eighty-two; also members of the Carteret family, daughters of M. Cougot, and others.

the ground floor and two above; each house having a separate entrance. They are built of red brick with stone dressings.

Account from 'Valor Ecclesiasticus.'

The return in the 'Valor Ecclesiasticus' of 1536 will afford some further notices of the hospital.

First, the manor of Gusyche (Gussage), Dorsetshire, worth £20, 13s. 4d. per annum. From this was to be deducted quit-rent to Sir Edward Willoughby, 3s. 4d.; also payment to Geoffrey Rudde, receiver of the hospital on the manor, 13s. 4d.; and to John Mylle, seneschal, 20s.—leaving a clear £18, 16s. 8d.

From the manor of Cosseham, Isle of Wight, £5, 6s. 8d.

Manor of Warror, Isle of Wight, £5, 2s.

County of Southampton: two tenements at Ewksbury (Exbury) and Hamley, 11s. 8d.

Manor of Hekeley (Hickley), £3, 16s. 10d.; from which was to be deducted a quit-rent of 10s. belonging to Netley Abbey.

A garden in Winchester, 1s. 4d.

The Priory of Monks Sherborne—appropriated to the hospital—£58, 7s. 4½d.; from this was to be deducted, as arranged by the statutes governing appropriations, payment for one priest to pray for the founders and benefactors of the Priory, £6; to the poor of the said Priory by the same authority of Parliament, £1, 3s. 4d.; to the king for rent in chief, 17s. 9½d.; to the vicar at the Priory, by the above authority of Parliament, for the pension of old assigned, £1, 14s.; to the Archdeacon of Southampton for procurations, £1, 11s.; to Richard Sands, seneschal at the Priory, £1, 6s. 8d.; to Christopher Wrangwyche, receiver, £1, 6s. 8d.; to John Askard, bailiff, £1; to maintenance and sustentation of the priory, church, and furniture, on average, £3, 12s. 4d.

Tenements and rents in and near Southampton and suburbs, £67, 8s.; to be deducted, quit-rents to the mayor and bailiffs of Southampton, 6s. 8d.; quit-rent to Walter Bacar, 1s.; annual pension to the Church of St. Cross, 3s. 4d.; to Thomas Asheley, receiver at Southampton for the hospital, £1, 6s. 8d.; to Geoffrey Rudde, seneschal, £1, 6s. 8d.

The sum total of the possession of the hospital, in gross, was thus £161, 7s. 2d. per annum.

On account of the hospital itself further deductions were to be allowed.

Thus to the three priests appointed by order of the founder and of King Edward IV. to pray for the souls of the founder, Edward IV., Richard, Duke of York, Richard, Earl of Cambridge, who was buried there, and for the souls of other benefactors of the hospital, £18. The three priests were Sir Geoffrey Rudde, Sir Thomas Asheley—who also had other offices (see above),—and Sir William Gy. Also to ten poor brothers and sisters (named) of the said hospital, by order of the founder and of Edward IV., for food, clothing, and other necessaries, £24; also by order of the founder, to the support and maintenance of seven beds for hospital accommodation of poor and infirm mendicants, for their nursing and burial, £20; also by order of the founder, to the keeping hospitality to poor strangers coming daily by land or sea, and in daily distribution to mendicants and poor inhabitants of the town and neighbourhood, £28. **Doles.**

Beyond these deductions the Commissioners asked that the following allowances might be made:—

To commons for the butler, cook, and under-cook at the hospital, £6; to stipend of butler, £1, 6s. 8d.; same of cook, £1, 6s. 8d.; under-cook, 13s. 4d.; barber, 8s.; washerwoman, 16s. For chapel expenses: wax, wine, breads for celebration, and other necessaries, £1, 13s. 4d.; to utensils in hall, pantry, and kitchen, on average, £1, 6s. 8d.; to necessaries and daily repairs within the town of Southampton, £18; to void houses, on average, £6; to fuel, wood, and coal in hall and kitchen, on average, £2, 13s. 4d.; to travelling expenses on business of the hospital, on average, £3, 13s. 4d.

**God's House never suppressed.**

This hospital, owing to its custody being vested in Queen's College, was not suppressed at the dissolution of colleges, chantries, &c., in 1 Edward VI., 1547, the colleges of the universities and certain other foundations being exempted from the operation of that Act, the only return concerning God's House made by the Commissioners of that time being to the effect[1] that there were therein three stipendiary priests, whose office was to celebrate and minister to the poor of the hospital, and that they received each of them a salary of 53s. 4d. from Queen's College, Oxford, besides meat, drink, lodging, barber, and laundry; the salaries and allowances thus paid by the college amounting to £20 per annum. It seems[2] that a proposal was made, nevertheless, to lay hands on this £20 per annum; but on petition of the College it was ordered November 27, 1549 (3 Edw. VI.), that the Provost and Fellows should 'not be molested, vexed, or troubled by the king's ministers for the said yearly sum of £20.' Matters went on as heretofore. In the Computus of 1568–69[3] the senior priest was seneschal; the house still paid a pension of 3s. 4d. to the vicar of St. Cross, and fourpence to the sacristan, and was still celebrating the exequies of Edward IV., and Richard, Earl of Cambridge, of Master Pereson, and the founders gene-

1 Chantry Certificates, Roll 52, No. 61.

2 Information of the Provost of Queen's, from document.

3 *Penes* Rev. J. L. Carrick.

rally, each at a cost of four shillings. The pauper inmates were, brothers and sisters, eight in number all told, and their cost was £41, 12s.

Present establishment.

The present establishment within the hospital consists of four poor brethren and four poor sisters, who each receive an allowance weekly from Queen's College; they also participate in some of the town charities (see p. 306). There is no provision for a larger number of inmates. The chaplain of the hospital is Rev. J. Aston Whitlock, vicar of Holy Rood, appointed by the College in 1873.

In Dr. Speed's short notice of this house, not otherwise produced, occurs the following extraordinary statement, which appears to be utterly without foundation, but may yet be capable of some explanation:—

"The hospital was in the hands of the crown in Queen Elizabeth's "time . . . but in that Queen's reign Francis Mylles, Esq. [described "in a family Bible as of Bittern and God's House], who had been edu- "cated at Queen's College, and afterwards became secretary to Sir "Francis Walsingham, by his interest got it, with all its appurtenances, "restored to the College by a new grant from that Queen."

*Provosts, Priors, or Wardens.*[1]

Roger.[2]

William was Prior in 1195, 6 Rich. I.

Fulient (sic.), 1200, 2 John.

Vincent.[3]

Warin, a Canon of St. Denys, appointed[4] by Bp. Peter de Rupibus (1206–38).

John Chilbaton,[5] chaplain to Bishop, appointed by Bishop William de Ralegh[4] (1244–50).

Nicholas Rokeland, appointed by Bishop William de Ralegh.[4]

William Cherubyne, or William of York, appointed by Bishop John de Exon 1262–68,[4] 1262, 47 Hen. III.

Robert Knowell or Cnobel, appointed by Bishop John de Exon;[4] he was custos before 1267 (Addit., 15,314 f. 78); died Dec. 1285, 14 Edw. I.

Robert Stokes, appointed by Queen Eleanor, December 1285.

John le Flemang, appointed by Bishop John de Pontissara, January 3, 1285–86.[6]

Roger de Multon, appointed by Bishop John de Pontissara, July 11, 1286.[6]

Robert Stokes or le Stock or le Aumoner, reinstated by process of law, and confirmed by king, May 1290.

Henry de Bluntesdon, 1297, 25 Edw. I. (died 1316).

Gilbert Wigton, installed 1318, 12 Edw. II.

Robert Eglesfield,[7] 1340, 14 Edw. III.

John de Hotham, about 1343, 17 Edw. III.

---

1 The names are from transcript from St. Julian's Register, except where otherwise specified.

2 See above, p. 450.

3 Vincent occurs as custos in a deed of this period (Appendix to Report, p. 254).

4 Reg. Pontiss., f. 192.

5 This and the following two names are placed according to the dates given in the Register.

6 Reg. Pontiss., ff. 4, 5.

7 The founder of Queen's College. All the following Priors or Wardens were Provosts of Queen's Hall or College.

Henry de Whitfelde, about 1361, 35 Edw. III.
Thomas de Carlile, 1378, 1 Rich. II.
Roger Quelpdale, about 1420, 7 Hen. V.
Walter Belle.[1]
Rowland Bires, about 1427, 5 Hen. VI.
Thomas Eglesfield, occurs in 1440, 18 Hen. VI.
William Spencer, 1442, 20 Hen. VI.
John Pereson, 1459, 37 Hen. VI.
Henry Boost, 1483, 22 Edw. IV.
Thomas Langton, 1489, 4 Hen. VII.
Christopher Bainbrigge, 1495, 10 Hen. VII.
Edward Rigge, 1508, 23 Hen. VII.
John Pantree, resigned in 1534, 25 Hen. VIII.
William Denison, 1534, 25 Hen. VIII.
Hugh Hodgson, 1558, 4 and 5 Phil. and Mary.
Thomas Francis, 1561, 3 Eliz.
Lancelot Shawe, 1563, 5 Eliz.
Alan Scott, 1565, 7 Eliz.
Bartholomew Bousfield, 1575, 17 Eliz.
Henry Robinson,[2] 1581, 23 Eliz.
Henry Airay, 1598, 40 Eliz.
Barnaby Potter, 1616, 14 Jas. I.
Christopher Potter, 1626, 2 Chas. I.
Gerard Langbaine, 1645, 20 Chas. I.
Thomas Barlow, 1657, 9 Chas. II.
Timothy Halton, 1677, 29 Chas. II.
William Lancaster, 1704, 2 Anne.
John Gibson, 1717, 3 Geo. I.
Joseph Smith, 1730, 4 Geo. II.
Joseph Browne, 1756, 29 Geo. II.
Thomas Fothergill, 1767, 7 Geo. III.
Septimus Collinson, 1796, 36 Geo. III.
John Fox, 1827, 8 Geo. IV.
William Thomson (present Archbishop of York), 1855, 18 Vict.
William Jackson, 1862, 25 Vict.
John Richard Magrath, D.D., 1878, 42 Vict.

[1] So the transcript; this name does not occur among lists of the Provosts of Queen's.

[2] The last name in the Register.

# CHAPTER IX.

## *EVENTS TILL THE PRESENT TIMES.*

THIS last chapter will contain notices of the chief locally remarkable events not otherwise recorded in this work.

The period before the Domesday record has been sufficiently dealt with. Not to dwell on the visits of Robert of Normandy or of Henry I., under whom the men of Hampton 'had their guild' (p. 152), or the submission of Baldwin de Redvers to King Stephen at this place, or the wrath of Earl Robert of Gloucester against the burgesses, we pass to the close of the reign of Stephen (1153), when, all parties being tired of strife, the claims to the throne were settled at Winchester, and it was provided under the articles which secured the crown to Stephen that the Bishop of Winchester should give security for delivering up the fort of Southampton and the castle of Winchester to Prince Henry in the event of the king's death, like pledges being required of the keepers of the other royal fortresses—the Tower of London, the moats of Windsor and Oxford, the fortress of Lincoln.

Henry I.

Stephen.

Henry II.

King Henry II., who before his accession had been no stranger to our port, was here in 1157. The queen and her children had landed from Normandy about February, and the king from Barfleur two months later (see p. 30). Under 1162 we have accounts of the young Prince Henry being here, payments occurring for his keep, and for his yacht (esnecca); and in January 1163 the king himself landed from Barfleur, being met by his Chancellor, Archbishop Beket, with the Prince. Several other traces exist of the king's presence at Southampton on his passage to and from Normandy. One memorable occasion was on July 8, 1174, when he again landed from Barfleur, at a crisis for his kingdom. He had with him Queen Eleanor as his prisoner, and others, all of whom he consigned on landing to safe keeping; then he set forth to perform his vow in the city famous already for the reputed miracles at Becket's shrine.

Such was the earliest notable pilgrimage from our town to Canterbury, the first traversing of a way henceforth much to be frequented by devotees from Normandy, Anjou, and Brittany. The road led either through Winchester, or over the Itchen at Stoneham, through Bishops Waltham and Alton to Farnham, thence along the ridge eastward through Guilford. A trace of their starting-point in our town may perhaps be detected in the name 'Pilgrims' Pit,' near Biddlesgate, which was close to the ancient quay at which they would land (p. 86). No further mention need be made of royal visits in this reign; the last was apparently in April 1186.

Richard I.

King Richard I. was here previously to his coronation, preparations for that event causing much stir at Southampton, the port being alive with the transit of great folk (see above, p. 31).

In the time of this king, Bishop Godfrey de Lucy (1189–1204) commenced, and finished at the beginning of the following reign, his great work of restoring the navigation of the Itchen from the port of Southampton to Winchester and Alresford, obtaining from King John, for himself and his successors, the royalty of the river from the lake of Alresford, which he had constructed, down to the sea, as also a charter for collecting duties on the navigation.

John.

The worst of all our monarchs was certainly a frequent visitor at Southampton. For the worth of the traditions respecting him, see page 91. In several years of this reign naval preparations were made here under the direction of William de Wrotham, Archdeacon of Taunton.

The Edwards.

No special notice seems required of the reign of Henry III. In those of the Edwards the town took its full and prominent share in the warlike levies of the period. One year must be dwelt on—the saddest, as it has always been accounted, in Southampton annals. War had been declared with France, and King Edward had sailed on July 16, 1338. Early on Sunday morning, October 4, a numerous fleet of galleys, crowded with Normans, Picards, Genoese, and Spaniards, landed its horde at the south-western quarter of the town while the inhabitants were at mass. The burgesses fled before them; the town was at their mercy. They plundered and burnt at pleasure, and hung some of the townsfolk in their own houses; but on the following morning a rally took place, and the 'aliens' were driven to their ships. According to Stowe and others, a son of the king of Sicily was killed among the marauders, felled by a countryman with his club, who mistook the cry of rançon for Françon, and belaboured him to death with these words, 'Yea, I know thou art a Françon, and therefore thou shalt die.'

Elsewhere we have given some details of this singular destruction (see pp. 79, 456), to which the following may be added. Brother Philip de Thame, Prior of the Hospitallers in England, in his account[1] of the estates of his order for 1338, shows that property in Southampton and Portsmouth which had produced £20, 3s. 4d., now, since the burning of

1 Printed for Camd. Soc. in 1857.

those towns —for Portsmouth had also suffered about or just before this time—only yielded £14, 10s. In other directions, the Prior of Carisbrook could not get the rent, £9, 5s., for the Abbey of Lire, charged of old on the fee-farm,[1] nor could Queen Isabella get her £201, 3s. 2d. from the same source, or other dues owing from the town; in consequence of which all the profits of the town were made over to her, dating from its capture by the enemy.[2] There was also a difficulty as to the payment of ninths and fifteenths granted by Parliament in 1340 for the next two years for the good keeping of the realm.

Still the disaster is not to be exaggerated. Its results we have seen elsewhere in the busy erection of walls and improvement of the town, but it was a heavy blow to English prestige, sadly mourned over in the official documents of the time. The conduct of the burgesses had brought disgrace not only on the town, but on the whole king's realm, and the town had accordingly been taken from them. Minot, the contemporary rhymer, thus minimises the damage done, and does credit to native bravery:—

'At Hamton, als I understand,
Come the gaylayes unto land,
And ful fast thai slogh and brend,
But noght so makill als sum men wend.
For or thai wened war thai mett
With men that sone thare laykes lett.
Sum was knokked on the hevyd,
That the body thare bilevid;
Sum lay stareand on the sternes;
And sum lay knoked out thaire hernes:
Than with tham was non other gle,
Bot ful fain war thai that might fle.
The galay men, the suth to say,
Most nedes turn another way;
Thai soght the stremis fer and wide
In Flandres and in Seland syde.'

—*Polit. Poems*, i. 64, *Rolls Series.*

In 1340 one squadron of the fleet was victualled here under the Seigneur John de Wattenhull,[3] and six years later the king was at Southampton along with the Black Prince, then in his seventeenth year, about to embark at the head of the fleet.[4] He sailed on July 14, and Crecy was fought on August 26.

In 1349 the first of the three[5] terrible pestilences of the fourteenth century entered our port. The date assigned for its prevalence in the kingdom is from May 31 to September 29; it is supposed that nearly

[1] Rot. Parl. ii. 188.
[2] Rot. Orig. Abbrev., 14 Ed. III. (1340).
[3] Rot. Parl. ii. 116.
[4] Froissart, c. 120.
[5] The second was from August 1361 to May 3, 1362; the third from July 2 to September 29, 1369.

half the population were carried away. The business of the kingdom was stopped, lands were thrown out of cultivation, the price of labour became enormous. Nor were the flocks and herds spared. The neighbourhood of Southampton and Winchester suffered deeply in the general calamity, but no special details appear to have survived

The King and Prince were again at Southampton in 1372, bent on the relief of Thours.

Richard II.

The first year of Richard II. is memorable in Southampton's story. A few days after the death of Edward, which occurred on June 21, Rye had been burnt by the French. Upon this the Earls of Cambridge and Buckingham had been ordered to Dover, and the Earl of Salisbury and Sir John Montagu to the country near Southampton. After their exploit at Rye, the enemy had plundered the Isle of Wight and partially destroyed Poole, thence coasting towards Southampton, followed along the shore by the Earl of Salisbury, who frustrated their attempts at landing. The fleet now stood up the Southampton Water, menacing the town itself, but the brave governor was well prepared to receive them (see p. 82), 'otherwise the town would have been taken.'[1]

In August 1378 (2 Rich. II.), John of Gaunt, Duke of Lancaster, at the head of an army raised for service in Brittany, sailed from Southampton to St. Malo; but having consumed valuable weeks in the fruitless siege of that town, he returned back, to the great displeasure of the English people, landing at Southampton to learn that Sir John Arundel, the governor, whose guard was at this time two hundred men-at-arms and four hundred archers, had gone to reinforce the garrison at Cherbourg. After revictualling the fortress, and leaving behind an English garrison, Sir John returned to Southampton after remaining fifteen days at Cherbourg.[2]

The following year (1379) witnessed the arrival at our port of knights from Brittany recalling the Duke, then resident in England, to his dominions, preparations for his departure being made at Southampton. A few months later Southampton lost its brave governor in the expedition designed to assist the Duke, a force having been placed under his command for that purpose. On leaving port the weather was fair, but in the evening the wind shifted, and the ships were driven towards the Cornish coast. The next day the storm increased, and three of the vessels were sunk, in one of which perished the commander-in-chief with eighty men-at-arms. The remnant of the squadron, after beating about some time, made Southampton again with sad tidings for the king and council. This was in December 1379.[3]

[1] Froissart, c. 328.

[2] Ibid., ii. c. 17 and 21.

[3] Ibid., ii. c. 43.

It is not to be supposed that the constant presence of armaments, the coming and going of great nobles, their knights and retainers, were without drawbacks on the well-being of the town and neighbourhood, especially in a coarse and cruel time; for the ages of chivalry were by no means those of civilisation and refinement. In the impeachment of John, Lord Neville, in 1376 (50 Ed. III.), the unrestrained conduct of his troops at Hampton, their villany, rapacity,[1] and horrible licentiousness, were alleged against him as seriously as the charges of having lost many fortresses in Brittany.

Henry IV. The condition of life at this period must have been sufficiently exciting, when not only were armed forces constantly passing through the port, but the movements of the enemy were sometimes near enough to be unpleasant. In 1404 the French under the Count Waleran de St. Pol had landed some 1500 men in the Isle of Wight, merely, however, to burn a few miserable villages and fly to their ships.[2] All the south-western coast had been under the apprehension of petty invasions. Plymouth and a few other places had actually suffered; Southampton had again been menaced.

Henry V. The following reign was perhaps that of greatest brilliancy in the annals of Southampton. Henry V., prosecuting his claim to the crown of France, made this port one of his chief places of rendezvous. In April 1415 (3 Hen. V.), orders were issued for arresting all vessels of twenty tons and upwards in the various seaports, as well as such as should arrive before May 1, and assembling them at the ports of Southampton, London, and Winchelsea, by the 8th of May at the latest; and on the 27th the sheriff of the county was desired to cause bread and ale to be provided in Southampton, Winchester, and the places adjacent, by the time the king should arrive.

1415. On June 18 the king left Westminster for Southampton. On the 26th, and for some followings days, he was at Winchester, where on the 30th he gave audience to the French ambassadors. On the 12th of July he was at Southampton—a letter from John Cheney, Esq., to Sir John Pelham, Knight, asking a loan of money, being dated from Southampton on that day, and referring to the king and nobles as being there and well. The king remained in the town or in the neighbourhood till his embarkation on August 10. Writs were tested by the king at this town on July 20, on the 24th, when he dated his will; on the 27th and 28th, on this latter day he dated his letter to the King of France, 'our cousin and adversary,' 'en nostre chastel de

[1] See also petition to Parliament (1379) from Hants and maritime ports obtaining the concession that captains were to indemnify for losses, provided the complaints were made at once. Rot. Parl. ii. 329, iii. 80. See also similar complaints in 1442.

[2] Monstrelet, i. xix.; Wavrin, ii. 93.

Hantonne au rivage de la mer.'[1] On August 1 he dates from Westminster; from Southampton again on August the 2d, the 5th, 6th, and 7th. Later in the same day he was at Porchester; from Waltham he dated on the 10th; from Portsmouth on the 11th, the day the expedition sailed; and another document was tested at Southampton on the 14th,[2] an unexplained error.

The king while at Southampton was engaged in the last preparations. Ships had been built here to his order (see p. 263), of a larger construction than had been attempted hitherto. In the 'Libel of English Policy,' Henry's energy is thus sung :—

'And yf I shulde conclude al by the kynge,
Henry the fifte, what was hys purposynge,
When at Hampton he made the grete Dromons,
Which passed other grete shippes of alle the comons,
The Trinité, the Grace Dieu, the Holy Goste,
And other moo which as now be loste,
What hope ye was the kynges grette entente
Of tho shippes, and what a mynde he mente ?'

And farther on :—

'And if he had to this time lyved here,
He had bene prince named wythoutene pere.
His grete shippes shulde have bene put in preffe
Unto the ende that he mente of in cheffe.
Ffor doute it nat, but that he wolde have be
Lorde and master about the rounde see.'[3]

Immediately after the king's arrival at Southampton the conspiracy against his crown and person by Richard of York, Earl of Cambridge, Henry, Lord Scrope of Masham, and Sir Thomas Grey of Heton, was brought to light, possibly through information of the Earl of March, who, according to the Earl of Cambridge's confession, had been himself implicated in the plot. A jury was summoned at Southampton on August 2, and verdict was given against the three conspirators. The two peers claimed to be tried by their peers; but sentence was executed the same day upon Sir Thomas Grey, who was led on foot from the Watergate to the North Gate, outside which he was beheaded. Three days later, on August 5, a court or parliament of peers, presided over by the Duke of Clarence at Southampton, affirmed the judgment previously given against the two peers. The Earl, on account of his royal blood, was permitted to walk through the town; but Lord Scrope was drawn on a hurdle to the place of execution, outside the North Gate.[4] The action of this 'pretended session' was of course annulled in the

[1] Wavrin, ii. 174, 175.
[2] Nicholas's Battle of Agincourt, p. 19.
[3] Political Poems, ii. 199.
[4] Rot. Parl. iv. 64, &c.

first year of Edward IV.[1] The heads of Lord Scrope and Sir Thomas Grey were ordered to be fixed up at York and Newcastle, and the body of the Earl[2] was buried within the chapel of God's House.

The embarkation of the troops under the king occupied some days. During this time a story is told of his rejecting at Southampton the services of a gentleman named Olandyne, who had brought with him twenty men-at-arms, on account of his having been once a monk of the Charterhouse who had broken his profession. Rejected thus on account of his 'life and conversation,' Olandyne went over to the enemy, and was slain at Agincourt.

In the following year (1416) a French fleet with Genoese auxiliaries menaced Henry's ships in the Southampton Water and the Solent. In June the king was himself in the town, orders being issued to the sheriff of the county to provide in the usual way for the defence of the coast, and the Duke of Bedford, by commission dated at Southampton, July 22, was put in command of the English ships. The Channel was now cleared, a decisive naval battle being fought not far from Southampton, which led to the relief of Harfleur.

The king was again in Southampton towards the end of April 1417, in preparation for another invasion of France. Ships had been built, and on July 12 he renamed three carracks which had been taken from the French by the Earl of Huntingdon.

When all was in readiness, the king went on board a royally-decked carrack, called the 'King's Chamber,' the sail of which was of purple silk, beautifully embroidered with the arms of England and France: a consort was in attendance of like apparel, surnamed the 'King's Hall.' Anchor was weighed, and the harbour of Southampton left amid the inspiring music of trumpets and clarions, and with minstrel song.

Reinforcements and stores for the army now passed through our port; among the latter, books, vestments, and ornaments for the king's chapel; prisoners also were sent over in batches.

In April 1422 the queen herself embarked from the town, under the escort of the Duke of Bedford, with an army of relief of 20,000 men.

Henry VI. The short but glorious reign of Henry V. reflected its splendour on the town; his son gave it the benefit of incorporation in the completest form (p. 155).

The infant king was at Southampton the third year of his reign (1425), no doubt under the guardianship of the Earl of Warwick, a

[1] Rot. Parl. v. 484.

[2] I am not aware that it is anywhere stated in ancient sources that the bodies of the others were buried there.

royal grant being dated from the place on July 27 that year.[1] A few years later (July 1429), Cardinal Beaufort, with his 4000 men, embarked from our port to give help to the Regent in France. Later again, from a royal letter to the Chancellor of France and the English council at Rouen dated January 28, 1435–36, we gather that the troops were massed at Southampton, and that a fleet in its capacious harbour was awaiting better weather outside to carry relief across the Channel.[2]

In the year which was eventful for the incorporation of Southampton, namely, in 1445, the town gave its welcome to Margaret of Anjou, the bride of Henry VI., soon after her arrival in this country. Having rested (April 9) for the night at the Maison Dieu, Portsmouth, she was conveyed the following day to Southampton in great state by water, and lodged at the Hospital of God's House. While here some troublesome cutaneous malady developed itself, and she does not appear to have met the king till four days later, namely, on Wednesday, April 14, when with her whole suite she was admitted to his presence in Southampton. Eight days after this the royal marriage took place at Titchfield (April 22) by the Bishop of Salisbury, the queen being specially fitted out for the occasion by a London dressmaker summoned to Southampton. On the 30th of the month following, her coronation was celebrated at Westminster. 1445.

During the remainder of this reign the succours demanded by the wars affected the town in various ways; it had to find its contingents of archers and to relinquish its ships.

About this period our town became the resort of wealthy Italian merchants, driven from the metropolis by the jealousy of the citizens, excited anew by one of those passing 'frays' which so constantly enlivened old town-life. It appears that in May 1456 an outbreak occurring in Cheapside, the quarter of the mercers, grew to such dimensions that the Italian merchants left London in a body and sought refuge in Southampton and Winchester, making a byelaw among themselves against any future trade with London, an ordinance ratified by the Venetian senate. It is to be presumed that Southampton was found the more convenient place for residence and trade, since, to the discredit of the foreigners, it is alleged that they took 'grete old mancyons' in Winchester, and put the landlords to heavy expense in repairs, but never went there after all.[3]

During the Yorkist and Lancastrian struggles Southampton was inevitably in a state of excitement. About the middle of 1460 the Earl

1 Rot. Parl. v. 294.
2 Wars of the English, Rolls Series, i. 424.
3 Gairdner's 'Three Fifteenth-Century Chronicles' (Camd. Soc.), Introd. viii.; Gregory's Chron., p. 199; Falyan., p. 459, &c.

of Wiltshire (James Boteler), Treasurer of England, after inflicting terrible severities on the Yorkist town of Newbury, threw himself into Southampton, ostensibly to intercept the Earl of Warwick, but in reality to make good his retreat from the realm. There were at that time five carracks of Genoa in the port; these he seized and filled with his soldiers, victualling them, as if for the royal service, at the king's prices, without payment; he secured also his own treasure, then put to sea, and carefully avoiding the Earls of Warwick and Salisbury, arrived in the Netherlands, and sent his soldiers back.

Edward IV.

Edward IV. visited Southampton in the autumn of 1461, the first year of his reign, riding along the coast from Sandwich. On this occasion the new charter was negotiated, the king receiving a pipe of wine worth £4 as a present from the town.[1]

A few years later (April 1470) the king was again at Southampton after the defeat, under the Lord Scales, of the Duke of Clarence and the Earl of Warwick, who had attempted to cut out from Southampton a large ship called 'Le Trinité,' which had belonged to the latter. The king had committed the unfortunate Lancastrian gentlemen and yeomen taken prisoners, twenty in number, to the tender mercies of Tiptoft, Earl of Worcester, whose manners had not been softened by his scholarship; by him they were adjudged to be drawn, hanged, and beheaded, and their remains treated in a barbarous fashion, to the disgust of the town's folk, before whose eyes this exhibition of savagery was exposed some three weeks.[2] After the above skirmish the Lord Scales and other notables seem to have been feasted and to have received presents in the town; the mayor of Winchester 'and his fellowship' had also come to aid in a possible emergency.

During the king's sojourn at Southampton he visited Chichester on horseback: 'Item, payde to Watkyn Latham, towne clerke of this townne, the xxij[d] day of May, when he rode w[t] the kyng to Chichester to have a wrytyng of the money þ[t] the kyng had granted to the towne.'

Scenes of festivity were mingled ever with those of bloodshed and war, and the accounts of this time abound in such notices. They also contain (see p. 109) payments for the making of bulwarks and the repairs of ordnance. They have also the following notice of soldiers sent, presumably from the Southampton garrison, on special service: 'Item, payde to the sowdyers that where sent to the kyng into the northe countrey by the town; when they where come home agen they asked alowaunse, and the maire by the assent and avysement of his bretheryn in the churche of Holy Rodes alowed them xxvj[s.] viij[d.]'

---

1 Steward's Book.
2 Stowe, 422; Steward's Book, 1469–70.

On April 14, 1471, the very day of the battle of Barnet, fatal to the great Earl of Warwick and to the cause of Henry VI., a record occurs of 'costes done upon my Lady of Warwick,' who had probably at the time landed at Southampton to learn the heavy tidings that awaited her;[1] she took sanctuary at Beaulieu.

It seems that about this time Edmund, Duke of Somerset, a strong adherent of the Lancastrian cause, or some of his people, were lodging at the Angel Inn. He was himself, however, at Barnet field, and was killed after the battle of Tewkesbury.

It was in Southampton (September 1471) that Thomas Nevill, bastard of Fauconbridge, formerly vice-admiral under the Earl of Warwick, then captain of a fleet of adventurers who had attempted the rescue of Henry VI. from the Tower, fell into the hands of Richard, Duke of Gloucester, and in consequence lost his life.

Two years later (1473) we find Earl Rivers sailing from Southampton on a pilgrimage to Compostella.

In connection, no doubt, with the alliance of Edward IV. with the Duke of Burgundy, formed in July 1474, the Bastard of Ravenstein was at Southampton on November 9th that year, a reward of ten shillings for guiding him to London being paid by command of the mayor.[2]

It seems that in June 1475 French ships cruising about the south coast and the Isle of Wight had ventured up the Southampton Water and seized a Portuguese vessel, but had been beaten off by the town lieutenant, Richard Gryme. On June 20 news was brought him of the ships being at Portland; then, as danger neared, he sent to 'Master Cooke, lieutenant of the Isle of Wight,' desiring him to signal the king's ships, and hurried off a messenger to the king himself at Sandwich. From Winchester he summoned the usual help; powder was served out to the Lord Audley's[3] gunners, that nobleman having been retained to serve the king in Normandy, and chancing apparently to be in the town.

The town guns were scarcely fit for use when the ships hove in sight, and sadly wanted putting in order when the fray was over. Two 'forlokkes' had to be provided for 'Thomas with the beard,' and serious repairs for the 'organs' and other guns, sufficiently curious. It appears that the ordnance was generally kept in store till actually wanted for use. Thus we have accounts here of the 'organs' being carried to the quay and to Adrian's House, other guns to the Long House, and of their being carried from the storehouse to the quay when

[1] Steward's Book, 1470–71. [2] Ibid., 1474–75.

[3] About this time he received a pension of £100 a year from the customs of Southampton.

the ship was taken. Among the hasty repairs in action was finding 'a cord for the safeguard of the stock of Thomas of the Beard, which brake in shooting at the taking of the Portingalle.' It is not altogether easy to understand this little unrecorded fray; but the act must have occurred close to the town, or the 'organs' would have bellowed and 'Thomas' shaken his fiery beard in vain.

The following entry also occurs as to the detention of ships:—'Item, paid to John Roper for his going with a boat to arrest the carracks by the commandment of Richard Gryme, lieutenant, xx^d.' Preparations for a visit from King Edward IV. were made towards the close of 1481: he seems to have been in the town in the following spring, and on March 1 a tun of sweet wine worth £7 was given him.[1]

The king died on April 9, 1483. In the following month occurs an entry about preparations at Beaulieu for the Marquis of Dorset, Thomas Grey, the son of Edward IV.'s queen by her previous marriage with Sir John Grey, who took sanctuary with the queen at Westminster in May 1483, and was apparently expected at Beaulieu.

Richard III.

At the beginning of a new reign favours were generally sought, and sometimes bought. Thus on December 3, 1483, the town-clerk, with two burgesses and their attendants, rode to London 'to the king's good grace, to show and defend the town privileges as granted by the king's noble progenitors,' doubtless with a view to confirmation of the charter. On their way the deputation were detained at Guilford by great frost and snow.

The next year the town was engaged in one of its lawsuits[2] (see p. 61), when 'there was ayenst us ij sergeauntez and iiij prentez w^t all the help of my lord tresorer and favoure of iij barons ayenst all the ordre of lernyng, right, and lawe.'

Henry VII.

In the first year of Henry VII. (August 22, 1485–86) the ambassadors of Francis, Duke of Brittany, who had arrived in England to ask assistance in the contest with France, were entertained by the Corporation, 'as the kyng commanded us by Richemond, kyng of heraldes, that we shold do them chere.'[3] This Richmond herald was Roger Machado, who had a house in the town, and was about this time—namely, September 21, 1485—made searcher in the port of Southampton and its dependants.[4]

In the following year (August 1486) the king, who had recently made a progress through the kingdom, visited Southampton, receiving a present of a tun of wine worth £6, a couple of oxen, twenty sheep,

1 For a circumstance connected with this visit, see under 'Guild Priest.'
2 Steward's Book, 1483 (rather 1484).
3 Lib. Remembranciarum H., sub anno.
4 Materials for Hist. of Hen. VII., Roll's Series, p. 28; Steward's Book.

and twenty couple of capons, making the 'reward unto his welcome' amount to £10. The town also presented an address: 'Paid for a quart of white wine in the Audit-house to Mr. Mayor and his brethren when ye made your petitions unto the king's grace 2$^{d.}$ Paid for red wax for sealing the indentures between the king and the town, 3$^{d.}$ Rushes for the court hall, 8$^{d.}$' It appears that the town borrowed money to entertain the king.

Prince Arthur, the future first husband of Catherine of Arragon, was born at Winchester early on September 20 (1486), announcement being made in Southampton the same day to the mayor and his brethren by John Burnard, yeoman of the queen's chamber; upon which, in obedience to the king's commands, all the curates, priests, and clerks of the town went in procession and sang *Te Deum*.

The king was again in the town receiving further presents early in 1487, when Master Jay 'sat upon a special sessions and gaol-delivery,' and also in September.[1] In August 1488, or the following year, he was cruising about in the neighbourhood, and on the 20th of that month wine was presented to him on board the 'Sovereign' by the mayor and his brethren.[2]

The following strange encounter is related between English and Venetian ships. On Christmas Day 1488, when the Doge was in church, a letter from London, dated November 3, addressed to the Florentine Giovanni Frescobaldo, the money-changer and usurer, stated that the Flanders galleys, which left Antwerp for Hampton on October 26, fell in with three English ships off St. Helens, and were commanded to strike sail. The galleys hove to and explained that they were friends; but finding mischief meant, the master blew his whistle and beat to quarters; and having killed eighteen English, made his way into the Southampton Water, pursued by the ships. The captain of the galleys then complained to the king, who sent the Bishop of Winchester with the episcopal message that he need not fear, as those who had been killed must bear their own loss, and that a pot of wine would settle the matter.[3]

A few years later (1495), the captain of the galleys and other Venetian subjects having been seized in Southampton harbour by French or Bretons, the Doge complaining to Henry VII., advised reprisals on French subjects.[4]

On December 21, 1488, the embassage to Spain and Portugal, commissioned by Henry VII., consisting of the herald Machado and others, sailed from Southampton in two Spanish ships on January 19. At

1 Lib. Remembranc. H., ff. 161 b, 167–174 b.
2 Steward's Book. 3 Cal. State Papers (Venetian). 4 Ibid.

the expiration of the embassy, Machado returned to his house at Southampton, July 25, 1489, remaining there till the 27th, after which he reported himself at Windsor. The next year, June 12, 1490, he was sent into Brittany, in company with Sir Robert Clifford. They left the king on the 14th. Richmond had to arrange for the passage; but when Sir Robert arrived, and saw the boat intended for them and their horses, his heart misgave him, and he refused to go—it was only sixteen tons burden. But by help of a king's missive to Portsmouth, a more suitable bark of sixty tons was provided—the 'Magdalene of Portsmouth,'—a good, fine vessel, and well furnished.[1]

In January 1492 the king's arsenal at Southampton caught fire, and, as was reported to the Doge at Venice, 'Ser' Filippo Morosini going in to see the fire, was suspected of having caused it, but was cleared.[2]

The town took its part in the preparations against Scotland in the winter of 1495.

In the following year the town books bear some traces of the progress of the Cornish insurgents through Salisbury and Winchester into Kent; soon after which Perkin Warbeck, deprived of the protection of Scotland, and probably encouraged by the tone of the Cornishmen, landed in Cornwall on September 7. His cause was thoroughly broken up and himself in flight for sanctuary at Beaulieu by September 20. On that day rewards were paid to John Elmes for riding to Master Dawtrey and to Master Controller to have tidings of Perkins, and for others 'to spy of Perkins' ill demeanour.'

I have not been able to verify the following statement of Dr. Speed; John Godfrey, moreover, went out of office in September, while Perkin surrendered in October:—"It appears in an old register book of the "Corporation that John Godfrey, then mayor, gave the Corporation "credit for £40 which he had received of the king's grace as a reward "for taking Perkin Warbeck."

In February 1497 the Princess Margaret of Austria arrived in the Southampton Water. The king wrote offering hospitality in the town, and proposing to visit her if her stay allowed it.[3] The honour of receiving the Princess Catherine had been also designed for Southampton, a programme of splendour by land and water being arranged for August or September 1501. However, the princess landed at Plymouth at the beginning of October.[4]

Henry VIII.

In the month of May 1512 (4 Hen. VIII.) the expedition under

[1] Journal of Roger Machado, Rolls Series, pp. 157, 200.
[2] Cal. State Papers (Venetian). [3] Ibid.
[4] Letters Illustrative of Reign of Hen. VIII., Rolls Series.

Thomas Grey, Marquis of Dorset, in aid of King Ferdinand of Spain against the French, brought many notable names to Southampton, an army of 10,000 men being mustered here, and the king himself being present to review his troops and fleet.

The king was expected, and appears to have visited the town in 1513, when work was carried out on the walls and ditches, and at one of the posterns by the king's command. In the same account we find a certain Baltyzar employed in making gunstones and on other work for the guns. Mention is also made of 'haylle schotte.'

It appears that a landing of the French on the Hampshire coast—probably after the death of Sir E. Howard and the discomfiture of the fleet (April 25)—had put the town on the alert, the mayor of Christchurch's servant having been rewarded for bringing the tidings.[1]

The account of the next year (Mich. 1513 to Mich. 1514) again mentions 'the coming of the king's grace.' Various cleansings went on in preparation, and all the guns of the town were charged. In the next year the king was in the town on August 10.

Something of a local tradition connects the visits of the king with the interesting timber house of the Tudor period in St. Michael's Square, opposite the west end of the church.

During one of these visits he wrote a singular letter, assigned to December 1517,[2] to the widow Cowart of Southampton, recommending her a second husband in the person of William Symonds, one of the sewers of the chamber, urging the suit right vigorously, and enclosing a token. The letter has been several times printed, and was successful in securing the lady's consent. We find also the king thanking Sir John Daventry for having interfered in the same matter.[3]

At the close of 1517 (December 10) Sebastian Guistinian, writing to the Doge and reporting a serious storm on St. Andrew's Day, said that the Venetian galleys were anxiously looked for, that they would have a good market, and that the king himself intended to come and make purchases. Henry was in the town in June 1518, and on the 16th Sebastian Guistinian described the king's reception by the captain of the galleys. 'On the 10th the captain, with the masters and myself, went out of the town to meet his Majesty, and on coming up with him, the most noble captain delivered a brief Latin oration on horseback, surpassing his entire auditory, which had no idea that a professor of navigation and commerce could prove himself so able a rhetorician.' Henry ordered a councillor, one of his finest scholars, to reply; he then partook of a banquet on board one of the galleys, at which he was

[1] Steward's Book, 1513. [2] Brewer's Letters, &c.; Hen. VIII.
[3] Halliwell's Letters, i. 347.

highly delighted. After this, feats were performed on slack ropes suspended from the masts, to the immense admiration of the spectators, who were unaccustomed to such exhibitions of skill. Next day the king chose to have all the guns fired again and again, to mark their range; and on Saturday (12th) left for the Bishop's palace.[1]

The Venetian galleys were again daily expected on January 13, 1519, but were detained in Flanders; and on the 10th March we find the merchants busily engaged at Hampton in relading them.[2] About this time the town was suffering again from the plague.

The Emperor Charles V. was at Southampton for some days in 1522, at the end of his lengthened visit to England, his fleet of 180 sail awaiting him at Southampton. Having taken leave of the king at Winchester, he arrived at this port on July 1, if not three days earlier; expenses occurring for 'dressynge of the town yattes (gates) ageynst the commynge of the Emprower the xxviij day of June.'[3] Here the Emperor waited a favourable wind and the convoy of the Earl of Surrey, the English admiral, whom the Emperor had also made his own by a special instrument dated June 8. The Earl, directly after his commission, had made successful descents on the French in Normandy and Brittany; and having knighted some of his officers for good service, and left his vice-admiral to scour the seas, returned to Southampton for the Emperor.[4]

It seems that the Venetian galleys then unlading at Southampton had been requisitioned to form part of the Emperor's convoy. Surrey wrote to the king on the 13th June that they were not over-willing to serve him, and in the end they seem to have prevailed through constant demands for wages and time.

At length, all preparations being completed, the Emperor embarked on Sunday, July 6, at two o'clock in the afternoon.

Later in the same year (November 23, 1522) a complaint of the Venetian ambassador, Suriano, was made to Wolsey of the detention of the galleys at Southampton. The sailors were deserting, and the ships were being spoiled by worms. He begs they may be allowed to go back.[5]

During the mayoralty of Henry Huttoft (Michaelmas 1525–26) Queen Catherine visited the town. Her approach was announced by a royal salute from the Bar Gate, where wine was presented to her. Provision was also made for her consumption during her stay. The

[1] Brewer's Letters, &c., of Henry VIII. [2] Ibid.
[3] Steward's Book.
[4] Lord Herbert, Life of Henry VIII., pp. 124–131; Stowe, 516.
[5] Brewer's Letters of Henry VIII., also Venetian papers.

expenses of the royal kitchen were also in part provided by the town.[1]

In 1527 (1st November) the mayor writes to Wolsey that three great Flemish ships had entered the port and boarded and taken out a Breton ship, in spite of the protests officially made by four of the Corporation. They had, however, no force with which to back their words.

A note of the time occurs under the 21 Hen. VIII. (1529–30) in a payment 'to the pursevant that brought the kynge's proclamacon ageynst the false and erryneous oppenyons of Lewter [Luther] iij$^{s.}$ iiij$^{d.}$'[2]

In 1531 the Act of Parliament was passed releasing the town from the payment of forty marks of the fee-farm (see pp. 33, 38). Among the recorded acknowledgments are these:—'For glasses given for presents to the Barons of the Exchequer and other officers there for their lawful favours; first, to Baron Hales, 9$^{s.}$, for Baron Scott, 5$^{s.}$, for Mr. Smyth, 8$^{s.}$, for Mr. Hide, 5$^{s.}$, for Mr. Attorney, 10$^{s.}$' In addition a present was 'given to my Lady Fitz William, because her husband was very good in helping the town to the new act, £7, 3s. 3d. Item, more to James Stoner for four boxes mermelade for her, 9$^{s.}$ 4$^{d.}$' Also 'paid for a barrel of sweet oil given to the Duke of Suffolk in remembrance of his favour to the town's business, and as many glasses as cost all, 49$^{s.}$ 8$^{d.}$ Item, to Sir Harry Gifford, controller of the king's house, for the like cause, a barrel of oil and as many glasses as cost 41$^{s.}$' Various other presents were made.[3]

In the session of Parliament in November (26 Hen. VIII.) 1534, the Act (cap. 14) for the nomination and consecration of suffragans was passed: Southampton being one of the twenty-five places for which it might be lawful to appoint a suffragan bishop.

It is strange to read of the insecurity of the seas round the English coasts; yet pirates swarmed and open enemies fought their battles close to English towns and in the mouths of English rivers. In 1536 the French cut out a Flemish ship from Southampton and another from Portsmouth;[4] Calshot Castle, to guard the Southampton Water, being erected in the following year as part of a system of coast defence. Under the account for 1543 we find 'expensys uppone the takynge of vi Frenshe shyppes under Wyghte.'

In 1549 the Duke of Somerset received presents from the town, probably in July, during his progress, as we learn from King Edward's Edward VI.

[1] Temp. Thomæ Overey, sub anno.
[2] See Collier's Church Hist., ii. 48.
[3] Steward's Book, 1530–31.
[4] See Froude, iii. 65.

Journal, 'to set order in Oxfordshire, Sussex, Wiltshire, and Hampshire.'

From Southampton he went over to Calshot, a boat being specially prepared for him with 'benches' in it; it was also provided with 'bails.' But the town was not without recompense, for there follows next 'the charges of bakyng of the iiij buckes gevyn by the Duke's grace of Somersett.'[1]

In August 1552 the young King Edward VI. with about a hundred and fifty attendants visited the town. He had been at Portsmouth on the 8th. On the 10th he removed to the Earl of Southampton's house at Titchfield, and from thence to Southampton on the 14th. While here on the 16th he gave audience to the French ambassador, leaving the same day for Beaulieu. The town had been brightened up for the royal visit. 'The citizens had bestowed for our coming great cost in painting, repairing, and rampairing their walls. The town is handsome, and for the bigness of it as fair houses as be in London. The citizens made great cheer, and many of them kept costly tables.'[2]

For the arrival of Philip of Spain, see p. 357.

Queen Elizabeth visited the town (see p. 385) on August 13, 1560, coming from Netley Castle, where she had been entertained by the Earl of Hertford. She left for Winchester on August 16.

The plague of 1563 was heavy in the town, and the usual expedients were resorted to for avoiding contagion. The painter's wife in East Street was employed on 18th September—but not for the first time—in making crosses on the house-doors of infected persons; and such unfortunate people were obliged to carry white rods in their hands, 'to knowe the syke from the whole.' The town employed (Oct. 1) six men and women as 'keepers and bearers' of the sick people, that is, no doubt, to nurse them during their sufferings, and carry them to their graves: each of these attendants received one shilling a week. Such payments continued at least till December, when the fragment breaks off, at which time also the town gave relief to the sick people who cried out for famine.[3]

The queen was again in the town in 1569 on her way from Titchfield to Basing, dating a writ (displacing the mayor of Coventry) on September 8, 'at our tower of Southampton.'

In 1583 the town was afflicted with the plague, which lasted the whole of the summer (see p. 408).

---

1 Temp. Thomæ Overey, sub anno.

2 Edward's Journal and Letters.

3 Paper in Temp. Thomæ Overey (a fragment). A similar plan was followed in London.

Pirates had for some time infested the neighbourhood of Southampton.

In 1584 M. de Segur, Henry of Navarre's ambassador, was forced to wait on his return at Southampton till an armed escort could be provided. In a letter to Walsingham the ambassador complains that he could not have found a worse place for embarking. Only yesterday—he wrote on December 15—a Jersey boat had been attacked and driven back by pirates, who closely guarded the mouth of the water. The Solent was swarming with them, and so was all the water as far as Poole: a few of the queen's ships at Portsmouth kept some kind of guard there, but this only made matters worse for other places, such as Southampton, to the very quays and walls of which these marauders penetrated to plunder the merchants.[1] Many notices of piracies occur in the town books of this period.

The year 1588, that of the Armada, was of course eventful for Southampton. The port possessed at this time eight vessels over 100 tons, seven under 100 but over 80, and forty-seven under 80 tons. These figures are more instructive by a little comparison. The port of London, which had by far the largest number of ships, owned 62 of the first class, 23 of the second, and 44 of the third. Devon possessed in the same classes, seven, three, and a hundred and four. Bristol and Somerset, nine, one, and twenty-eight. Dorset, nine, one, and fifty-one. The Isle of Wight had only twenty-nine vessels, these all under eighty tons. The total amount of ships in the realm being 183, 180, and 1392 of the three classes.[2] The royal navy, at this period, consisted of thirty-eight vessels, including small cutters and pinnaces, only thirteen of the ships being over 400 tons.[3] In the country's emergency the ports sent the best ships they could (see p. 259); Southampton also supplied her ammunition, and kept watch by land and sea; and when the Armada was fairly under weigh, the fire-beacon from the castle tower flashed on the signal which had been received. To tell of the dissolution of this mighty armament does not come within the bounds of our story.

In 1599, under the special alarm of a second Armada, Southampton, in common with some other ports, was required to send a 'nimble vessel' to spy out the Spanish fleet, and to keep a vessel at sea for six weeks.[4]

Queen Elizabeth visited the town with all her court on September 4, 1591, leaving on the 7th (see p. 408). Her visit cost the town £98.[5] The gilding of the civic mace cost £1, 1s., and a purse which cost £1, 9s. contained a welcome present of £40 inside.

1 Froude, xi. 471. 2 Bree, 358, 359. 3 Froude, xii. 357.
4 Harl., 168, f. 149, 150. 5 Liber. Debitorum, fol. 133.

James I.

Queen Elizabeth died on the 24th March 1603; on the 27th her successor was proclaimed at Southampton, between the hours of 9 A.M. and 10 A.M., in the open market before Mr. Cornellis's door. The proclamation was read by Mr. Aspden, the mayor, and 'openly pronounced and divulged' by the town-clerk, John Friar—as he tells us himself—'with the greatest exaltation of my voice that I could, and with my heart's joy and comfort. Vivat Rex Jacobus.'[1]

Towards the end of this mayoralty in September 1603, King James I. and his queen, Anne of Denmark, were welcomed with a verbose address and a small present. The more important sentences were as follows:—

> 'This poor town hath already received, besides these general blessings to all your subjects, a most singular benefit by your Majesty's taking away diverse monopolies, whereby the trade of all foreign merchants being open to this your Highness's port of Southampton, the same is in all good possibility to wade out of their poverty, and by honest traffic with all foreigners to grow in short time unto wealth, whereby they may be able to serve your Highness. But repair to this town without warning to the same, and the majesty of your royal presence astonishing me, I am forced suddenly to break off my speech with this most humble prayer to God, that He will long preserve your Sacred Majesty in your reign over us, if it be His holy will, to double the happy years of our late Queen.'[2]

The king had sought the town as the healthiest refuge from the plague. Here he was surrounded by his court and the ambassadors from foreign states; bull-baiting and dancing being provided for the common amusement.[3]

In October 1605 we find the town suffering, as was so common, from impecunious troops. An Irish company from Flushing in great want beg from the House an order for their victualling; when it was thought best rather to 'rid them out of the town, and bestow upon them forty shillings in money, with a passport to go to London.'[4]

In the summer of 1609, the king being at Beaulieu, an order was received by the mayor for an increased bodyguard of twenty-four men fully equipped and armed, to report themselves on Saturday, August 5th, and attend the king's person; a like number being provided for the Sunday and Monday. On the receipt of this warrant, demanding so many men out of the town and county as compared with those afforded by the shire, and that upon no special emergency, John Friar, the town-clerk, was ordered to ride to Beaulieu with a letter to Sir Thomas Lake, the Secretary of State, and a native of St. Michael's parish, Southampton, with a view to his opinion on this strange requisition. The town-clerk succeeded so well with his errand that the town was discharged of this duty, and the men were levied on the shire.[5]

---

[1] Journal. [2] Vespasian F. ix. f. 156.
[3] Cal. State Papers, September 21-29. [4] Journal. [5] Ibid.

In 1620 the 'Pilgrim Fathers,' as they were afterwards called—a body of Independents forced under Elizabeth to seek refuge in Holland—returned to this port, and set sail on August 5th for the New World in two small vessels; one of these, the 'Speedwell,' put back after reaching Plymouth; but its companion, the 'Mayflower,' a bark of 180 tons, stood out (Sept. 6), and carried its freight of forty-one emigrants with their families—in all, about one hundred souls, whose names are preserved—to Massachusetts. They landed in November at a spot to which they gave the name of Plymouth, in memory of the last English land on which they had touched.[1] Other emigrants 'for the Barbathoes' and elsewhere sailed from the port in 1638 and 1640. For those of the former year the 'Bevis of Hampton,' 150 tons, was prepared; those of 1640 shipped in the 'Virgin of Hampton,' 60 tons.

In June and July 1623 great preparations were made in Southampton for receiving Prince Charles and the Infanta of Spain. The lords of the council were here, together with Inigo Jones and 'Allen the old player,' who would have done just as well, we are told, without so many lords, 'but we must show our obsequiousness in all that concerns her.' However, the unpopular marriage never came off.

King Charles, who had ascended the throne on March 27, was proclaimed in the town on Thursday, March 31, 1625. Charles I.

A few months later he was in Southampton. The plague was raging in the metropolis in the early summer, and the Parliament had been adjourned to Oxford, where it sat a few days at the beginning of August. From that city the king and his council came to Southampton, several orders of council in August being dated from this town; they were here also some portions of September. No. 17 in the High Street, which contains a good specimen of wood-carving, is said to have been the king's abode. During this interval an alliance, defensive and offensive—the 'Treaty of Southampton,' dated September 7, 1625—was concluded with the ambassadors of the United Provinces.[2] The king was not only resident some little time in the town, but was indebted to the Corporation, as also to that of Salisbury, for the loan between them of £3000 for the wants of his household.

At this time the town, as so often, was seriously oppressed by the billeting of soldiers. In January 1626 the mayor asks Secretary Conway what to do with the soldiers—a part of Colonel Bruce's regiment—now in town and fit for service; he had built them a court of guard near the market-place for practice. This detachment eventually, at the mayor's request, on September 5 occupied the town. In June he had

[1] See Hotton's Original Lists of Emigrants, Introd. xxiv., &c.; Bartlett's 'Pilgrim Fathers,' 109–122.

[2] Rushworth, i. 228, and Cal. State Papers.

written to Sir Benjamin Tichborne, Sir Richard Norton, and Sir Thomas Jervoise, commissioners for soldiers billeted in the town, begging a pecuniary supply to avoid mutiny, otherwise he must himself fly the town, as he could not endure the strain. In July he had reported to the council that they had done what they could to repair the ordnance, but were unable to fortify the town without help, recommending also that the castles in the neighbourhood should be put in repair. In the following April (1627), the captains of the town were reduced in pay, and the troops were ready to break out. In May Colonel Conway's regiment was stationed in the town and at Romsey.

The king came again to Southampton on June 18, 1627. He was received at the Bargate by the mayor, Mr. Francis Knowles, and the aldermen, who presented him with a covered cup—what was in it the observer could not say—and also with the keys of the town, which latter he returned. His Majesty then passed down the street through a file of soldiers to Sir John Mill's house, where he dined; after which he reviewed the troops in the Saltmarsh, and then took 'koch'—coach—for Titchfield, where he remained the night.[1]

In April 1628 two companies lately from Ireland and part of Lord Morton's regiment were billeted in the town; and in May the mayor begged for their removal to Lymington, as the town had been oppressed beyond bearing, and the inhabitants were ready to leave their homes; added to which the companies which had been with them since November 17 had only received ten weeks' pay. By November 1630 a long bill had been run up for billeting soldiers, and the town sent Nathaniel Mill to treat on the matter. Five years later (Dec. 1635) the heavy amount of £905 was owing to the Corporation on this account.[2]

Among the writs for ship-money in 1635 and 1636 we find Southampton charged £195 towards the sum of £6000 laid on the whole shire, for providing a ship of 600 tons with 240 men; the quota for Winchester was placed at £190—this in 1637 fell to £170; for Portsmouth £60; other towns in proportion.[3]

In 1640, on November 28, William Prynne, barrister of Lincoln's Inn, the learned Puritan and most voluminous writer, together with Henry Barton, clerk in holy orders, a lecturer of London, and formerly a closet-keeper of the king when Prince of Wales, who had both some time previously been censured by the Star Chamber for libellous productions, and then banished—the former to Jersey, the latter to Guernsey—were brought back to England and landed at Southampton. Here they were well received by an enthusiastic crowd; their expenses

[1] Egerton, 868. [2] Cal. State Papers.
[3] Rushworth, ii. 338, and Cal. State Papers.

were paid, and liberal presents made them. The like fortune attended their journey to the capital, numbers meeting them in every town. At Charing Cross they were greeted by a multitude of 10,000 persons, flowers being strewn in their way to the city. John Bastwick, a doctor of medicine, who had been banished to Scilly, returned through Dover a few days after, meeting with the like reception in his progress through Kent and in London.[1]

In the troubles of this period the authorities of the town seem to have sympathised generally with the Royalists. It appears, however, that a rising in the opposite interest took place on November 7, 1642; on pretext of which, on November 8, Colonel Whitehead sought entrance for his troops, agreeing to be responsible for their payment, whether he brought three, four, or five hundred men for the quiet of the town.

On the 13th November a hundred men were sent by sea from Portsmouth, and were received by the mayor at the Water-gate; the 'Mayflower' also was anchored in the river, while within the walls the usual guard of burgesses was set in the wards, who had authority to sound the alarm and raise the inhabitants by beating drums at any threatening of assault.

The authorities of the town on December 7 respited the inquiry into the commotion of November 7, for fear of another rising, which might bring forces on the town from the ships of war at hand in the Parliamentary interest.[2]

On the following Saturday (December 3), the mayor and Corporation received the following summons from Captain Swanley, of H.M. ship 'Charles,' in which he advises the town to submit to the commands of Parliament and the direction of the Governor of Portsmouth:— Town threatened.

'Mr. Mayor and the rest of your Corporation,—You well know in what distractions this kingdom is in at this time. I am placed here by authority of Parliament for the quiet and peace of this part of the kingdom, which I shall endeavour to maintain as far as my ability of life and fortune may extend. Your town is a considerable place of merchandise, and by reason thereof are men amongst you of very good fortune and estates, and to preserve their estates, and so in general through the whole kingdom with their religion and liberty, is the only aim of the Parliament; and no question those that shall oppose either of these are unfit to enjoy either, but to be branded with baseness. There are divers reports in the country of your forwardness in opposing the Parliament herein, but I hope you wish your own peace herein better than so; if you should, there can nothing befall you but ruin and destruction. To know the truth of this I have sent my letter unto you, as likewise whether you will submit yourselves obedient to the commands of Parliament, and so consequently to the directions and commands of the Governor of Portsmouth, and the committee there authorised by both Houses of Parliament for the peace of this part of the kingdom. I have

[1] Clarendon (edit. 1707), vol. i. pp. 199-202.
[2] Journal sub dat., and Egerton, 868.

seized Calshot Castle, disabled St. Andrew's Castle and Netley Castle. I have seized all the boats of Huth [Hythe] and thereabouts. I have given orders to stop all provisions from coming out of the Isle of Wight: all which I have done by the commands of the committee at Portsmouth. I have also authority to summon you and that town to your obedience to the Grand Council of England, to which I desire an answer; if no answer, shall take it as a denial, and then if any unhappiness befall you, thank yourselves, for I shall to my uttermost endeavour use all my power to bring you thereunto. I pray you let this letter be known to the Commons as to yourselves. Thus expecting an answer by this messenger,—I rest, yours as you use yourselves,

'RI. SWANLEY.

'From aboard His Majesty's ship the "Charles,"
the 2d of December 1642.'

On the receipt of this letter, about one o'clock, the mayor immediately called the Council together, and after much deliberation, the following answer was returned:—

'SIR,—Yours of this month we received this day, about one of the clock, the contents whereof cannot be communicated to the inhabitants of this town until Monday next; in the meantime, we cannot but marvel that reports of our disaffection to the Parliament should be spread of us, not knowing that we have done any act to deserve the same. A more full answer to your letter you shall receive some time the next week. This, with our hearty commendation to you remembered,—We remain, your very loving friends,

'PETER SEALE, *Mayor, &c.*[1]

'Southton., 3d December 1642.

'To our very loving Friend, Captain Swanley, aboard the "Charles," riding at anchor near Cowes, these presents.'

On the following Monday, at seven o'clock in the morning (December 5), two letters were agreed on, one to the committee at Portsmouth, the other to Captain Swanley; both were intrusted to deputations of burgesses. That to Captain Swanley simply contained a copy of the letter to Portsmouth, which was as follows:—

Town declares for Parliament.

'WORTHY SIRS,—It may please you to take notice that we lately received from Captain Swanley a letter which we thought fit herewith to send you. We are heartily sorry that such suspicions should lie upon this town, being confident that there will appear no just cause for the same. Mr. Mayor has summoned the inhabitants of the town according to directions, and they whose names are hereunder written do cheerfully and unanimously consent and agree to submit themselves in obedience to the commands of the King and Parliament, according to the protestation by them taken, and to the directions of the committee authorised by the Parliament for the county of Southampton. Our due respects presented, we humbly rest, your affectionate servants,

'PETER SEALE, *Mayor*
(*with the Aldermen, &c., in all* 96 *names*).[2]

'Southton., 5th December 1642.

'To the ho$^{ble.}$ the committee for the county of Southton. at Portsmouth, these presents.'

[1] And ten other names, but the paper is decayed, and the list cut short.
[2] Corporation Journal under date.

On the following Thursday (December 8), the mayor and his assistants having had under consideration certain directions from the committee at Portsmouth, sent the following answer by Mr. Peter Le Gay:—

'WORTHY SIRS,—May it please you to be advertised that we whose names are subscribed, having considered of the propositions received from you, as first, for setting the town in a posture of defence, such as may secure the town in these times of trouble from the attempts of them that shall trouble the public peace, and to observe such directions therein as shall be sent from both Houses of Parliament, or such as are, or shall be, lawfully authorised from them; secondly, to take care of advancing what monies we can upon the propositions set forth by both Houses of Parliament for the public safety; thirdly and lastly, to assist the apprehending of delinquents against the power of Parliament, according to the protestation; do, with a willing and ready consent, promise, as much as in us lyeth, to put the premises in execution, being now in agitation for the subscriptions for money and plate to be raised in this town and county. And we do hereby desire your assistance by furnishing us with some able and experienced men to direct us for the better defence of this town; desiring also that such monies as shall be raised in this town upon the provisions set forth by the Houses of Parliament for the loan of money, may be by your approbation employed for the better strengthening of the same, and the sooner because we hear of the violent proceedings of the Cavaliers against Marlborough. Also we are informed that there is an order of Parliament for the sending of two ships to lie before this town for the defence of the same, which we desire may be effected with all convenient speed. Thus, with our true respects unto you, we humbly remain, yours in all due observance,

'PETER SEALE, *Mayor*
(*and* 47 *others*).

'Southton., viij° December 1642.

'To the hoble. the committee for the county of Southton. at Portsmouth, these presents.' [1]

Southampton was by this time secured, as a matter of self-interest, to the Parliamentary cause. It is not to be supposed, however, that the town altogether escaped trouble. Serious levies of money were extorted, especially from the more wealthy and suspected burgesses; the town had to be kept in a posture of defence, and the evils of violent partisanship had to be endured within its walls. During 1643 the town was threatened by the Royalists, the Cavaliers under Lord Crawford being in possession of the country round, and skirmishes occurring with equal fate on either side. A Royalist garrison had been placed in Romsey, and apparently on December 12, 'our Colonel Norton, with our Major Murford, Captain Bowen, and about 200 men, surprised Romsey, took 140 horses, and brought away 40 prisoners, among whom was the colonel's brother, Captain Norton.' [2]

In the town itself little need was likely to occur for powder and shot, and we find Colonel Ludlow, who surrendered Wardour Castle to

[1] Corporation Journal under dates.

[2] Egerton, 868, sub 1643-44.

the Royalists on February 18, 1644, buying up as much ammunition as could be spared, with a view to his defence. During this period, in January Ludlow's troop of horse was lying between, and keeping communication with, the garrisons of Poole and Southampton, the prize of £700 or £800 being held out to these garrisons for relief. On one occasion his cornet, afterwards Major William Ludlow, was seriously wounded and carried into Southampton. Later on, after a defeat near Salisbury, he was himself a fugitive to the town with the remnant of his troop, where he relieved Colonel Norton, who was then before Winchester. The town was at this time pretty full of wounded and of prisoners.[1] In the same year Southampton received and supplied the wants of some of the Earl of Essex's starving troops from Fowey, in Cornwall, who, beaten by the Royalists, had been permitted to march to Southampton on leaving their arms, ammunition, and ordnance. Dejected and forlorn as they were, they had been plundered by the common people. 'My poor naked foot,' the Earl of Essex wrote, September 14, 'came last night to Southampton.' They were speedily provided with necessaries, and by October 17 were fit to take the field.[2]

A double stream of feeling is to be detected in the town during these years; the authorities sat loosely to the Parliamentary cause, and, as opportunity occurred, quietly fined those who maligned the king and queen. The soldiers quartered in the town were a source of great annoyance, and money was constantly advanced for their needs.

With the death of King Charles, January 30, 1649, we are not locally concerned.

Commonwealth.

Before the municipal elections of September 1649 the Council of State wrote to the governor and the mayor desiring that the tests prescribed by Parliament might be put to the officers to be elected, Parliament looking on the town as a place of great importance. Peter Seale, jun., had been summoned to appear before the council on August 24, and there was evidently a strong spirit of opposition. The mayor took no notice of the above command, and on September 29 the council called him to account, requiring the names of those who should refuse. He then took action, but on October 11 the council objected to the manner in which he had proceeded, and further to the limitations which many of those who had taken the oath put upon it, and required that the oath should be tendered again. On the 27th they wrote to

[1] Ludlow's Memoirs, i. 71, 85, 111, 117, 143.

[2] Memoir of Colonel Birch, 93, 94; Thurloe State Papers, i. 49; Godwin's 'Civil War in Hampshire' (1642–45) contains most of the intricate history of these years.

the governor and to Alderman Le Gay requesting definite information on what had taken place.

Governor Murford[1] had been employed in fortifying the town in the autumn of 1643 and subsequently, and in June 1650 (see p. 106), the walls having been certified as in a bad condition, a warrant for £250 was given him (August 14) for their repair. Two days before this (August 12) the children of the late king, the Lady Elizabeth and Henry, Duke of Gloucester, were 'entertained' by the governor, and the next day taken by him to Carisbrook, 'to be kept close' till further arrangement should be made. There on September 8 the Lady Elizabeth died in her fifteenth year; she was buried on September 24, in the presence of the mayor and Corporation, at St. Thomas's Church, Newport, where a monument has been erected to the poor heartbroken little princess by Queen Victoria.

About October 9, 1651, the town garrison had been disbanded by order of Parliament, when Murford was apparently dismissed; three companies of Colonel Pride's regiment, however, came the next week, and remained for a month, under the command of Captain Andrews. In the following June (1652) the guns and ammunition were removed, and the guardhouse which had been built by the town near the Bargate for the garrison was pulled down, Murford, who was again in authority, and at this time or soon after a justice of the peace, doing with the timber-work as he pleased.[2]

Early in 1651 the monotony of war and discord was somewhat relieved by the presence of the Portuguese ambassador, on his way to London, who made an eight days' sojourn in the town; and in March the Lords' ambassadors to Holland, St. John and Strickland, were here with a considerable retinue: they appear to have sailed on Sunday, March 9.[3]

In the winter of 1652 the mayor received an order, in common with the mayors of Weymouth, Poole, and Bristol, to impress 300 seamen, an equal number from each town; but on the 4th of February next year (1653), a sorry list of twenty-one impressed men was sent from our town, with the apology that, owing to the lack of trade and but few ships arriving, seamen were not to be had; and at the same period various merchants petitioned urgently for immunity from impressment for their crews, such a practice being fatal to trade.

On Friday, 18th February, this year (1653), an engagement, which lasted till Sunday the 20th, took place between the Dutch and English

[1] He is said to have been a tailor, and was apparently a coarse despot. In 1643 he turned Bugle Hall into a prison for Royalists, and at one time confined the mayor within the town walls.

[2] Journal, and Egerton, 868.

[3] Whitelock, 465.

fleets between the Isle of Wight and Portland, when a considerable number of the Dutch fleet was destroyed, fifty well-laden merchant vessels were taken, and 1500 prisoners. Of these, no less than 1100 were provided for in Southampton early in March, in spite of the protests of the mayor and the governor that the town was already sickly; that other places would be more convenient; that sick and wounded were already quartered in private houses, the few inns barely sufficing for travellers; that a pestilence had broken out when in 1644 the Earl of Essex's regiments were crowded into the town; only such numbers should be sent as could be secured in warehouses, and guarded by the small company of sixty men. Other entries occur about these prisoners, together with their doctor's bill (1654), which amounted to £106, 3s. 6d. No one could check it, for no one would go near the doctor, who had moreover lost his wife and two assistants by the contagion.[1] A great deal of shipbuilding was going on at this port in these years.

The following indignant complaint of the mayor and council to the Protector is a further illustration of the times, and is not without its ludicrous aspect. On notice of the late disturbances at Sarum, they had placed a treble guard throughout the town, but on the 15th March 1655, one Captain Martin Jubbs with his company had arrived from the deputy-governor of Portsmouth, to render help if required, had demanded the keys of the town on the 19th, and even made the authorities prisoners in their own council-chamber till the keys were delivered up. The council on the same day dispatched a special messenger with their complaint, who would also detail 'some other actions unhandsomely committed.' They begged the company might be removed, assuring the Protector of their devotion. The letter was signed by William Higgins, mayor, William Horne, Edward Exton, Henry Pitt and others.[2]

The immediate upshot of this does not appear, but the deposition of the mayor and others occurred in August (see pp. 168, 179). From a letter of Lord President Laurence, dated Wednesday, August 15, 1655, we learn that 'His Highness and the council having taken into consideration the miscarriage and misdemeanours of William Higgins, mayor of the town of Southampton, William Stanley, alderman, and Edward Downer, late high sheriff of that Corporation, appearing by several examinations, have resolved' on their deposition, and the Corporation was ordered 'forthwith to proceed to the election of the fit persons in their respective places, men of integrity, and well affected to the present Government.' In obedience to which letter and commands, on the 22d August, William Horne was elected mayor, Thomas

[1] Cal. State Papers, Domestic, under date. [2] Thurloe, iii. 273.

Cornelius, justice of the peace, and Edward March, sheriff. In the Journal this minute is immediately followed by an entry subsequently made:—'August 20, 1662. We, his Majesty's commissioners for regulating this Corporation, do hereby restore the above-named William Stanley, William Higgins, and Edward Downer, to their respective burgesships, to have and to hold the same in as full and ample manner as if the above-written order had not been made, and to enjoy their places of seniority accordingly. Given, &c. Thomas Knollys, Richard Goddard,' &c., &c.

In spite of the above deposition and severities, the old spirit of the town magistracy was not put down. Major-General Goffe, writing to Secretary Thurloe from Winchester on May 5, 1656, says:—'Being yesterday at my Lord Richard Cromwell's, I met with very sad complaints concerning the unworthy carriage of the magistrates of the town of Southampton against the godly party. The mayor has gone to London, it is to be feared on some ill design (they say town business). My Lord Richard Cromwell and Mr. Major are very sensible of the wicked spirit of the magistrates, and do judge it absolutely necessary that something be done against this.'[1]

On November 26, 1658, 'her Highness, the Lord Richard Cromwell's lady, came to her father's, Mr. Richard Major's, at Hursley, to visit him and her mother;' upon which the town sent her a present of a hogshead of new claret, and another of new white wine, for her entertainment while there.[2]

Amid the confusion of parties immediately before the Restoration the town had to steer its wary course. A letter dated from Wallingford House, on November 12, 1659, from Lord Fleetwood, the commander of the army, directed the mayor and Corporation to provide thirty or forty fire-arms for recruits, whom it was necessary to add to Major Cadwell's company for the security of the town, the arms to be restored in due course. In answer, Mr. Capelin, the mayor, and twenty others, afforded each, with three exceptions, a musket and bandoleer, which were duly acknowledged as received at the Audit-house by Major Cadwell, December 1, 1659. A few days later a letter (Dec. 11) was received from Sir Arthur Haselrig, who, with Colonels Walton and Morley, had been admitted with their troops into Portsmouth by the governor, Colonel Whetham, and had immediately declared for the Parliament, ordering more forces to their assistance, and intitling themselves 'commissioners of Parliament.' 'God in His providence,' they say, 'having brought us hither to the town of Portsmouth, this garrison hath declared for the Parliament, and we are now considering

[1] Thurloe, iv. 764. [2] De la Motte in Egerton, 868.

how the forces and garrisons of the Commonwealth may be disposed of and settled; and having business of great importance to advise with you about,' they desire that, at least, a deputation may come at once to Portsmouth to consult on the public good and welfare of the town. The mayor and council returned a cautious answer, and did nothing. 'This town is and hath been for a long time under the command of a major and company of foot-soldiers, sent hither by desire of Parliament, who have the keys of the gates in their possession, and of late they are reinforced with some horse and foot which quarter in the town, so that at present the chief magistrate hath not in power or capacity to answer your honours' desire in waiting on your honours in order to any treaty about it; and we, therefore, humbly beg your honours' charitable opinion of us and this town and your favourable excuse of us herein, desiring and praying that God may dispose your honours' hearts and all other of the nation to a general and settled peace; which hath been, is, and shall be, the daily and continued prayer of, &c., James Capelin, mayor,' &c., &c.[1]

Major Cadwell and his party marched out of the town—thus 'freed from the usurping Rump'—about December 27, 1659, on which day the keys of the seven gates were taken charge of, according to ancient custom, by the burgesses whose names are recorded, the mayor having the special custody of Bargate; and the ammunition was removed from the Town Hall (at Bargate) to the Audit-house (opposite Holy Rood Church) for safe custody.

On January 10, 1660, a letter from the Corporation to the commander of the army informed him that all the arms and ammunition left by Major Cadwell had been secured for the use of the Commonwealth; complaining, at the same time, of the debts of the troop, as by enclosed list, which 'the cries of our poor inhabitants' desire may be satisfied. They pledge their sincere attachment.

A few weeks later a letter from Colonel Norton, dated February 23, conveyed an order for revocation of the malitias of the respective counties, and of the levy of money; in the next month fresh captains were chosen under the empowered commissioners:—James Capelin, mayor; Edward Exton, Colonel Norton, Mr. Knollis, Mr. Buckley, Mr. Gollop, &c.; William Horne and James Clungeon having companies, Edward Downer and Arthur Bracebridge being lieutenants.

Events were now hastening on to the Restoration. Stanley and Richbell, the town M.P.'s, were keeping the Corporation well informed of what was transpiring in the House; and under May 3 we have the following entry, cautious as usual:—'Upon reading of a letter from

[1] Corporation Journals; Egerton, 868.

Mr. Stanley and Mr. Richbell in relation to His Majesty, it is conceived convenient that the inhabitants of the town doe make bounfyers this night, yf they please, and that the bells doe ring all the day.' Restoration.

The town received with becoming gratitude the pardons of the restored monarch, 'given under His Majesty's sign manual and privy signet at his court at Breda, the 4-14th April last past, and upon the first day of May last ordered by the Commons in Parliament to be printed and published,' the Corporation declaring that with all thankfulness they laid hold upon His Majesty's 'saye free and general pardon,' and pledging themselves to continue His Majesty's loyal and obedient servants. Dated at Southampton the 8th day of June in the year of our Lord 1660, and in the twelfth year of the reign of our sovereign Lord King Charles.' Signed by James Capelin, mayor, and seventy-three others.[1]

The restored monarchy had to contend from the first with the difficulties of poverty. The Parliament which commenced at Westminster on May 8, 1661, voted a free and voluntary present to his Majesty,[2] under which commissioners were appointed for the various counties and towns, with a view to raising £1,260,000, spread over eighteen months, and assessed for each district by the Act itself. The county of Southampton with the town and county of the town were assessed at £2022, 4s. 4d. for each month, the town's share not being specified, and the commissioners being taken both from the shire and the town. Arising out of this Act we find subscriptions taken at the Guildhall 30th October 1661.

It will give an idea of the relative importance of the wards to set down the amount gathered from each:—Holy Rood contributed £92, 17s. 4d.; St. Lawrence, £28, 1s.; St. Michael, St. John, £16, 1s.; All Saints Within Bar, £7, 13s.; All Saints Above Bar, £4, 14s.; East Street and Bagg Row, 10s.; Portswood, £2, 3s. 6d. In all £151, 19s. 10d.; or deducting the brass money (£3, 2s. 4d.), £148, 17s. 6d. This amount was returned to the Exchequer in Michaelmas term 1662.

The largest contribution was that of William Stanley, the mayor, £20. The next was that of his successor, Robert Richbell, £15. William Horne and George Stanley each gave £10. The total number of contributors was 135.[3]

Tuesday, April 23, 1661, being appointed for the coronation, the

---

[1] Journal. In the following December the old arms stored in the Audit-house were sold to Bat. Kempster, celebrated by Dr. Speed in 'Batt upon Batt,' for fifteen shillings and tenpence.

[2] 13 Car. II., cap. 3.

[3] Subscription for His Majesty (Corporation Papers).

town council on April 18 ordered that the members of the House should attend the mayor that day in scarlet, and the rest of the burgesses in their liveries, and proceed to Holy Rood in the morning. The militia were to be under arms by nine o'clock, ready to attend the direction of the mayor and aldermen; the four conduits of the town were to run with claret, and the great guns were to be got ready.

In the next year (1662) the king intending a visit to the town, it was ordered on May 14 that a present of £50 in gold be given to his majesty, and that Mr. Mayor 'procure the fifty pieces of goold on ye best termes he cann,' His Majesty being expected within two or three days. On the 16th powder was procured for the great gun, and on the same day 'sixty ounces of the town plate, such as is most unfashionable,' were ordered to be melted down and made into a handsome mace, to be carried before the mayor. The king's marriage with Catherine of Braganza was celebrated at Portsmouth on the 21st May, and it does not appear that the visit was paid.

The royal cause within the town had not universally been favoured. In January 1661 a seizure of arms and disaffected persons had been reported by Sir Humphrey Bennet to Secretary Nicholas; there had been also a suppression of sectaries. These measures had not purged the unruly leaven; and in a letter dated June 23, 1662, the king, anxious to recover the town from the effects of the late disorders, desires the names of those 'forward and obstinate persons who continue to disturb the government of the town and obstruct wholesome contributions' may be sent to the council for discountenancing the spirit of faction.[1]

The expulsion of James Capelin from the Corporation followed in August, when Stanley, Higgins, and Downer were restored. The following papers[2] relate to the expulsion:—

'At the commission for regulating the Corporation of Southampton, sitting the 20th August 1662, oath was made unto the commissioners, ther beinge present, Wm. Stanley, Richd. Goddard, Thos. Knollys, Roger Gollop, Thos. Mill, Edw. Hooper, Petr. Clungeon, Robt. Richbell, Wr. Horne, Edw. Downer, that James Capelin, beinge mayor in the tyme of the Rump, did charge divers persons with arms, especially Thos. Farr with twelve musketts, with all things belonging to them, to assist Major Cadwell, then a commander for the Rump, and told the sd Thos. Farr that the king was coming in with a forraine power, and wou'd bring in Popery with him, wch he wou'd oppose with the best bloode in his body. And was heard say publicquely in the open streete with a lowd voice that the king was cominge in, and wou'd bring in Popery, and charged Henrie Merifeild, a gunsmith, to gett what armes he had to be ready fix'd. This John Speering heard him saie, though at a greate distance from him in the streete.

[1] Journal.

[2] Given by Dr. Speed in his Appendix.

On the oath of Thos. Farr, and the affirmation and testimony of John Speering, it was put to the vote, and of the ten commissrs there were eight voted that James Capelin shou'd be expung'd out of this Corporacion.

There were other articles exhibited against him, as—

I. That James Capelin was in armes against the late king, and was captain of a foot company in the garrison of Southampton, either as a voluntier or bie commission.

II. That in 1653 the mayor was inhibited the appointeinge orthodox ministers to preach the Thursdaies lecture in that toune by Oliver Cromwell, and other men of different sects apointed to preach that lecture, and that James Capelin went ordinarilie after that alteration to heare them at their lectures.

III. That James Capelin, being mayor in 1660, did, without the consent of the major part of the Corporacion, of his own arbitrarie will, elect and sweare twelve burgesses, without a penny fine or benefit to the Corporacion for any one of them, that only thinge being 500l prejudice unto it, for that soe much many men have given, and offer'd soe much for the same fredomes, and severall of those men chosen of differinge judgments from the maine body of the Corporation.

IV. That James Capelin, during the time of his mayoraltie, after the results of the comon counsell held at the Audit House, had imediately after privat consultacions at his oune house with a cabbal of persons of other judgments, and had communicacion with such among them as were not of the Corporacion.

V. The same as the articles sworn to.

VI. That James Capelin is not serviceable to the Corporacion by his assistance to the mayor and comon counsel at such somons as he ought, and that he appears not at their meetings, though at all tymes warned by an officer, not so often as requir'd, but absents himself without any warrantable excuse, and soe for divers yeares past hath accustomed to doe.

VII. That James Capelin hath very often boasted how usefull he hath been, and what service he had done for the late Commonwealth, and tooke great delight in its relation, and that when he was a captaine he disarmed some persons well affected to the king.

All which being sommed up, from his first undertaking armes against the late king to his first knowledge of our present king's restoracion, doth make him visibly appeare to be a very disaffected person, and unworthy of any trust under him.

These articles were reade before the commissrs above nam'd, who gave sentence as above.

The two that voted in his favour were Wm. Stanley, Petr. Clungeon.'

In the following winter the town suffered from a scarceness of provisions, a mutiny occurring in February (see p. 265) which required the presence of the trained bands to enforce the persuasions of the mayor. These trained bands, under Captain Horne of Holy Rood, and Captain Clungeon of St. Michael's, had previously themselves engaged in a hot dispute as to priority, but the matter being referred to the House, decision had been given in favour of Holy Rood.

The plague of 1665 fell heavily on Southampton. About the middle of June a house was shut up under the terrible suspicion; the physicians declared it to be unfounded, but in another few days (26th June) it was only too evident that the malady was in Southampton. **Plague.**

On the 27th, eight houses were closed. According to De la Motte, the plague had been introduced June 6 by a child brought from London and placed under the care of a widow, who herself sickened and died with the rest of the household. De la Motte moved his family to Woolston on the 13th, and from thence by sea to Millbrook, where he took a house. On the 28th the town was panic-stricken, and on this same day the Corporation promised the next vacant porter's place to an individual who had volunteered to bury all who should die of the plague during the present visitation.

The sickness increased with terrible rapidity, and booths were erected outside the town as a further accommodation for the infected.

On Wednesday, July 5, the town was in so distressed a condition that the few members of the Corporation who could be got together decided on a general appeal for help.

'We cannot believe but that you are acquainted with the very sad and calamitous condition of our poor distressed town by reason of that malignant and pestilential disease which is broken in upon us, and still is raging, putting an utter period to our traffic, driving the richer sort out of the town, and affrighting the country from bringing in their accustomed provisions, insomuch that we seemed to be threatened with famine as well as pestilence, unless some provident course be taken; and not only so, but it is also much to be feared (if it please not God in some short time to withhold His afflicting hand) that the poorer sort of people wanting relief, and not finding it (there being very few persons of any ability remaining in the town), will be very hardly restrained from breaking forth and wandering abroad to the great danger of infecting the whole neighbourhood.'

They therefore beg of the justices assistance from the county at large, and the levying of such a tax on the adjacent parts, according to the Act in such cases provided, as might meet their absolute necessities. This letter, dated July 3d, was signed by Thomas Cornelius, mayor, James Clungeon, Thomas Clutterbuck, and Arthur Bracebridge.

On the following day a letter couched in similar terms was sent to Lord Ashley, Lord President of the Council. The Corporation, or rather the few remaining, were unable to relieve, manage, or rule the people, none of the chief inhabitants being left in the town, but 'only the mayor and one justice of peace more, who have so great a burden upon them that they must needs sink under the load or fly from it, unless some kindly course be taken for their encouragement and assistance.' They ask for a 'skilful chirurgeon or physician, or both, that will adventure to visit the sick.' Proper and timely help may possibly be 'a means to prevent that which we have but too just a cause to dread, even the utter ruin and desolation of this place and people; out of a deep sense whereof we have thought fit to advertise your Lordship hereof, not doubting but to find so much Christian compassion in your breast as that you will be pleased to acquaint the Rt. Honble. the Lord Treasurer and the rest of the most Honble. Council with our very sad condition, that so they may consult of some means for our better relief, and advise us in that we are not able to advise ourselves.' The letter was signed by Thomas Cornelius, mayor, James Clungeon, Edward Downer, Thomas Clutterbuck, Arthur Bracebridge. It was probably written by William Bernard, vicar of Holy Rood, whose name is signed at the side; it was dated July 4, 1665.

The reply was as follows:—'After our hearty commendations, the Lord Ashley hath acquainted his Majesty and the Board with your letter of the 3d of this month, representing the sad condition of your town, which his Majesty doth very much commiserate.' The king had appointed the first Wednesday in every month to be observed as a fast during the visitation; on these days special collections would be made everywhere in aid of places infected; special directions had been given that Southampton should be relieved. Letters had been written to the justices directing that provisions should be sent from the county to supply the town from time to time; the Lord Treasurer and the Lord Ashley had also been directed to send a physician at the king's expense. Dated Hampton Court, July 11, 1665, and signed T. Southampton, Lauderdale, Ashley (and other members).

At the same time the mayor, Thomas Cornelius, and those who were with him—James Clungeon, Edward Downer, and Arthur Bracebridge—expressed their sense of the conduct of those who had deserted their posts. Mr. John Steptoe, mayor last year, and deputy mayor, justice in quorum, and sworn assistant for the present year, was fined for neglecting to give his assistance in this time of affliction £20; on the same day John Harwood, one of the churchwardens of Holy Rood, was fined £10 for deserting his office and leaving the town; James Parker and James Wheeler, the churchwardens of St. Michael's, for the same offence, £5 each; William Palmer, churchwarden of All Saints, £5; Joseph Read, one of the collectors for the poor in St. Michael's parish, £1; Thomas Fletcher, collector of St. John's parish, £10; Robert Elcock, collector of Holy Rood, £5; Mr. W. Newman, town steward, for the like offence, £10; Mr. W. Walliston, chief bailiff and sworn assistant, £5; Mr. W. Israel, water-bailiff and sworn assistant, £5; Christopher Smith, George Prince, and James Cross, discreets of the market, were fined, the first £2, the others £3 each; the three 'bidells,' Henry Norborne, gent., Erasmus Bradby, and William Herring, were each fined £3.

On Saturday, July 15, 'a certificate' of the 'sad and lamentable condition' of the town was issued under the seal of the mayoralty, addressed to all justices of the peace and charitable persons in the county of Hants.

They have done all that is statutable in rating and assessing[1] the inhabitants within the town for relief of the infected poor, but they find their poverty so great, and the poor so numerous and daily increasing, that it is impossible to meet the requirements. 'The wars abroad and the pestilence at home have put such a stop both to their merchandise and clothing, the only known ways of their subsisting, that many of those who lately contributed towards the relief of others are now reduced to that necessity as to need relief themselves.' The mayor therefore appeals for assistance to all the justices of the peace, and other charitable persons within the county of Southampton (Hants). 'The weekly charge,' he adds, 'beyond the ability of the place will, according to the best and nearest account that can at present be given, amount unto above £150 per week.'

A large sum was raised, the fund being received and accounted for by Aldermen W. Horne and W. Stanley. It will be interesting to note some of the contributions. The spiritual court at Winchester sent £6, while the Bishop sent £20. The Bishop of Norwich—of whom elsewhere—gave £20. The Cathedral body sent £12, and the College £10. Thomas, Earl of Southampton, Lord Treasurer of England, gave £50; the town of Dorchester, £50; Portsmouth, £57; the parish of Titchfield, £28; the town and county of Poole, £28, 6s. 7d.; Gosport, £14, 15s. 7d. Several contributions came from London. The town of Marlborough sent £46; Lymington, £36, 8s. His Majesty gave twenty tuns of French wine, whereof half a tun was distributed among the poor, the remaining 19½ tuns produced, at £12, 10s. per tun, £242, 15s. Thus Cornelius the mayor bought 9 tuns 3 hgs. for £121, 7s. 6d.; Edward Downer, 4 tuns 3½ hgs. for £60, 13s. 9d.; Arthur Bracebridge the same quantity for the same amount. Besides this, the king, who was then at Sarum, contributed £50 on the first day of general fast; the city of Sarum gave £70, while from the Close at Sarum came £41—this comprised, no doubt, offerings from the court; Exeter sent £55, 12s. 9d.; Andover, £14; Blandford, £30; Christ Church, £34, 15s. 4½d.; Sherborne, £21, 10s.; New College, Oxford, and some individuals, £36; Bristol, £83, 15s. 4¾d.; Fareham, £24; Netley, Bitterne, Botley, Bursledon, and Hamble, £18, 15s. 11d.

On July 18 the sickness was reported as somewhat less; still in August there was little abatement. In September it was on the increase.

The Corporation took charge of the property, whether in money, plate, rings, or other goods, of persons dying of the plague, with a view to their lawful distribution. In November 1670 we find the

[1] See 1 James I., cap. 31 (1603-4).

goods of one Roger Culliford ordered to be buried without being opened. They had been left for the last four years in bundles in the room where Culliford had died, which no one had since entered. We cannot doubt that all was done that could be suggested by the knowledge of those days to lessen the horrors of this frightful time.[1] Still the precautions taken involved extremest misery. The closing of a house supposed to be infected meant the compulsory herding together of the inmates, all egress being forbidden. We cannot wonder that fears were entertained of people 'breaking out' from such restraint, and that attempts were made to elude the vigilance of the watch. In October a mother living at Cowes hired two young sailors to go to Southampton and rescue thence her daughter from a house wherein all but she had died. They did it, but were taken; and the girl and one seaman were shut up again by the authorities, and the other man, who had escaped on shipboard, reserved for a court-martial by Sir W. Berkeley.

In December the sickness slackened, and the people began to revisit their deserted houses;[2] but the plague returned, though with diminished force, in the next year. Commissioner Middleton, writing to Samuel Pepys on August 7, 1666, reports the plague as abating at Portsmouth, while in Southampton only two had died of all distempers in the past month. On November 29 we hear from Whitehall that Southampton is so free from sickness that the Prize Office is to be brought thither from Cowes next week. The removal took place, and caused a greater resort to the town: at the same time the Commissioners of Prizes (December 14, 1666) warned the Corporation not to stand too rigidly on their ancient privileges as to buying and selling and the employment of labour, as such might be disadvantageous to the king, and so to them. From this time notices of the Prize Office are frequent.

In the month of June 1667 the Dutch fleet under De Ruyter created much alarm in the town. On Sunday the 16th breastworks were thrown up on the quay and platform by order of the mayor, and the sailors in the harbour were employed in mounting guns in position. All the townspeople worked with a will, the excitement continuing through the next day. The Dutchmen were really after the shipping at Portsmouth; and having demonstrated before Southsea Castle, they put out to sea, but had come near enough to Southampton to be seen 'from the turret.'[3]

The king purposing to visit the town, it was agreed on August 27, 1669, to present him on his arrival with fifty gold pieces in a purse, and

[1] Journal. [2] Egerton, 868. [3] Ibid.

twenty pieces to the Duke of York, should he accompany the king, but not otherwise. This £50, with the usual fees belonging to a royal progress, would amount to the sum of £100.[1] His Majesty arrived at the Bargate about six o'clock P.M. on Monday, August 30, accompanied by the Dukes of York, Monmouth, and Buckingham, the mayor and Corporation meeting him at the gate. Roger Gollop, the recorder, made a speech on his knee, his Majesty giving 'good attention;' the mayor then produced the purse with 150 guineas,[2] which he presented, together with the keys of the town and the maces: these latter the king touched and returned. A procession was then formed, the members of the Corporation in scarlet going first, then came the mayor—Kingston Fryar—bearing the great mace before the king; the life-guards followed. They went down the High Street to Mr. Richbell's house, where the king dismounted and took up his quarters; the Duke of York went to Mr. Stanley's, Monmouth to Mr. Cornelius's, Buckingham to Mr. Downer's. On Tuesday the 31st the king rode early to the forest and killed a stag, returning to dinner; after which he took boat and sailed to Calshot Castle, and was in the town again by seven o'clock. Early on September 1 he went over to Hythe, and so to Beaulieu, where he hunted, then dined and returned to the court. On Thursday, September 2, he went to Lyndhurst, and dined 'at the Lord St. John's cost.' On Friday morning, September 3, he started early for the forest, but came back to dinner, after which he took water and went again to Itchen Ferry, returning to the town at eight o'clock. 'The town gave him a salute with divers guns out of the tower at his arrival. Then he received news[3] of the death of the queen mother, which gave sadness to the court.' On Saturday, September 4, the Duke of Monmouth left for Hampton Court. On Sunday, September 5, 'his Majesty went not to church, but after sermon he, with the Duke of York, took boat. Sir Robert Horne was steerman.' They rowed into the Itchen and up as far as St. Denys, and returned to supper. On Monday the 6th, the king and the Duke of York rose before day and took coach by four o'clock, and went hence for Hampton Court. 'God be his good friend.'[4] The town had intended a banquet, 'but through his Majesty's sudden departure this was omitted.'[5]

In 1681 the town joined in the expressions of confidence bestowed upon the monarch from every quarter, in answer to his Majesty's declaration, dated April 8, touching the causes which induced him to

[1] Journal.

[2] So De la Motte. Whether the Duke of York got his money we are not told.

[3] De la Motte appears to mean that he received the news on September 3, but Queen Henrietta Maria had died on Tuesday, August 31, at her chateau, near Paris.

[4] Egerton, 868.

[5] Journal.

dissolve the two last Parliaments. The declaration was read at the general sessions of the peace, May 6, and the address of thanks voted by the common council was ordered to be presented by their two late members, Wyndham and Newland. The address speaks of the 'miraculous preservation of Tangier,[1] by which the chiefest trade now left us (since the prohibition of French goods) receives much security and encouragement.'

After the discovery of the Rye House Plot in June 1683, and consequent proclamations and arrests, the town agreed on an address to his Majesty at the sessions of peace held in the Guildhall on July 13:

> 'We were in good hopes that the late abhorrency so generally declared by all the counties, corporations, and societies of good men against the association had sufficiently discouraged that treasonable project, and deterred the conspirators from any further machinations. But, to our astonishment, we find these pretended patriots of their country are still plotting the ruin of it, and whilst they style themselves true Protestants and zealots for religion, are contriving what no Turk or Jew, or any but the most profligate atheists possessed with ambition, malice, and revenge, durst attempt. At the thought of which we cannot but tremble, being sensible that in such a hellish enterprise the massacre of all good subjects, as well as of their Prince, must be designed.'

The king was expected to embark from Southampton for Portsmouth and the Isle of Wight on Wednesday, September 5, and to be in Winchester by Saturday, the following day being appointed for the general thanksgiving for his deliverance. The town of course resolved to entertain his Majesty, and made hospitable preparation for his reception.

King Charles II. died on February 6, 1685. On the same day an address of loyalty to the new monarch was signed, and the mayor was desired to take it to London with such of his brethren as he should think fit. The proclamation of James II. was made in the town on February 9. **James II.**

In August the following year the king was expected on a sudden, and a 'certain homage' had to be presented; moreover, several fees due to the royal servants, amounting to £36, had to be raised forthwith. It was therefore ordered (August 25, 1686) that £30 should be advanced out of the Michaelmas rent of petty customs.

In the August following (1687) the king was again in the town, leaving by yacht for Portsmouth on the 30th.

The proclamation of William and Mary was made in the town on or immediately after February 16, 1689, their accession dating from the 13th. The death of the queen happened on December 28, 1694, **William and Mary.**

[1] Tangier was abandoned and its works destroyed by Charles II. in 1684.

and on January 9 the town offered condolence to the king in terms which have been thought to be specially happy.

Anne. On March 14, 1702, Queen Anne was proclaimed in the town: she had succeeded on March 8.

Nine guns were fired, and six dozen of wine were ordered to the Audit-house, with 'other conveniences' as Mr. Mayor should think fit.

On June 27, 1706, the day appointed for thanksgiving for the successes in the Low Countries under Marlborough, the usual festivities were provided for in the Audit-house, and thirteen guns were fired.

George I. On April 30, 1725, the town petitioned with success for the regular holding of assizes in the town, and to be included among the counties of the Western circuit; and on the 25th June the mayor was authorised to entertain the judges.

George II. The Corporation addressed the king in reference to the Pretender on March 6, 1744, and the rebellion being crushed, and Thursday, October 9, 1746, appointed as the thanksgiving day in consequence, the occasion was observed as usual in the town; the mayor being desired to entertain the Corporation at the Audit-house in the evening, and to provide illuminations.[1]

On December 14, 1750, the Prince of Wales, on his visit to the town, was presented with a copy of his freedom in a gold box, the cost of which was ultimately allowed at £35, 11s.

On May 15, 1756, eight regiments of Hessian troops in British pay landed at Southampton, with a train of 114 pieces of cannon, under Count Isenburg, and were quartered in all the neighbouring towns, strict discipline being kept. Some difficulty subsequently occurred, and the Hessian generals were ordered in November to build huts for their troops, the innkeepers refusing them winter quarters. However, provision as to the quartering of the foreign troops was made by Parliament in December, and on the breaking up of the camp within a few days, the grenadier regiment was moved to Southampton.[2]

George III. Upon the marriage of George III., the Corporation, on September 15, 1761, in a special address, desired to 'mingle with the shouts of loud applause the gentle voice of piety,' with which they prayed for blessings on the union, and for a line of princes who, emulating the glory of their ancestors, might reign the perpetual fathers of these nations.

The Dukes of York and Cumberland have left their names in the place. On a visit of the latter, then in his twenty-fifth year, on August 14, 1770, the mayor and Corporation, in their formalities, addressed him in the usual style.[3]

[1] Journal.

[2] 'Gentleman's Magazine' for year.

[3] The 'Gentleman's Magazine' for the month preserves a local lampoon on this occasion.

In 1789 the king and queen visited Southampton from Lyndhurst, on their way to Weymouth and Plymouth, having left Windsor at seven o'clock on the morning of Thursday, June 25, reaching Lyndhurst about ten minutes past three. On the following day (June 26) their Majesties arrived at Southampton about eleven o'clock; the king on horseback, attended by the Duke of Gloucester, Lord Delawarr, Lord Courtown, Colonel Goldsworthy, and Colonel Gwynn; her Majesty with the Princess Royal, the Princesses Augusta and Elizabeth, and attended by Lady Courtown and the two Ladies Waldegrave, in carriages. They were received at the steps of the Audit-house by the mayor, bailiffs, sheriff, and town-clerk, and conducted to the 'great room'—the present council-chamber—where the Corporation were assembled. An address was read by the town-clerk, in which, of course, reference was made to the king's restoration to health from the serious attack which had fallen on him in June the previous year, and from which, under the care of Dr. Willis, he had recovered completely by the end of February. The Corporation had the honour of kissing hands. Their Majesties, after partaking of refreshments, went to the quay, and walked thence to the platform; after which, expressing their delight at the 'grandeur' of the views, which were enriched by a full tide, they drove round the beach, and having honoured Colonel Heywood with a call, returned to Lyndhurst.

On December 3, 1792, the Corporation adopted the resolutions of the City of London (November 29) on the duty of supporting the king and constitution, as a necessary action on their part 'in the present state of affairs.'

The Prince of Wales visited the town and was elected a burgess on September 22, 1795, receiving a suitable address. On Sunday, January 31, the following year, the Duke of Gloucester arrived in the town, then full of distinguished company, and honoured the ball at the Dolphin on the following Tuesday.

Under 1795 we may mention the unfortunate scheme of the Southampton and Redbridge Canal. An Act of Parliament was obtained this year for cutting a canal from the platform into the Andover Navigation, to be extended from Kimbridge Mill to Salisbury; also a collateral cut from Houndwell, the centre of Southampton, to Northam, 'where merchant vessels of any tonnage may come and lie close to the first lock of the canal in one of the finest harbours in Europe.' A second Act was obtained in 1800. As far as immediately concerns our town, the efforts of the company were expended in carrying a canal along the old ditch or moat on the east side of the town walls, having its mouth under the south castle by the old flood-gates: northward, it passed across the Houndwell, destroying the springs there, through a tunnel which has now long been utilised by the Southampton and Salisbury railway, and thence along the shore to Redbridge.

This scheme, though it was regarded with considerable favour in the town, and called forth some capital, soon became a laughing-stock in the commercial world; and in September 1800 the following lines of the poet-laureate Pye appeared in the 'Gentleman's Magazine;' they may have been in circulation previously:—

> 'Southampton's wise sons found their river so large,
> Tho' 'twould carry a *ship*, 'twould not carry a barge.
> But soon this defect their sage noddles supply'd,
> For they cut a snug *ditch* to run close by its side.
> Like the man who, contriving a hole through his wall
> To admit his two cats, the one great, t'other small,
> Where a *great hole* was made for *great puss* to pass through,
> Had a *little hole* cut for his little cat too.'

The works soon after this became suspended as money fell short—'the natural consequence of the war,' it was said in the town. In 1805 attempts were made to bolster up the languishing works; three years later the affair collapsed.

At this time, and for some years previously, Southampton had been in a constant excitement of naval and military preparations. Immediately on the declaration of war with Holland (December 21, 1780), vessels had been purchased here by different adventurers and fitted out with all speed as privateers, and in January and the following months we have several accounts of rich Dutch prizes being brought into port. On the news of the French descent upon Jersey, which occurred on January 6, 1781, and ended victoriously for the British under the brave Major Pearson, who was mortally wounded, the Dorsetshire militia, then in quarters in Southampton, petitioned Lord Rivers, their colonel, to be sent over to defend the island; while the masters of Jersey trading vessels in the port offered themselves as pilots. Alarming reports were now spread as to further threatened descents, and in April the most opulent inhabitants of Jersey and Guernsey came over to our town till the return of the grand fleet, which, they allowed, would dispel their fears.

In October and November Spanish and French prisoners were lying on board three cartels in the river, and precautions had to be taken for their management; one was the preparation of a fireship in case of extremities. The Northumberland militia were in this latter month marched into the town for winter quarters; the East Kent had succeeded the Dorsetshire in the early part of July.

In the month of April 1782, the Channel was reported full of French and Dutch privateers, who cut the merchantmen out of our ports, while, as the complaint went, few or no cruisers were sent after them. The Government express-packet from this port to Jersey was chased for several hours on Sunday, April 21, by a Frenchman of ten guns: a few days before, the 'Childers' passenger cutter somewhere about the Needles fell in with a Dutch privateer of sixteen guns, to which she was forced to strike. However, while the Dutchman was lowering his boats, the cutter slipped off, and being a fast sailer, escaped to port after a three hours' chase, during which she was the target for over a hundred shots.

On Monday, July 1, the 51st and 61st regiments from Minorca marched into the town, to remain till the breaking up of the camp; they numbered no more than 700, many being very old and destined for Chelsea. They had come over in twenty-one Spanish cartels, which remained in the roads waiting to take back in exchange Spanish prisoners. By August 10 about 1200 had embarked. They came mostly from Winchester and Bristol.

On September 17 the 51st regiment, who had been made prisoners at Minorca, received their arms and accoutrements on the parade, and two days later left the town for Leeds. In October great preparations were made for receiving Lord Rodney, and on December 27 Lord Howe, Lord Rodney, and his excellency General Elliot, governor of Gibraltar, were elected burgesses.

On the breaking out of war with France again, under February 1793, we find the Corporation and inhabitants of the town encouraging volunteers for the royal navy by establishing a fund to bestow a bounty of three guineas to every able seaman, two guineas to every ordinary, and one and a half guinea to every landsman, in addition to the royal bounty. The Commercial Society gave their support; and the committee consisted of Major-General D'Auvergne, Colonel Heywood, Captain Scott, R.N., the Mayor, Sir Yelverton Peyton, Bart. (late mayor), and several others.

Under June 15 we hear of the publicans of the town making interest, through the application of the Corporation and members of Parliament for the town, to obtain from Government the erection of barracks for their relief, since—as had always been the case—they were oppressed by the number of soldiers quartered at their houses, while their families suffered considerably.

The army of the Earl of Moira, who has left his name in the place, embarked from this port in 1794, after having been encamped on Netley Common. The mercenaries also for Quiberon sailed from here in 1795.

In February 1796 barracks were being fitted up in the town and neighbourhood for the reception of 10,000 French emigrants and other foreign troops, expected by the first fair wind. Three regiments—the 31st, 42d, and 80th—had lately disembarked at the port; two others, the 19th and 29th, were remaining at the new barracks, but were to give place on the arrival of the foreigners. Stables were being made ready for 500 horse, which were also expected shortly; Southampton, therefore, in a few months would have 'more the appearance of a garrison town than of a fashionable watering-place.' The Duke of York's own regiment, the York Hussars, whom the Prince of Wales had reviewed a few weeks before, and whose uniform had so pleased him that he ordered his own regiment to wear the same, were also in barracks near the town. At the beginning of March, those at Half-way Barn, fitted up for the French emigrant artillery, were burnt down. On the 18th of the same month the large number of foreign troops which had now for some time been quartered in the town and neighbourhood were embarked, mostly for the West Indies.

After this there was a slight cessation of martial movement, the town being left remarkably quiet and dull. Then the 37th regiment passed through for Poole, after which the 90th came into quarters here at the beginning of April; the 12th regiment was expected within a few days, and would remain till transports arrived.

In 1799 the troops for the Helder expedition were in the first instance encamped on Shirley Common, but were summoned to Yarmouth for embarkation. In the next year (1800) another body of troops were in camp on Netley Common, and soon after embarked here for Egypt, forming part of the gallant army which so greatly distinguished itself. There is a record of a duel fought near the camp between Lieutenant Smith and Ensign O'Brie, of the 9th regiment. Smith, the challenger, died on the spot; a verdict of manslaughter being brought by a Southampton jury against O'Brie, who had been apprehended at Winchester and brought back to this town. Smith was buried at Peartree Green.

The volunteer movement had been followed in Southampton with great spirit. There was a troop of cavalry, then of infantry, a company of associated householders composed of substantial men, another of younger men, a third raised and trained at the sole expense of Walter Taylor, Esq., of the Navy Block Manufactory at Wood Mills, then a flourishing concern; and besides these was a company of Sea Fencibles. The cavalry were drawn out for the first time under Captain Smith on February 18, 1797; they were composed of the principal tradesmen, more than fifty of whom had banded themselves 'at this perilous crisis.' They were well mounted, and had a handsome blue uniform. On July 11, 1798, they went to All Saints Church with the mayor and Corporation for 'the consecration of their standard.' On October 18,

1800, the whole of the volunteer troops, the cavalry, the infantry of associated householders, and the corps of Walter Taylor, Esq., between 300 and 400 men, were reviewed by General Cowell, who expressed himself highly satisfied, especially with the cavalry.

The above memoranda will give an idea of the stir and movement in the town in a military point of view: the fiscal arrangements of the time, under the exigencies of the war, were entered into as readily. In 1796, in answer to Pitt's address to the Bank of England (November 30), and to the Lord Mayor (December 1), the public loan of that year, called the 'Loyalty Loan,' amounting to £18,000,000, was opened on December 1, and completed before twelve o'clock December 5, with unexampled rapidity, many of the public companies not being able to get their names entered at all, while the Corporation of London could only be admitted to subscribe £100,000. The Corporation of Southampton advanced £1000 on December 3d. It was a time for effort in every direction; and on February 23, 1798, the Corporation determined to suppress all expenses at their meetings, in order the better to contribute in the present emergencies to the aid of Government. A subscription had been raised at the Royal Exchange on February 9th, for the service and defence of the country, and by September 28th the voluntary contributions amounted to over £1,500,000. The Corporation of Southampton at the above meeting resolved to subscribe £200 towards this aid, and £100 per annum during the war. But on February 22d in the following year (1799), after Mr. Pitt's Income Tax Act of January, the above resolution of contributing £100 a year was rescinded, and the income of the Corporation ordered to be returned, with the expression of their readiness to pay £50. According to the report of the committee of accounts, August 8, 1800, the corporate revenues for the last preceding fourteen years, ending at the close of 1799, amounted to £1040, 6s. 7¼d.; while the outgoings, consisting of interest on money, law charges, charities, and other expenses, were £962, 11s. 11¾d., leaving a balance in favour of the Corporation of £77, 14s. 7½d., a sum which appeared to the committee to be an increasing fund.[1]

Amusements.

From war and its costs we may now turn to the amusements of the town, a paragraph essential to an account of Southampton at this period. The town commenced to be fashionable in the early part of the reign of George III., as we have already seen (p. 86) under the notice of the Long Rooms at West Quay and elsewhere.

First there were the assemblies in the summer at the Long Rooms,

[1] All the above particulars are derived from the town journals and local papers of the time.

in the winter at the Dolphin. And 'it being absolutely necessary in all polite assemblies to have some regulations established, without which no order or decorum can be preserved,' we will look at those for the summer meetings signed by William Dawson, Esq., master of the ceremonies (1781). (1.) Gentlemen were not to appear in the rooms on Tuesday, Thursday, or Saturday evening in boots; (2.) They were always to leave their swords at the door; (3.) The balls were to begin as soon as possible after seven o'clock and finish precisely at eleven o'clock, even if in the middle of a dance; (4.) Gentlemen and ladies dancing down a country dance were not to quit their places till the dance was finished, unless they intended to dance no more that night; (5.) Dancing in coloured gloves was not allowed; (6.) 'That after a lady has called a dance and danced it down, her place in the next is at the bottom;' (7.) No tea-table was to be carried into the card-room. The winter assembly at this period, presided over by Thomas Prescott, Esq., M.C., commenced at seven o'clock, and ended rigorously at twelve o'clock. The same general code as the above seems to have prevailed. The subscription for the season was five shillings, or for separate nights two shillings and sixpence. Tea was paid for each night on entry at sixpence a head. Every card-table, with two packs of cards, 'paid' seven shillings and sixpence; a single pack for a round table was five shillings, and a single pack used for any other game four shillings.

The master of the ceremonies was an official hardly second in importance to the mayor himself. It was his duty to call upon all newcomers to the place, and act as the sifter to 'polite society;' his word was law, and his introduction perfectly satisfactory. The rules of precedence, as ordered by the heralds, were printed and strictly observed on all occasions, yet not to the interruption of a dance which had commenced. Little points of dispute and etiquette had to be arranged by the great official, who was always a most agreeable gentleman and ruled with honied words, while his authority had naturally, by rule and custom, that of the subscribers to back him. Meetings for the election of an M.C. caused a general flutter among the élite. That of January 21, 1786, when Mr. Dawson's place had to be filled, was the 'fullest and most respectable ever seen upon almost any occasion,' and great expectations were entertained from the return of Mr. Haynes. A little after this W. Lynne, Esq., filled the office; and there are many now alive who must remember his successor, the courteous old gentleman, Peter Dickson, Esq., who ended his days in the town, the last of the M.C.'s. This functionary had, as a rule, one or two benefit balls. For the conveyance of guests there was a service of assembly chairs, the charge for which was generally sixpence; in later years the fares were raised.

On Tuesday, March 24, 1789, a special ball and supper were given at the Long Rooms in honour of the restoration to health of George III., where all the nobility and gentry of the town and neighbourhood assembled at nine o'clock. Minuets were danced till after ten; then came country dances till twelve, at which hour the supper-room was thrown open, and the company were saluted on their entrance with 'God save the King.' The room presented a brilliant appearance, the table being laid for 250 guests. There was always a ball on the King's birthday, June 4. On this occasion, in 1796, the local chronicler, finding the town possibly a little flat after the late removal of troops, observes that 'the gentility of the inhabitants of the town and its environs can form a more splendid assembly than many public places even at the height of their season.' Nothing was to be seen of that hurry and bustle which lately pervaded the streets, and the town had resumed its wonted tranquillity. A good season was anticipated, as more troops were coming.

Southampton was a watering-place in all the usual senses. There were sea-bathing for the robust and baths and mineral waters for the invalids. On the former subject Dr. Speed himself wrote a Latin treatise, commended by all, but read, it is presumed, by few of the élite; it appeared, however, afterwards in an English dress. Baths.

Contiguous to the Long Rooms were Martin's, Seward's, and Simcox's baths, all highly attractive and 'commodious for people of fashion.' There were also the baths at Cross House, the Gloucester, and others.

For the mind there were circulating libraries, Ford's next the market-house, from whence Ford's 'Guide' emanated, and where in 1781 the 'Morning Chronicle' and 'Morning Herald' might be procured at threepence each, and where the following evening papers were supplied at twelve shillings per quarter, and generally twelve hours sooner than by post:—'The Ledger,' 'London Packet,' 'Lloyd's Evening Post,' 'English Chronicle,' 'General Evening Post,' 'Lloyd's List,' 'New List,' 'London Gazette,' 'London Evening Post,' 'London Chronicle,' 'Middlesex Journal,' 'St. James's Chronicle,' 'Whitehall Evening Post,' 'Craftsman,' 'Price Current;' the 'Hampshire Chronicle, or Portsmouth, Winchester, and Southampton Gazette,' were also supplied. There was a reading-room attached. Baker's was two doors above Butcher's Row; from this establishment also a 'Guide' was produced; here also all kinds of books were sold, and the 'Morning Post' (daily) at the same price as in London. A little later was Skelton's Library, 22 High Street, and reading-rooms; from this house came also a well-known guide-book, successor to Ford's. There was also a subscription coffee-house near Holy Rood Church, Libraries.

open from nine in the morning till nine at night, where certain papers were always to be seen.

Spa. Then there were the mineral springs, one at Houndwell, good for the eyes, and, long surviving that, the chalybeate water to the west of the Bargate at the bottom of Orchard Street, famous for numberless remarkable cures, into which we need not enter. The Spa had for many years been leased by Mr. Bernard: in 1817 the Corporation refused to renew, but reconsidered the matter next year, stipulating, however, that the Spa should be preserved and kept open for the good of the public; before this the water had been open to the poor with the mayor's certificate. Adjoining this were 'Cherry Gardens or Spa,' originally granted to Robert Ballard, and in 1808 renewed to the Marquis of Lansdowne. The comparatively modern Victoria Rooms now overlook these old gardens: the virtues of the Spa are quite forgotten.

Theatre. Again there was the theatre. Originally built by subscription shares in 1766 a little to the south of the late theatre in French Street, it was enlarged in 1780 under the management of Mr. Collins, who in 1798 bought the old St. John's Hospital, and erected on its site a new theatre, which, after various improvements, has now been superseded by the Prince of Wales's, Above Bar.[1] It was well frequented during the season; and about the end of the last century performances commenced in August, and were continued three times a week during the fashionable months. On August 27, 1791, the old house was full of rank and fashion. The Duchess of Bolton and others of the nobility were present, as also Prince William, who came over from Lyndhurst, where he was staying. On September 24, 1793, Mrs. Inchbald's new comedy of "Every One has His Faults" was performed for the benefit of the Sunday-schools. But these notes need not be extended.

Archery. Then there was archery, the headquarters of which were at Archers' Lodge, near the entrance to the Avenue. Under August 1791 we find reports of the town rapidly filling, and the balls being well attended, while new houses were being built with views of the river and the Isle of Wight. At the same time archery and cricket were the prevailing amusements. Once a fortnight the Royal Southampton Archers gave a cold collation to their friends at the Lodge. These meetings were attended by most of the ladies of rank and fashion, whose vocal powers were called in requisition after the repast. On target-days the members gave also a breakfast and dance to the ladies; they also had regular balls at intervals.

[1] The Prince of Wales's Royal Theatre, Above Bar, on the Ogle property, has every modern improvement, and is under the management of Mr. J. W. Gordon, who has already been before the public for over twenty-five years.

Roving celebrities of all kinds resorted to the town. In August 1796 the Chevalier d'Eon, then called Madame or Mademoiselle d'Eon, formerly ambassador from the court of France, but who, at the time we speak of, had assumed female attire for about twenty years, was in the town exhibiting proficiency in the art of fencing, thus adding to the 'numerous entertainments in this fashionable watering-place.' One day, while fencing, the button of her antagonist's foil broke off, D'Eon receiving a severe wound; as some compensation for which a subscription was raised in the place. The true sex of this most extraordinary character was not known till his death in 1810, before which event it was supposed that he had falsely represented himself as a man during his political career. He must have been, at the time of the above incident, about sixty-nine years of age.

The water was also an attraction, as it must always be at Southampton; but let us look at the ordinary water passenger traffic at this time.

Under 1781 we find there was a swift-sailing cutter stationed here by Government, which sailed every fortnight for Guernsey and Jersey, conveying passengers and small parcels. Packet-boats—not, of course, *steamers* as yet—went to the Isle of Wight every evening except Monday; a hoy sailed for Portsmouth generally three times a week, returning the following day. Yachts, boats, &c., could be hired privately at any time. After the commencement of the present century additional accommodation was being afforded. A packet sailed every Tuesday for Havre 'in time of peace,' fare, £1, 11s. 6d. Two smart-sailing cutters left every Thursday for Guernsey, and two for Jersey every week. The fare was twenty-one shillings. Trading vessels of from twenty-five to sixty tons, which were constantly going to and fro, had also accommodation for passengers. The Isle of Wight packets sailed in the morning instead of in the evening. It appears also that two other vessels were available for French ports—one regularly—at all events in 1802—on Saturdays for Havre; the other for any French port in the Channel, at any time when hired. Travelling.

From water we turn to land travelling. In 1781 for London there were—From the Coach and Horses, Rogers's London machine every morning, except Sundays, at five o'clock; Rogers's London diligence, or 'dilly,' every morning at six; from the George, Brookman's common stage waggons on Monday, Wednesday, and Friday, returning the following days; from the Royal George, Aslett's London waggon, every Wednesday and Saturday at ten, arriving on Fridays and Tuesdays at twelve, and returning Tuesday and Friday evenings; from the Star, Cottier's London coach, every morning at five; from the Vine, a London diligence every morning at five, Sundays *not* excepted, also from the same house a London waggon started three times a week. There was also communication with Bristol; Rogers's Bristol diligence left every Monday, Wednesday, and Friday, at five, through Salisbury and Bath, returning on the following days; a Bath and Bristol waggon left the Royal George three times a week at eleven. Oxford was reached through Winchester, Whitchurch, Newbury, and Abingdon, by Calcutt's Oxford waggon, which also went on to Birmingham. It started every Thursday. All the neighbouring towns were to be reached by coach, waggon, or cart; and there seems to have been a regular service for the conveyance of fish.

In 1803 the inducements to travel were set forward as follows: The mail-coach from London to Poole carried four inside passengers at £1, 11s. 6d., and one outside, 18s. It arrived at Southampton at seven in the morning and returned at half-past eight in the evening. Two places were constantly secured for Southampton passengers at the above fares. The stage to Lymington carried four inside passengers at 6s., outsides 3s. 6d., leaving the Coach-and-Horses every morning at eight. Stage-coaches for London left the above house, the Star, the Vine, and Royal George inns, at five o'clock, returning the same evenings: inside, 21s.; outside, 14s. Night stage-coaches ran every Tuesday, Thursday, and Sunday at seven o'clock from the Coach-and-Horses and Fountain inns: fares—inside, 18s.; outside, 12s. The Oxford stage ran from the Coach-and-Horses every Monday, Wednesday, and Friday morning at six o'clock: inside, 26s.; outside, 16s. The Bristol stage, from the same house every morning at seven: inside, 24s.; outside, 14s. A Bath stage, from the same, through Salisbury, every morning (except Saturday) at seven o'clock: inside, 24s.; outside, 14s. The Portsmouth stage, from the same, every Monday, Wednesday, and Friday morning at seven; and the Gosport stage, every Tuesday, Thursday, and Saturday at the same hour: inside to Portsmouth 8s., outside 5s.; to Gosport, inside 7s., outside 4s. 6d. 'Vans[1] to and from Portsmouth, Gosport, Winchester, Romsey, Salisbury, &c., were 'to be heard of' at the Nag's Head, Red Lion, Fountain, and White Hart inns. There being 'no hackney coaches, the gentry' were 'accommodated with sedan-chairs on reasonable terms.' Such was the state of things in the first decade of this century, at which period the population of our town amounted to something over eight thousand.

Southampton was honoured with another royal visit on July 1, 1801. The king and queen, attended by their royal highnesses the Duke

[1] At this time generally so printed, its abbreviation from caravan not being forgotten. The word occupied the same position as 'bus' does with ourselves; it was scarcely received.

of Cumberland, Prince Adolphus, the Princesses Augusta, Elizabeth, Mary, Sophia, and Amelia, and the Princess Sophia of Gloucester, were received by the mayor and Corporation at the Audit-house, after which they took refreshment at the mayor's house, Above Bar, and returned to Cuffnells, the seat of George Rose, Esq., where they were staying. On this occasion, Prince Adolphus Frederick, seventh son of the king, was elected a burgess, and being present, was sworn in, their Majesties and the royal family being also present.

The king and queen, accompanied by the Dukes of Cumberland and Cambridge, and the Princesses Elizabeth, Mary, and Sophia, again honoured the mayor and Corporation with their presence at the Audit-house on Thursday, October 31, 1804, receiving an address from the recorder. They returned afterwards to Cuffnells.

The victory of Trafalgar was won on October 21, 1805, the town being illuminated for the occasion on November 11; and on November 25, an address, signed by three hundred and seventy-nine of the inhabitants, was forwarded to the king; the freedom of the town being voted to Lord Barham, First Lord of the Admiralty, and Lord Collingwood.

At the beginning of the century the chief artery of communication eastward of the town was through East Street; by Holy Rood Church there was only a narrow lane called Pitt's Lane. The present Bridge Street, since again much improved, took its origin in a proposal of the Messrs. Bernard (September 25, 1807) to produce £350 towards the construction of a street through Pitt's Lane, and a good bridge over the canal (the Ditches). The Corporation fell in with this offer, and it was further agreed that the street should be made as far as Orchard Lane, which ran at right angles with its line. The Canal Company agreed to permit the bridge to be built provided the Corporation made it substantial and kept it in repair. The upper part of the street as far as the bridge was to be called Bridge Street; on the other side as far as Orchard Lane the street was called, after the original projectors, Bernard Street.

On December 31, 1811, the Duke of Clarence was sworn a burgess and received an address. On November 27, 1812, a letter was received from the Duke (then Marquis) of Wellington, dated from Rueda in Spain, thanking the Corporation for a similar compliment.

Under December 16, 1815, we find that the projectors of steam- Steam. boats were said to be contemplating an establishment of 'this useful invention' between the town and the Isle of Wight.

The usual addresses had been presented by the Corporation on incidents of moment in the royal family, *e.g.*, May 8, 1816, on the marriage of the Prince Regent's daughter, Charlotte Augusta, with the

Prince of Coburg; November 21, 1817, on her death; November 30, 1818, on the death of the queen, which had happened on the 17th. George IV. At length there was one to George IV., whose accession was proclaimed from the balcony of the Audit-house, at the outside of the Bargate, and at the custom-house, with the usual solemnities, on Wednesday, February 2. The old king had died on Saturday, January 29. The town seal was affixed to the address on February 22, 1820.

In November 1820 an address was voted to the king, condemnatory, like so many other petitions from various parts of the country, of the proceedings in reference to Queen Caroline: 'We humbly implore that your Majesty will not authorise your official servants to reagitate a question which can only tend to alienate the affections of your dutiful and loyal subjects.'

On November 13 the town was illuminated, and on the 20th a dinner was announced for celebrating the happy termination of proceedings against the queen. An address to the queen from the town in October had received 3000 signatures.

The Southampton races date from June 14, 1822, when the Corporation gave permission for the marking out sufficient ground for the purpose on the common.

Gas. On the introduction of gas into the town in 1820—by September 4 a gasometer eighty-four feet high had been erected, and in a few weeks the town would be lighted—the iron pillars for supporting the public lights were presented by W. Chamberlayne, Esq., of Weston Grove, one of the M.P.'s for the borough, to commemorate which munificence the Corporation and inhabitants erected the Chamberlayne column (August 1822). The column was at first placed at the corner of Northam Bridge Road, and afterwards (1829) moved to the quay, where it served as a useful sea-mark. It was noted among the improvements of the town in 1822, during which year also upwards of a hundred new houses had been built, and all the line of the canal from Hanover Buildings had been taken in and appropriated for gardens, houses, or for mercantile purposes.

George IV. having intended coming within the limits of the port in his yacht in August 1823, the Corporation readily accepted the offer from Mr. Wyon of the Mint (hon. burgess, September 20, 1823) to present them with the die of a medal to commemorate the event. However the king never came; the weather was bad and he was indisposed; so the Corporation struck a gold medal from the above die and forwarded it with an address expressive of 'veneration' for the royal person and gratitude for blessings enjoyed under his 'most auspicious and parental reign.' To this the town seal was affixed on August 23, 1823.

The Chain Pier was projected by private subscribers in 1824, who obtained from the Corporation a lease of the necessary land near the platform for forty years, at a fine of £1, 1s., quit-rent £1, 1s., and 4s. (as was usual in town rents) for capons. The land or mud was a strip 30 feet wide to low-water mark, with a breadth of 60 feet at the extreme end.

On February 2, 1828, the town seal was affixed to a memorial to the Lords of the Treasury, requesting them to reconsider the late classification in which they had placed Southampton in the third list of ports, when by comparison of its foreign trade with that of other ports it seemed entitled to be ranked in the second class.

Later in the same year the Corporation encouraged scientific investigations by subscribing (September 22) £2, 2s. towards Mr. Graham's ascent in a balloon from Baker's sawmill yard.

On the death of George IV., on Saturday June 26, 1830, the usual proclamations of his successor were made on Tuesday, June 29, pursuant to warrant of Privy Council, and an address was forwarded to the king and queen. William IV.

The coronation of William IV. on September 8, 1831, was celebrated, as in the highest quarters, on a modified scale. The committee appointed for raising funds reported to the mayor (September 6) that it would be 'impossible, from the increased population of the town, to give a public dinner, as at the last coronation.' The bells, therefore, were to be rung, the guns fired, and a display of fireworks made in the Marsh for the amusement of the people.

A visit from the Duchess of Kent and the Princess Victoria being expected on their way from Bath to Portsmouth in October, the Corporation directed the sheriff and the senior bailiff to wait upon their royal highnesses at the Star Inn, and ascertain whether it would be agreeable to them to receive an address. Accordingly, on the 25th October, the deputation waited on their royal highnesses, and were informed that an address would be received at noon on Wednesday the 27th. On that day a brilliant company of ladies were in waiting at the Audit-house, whither their royal guests were conducted by the mayor, recorder, and members of the common council. An address was read by the recorder, to which the Duchess replied. Among other things she said, 'As the happiness of the Princess's future life must depend on her meriting the continuance of such attachment, it is therefore the ardent wish of my heart to bring her up so as to realise the expectations formed, and to qualify her to fill the great station that seems to await her under the will of Providence, but which I fervently hope may be her lot at a very distant day, in our great, free, and enlightened country.'

The several members of the Corporation and the clergy were then presented.

The opening of the newly constructed pier (see above, and p. 113) was honoured by the presence of the Duchess of Kent and the Princess Victoria, who were then residing at Norris Castle, on July 8, 1833; they had at first been compelled to decline the invitation (June 28), on account of which the ceremony had been slightly postponed. On the day appointed a deputation of seven gentlemen, representing the Corporation, the commissioners, the gentry and merchants of the town, accompanied by the town-clerk, in a state barge, at the bow of which the silver oar, the badge of the town's admiralty, was conspicuously displayed, waited upon their royal highnesses on board the 'Emerald' royal yacht, inviting them to land. The Duchess expressed the satisfaction she felt at complying with the request, and gracefully referred to their former reception. Their royal highnesses, steered by Admiral Tinling, deputed for that purpose by the mayor as admiral of the port, were received at the foot of the pier stairs by the mayor and Corporation, and conducted to a marquee at the pier-head, where refreshments were served, and the Duchess, at the request of the town-clerk, in the name of the Corporation, named the pier:—'It affords me great pleasure to name the pier the "Royal Pier," and I am to add our sincere good wishes that it may promote the prosperity of the town.' The proceedings were said to have been witnessed by some 25,000 persons. The work itself, under the superintendence of Mr. Betts, the engineer, had been accomplished in six months, at a cost of £10,000, raised in £50 shares. At this same time an extension of the quay eastwards to the platform was carried out and called the Eastern Pier.

In November the Duchess and Princess, on their way from the Isle of Wight to Kensington, were again received (November 6) by the mayor and Corporation, and entertained with a breakfast in the rooms at the pier-head,—the good Duchess, in reply to an address, saying, 'I feel I cannot better ensure to the Princess the love of the nation than by leading her, as I do, to mix freely with the people, that she may by such intercourse have the means of knowing their interests and opinions.'

The great event of this reign in relation to the history of Corporations—the Act of 1835—has already been several times mentioned.

William IV. died on June 20, 1837, and Queen Victoria was proclaimed on Thursday, June 22, at the Audit-house, outside the Bargate, and at the custom-house. Her Majesty and Prince Albert visited the town from Windsor on their way to France and Belgium on August 28, 1843. They were received at the railway terminus by Major-General Sir H. Pakenham and staff, and by the mayor and

Corporation, and at the end of the pier by the Duke of Wellington and other noble personages. Her Majesty has not since visited the town excepting on the occasion mentioned on page 283. Southampton received the Prince and Princess of Wales on their wedding-day, March 10, 1863, when an address was presented. The most noteworthy of remaining royal visits was that of the Prince and Princess in 1878 (see p. 343).

Southampton has had its agricultural shows, its loan exhibitions, has once received the Church Congress, twice the British Association, and has welcomed the great archæological and other societies. The last few years have been those of increasing prosperity; the town has extended its limits in all directions, though it has sacrificed thereby its old estates and mansions in the immediate vicinity. In 1861 the census gave 46,960; in 1871 the population was 53,747; in 1881 it was 60,051, namely, 28,382 males, 31,669 females. In 1871 the population of the suburbs was 32,203; in 1881 it was 40,950, making the population of the town and suburbs 100,866. Trade returns have shown fluctuations: the value of exports in 1882 was £7,763,882, against £8,946,281 in 1881, and £9,306,326 in 1880 (see p. 285): the value of imports in 1882 was £9,269,926, against £7,901,225 in 1881, and £9,205,183 in 1880. The gross amount of customs received in 1882 was £34,961, against £34,705 in the previous year. Southampton, as we have seen in the foregoing pages, has gone through many changes; it has risen, almost within living memory, from the sleepiness of a dull town with its 'season,' to being one of the prominent centres of life in the kingdom, while the beauty of its surroundings, the healthiness of its climate, its convenience for London, the Isle of Wight, and the Continent, and its ancient monuments, must always render it an attractive place of residence.

# INDEX.


ABERE, William, 122.
Above Bar, 295, 342, 396, 449.
Above Bar chapel, 307, 395, 428, 429.
Abyndon, Thomas de, 201.
Ace, Benedict, 163, 450.
Achard's, Acard's, Acorn bridge, 41, 42, 44, 45, 46, 49, 114, 436; fountain, 114, 117.
Adelard, Prior, 434, 440.
Adkins, Thomas, 429.
Admiralty court, 135, 159, 239–242.
Admiralty of town, 155, 156, 166, 196, 221–224, 239, 240, 246.
Aiulf, the chamberlain, 27.
Alberti of Florence, society of the, 253.
Albion chapel, 430.
Albion steps, 73.
Alderman, the, 136, 137, 139, 143, 144, 147, 208.
Aldermen, 158, 162, 208, 209.
Aldermen of wards, the, 134, 137, 146, 147, 208, 213, 235.
Alderney, 267.
Alcocke, Griffyn, 192.
Aliz, William, 436.
Allcobasse, Peter de, 348.
Allington, Aldinton, 329, 332, 333, 453.
All Saints parish, 48, 271, 293, 296, 300, 302, 456; church, 115, 117, 329, 330, 331, 332, 333, 334, 340, 341, 394–402, 507.
Almshouses, 293, 294, 300.
Almshouses, Thorner's, 307–309.
Alresford, 465.
Alton, 274, 464.
Alum, 255.
Alyn, John, 335, 336, 348.
Ambly, Mikarly de, 252.
Ambrose, Christopher, 53, 244, 272.
Amesbury, Abbess of, 37.
Amyatt, James, 206, 207.
Angel inn, 473.
Anglesea place, 398.
Anglicus, William, 37.
Anne, Queen, 70, 71, 502.
Anschil the priest, 26.
Anschital, 27.
Antwerp, 257, 475.
Apparel, 193, 194, 234–236.
Appelby, Thomas, 201.
Arcade, the, 59, 85, 87–90.
Archery, 510; butts, 216.
Armada, the, 259, 481.
Arnewode, Ernewode, Richard, 323, 368.
Arnewode, Thomas, 441.
Armorer, Thomas, 168, 173, 202
Arms of the town, the, 245.
Arragon, 250, 254.
Arsenal of Southampton, 476.
Arthur, Prince, 475.
Arundel, Earl of, William Fitz Alan, 37, 126; Thomas, 61.
Arundel, Sir John, 61, 75, 82, 467.
Arundel, Sir John, 37.
Arundel tower, 61, 62, 72, 73.
Arundel, William de, 393, 438.
Ascapart the giant, 65, 66, 71, 247.
Asheley, Thomas, 460.
Ashley, Lord, 496.
Assistants (also Discreets), the, 137, 143.
Assize of victuals, 154.
Atherley, Arthur, 207; Arthur, junior, 207.
Audit-house, 42, 125–128, 164, 192, 194, 270, 296, 353, 446, 475, 492, 503, 513, 515, 516.
Aude, Walter, 393; William, 393.
Audley, Lord, 473.
Aulnager, 166, 213.
Auncell weight, 249.
Avenue, the, 51.
Aylward, Robert, 173, 174; Walter, 164, 174.
Aylesby, Richard, 250.
Ayres, John, 71.
Ayscough, James, 197.
Aysche, Assche, Richard, 157, 202, 215.
Azo, accounts for farm, 32.
Azon of Hampton, 452.
Azon, Benedict, 170, 437, 443; John, 437.

BACHELOR, John, 228.
Back-of-the-walls, 106, 398, 456.
Bacon, Francis, 204.
Bacon, John, 98.
Bacoun, Bacon, William, 201.
Baddesley, 332, 424.
Bagge, Richard, 322.
Bagge family, 376.
Bag row, 271, 342.
Bailiff of the court, 134, 209, 232.
Bailiff, water, 134, 209.
Bailiffs, 34, 137, 143, 144, 158, 163, 164, 169–174, 194, 209, 210, 235.
Bainbrigge, Christopher, 53, 54.
Bakers' corporation, the, 264, 265, 295.
Baker, Mary, 345.
Baker, Arthur, 116.
Baker, Bacar, Walter, 105, 167, 176, 460.
Balvair, Balvayr, Roger, 400; family, 456.
Balweys, William, 448.
Banester, Thomas, 393.

Bangor, Bishop of, William Barrowe, 263; Thomas Skevington, 198, 256.
Banister's farm, 43, 44; court, 43, 45.
Banister, Sir Edward, 43.
Banister, Nicholas, 254.
Banke, Richard, 323.
Bankesford, John, 427.
Baptists, 432.
Barbers, the, 265, 266.
Barbican, 59, 89, 111.
Barbflet, Nicholas de, 114, 249, 445, 447.
Barbot, Jean, 412, 415.
Barbur, Barber, Robert le, 170, 228, 322, 457; John le, 186, 200; Thomas le, 400.
Bareflet, Richard de, 171, 322.
Barfleur, 464.
Bargate, 41, 42, 44, 59, 61, 63–72, 105, 107, 108, 116, 119, 120, 122, 147, 337, 469.
Bargate, Walter, 164.
Baril, Barrell, Bercher, 169, 196, 398.
Barkstead, John, 11, 427.
Barnouin, J. Jean de, 419, 422.
Barre, Robert atte or de la, 79, 171, 200.
Barre, John de la, 199, 457.
Barry, Roger, 380.
Barton, Henry, 484.
Barton, John, 360.
Basariotts, 271; perhaps Levanters.
Basingstoke, 280.
Basset, Walter, 436.
Bassingrom, Petronilla, 320, 321; Matilda, 320, 321, 322; William, 170, 200, 320, 321, 455.
Bastide, George, 197.
Bastwick, John, 485.
Bathe, Mr., 312.
Baths, 509.
Baudewyne, F., 190.
Bayeux, Bishop of, 31.
Bayly, Joceus, 393.
Bayonne, 253.
Bagworth, Robert, 36, 164.
Beacon, Thomas, 358.
Bearers, 213.
Beatrice, the Princess, 283.
Beauchamp, John de, 81.
Beauflour, Ralph, 201.
Beaufort, Cardinal, 36.
Beaulieu, 224, 264, 482.
Beaulieu Abbey, 220, 332, 473, 474, 480; Abbot of, 198, 240.
Becford, Thomas de, 347, 353.
Beche, Edmund de la, 79.
Bechefounte, Robert, 323.
Bedford, Duke of, John Plantagenet, 470.
Bekingham, Beckingham, Thomas, 203, 236.
Beel, Richard, 188.
Beer, 248, 267.
Beere, Montague, 186.
Beggars, 294, 297.
Behaute, Mr., 359.
Beket, Thomas, Archbishop, 434, 464.
Beket, Nicholas, 425, 426, 437.
Belhous, Robert, 119.
Bell street, 53.
Belleau, Lewis de, 421, 459.
Belvedere chapel, 430.
Benefactions, 300–309.
Bennett, Beneyt, John, 115, 173.
Berd, Robert, 263.
Bere, forest of, 41, 51.
Bernard street, 53, 513.
Bernard, William, 313, 359, 360, 365, 370, 407, 497.
Bernard's land, 453.
Bertram, John, 429.
Bettridge, William, 402.
Betts, Thomas, 46.
Bevois mount, 2, 6, 342, 365.
Bevois or Bevis, Sir, 6, 65, 66, 71, 247.
Bible Christians, 432.
Biddles gate, 63, 72, 73, 84, 85, 86, 88, 90, 106, 465.
Bidelles, the, 134, 211, 213.
Bingham, Peregrine, 186.
Birchmere, Mr., 220.
Bird, Elizabeth, 306, 307.
Bishop's charity, 367.
Bisse, Henry, 350.
Bitterle, Stephen de, 60, 79, 80.
Bittern, 3, 4, 6, 8, 9, 10, 329, 365.
Bittern park, 11.
Blackford, Richard, 406.
Blackworth, 42.
Blanc, Richard le, 411, 412, 415.
Blancbully, John, 49.
Bleby, John de, 347.
Blewet, Bluet, Robert, 36, 53, 202.
Blount, Thomas le, 400.
Blue Anchor gate, 63, 89; court, 88, 91; lane, 90, 91, 385, 438.
Blunt, Sir Michael, 46, 47.
Bluntesdone, Henry de, Archdeacon of Dorset, &c., 114, 445, 447, 457, 462.
Bockland, 449.
Bohun, Humphrey de, 436.
Bokland, John de, 79.
Bolar, William, 429.
Boldre, 242.
Bole, William, 201.
Bolehusse, Bolehouse, Bolehuge, Bulehuse, Simon de la, 170; John de la, 146, 147, 436; Bartholomew, 436.
Bolton, Duke of, Charles Pawlett, 67; Charles, 67, 224.
Bonde, Thomas, 204.
Bonhait, Roger, 37.
Bonhayt, Robert, 425.
Boothby, Martin, 159.
Bordeaux, 248, 250, 253.
Bosco, Hugo de, 32; Sir Ernald de, 41.
Boston, 248, 255, 260.
Botley, 241, 332, 333.
Bottlesham, Stephen de, 380.
Bourgogne, John de, 322.
Bourne, Robert de, 334, 393.
Bowling-green, 54, 456.
Bowman, Alderman, 69.
Bowyer, William, 191.
Brabason, 338.
Bracebridge, Arthur, 179, 492, 496, 497, 498.
Brackelye, Walter de, 171, 322, 456; Joanna de, 322.
Bradeway, Richard, 201, 376, 377.
Bradsell, Mr., 302.
Brambles, the, 221.

Bramston, Sir Mountford, 360.
Brande, Brenne, Brende, James, 185, 203.
Brannon, Philip, 75, 433.
Breauté, Fulk de, 252.
Brent, Sir Nathaniel, 409.
Breton, William, 310, 311.
Bretun, Richard le, 450.
Brett, Richard, 205.
Bretville, Gilbert de, 27.
Brewery and block manufactory, 246.
Brewers, the, 149, 266–268, 295.
Brickmaker, the town, 215, 216.
Bridge street, 53, 125, 361, 513.
Bridge, Free Cobden, 291.
Bridge, London and S.-W. Company's, 292.
Brideoake, Ralph, 342, 343, 349, 388.
Bridewell, *see* 'Prison.'
Briewere, William, 32, 34, 41, 78.
Brinton, George Simon, 69, 352.
Bristol, 227, 250, 253, 254, 255, 256, 257, 259, 260, 264, 274, 284, 286, 287, 481, 489.
British Association, 118, 292.
Brittany, 257, 274, 467, 468; Duke of, 474.
Britton, Frederick, 196, 386.
Britton street, 53.
Broad lane, 456.
Brock, William, 185.
Brokers, the, 134, 135, 150, 212.
Broke, Richard, 54.
Brougham, Bernard, 370, 372, 381.
Broun, William, 200.
Bruges, 257.
Brunage, 242.
Brunswick place, 366; square, 53.
Brut, Maurice, de Sydenham, 380.
Brya, Henry, 147.
Budworth, William, 394.
Bugle, Bull, street, 94, 147, 318, 321, 386, 387, 456.
Bugle tower, 63, 85, 86, 93.
Bulehus, Thomas de, 37, 252.
Bull or Bugle hall, 93, 299, 316, 386, 455.
Bullar, John, 3, 6.
Burgess, Burgers, street, 42, 46.
Burgesses, the, 134, 135, 152, 153, 154, 156, 165, 190–199.
Burgesses, honorary, 138, 191, 197, 198.
Burgundy, Duke of, 473.
Burlestone, the, 41, 42, 46, 49.
Burry, Henry, 200.
Burton, William, 349.
Bury, Friar John, 76.
Bussilden (Bursledon), 240, 241, 242.
Butchers, 135, 145.
Butchers, the, 268–270.
Butler, Thomas, 313, 388, 394, 407.
Butler, Stephen, 350.
Buttler, Richard, 176, 203, 293.
Butts, the, 77, 108.
Bygard, John, 201.
Bynedon, John de, 170; Thomas de, 171, 200, 253, 353.
Byrt or Burde, William, 381.

CABOT, Francis, 411.
Cadlands, 240.
Cadwell, Major, 491, 492.
Cæsar, Sir Julius, 258.
Cake, Philip, 201.
Calais, 251, 254, 255.
Caldwell, Benjamin, 196.
Calshot, Calchesores, 148, 261.
Calshot castle, spit, 2, 83, 223, 242, 365, 486.
Calvert, John, 401.
Calwell or Colwell fountain, 114, 445, 447.
Cambridge, Duke of, 513.
Cambridge, Duke of, 283.
Cambridge, Earl of, Richard de Coningsburgh, 82, 455, 459, 460, 461, 469.
Cambridge, University of, 295.
Camden, his account, 3, 15, 260.
Canal, 100, 109.
Candy (Candia), 258.
Cannon, 100, 101, 214, 215, 473, 474.
Canshut lane, 450.
Canterbury, 250, 464.
Canterbury, Archbishop of (Dr. Tait), 344.
Canterbury, French church at, 411.
Cantilupe, Robert de, 77.
Canute's palace, 94, 95.
Caplen, Capelin, Caplyne, &c., John, 38, 39, 105, 176, 203, 314; Nicholas, 203, 229, 406; Henry, 193; James, 167, 193, 491–492, 494, 495.
Capon, John (Bishop of Bangor, Salisbury), 310, 349, 372.
Capon, William, 310, 311, 336, 338, 349.
Cappers, the, 270.
Carausius, 8, 9.
Cardiff, 286, 287.
Cardonnel, Adam de, 67, 406, 411, 413, 459.
Cardonnel, Adam de, 67, 68, 205, 406.
Carisbrook priory, 370, 466; castle, 489.
Carlton chapel, 432.
Carlton crescent, 402.
Caroline, Queen, 514.
Carpenter, the town, 215.
Carriers, 212, 216.
Carteret, Philippe de, 407.
Carteret, Philip, 398, 407.
Cary, James Walter, 318, 402, 403.
Castanier, Anne, 422.
Castle, the, 29, 30, 32, 35, 59, 74–84, 91, 253, 464, 468; chantry in, 333.
Castle gardens, 74; lane, 74, 75.
Castle green, 76, 77.
Catalonia, 250, 254.
Catchcold tower, 62, 72, 73, 105.
Catherine of Arragon, 475, 476, 478.
Catholic Apostolic Church, 433.
Cemetery, the, 50, 51.
Cerdic, 13, 14.
Ceremonies, master of the, 508.
Chacombe, Richard de, 440.
Chalke, Walter de, 435, 436.
Chamber, Edward, 380.
Chamberleyn, Chaumberleyn, Chamberlayne, William, 202; Thomas, 202; William, 207.
Chandlers, the, 270.
Chandos street, 53.
Channel Islands, 261, 263, 414, 417.
Chantries, 422–427.
Chantry of St. Mary's, 333, 335, 336.
Chapel, 52, 230, 231, 232, 237, 342.
Chaplain of the Guild, the, 136, 139.

Chapman, Edwin, 433.
Charities, 293–309.
Charles I., 39, 158, 483, 484, 489.
Charles II., 39, 40, 160, 373, 493, 494, 497, 498, 499, 500.
Charles V., Emperor, 478.
Charlotte street, 53.
Charters, the town, 151, 152–163.
Chekehull, Hugo de, 436.
Chekehull, Isabella de, 444, 445, 446.
Chelegrave, William de, 452.
Cheney, John, 468.
Cherbourg, 467.
Chester, 260.
Chester, constable of (Roger de Lacy), 152.
Chewe, John, 76.
Cheyne, Le, 94.
Cheyne, Sir John, 82.
Chichester, 186, 250, 255, 472.
Chilworth, Coleworth, 81, 332, 436.
Chimney-sweep, 124.
Chippenham, Henry de, 368, 380.
Christchurch, 224; castle, 82; head, 221.
Christchurch, Northam, 351.
Christchurch, Portswood, 352.
Chopin, Chopyn, John, 49; Robert, 455.
Cinque ports, 153.
Claremunde, Cleremond, the Lady, 150, 437.
Clarence, Duke of, Thomas, second son of Henry IV., 469, 472.
Clarence, Duke of, 513.
Clarke, Joseph, 313.
Clarke, Mrs., 47.
Clausentum, 2–12.
Clayton, George, 429.
Clerk, John, 76.
Clerk, John le, 201, 322, 323.
Clerk, John, 200.
Clerk, Walter, 202.
Clerke, Richard le, 200.
Clerke, Thomas, 185.
Clifford, Henry, 188.
Clifford, Mr., 341, 395, 401.
Clifford, Sir Robert, 476.
Clobery, Sir John, 219.
Clothworkers, the, 271, 272.
Cloth-house, 126.
Clungeon, John, 391, 409; Peter, 110, 222; James, 167, 228, 406, 492, 496, 497.
Clutterbuck, Thomas, 313, 341, 342, 349, 496, 497.
Cnut, King, 18, 23, 24, 25.
Coaches, 511, 512.
Cobblers, 135; corporation of, 272.
Cockburn, Sir A. J. E., 186, 208.
Cockys, George, 240.
Coinage, Southampton, 20; tokens, 246.
Coins, Roman, 4, 6, 8, 9, 17; old English, 16, 17.
Cole, Hugo, 451.
Coles, Francis, 188.
College street, 53.
Coleshull, Richard de, 335, 347.
Colles, Cristina, 377.
Collins, Sir John, 196.
Collis's court, 63, 85.
Colrithe, Thomas, 219.
Combe, La, M., 411.
Comfort, John, 219.
Common, the, 44, 48, 55, 215.
Commoners, the, 134.
Common lands, 51–52.
Commonwealth, the, 39, 166, 488–492.
Companies, steam-ship, 289–291.
Company, Southampton and Itchen bridge, 291.
Condray, Thomas, 79.
Conduit, John, 206.
Conduit Hede, Le, 114, 115.
Conduits and waterworks, 114–119.
Connaught, Duchess of, 283.
Constables, 134, 215.
Constables of castle, 77–84, 163.
Cooke, William Major, 186.
Coopers' corporation, the, 272.
Cormeilles, abbey of, 27, 29, 30, 35.
Cornelius, Cornellius, Cornellis, Richard, 168, 177, 482; Thomas, 167, 178, 179, 491, 496, 497, 498, 500.
Cornish, John, 301.
Coroners, 134, 153, 158.
Correction, house of, 297.
Corvesers, cordwainers, 273.
Coryngdon, John, 348.
Cosham, Isle of Wight, 460.
Cosne, Pierre de, 414, 415.
Cougot, Antoine, 411, 413, 414, 415, 416, 417, 422.
Courand, Jean, 407, 422; Paul, 411.
Council, common, town, 136, 158, 159, 160, 162, 165, 166, 189, 192, 195, 197, 198, 199, 209, 212.
County, town made a, 155, 156, 158, 166.
Court, admiralty, 239–240.
Court, county, 156, 158, 209, 238.
Court, justices', quarter sessions, 156, 158, 238.
Court leet, 43, 44, 45, 46, 47, 154, 156, 158, 191, 210, 233–237.
Court, orphans, 239.
Court, pavilion, 243–245.
Court, pie-powder, 156, 231, 242.
Court, town, 153, 154, 156, 166, 237.
Courtney, James, 98.
Coventry, 228.
Cowart, the widow, 477.
Cowarte, Nicholas, 115, 175.
Cowes, port of, 222, 223.
Cowherds, the, 304.
Cox, Henry, 359, 385, 400.
Crabbe, Rev. J., 84, 327.
Craddock, Michael, 65.
Crampe lane, 52, 54.
Croke, John, 401.
Croucheston, Richard, 381.
Croc, Rainald, 27.
Crocker, 336; Alexander, 65; Walter, 65.
Cromwell, Oliver, 134, 168, 193, 495.
Cromwell, Richard, 360, 491.
Cromwell, Thomas, 38, 338.
Crook, John, 203, 251.
Crop, William, 109.
Cross house, 42, 52, 53, 109, 110, 232, 342.
Cross street, 53.
Crosse, James, 161.
Crosse, Thomas de, 347.

Crowe, Mitford, 205.
Crunden, John, 127, 442.
Cucking-stool, 108, 323.
Cuckoo lane, 93.
Culloden, battle of, 51.
Cumberland, Duke of, 502, 513.
Cummin, William, 29.
Curry, William, 189.
Curtis, Sir Lucius, 281.
Cushen's gift, 368.
Custom-house, 98.
Customer, petty, 134.
Customs, lease of, 33.
Customs, petty, 198, 225–230, 261, 280.
Cut-thorn, 41, 42, 43, 45, 47, 48, 49, 50, 194, 435.
Cynric, 13.

DAMAN, William, 189.
D'Amory, Sir N., 253.
Dancing-school, 273.
Danes, 19–25; Danish vessel, 25.
Darcy, Sir A., 446.
Darsset, William, 336, 348; William, 393; Thomas, 348, 393.
Dartmouth, 253, 289.
Daunger, Thomas; Matilda, 437.
D'Aussey, Charles, 307.
D'Auvergne, James, 182, 196, 386, 398, 505.
Davisson, William, 312.
Dawkins, Henry, 113, 206.
Dawtrey, Francis, 442; Sir F., 216; John, 112, 115, 203, 244, 444.
Dawtrey, Lady, 42, 50.
Deacon, Charles Edward, 189.
Deanery, the, 344, 346.
De Crespigny, Sir W. C., 207.
De la Motte, Philippe, 422; Joseph, 167, 272, 407, 496; Mrs., 302.
Delawarr, Earl, John West, 459; John Richard, grandson of last, 503.
Delmé, Peter, 206, 362.
Demichevalier, Thomas le, 322.
Denmark, 257.
Depeden, Walter de, 226, 227.
Deryng, John, 201.
Dey, Nicholas, 203.
Dibden, 242, 332, 333.
Diganson, Thomas, 311.
Discreets (prodeshommes), 137, 168.
Discreets, the twelve, 137, 141, 143, 144, 146.
Discreets of market, 134, 137, 143, 144, 211.
Disfranchisement, 192, 193.
Dispensary, the, 309.
Ditches, the town, 107, 108, 513.
Dixon, Thomas, 197.
Dobree, Peter, 323.
Docks, the, 280–284.
Doge, the, 251.
Dogra, Demagrine, Nicolyne, 38.
Dolphin, the, 221, 364, 503, 508.
Domesday, 14, 26–28, 328.
Donys, William, 400.
Dorset, 257.
Dorset, Darset, William, 391.
Dorset, Marquis of, 474, 477.
Dottin, Abel Rous, 207, 386.
Dowman, John, 348.
Downer, Edward, 490, 491, 497, 498, 500.
Drake, John, 312, 401.
Draper, B. H., 431.
Du Boulay, B. F. H., 459.
Dulamon, Jacques, 422.
Dumaresque, Philip, 196.
Dummer, Thomas, 219; Thomas Lee, 206; Thomas, 111.
Duncan, Viscount, 207.
Dunch, John, 298, 299.
Dunstan, John, 400.
Dupré, Edward, 419, 422.
Durand de Gloucester, 27.
Dutch, the, 160; ship, 223; fleet, 160, 490, 499; prizes, 504.
Duthy, John, 91.
Duval, David, 419, 422.
Dyggs, Thomas, 203.
Dymock, Thomas, 240, 244.
Dyndbeth (Denbigh?), 229.

EDWARD the Confessor, 25, 26, 28.
East Meon, 274.
Eastley, Esteley, 329, 332.
East street, 38, 53, 123, 146, 271, 293, 300, 337, 431, 432, 480.
Eastgate, 63, 103, 104.
Echevins, the, 136, 137, 139.
Edmundson, Henry, 218, 369.
Edward I., 33, 35, 153, 249.
Edward II., 35, 153, 249.
Edward III., 35, 60, 154, 342, 452.
Edward, Black Prince, 79, 466.
Edward IV., 34, 61, 156, 157, 217, 243, 454, 457, 460, 461, 472.
Edward VI., 38, 39, 62, 157, 158, 257, 261, 402, 461, 480.
Edward, Symken, 255.
Eglesfield, Robert de, 452, 462.
Eleanor, queen of Henry II., 248, 252, 464.
Eleanor, queen of Henry III., 35, 457.
Election of mayor, &c., 164.
Eling, 242, 332, 333.
Elizabeth, queen of Edward IV., 36.
Elizabeth, Queen, 65, 92, 158, 231, 259, 261, 373, 385, 403, 405, 408, 480, 481.
Elliott, W. J., 71.
Ely, Bishop of, Geoffrey Ridel, 31; Eustace, 152.
Emmory, Emery, John, 201; John, 173.
Englefield, Sir Henry, 3, 6, 7, 9, 11, 12, 60, 74, 86, 87, 88, 89, 95, 104, 391.
Engleis, Bartholomew le, 200.
English street, *see* 'High street.'
Erdington, Thomas de, 78.
Ernewode, Richard, 368.
Erneley, William, 187, 240.
Eschaetor, the mayor, 155, 158, 166.
Essex, 257.
Essex, Earl of, Henry Bourchiere, 41; Robert Devereux, 488.
Estcote, Walter de, 79; Hugo de, 81.
Esteney, William, 219.
Etuer, Estur, Richard, 245, 373, 406.
Exbury, 240, 242, 460.
Exeter, 250.
Exton, Edward, 104, 109, 204, 490.
Eyre, Sir Giles, 185; Sir Robert, 165, 186; Robert, 186, 206; William, 186, 241.

Evreux, Count of, 27.
Ewerly, John, 255.

FAIRS, 230-233; Above Bar, 56; Trinity, 194, 195, 210.
Falbergh, Robert, 323.
Fall, Philip, 398.
Falmouth, 289.
Falvey, Timothy, 75.
Farbrother, Roger, 370.
Far[e]ham, Simon de, 347.
Farnham, 274, 464.
Farr, Thomas, 193.
Fashin, George, 388.
Fasshyn, Thomas, 203.
Fawley, Fallele, 301, 332, 333.
Fawne, John, 354, 369.
Fee-farm, 29-40, 152, 155, 157, 158, 160, 221, 225, 479.
Feryng, Geoffrey de, 333.
Fessant, J., 202.
Fetplace, Walter, 173, 377; Walter, 174, 164, 202.
Few, William Jebb, 351.
Fifield's gift, 305.
Fire, precautions against, 124.
Fish street, 455.
Fishermen of Itchen, &c., 222, 223.
Fishmarket, 126.
Fishmongers, the, 273.
Fishmark, John, 201.
Fitz-Osbern, William, 370.
Fitz-Ralph, William, 152.
Fitz-Warren, Ivo, 82.
Fleet prison, the, 37.
Fleetwood, Sir Gerard, 339; Lord, 491.
Fleming, Flemang, Flamang, Walter, 37, 170; Henry le, 170; Walter le, 149, 425, 437, 443, 444; Sir William le, 320; Giles le, 426; John le, 199, 200, 457; Robert le, 453; Henry le, 200, 445; John, 202; John, 53, 115, 203; Sir Thomas, 68, 134, 185, 204, 219; Sir Francis, 203, 357; Sir Thomas, 68, 204; Edward, 68, 205; Richard, 205; John, 206.
Flete, John de, 79; John, 172, 201.
Florans, Floryse, Robert, 173, 424, 426, 427.
Fogge, Sir John, 36.
Foran, Walter, 59.
Ford, Sir Richard, 204.
Ford, John, 431.
Forester, John le, 445.
Forst, John, 200.
Forster, Henry, 200.
Foster, John, 441.
Fortifications, the, 59-110.
Fortin, Walter, 77, 170, 452; Denys, 37, 453; Amise, 49; Alice, 437; Michael, 437; John, 227.
Fotheringay, 35.
Foxle, John de, 82.
Foxholes, John, 254.
Fowel, Fowell, Fughel, Fulghel, 26, 170, 186, 199, 200, 322.
Fowey, 253, 488.
Foyle, John, 219.
Fradin, François, 421.
Franceis, Richard le, 437.
Francfort, 257.
Franchisers, freemen, the, 138, 139, 141.
Francis, Henry, 429.
Free towns, list of, 229, 230.
Freeman, George, 246; William, 209; William, 304.
French church, 302, 306, 374, 403-422.
French street, 94, 147, 149, 298, 318, 321, 456.
Frescobaldo, Giovanni, 475.
Friar, John, 187, 482.
Friars' head (also le Conduit hede), 43, 116.
Friary, Friars, the, 63, 103, 105, 114, 115, 117, 139, 215, 269, 364, 437, 442-447, 458.
Fryar, Kingston, 500.
Fulham, George, 349.
Fuljambe, N., 241.
Fuller, John, 206.
Full flood, 147, 449, 455.
Fuzewells, 41, 47.
Fysch, John, 186.

GALFRID, son of Azon, 21.
Gallows, the, 50.
Gardiner, Thomas, 232.
Gardyner, Richard, 348.
Gariot, Thomas, 415.
Garland, John, 40.
Garnard, Richard, 83.
Garstons, the, 437, 449, 455.
Gas, 514.
Gascony, 253, 257.
Gates, the, 63.
Gaucourt, the Lord, 254.
Gefferey, William, 230.
Geffrey, Thomas, 381.
Genoa, 253, 254, 257; carracks of, 39, 157, 251, 257, 276, 472.
Genoese trade, 250, 255.
George II., 502.
George III., 39, 69, 70, 502, 509, 512, 513.
George IV., 514, 515.
George, the, 116.
Gerard, the canon, 440.
Gerard le Grue, 243.
Gerard, the Lord, 106.
Gerneys, Robert, 392.
Gernyngton, William, 381.
Gervase, Gervaise, le Riche, 31, 320, 437, 450, 451, 452, 456.
Gibbon, Edward, 206.
Gibbons, Sloane, 306.
Gibson, Edmund, Bishop of London, 262.
Giddy bridge, 366.
Gifart, Osbern, 27.
Gignoux, Isaac, 422.
Giles, John, 186; Alfred, 208, 281.
Glapion, Gavin de, 152.
Gloves, the, 274.
Gloucester, Duke of, Humphrey, 82, 256; Richard, 473
Gloucester, Duke of, 503.
Gloucester square, 443.
Glynne, John, 203.
Goce, præpositus, 452, 453.
Goddard, Richard, 204, 210; Thomas, 203, 357.

Godeston, Godestowe, John, 381.
Godfrey, John, 188, 189, 241, 364, 476.
God's House, 52, 53, 54, 63, 99, 109, 117, 123, 139, 305, 320, 321, 353, 405, 425, 437, 450–463, 470, 471.
God's House gate, 61, 63, 96, 98, 99, 107.
God's House tower, 70, 99, 100, 101, 102, 103, 104, 105, 215.
God's House meadow, 52, 53, 54.
Godwin, 26.
Golden grove, 342.
Goldsmyth, William, 381.
Gollop, Gallop, George, 83, 194, 204, 301; Peter, 83; Roger, 185, 204, 500.
Gomesester (?), 229.
Good, Richard, 161.
Goswell, Gosling, lane, 115, 116, 436, 437, 450.
Grammar school, the, 38, 300, 301, 302, 310–320.
Grane, John Willis, 351.
Granger, John, 381.
Gravel, the, 94.
Gray, Michael, 363.
Gregory, John, 234.
Grentmesnil, Hugo de, 27.
Greville, Fulk, 203, 258.
Grey, John, 376.
Grey, Sir Thomas, 82, 459, 469, 470.
Griffith, Jermain, 192; John, 269, 384; Charles Tapp, 315, 316, 394.
Grimpé, Paul, 410.
Grosvenor square, 114.
Grossard, Susanna Louise, 419; Henry, 419.
Grove, John, 113, 229.
Grove street, 16, 293.
Gruchy, De, M., 411, 412.
Grymold, John Baptist, 250.
Gryme, Richard, 37, 38, 101, 107, 164, 174, 425, 473, 474.
Grysthwayt or Gristwood, Thomas, 380.
Gubbs, Thomas, 313.
Guernsey, 34, 191, 261, 263, 267, 410, 504.
Guidotti, Anthony, 167, 168; Lady, 168.
Guienne, 255.
Guild merchant, the, 32, 132–151, 190, 191, 217, 294; ordinances of the, 37, 121, 139–151.
Guildsman, the, 135, 137, 139, &c.
Guild priest, the, 217, 218.
Guildhall, the, 50, 63, 71, 72, 154, 164, 240, 241.
Guild meetings, 137, 147, 151.
Guilds, craft, 136.
Guilford, 274, 465, 474.
Guilford, Earl of, Francis North, 343, 346, 349.
Guillaume, M., 411; Thomas, 50.
Guistinian, Sebastian, 477.
Gunner, the town, 214, 215.
Gunner, Thomas, 186.
Gunpowder, 214, 215, 473.
Gunter, William, 174, 424, 426.
Gurney, Russell, 208.
Gussage, Guersich, &c., 451, 457, 460.
Guy, Sir, of Southampton, 247.

HACKNEYMEN, the, 274.
Hadewis, the abbess, 435.
Halton, Miles, 363, 370.
Halveknyght, Thomas le, Cristina, John, Thomas, Roger, Walter, 320, 321; Roger, 455; William, 377.
Halveknyght lane, 321, 322.
Hammond, George, 388; Charles Hilgrove, 186, 307.
Hampton, Hanton, Hantune, Heantun, &c. (*see* 'Southampton'), 13, 14, 17, 18, 19, &c., 26, 337.
Hampton court, 274.
Hampton court, Little Hampton, &c., 448.
Hampton, Roger de, 450; Roger de, 437, 451, 452; John de, 79.
Hamble, Hamele, Hamullryse, &c., 33, 135, 224, 225, 240, 241, 242, 253.
Hancock, Thomas, 383, 384; William, 188.
Hanover buildings, 109.
Hanydon, Robert de, 393.
Harbour commissioners, 94, 113.
Hardley, 240.
Hardwin, Robert, 32, 59.
Harfleur, 470.
Harpesfelde, Nicholas, 357.
Harris, John, 297, 298; Roger, 205.
Harrison, John, 196.
Harrison, Thomas, 323.
Harrison, William Dann, 329, 352.
Hartley, Henry, 129; Henry Robinson, 129.
Hartley Institute, the, 127, 128–131, 245, 246, 261, 301, 320.
Haselrig, Sir Arthur, 491.
Hashert, Giles, 167.
Hatfield, 40.
Haven stone, 42, 44, 46, 47.
Hayward, Harvey, 190.
Haywode, Andrew, 200.
Haywoode, Roger, 438.
Heath, the, *see* 'Common.'
Heathcote, Sir William, 206, 363.
Heg stone, 42, 46.
Henderson, Colonel, 280.
Henley, Anthony, 206.
Henry I., 152, 243, 433, 434.
Henry II., 29, 59, 152, 248, 434, 464.
Henry III., 33, 35, 41, 59, 153, 243, 452.
Henry IV., 35, 61, 154, 449.
Henry V., 35, 61, 154, 256, 459, 468.
Henry VI., 154, 155, 157, 245, 255, 470, 471, 473.
Henry VII., 43, 61, 157, 230, 447, 474.
Henry VIII., 36, 157, 231, 477, 478.
Hereford, 39.
Hermitage, the, or chapel, 232.
Hersent, David, 360.
Hertford, Earl of, Edward Seymour, 312, 480.
Heton, Thomas, 204.
Hervart, Philibert d', 417, 418, 421.
Heywood, Nathaniel, 182, 196, 386, 503, 505.
Hickley, Heckeleia, &c., 451, 452, 453, 460.
High or English street, 70, 94, 95, 96, 106, 113, 115, 117, 119, 125, 126, 149, 353, 483.
High, Arthur, 428.
Higgins, Higgens, William, 168, 179, 228, 490, 491.
Hildesly, Hildesley, John, 184, 359, 360.
Hill, village of, 42, 43, 44, 45, 50, 114.

Hill head, Helhead, 221, 242.
Hill, Hugh, 368, 370; Ann Lance, Bridget Lance, 368.
Hill, Nicholas, 76.
Hillyard, John, 349.
Hitchcock, Mr., 358, 384.
Hoadley, John, 342, 345, 349.
Hoare, Peter Merrik, 208.
Hode, Hood, cross, 42, 44, 45, 46.
Hodges or Hegge, Richard, 381.
Hodges, Eleanor, 219.
Hodgson, Isaac, 315.
Hogheles, Geoffrey, 249, 250.
Hoglands, 51, 52, 55, 436.
Holand, John, 348, 381.
Holbery, John de, 322.
Holbury, 242.
Holden, Alexander, 381.
Hollis, Peter, 428; Thomas, 308.
Holmehegge, Nicholas, 164, 174, 202, 422, 423, 426, 427; Joanna, 423.
Holmes, Sir Robert, 39, 223, 224.
Holy Rood, parish, 48, 129, 271, 293, 300, 302, 456; church, 105, 115, 117, 125, 150, 262, 296, 324, 329, 330, 332, 334, 340, 341, 353–370, 417, 427, 438, 472.
Hook, 253.
Hookey, John, 397.
Hooper, Mr., 185.
Hope, George William, 208.
Hopkins, Henry, 369, 380, 406.
Hopton, David, 348.
Hordyer, Horder, William le, 455; Adam le, 170, 322, 436, 455; Robert le, 322; Agnes le, 86, 104, 345.
Horewoode, Robert, 115.
Horlock, John, 311.
Horn, John, 333.
Horne, Edward, 375, 382
Horne, William, 167, 179, 313, 365, 490, 492, 493, 498.
Horsey, Edward, 203.
Hose, Geoffrey de, 435, 436.
Hotham, Galfrid de, 347.
Hoton, John, 82.
Houndwell, the, 51, 52, 55, 56, 117, 450, 510; cross, 437, 450.
Houses, the king's, 59.
Howard, Sir Edward, 477; lord, of Effingham, 259.
Howse, Reynold, 126.
Hoy, James Barlow, 207.
Hubert de Burgh, 252.
Hull, 250, 254, 255, 257, 260, 264, 284, 285, 286, 287.
Hulton, William Preston, 346, 402.
Hurnet, Richard de, 152.
Hun, Hane, Hound, 228, 332, 333.
Hunderlythe, William, 381.
Huntington, Earl of, John Holland, 470.
Hunton, 83.
Hurne, Roger atte, 200.
Hurst, 34, 148, 221, 226, 242.
Husband, Azariah, 39.
Husee, John, 115.
Husse, Thomas, 380, 384.
Huttoft, Henry, 105, 167, 445, 478,
Hyde, Abbot of, 80, 81.
Hyll, Richard, 115.
Hythe, 224, 240, 242; ferry, 62, 223, 291.

Ikelyngton, John, 348.
Imberd, Richard, 172, 200, 201.
Incent, John, 348, 401.
Incorporation of town, 155, 158, 166, 470, 471.
Infirmary, the, 309.
Ingoldsby, John, 38, 98, 185.
Inscriptions, Roman, 6, 7, 8, 9.
Inweys, Ineys, Adam, 200.
Invasions of town, 60, 78, 94, 109, 382, 465, 466.
Ipswich, 250, 255, 264, 338.
Irwine, Alexander, 196.
Isabella of France, queen of Edward II., 35, 466.
Isembart, Isembard, Ralph, 170; James, 170, 452.
Italian merchants, 255, 257, 471.
Itchen, 242; bridge road, 56, 291; cross, 54, 109—*see also* 'Cross house;' ferry, 53. 54, 111, 222, 223, 291, 302, 365, 500; river, 1, 41, 46, 54, 109, 222, 465.
Itchenworth, 42, 110.

Jackson, Josias, 207.
Jacomin, Mr., 302.
James I., 36, 83, 158, 261, 278, 482.
James II., 161, 162, 373, 501.
James, Jamys, Andrew, 101, 164, 174, 202, 255.
James, John, 425.
James, Peter, 173, 154.
Jardyn, John, 201.
Jeffrey, Sir John, 204.
Jenkins, Sir Lionel (Leoline), 160, 161.
Jersey, 34, 191, 261, 263, 267, 410, 504, 505.
Jesus chapel, 302, 340, 341, 506.
Jew's house, the, 456.
Joanna of Navarre, queen of Henry IV., 35.
John the controller, 29.
John, King, 41, 42, 91, 152, 221, 436, 452, 465; his palace, 89, 91; his pond, 91.
John-a-Guernsey's cross, *see* 'Padwell.'
Johns, Abraham, 428.
Jolliffe, William, 246.
Jubbs, Martin, 490.
Jurden, John, 200.
Justice, William, 444.
Justices, the, 134, 154, 156, 158, 162.

Kampeline, Isabella, 452.
Karron, Walter de, 91.
Kell, Edmund, 75, 327, 433.
Kelsale, Roger, 61, 202.
Kempster, Bartholomew, 493.
Kene, Richard, 190.
Kennington, 79.
Kent, 257.
Kent, Duchess of, 515, 516.
Kerby, Cranley Thomas, 186.
Keten, Robert, 393.
Keton, John, 345, 348.
Keyhaven, 33, 135, 222, 224, 225, 240, 242.
Kibolis Evanton (?), 230.
King, Sir Richard, 196, 366.

Kingherne, *see* 'Langherne gate.'
Kingsbury, William, 397, 429.
Kingsfield chapel, 430.
King's houses within the castle, 32, 33, 91.
King's houses, 91, 92.
Kingsland, 32, 41, 51, 328, 329, 342, 434, 435, 436.
Kingsman, William, 315, 392, 394.
Kingsmill, Mr., justice, 54.
Kingston-on-Thames, 274.
Kirkeby, John, 202.
Knaplock, Robert, 98, 187, 295, 311.
Knapton, Ferdinand, 188; John, 188, 189.
Knight, Alderman, 304.
Knight, Mr., 50; William, 105.
Knollys, Knollis, Knowles, Thomas, 204, 222, 491; Francis, 484.
Knowell, Robert de, 457, 462.
Knowles, Mrs. Avis, 303.
Knutswood, 91.
Kotterorne, *see* 'Cut-thorn.'
Kyngeston, Richard de, 353, 368.
Kyngton, Thomas de, 201.

LACEMAKING, 274.
Laishley, George, 79.
Lake, Sir Thomas, 258, 482.
Lamb, Andrew, 432.
Lambert, Walter, 122, 338, 339; Elizabeth, 339; Sir Oliver, 339; Charles, Lord Lambert, 339, 340.
Lambert, Thomas, 204.
Lame, Andrew, 442.
Lamplough, Thomas, Archbishop, 341, 362, 369, 395.
Lancaster, Duchy of, 229.
Lancaster, Duke of, John of Gaunt, 467.
Land, Sir Robert, 83.
Lange, Walter, 201, 202.
Langetot, William de, 77.
Langherne gate, 42, 44, 46, 47.
Langley, John, 403.
Langston, 34, 148, 221, 222, 226, 242.
Lanham, Edward, 69.
Lansdowne, Marquis of, John Henry Petty, 70, 84.
Lansdowne place, 84.
Lark, Thomas, 187.
Latham, Watkyn or Water, 186, 472.
Latimer street, 53.
Lavand, M., 411.
Law-day, the, 47, 58, 194.
Lawrence, Lord President, 490.
Le Cras, Noah, 196, 386.
Leeds, Duke of, Thomas Osborne, 40; Thomas, great-grandson of last, 40.
Lee, John, 428.
Lee, Henry, 208.
Lee, Lord Chief-Justice, 66; William, son of, 66.
Le Feuvre, George, 419, 422.
Le Gay, Peter, 167, 360, 487; Charles, 189.
Legg, William, 204.
Legh, Anthony, 250.
Leicester, Earl of, Robert Dudley, 259.
Leicester, Richard de, 32, 252, 425.
Leigh, Sir John, of Testwood, 68; Thomas, Philip, 68, 219; Edward, 68; Mary, 219.
Lekford, John de, 393.
Leland, his account, 3, 15, 17, 18.
Lemon, James, 128.
Lepe, Leape, 135, 215, 240, 242.
Lepers' hospital, the, 30, 31, 139, 331, 437, 448, 455, 456.
Le Scrope of Masham, Henry, Lord, 82.
Letley, *see* 'Netley.'
Levant trade, 251, 256, 258, 261.
Levedon, Lufeledon, &c., 436.
Levingston, Thomas, 184, 185, 204.
Lewis, Thomas, 205, 365.
Lexington, Robert de, 49.
Liberties or precincts, 41–48.
Libraries, 509.
Liggins, Joseph, 281.
Lighting, 120.
Limesey, Richard de, 30.
Lincoln, 250.
Lincoln, Earl of, Henry de Lacy, 114.
Linen hall, 275.
Lire, Abbey of, 29, 30, 31, 35, 370, 380, 381, 466.
Lisle, John, Lord Commissioner, 184, 185, 188, 204.
Lisle, Sir William, 219.
Liverpool, 264, 284, 285, 286, 287.
Lobery, John William, 155; Walter, 155.
Lobery mead, 51, 114, 115, 437.
Lockerley, 436.
Lockhart, Allan, 188.
Lombardy, 257.
London, 34, 36, 37, 160, 192, 216, 217, 248, 253, 254, 255, 256, 257, 262, 274, 284, 285, 286, 287, 468, 471, 474, 481.
London, Tower of, 79.
London, John de, 190.
London and S.-W. Steam-Packet Co., 290.
Longhouse, the, 101.
Long Rooms, 86, 507.
Longe, Nicholas, 200.
Louis of France, 252.
Lowsley, 453.
Lucy, Geoffrey de, 34; Philip de, 330, 331, 347.
Lubery cross, *see* 'Padwell,' 449.
Lubery street, 147.
Ludlow, Edmund, 487, 488; William, 488.
Ludlowe, Richard, 377.
Lym, Henry de, 171, 200, 322, 353, 455.
Lymington, Linnentone, 33, 135, 221, 222, 224, 225, 226, 227, 241, 242, 253.
Lynch, William, 301.
Lyndhurst, 35, 78, 81, 500, 503.
Lynn, 250, 254, 255, 260.
Lyons, Peter de, 33, 170, 199, 225, 228, 322.
Lyster, Sir Richard, 383, 384, 385, 389, 390.
Lyster, Thomas, 38, 175, 293.

MACHADO, Roger, 474, 475, 476.
Magdalene, Nicholas atte, 79, 80.
Magdalens, *see* 'Marlands.'
Maison Dieu gate, 42, 44.
Maister, William, 234.
Major, Richard, 297, 359, 360, 491.
Malmand, 453.
Malmeshull, Peter de, 382, 393.

Malmeshull, Malmesylle, Maunsell, William, 173, 201, 424, 426, 427.
Malortie, Isaac, 293.
Mansbridge, 81, 119, 453.
Mant, Richard, 315, 372, 397, 401.
Mapel, William, 201.
March, Adam, 425, 427.
Marche, William, 202.
Marche, Thomas de la, 200, 456.
Marchwood, 242.
Margaret of Anjou, queen of Henry VI., 35, 471.
Margaret of Austria, 476.
Margaret of France, second wife of Edward I., 35.
Market, clerk of the, 154, 155, 158.
Markets, 126–128, 138, 143, 211.
Marlands, Magdalens, Maudlin, East and West, the, 51, 52, 55, 56, 437, 449, 450.
Marlborough, 227.
Marleburgh, Thomas, 201, 202.
Marsh improvements, 55.
Marsh lane, 52, 53, 56, 346.
Marsh, Margery, 425, 427.
Marsh, Thomas, 105.
Marsh, the great, 54; the little, 53, 54.
Marmesfield, John, 75.
Mart, free, 257, 258.
Martin, Mr., 86.
Martin, Sir Henry, 206.
Martyn, Charles Cecil, 207.
Mary, Queen, 258, 261.
Mason, Adrian, 381.
Mason, Robert, 185.
Mason, Thomas, 88, 110, 230.
Mascall, John, 115, 171, 376, 377, 424.
Mascall, Roger, 201, 322.
Matcham, Cornelius, 246.
Matilda, queen of Henry I., 337.
Maudeleyne, &c., *see* 'Lepers' hospital.'
Mauncell, William, 249.
Mauleon, Savaric de, 34, 252.
Mawardyn, Richard, 61.
May, Walter, Prior, 335, 441, 442.
Mayjor, Major John, 204, 297, 298.
Mayor, Lord, of the Buckinges, 44.
Mayor, the, 133, 134, 155, 156, 158, 162, 163–184, 195, 197, 232, 235, 244.
Mears, Thomas, 50.
Mears, Thomas, 218, 382, 385, 394, 401.
Measurers of cloth, 134; of salt and corn, 134.
Medical charities, 309.
Mees, Laurence de, 171, 200, 250.
Meggott, Richard, 354.
Melcombe, 263.
Melton, John, 254.
Mercer, Mercier, Paul, 306, 403, 408, 421.
Mercer, Robert le, 33, 170, 225, 228, 322, 444, 445, 447, 457.
Mercers, the, 275.
Mercyer, Peter, 459.
Merton, William de, 330.
Metals, staple of, 255.
Mey, Richard, 201.
Michell, Thomas, 377.
Middleton, 81.
Mildmay, Humphrey St. John, 207.
Milford, 242, 301.
Mill, Sir John, 68, 204, 219, 484.
Millbrook, 80, 149, 242, 332, 333, 345, 365, 401, 407, 413, 417, 496.
Millhouse, the, 100.
Mille or Mylles, John, 106, 185, 187, 203.
Mille, Thomas, 185, 203, 311, 357.
Miller, Henry, 246.
Millet, John, 191.
Mills, John, 236.
Mills, Mill, Nathaniel, 178, 228, 302, 303, 484.
Millstone point, 42.
Milverton, Robert de, 380.
Minstrels, the town, 216.
Mint at Hampton, 19, 20.
Minchin Hampton, 249.
Missing, Thomas, 205, 362.
Moffatt, George, 207.
Moira, Earl of, Francis Rawdon, 505.
Mompesson, Roger, 184, 185, 205.
Mompesson, Thomas, 219.
Monckton, John, 50.
Montacute, John de, 31.
Montagu, Sir John, 467.
Montsent (Mottisfont), Prior of, 53.
Moody, Henry Vernon, 246.
Morley, Francis, 354.
Morrell, William, 380.
Morris, J., 431.
Mortain, Earl of, 27.
Mortemer, Ralph de, 26, 27.
Moundelard, Richard de, 250.
Mount street, 53.
Moxins, 392.
Moyen, Lawrence, 255.
Muleton, Sir Thomas de, 49.
Multon, Roger de, 457.
Munday, Andrew, 219.
Municipal Corporations Reform Act (1835), 137, 165, 198; (1882), 199.
Municipal offices, 163, 218.
Munkelonde, 329.
Munn, Nicholas, 312.
Murages, 59, 60, 89.
Murford, Peter, 83, 360, 395, 487, 489.
Musard, Ralph, 49; William, 436.
Musters, 121, 123.
Mydlington, Middleton, Thomas, 112, 201, 202.
Mylles, Richard, 377, 426; Bessamy, 426.
Mylles, Francis, 4, 462.
Mylles, James, 111.

NANTES, Edict of, revocation of, 410.
Naunton, Secretary, 258.
Navy block manufactory, 506.
Needles, the, 1, 62, 221, 505.
Netherlands, 257.
Netley, 240, 241, 242, 332, 385; common, 506; Abbey, 220, 228; castle, 480; Abbot of, 53, 62.
Neville, John, Lord, 468.
Neville, Thomas, of Fauconbridge, 473.
New Forest, 35, 81, 83, 113; bailiff of, 444, 446.
Newbye, Nicholas, 298.
Newcastle, 250, 260.
Newfoundland trade, 261, 263.

Newland, Sir Benjamin, 69, 160, 204, 205, 410, 501.
Newman, John, 401.
Newport, 222.
Newport, John, 449.
Newton, John, 381.
Newton, Thomas de, 440.
Newtown, 147, 443, 453, 455, 456.
Newtown lane, street, 53, 147, 437.
Neyre, Stephen le, 249.
Nicholas, Dean of Southampton, 333, 347.
Nicholas, Prior, 333, 440.
Nicholson, William, 380.
Nigel the physician, 27.
Noble, Edward, 127.
Noble, William, 380.
Noel, Roger, 227.
Noel, Viscount Campden, Edward, 66; Wriothesley Baptiste, 67.
Norbonne, Henry, 246.
Norbury, William, 401.
Normandy, 254, 257, 274, 464, 473.
Norman Conquest, &c., 26, 248.
Norman houses, 89, 90, 91, 95.
Norman, Normaund, Roger, 80, 171, 200, 253, 353.
Norman, Walter, 381.
Norman, William, 441.
Northam, 49, 119, 264, 283, 333, 342, 434.
Northam bridge, 3, 12, 56, 233, 291, 514.
Northam docks, 5; fort, 6.
Norton, Richard, 359, 360, 487, 488, 492.
Norton, Sampson, 203.
Norway, 257; trade, 261.
Norwich, 250, 255.
Nowell, Robert, 358.
Nursling, Nusshelyngges, 332, 333.
Nutley, Mr., 187, 188.
Nutson, Thomas, 61.
Nycoll, William, 173, 423, 424, 426, 427.

OATHS of office, 168, 185, 189, 197, 211.
Ocle, Thomas de, 347.
Officials unmentioned in charters, 213, &c.
Ogle, Newton, 346, 349.
Olyver, William, 380.
Orchard, King's, Queen's, 54; lane, 52, 53, 342, 437, 455; street, 108, 510.
Orchiere, Orcherd, Robert, 323.
Ordnance Survey office, 131.
Orphans, court of, 159.
Orpit, John, 191, 393, 401.
Osbern, Thomas, 255.
Osey, William, 83.
Ouchterlony, Sir James, 83.
Overey, Mr., 244; Thomas, 42, 134, 403, 444; William (mayor), 133, 202, 276; William (town-clerk), 133, 187.
Ower, Oure, 240, 332, 452.
Owers, Richard, 431.
Oxford street, 53.

PACE or Pacye, Thomas, 311, 357.
Packers, 212.
Packet-boats, 511.
Padwell, Padwell cross, 51, 451.
Palk, Edward, 327.
Palmer's gift, Alice, 399.
Palmerston, Henry, Viscount, 206.
Palshid, Palshed, Richard, 98, 115, 185, 187.
Palton, John de, 79.
Pancevolt, Bernard, 26.
Parker, James, 389.
Parker, Thomas, 312.
Parker's annuity, 378.
Parkins, Sir Christopher, 223.
Parkinson, Bridget, 301.
Parkinson, Captain, 77, 83.
Parks, the, 56.
Parliament, burgesses of, 199–208.
Patrick, Simpkin, 37.
Pavement commissioners, 64, 70.
Pavilion, Powlyn, Paulyn, &c., *see* 'Courts.'
Paving, pavement, 93, 119, 120.
Paxbread, the, 132, 133, 191, 192.
Payn, John, 202, 424; John, jun., 164; Thomas, 164, 174.
Payn, John, 347.
Payne, Sampson, 75.
Peartree, 4; green, 223; church, *see* 'Jesus chapel.'
Peck, Sir Robert, 53.
Pecock, Gilbert, 446.
Pedeland, 437, 449.
Pedley, Roger, 39, 116.
Pelham, Sir John, 468.
Pembridge, Richard, 81.
Pemerton, George, 306.
Pembroke, Earl of, William Mareschall, 152.
Pengelly, Mr. Serjeant, 63.
Pengeston, John, 201, 202.
Peniton, 81.
Penbroke, John, 323, 381, 393.
Penleaze, John Storey, 207.
Pennington, Pennehall, 240, 242.
Peninsular and Oriental Company, 288, 289.
Penruddoke, John, 184, 185, 203.
Pentiz, Nicholas de la, 451, 453.
Peperyng, John, 75.
Pepper alley, 249.
Pepys, Samuel, 66, 499.
Perchard, John, 58.
Pereson, John, 52, 462.
Perkins, Daniel, 370.
Perkins, Sir Frederick, 70, 103, 208.
Pescod, Nicholas, 406, 459; Marie, 406.
Peterborough, Charles Mordaunt, Earl of, 6, 442.
Petersfield, Roger de, 438.
Petithome, Hosbert, 252.
Pett, Simon, 393.
Petty session, 369.
Peule, Richard de, 79.
Peverel, Andrew, 438; Sir Thomas, 438; Henry, 81.
Peyton, Sir Yelverton, 181, 182, 397, 398 505.
Pharewyse ford, 453.
Philip and Mary, 158, 357.
Philip of Spain, 258, 357.
Phillater, Edward, 187.
Philpot, John, 157.
Piacle, John, 249.
Pidgeon, Richard, 187.
Pie-powder, *see* 'Courts.'
Pier, the, 113, 515, 516.

Piggott, Humphrey, 380.
Pilgrim fathers, the, 483.
Pilgrim's pit, 86, 465.
Pinhorne, John, 313, 401.
Pinsun, Daniel, 412, 414, 415.
Pits, rubbish, 15, 16, 17.
Pitt, G. F., 127, 198.
Pitt, Henry, 167, 179, 490.
Pittis, Mr., 187.
Pittis, Thomas, 360, 370, 381, 407.
Pitt's lane, 361, 513.
Plague, the, 160, 385, 407, 408, 466, 480, 482, 483, 495–499.
Platform, the, 109, 110, 112, 113.
Players, stage, 216, 217.
Plummer, Nicholas, 401.
Plundered ministers, committee of, 339, 341.
Plymouth, 253, 254, 468.
Pocock, Richard, 314, 401.
Pocock, Richard, Bishop of Meath, 315.
Pocock, William, 188.
Poitou, 34, 35.
Poleyn, Nicholas, 380.
Polygon, the, 114, 436.
Polymond, John, 81, 104, 172, 201.
Polymond tower, *see* 'St. Denys.'
Pontearch, William de, 433.
Poole, Anthony, 370, 381.
Poole, J. G., 70, 433.
Poole, 253, 255, 260, 263, 481, 489.
Poor, care of, 294–300.
Popham, John, 82.
Porchester, 469.
Port, Hugh de, 27; Henry de, 454; Adam de, 78,
Porters, the, 149, 212.
Porter's lane, 94.
Porter's meadow, 53, 54.
Portland chapel, 431.
Portland terrace, 392.
Portsmouth, Portesmue, &c., 32, 33, 34, 77, 106, 152, 153, 155, 158, 214, 215, 221, 222, 224, 225, 226, 242, 252, 253, 259, 274, 451, 465, 469, 471, 476, 479, 481, 485–487, 491.
Portswood, 2, 30, 32, 41, 47, 49, 50, 329, 434, 435, 436; Alderman of, 47, 123, 134, 211.
Portuguese trade, 261.
Pottery, Roman, 6; old English, 17.
Poultry market, 126.
Poynet, Bishop, 10.
Prentyse, William, 348.
Priaulx, Robert, 379.
Prideaux, Roger, 442.
Pride, Colonel, 489.
Prince Consort, statue of, 103.
Prisage, 193; exemption from, 219, 220.
Prise, Philip de la, 146; Richard de la, 146, 147.
Prisons, 70, 101, 102, 159, 391, 455.
Private nomination, the, 164, 165.
Proclamation house, 361, 362.
Prodeshommes, *see* 'Discreets.'
Prussia, 257.
Prynne, William, 484.
Pugh, S. S., 431.
Pugnant, Richard, 27.
Pullar, Thomas, 430.
Pulmound, *see* 'Polymond.'
Pulsford, John, 431.
Purbeck, Alderman, 127.
Purbeck, William, 401.
Purkis, Peter, 275.
Puteo, John de, 170, 322.
Puteo, Robert de, 368, 448.
Putton, William, 445.
Puytz (De Puteo), Sampson del, 150.
Pye, H. J., 397, 504.
Pyne, William, 381.

QUATE, Peter, 50.
Quayages, 59, 89, 154.
Quay, castle, 74, 91, 111; water-gate, 107, 112, 113; west, 85, 86, 93, 111, 112, 147, 149, 437, 456.
Queen's College, Oxford, 130, 355, 356, 357, 405, 409, 414, 415, 453, 454, 455, 461, 462.
Queen's street, 53; terrace, upper and lower, 53.
Quo warranto, 159, 161, 162.

RACES, 514.
Railways, the, 55, 280, 282, 291, 292.
Ralph de Todeni, 27.
Ravenston, William, 97.
Ravenwyke, Peter de, 400.
Raymond, Richard, 66.
Raynolde, Robert, 349.
Reade, Samuel Figgai, 189.
Reading, convent of, 78, 81.
Recorder, the, 134, 158, 184–186.
Redbridge, 35, 78, 81, 222, 224, 242, 261.
Redford, Edward, 401.
Redvers, Baldwin de, 464.
Redvers, Margery de, 452.
Redvers, William de, Earl of Devon, 452.
Regalia of the town, the, 246.
Regent street, 450.
Religious houses, 433–463.
Renawd, John, 173, 345, 364, 426.
Rennie, Mr., 280.
Reservoirs, 119.
Restoration, the, 159, 192, 261, 493.
Retimo, 258.
Reveley, John, 397.
Reyneger, Robert, 357.
Reynold, Thomas, 202, 203; Robert, 190.
Reynolds, Catherine, 301.
Reynolds, Edward, 313.
Reynolds, Edward, Bishop of Norwich, 314, 498.
Richard I., 31, 41, 152, 434, 450, 451, 465.
Richard II., 60, 64, 97, 154, 243, 445.
Richard III., 34, 157.
Richbell, Robert, 204, 493, 494, 500.
Richerius, 328, 329, 347.
Richerius de Andeli, 27.
Ridding, Thomas; Thomas, 189.
Ridley, Sir Thomas, 122.
Ring, Richard, 430.
Ringwood, 83.
Rivers, Earl, Anthony Widvile, 473.
Robert, precentor, 347.
Robert the talliator, 37.
Roberts, William, 430.
Robinson, Christopher, 310.

Robinson, George, 129.
Robinson, Nathaniel, 307, 341, 359, 360, 374, 379, 381, 395, 400, 401, 428, 429.
Robyns or Revys, Thomas, 441.
Rochel lane, 456.
Rockesdone William de, 437, 453.
Rockstone gate, 123.
Roger the chanter, 333, 347.
Roger, son of Folcher, 29, son of Marcus, 452.
Rogers, George, 196.
Rogers, W. H., 128.
Rolle, Lord Chief-Justice, 44.
Rollestone, Samuel, 196.
Romsey, 252, 301, 428.
Ronde, John de, 200.
Rooke, Robert, 394, 401.
Roper, John, 323.
Roque, David, 421.
Rose, George Henry, 207, 513.
Rose, William Anderson, 208.
Rosse, Alexander, 302, 312, 369, 401.
Rouen, 471; Archbishop of, 152.
Rought, Walter, 340, 341, 349, 359.
Rowcliffe, Edward, 430, 431.
Rowlandson, James, 369, 380.
Royal Mail Company, 283, 289.
Rudde, Geoffrey, 460.
Rueland, Prior, 330, 333, 440, 449.
Rufane, Duchesne, 414, 415.
Rumbridge, 33, 225.
Russell, Mary, 219.
Russhall, William, 381.
Russian trade, 261.
Rutland, Earl of, Edward de Langele, 82.
Ryall, John, 441.
Rye, 467.

Sadleir, Richard Vernon, 305.
Salisbury assizes, 42, 43, 44; corporation of, 310.
Salisbury, Earl of, William Longespée, 33; John de Montacute, 467; Richard Nevill, 472; James Cecil, 40; Ann, Countess of, 40.
Salisbury, New Sarum, 228, 274.
Salmon, Massias, 175, 377.
Saltmarsh, the, 51–59, 267, 451.
Sambrooke, Elizabeth, 314.
Sampson, Hugo, 171, 200, 249, 250, 322, 334, 353, 456.
Sandes, Sir William, 58, 83.
Sandwalkers, 214, 242.
Sandwich, 109, 251, 255, 263, 472, 473.
Saravia, Christopher de, 406; Adrian, 311, 312, 406, 422.
Sauvage, Daniel, 409, 422.
Savoy, French church, the, 410, 416.
Saxon shore, Count of, 10.
Saxons, landing of, 13.
Say, Giles, 384, 385, 394.
Scales, the Lord, Anthony Widvile, 101, 472.
Scarlet, John, 201.
Scavage-money, 124.
Scavenger, 215.
Scharprixe, 33, 225.
Schools, 325–327.
Scotland, John, 351.
Scott, Alexander, 182, 196, 505; James, 381; William, 315, 401.
Scrope of Masham, Lord Henry, 459, 469, 470.
Scudamore, John, Viscount, 219.
Scures, John de, 79.
Scurlag, Geoffrey, 226.
Seale, Peter, 167, 178, 303, 400, 409, 486, 487; Peter, jun., 179, 303, 488.
Seals of the town, the, 245.
Searle, Richard, 304.
Seggewicke, Nicholas, 190.
Sendy, Lawrence, 293, 300; William, 300.
Sergemakers, sergeweavers, 275.
Serjeants, the, 134, 139, 159, 211, 212.
Sevenhampton, Walter de, 347.
Seymour, William Digby, 208.
Shadwell, John Emylius, 401.
Shamblehurst, 453.
Shapcott, Thomas Lawes, 85, 316, 389, 392, 394.
Sharpe, Giles, 193.
Shene, 35.
Sherborne, Priory of, 454, 455, 460.
Sherfield, Sherfeild, Henry, 185, 204.
Sheriff, the, 134, 156, 158, 164, 166, 174–184, 194, 209, 235.
Sherwynd, Nicholas, 201.
Shipbuilding, 283, 284, 469, 470.
Ships of Southampton, 163, 259, 260, 263, 264, 281, 284.
Shirley, 41, 48, 332, 438, 506.
Shirlie, Schirlye, John de, 170, 199, 200, 321, 322, 455; Felicia de, 322.
Shoemakers, 135, 196 (also Corvesers).
Shrewsbury, Earl of, John Talbot, 255; Margaret, Dowager-Countess, 36.
Shropshire, John, 203, 425.
Shypton, John, 202.
Sidford, 45.
Silk-workers, silk-weaving, 276, 409, 410.
Simnel street, 147, 249, 301, 322, 455.
Sims, John, 430.
Skelton, Alfred, 442.
Slatter, John, 393.
Sleddale, Adam, 323.
Smale, Thomas, 424.
Smirke, Sir Edmund, 132, 151, 186.
Smith, Richard, 223.
Smith, John, 205.
Smith, Charles Roach, 4, 6, 7.
Smith's charity, Henry, 367, 368.
Smyth, William, 380; Thomas, 380.
Society of Friends, 432.
Somerset, Duke of, Edmund Beaufort, 473; Edward Seymour, 479.
Soper, William, 97, 98, 173, 202, 254, 263.
Sorell, Elizabeth, 61.
Sorré, Jean, 412.
Soteshal, Shotshale, &c. (Satchell), 228, 240, 241.
Sotheby, William, 196.
South castle, *see* 'Godshouse tower.'
South, Thomas, 197.
Southampton, prehistoric, 1; British and Roman, 2; origin of, 13; name, 14; old site, 15–17; removal of site, 18; notices of, 19–25; Domesday account, 26–28;

prosperity of, 28 ; fee-farm of, 29-40 ; liberties or precincts, 41-48 ; the common and common lands, 48-51 ; salt marsh, 51-55, 56-58 ; marsh improvement, 55-56 ; fortifications of, 59-63 ; walls, gates, towers, 63, &c. ; Bargate, 63-72 ; castle, 74-84 ; arcade, 87-89 ; Norman houses, 90, 91 ; West gate, 92 ; Water-gate, 95-98 ; God's House gate, 99 ; spur-work and tower, 99-103 ; East gate, 104 ; decay of walls, 106 ; ditches, 107-109 ; platform, 109 ; cross house, 110 ; quays, 111-113 ; waterworks, 114-119 ; artesian well, 118 ; pavement, 119 ; watching, 120-123 ; streets, 123 ; modern Acts, 125 ; markets, 125-128 ; Audit-house, 125, 127, 128 ; the Hartley Institute, 129-131 ; ordnance office, 131 ; guild merchant of, 132-139 ; ordinances, 139-151 ; charters of, 152-163 ; incorporation of, 155 ; made a county, 156 ; quo warranto against, 159, 161 ; renewal of charter considered, 159-163 ; mayors of, 163-184, 490 ; recorders of, 184-186 ; town-clerks, 186-189 ; burgesses, 190-199, 491, 495 ; members of Parliament, 199-208 ; aldermen, 208 ; sheriff, 209 ; bailiffs, 209, 210 ; steward and treasurer, 210, 211 ; other officers, 211-218 ; the staple of, 219 ; exempt from prisage, 219-220 ; admiralty of, 221-224 ; head port and harbour of, 224, 225 ; petty customs of, 225 ; disputes about, 225-228 ; value of revenue, 229 ; abolished, 229 ; towns free of, 229, 230 ; fairs, 230-233 ; court leet, 233-237 ; town court, 237 ; county court, court of quarter sessions, 238 ; orphans, 239 ; admiralty, 239-242 ; piepowder, 242 ; pavilion court, 243-245 ; seals, arms, coinage, Sir Bevis, 245-247 ; trade of, wine, 248 ; wool, 249-250, 255 ; Venetian, 250-251, 475 ; hindrances of, 252, 253 ; prominence of, 253, 254, 471 ; loans from, 254, 255 ; tin and metals at, 255, 256, 261 ; assignments on customs of, 256 ; falling off of trade, 256 ; free mart proposed, 257, 258, 261 ; sweet wine grants, Turkey Company, 258, 259 ; decay of port, 259-261 ; efforts to restore trade, 262 ; Channel trade, 263 ; shipbuilding, 263-264 ; trade regulations—bakers, 264, 265 ; barbers, 265, 266 ; brewers, 266-268 ; butchers, 268-270 ; cappers, 270 ; chandlers, 270-271 ; cloth-workers, 271, 272 ; coopers, 272, 273 ; corvesers, 273 ; dancing, 273 ; fishmongers, 273 ; glovers, hackney-men, lace-making, 274 ; Linen hall, mercers, sergemakers, 275 ; silk-workers, 410, 411 ; surgeons, 276 ; tailors, 276, 277 ; tipplers (tavern-keepers), 277-279 ; tobacco, vintners, wool, 279 ; modern trade, railways, 280, 291, 292 ; docks, 280-284 ; growth of trade, 284-288, 517 ; steam-ship companies, 289-291 ; charities, alms-houses, 293, 294 ; care of poor, 294-296 ; workhouse, 297 ; St. John's hospital, 298 ; union, 299, 300 ; benefactions, 300-308 ; medical charities, 309. Educational — grammar school, 310-320 ; West hall, 320-323 ; Taunton's school, 323-325 ; other schools, 325-328. Ecclesiastical—St. Mary's, 328-350 ; Holy Trinity, St. Luke's, 350 ; Christ Church, Northam, St. James's, Bernard Street, 351 ; St. Matthew, Christ Church, Portswood, St. Denys, 352 ; Holy Rood, 353-370 ; St. Lawrence and St. John, 370-382 ; St. Michael's, 382-394 ; All Saints, 394-402 ; St. Paul's, 402 ; St. Peter's, 403 ; French church, 403-422 ; chantries, 422-427. Nonconformists—Above Bar, 428-429 ; Albion, Kingsfield, Belvedere, 430 ; Baptists, 430-432 ; Presbyterians, 432 ; Friends, Synagogue, 432 ; Methodists, 432 ; Free Church, Catholic Apostolic, Roman Catholic, 433. Religious houses—St. Denys, 433-442 ; Friary, 442-447 ; Lepers' hospital, 448-450 ; Godshouse 450-463. Southampton after Domesday 464 ; Henry II. at, 464 ; Richard I., John, the Edwards, 465 ; invasion of town, 465-466 ; under Richard II., 467 ; under Henry IV. and Henry V., 470 ; shipbuilding, 468, 469 ; conspiracy at, 469, 470 ; under Henry VI., 470-472 ; town incorporated, 471 ; resort of foreign merchants, 471 ; under Edward IV., 472-474 ; under Henry VII., 474-476 ; under Henry VIII., 477-479 ; under Edward VI., 480 ; under Elizabeth, 480-481, 259-260 ; James I., 482-483 ; Charles I., 483-488 ; town threatened and submits to Parliament, 485-488 ; Commonwealth, 488-492 ; Charles II., 493-501 ; plague, 495-499 ; alarm from Dutch fleet, 499 ; king at, 500 ; James II., 501 ; under the Georges, 502-515 ; abortive canal, 503, 504 ; movement of troops, 504-506 ; volunteers, 507 ; amusements, 507-511 ; access and egress, 511-512 ; steamboats, 513 ; gas, 514 ; the pier, 515 ; revival of town in present century, 517.

Southampton, Earl of, Henry Wriothesley, 313.

Southampton, Walter, 1, 24, 147, 221, 467, 470, 473, 475, 476, 479, 481.

Spa, the, 310.

Spanish burial-ground, 93 ; prison, 95 ; prisoners, 504, 505.

Spanish merchants, 249, 257, 261.

Speed, John, "Batt upon Batt," 160, 161, 179, 180, 262, 313, 389, 396, 410.

Spicer, Richard, 82.

Spinks, Sarah, 306.

Spinola, Hortensio, 75.

Square tower, 93, 94.

Stakepolle, Adam, 380.

St. Amand, Almaric de, 81.

St. Andrew's chapel, 331, 332, 335.

St. Andrew's Presbyterian church, 432.

Stanford, Henry, 201.

Stanley, Richard, 135, 187 ; William, 204, 490, 491, 492, 493, 494, 498, 500 ; George, 493 ; Hans, 113, 206.

Stanswood, 242.

Stapenhull, Ralph de 380.

Staple, mayor of, 155, 158, 166, 219; constables of, 134, 155, 166.
Staple of metals, 255.
Staple, the, 219.
Staunford, Stamford, Richard de, Prior, 440; John, 441, 449.
Staunford, Nicholas de, 200.
Staunton, John de, 347.
Staveley, John, 203, 239.
Staward, Walter, 393.
Stawell, John, 380.
St. Barbara's tower, 94, 105.
St. Barbe, Alexander, 196.
St. Cross church, *see* 'Holy Rood.'
St. Cross, Winchester, 36.
St. Denis, Pierre Deneveu de, 416–419, 422.
St. Denys's priory, 79, 220, 232, 320, 321, 330, 353, 354, 371, 433–442, 448; canons of, 30, 31, 32, 41, 47, 329; Little, 448.
St. Denys's tower, 61, 72, 73.
St. Denys's church, 342.
St. Dionyse oldehouse, 442.
Steamboats, 513.
Stebbing, Joseph Rankin, 75.
Steere, Thomas, 384, 401.
Stenigg, Robert, 445, 447.
Stephen, King, 59, 243, 434, 464.
Stephen of Reims, 329, 347.
Stephen (the) Stirman, 27.
Steptoe, John, 179, 298, 301, 314, 497.
Steuart, Simeon, 205.
Steward, the, 134–137, 139, 144, 210.
Stewart, John, M.D., 196.
St. George, chapel of, 76.
St. George's market, 128.
St. Helen's, 475.
Stibbert, Giles, 442.
St. James's, Bernard street, 351.
St. John, parish of, 48, 271, 296, 300, 302, 324, 370–372, 380, 381, 456; church, 321, 328, 332–334, 340.
St. John's Free church, 433.
St. John's hospital, 298, 299.
St. John, William de, 78.
St. Joseph's Roman Catholic church, 433.
St. Julian's, *see* 'God's House.'
St. Lawrence's cross, 126.
St. Lawrence, parish of, 48, 77, 123, 293, 297, 300, 302, 486; church of, 126, 329, 330, 332, 334, 340, 341, 355, 370–382.
St. Lawrence, Richard de, 30; Cecilia, 31.
St. Lawrence, Simon de, 37, 252, 452.
St. Lawrence, William de, 170, 452.
St. Luke's church, 350.
St. Malo, 467.
St. Mary church, 15, 16, 18, 19, 328–350, 353.
St. Mary's Litton (churchyard), 232, 293, 299.
St. Mary of East Gate, chapel of, 104.
St. Mary de Graces, chapel of, 232.
St. Matthew's church, 19, 351.
St. Michael's, parish of, 48, 126, 271, 296, 300, 302, 456; church, 115, 150, 329, 330, 332, 334, 340, 341.
St. Michael's prison, 391, 455.
St. Michael's square, 433, 477.
St. Nicholas, chapel of, 337.
Stokesley, John, 335, 348.
Stonard, Stoner, John or James, 203.
Stone, 242.
Stone, Thomas, 322.
Stone, William, 202.
Stoneham, North, 332, 333.
Stoneham, South, church, 329, 333; farm, 46; manor, 47, 328; mill, 47, 464; rectory, 346.
Stoneham, Peter, or Robert de, 440.
Stowe, Christopher, 203.
St. Paul's church, 402.
St. Peter's church, 114, 403.
St. Pol, Waleran de, 468.
St. Quintin, George Darby, 350.
Strand, the, 147, 436, 437, 450.
Stranger, 'foreigner,' 138, 141–145, 155.
Streets and sanitation, 123.
St. Swithin's, prior of, 80, 81; monks of, 328.
St. Thomas of Canterbury (Beket), 86.
Studley, Andrew, 193.
Stut, Thomas, 322.
Stydolf, Thomas, 36.
Sudhanton, &c., *see* 'Southampton.'
Suffragan Bishops' Act, 479.
Sugarhouse lane, 443, 447.
Sugar-refinery, 283.
Sunderland, 286.
Sunnynges, Adam de, 368.
Surgeons, 276.
Surlie (Shirley), Nicholas de, 49, 114.
Surrey, 257.
Surrey, Earl of, Thomas Howard, 478.
Surteys, William, 400.
Surveyors of highways, 124.
Sussex place, 56.
Sutton, Richard de, 200.
Swanley, Richard, 485, 486.
Swansea, 286, 287.
Swanton, M., 188.
Swanwick, 242.
Sweden, 257.
Swein, Roger, 37.
Sweyn, William, 381, 393.
Swymmer, Anthony Langley, 206.
Swyna, William de, 400.
Sylder, John, 425, 427.
Synagogue, the, 432.

TADCASTER, John de, 393.
Taillour, Ralph, 201.
Tailors, company of, 276, 277.
Talbot, Sir Richard, 80.
Tangier, 501.
Taunton, 248.
Taunton, Richard, 303, 304, 324, 325, 355, 361, 372.
Taunton's school, 303, 323–325.
Tawley, Robert, 76.
Taylor, Walter, 246, 506, 507; John, 316.
Tellar, Thomas, 364.
Teller of leather, 134.
Templars, knights, 29, 30, 31.
Tempull, William, 109.
Terminus terrace, 53.
Test, river, 1, 222.
Testwood, 68, 222.

Tetricus, 7, 8.
Thame, Philip de, Prior of Knights Hospitallers, 79, 80, 465.
Thames, the, 253.
Theatre, 298, 510.
Thenelin, Wallerand, 406, 422.
Thomas, J. Blount, 128, 363.
Thomas, Thomas, 53, 83, 203, 444.
Thorley, William, 203.
Thornburgh, John, 70.
Thorner, Robert, 307, 428.
Threefield lane, 53.
Threkyngham, Lambert, 393.
Tilbury, 242.
Tilney, Frederick, 205.
Timber house, 93.
Tin, 135, 255, 261, 262.
Tipet, John, 82.
Tipplers (tavern-keepers), 277–279.
Titchfield Abbey, 220, 221, 471, 480.
Tobacco-cutters, 279.
Toms, John, 341, 384, 394, 395.
Tomson, William, 393.
Tonellario, Roger de, 252.
Tonge, John, 400.
Totington (Totton), 228.
Totton, 242.
Towers, several mentioned, 63, 72, 101, 104, 105, 106.
Town-clerk, the, 134, 159, 186–189, 234.
Trade of town, 248–292.
Tramways Company, 291.
Treasurer, the, 210.
Trenchmere, Alan, 31.
Trentegeruns, William, 29, 30.
Trim, Mary, 368.
Trinity, chapel of the Holy, 54, 330, 332, 334, 335, 337.
Trinity church, Holy, 350.
Troys, Thomas, 250.
Turkey Company, 258, 259.
Turner, Roger, 341.
Turner, Peter, 430.
Turstin, chamberlain, 27; the engineer, 27; the sheriff, 30.
Twiste, Mr., 312.
Tyler, Stephen, 348.
Tylney, Frederick, 67.
Tyne ports, 286, 287.

UNION Steamship Company, 289.
Union street, 53.
Union workhouse, 300.
Unitarian church, 433.
Upton, John de, 368, 400.
Usher, the, 136, 137, 139.

VALLÉE, De, M., 414.
Vallibus, John de, 249.
Vasse, Thomas, 76.
Vaughan ap Griffith, John, 381.
Vaulted chambers, 74.
Vaus, John de, 170, 200.
Venetian trade, 250, 254, 475, 477.
Venice, galleys, merchants of, 39, 157, 250, 251, 257, 276, 475, 477, 478.
Venyng, Stephen, 381.
Vere, Ver, Henry de, 78.
Vernon, George, 393.
Veule, Adam de, 411.
Victoria, Princess, 515, 516.
Victoria, Queen, 283, 516.
Victoria rooms, 510.
Vienne, John de, 249.
Vincent the warden, 452.
Vincent, Frederick, 420, 422.
Vincent, George, 196.
Vintners, 279.
Vyes (Devizes), 230.

WALES, 253, 257.
Wales, Prince and Princess, 283, 343.
Waleys, Adam, 400.
Walkelin, Prior, 437, 440.
Walker, John, 38, 52, 202, 203.
Walker, Sir John, 101.
Walleston, Christopher, 167.
Walloons, 403, 404.
Walloon church, Threadneedle street, 414, 415.
Wallop, William, 204, 241, 300.
Wallope, Sir Henry, 203.
Walls, the, 63, &c., 160.
Walonfolling (?), 228.
Walpole, Sir Robert, 227.
Walsh, John, 98, 240, 444.
Walsingham, Sir Francis, 187, 259.
Waltham Bishops, 10, 244, 465, 469, 478.
Walwyn, Robert, 380.
Wandesford, Sir George; Mary; William, 221.
Warbeck, Perkin, 476.
Ward, Jacob, 246.
Ward, 121, 124, 146, 147, 208.
Ware, John de, 335.
Wareham, Thomas, 313.
Warenne, Gundred de, 436.
Warcwyk, William, 201.
Warham, William de, 440.
Warsash, 241, 242.
Warwick, Earl of, Thomas Beauchamp, 79; Guy, 249; Thomas; Thomas; Richard, 250, 470; Henry; Edward, 250; Richard Nevill, 36, 472.
Waryn, Gilbert, 392.
Wastes, grant of, 154.
Watch-bells, 70, 97.
Watch-tower, 95, 98.
Watching, 120–125, 135.
Water-gate, 63, 93, 95, 96, 97, 98, 112, 119, 122, 240, 456; of castle, 63.
Waterhouse lane, *see* 'Goswell.'
Waterworks, *see* 'Conduits.'
Waterton, Richard, 187.
Watkins, Father, 433.
Watt, Alexander, 350.
Wattenhull, John de, 466.
Watts, Isaac, 212, 308, 428; Isaac, 315, 448.
Waverley Abbey, 220.
Waynflete, John, 348.
Wegge, Richard, 200.
Weguelin, Thomas Matthias, 208.
Weighing, 135, 159, 166.
Well on the common, 118.
Wellington, Duke of, 513, 517.

Wenda, William de, 330.
Wenlock, Lord John, 73,
Werrore, 451, 452, 460.
Wesley, John, 432.
Wesleyans, 432.
West hall, 38, 311, 314, 316, 320, 321–323.
West gate, 63, 92, 93, 386.
West street, 392.
West, Thomas de, 78.
West, William, 187.
West, George, 241.
West, Sir Thomas, 222, 312.
Westcarre, Bishop, 394, 400.
Western circuit, 188.
Westminster, 250.
Weston, 187, 242.
Weston, William de, 80.
Weston, John de, 200.
Weston, Robert, 358.
Wete, Cecilia la, 333.
Wetherick, Robert, 223, 224.
Weymouth, 249, 250, 260, 489.
Wherwell, Abbess of, 27.
White, Richard, 209.
White, Sir Thomas, 300.
Whitehead, Master, 42, 43; Mistress, 42; Sir Henry, 43; Thomas, 380.
Whiteling, William, 348.
Whittaker, George, 315.
Wight, Isle of, 1, 62, 106, 222, 223, 253, 468, 473, 479, 481, 490, 513.
Wigram, Joseph Cotton, 343, 350.
Wilcok, John, 191, 369.
Wilcox, Brodie M'Gie, 208.
Wilderne, Nigel de la, 170.
Wilkes, Sir Thomas, 204.
Willet, Henry, 380.
William the Conqueror, 26, 28, 243.
William Rufus, 243.
William and Mary, 501.
William IV., 515.
William, John, 202.
William, son of Stur, 27.
Willmott, Edward, 203.
Wilson, William, 361, 370.
Wiltshire, Earl of, 472.
Winchester, 4, 13, 41, 78, 111, 196, 218, 243, 250, 254, 268, 280, 385, 465, 467, 468, 471, 473, 475, 478.
Winchester road, 49, 50, 449, 450.
Winchester terrace, 53.
Winchester, bishop of, Ælfwine, 328; Walkelin, 243; William de Giffard, 433; Henry de Blois, 434; Godfrey de Lucy, 329, 406, 465; Peter de Rupibus, 252; Ethelmar, 243, 333; John de Exon, 243; John de Pontissara, 448, 457; Woodlock, 10, 228, 333; John de Sandale, 114, 444; John de Stratford, 334, 353; Adam de Ortton, 80, 234, 440; Wykeham, 335, 345; Beaufort, 256, 353, 471; Waynflete, 244, 354; Peter Courtenay, 198, 244, 475; Thomas Langton, 244; Richard Fox, 441; Wolsey, 256; Gardiner, 383; Horne, 404; Cooper, 409; Andrewes, 122; Morley, 316, 354; Mew, 413; Trelawney, 371; Sumner, 343; Wilberforce, 343, 344, 357; Harold Browne, 344.
Winchester, Thomas, 441.
Winchelsea, 468.
Winchelsea, Earl of, Heneage Finch, 219.
Winder, John, 360.
Windmill lane, 450.
Windsor's gift, Andrews, 379, 394, 399.
Wine, 163, 223, 224, 248, 258, 259.
Winkle street, 95, 96, 98, 99, 314, 411.
Winterbone, Thomas, 115.
Wintershull, Master, 42.
Winton, Adam de, 78.
Witch (Droitwich), 230—the basis of the ancient salt way to Southampton (Mr. Thomas Kerslake).
Witchcraft, 236.
Wode or Wodd, Robert, 441.
Wood, Thomas, 442.
Wood mill, 118, 119, 222, 224, 506.
Woodside, 242.
Woodstock, Viscount, 205.
Wool, weigher of, 213, 249, 250.
Wool trade, 249, 255, 263, 279.
Wool street, wool-house, wool-bridge tower, 74.
Wool-combers, 275.
Woking common, 289.
Wolgar, William, 49.
Wolsey, Cardinal, 58, 256, 335.
Worcester, Earl of, 472.
Worgan, John de, 201.
Workhouse, the, 297–300.
Wormenhall, John de, 335.
Wriothesley, Sir Thomas, 83.
Wroth, Robert, 167, 360.
Wrotham, William de, 248, 465.
Wryght, Robert, 244.
Wulfris charity, 365, 366.
Wybert, the official, 334.
Wychford, Robert de, 347.
Wygayn, John, 201.
Wyld, Joseph W., 430.
Wylderne, Nigel de la, 200, 322.
Wyncestre, John de, 156.
Wyndham, Sir Charles, 68, 69, 205, 501; John, Thomas, 185.
Wynne, Owen, 161.
Wystard, Richard, 61.
Wyte, John de, 149.
Wytegod, John, 201.

YARMOUTH, 250, 254, 255.
York, 250.
York gate, 63.
York buildings, 293, 300.
York, Duke of, Richard, 254, 455, 460.
York, Duke of, 502.

ZION chapel or hall, 84.

PRINTED BY BALLANTYNE, HANSON AND CO., EDINBURGH AND LONDON.